TRUCKING

Tractor-Trailer Driver
Handbook/Workbook

THIRD EDITION

TRUCKING:

Tractor-Trailer Driver Handbook/Workbook

ALICE ADAMS

THOMSON

DELMAR LEARNING™

Australia Canada Mexico Singapore Spain United Kingdom United States

Trucking: Tractor-Trailer Driver Handbook/Workbook Third Edition

Alice Adams

Vice President, Technology and Trades PBU:
Gregory L. Clayton

Director of Learning Solutions:
Sandy Clark

Product Development Manager:
Kristen Davis

Product Manager:
Kim Blakey

Marketing Director:
Beth A. Lutz

Channel Manager:
Erin Coffin

Marketing Coordinator:
Marissa Maiella

Production Director:
Mary Ellen Black

Senior Production Manager:
Larry Main

Project Editor:
Christopher Chien

Production Coordinator:
Benj Gleeksman

Art/Design Specialist:
Mary Beth Vought

Technology Project Specialist:
Jim Ormsbee

Editorial Assistant:
Vanessa Carlson

Library of Congress Cataloging-in-Publication Data:
Adams, Alice.
   Trucking:tractor-trailer driver handbook/workbook / Alice Adams.—3rd ed.
      p. cm/
   Rev. ed. of: Trucking, 2003.
   Includes index.
   ISBN 1-4180-1262-9
1. Truck driving—Handbooks, manuals, etc. 2. Truck driving—Examinations—Study guides. I. Professional Truck Driver Institute of America. II. Trucking. III. Title.
   TL230.3.T79 2006
   629.28'44—dc22

Card Number: 2005027452
ISBN: 1-4180-1262-9

NOTICE TO THE READER

The sale, distribution, or use of this publication by a truck driver training program should not be construed to mean that the training program has been certified by The Professional Truck Driver Institute, Inc., or that an application for certification is pending. Users are responsible for independently determining whether any such certification exists.

Publisher does not warrant or guarantee any of the products described herein or perform any independent analysis in connection with any of the product information contained herein. Publisher does not assume, and expressly disclaims, any obligation to obtain and include information other than that provided to it by the manufacturer.

The reader is expressly warned to consider and adopt all safety precautions that might be indicated by the activities herein and to avoid all potential hazards. By following the instructions contained herein, the reader willingly assumes all risks in connection with such instructions.

The publisher makes no representation or warranties of any kind, including but not limited to, the warranties of fitness for particular purpose or merchantability, nor are any such representations implied with respect to the material set forth herein, and the publisher takes no responsibility with respect to such material. The publisher shall not be liable for any special, consequential, or exemplary damages resulting, in whole or part, from the readers' use of, or reliance upon, this material.

Contents

5

Basic Control 107

6

Shifting 122

7

Backing 140

8

Coupling and Uncoupling   151

9

Sliding Fifth Wheels and Tandem Axles   163

10

Preventive Maintenance and Servicing   177

11

Recognizing and Reporting Malfunctions 193

12

Communication 212

16

Night Driving 257

17

Extreme Driving Conditions 268

18

Skid Control 291

19

Hazard Awareness 304

20

Railroad Crossings 320

24

Handling Cargo   385

25

Cargo Documentation   414

26

Trip Planning 430

27

Hours of Service 446

28

Driving International Routes 461

29

Transportation Security 475

30

Public Relations and Job Search 487

31

Professional Driver Health, Safety, and Security 503

32

Hazardous Materials 531

33

Transportation Technology   552

34

Whistleblower Protections for Professional Drivers   565

35

The Commercial Driver's License   576

APPENDIX A

Troubleshooting Guide

Preface

As you read this, more than 3 million professional tractor-trailer drivers are moving the economy of the United States up and down the highway every day of the year. These professionals represent men and women of all ages and all ethnicities as they supply the food, clothing, furniture, medicines and medical supplies, electronics, household goods, and the various elements that go into the manufacture of every consumable item necessary for today's lifestyle.

Without professional drivers, this country's economy would come to a halt, with little ability to make progress in any area, including medical research and other technologies that now save labor and time in our everyday lives.

Without realizing it, the entire U.S. population depends on the commitment, skills, and dedication of professional drivers to do their jobs and do them as safely and efficiently as possible.

As you use this textbook to prepare for your career as a professional driver, do not lose sight of the generations of drivers who have brought the profession to where it is today. As you take your place behind the wheel of a tractor-trailer rig, remember those dedicated individuals who spent countless, lonely hours on the road, driving vehicles without heat or air conditioning, loading and unloading shipments onto makeshift docks in all kinds of weather, without the communications technology and improvements commonly found on tractor-trailer rigs today.

Unlike the early days of the transportation industry where anyone could drive and drivers were expendable, today's focus remains on getting the job done but getting it done safely with the driver's health, lifestyle, and security top priority.

As you take this step into a new career and new opportunities, the gratitude of an entire nation goes with you. You will soon join the ranks of elite professionals, a strong fraternity of dedicated professionals with a proud tradition who see their first priority as the safe and efficient movement of goods from origin to destination and, ultimately, the end user.

This textbook has been designed to help make your transition from where you are now to where you hope to be as a professional driver as easy and as efficient as possible. Yours will be an important job. Do it safely and do it well. This country is depending on you, every day you are on the job.

It is a huge responsibility. Good luck and safe driving!

Supplements

Used in conjunction with this textbook, the following supplements provide a comprehensive, turnkey curriculum for tractor-trailer driver training.

Trucking: Tractor-Trailer Driver Handbook/Workbook E-resource.

The e-resource provides everything an instructor needs to support classroom teaching. This all-in-one CD contains an Instructor's Guide with overviews of each chapter, suggested learning activities, discussion starters, and answers to all workbook review questions. The CD also contains PowerPoint presentation slides, a computerized test bank, an image library, and digitized video clips.

Trucking: Tractor-Trailer Driver Handbook/Workbook Video Series.

Created in cooperation with the Professional Truck Driver Institute, Inc. (PTDI), these videos can be used as part of the Trucking: Tractor-Trailer Driver training system or as part of an existing driver-training program.

Trucking: Tractor-Trailer Driver Handbook/Workbook Web Tutor.

Web Tutor is a content-rich, web-based teaching and learning aid that reinforces and clarifies concepts covered in the textbook. Web Tutor helps instructors organize their courses and students maximize their understanding. It includes a course calendar, chat, e-mail, and threaded discussions. Instructors can monitor student progress and participation, and students receive immediate feedback when they take chapter quizzes.

Acknowledgments

The development and publication of this book was made possible by many individuals. Special thanks to Alice Adams for her tireless effort updating, revising, and expanding this third edition. We also thank the following reviewers for their contributions:

John Moore—Ruhl Forensic, Inc., Scottsdale, Arizona

Gail Swiger—ABF Freight System, Inc., Atlanta, Georgia

Bob Watkins—Consolidated Safety Services, Inc., Fairfax, Virginia

Thank you also to:

Accent Photography by Terra—Contract Freighters, Inc.

Freightliner Trucks, a division of Freightliner LLC.—Freightliner LLC is a division of DaimlerChrysler Company.

Peterbilt Motors Company

Volvo Trucks North America

Erik Berthelsen Photography

Features of the Text

Objectives

Objectives are listed at the beginning of each chapter. They provide clear direction to students as to what they should understand when they have completed the chapter.

Introduction

The Introduction follows the Objectives in each chapter. It gives a summary of the content that will be covered in the chapter and the key concepts and topics that will be taught.

Color Blocks

There are Green, Yellow, and Red color blocks throughout the book that emphasize workplace safety and highlight key concepts. The Green "Go!" blocks highlight information that makes the student "ready to go" once he or she has a clear understanding of it. Yellow "Caution!" blocks highlight information on concepts or techniques that, for reasons of safety, require the student to exercise caution when putting them into practice. Red "Stop!" blocks draw the students' attention to the most serious safety concerns.

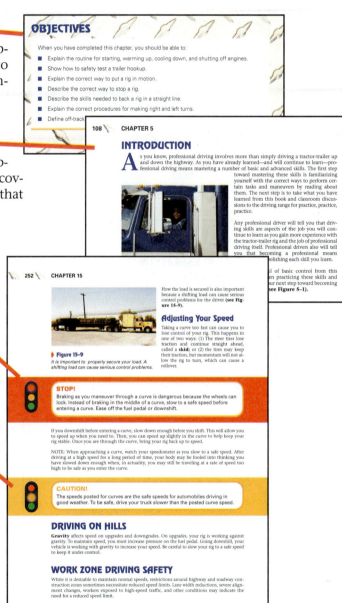

OBJECTIVES

When you have completed this chapter, you should be able to:

- Explain the routine for starting, warming up, cooling down, and shutting off engines.
- Show how to safety test a trailer hookup.
- Explain the correct way to put a rig in motion.
- Describe the correct way to stop a rig.
- Describe the skills needed to back a rig in a straight line.
- Explain the correct procedures for making right and left turns.
- Define off-track

108   CHAPTER 5

INTRODUCTION

As you know, professional driving involves more than simply driving a tractor-trailer up and down the highway. As you have already learned—and will continue to learn—professional driving means mastering a number of basic and advanced skills. The first step toward mastering these skills is familiarizing yourself with the correct ways to perform certain tasks and maneuvers by reading about them. The next step is to take what you have learned from this book and classroom discussions to the driving range for practice, practice, practice.

Any professional driver will tell you that driving skills are aspects of the job you will continue to learn as you gain more experience with the tractor-trailer rig and the job of professional driving itself. Professional drivers also will tell you that becoming a professional means polishing each skill you learn.

...level of basic control from this...when practicing these skills and...your next step toward becoming...(see Figure 5–1).

252   CHAPTER 15

Figure 15–9
It is important to *properly secure your load*. A shifting load can cause serious control problems.

How the load is secured is also important because a shifting load can cause serious control problems for the driver **(see Figure 15–9).**

Adjusting Your Speed

Taking a curve too fast can cause you to lose control of your rig. This happens in one of two ways: (1) The steer tires lose traction and continue straight ahead, called a **skid**; or (2) the tires may keep their traction, but momentum will not allow the rig to turn, which can cause a rollover.

> **STOP!**
> Braking as you maneuver through a curve is dangerous because the wheels can lock. Instead of braking in the middle of a curve, slow to a safe speed before entering a curve. Ease off the fuel pedal or downshift.

If you downshift before entering a curve, slow down enough before you shift. This will allow you to speed up when you need to. Then, you can speed up slightly in the curve to help keep your rig stable. Once you are through the curve, bring your rig back up to speed.

NOTE: When approaching a curve, watch your speedometer as you slow to a safe speed. After driving at a high speed for a long period of time, your body may be fooled into thinking you have slowed down enough when, in actuality, you may still be traveling at a rate of speed too high to be safe as you enter the curve.

> **CAUTION!**
> The speeds posted for curves are the safe speeds for automobiles driving in good weather. To be safe, drive your truck slower than the posted curve speed.

DRIVING ON HILLS

Gravity affects speed on upgrades and downgrades. On upgrades, your rig is working against gravity. To maintain speed, you must increase pressure on the fuel pedal. Going downhill, your vehicle is working with gravity to increase your speed. Be careful to slow your rig to a safe speed to keep it under control.

WORK ZONE DRIVING SAFETY

While it is desirable to maintain normal speeds, restrictions around highway and roadway construction zones sometimes necessitate reduced speed limits. Lane width reductions, severe alignment changes, workers exposed to high-speed traffic, and other conditions may indicate the need for a reduced speed limit.

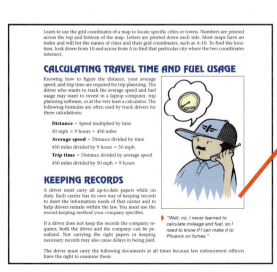

Learn to use the grid coordinates of a map to locate specific cities or towns. Numbers are printed across the top and bottom of the map. Letters are printed down each side. Most maps have an index and will list the names of cities and their grid coordinates, such as A-10. To find the location, look down from 10 and across from A to find that particular city where the two coordinates intersect.

CALCULATING TRAVEL TIME AND FUEL USAGE

Knowing how to figure the distance, your average speed, and trip time are required for trip planning. The driver who wants to track the average speed and fuel usage may want to invest in a laptop computer, trip planning software, or at the very least a calculator. The following formulas are often used by truck drivers for these calculations:

Distance = Speed multiplied by time
50 mph × 9 hours = 450 miles

Average speed = Distance divided by time
450 miles divided by 9 hours = 50 mph

Trip time = Distance divided by average speed
450 miles divided by 50 mph = 9 hours

KEEPING RECORDS

A driver must carry all up-to-date papers while on duty. Each carrier has its own way of keeping records to meet the information needs of that carrier and to help drivers remain within the law. You must use the record-keeping method your company specifies.

If a driver does not keep the records the company requires, both the driver and the company can be penalized. Not carrying the right papers or keeping necessary records may also cause delays in being paid.

The driver must carry the following documents at all times because law enforcement officers have the right to examine them:

"Well, no. I never learned to calculate mileage and fuel, so I need to know if I can make it to Phoenix on fumes."

Good Buddy

Good Buddy cartoons appear throughout the book, adding humor and visual interest, while at the same time providing tips to students and reinforcing concepts presented.

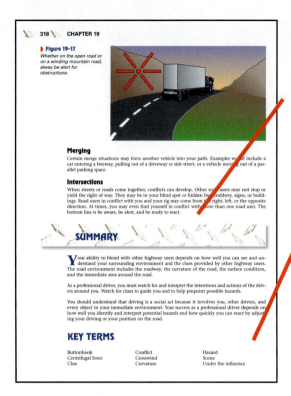

Summary

The summary appears at the end of each chapter prior to the list of Key Terms. It can be used to review the chapter and stimulate discussion.

Key Terms

Key Terms from each chapter are listed at the end of chapters. This list can be used as a quick review of the most important terms or concepts presented.

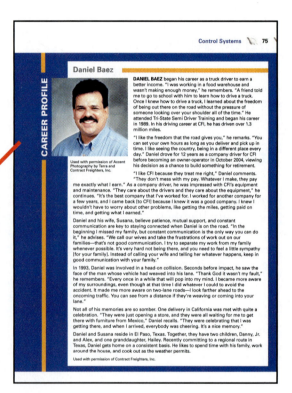

Driver Profiles

Profiles of professional drivers and driving teams showcase top drivers and driving teams, illustrating how successful and rewarding a truck driving career can be.

Review Questions

Multiple choice-style Review Questions appear at the end of each chapter. The review questions will help measure students' knowledge of each chapter; determining which areas of study they have a thorough understanding of and which areas need further review.

1

An Introduction to Trucking

OBJECTIVES

When you have completed this chapter, you should be able to:

- Have a working knowledge of the evolution of trucking transportation.
- Explain why the trucking industry is vital to our nation's economy.
- Explain the rules and regulations under which the industry operates.
- Understand the main components of tractor-trailer rigs.
- Describe the professionalism required of today's drivers.

INTRODUCTION

Trucking: Tractor-Trailer Driver Handbook/Workbook begins with the fundamentals. Developed as a step-by-step guide for training those individuals who wish to enter the trucking industry as tractor-trailer drivers, this book provides a solid foundation of entry-level knowledge and skills. As an aspiring driver, you will find this book to be the best source of information and instruction available.

▶ **Figure 1-1**

Professional drivers help keep the nation's economy moving.

As you work through this book, each chapter will provide you with basic knowledge on a variety of topics as well as the characteristics of a professional driver and the skills needed to perform the important work required of transportation professionals. You will learn basic laws, how to establish goodwill with the public, how to maintain the records necessary in your job, and how to perform every aspect of professional driving safely.

Because professional drivers provide the momentum behind America's economy, you also will learn how to maintain your health and physical stamina as well as how to safely handle the demanding job of professional driving. Your presence on America's highways means the nation's economy is moving and still growing **(see Figure 1–1).**

It has been said, "If you have it, a truck brought it," and this, in a nutshell, captures the true importance of professional drivers. An entire nation's economy depends on the legions of professional drivers who move freight over our highways each day. Without professional drivers and the trucking industry, no city, no neighborhood, no family, and no individual in the United States could enjoy the comforts and quality of life available today.

Trucks transport almost everything we eat, wear, use, or need from origin to final destination **(see Figure 1–2).**

Oh the joy of the open road

▶ *Welcome to my world—the joy of the open road . . . where it takes a true professional to make the grade!*

▶ **Figure 1-2**

Trucks transport almost everything we eat, wear, use, or need from the point of origin to the final destination.

The needs of families, business, industry, farms, the medical community, government, and education are served by trucks—trucks that haul farm products from the field to the processing plant and then to the market.

Trucks also move crude oil from the oil field to the refinery or from barges to petrochemical plants, and then from these plants to service stations or homes. Companies that mine raw materials—such as coal, ore, and chemicals—rely on professional drivers for transport from mines to processing plants and from plants to manufacturers and, finally, to the retail market **(see Figure 1–3).**

Figure 1–3

Trucks move crude oil from the field to the refinery.

This country's 2 million-plus fleet of tractor-trailers hauls 3 of every 4 tons of goods in this country each year. This means 735 billion ton-miles of freight are carried over America's highways by professional drivers every year (1 ton-mile equals 1 ton of goods carried 1 mile).

More than 8 million Americans work in the trucking industry, including drivers, dock workers, dispatchers, safety directors, administrative support, and sales personnel. Almost 13 percent of all Americans depend on employment within the trucking industry—more than 33 million people.

Figure 1–4

Professional truck drivers transport the basic necessities of life as well as the luxuries.

"Good stuff—trucks bring it," the center-piece statement of the American Trucking Association's current image campaign, is a true statement **(see Figure 1–4).** It is also true that without the efforts of a professional truck driver, you would not have access to the basic necessities of life.

THE U.S. TRUCKING INDUSTRY

Firms of all kinds rely on trucks for pickup and delivery of goods because no other form of transportation can deliver goods door to door. Goods carried by ship, train, or airplane usually reach their final destinations by trucks **(see Figure 1–5).**

Figure 1–5

The professional driver is a skilled and safe tractor-trailer operator.

In the beginning, goods were transported from town to town or from factory to consumer by horse-drawn wagons. Because teams of horses were often used, the drivers were called teamsters. At the turn of the 20th century, a typical teamster's day included 12 to 18 hours of work, 7 days a week. The average wage was $2.00 per day. If a load was damaged, lost, or a customer refused to pay, company owners would take the costs out of the team-driver's meager wage. In 1912, the first transcontinental delivery of goods was made by motor truck. Soon after that, horses were put out to pasture, the wagons disappeared, and the rest, as they say, is history.

Today, new technologies are changing the way truck drivers work, especially long-distance truck drivers. Satellites and global positioning systems (GPSs) link many trucks with company headquarters. Troubleshooting information, directions, weather reports, and other important communications can be delivered to the truck, anywhere, within seconds. Drivers can easily communicate with the dispatcher to discuss delivery schedules and courses of action in the event of mechanical problems. The satellite linkup also allows the dispatcher to track the truck's location, fuel consumption, and engine performance. Many drivers also work with computerized inventory tracking equipment.

Over the years, as new technology has been developed, truck driving has become less physically demanding, because most trucks now have comfortable seats, proper ventilation, and improved, ergonomically designed cabs.

In 2002, there were about 3.2 million truck drivers moving freight down America's highways **(see Figure 1–6).** Of these workers, 431,000 were driver/sales workers and 2.8 million were truck

FACTS YOU NEED TO KNOW ABOUT TRUCKING

- The U.S. trucking transportation industry expands by approximately 5 percent every year.

- Approximately 70 percent of all U.S. communities depend solely on trucking for delivery of their goods and commodities.

- Approximately 300,000 new drivers will be needed to support the current transportation system every year for the next 10 years.

- It is projected that by 2008, the trucking industry will haul 9.3 billion tons, or over 64 percent, of total U.S. freight.

- In the United States, approximately 15.5 million commercial trucks are in operation, including 1.9 million combination units.

- Approximately 9.5 million people are employed in jobs directly related to trucking.

- There are approximately 3.08 million truck drivers in the United States. Of that number, approximately 5.7 percent are female.

- In 1999, there were 9.5 million commercial driver's license holders.

- Trucking transportation employs more than 9 million people, more than the population of forty-two of the fifty American states.

- The total distance driven by commercial trucks each year in the United States exceeds 150 billion miles, the equivalent to about 640 trips from the earth to the moon.

- In the year 2000, professional drivers in the United States drove 200 billion miles, a distance equal to 1,000 round trips to the sun.

- As of 2004, the U.S. trucking industry carried 11.6 billion tons of freight, generating $574 billion in revenue.

- In the United States, the average truck travels 64,200 miles per year, a distance equivalent to two and one-half trips around the world.

- A single truck averages 420 miles per trip.

- Speeding was a factor in about 17 percent of all injury crashes and 20 percent of all fatal crashes that involved a tractor-trailer.

▶ **Figure 1–6**

Trucking is an essential part of America's economy.

drivers. The truck transportation industry employed almost one quarter of all truck drivers and driver/sales workers in the United States. Over 10 percent of all truck drivers and driver/sales workers were self-employed. Of these, a significant number were owner-operators who either served a variety of businesses independently or leased their services and trucks to a trucking company.

The trucking industry continues to be an essential part of America's economy. The lives of every citizen of every age are affected by professional drivers moving freight from one point to another—across the city, across the state, and across the nation **(see Figure 1–7)**.

▶ **Figure 1–7**

Truck drivers are essential to America's economy.

Tightly regulated by federal and state laws, U.S. motor carriers seek drivers who are not only skilled and safe tractor-trailer rig operators, but are also professionals in their attitudes and approach to every job. In addition, carriers of every size continually work to improve safety in the workplace as well as driver safety on the nation's streets and highways **(see Figure 1–8)**. Many companies annually reward drivers earning safe driving records for their professional performance.

America's trucking industry has evolved over more than 100 years of service and is divided into two distinct categories of operation. Carriers that operate within the borders of one state are known as **intrastate carriers** and are subject to that particular state's rules and regulations. Carriers that move cargoes from one state to another are known as **interstate carriers** and are subject to federal regulations as well as the regulations of the state in which they operate. State regulations are generally the same as federal regulations but often impose their own cargo size and weight rules as well as insurance requirements.

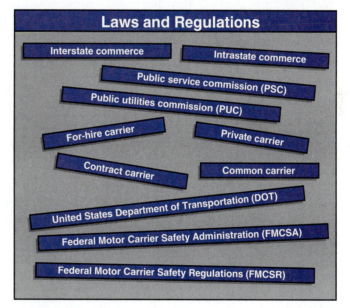

Laws and Regulations

- Interstate commerce
- Intrastate commerce
- Public service commission (PSC)
- Public utilities commission (PUC)
- For-hire carrier
- Private carrier
- Contract carrier
- Common carrier
- United States Department of Transportation (DOT)
- Federal Motor Carrier Safety Administration (FMCSA)
- Federal Motor Carrier Safety Regulations (FMCSR)

▶ **Figure 1–8**

The trucking industry is regulated by federal and state laws and regulations.

Carriers can be classified as for-hire carriers and private carriers.

> **For-hire carriers** are companies that haul cargo for their clients by truck.

> **Private carriers** are corporations that use trucks to transport their own goods with their own fleet of trucks.

For-hire carriers can further be divided into common carriers and contract carriers.

> **Common carriers** are motor carriers that offer services to all individuals and businesses.

> **Contract carriers** are motor carriers that are under contract to transport the freight of a customer. The contract sets the rates and other terms of service.

Any common carrier transporting cargo by truck in interstate or foreign commerce must first receive authority to operate from the **U.S. Department of Transportation (DOT).** That carrier must also file the rates it charges customers to haul their freight with the DOT. Contract carriers and private carriers do not have to file rates.

HOW THE TRUCKING INDUSTRY IS REGULATED

More than 80,000 various government entities regulate the trucking industry. These include federal, state, county, and city authorities. Federal laws regulate commerce that crosses state lines. State governments, including counties, cities, towns, and villages, regulate routes, speed limits, truck loading, and parking zones. State laws also regulate commerce within each state **(see Figure 1–9).**

KNOW YOUR STATE REGULATIONS

1. What is the speed limit for commercial vehicles on interstate highways? County and local roads?

2. What is the maximum weight limit for a combination of vehicles such as a tractor-semitrailer? Straight truck pulling a trailer?

3. Who should you contact for an overweight or oversize vehicle?

4. What is the maximum legal length for a combination truck and single trailer? Double trailers, if allowed? Triples?

5. What is the maximum vehicle height allowed without a permit?

6. What is the maximum width allowed for a commercial vehicle?

7. How far can rearview mirrors extend from the side of the vehicle?

8. How far can a load extend from the vehicle?

9. How many hours can you legally drive?

10. How many hours can you legally be on duty?

11. If your vehicle is involved in an accident, what must you do?

12. What items do you need to bring to the licensing office to apply for your CDL?

13. Which commercial drivers need a CDL?

14. What class of CDL will you need?

15. Do experienced commercial drivers with a good driving record need to take the CDL knowledge (written) and skill (driving) tests to get their new CDL? Can you obtain a waiver?

16. What type of CDL endorsements do you need?

17. What group of drivers are exempted by state law from having to obtain a CDL?

▶ **Figure 1–9**

Professional drivers must know and obey the laws in the states where they travel.

The Motor Carrier Act of 1935

In 1935, the Motor Carrier Act was passed by the U.S. Congress. This legislation created the Bureau of Motor Carriers of the Interstate Commerce Commission to develop and enforce safety regulations in the trucking industry. The safety regulations developed by the Interstate Commerce Commission are entitled the Federal Motor Carrier Safety Regulations (FMCSR).

The Commercial Motor Vehicle Safety Act of 1986

The **Commercial Motor Vehicle Safety Act of 1986 (CMVSA/86)** ensures that all commercial vehicle drivers are qualified to drive. The act also prevents professional drivers from having more than one **commercial driver's license (CDL)** and disqualifies drivers from driving if they commit certain traffic law violations. The CMVSA/86 applies to:

- Interstate drivers and carriers
- Intrastate drivers and carriers
- **Commercial motor vehicle (CMV)** drivers who drive vehicles with a **gross vehicle weight rating (GVWR)** of more than 26,000 pounds
- Drivers of vehicles carrying 16 or more passengers (including the driver)
- Drivers of any vehicles transporting hazardous materials requiring placards

CMVSA/86 states that employers shall not employ any driver of a CMV who has more than one CDL, whose CDL has been suspended, revoked or cancelled, or who has been disqualified from driving under the FMCSR. The CMVSA/86 requires that drivers have only one CDL, notify their employer and the state that issued the CDL within 30 days of conviction of any traffic violation (except parking violations), and provide every employer with information about all driving jobs held during the past 10 years. The FMCSR requires drivers to notify their employers at once if their CDL is suspended, revoked, or cancelled, even though the CMVSA/86 does not require this.

The Motor Carrier Safety Improvement Act of 1999

The purposes of the Motor Carrier Safety Improvement Act of 1999 (MCSIA/99) are to:

1. Establish a Federal Motor Carrier Safety Administration (FMCSA)
2. Reduce the number and severity of large-truck involved crashes through more CMV and driver inspections and carrier compliance reviews; stronger enforcement, expedited completion of rules, and sound research; and effective CDL testing, record keeping, and sanctions

Key provisions of the MCSIA/99 are:

Establishment of the Federal Motor Carrier Safety Administration:
- The act establishes the FMCSA (effective January 1, 2000) within the Department of Transportation.
- The act requires development of a long-term strategy to improve CMV, operator, and motor carrier safety which includes an annual plan and schedule. Progress must be assessed semi-annually and reported to Congress annually.
- The act allows the establishment of a Commercial Motor Vehicle Safety Advisory Committee. This committee will include representatives of the motor carrier industry, drivers, safety advocates manufacturers, safety enforcement officials, law enforcement agencies of border states, and others. No one group may constitute a majority. The advisory committee shall provide advice to the secretary of transportation on commercial motor vehicle safety regulations and other matters relating to the FMCSA.
- The act establishes department-wide safeguards against conflicts of interest in research.

Commercial Driver's Licensing:
- The act creates *new* 1-year disqualifying offenses for (1) driving a CMV with a revoked, suspended, or cancelled CDL or driving while disqualified and (2) conviction for causing a fatality through the negligent or criminal operation of a CMV. Lifetime disqualification is *required* for multiple violations or convictions.
- The secretary may disqualify drivers for up to 30 days if their operation of a CMV would create an imminent hazard.
- Criteria must be established for disqualifying a CDL holder (1) convicted of a serious offense involving a vehicle that is not a CMV that resulted in license suspension or revocation, or (2) convicted of a drug- or alcohol-related offense involving another type of vehicle.

- The list of serious traffic violations for which a CDL holder can be disqualified is expanded to include:
  - Driving a CMV without obtaining a CDL
  - Driving a CMV without a CDL in possession
  - Driving without a required endorsement
- The federal medical qualification certificate must be made part of the commercial driver's license requirements.
- A rulemaking for a special CDL endorsement for drivers of school buses must be conducted.
- The department must study the feasibility and merits of having medical review officers (MROs) or employers report positive drug tests of CDL holders to the licensing state and requiring prospective employers to check with the state.
- A uniform system must be developed to transmit data among states on convictions for violations of traffic control laws by CDL holders. This completes the process started by the CDL program, establishing one accurate, complete license for each driver.
- States are required to:
  - Request a driver's record from another state that has issued the driver a license before issuing or renewing a CDL
  - Include information on the underlying violation when reporting disqualification, revocation, suspension, or cancellation of a CDL
  - Include information on all violations of motor vehicle traffic control laws committed by CDL holders in the driver's record
  - Record information on traffic violations received from other states in a driver's record; states may not allow information on violations to be masked or withheld from the CDL holder's record
  - Notify the licensing state of violations by CDL holders within 10 days after violations are committed
- States may not issue special licenses or permits to CDL holders.
- Before issuing any motor vehicle operator's license, a state must check the National Driver Register and the Commercial Driver's License Information System (CDLIS).
- If a state is not substantially complying with federal CDL requirements, the secretary must prohibit the state from processing and issuing CDLs and withhold Motor Carrier Safety Assistance Program (MCSAP) funding increases until compliance is achieved.
- Permits emergency grants of up to $1 million to states having difficulty meeting CDL program requirements.

Motor Carrier Safety Initiatives:

- Progress in achieving the goal of reducing fatalities in truck and bus crashes by 50 percent must be reported to Congress by May 25, 2000.
- Recommendations of the DOT inspector general must be implemented and reports on progress must be made to Congress every 90 days.
- Staffing standards must be established for federal and state safety inspectors in international border areas; the number of inspectors may not fall below FY 2000 levels.
- The definition of *imminent hazard* is changed to refer to a condition that substantially increases the likelihood of serious injury or death.
- The General Accounting Office is required to study the effectiveness of enforcement of household goods consumer protection rules and other potential methods of enforcement. The limit for mandatory arbitration is raised from $1,000 to $5,000.

- The toll-free telephone hotline for reporting motor carrier safety violations is required to be operational 24 hours a day.

- Innovative methods of improving motor carrier traffic law compliance may be developed, including use of imaging technologies.

FEDERAL AND STATE REGULATING AGENCIES
Federal Regulating Agencies

The **Federal Motor Carrier Safety Administration** was established as a separate administration within the U.S. Department of Transportation on January 1, 2000, pursuant to the Motor Carrier Safety Improvement Act of 1999. FMCSA's primary mission is to reduce crashes, injuries, and fatalities involving large trucks and buses. Headquartered in Washington, DC, FMCSA includes more than 1,000 employees in the fifty states and the District of Columbia. The agency's goal is to improve bus and truck safety and to save lives.

To achieve its mission, FMCSA:

- Develops and enforces data-driven regulations that balance motor carrier (truck and bus company) safety with industry efficiency

- Harnesses safety information systems to focus on higher risk carriers in enforcing the safety regulations

- Targets educational messages to carriers, commercial drivers, and the public

- Partners with stakeholders including federal, state, and local enforcement agencies, the motor carrier industry, safety groups, and organized labor on efforts to reduce bus- and truck-related crashes

Key programs of the FMCSA are:

Federal Motor Carrier Safety Regulations (FMCSR)—FMCSA develops, maintains, and enforces federal regulations that promote carrier safety, industry productivity, and new technologies. These regulations establish safe operating requirements for commercial vehicle drivers, carriers, vehicles, and vehicle equipment.

Hazardous Materials Regulations (HMR)—FMCSA enforces these regulations, which are designed to ensure the safe and secure transportation of **hazardous materials.** These rules address the classification of hazardous materials, proper packaging, employee training, hazard communication, and operational requirements.

Commercial Driver's License Program—FMCSA develops, monitors, and ensures compliance with the commercial driver licensing standards for drivers, carriers, and states.

Motor Carrier Safety Identification and Information Systems—FMCSA provides safety data state and national crash statistics, current analysis results, and detailed motor carrier safety performance data to industry and the public. This data allow federal and state enforcement officials to target inspections and investigations on higher risk carriers, vehicles, and drivers.

New Entrant Safety Assurance Process—FMCSA ensures that new entrant motor carriers (carriers applying for a new USDOT number) are knowledgeable about applicable federal motor carrier safety and hazardous materials regulations.

Motor Carrier Safety Assistance Program (MCSAP)—A federal grant program that provides states with financial assistance to hire staff and implement strategies to enforce FMCSR and HMR. Funds for this program are used to conduct roadside inspections and review motor carriers' compliance with FMCSR and HMR. The program's funds promote detection and correction of commercial motor vehicle safety defects, commercial vehicle driver deficiencies, and unsafe motor carrier practices before they become contributing factors to crashes and hazardous materials incidents.

Performance and Registration Information Systems Management (PRISM)—A federal–state partnership that makes safe performance a requirement for obtaining and keeping commercial vehicle registration. PRISM links federal motor carrier safety records with the state's vehicle registration system. The USDOT number of the carrier responsible for safety is identified at the vehicle level, allowing the state to determine a carrier's safety fitness before issuing license plates. Safety performance is continuously monitored, and carriers prohibited by FMCSA from operating in interstate commerce may have their ability to register vehicles denied. PRISM plays a key role in FMCSA's effort to remove high-risk carriers from our highways.

Research and Technology (R&T)—R&T work is aimed at gaining fundamental and applied knowledge in order to develop new methods and technologies to enhance truck and bus safety and security.

Border and International Safety—FMCSA supports the development of compatible motor carrier safety requirements and procedures throughout North America. FMCSA works closely with the governments of Canada and Mexico to ensure that these countries' motor carriers, drivers, and vehicles operating in the United States meet the same safety standards as U.S. carriers.

Safety Education and Outreach—FMCSA implements educational strategies to increase motor carrier compliance with the safety regulations and reduce the likelihood of a commercial vehicle crash. Messages are aimed at all highway users including passenger car drivers, truck drivers, pedestrians, and bicyclists.

Household Goods Program—FMCSA regulates interstate household goods movers and requires them to register with the agency. FMCSA has developed a website (http://www. fmcsa.dot.gov/factsfigs/moving.htm) to assist consumers moving across state lines.

For more information about FMCSA's safety programs, contact the Federal Motor Carrier Safety Administration, 400 Seventh Street SW, Washington, DC 20590. Phone: 202-366-2519. Internet: http://www.fmcsa.dot.gov.

Other Federal Regulatory Agencies and Departments

The **Pipeline and Hazardous Materials Safety Administration (PHMSA)** regulates and classifies hazardous materials. It also sets standards for shipping containers, shipping documents, marking, labeling, and placarding **(see Figure 1–10).**

Hazardous material is also regulated by the **Environmental Protection Agency (EPA),** the **Nuclear Regulatory Commission (NRC),** and the **Occupational Safety and Health Administration (OSHA).**

The **National Transportation Safety Board (NTSB)** investigates accidents and offers solutions to prevent future accidents.

Placards

▶ Figure 1–10

Placards help fire and emergency personnel identify dangerous cargo in the event of an accident or spill.

The **Department of Homeland Security** is also involved in maintaining safety and security within all facets of the transportation industry. Beginning in 2005, the Department of Homeland Security will provide a $21 million grant for use in the American Trucking Association (ATA) Highway Watch® Program. This cooperative agreement with the ATA will expand the Highway Watch® program, which trains highway professionals to identify and report safety and security concerns on our nation's roads. The program will provide training and communications to prepare hundreds of thousands of transportation professionals to respond in the event they or their cargo are the target of a terrorist attack and to share valuable intelligence with Homeland Security if they detect potential threats.

At this time, because of an increased emphasis on safety and security in all American industries, new laws and regulations are being decided. To review the most up-to-date listing of rules and regulations for the trucking industry, go to www.fmcsa.dot.gov.

State Regulations

Every state in the United States regulates motor carriers and has established commercial motor vehicle laws. Each state's **Department of Motor Vehicles (DMV)** usually assists in making these laws, which:

- Decide maximum loads trucks may carry
- Decide maximum length, width, and weight of **Commercial Motor Vehicles (CMVs)**
- License drivers, including the testing required to issue the **Commercial Driver License (CDL)**
- Collect road and fuel taxes
- Set minimum insurance requirements

Professional drivers must know and obey all federal regulations and must know and obey the state laws in the states they travel.

COMMERCIAL MOTOR VEHICLES

As a professional driver, you may be required to drive any number of commercial motor vehicles. The following basic terms and descriptions will help to acquaint you with an assortment of CMVs on the road today.

Truck Tractors

A **truck tractor,** or **tractor,** is used to pull one or more vehicles **(see Figure 1–11).** Tractors may pull semitrailers, tankers, flatbeds, lowboys, carhaulers and other types of vehicles. The tractor is built to carry only part of the load of the vehicle it pulls.

Conventional tractors house the engine under the tractor's hood and provide a smoother ride because the driver sits between the front and rear wheels. The conventional cab's longer wheelbase makes maneuvering in tight spaces more difficult **(see Figure 1–12).**

▶ **Figure 1–11**

A tractor is used to pull one or more vehicles, such as semitrailers, tankers, or carhaulers.

▶ **Figure 1–12**

A conventional tractor.

▶ **Figure 1–13**

Straight truck.

▶ **Figure 1–14**

A two-axle truck with a single drive axle.

▶ **Figure 1–15**

Tandem axle configuration.

Both **straight trucks** (single-unit vehicles with engine, cab, and cargo compartment all on the same frame) **(see Figure 1–13)** and truck tractors have a front axle and one or more rear axles. The front axle is the steering axle. The rear axle that is powered is called the **drive axle.**

A truck or tractor with only one axle in the rear is called a two-axle truck with a single drive axle **(see Figure 1–14).** The wheelbase of the single drive axle tractor is usually shorter, which allows easier turning in small spaces, but the shorter wheelbase also limits the amount of weight the truck can carry.

To carry heavier loads, another axle must be added to lengthen the wheelbase. The two axles are called a **tandem (see Figure 1–15).**

A **tandem axle tractor** usually has two drive axles, also called **twin screws.** Twin screws give the truck more traction in slippery or extreme conditions.

A driveshaft runs between the differential of the front drive axle and the differential of the rear drive axle. Many twin screws also have a differential lock to distribute power evenly to each axle. The lock is engaged only in slick, slippery conditions and at low speeds.

Some tandems have only one drive axle. The nondriven axle, when mounted behind the drive axle, is called the **tag axle.** When the nondriven axle is mounted ahead of the drive axle, it is called the **pusher axle.**

Wheels with tires mounted in pairs on each end of the axle are called **duals.** A single-drive-axle tractor with dual wheels on the rear axles has 10 wheels **(see Figure 1–16).** Some fleets use the

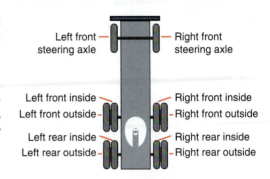

Figure 1–16
A dual axle tractor.

"super single" instead of duals. The super single is a large, single tire that has less rolling resistance than duals, resulting in better fuel economy.

Each wheel on a tractor is identified in **Figure 1–17.** When a driver reports a tire problem to the dispatcher or maintenance shop, these identifications are used, being sure to call each wheel by its proper name.

Left front steering axle — Right front steering axle

Left front inside — Right front inside
Left front outside — Right front outside

Left rear inside — Right rear inside
Left rear outside — Right rear outside

Figure 1–17
Tractor wheel identification.

Trailers

A **trailer** is a vehicle built for hauling cargo **(see Figure 1–18).** As the use of the combustion engine continued in its popularity, delivery vehicles were soon designed to sit on the Model-T chassis. By the 1930s, trailers were developed to be used in tandem with motor trucks, and by the end of that decade it became apparent that the semitrailer would become an integral part of modern truck transportation.

Today's trailers have one or more axles and two or more wheels. **Full trailers (see Figure 1–19)** are designed so that no part of the trailer's weight rests on the vehicle pulling it. The front of a

Figure 1–18
Trailers are vehicles designed to haul cargo.

Figure 1–19
A full trailer is designed so that no part of its weight rests on the vehicle pulling it.

Figure 1–20

A semitrailer has axles only at the rear of the trailer. The front of the trailer is supported by the tractor.

Figure 1–21

Fifth wheel.

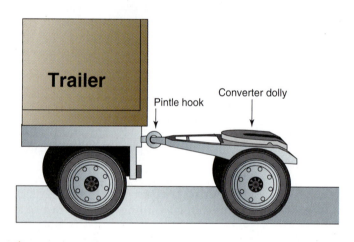

Figure 1–22

A semitrailer is made into a full trailer by coupling it to the fifth wheel on a converter dolly.

Figure 1–23

Different types of semitrailers.

semitrailer rests on a "fifth wheel" mounted over the rear axle of the tractor **(see Figure 1–20).** The **fifth wheel** has locking jaws in its center into which the trailer's kingpin fits **(see Figure 1–21).** This couples the units together. The fifth wheel is the pivot point between the tractor and the trailer and bears the weight of the front of the semitrailer.

A semitrailer can be made into a full trailer by coupling it to the fifth wheel on a **converter dolly (see Figure 1–22).** The dolly is hooked onto the rear of another trailer. When you put a dolly on a semitrailer, it becomes a full trailer.

There are many different types of semitrailers. Some of them are illustrated in **Figure 1–23.**

When a trailer is added to a tractor or a straight truck, it is called a **combination vehicle** or **combination rig.** Some of the many types of combination vehicles are shown in **Figure 1–24.** These combination rigs often have different types of wheel and axle arrangements.

Other types of combination vehicles include:

Rocky Mountain double —This rig has two trailers. The tractor has three axles and the rig has a total of seven axles. Rocky Mountain doubles are not allowed to run in some states.

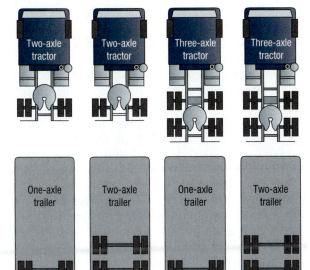

▶ **Figure 1–24**
Combination vehicles.

▶ **Figure 1–25**
A double trailer has a single axle trailer pulling a 28-foot semitrailer or 28-foot trailer.

Standard double—This rig consists of a single-axle tractor pulling a 28-foot semitrailer and a 28-foot trailer. These rigs are not legal in some states **(see Figure 1–25).**

Turnpike double—This rig consists of a tandem axle tractor pulling a 48-foot semitrailer and a 48-foot trailer. These rigs are not legal in some states.

18-Wheeler—This rig is the most familiar sight on the highway. It consists of a 10-wheeled tractor and a semitrailer with eight wheels. There are five axles on an 18-wheeler.

BECOMING A PROFESSIONAL

Truck drivers who are successful always drive responsibly and act in a professional manner. They:

- Know their jobs and are responsible for each detail
- Maintain clean, dependable vehicles
- Have a positive attitude
- Practice safety at all times
- Make responsible, independent judgments when necessary
- Are accountable for their driving and their actions
- Know and understand the equipment they use

Why does truck driving require professionals?

- It requires specialized knowledge, specific skills, and attitudes that result from intense preparation, training, and experience.
- It is based on a specialized body of knowledge, regulations, practices, and procedures.
- It requires that all driver personnel meet the requirements for the profession through licensing, physical examination, and other testing.

Professional drivers must conduct business in an ethical manner while on the road, handling cargo, or interacting with the customer.

Professionals in any field are expected to act and make independent judgments based on their knowledge, skill, and experience—in any situation to the best of their ability. Professional drivers are accountable for their behavior on the road, while handling cargo, in their interactions with customers and coworkers, and in their handling of required paperwork **(see Figure 1–26).** In every instance, professional drivers are expected to conduct business in an ethical manner and, in every way, to be committed to the public good, on and off the job.

Today's motor carriers work in a competitive environment where profit margins continue to shrink. Carriers want drivers who perform in a manner that is not only professional but also efficient. They entrust expensive equipment and valuable cargoes to the driver's care. Carriers also know that drivers present the company's corporate image to their clients and the public, on the road and in public places such as roadside parks, truckstops, and destination locations.

Competent, safe, courteous, and responsible drivers are invaluable to a company and are a credit to the industry. Drivers who become a hazard or a liability will have short careers in this vital service industry.

During the aftermath of the terrorist attacks on the World Trade Center in New York City and the Pentagon in Washington, DC, truck drivers became the lifeline for America. In this emergency situation, the entire country and the U.S. business community relied on professional drivers to keep the wheels of commerce turning—drivers with strong personal values, above-average commitment to their industry, and a can-do attitude in the face of tragedy.

Professional tractor-trailer drivers must also rank above average in the following areas.

Physical and mental abilities: The driver meets government, industry, and company standards.

Skill: The driver is qualified by training, experience, and desire to operate specific vehicle types (tractor-trailer, tankers, etc.).

Safety standards: The driver understands and practices safe driving methods, obeys the law, knows more, and is safer in all highway situations than the average driver. The driver remains concentrated on the highway environment, reading clues, and working to avoid hazards or accidents.

Tolerance and courtesy: The driver can accept negative traffic behaviors and blatant road rage from other drivers without becoming involved or attempting to get even; cooperate with other road users at all times; and communicate regularly with dispatchers.

Efficiency: The driver delivers cargoes on time and works courteously with others while obeying laws and regulations; recognizes a carrier cannot be successful unless schedules are met; and does everything possible to use fuel efficiently.

Knowledge: The driver knows government regulations and follows industry requirements for driving and handling cargo. The driver maintains a current knowledge of rule changes and new regulations that affect the professionals in the industry.

Professional drivers understand *they ARE the trucking industry* in the eyes of their customers and the motoring public. They know they must always perform at higher skill levels than the average drivers, and they realize that driving well is not enough. They must also conduct themselves in a courteous manner and practice the highest levels of safety on the road, at the dock, and wherever they drive. Professional drivers also know they must continually improve their skills and knowledge of the equipment they use and the technology that supports their industry.

A new generation of trained, responsible, professional drivers is critical to improving highway safety across the nation; and, as carriers hire the next generation of drivers, they continue to look for such individuals who will represent the best of the profession; men and women who consistently employ good judgment, common sense, courtesy, and safety in every situation.

SAFETY

Safety is the tractor-trailer driver's highest priority. The ultimate goal of the U.S. transportation industry is to move cargo from one point to another without damage to the equipment or cargo and without injury to the driver or those nearby.

Professional driving can be one of the most dangerous and demanding jobs in American transportation today. Because professional driving is such an integral part of this nation's economy, the transportation industry seeks personnel who consistently meet the highest levels of safety standards. Professional drivers today must not only know their vehicles and be highly skilled in every task, but they must also be skilled professionals who are trained to be constantly aware of their surrounding environment.

Accidents happen in the blink of an eye, and truck drivers must be constantly on guard, reading clues from other drivers, road conditions, weather conditions, and their own vehicles, so they can avoid difficult maneuvering situations.

Professional drivers must always think and look ahead to avoid hazards. They must use common sense, always work at the highest level of alertness, and have the training and experience it takes to avoid costly and dangerous situations.

TRAINING AND INSTRUCTION

Professional drivers are required to prepare themselves for their careers by earning their CDL and by taking training that will ensure their safe handling of tractor-trailer rigs in all situations, from highway driving and backing up to docks to defensive driving maneuvers and responding to emergencies of all types. The more driving skills gained from training schools and other training opportunities, the more attention drivers can pay to on-the-job learning experiences. Formal training and one-on-one work with an experienced instructor is invaluable when learning to drive a tractor-trailer rig.

A significant part of the training process is devoted to identifying individual driver strengths and weaknesses. Drivers who realize their weak points can devote time with an instructor to making that weakness a strength. Training also allows new drivers to understand the capabilities and limitations of the motor vehicle, particularly when training includes driving the motor vehicle in both good and difficult weather conditions and terrain (see Figure 1–27).

▶ **Figure 1–27**

Professional drivers are trained to drive safely in good and bad weather.

Driving experiences in a formal educational environment also allow drivers to identify hazards and to learn how to respond to these hazards with the guidance of an instructor. By identifying hazards before they become huge obstacles, professional drivers can learn to control many of the safety factors they will encounter in their over-the-road experiences.

Emergencies may happen, regardless of the expertise and skills of the driver, and may happen quickly. Some emergencies occur due to road conditions, traffic, or unsafe actions by drivers of other vehicles. In these situations, the professional driver should have the capability to analyze the possible hazards and determine the best and safest possible action.

According to safety statistics, most CMV drivers tend to have more accidents during the early months of their careers. Some of these accidents are due to lack of training or experience behind the wheel. For this reason, many carriers now offer new drivers the opportunity to ride with more experienced drivers the first few months of their employment. This provides the new driver with a wealth of knowledge and experience before occupying the driver's seat for the first time.

Improved vehicles, improved safety, more training opportunities, and formal education focus on making America's highways safe for professional drivers and all other highway users. One of the priorities for professional drivers across the nation is promoting courtesy over the road. Carriers are also working to make America's highways safe for their employees and the jobs they do.

As a new professional driver, learn as much as you can, ask questions of your instructors, practice what you learn, and make it your personal priority to make America's roads safe for yourself and the industry you will represent.

SUMMARY

This chapter begins your study and your understanding of the U.S. trucking industry and how it operates. You have become familiar with some of the agencies that regulate the transportation industry as well as the various types of carriers and how they operate with these regulations. You have also reviewed differences among the various types of commercial motor vehicles on the highway today and learned some of the terms and acronyms (abbreviations) for various regulatory agencies as well as for terms related to the industry itself.

Use this chapter as a foundation for your personal development as a professional driver, understanding the personal traits and values necessary to be a success behind the wheel and over the road.

KEY TERMS

Combination vehicle or rig
Commercial driver's license (CDL)
Commercial motor vehicle (CMV)
Commercial Motor Vehicle Safety Act of 1986 (CMVSA/86)
Common carrier
Contract carrier
Conventional tractor

Converter dolly
Department of Homeland Security
Department of Motor Vehicles (DMV)
Drive axle
Duals
18-wheeler
Environmental Protection Agency (EPA)

Federal Motor Carrier Safety Administration (FMCSA)
Federal Motor Carrier Safety Regulations (FMCSR)
Fifth wheel
For-hire carrier
Full trailer
Gross vehicle weight rating (GVWR)
Hazardous materials
Interstate carrier

Intrastate carrier
Motor Carrier Safety
   Assistance Program
   (MCSAP)
Motor carriers
National Transportation
   Safety Board (NTSB)
Nuclear Regulatory
   Commission (NRC)
Occupational Safety and
   Health Administration
   (OSHA)

Office of Hazardous Materials
   Transportation (OHMT)
Pipeline and Hazardous
   Materials Safety
   Administration (PHMSA)
Private carrier
Pusher axle
Rocky Mountain doubles
Semitrailer
Standard double
Straight truck

Tag axle
Tandem
Tandem axle tractor
Tractor
Trailer
Truck tractor
Turnpike double
Twin screws
U.S. Department of
   Transportation (U.S. DOT)

REVIEW QUESTIONS

1. Despite extensive deregulation of the trucking industry and transfer of licensing and monitoring of professional truck drivers to the states, the _____ remains the sole safety standard by which professional truck drivers and motor carriers are required to follow in the operation of commercial vehicles.

   a. Hazardous Materials Regulations (HMR)

   b. Federal Motor Carriers Safety Regulations (FMCSR)

   c. Motor Carrier Safety Assistance Program (MCSAP)

   d. Commercial Driver's License (CDL)

2. A tandem axle tractor has how many rear axles?

   a. three

   b. four

   c. none

   d. two

3. A single-drive-axle tractor has how many rear axles?

   a. two

   b. two in the rear and one in the front

   c. one

   d. none, as the term refers to tractors with front wheel drive

4. Wheels with tires mounted in pairs on each end of the axle are called _____.

   a. duals

   b. singles

   c. quads

   d. none of the above

5. The front of a semitrailer has _____ axle(s)?

   a. one

   b. two

   c. dual

   d. none

6. The device that connects a trailer to a tractor is called a _____.

   a. fifth wheel

   b. bypass

   c. dual wheel

   d. tandem

7. Regarding tractors with only one drive axle, the nondrive axle mounted behind the drive axle is called a _____.

   a. driver axle

   b. pusher axle

   c. tag axle

   d. steering axle

8. Single-unit vehicles with engine, cab, and cargo compartment all on the same frame are called _____.

   a. rigid trucks

   b. straight trucks

   c. truck tractors

   d. none of the above

9. Why does truck driving require professionals?

   a. It requires specialized knowledge, specific skills, and attitudes that result from intense preparation, training, and experience.

   b. It is based on a specialized body of knowledge, regulations, practices, and procedures.

   c. It requires that all driver personnel meet the requirements for the profession through licensing, physical examinations, and other testing.

   d. a, b, and c

10. To avoid hazards and difficult maneuvering situations, a professional driver must constantly be on guard, reading clues from _____.

   a. other drivers

   b. a, c, and d

   c. road conditions

   d. their own vehicle

Vehicle Inspections

OBJECTIVES

When you have completed this chapter, you should be able to:

- Describe a routine to use for a thorough and complete pretrip inspection.
- Recognize damaged, loose, or missing parts and system leaks.
- Explain the importance of correcting malfunctions before beginning each trip.
- Understand and use federal and state regulations for your inspection.
- Explain the steps for en route and posttrip inspections.

INTRODUCTION

As a professional driver, safety is your number-one priority. Safety is your first priority when your rig is being loaded, during your pretrip inspection, on the road, when you are delivering your cargo, and during your posttrip inspection **(see Figure 2–1).**

▶ **Figure 2–1**

Safety is the number one priority for a professional driver.

Because today's tractor-trailer rig has become increasingly more technologically advanced and complex, it requires consistent maintenance and constant attention, and also that professional drivers learn more skills for optimum performance.

Each of your rig's systems must be regularly inspected to assure that each part is intact and operating at maximum efficiency. Fluid levels must be constantly checked and refilled when necessary. Routine maintenance must be thoroughly and expertly performed.

The most critical key, however, to your rig's optimum performance is your timely, step-by-step pretrip and posttrip inspections.

This chapter will emphasize the critical nature of these inspections and will provide an efficient routine for you to follow each time you check your rig.

CAUTION!

No one in America has a more dangerous job than a CMV driver, and a professional driver is aware of the importance of safety from the minute he or she steps into the vehicle to the minute he or she steps out of the vehicle—for any reason. The safety of the motoring public is in your hands. A vehicle inspection is the first step toward ensuring the safe operation of your rig.

PRETRIP, EN ROUTE, AND POSTTRIP INSPECTIONS

State and federal laws require that you—the driver—conduct a thorough vehicle inspection each time you take your CMV onto the highway. **Federal Motor Carrier Safety Regulations Part 396** includes the requirement of a vehicle inspection. Further, the FMCSR, Part 392.7 states:

No motor vehicle shall be driven unless the driver thereof shall have satisfied himself that the following parts and accessories are in good working order, nor shall any driver fail to use or make use of such parts and accessories when and as needed:

- Service brakes, including trailer brake connections
- Parking (hand) brake

- Steering mechanism
- Lighting devices and reflectors
- Tires
- Horn
- Windshield wiper or wipers
- Rear-vision mirror or mirrors
- Coupling devices

The skills of a professional driver can first be measured in the thoroughness of each of his or her inspection routines **(see Figure 2–2).** Knowing that the "parts and accessories are in good working order" comes from a thorough vehicle inspection—before going on the road.

▶ **Figure 2-2**

It is important to perform a thorough inspection routine.

GO!

Inspections provide the driver with information about the rig, including:

- Systems and parts that are working properly
- Systems and parts that are not working properly
- Parts that are damaged, loose, or missing
- Systems or parts on the verge of failing
- Systems or parts in danger of failing or malfunctioning

By law, each rig must meet certain performance standards. It is your responsibility for your rig to meet these standards. You will have this knowledge by becoming familiar with the required equipment for your vehicle, how the systems work, how certain damage or defects keep the vehicle from operating properly, and how to load cargo properly.

▶ *The squeaky wheel should not only get the grease but also a good inspection before you hit the road.*

GO!

Professional drivers are responsible for knowing how to conduct three types of vehicle inspections:

Pretrip inspection: a systematic check of systems and parts done before each trip, including how the cargo is loaded and/or tied down

En route inspection: a systematic check of the rig's controls, instruments while driving, and other items such as cargo tie-downs, couplings, tires, and wheels at each stop

Posttrip inspection: a thorough check of the rig at the end of the trip and a written **Vehicle Condition Report (VCR)** listing any defect noted or reported to the driver during operation and inspection

It is also important that you be able to determine when problems occur while you are operating the vehicle.

Aside from the professional driver and those maintenance professionals assigned to maintain rigs, there is one other group that inspects commercial vehicles. These are federal and state inspectors who can conduct an inspection at any time. It may be at a weigh station or it may be while you are driving down the road. For these inspections, you either (1) have to stop at an inspection point or (2) the inspector pulls you over to conduct a roadside inspection anywhere in the country.

When these inspections occur, if the vehicle is found to be unsafe in any area, it can be put out of service (OOS). When you are OOS, you cannot go anywhere until the vehicle is repaired and is safe to go back to the highway.

WHAT MAKES A GOOD INSPECTION GREAT?

Any professional driver will tell you that learning to conduct a thorough vehicle inspection will make your job easier *and* may save your life and the lives of others **(see Figure 2–3)**.

FACT: You can only conduct a thorough inspection if you have the knowledge of your rig and its systems. But, more than that, you have to have the desire to operate safely and the discipline to do these inspections to the best of your ability every time. You also have to understand why you want to conduct a thorough inspection and what you are looking for.

▶ **Figure 2–3**

Learning to conduct a thorough inspection may save your life.

> **CAUTION!**
>
> As you learn to perform inspections of tractor-trailer rigs, you should:
>
> ■ Learn and follow a regular routine. By using the same routine each time you perform an inspection, you will cover the rig front to rear without missing critical points
>
> ■ Know what you are looking for
>
> ■ Report any problems so mechanics can easily identify the problem and repair the rig

More about Inspections

As the name tells you, *pretrip inspections* are conducted before each trip. These inspections are so important that you should record them in your logbook. During these inspections, look for problems and damage to the vehicle that could cause a breakdown or an accident. Any damage you find must be repaired before the vehicle heads for the highway. A "posttrip" inspection is conducted at the end of the trip—or if the trip lasts several days, then at the end of each day or at the end of each shift.

As any veteran driver will tell you, conducting a thorough inspection will ensure your personal safety and the safety of others. Then, by knowledge of your vehicle and its systems, watching gauges for trouble and using your senses (sight, hearing, smell, and feel) to check for any problems that may occur when on the road, you will arrive safely and on time at your destination, along with your load **(see Figure 2–4).**

Goals of Inspection

- **Goals**
  - To identify
    - A part or system that is malfunctioning or has already failed (or is missing)
    - A part or system that is in imminent danger of failing or malfunctioning
    - A part or system that is all right or is functioning properly
    - The legal requirements for various parts or system conditions
- **Driver Responsibility**
  - Safety of vehicle and cargo
  - Vehicle inspection

- **Basic Reasons**
  - Safety
  - Economy
  - Public relations
  - Legality
- **Three Elements of a Good Inspection**
  - Knowing what to look for
  - Having a consistent way of looking for it
  - Being able to report findings in a technically accurate way so that the mechanics will be able to identify and repair the problems
- **Types of Inspection**
  - Pretrip
  - En route
  - Posttrip

▶ **Figure 2–4**

The pretrip, en route, and posttrip inspections are pivotal to the performance of the rig and to the efficiency and effectiveness of the professional driver.

What to Look for During a Rig Inspection

The major reasons for performing regular inspections are, as stated earlier, (1) to maintain the rig properly, (2) to make operation of the rig as safe as possible, (3) to minimize breakdowns, (4) to maintain good public relations with other highway users, and (5) to make your job easier.

As a professional, you must know the following in order to make a thorough inspection:

- If a system is working properly
- When a system or part is in danger of failure or malfunction
- The difference between major and minor defects
- Defects/problems that will make your rig illegal to operate and could cause it to be put out of service during a federal or state roadside inspection

FMCSR 396.3(a)1 requires that every motor carrier systematically inspect, repair, and maintain, or cause to be systematically inspected, repaired, and maintained, all motor vehicles subject to its control. This requirement ensures that parts and accessories are in safe and proper operating condition at all times. These include any additional parts and accessories which may affect safety of operation, including but not limited to, frame and frame assemblies, suspension systems, axles and attaching parts, wheels and rims, and steering systems.

FMCSR 396.9(c) Motor Vehicle Declared Out-of-Service. This regulation prevents any driver from driving a CMV that is out of repair and *imminently hazardous to operate.* Safety defects considered imminently hazardous include:

- Defective steering system
- Brake shoes that are missing or do not work
- Cracked brake drums

- Serious air loss in the brake system
- Missing lights or ones that do not work
- Bad tires
- Cracked wheels, ones that have been welded, or ones that have missing lug nuts
- Fuel system leaks
- Cargo not properly secured
- Defective coupling system

This same regulation also states that a motor carrier cannot require or permit a driver to operate a vehicle that has not been regularly inspected or maintained.

Fluid Leaks

You may have previous experience with fluid leaks, such as in going out to your personal vehicle and finding puddles of leaking fluid on the driveway or ground under it. You may also know that serious engine damage or breakdowns can occur because of loss of fluids such as coolant or lubricants **(see Figure 2–5).**

▶ **Figure 2–5**

Serious engine damage or a breakdown can occur as a result of the loss of fluid.

During every inspection—pretrip, en route, and posttrip—always check every fluid level, including oil, coolant, and fuel. Also, check for signs of fluid loss under the vehicle and while you are driving, and keep a constant eye on the gauges that monitor these vital fluids.

Bad Tires

Like ever other American traveler, you have certainly driven down a highway and seen the remains of blown or damaged tires, usually 18-wheeler tires. Tire defects increase the chances of a blowout and can make any big rig dangerously difficult to handle. Federal regulations forbid professional truckers to drive with faulty tires.

> **CAUTION!**
>
> FMCSR 393.75 states (a) no motor vehicle shall be operated on any **tire** that (1) has body ply or belt material exposed through the tread or sidewall, (2) has any tread or sidewall separation, (3) is flat or has an audible leak, or (4) has a cut to the extent that the ply or belt material is exposed.

Careful inspections of each wheel and tire will make blowouts less likely and may prevent accidents as well as costly downtime **(see Figure 2–6).**

Wheels and Rims

Defective **wheels** or **rims** can cause a tire to come off and cause an accident. Use a lug wrench to check for tightness of lug nuts and look for:

- Cracks or damaged wheels or rims
- Dented or damaged rims or cracks starting at the lug nut holes **(see Figure 2–7),** which can cause tires to lose air pressure or come off the rim on a turn
- Missing spacers, studs, lugs, and clamps
- Damaged or mismatched lock rings
- Welding used to repair wheels or rims, note as defect

▶ **Figure 2–6**

Careful inspection of the tires will help reduce blowouts and may prevent accidents.

▶ **Figure 2–7**

Check for rust around the lug nut holes as well as rust trails and loose or missing lugs.

- Rust around wheel nuts, check for looseness with wrench
- Out-of-round (oval or egg-shaped) stud or bolt holes on rims
- Hub oil supply and possible leaks

TIRE INSPECTION

Whether you have driven for 2 or 20 years, you already know that it is dangerous to drive with bad tires. During your inspection:

- Look for worn treads and body ply or belts showing through the tread
- Look for separation of tread or sidewall
- Look for deep cuts or cracks that reveal ply or belt beneath

▶ **Figure 2–8**
ICD—Inflation—Condition—Depth

- Look for damaged or cracked valve stems, or missing stems and valve caps
- If tire is low or flat—or any of the above—get it repaired
- Listen for air leaks and look for bulges (could mean blowout)
- Check inflation pressure with tire gauge (especially during CDL test)
- Check for wear—need no less than 4/32-inch tread depth in every major groove on the front and 2/32-inch tread depth on other wheels
- Ensure that dual tires are not touching each other or another part of the vehicle
- Make sure all tires are the same size and type (radial and bias-ply tires should not be used on the same axle, which is forbidden in most states)
- Remove regrooved tires on the front of tractors with 8,000-plus-pound front axle rating

When checking your tires, remember the acronym ICD—inflation, condition, and depth **(see Figure 2–8).**

Tire Chains

According to another state-by-state requirement for driving in snow and ice, include **tire chains** in your equipment inspection and be able to mount and remove them if asked. Check regulations in both your home state and other states where you will be operating. Tire chains are usually required in the mountain regions.

INSPECTING MUD FLAPS/SPLASH GUARDS

A common state requirement is that **mud flaps (see Figure 2–9)** must be as wide or wider than the tires.

- Mud flaps should be no more than 6 inches from the ground with vehicle fully loaded. States vary so be sure to check your state's restrictions.
- Flaps should be mounted as far to the rear of the wheel as possible.

▶ **Figure 2-9**
Generally, mud flaps must be as wide or wider than the tires.

BRAKING SYSTEMS INSPECTION

You must be able to control the stopping and starting of your rig safely. To do so, your **brakes** must be in top shape. Inspect all four wheels in the following manner:

- Check wheel for cracks and hubs for any leaking fluid. Check lugs.
- Check brake lines for worn or weak spots.
- Make sure lines are not kinked or twisted.
- Check hydraulic fluid level in the master cylinder (when inspecting engine area). Use sight glass or visual and check manual for proper inspection method. Make sure fluid level reaches mark indicated. Leaks in this area mean trouble.

Check Air Pressure

You should not be able to hear any air leaks. The sound of air coming from any part of the air brake system means the system is defective and can be dangerous. To check the brake system, follow these steps:

1. Set the brakes (parking and trailer). Start the engine and let air pressure build until the system is fully charged, about 125 pounds per square inch (psi).

2. Turn off the engine and release parking brake and trailer brakes (puts air into the spring brake system). After the initial air pressure drop (about 10 to 15 psi), apply firm pressure (about 90 psi) to the service brake pedal (puts air into the remainder of the system). Hold this for 1 minute.

3. Watch the air pressure gauge. The air pressure should not drop more than:
   - 3 psi in 1 minute for tractor
   - 4 psi in 1 minute for tractor and trailer
   - 6 psi in 1 minute for a tractor and three trailers

Air leaks that can be heard or are more than the amounts listed should be repaired before the truck or combination is driven, because they are unsafe and violate safety regulations.

Check Brake Lines

You should not hear any air leaks and should check for air lines that are:

- Not secured properly
- Hardened or swollen

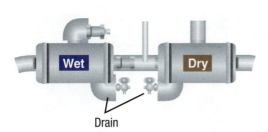

Figure 2-10

The air reservoirs should be bled each day.

- Chafed or worn so that fabric or steel braid is visible
- Cut or cracked
- Crimped, pinched, or restricted in any way
- Taped or not spliced correctly

Check Air Reservoir

The **air reservoir(s) (see Figure 2–10)** must be attached correctly to the rig. The reservoirs must be bled each day to remove moisture. A good time to bleed them is during the pretrip and posttrip inspections.

Check Parking Brakes

- Put your seat belt on.
- Put vehicle in gear and let it move forward slowly.
- Apply parking brake. Vehicle should stop. If it does not stop, get parking brake repaired before your trip.

Check Service Brake

- Go forward about 5 miles per hour.
- Push pedal firmly—if vehicle veers left or right, this could mean brake trouble.
- Any pause before brakes "catch" is another sign of a problem.
- If the brake pedal feels weird—takes too much time to catch or requires too much effort to push—then the brakes should be checked and repaired before any trip.

STOP!

Most units have redundant systems. Most failures happen over time and can be discovered during the pretrip inspection. Do not operate a unit that you cannot stop.

STEERING SYSTEM INSPECTION

Although this goes without saying, the professional driver must be in control of his or her rig at all times and in all situations. Lack of complete control may be the result of poor maintenance or system malfunction. The **steering system** provides the driver's most immediate control over the direction of a rig, and defects in this system create unsafe situations.

STOP!

Steering system defects may affect total control of the vehicle, and the higher the speed the rig is traveling when steering system problems occur, the more prone you become to a serious accident.

When conducting pretrip, en route, or posttrip inspections, look for:

- Bent, loose, or broken parts such as the steering column, steering gear box, tie rods, Pitman arms, and drag link
- Missing nuts, bolts, cotter keys, or other securing devices
- Damaged hoses and pumps
- Proper fluid level in the power steering reservoir
- Air and fluid leaks
- Anything shining to indicate something is loose
- Check the steering wheel for **steering wheel lash (see Figure 2–11),** looseness or play in the steering wheel's movement. (For power steering, if there is more than 5-¾ inches of play, the rig should be placed out of service until this is corrected.)

Steering Wheel Diameter	Manual Steering System	Power Steering System
16 inches or less	2 inches	4-½ inches
18 inches	2-¼ inches	4-¾ inches
20 inches	2-½ inches	5-¼ inches
22 inches	2-¾ inches	5-¾ inches

▶ **Figure 2–11**

Parameters for Steering Wheel Lash (FMCSA 393.209).

To check the steering system, make sure the steering column is securely mounted and the steering wheel is secure, moves easily, and is free of cracked spokes.

- Steering wheel lash or free play (the number of turns the steering wheel makes before wheels move) should be no more than 10 degrees or 2 inches on the rim of a 20-inch steering wheel according to FMCSR Part 393. If free play exceeds limits, vehicle will be difficult to steer.
- Check U-joints for wear, slack, damage, or signs of welding repair (not acceptable for U-joint repair).
- Gear box is free of damage and bolts and brackets are in place and secure.
- Pitman arm is secure.

For vehicles with power steering:

- All parts should be free of damage and in good operating order.
- Belts that are frayed, cracked, or slipping should be replaced or adjusted.
- Look for leaks in lines and tank and make sure tank contains ample power steering fluid.
- If you see missing nuts, bolts, cotter keys, or other damaged parts, replace immediately, as well as damaged, loose, or broken steering column, gear box, or tie rod.

SUSPENSION SYSTEM INSPECTION

The **suspension system** supports the rig's load and maintains axle attachment and alignment. Failure of this system can have tragic results. Check for:

- Cracked or broken torque arms and U-bolts
- Hangers that allow the axle to move from its proper position
- Missing or broken leaves in a spring leaf cluster **(see Figure 2–12).** (The rig will be put out of service if one fourth or more of these leaves are missing. Any broken or missing leaves can be dangerous.)
- Leaking or faulty shock absorbers
- Missing or damaged spring hangers
- Cracked or broken spring hangers
- Damaged or leaking air suspension systems

▶ **Figure 2–12**

Check for broken or missing leaves in a spring leaf cluster.

- Broken leaves or leaves that have shifted and are touching the tires, wheels, frame, or body
- Missing or broken torque rods
- Loose, cracked, broken, or missing frame members

CAUTION!

On every inspection, check the vehicle's frame for loose, cracked, sagging, or damaged frame.

- Check for missing bolts.
- Replace any broken bolts on the frame.
- Check that all bolts and rivets are tight and in place.

EXHAUST SYSTEM INSPECTION

Faulty **exhaust systems** can lead to harmful—even deadly—fumes in the cab or sleeper berth.

- Check for broken, loose, or missing exhaust pipes, mufflers, tailpipes, or stacks.
- Look for loose or broken mountings, missing brackets, bent clamps, or missing or broken nuts and bolts.
- Check to make sure no parts of the exhaust system are rubbing against parts of the fuel system.
- Check for broken, worn, or frayed hoses, lines, and wires.
- With your hand close (but not on it because you will burn yourself) to the exhaust manifold, check for leaks. You will feel them.
- Never patch or wrap the exhaust system. Note any such repair work on your inspection as a defect and have it fixed.

COUPLING SYSTEM INSPECTION

Failure of the **coupling system** (upper or lower **fifth wheel**) can cause cargo damage or serious accidents **(see Figure 2–13).** The coupling system includes saddle mounts, tow bars, king pins, pintle hooks, and safety chains used in tow-away situations.

Check for:

- Too much slack in the fifth-wheel locking system
- Bends or warping, cracks, or breaks in all parts used to couple vehicles
- Safety chains with broken or twisted links
- Missing pins or other defects in the slide mechanism of the sliding fifth wheel
- Bent, cracked, or worn king pins
- Lights, reflectors, steering, and brakes, which must work on the vehicle when towing or when being towed
- Missing U-bolts, cracked or broken welds, or other defects in the fifth-wheel mounting devices
- More than ⅜-inch horizontal movement between the pivot bracket pin and the bracket
- Pivot bracket pin missing or not secured

▶ **Figure 2–13**
Fifth wheel.

CARGO INSPECTION

Safely loaded cargo (no room for shifting or falling) should be inspected and the following should be in good working condition **(see Figure 2–14):**

- Tailgate
- Doors

- Cab guard or header board (headache rack)—free of damage and securely in place
- Stakes/sideboards (if necessary)
- Tarps tied down and tight
- Spare tire
- Binders
- Chains
- Winches
- Braces and support
- Curbside doors secured and locked

Figure 2-14

Cargo should be safely loaded so there is no room for shifting or falling.

Cargo must be loaded without blocking view or impeding driver's arms and legs.

- If you haul sealed loads, then you need security seals on doors.
- If you haul hazardous materials, then you need placards, proper paperwork, and the HazMat Endorsement.

STOP!

Remember: Anything you find on your inspection of the vehicle that is broken or not functioning properly must be repaired before you take the vehicle on the road. Federal and state laws forbid operating an unsafe vehicle.

STEPS FOR A PRETRIP INSPECTION

You have a moral, professional, and legal duty to your employer, other motorists, and yourself to conduct a thorough pretrip inspection of any rig you drive. It takes much longer to learn how to perform a quality pretrip inspection than it takes to do one. After much practice, you will be able to do a thorough inspection in less than 15 minutes.

The secret to making an efficient and accurate inspection is to learn the step-by-step **inspection routine.** If you inspect your rig the same way every time, you will be able to do it quickly and efficiently without a chance of overlooking a key system or part. The seven-step pretrip inspection is, by far, the most used of the routines **(see Figure 2–15).**

NOTE: Many companies have specific policies on vehicle inspection. Some carriers require drivers to conduct more extensive inspections while other carriers prohibit certain checks. All drivers should establish an inspection procedure that is consistent with company policy.

Step 1: Approach the Vehicle

While walking toward the rig, look for signs of damage. Also look for anything that may be in the way when you try to move the vehicle. As you approach the rig, look at the following:

Vehicle posture—a truck sagging to one side may mean flat tires, overloading, shifted cargo, or suspension problems.

Seven-Step Pretrip Inspection Checklist

1. Approach vehicle — look for leaks

2. Check under hood or cab

3. Start engine and check inside cab

4. Check headlights

5. Conduct walkaround

6. Check signal lights

7. Check air brake system

Cargo—the trailer or **cargo compartment doors** should be closed and properly fastened. For flatbed trailers and other open cargo compartments, make sure the cargo is not hanging over the side and that restraints can stand 1-½ times any pressure from the load **(see Figure 2–16).**

Damaged, loose, or missing parts—check for cracked glass, dents, or missing parts such as fenders, mud flaps, and lights. Check for loose parts such as a fuel tank hanging with unsecured straps.

Leaks—check under the truck for puddles of fresh oil, engine coolant, grease, or fuel. Look for any other signs of leakage and also be sure to listen for air leaks.

▶ **Figure 2-16**

Check cargo restraints to ensure the load is secure.

Area around vehicle—look for anything that may be damaged by the rig or will damage your rig as you drive away. Be on the lookout for anything on the ground, such as glass or boards with nails. Look up to check for low-hanging branches, utility wires, and any other overhead objects that may be hit by the tractor or trailer.

Most recent pretrip and posttrip vehicle inspection reports—if items listed affect safety, check to make certain mechanic's certification indicates repairs were made or no repair was needed. Then, inspect these areas yourself to find out what was done about problems noted on last inspection.

Step 2: Check under the Hood

With parking brakes on, check the engine compartment to ensure the vehicle has been properly serviced. Look for signs of damage or possible problems with the engine, steering mechanism, and suspension system. Most tractor hoods are equipped with safety latches and are designed to prevent the hood from falling on the person checking the engine compartment. Perform a thorough check of the following:

Fluid levels—check engine oil level (should be above "low" or "add" marks) on dipstick. Check coolant level (should be above "low" mark). Check radiator shutters (if you still have them), remove any ice, and check to see if winter front is open. Inspect the fan to ensure blades are undamaged and hoses and wires are out of the way. Check other fluid levels such as automatic transmission fluid, windshield washer fluid, and engine oil in the makeup reservoir. Be sure all fluids are at the right levels before starting the engine, and that hoses are in good condition.

Leaks—look for leaks such as oil, water, or hydraulic fluid in the engine compartment. Check around the entire compartment for grease, soot, or other signs of fluid leaks. Inspect the exhaust manifold for signs of leakage, and if your rig's main air tanks are under the hood, listen for the hiss of leaking air.

- For windshield washers, check fluid level.
- Automatic transmission? Check fluid level (may do this with engine running)

Check electrical system—make sure the battery is secured and terminals are not corroded. Check for loose electrical wires and check all wires for wear. If your rig has spark plugs, check for secure electrical connections.

Belts and pulleys—inspect alternator, air compressor, and water pump belts for cracks or fraying. Test belts for tension and slippage. If you can slide a belt over a pulley, it is too loose and should be tightened or replaced.

Cooling system—check radiator, shroud, and shutters to make sure they are structurally sound and free or dents or damage. (Newer systems have thermostatic fans that eliminate shutters.) Make sure all parts of the cooling system are properly secured. Check hoses for cracks, breaks, or other damage. Inspect the fan for missing blades and look for hanging wires or hoses that can catch on the blades **(see Figure 2–17).**

Steering system—check steering linkage and gear box closely. Make sure they are secure and look for signs of wear, such as paint that has been rubbed off. If the rig has power steering, make sure these lines are securely connected and there are no leaks. Look for leaking or defective shock absorbers. If the rig has an air suspension system, make sure air bags are not leaking or damaged.

Exhaust system—examine the muffler. Be sure it is securely connected and has no holes, large dents, or is crushed. Make sure all lines and hoses are securely fastened. Report any damage found before your trip. Be sure fuel and electric lines will not come too close to any part of the exhaust system that gets hot.

Braking systems—look for cracked brake drums, missing brake shoes, and missing or disconnected hoses and slack adjusters. Make sure air intake screen for air brakes is not clogged with debris. Open air tank petcocks and drain tanks. Check for oil contamination, but be sure to close petcocks when you have completed this part of the inspection.

Figure 2–17
Inspect fan.

Suspension system—check U-bolts, spring pins, spring brackets, and torque arms for cracks, bends, or missing bolts. Check axles for signs of rubbing. If the truck has adjustable axles, make sure all locking pins are in the proper position and fully engaged. Make sure all safety clamps holding locking pins are securely in place. Then check for cracks in the truck's frame and cross members. Check entire suspension system for rust or shiny spots that may indicate excessive wear. Look at all leaf springs for missing, out-of-place, or broken leaves. Leaves sticking out from a leaf spring may touch the tires, rims, or frame.

Step 3: Start the Engine and Check Inside the Cab

After checking the engine, climb into the **cab** and prepare to start the engine. For the professional driver, the cab is a home away from home, of sorts; therefore, it should be kept orderly and clean. Check to make sure:

- All controls and instruments are in working order
- Doors open and close easily and securely
- There are no loose, sagging, or broken parts
- Seats are secured firmly in place
- Front bumpers are secure
- Rear bumpers are firmly on if vehicle is higher than 30 inches from the ground (empty).

Perform a thorough check of the following:

Vehicle entry—check that the ladder, grab handle, and door handles are secure and free of dirt, grease, or ice. Make sure doors latch securely.

Emergency and safety equipment—make sure you have all the required emergency and safety equipment **(see Figure 2–18).** Check to see that:

- The fire extinguisher is securely mounted with easy access, which should be checked as part of the inspection. Most vehicles require a 10 B:C rating. Is the nozzle clear and the tip of ring pin in place? Check pressure gauge to be sure needle is in the green area.
- You know how to use the fire extinguisher.
- There are three reflective emergency triangles (see FMCSR 393.95 for full description and options).
- You have spare fuses and know how to install them, unless your vehicle has circuit breakers.
- You have an accident notification kit (for example, keep a disposable camera in the accident kit to visually record damages) and emergency phone numbers.

▶ **Figure 2-18**

Required by law, each truck should have a fire extinguisher and reflective triangles.

▶ **Figure 2-19**

Check windshield wipers and mirrors.

Mirrors and glass—always check all windows and panes of glass before you drive **(see Figure 2-19).** Viewing area must be clean—free of stickers, dirt, discolorations, and only factor tints to reduce glare are allowed.

- Apply only required stickers at the bottom of the windshield, no more than 4-½ inches into the viewing area.

- Do not allow cracks (longer than ¼ inch) or dings in the glass.

CAUTION!
Run your hand along the windshield wiper blades to check for worn spots. Rubber should be soft and pliable.

- Make sure mirrors are securely mounted.

- Adjust the seat into a comfortable driving position.

- **Rear-view mirrors** on each side of cab should be adjusted when in the driver's seat. You should be able to see down both sides to the rear of the vehicle. Mirrors should also be clean and free of damage.

Engine startup—once you climb into the cab, look around and inspect the inside area. Put on your seatbelt. Make sure the parking brake is on and the vehicle is in neutral or park. Start the engine at zero throttle. Do not crank for more than 15 seconds. Listen for any unusual pinging, skipping, or other noises. With the engine running (all readings should register a few seconds after starting the engine), check the following:

- Gauges—oil pressure goes to normal in seconds

- Ammeter and voltmeter display readings—needle should jump, flutter, and then register "charge" or "+" for a normal reading

- Coolant temperature—should start "cold" and gradually rise to normal

- Engine oil temp—slowly to normal

- Oil, coolant, and charging circuit warning lights come on and should go off almost immediately (unless a problem exists)

- Low air pressure warning buzzer—should sound until air pressure builds to about 60 psi, then the buzzer or alarm should stop

- Air pressure gauge—should build steadily (Check the time needed for the pressure to build to 125 psi. If it is within 45 seconds, the buildup is adequate. Buildup can take longer with oversized air tanks.)

- Air pressure governor cut-off—should stop between 115 and 125 psi (If it stops above or below this range, adjustments are needed.)

- All controls in working order—check loose or sticking controls, any damage or improper readings or settings

- Mirrors, windshield for defects, problems

- Required emergency equipment that is in good working order

- Items required by state laws, such as mud flaps and tire chains

NOTE: In trucks with electronically controlled engines, the needles on all gauges will make a full seep after ignition. This self-check function ensures that all gauges are working.

CAUTION! NEW LAW

In July 2004, the California Air Resources Board (ARB) adopted a diesel air tax control measure that requires big rig truck and interstate bus operators to shut their engines down after 5 minutes of nonessential idling. The new regulation affects the more than 400,000 heavy-duty diesel trucks and buses registered in California and all out-of-state trucks and buses operating in California. The regulation will eliminate 166 tons of particulate pollution per year and about 5,200 tons per year of smog-forming nitrogen oxide emissions from the state's air. As a result of the new measure, California truck and bus operators will each save about 125 gallons of diesel fuel per year, or collectively over 1 million gallons each week. Bus operators may idle for 10 minutes prior to entering passenger service in order to prepare their vehicles for customer use.

Primary Controls—with the engine still running, check the vehicle's main controls:

- **Steering mechanism**—check for **free play** or lash in the steering wheel. Open the cab door and lean out so you can see the left front tire of the truck. While watching the tire, turn the wheel until the tire starts to move. Refer back to Figure 2–11 for unsafe levels of free play for manual and power steering wheels.

- **Clutch**—depress the clutch until you feel a little resistance. For most clutches, 1 to 2 inches of free play is normal. Too much or too little free play can cause difficult shifting, gear clashing, and clutch or transmission damage. To check the clutch brake, push the pedal to the floor. The pedal should stop before reaching the floor.

- **Transmission**—with the clutch depressed, check to see that the transmission allows you to shift freely from neutral into other gears.

- **Gas and brake pedals**—check both pedals for looseness or sticking. Be sure there is no dirt buildup underneath each pedal.

Secondary controls—the following are secondary controls that should be checked prior to beginning each trip to ensure that they are in working order:

- Defroster
- Fan
- Horn
- Interior lights
- Turn signals
- High-beam indicator

- Heater and air conditioner
- Lanyard to the air horn
- Windshield washers and wipers
- Dashboard lights
- Four-way flashers
- Steering tilt

Preparing to leave the cab—when air pressure has built to the governor cutout pressure, turn the engine off. If the engine shutoff is the pull-out type, leave it in the pulled out position until you start the engine again. Put the rig into the lowest forward gear. Set the parking brake. Turn on low-beam headlights and **four-way flashers.**

STOP!

Remove starter switch key and place it in your pocket to prevent someone else from moving the rig while you are making the outside inspection.

Step 4: Check Lights and Mirrors

Get out of the cab and go to the front of the rig to check the:

▶ **Figure 2–20**
Clean and clear headlights.

- Low-beam headlights—do they work and are they aligned? **(See Figure 2–20.)**
- Four-way flashers—do both work?

Reach into the cab and switch the lights to high beam.

- Do the high beams work? Are they aligned?
- Inspect mirrors—are they clean? Adjust if necessary.

Step 5: Conduct a Walkaround Inspection

Go back to the cab. Turn off the headlights and four-way flashers. Turn on right turn signal, leave the cab and begin the walkaround inspection—a 14-point routine **(see Figure 2–21).** During this part of the pretrip inspection, you will be looking at vehicle parts outside the cab. Start with the driver's side of the cab and cover the front and then work down the opposite side. Go over the rear of the vehicle and back to the driver's side of the cab.

Walkaround Sequence

1. Left side of cab area
2. Front of cab area
3. Right side of tractor area
4. Right saddle tank area
5. Coupling system area
6. Right rear tractor wheels area
7. Rear of tractor area
8. Front of trailer area
9. Right side of trailer area
10. Right rear trailer wheels area
11. Rear of trailer area
12. Left rear trailer wheels area
13. Left side of trailer area
14. Left saddle tank area

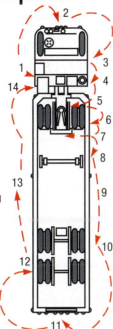

▶ **Figure 2-21**
Make a copy of this guide and use it as a reference when performing inspections.

CAUTION!

In some states, the driver is expected to perform the walkaround sequence beginning on the left side of the vehicle and proceeding along the left side to the rear and then up the right side. This is done so the driver is facing traffic, to ensure his or her safety. Be sure to check your state's requirements for performing the walkaround inspection.

General Tips

■ Walk around and inspect as you go.

■ Clean all lights, reflectors, and glass as you walk around the vehicle.

Left Side of Cab

■ **Driver's door glass**—should be clean and locks in working order.

■ **Wheels, rims, and tires**—should be in good condition with no missing, bent, or broken studs, clamps, or lugs. (a) Tires are properly inflated, with valve stem and cap in place. No serious cuts, slashes, bulges, or signs of tread wear. (b) Test lug nuts for looseness (rust streaks coming from the lug nuts also indicate looseness. (c) Hub oil level is good, with no leaks.

CAUTION!

If rims have more than one piece, they are under extreme pressure and can explode from the wheel if damaged, mismatched, or mounted improperly. Always have experts adjust them. These adjustments are regulated by standards set by the Occupational Safety and Health Administration (OSHA).

- **Check for improperly mounted tires and loose or missing lugs**—which can put too much stress on remaining lugs. Look for a rust trail around the lugs. This tells you the lug nuts may be loose. Always use a lug wrench to check lugs.

- **Look for signs of lubricant leaking from wheel seals**—lost lubricant can cause a wheel to lock up. Check the hub oil level.

- **Left front tire**—check air pressure (always use a gauge), general condition, and tread depth (should not be less than $\frac{4}{32}$ inch). Low tire pressure makes the rig hard to handle and can increase the possibility of blowout or tire fire. It also reduces a tire's life. Bald tires or worn out treads cause hydroplaning on wet surfaces.

- **Left front suspension**—check the condition of springs, spring hangers, shackles, U-bolts, and shock absorbers.

- **Left front brake**—check the condition of drum and hoses, and shoes (if they can be seen). Linings should not be less than ¼ inch.

- **Check brake chambers** and slack adjusters.

- **Air tanks**—drain according to specification.

Figure 2-22

Check the condition of the front of the cab.

Front of Cab (see Figure 2–22)

- **Front axle**—check for cracks or other problems.

- **Steering system**—check for loose, worn, bent, damaged, or missing parts and test for looseness.

- **License plates**—are on tight and check to make sure all legally required inspection stickers, tax plates, decals, and any placards are in place.

- **Windshield**—should be free of damage and clean. Wipers should be in good working order—check for proper spring tension in wiper arm. Check blades for stiff rubber and that they are secure.

- **Parking, clearance, and identification lights**—should be clean, operational, and the proper color (amber in front and red in rear).

- **Reflectors**—should be clean and undamaged.

- **Right turn signal light**—must be clean, operating, and the proper color (amber or white in front and red in rear).

Right Front

- **Right side of cab**—check all items as you did for the left front of cab.

Right Saddle Tank Area

- **Right fuel tank**—should be securely mounted with no leaks. Fuel crossover lines are secure, there is adequate fuel in tank for trip, and caps and gaskets are in place and secure.

- **Engine**—check condition of visible parts such as rear of engine with no leaks, transmission not leaking, exhaust system secure and not leaking or touching wires or lines, no cracks or bends in frame and cross members.

- **Driveshaft**—should be in position and secured, both in front and on the rear.

- **Exhaust system**—brackets, pipes, and other parts should be secure and free of leaks. Be sure no fuel lines or wires are in contact with exhaust parts. Look for soot, fluids, or burned areas which indicate leaks.

- **Frame and cross members**—look for bends and cracks in the parts of the frame you need.

- **Air lines and electrical wiring**—check for snagging, rubbing, or wearing.

- **Spare tire carrier**—check for damage and check spare tire/wheel is the right size at proper inflation.

- **Spare tire and wheel**—make sure they are sturdy and strong enough to carry the load and are not damaged. They should be chained.

- **Cargo secure**—cargo is blocked, braced, tied, and chained. Header board secure, sideboards and stakes free of damage and properly placed, canvas or tarp secured to prevent tearing, billowing, or blocking mirrors.

- **Oversized loads**—should have required signs properly mounted and all required permits in driver's pouch.

- **Curbside cargo compartment doors**—check that they are closed and latched with all required security seals in place.

Coupling System

- **Lower fifth wheel**—is it properly lubricated? Is it firmly mounted to the frame? Are any parts missing or damaged? You should be able to see no space between the upper and lower fifth wheels. Be sure the locking jaws are securely fastened around the shank of the kingpin. **Never leave them around the head of the kingpin!** The release arm must be properly seated and the safety latch/lock must be engaged.

- **Upper fifth wheel or apron**—guide plate should be firmly mounted on the trailer frame. Kingpin should not be bent, worn, rusted, or damaged.

- **Air and electrical lines to trailer**—should be in good condition **(see Figure 2–23)**. Be sure they are not tangled, snagged, or rubbing against anything. These lines should be free of oil, grease or damage. The air lines must be properly connected to glad hands. (Glad hands are air hose connections between the tractor and the trailer.) Check for leaks. Electrical lines should be firmly attached and locked into place.

- **Sliding fifth wheel (if rig has one)**—should not be worn or damaged. Make sure there are no missing parts. It should be properly lubricated and all lock pins should be locked into place. The in-cab lever should be in locked position. If it is air powered, make sure there are no leaks. The fifth wheel should not be too far forward. If it is, the trailer could hit the cab, the tractor frame, or the landing gear during turns.

▶ **Figure 2–23**
Check air lines to trailer.

STOP!

When checking the coupling of a tractor-trailer or inspecting the kingpin of the trailer and the jaws of the fifth wheel, be sure to remove the ignition key from the tractor before crawling under the rig to check the coupling.

Right Rear Tractor Wheels

- **Dual wheels and rims**—check the condition of wheels, rims, and tires for missing, bent, or broken spacers, studs, clamps, or lugs.

- **Dual tires**—should be evenly matched, of the same type (no mixing of radial and bias types), and properly inflated with valve stems and caps in place. No cuts, bulges, or tread wear. Tires should not be rubbing and should be clear of debris. Wheel bearing/seals should not be leaking.

- **Suspension**—check condition of springs, spring hangers, shackles, and U-bolts. Axle is secure and drive axle(s) not leaking gear oil.

- **Torque rod arms and bushings**—should be in good condition.

- **Shock absorber(s)**—should be working properly.

- **Retractable axle**—check lift mechanism. If air powered, check for leaks.

- **Brakes**—brake drums should be in good condition and hoses checked for wear, rubbing, and so forth.

- **Brake chambers and slack adjusters**—most slack adjusters are self-adjusting. If not, check them on disc S-cam brakes by parking on level ground and turning off the parking brakes so you can move the slack adjusters. Wear gloves. Pull hard on each adjuster you can reach. They should move less than 1 inch where the push rod attaches to it. Adjust them or have them adjusted if they move more than 1 inch. Too much brake slack can make a rig hard to handle.

- **Lights and reflectors**—side-marker lights should be clean and operating; red lights at rear and others are amber. Same for side-marker reflectors.

Rear of the Tractor

- **Rear clearance and identification lights**—should be clean, operating, and red at rear.

- **Reflectors**—should be clean and red at rear. Tail lights should be clean, operating, and red at rear.

- **Turn signals**—should be operating and the proper color (red yellow or amber at rear).

- **License plates**— should be present, clean, and secure.

- **Splash guards**—should be properly fastened, undamaged, and not dragging or rubbing tires.

- **Air and electrical lines**—should be secure, undamaged, and not rubbing on any other part of the equipment.

- **Cargo**—should be properly blocked and braced, tied, and chained.

- **Tailboards**—should be up and secure. End gates should be free of damage and secured in stake sockets.

- **Canvas or tarps**—should be secured to avoid billowing, tearing, blocking rear-view mirror, or covering rear lights.

- **Overlength or overwidth loads**—have all signs and additional flags/lights in proper position and have all required permits.

- **Rear doors**—check that they are closed and locked.

Front Area of Trailer

- **License/registration holder**—should be in place, contain the current registration, and be firmly mounted with the cover closed.

- **Header board**—should be undamaged and securely mounted.

- **Canvas or tarp (if applicable)**—should be damage free, securely mounted, and secured to the carrier.

- **Clearance and ID lights**—should be in working order, the proper color, clean, and in good condition.

- **Reflectors**—should be clean and damage free.

Right Side of Trailer

■ **Front trailer support (landing gear or dolly)**—should be fully raised with no parts bent, damaged, or missing **(see Figure 2–24).** The crank handle should be present, properly secured, and in low gear if possible. If the crank handle is power operated, there should be no air or hydraulic leaks.

■ **Spare tire carrier or rack**—should be in good condition, secure enough to carry the load, and the load should be chained.

▶ **Figure 2–24**
Inspect the trailer.

■ **Spare tire and wheel**—make sure they are sturdy and strong enough to carry the load and not damaged. They should be chained.

■ **Lights and reflectors**—side-marker lights should be clean, operating, and the proper color (red at rear; others amber). Same for side-marker reflectors.

■ **Frame and body**—frame and cross members should be free of bends, cracks, traces of rust, and damage. There should be no missing cross members.

■ **Cargo**—should be properly blocked, braced, tied, and chained. Sideboards and stakes should be in good condition and secure. Canvas and tarps should be properly tied down to prevent water damage, blowing, or blocking the driver's view.

■ **Doors**—should be secure and in place.

Right Rear Trailer Wheel Area

■ **Dual wheels and rims**—check the condition of wheels, rims, and tires for missing, bent, or broken spacers, studs, clamps, or lugs.

■ **Dual tires**—should be evenly matched, of the same type (no mixing of radial and bias types), properly inflated with valve stems and caps in place. Check for cuts, bulges, or tread wear. Tires should not be rubbing and should be clear of debris. Wheel bearing/seals should not be leaking.

■ **Suspension**—check condition of shock absorbers, torque rod arms, and bushings. Check springs, spring hangers, shackles, and U-bolts to make certain they are in good condition. The axles should be secure and drive axle(s) should not be leaking gear oil.

■ **Check brake chambers and slack adjusters**—inspect all brake chambers, making sure everything is connected and is in good working order. Where you can see them, check to make sure brake drums are free of cracks, rust, and wear. Brake shoes should be evenly adjusted. Although most slack adjusters are self-adjusting, check those that are not by parking on level ground and turning off the parking brakes so you can move the slack adjusters. Wear gloves. Pull hard on each adjuster you can reach. They should move less than 1 inch where the push rod attaches to it. Adjust them or have them adjusted if they move more than 1 inch. Too much brake slack can make a rig hard to handle.

Rear of Trailer

■ **Lights and reflectors**—side-marker lights should be clean, operating, and red at rear and others amber; same for side-marker reflectors **(see Figure 2–25).**

▶ Figure 2–25

Inspect the back of trailer with the lights on.

■ **Frame and body**—frame and cross members should be free of bends, cracks, traces of rust, and damage. There should be no missing cross members.

■ **ICC underride prevention bumper**—should be in place and in good condition.

■ **License plates**—should be in place, current, and securely attached.

■ **Splash guards**—should be undamaged and securely attached.

■ **Cargo**—should be properly blocked, braced, tied, and chained. Sideboards and stakes should be in good condition and secure. Canvas and tarps should be properly tied down to prevent water damage, blowing, or blocking the driver's view.

■ **Doors**—should be secure and in place.

Left Rear Trailer Wheel Area

■ Inspect the same things you inspected on the right, except the air tanks.

Left Side of the Trailer

■ Inspect the same items you inspected on the right side.

Left Saddle Tank Area

■ Check the same items you checked on the right side tank area, except the spare tire. Also check:

   ● **Battery box**—see that it is firmly mounted to the vehicle and its cover is in place.

   ● **Battery** (if not mounted in the engine compartment)—be sure it will not move and the case is not broken or leaking.

Step 6: Check Signal Lights

■ Return to the cab.

■ Turn off all lights.

■ Walk around the vehicle.

■ Check the left front and rear of the tractor.

■ Check the left rear trailer turn **signal lights.** Make sure they are clean, the right color, and in working order.

■ Check tractor and trailer stop lights.

Step 7: Check the Air Brake System

■ Return to the cab.

■ Turn off all lights.

■ Make sure you have all trip manifests, permits, and required documents.

- Secure all loose articles in the cab so they will not be in the way while you are driving or become missiles in case of accident.
- Fasten your **seat belt (see Figure 2–26).**

▶ **Figure 2-26**

Once you have completed your pretrip inspection, buckle up and you're ready to go.

GO!

The air brake system check is sometimes combined with the air loss check and the cab check. Now you are ready to test the air brake system. Be sure to check each item carefully.

Low-Pressure Alarm and/or Light

Start "fanning" off the air pressure by rapidly applying and releasing the treadle valve. At approximately 60 pounds, the low air pressure warning alarm should sound and/or the light should go on.

Tractor Protection Valve

Continue to fan off the air pressure. Emergency spring brakes should apply at no less than 20 pounds and no more than 45 pounds. This action must cause the trailer brakes to lock. If they do not, there is a defect in the system **(see Figure 2–27).**

Air Pressure Buildup

With the engine at operating rpm, the pressure should build from 85 to 100 psi within 45 seconds in dual air systems. If air tanks are larger than minimum, buildup time can be longer and still be safe. In single air systems, pressure should build from 50 to 90 psi within 3 minutes with the engine idling at 600 to 900 rpm.

Parking and Trailer Hand Valve Brakes

1. Set (lock) the tractor spring brakes and release trailer spring brakes. Then tug against the brakes.

2. Set the trailer and the tractor spring brakes, then tug.

3. Release all spring brakes, apply the trailer hand valve, and tug against the trailer service brakes. Move the truck forward, disengage the clutch, apply the service brake, and stop evenly.

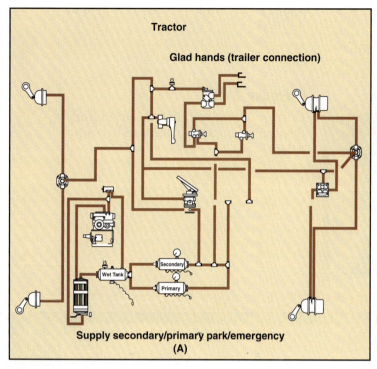

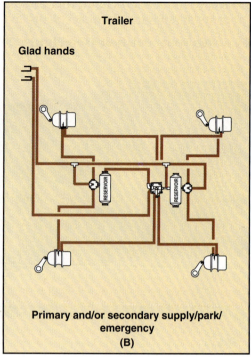

Tractor

Glad hands (trailer connection)

Supply secondary/primary park/emergency
(A)

Trailer

Glad hands

RESERVOIR

RESERVOIR

Primary and/or secondary supply/park/
emergency
(B)

▶ **Figure 2–27**

Air brake system.

CAUTION!

If the trailer is empty, it is possible to pull it with the brakes locked, but this causes undue wear. The fifth wheel can also be pulled out from under the trailer if it is not properly latched during this maneuver.

Too Much Slack in the Fifth Wheel

Put on the trailer brakes. Then carefully rock the tractor into first gear. Listen and feel for too much slack at the kingpin's locking jaws. If there seems to be too much slack, have it inspected by a mechanic. Be sure the clutch is working properly during this procedure.

Brake System Balance and Adjustment

In an off-street area, build the vehicle speed up to 5 to 7 miles per hour. Put on the service brakes sharply **(see Figure 2–28).** Note if the rig is pulling to one side or the other. If the stopping rate or the adjustment of the brakes does not feel right, have a mechanic check it right away. **Do not drive the rig until you are certain the service brakes are working properly.**

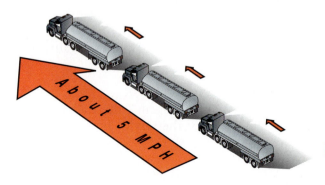

About 5 MPH

▶ **Figure 2–28**

Testing the service brakes.

EN ROUTE AND POSTTRIP INSPECTIONS

En Route Inspections

En route inspections are required by the Federal Motor Carrier Safety Regulations (FMCSR).

FMCSR 392.9—En Route Inspections

According to this ruling, a driver may not operate a commercial motor vehicle unless:

- The commercial motor vehicle's cargo is properly distributed and adequately secured

- The commercial motor vehicle's tailgate, tailboard, doors, tarpaulins, spare tire, and other equipment used in its operation, and the means of fastening the commercial motor vehicle's cargo, are secured

- The commercial motor vehicle's cargo or any other object does not obscure the driver's view ahead or to the right or left sides (except for drivers of self-steer dollies), interfere with the free movement of his/her arms or legs, prevent his/her free and ready access to accessories required for emergencies, or prevent the free and ready exit of any person from the commercial motor vehicle's cab or driver's compartment

Drivers of trucks and truck tractors must:

- Make sure he or she has complied with the provisions of this section before driving that commercial motor vehicle

- Inspect the cargo and the devices used to secure the cargo within the first 50 miles after beginning a trip and cause any adjustments to be made to the cargo or load securement devices as necessary, including adding more securement devices, to ensure that cargo cannot shift on or within, or fall from the commercial motor vehicle

- Reexamine the commercial motor vehicle's cargo and its load securement devices during the course of transportation and make any necessary adjustment to the cargo or load securement devices, including adding more securement devices, to ensure that cargo cannot shift on or within, or fall from, the commercial motor vehicle

- Reexamine and make any necessary adjustments when the driver makes a change of his/her duty status, the commercial motor vehicle has been driven for 3 hours, or the commercial motor vehicle has been driven for 150 miles, whichever occurs first **(see Figure 2–29).**

▶ **Figure 2-29**
Conduct a walk around to inspect your vehicle every 3 hours or 150 miles.

FMCSR 397.17—Required Inspections While Hauling Hazardous Materials

According to FMCSR 397.17, the driver must examine each tire on a motor vehicle at the beginning of each trip and each time the vehicle is parked.

If a tire is found to be flat, leaking, or improperly inflated, then the driver must have the tire repaired, replaced, or properly inflated before the vehicle is driven. However, the vehicle may be driven to the nearest safe place to perform the required repair, replacement, or inflation.

If, as the result of an examination, a tire is found to be overheated, the driver shall immediately have the overheated tire removed and placed at a safe distance from the vehicle. The driver shall not operate the vehicle until the cause of the overheating is corrected.

GO!

Each time you stop to inspect your vehicle en route, check the:

- **Tires**—check air pressure and temperature
- **Brakes**—check adjustment and temperature
- **Cargo**—check doors and make sure cargo is secure
- **Coupling device**—check to make sure attachments are secure (remove the key from the ignition before checking coupling)
- **Lights**—check lights at sunset and at every stop if driving at night

Posttrip Inspection

After every trip, you will be required to:

- Drain moisture from the air tanks and fill fuel tanks as instructed by your employer
- Identify any problems found during the en route inspection, such as unusual noise and vibrations
- Inspect rig to further identify or locate problems and to locate any developing problems
- Identify and diagnose the source of problems (this is covered in a later chapter)
- Complete an accurate and readable vehicle inspection report or Vehicle Condition Report (VCR)

Reporting Findings

Inspections have no meaning unless you take action. As a professional driver, you are required to:

- Report findings to your supervisor and/or maintenance department, as your employer directs
- Report any problems you find to your mechanics
- Prepare an accurate and readable report (required by law) for each rig you drive through your workday or during your shift

VEHICLE CONDITION REPORT

A written vehicle condition report at the end of a trip is required by law for companies in interstate or foreign commerce (FMCSR 396.11). This report must cover the following:

- Service brakes, including trailer brake connections
- Parking brake
- Steering mechanism

- Lights and reflectors
- Windshield wipers
- Rear-view mirrors
- Wheels and rims
- Tires
- Horn
- Coupling devices
- Emergency equipment

The **Vehicle Condition Report (see Figure 2–30)** serves as a record of what the driver finds during inspections of the rig. The law requires that one copy of the report be kept in company

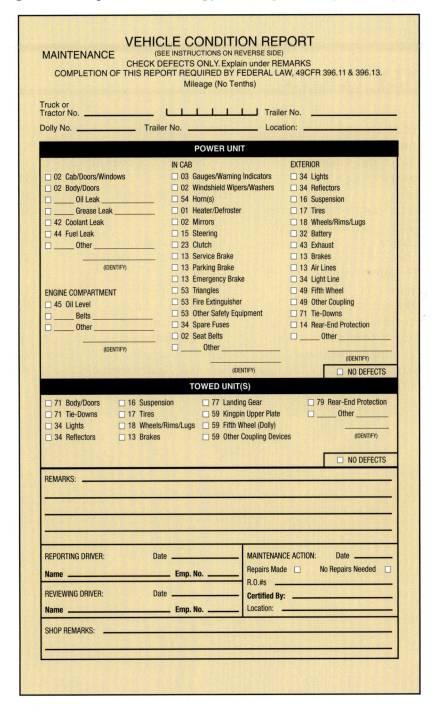

VEHICLE CONDITION REPORT

MAINTENANCE
(SEE INSTRUCTIONS ON REVERSE SIDE)
CHECK DEFECTS ONLY. Explain under REMARKS
COMPLETION OF THIS REPORT REQUIRED BY FEDERAL LAW, 49CFR 396.11 & 396.13.
Mileage (No Tenths)

Truck or
Tractor No. _____ |__|__|__|__|__|__| Trailer No. _____

Dolly No. _____ Trailer No. _____ Location: _____

POWER UNIT

	IN CAB	EXTERIOR
☐ 02 Cab/Doors/Windows	☐ 03 Gauges/Warning Indicators	☐ 34 Lights
☐ 02 Body/Doors	☐ 02 Windshield Wipers/Washers	☐ 34 Reflectors
☐ _____ Oil Leak _____	☐ 54 Horn(s)	☐ 16 Suspension
☐ _____ Grease Leak _____	☐ 01 Heater/Defroster	☐ 17 Tires
☐ 42 Coolant Leak	☐ 02 Mirrors	☐ 18 Wheels/Rims/Lugs
☐ 44 Fuel Leak	☐ 15 Steering	☐ 32 Battery
☐ _____ Other _____	☐ 23 Clutch	☐ 43 Exhaust
	☐ 13 Service Brake	☐ 13 Brakes
(IDENTIFY)	☐ 13 Parking Brake	☐ 13 Air Lines
	☐ 13 Emergency Brake	☐ 34 Light Line
ENGINE COMPARTMENT	☐ 53 Triangles	☐ 49 Fifth Wheel
☐ 45 Oil Level	☐ 53 Fire Extinguisher	☐ 49 Other Coupling
☐ _____ Belts _____	☐ 53 Other Safety Equipment	☐ 71 Tie-Downs
☐ _____ Other _____	☐ 34 Spare Fuses	☐ 14 Rear-End Protection
	☐ 02 Seat Belts	☐ _____ Other _____
(IDENTIFY)	☐ _____ Other _____	(IDENTIFY)
	(IDENTIFY)	☐ NO DEFECTS

TOWED UNIT(S)

☐ 71 Body/Doors	☐ 16 Suspension	☐ 77 Landing Gear	☐ 79 Rear-End Protection
☐ 71 Tie-Downs	☐ 17 Tires	☐ 59 Kingpin Upper Plate	☐ _____ Other _____
☐ 34 Lights	☐ 18 Wheels/Rims/Lugs	☐ 59 Fifth Wheel (Dolly)	
☐ 34 Reflectors	☐ 13 Brakes	☐ 59 Other Coupling Devices	(IDENTIFY)

☐ NO DEFECTS

REMARKS: _____
_____
_____
_____

REPORTING DRIVER: Date _____ | MAINTENANCE ACTION: Date _____
Name _____ Emp. No. _____ | Repairs Made ☐ No Repairs Needed ☐
| R.O.#s
REVIEWING DRIVER: Date _____ | Certified By: _____
Name _____ Emp. No. _____ | Location: _____

SHOP REMARKS: _____
_____

 **Figure 2-30**

Example of a driver's inspection report.

files for at least 3 months. Another copy must be kept in the vehicle until the next VCR is completed. This will tell the next driver about defects or problems, which should be repaired by this time. As a professional driver, you must, by law, review the previous driver's report and sign it if safety-related defects are listed.

SUMMARY

Upon completing this chapter, you should be able to describe ways to make a thorough and accurate pretrip inspection. You should also be able to explain the importance of correcting vehicle malfunctions quickly and should have a working knowledge of federal regulations for inspections. You should also be able to explain the purpose and procedures for en route and posttrip inspections.

KEY TERMS

Air reservoir
Binders
Braces and supports
Brakes
Cab
Cargo compartment doors
Cargo securement devices
Chains
Checklist
Coupling system
Defrosters
Dimmer switch
Emergency equipment
Engine compartment
En route inspection
Exhaust system
Fifth wheel

FMCSR Part 396
FMCSR Part 396.9c Motor
    Vehicle Declared Out of
    Service
Four-way flashers
Frame
Free play
Inspection routine
Instruments and gauges
Lights
Pretrip inspection
Posttrip inspection
Rear-view mirrors
Retarder controls
Rims
Seat belts (safety belts)

Signal (or identification)
    lights
Splash guards (mud flaps)
Steering system
Steering wheel lash
Suspension system
Tarps
Tires
Tire chains
Tire pressure
Trailer hand valve brake
Vehicle Condition Report
    (VCR)
Winches
Windshield wipers
Wheels

Three-Axle Tractor With Two-Axle Trailer Pretrip Inspection Routine
Review Checklist

Use this checklist to review the items to be inspected on your rig. Do you know the check points for each of the items listed? If not, mark or check the item for further review.

Note: In Kansas, the preferred sequence for inspecting the rig is to start on the left side of the tractor and proceed along the left side of the trailer facing traffic, then inspect the rear of the trailer and proceed up the right side of the rig. Be sure to check with your state department of motor vehicles for the preferred sequence in your state.

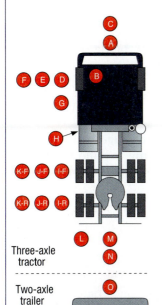

Three-axle tractor

- - - - - - - - - -

Two-axle trailer

A.   ENGINE COMPARTMENT
— Oil Level
— Coolant Level
— Power Steering Fluid
— Water Pump
— Alternator
— Air Compressor
— Any Leaks

B.   ENGINE START
— Clutch/Gearshift
— Air Buzzer Sounds
— Oil Pressure Builds
— Ammeter/Voltmeter
— Air Brake Check
— Steering Play

— Parking Brake
— Mirrors—Windshield
— Wipers
— Lighting Indicators
— Horn(s)
— Heater/Defroster
— Safety/Emergency
     Equipment

C.   FRONT OF TRACTOR
— Lights
— Steering Box
— Steering Linkage

D.   FRONT SUSPENSION
— Springs
— Spring Mounts
— Shock Absorber

E.   FRONT WHEEL
— Rim
— Tire
— Lug Nuts
— Hub Oil Seal

F.   FRONT BRAKE
— Slack Adjuster
— Chamber
— Hoses
— Drum

G.   DRIVER/FUEL AREA
— Door, Mirror
— Fuel Tank
— Leaks
— Battery/Battery Box

H.   UNDER TRACTOR
— Drive Shaft
— Exhaust System
— Frame

**I-F.   REAR WHEELS
          (FRONT AXLE)**
— Rims
— Tires
— Axle Seals
— Lug Nuts
— Spacers

**I-R.   REAR WHEELS
          (REAR AXLE)**
— Rims
— Tires
— Axle Seals
— Lug Nuts
— Spacers

**J-F.   REAR SUSPENSION
          (FRONT AXLE)**
— Springs
— Spring Mounts
— Torsion, Shocks
— Air Bags
— Torque Arm

**J-R.   REAR SUSPENSION
          (REAR AXLE)**
— Springs
— Spring Mounts
— Torsion, Shocks
— Air Bags
— Torque Arm

**K-F.   REAR BRAKES
          (FRONT AXLE)**
— Slack Adjuster
— Chamber
— Hoses
— Drums

**K-R.   REAR BRAKES (REAR
          AXLE)**
— Slack Adjuster
— Chamber
— Hoses
— Drums

L.   COUPLING SYSTEM
— Mounting Bolts
— Safety Latch
— Platform/Catwalk
— Release Arm
— Kingpin/Apron
— Air/Electric Lines
— Locking Jaws
— Gap
— Guide Plate
— Fifth Wheel Plate

M.   SLIDING FIFTH WHEEL
— Locking Pins

N.   REAR OF TRACTOR
— Lights, Reflectors
— Signal/Brake Lights
— Splash Guards

O.   TRAILER FRONT
— Air/Electric Connect
— Header Board
— Lights, Reflectors

P.   SIDE OF TRAILER
— Landing Gear
— Lights, Reflectors
— Doors, Ties
— Frame
— Tandem Release

Q-F.   WHEELS (FRONT AXLE)
— Rims
— Tires
— Axle Seals
— Lug Nuts
— Spacers

Q-R.   WHEELS (REAR AXLE)
— Rims
— Tires
— Axle Seals
— Lug Nuts
— Spacers

**R-F.   SUSPENSION
          (FRONT AXLE)**
— Springs
— Spring Mounts

**R-R.   SUSPENSION
          (REAR AXLE)**
— Springs
— Spring Mounts

S-F.   BRAKES (FRONT AXLE)
— Slack Adjuster
— Chamber
— Hoses
— Drums

S-R.   BRAKES (REAR AXLE)
— Slack Adjuster
— Chamber
— Hoses
— Drums

T.   REAR OF TRAILER
— Lights, Reflectors
— Doors, Ties
— Splash Guards

REVIEW QUESTIONS

1. The best way to check for loose lugs is to_____.

   a. look for rust around the lug nuts

   b. rely on the mechanic when the rig is given its annual inspection

   c. use a lug wrench

   d. use your hand

2. Which of the following is the best method to check tire pressure?

   a. kick the tires

   b. use an air gauge

   c. rely on the semiannual rig inspection by a mechanic

   d. look at the stance of the rig

3. To check steering wheel play (lash) on a rig that has power steering, the engine _____.

   a. need not be running

   b. needs inspection

   c. needs to be warmed up

   d. must be running

4. Regarding the buildup of air pressure as reflected by the air pressure gauge, if the buildup of air pressure is okay (adequate), the time needed for the air pressure to build from 85 to 100 psi is _____.

   a. not important

   b. within 45 seconds

   c. air pressure should not go over 95 psi

   d. 2 to 3 minutes

5. Rust around the lugs is most often a sign _____.

   a. the lugs are loose

   b. the rims are bent

   c. the rig has been driven along the Gulf Coast

   d. for the shop to be concerned with

6. When inspecting the tractor rear dual tires, which of the following is not a true statement?

   a. Valve stems and caps should be in good condition.

   b. All tires should be the same size and type.

   c. *Thumping* a tire with a tire iron is an accurate method to check for proper air pressure.

   d. Nothing should be stuck between the tires.

7. For a vehicle with a power steering system and a 20-inch steering wheel, if steering wheel lash is _____, the vehicle will be considered out of service.

   a. 5-¼ inches or greater

   b. 2 to 4 inches

   c. 3 to 5 inches

   d. 4 to 5 inches

8. To check for air pressure loss in the brake system, watch the air pressure gauge while you put on the foot brake _____.

   a. with the engine running

   b. with the engine not running

   c. with the shop foreman present as this is the responsibility of the shop

   d. with the dispatcher present so the condition of the brake system can be recorded

9. The proper way to inspect the air tanks for oil is _____.

   a. to check the oil level of the engine to see if the oil level has gone down

   b. to have a mechanic check for oil as this is not a driver responsibility

   c. to drive to the nearest shop and have the tanks checked by a mechanic

   d. to open the petcocks and allow the tanks to drain

10. After the air brake system is fully charged, with the engine off, the parking brake and trailer brakes released, and firm pressure (about 90 psi) applied to the service brake pedal for 1 minute, for a tractor and trailer the air pressure drop should be _____.

    a. zero

    b. tested by a mechanic

    c. no more than 15 psi

    d. no more than 4 psi

11. According to FMCSR, the steering wheel play (lash) in a tractor with a manual steering system and a 20-inch steering wheel should be _____.

    a. checked daily by a certified mechanic

    b. between 4 and 5 inches

    c. no more than 2-½ inches

    d. no more than 1-½ inches

12. According to FMCSR, a driver must stop to examine the cargo securing devices _____ of the start of a trip.

    a. within 50 miles

    b. at some time

    c. between 100 and 150 miles

    d. after 12 hours or 300 miles

13. According to FMCSR, if you are hauling hazardous material and your vehicle has dual tires on any axle, you must check the tires _____.

    a. only at the beginning of the trip

    b. only at the end of the trip

    c. only after each 300 miles of the trip

    d. before beginning a trip and each time you stop during a trip

14. The tractor protection valve should automatically go from the *normal* to the *emergency* position when the air pressure is _____.

    a. no less than 20 pounds and no more than 45 pounds

    b. normal

    c. at more than 100 pounds

    d. at 75 pounds

15. You must stop and do an en route walkaround safety inspection _____.

    a. each 100 miles of a trip

    b. every 4 hours of a trip

    c. every 150 miles or 3 hours (whichever comes first) during a trip

    d. every 400 miles or 8 hours (whichever comes first) during a trip

16. For most clutches, _____ inches of free play is normal.

    a. 0

    b. 1 to 2

    c. 4 to 5

    d. 6 or more

3

Control Systems

OBJECTIVES

When you have completed this chapter, you should be able to:

- Describe the role and function of engine controls, primary vehicle controls, and secondary vehicle controls.

- Name, locate, and describe the control functions for (1) starting the engine, (2) shutting down the engine, (3) shifting, (4) accelerating, (5) braking, and (6) parking.

- Locate the controls for lights, signals, and comfort.

- Understand the importance of using seat belts.

- Describe the acceptable operating range for the fuel, oil, air, cooling, exhaust, and electrical systems.

- Discuss how checking these systems often can help you spot problems early.

- Understand the function and importance of warning devices.

INTRODUCTION

I f you have ever seen the cockpit of an airplane, you know there is a vast difference between the console of an aircraft and the dashboard of your personal vehicle. Because the workload of a big rig is much different than that of a smaller truck or an automobile, the controls and instrumentation will also be different **(see Figure 3–1).** The objective of this chapter is to introduce the basic controls and functions of today's tractors and straight trucks.

Figure 3–1

Instrument panel.

VEHICLE CONTROLS

Let's begin with the basics and build from there.

The three types of controls found on big rigs are:

1. **Engine controls**—start the engine and shut it down
2. **Primary vehicle controls**—provide driver with control of vehicle
3. **Secondary vehicle controls**—assist driver with vision, communication, comfort, and safety but do not affect the vehicle's power

Engine Controls

Engine controls start the engine and shut it down. Engine controls do not control movement. Although they are similar in most vehicles, differences depend on the type of engine, fuel used, and starter mechanism.

Engine Control Switch

The engine control switch starts the engine. This switch is much like a gate through which an electrical current must pass before the engine cranks. The switch must be in the "on" position for the engine to start.

Today's rigs continue to be more technical—but some of the basics remain the same.

Starter Button

Some trucks may have a **starter button.** To start the engine in this type of vehicle, turn the key to the "on" position and push the starter button.

Other Engine Controls

Other controls that relate to starting or stopping the engine include the following:

Engine stop control knob—used in some diesel engines to shut off the engine. Operates by pulling out the knob and holding it until the engine stops.

Computerized idle timer—as a function of the engine's electronic controls, it will shut down the engine in a prescribed amount of time after the truck has come to a complete halt.

Figure 3-2

Cruise control is available in most newer trucks.

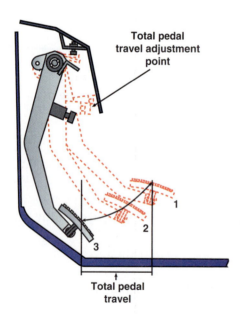

Figure 3-3

Primary vehicle control.

Figure 3-4

The three basic clutch pedal positions are (1) engaged, (2) free play, and (3) disengaged.

Emergency engine stop control—shuts down the engine. Use this control in emergency situations only. Many companies insist that it be reset by a trained technician after each use.

Cruise control—enables the driver to maintain a constant speed without having to depress the accelerator **(see Figure 3–2).**

Primary Vehicle Controls

The **primary vehicle controls** do exactly what their name implies: They allow the driver to control the vehicle. Primary vehicle controls include the clutch pedal, transmission control, accelerator pedal, steering wheel, and brake control. As a professional driver, you must not only know where these controls are found in the cab of a truck but also how to operate them **(see Figure 3–3).**

Clutch Pedal

To start the engine or to shift gears, you must use the **clutch pedal.** There are four basic pedal positions **(see Figure 3–4):**

1. **Disengaged**—the pedal is pushed within 2 inches of the floor. When the pedal is in this position, the engine and drive train are separated. The clutch must be disengaged to start the engine and shift gears.

2. **Free play**—this is the amount of pedal movement possible at the top of the stroke without engaging or disengaging the clutch. It should be between ½ and 2-½ inches.

3. **Engaged**—the pedal is fully released. The driver is not applying any pressure. The word *engaged* means the engine and drive train are connected and moving together.

4. **Clutch brake**—most transmissions use a clutch brake to stop and control the speed of the transmission input shaft and countershaft. The clutch brake is used to engage only the first gear or the reverse gear when the vehicle is stopped. It works when the pedal is within 1 or 2 inches of the floor, depending on the adjustment **(see Figure 3–5).**

Transmission Controls

Transmission controls vary with the different types of transmissions. Some tractors have manual transmission with both a clutch and a gear lever. All gear changes are controlled by the driver. Some tractors have semiautomatic transmissions, which include a clutch and gear

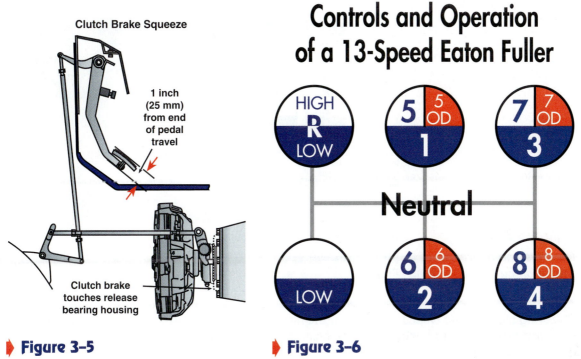

> **Figure 3–5**

Mechanics of the clutch brake.

> **Figure 3–6**

Diagram of a manual transmission.

lever, but some of the gear changes are controlled by an onboard computer. In recent years, more trucks are on the highway with fully automatic transmissions with just a gear lever and no clutch. All gear changes are controlled by computers or by hydraulics on these vehicles.

Controls Found on a Manual Transmission Gear Lever. Typically, a range change lever on the front of the gear lever allows you to switch between ranges. The lever is in the down position for the low range (usually the bottom four or five gears) and in the up position for the high range (the top four or five gears).

Splitter Valve. Some transmissions—like the 13-speed or 18-speed Eaton Fuller—use a **splitter valve** to split gears into overdrive **(see Figure 3–6).** This valve is controlled with a button on top of the gear shift knob.

Automatic Transmissions

More commercial motor vehicles today are equipped with automatic transmissions. Following are some basic suggestions for driving tractors or trucks with automatic transmissions. For the purposes of this instruction, the Eaton Fuller Automated Mechanical Transmission is used.

Proper Startup. To start a truck or tractor equipped with an automatic transmission, the following steps are suggested **(see Figure 3–7):**

1. Make sure the shifter is in neutral "N" and the parking brake is set.
2. Depress the clutch pedal and turn the ignition key to "on."
3. Wait for the service light on the shifter to go out and a solid "N" appears on the gear display.
4. Start the engine and let out the clutch pedal to register proper input speed. If the proper input speed is not registered, the engine will not shift into the initial starting gear.
5. Always return shifter to "N" before turning engine off.

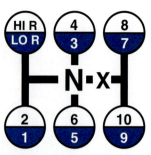

With the auto-range feature, the actual number of conventional lever shifts is half that of conventional ten-speeds. The range shift is triggered automatically at "X" location as the operator moves the lever toward the third rail.

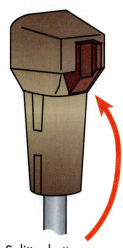

▶ **Figure 3-7**

Controls and operation of the Eaton Fuller Super Ten.

When starting in first gear, preselect the next gear with the splitter button, release the throttle, and accelerate when you are in gear.

Splitter button

Selecting the Starting Gear. Once the engine has been properly started, the next step is to select the starting gear. The following steps are suggested:

1. Select "D," "H" for manual mode, or "L" for low mode.

2. Depress the clutch pedal. A solid number on the gear display indicates that the gear is fully engaged. If flashing down arrows appear on the gear display, this indicates the input shaft has not slowed enough to get into gear.

3. Continue to depress the clutch pedal until the arrows are off. If down arrows are off and the gear number continues to flash slowly, let up on the clutch pedal to fully engage the gear.

4. Depending on how your vehicle is programmed, you can select different starting gears while in "D" or "H" (manual) by using up and down buttons. Remember to choose the correct starting gear for your load and grade.

5. Let out the clutch.

Available Gears.
"H" = Manual Mode

1. Can be selected while moving or from a stop.

2. Must use the up and down buttons to shift.

3. Shifter will "beep" if shift cannot be completed due to engine rpm and road speed.

"L" = Low Mode

1. Can be selected while moving or from a stop.

2. Selecting "low" from a stop engages and maintains first gear.

3. Selecting "low" while moving will allow for downshifts only and downshifts will be performed at a higher rpm.

"R" = Reverse Mode

1. Selecting "reverse" from "neutral" will engage "low reverse" and an "R" will appear on the gear display.

2. Transmission models with multiple reverses must use the up and down arrows to select other reverse gears. Remember to select the proper reverse gear for your load and grade condition.

3. All reverse gears can only be engaged at less than 2 mph.

Proper Shutdown Procedure.

1. Remember to depress the clutch when stopping the vehicle.

2. Before shutting the vehicle off, you must select "neutral" on the shifter and make sure a solid "N" is on the gear display.

3. Turn the key off, release the clutch pedal, and set the parking brake.

CAUTION!

It is very important that you DO NOT shut the truck off or stall the engine while the transmission is in gear. This will cause the transmission to lock in gear and the engine will not restart.

Tips for Drivers—Automatic Transmissions

The following general suggestions are provided by Eaton Fuller regarding the Automated Mechanical Transmission:

1. The clutch is only needed at startup, when selecting a starting gear, and when stopping. "D," "H," or "L" can be selected at any speed.

2. When first starting the engine after changing loads, AutoShift needs to adapt to the changing conditions of the vehicle. If the transmission holds a gear while in "D," simply push the "up" button and the shift will be completed. This may have to be done several times before the transmission "remembers."

3. "H" should be used when you want to control the shifts, such as moving around the yard, going up a grade, or in poor traction situations.

4. "L" should be used anytime you want to maximize the engine brake, such as going down a long grade or when coming to a stop.

5. The service light will come on and go off during powerup. If the service light comes on and stays on or comes on while you are driving, the transmission (AutoShift) has detected a fault in the system. Note the conditions when this occurs—hot/cold, wet/dry, on a grade/flat terrain—and get the vehicle to a service facility. Some faults prevent the transmission from shifting into other gears.

TIPS

Shifting Tips for Professional Drivers

- Always select an initial starting gear that provides sufficient reduction for the load and terrain.

- In order to shift from a higher starting gear to a lower starting gear, press the service brakes (e.g., "3," press brakes—3rd gear start).

- For normal driving, place the shift lever in D. You should not have to move the shift lever again unless driving conditions change.

- For manual control of upshifts, place lever in "3," "2," or "1." When upshift is desired, move gear selector to D and then back to "3," "2," or "1."

TIPS

- Under severe conditions, for the best operation and increased transmission cooling when driving up a long, steep grade, move the gear selector to "3," "2," or "1" from D. Select proper gear before starting uphill.

- To increase downshift points for optimal uphill driving, move the shift lever into "3," "2," or "1."

- Never coast with the gear shift lever in the neutral position.

- To inhibit upshifts during downhill driving and for optimal engine braking, move the gear selector to "3," "2," or "1." There will be no further upshifts, except to protect engine from overspeeding. The gear selector can be moved at any speed.

- For maximum downhill engine braking, move the gear selector to "1," depress the service brake, and operate the vehicle below 3 mph.

- When driving through adverse conditions, such as deep sand or mud, move the gear selector to "3," "2," or "1." To engage these gears while moving, the vehicle must be slowed to less than 3 mph.

- When parking the vehicle, move the shift lever to N and set the parking brake. If you stop on an incline, for safety reasons, block the wheels.

- There is a speed limit on reverse engagements, yet the driver can effectively rock the vehicle by moving the shift lever from reverse to drive and drive to reverse.

Other Controls

Fuel pedal—controls the amount of fuel entering the combustion chamber. Controls the vehicle's road speed (mph). Push the fuel pedal down to increase speed and ease off to reduce speed.

Steering wheel—used to determine direction of the rig. The steering wheel of a CMV is 6 to 12 inches larger across (diameter) than the steering wheel of a car. The larger size gives the turning leverage needed to control big rigs.

▶ **Figure 3-8**

Foot brake control.

Brake controls—used to slow or stop the rig. Learning how to use the brake controls includes the use of the following:

- **Foot brake control valve**—also called the foot valve or treadle valve, this valve operates the service brakes on both the tractor and the trailer. When pushed in, it supplies air pressure to all tractor and trailer service brake chambers **(see Figure 3–8).**

- **Trailer brake control valve**—also called the hand valve, trolley valve or independent trailer brake, this operates the service brakes on the trailer only in special situations. This valve should not be used to hold the rig when it is parked.

- **Parking brake control valve**—a flip-switch or push-pull knob that allows the driver to put on the parking brake. The parking brake should be put on only after the rig is stopped.

- **Trailer air supply valve**— in the open position, it provides air to the trailer brakes. In the closed position, it shuts off the air supply to the trailer. It is closed, or pulled out, when there is no trailer. NEVER use this valve as a parking brake. If you do so, loss of air will occur **(see Figure 3–9).**

CAUTION!

When the air supply drops to 20 to 45 psi, the valve closes automatically. This stops the flow of air and protects the tractor's air supply. The trailer's air supply valve triggers the emergency relay valve that puts on the trailer brakes.

▶ **Figure 3–9**

Trailer air supply valve.

■ **Trailer emergency relay valve**—activates when the air supply is lost, as with severed air line(s) or diaphragm failure. The spring brake will remain locked/parked until the chambers are caged with a caging tool and/or air supply lines are replaced or repaired and the air supply is restored.

■ **Antilock brake systems (ABS)**—an electronic control system that prevents wheels from locking. This makes it possible to prevent jackknifing and loss of vehicle stability **(see Figure 3–10)**. ABS works because special sensors monitor wheel speed at a rate of 100 times per second. If the system detects that any wheel is overbraked for existing conditions, the electronic control unit signals a valve that will reduce braking forces at that wheel until the threat of a skid is eliminated.

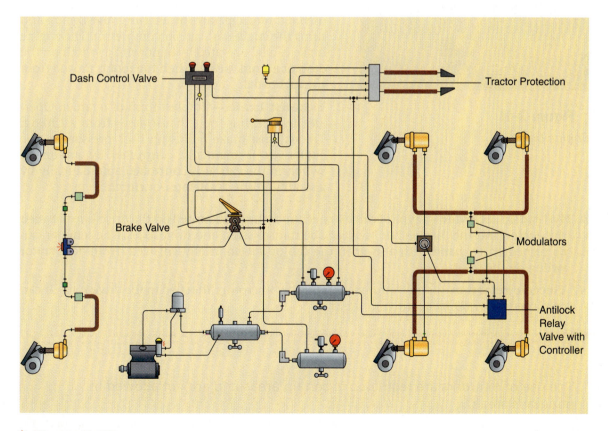

▶ **Figure 3–10**

Antilock brake system (ABS).

Tips for Driving with ABS

TIPS

1. With ABS, you do not have to brake any differently. If necessary, ABS automatically modulates braking while the driver maintains brake pressure.

2. Do not pump the brakes—ABS will control braking for you.

3. Even though your vehicle is equipped with ABS, you should not avoid taking unnecessary risks. Be cautious and use good driving skills such as maintaining adequate distances between you and the driver ahead.

4. Use your mirrors to watch your trailer during emergency braking if your vehicle is equipped with ABS. Apply your brakes as necessary to keep your vehicle in line. Tractor ABS will help prevent jackknifing but it will not keep the trailer from swinging out of control.

5. Only if your trailer has ABS will you maintain control when applying your brakes as necessary, to keep your rig in your traffic lane. Trailer ABS will prevent trailer swing but it will not keep your tractor from jackknifing.

▶ **Figure 3–11**

Engine brake.

Engine brakes and retarders—slow the rig without using the service brake system. The function of engine brakes and retarders is to keep the rig operating at a reasonable speed. Many towns and cities restrict the use of retarders because of the noise. There are four types of auxiliary brakes or retarders:

1. **Engine brake (see Figure 3–11)**—most widely used retarder. Operates by altering valve timing and turns the engine into an air compressor. The engine brake can be operated by hand with a switch on the dash or automatically when the foot is moved from the fuel pedal.

2. **Exhaust brake**—simplest form of retarder. Operates by keeping the exhaust gases from escaping. The exhaust brake builds up back pressure in the engine. It is manually controlled by an on/off switch in the cab. It is controlled automatically by a switch on the accelerator or clutch.

3. **Hydraulic retarder**—a type of drive line retarder that is mounted on the drive line between the engine and the flywheel or between the transmission and drive axles. The retarder can be turned on by hand with a lever in the cab or automatically engaged by an accelerator switch on the floor.

4. **Electric retarder**—uses electromagnets to slow the rotors attached to the drive train. It can be turned on or off by a switch in the cab.

CAUTION!
The use of retarders are restricted in certain areas and are not allowed in populous areas.

▶ Figure 3–12

Interaxle differential in the normal position.

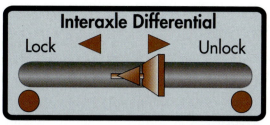

Interaxle Differential
Lock ◀ ▶ Unlock

Unlock
Normal position

Interaxle differential lock control (or power divider)—locks and unlocks rear tandem axles. Unlocked, the axles turn independently of one another on a dry surface **(see Figure 3–12)**. In the locked position, power to the axles is equalized to help keep the wheels without traction from spinning. This position is used on slippery roads.

STOP!

The interaxle differential lock control should *never* be engaged or disengaged while wheels are spinning. The control should be locked before wheels begin to spin.

Secondary Vehicle Controls

Secondary vehicle controls do not affect the rig's power or movement, but play important roles as they assist with safety:

- **Vision**
  Lights
  Windshield wipers
  Defroster

- **Comfort**
  Seat position
  Air vents
  Air conditioner and heater

- **Communication**
  Horns
  Radio
  Lights (headlights, brake lights, four-way flashers)

- **Safety**
  Seat belts
  Door locks

Other controls not related to driving include those for fifth-wheel lock assembly. Most of these controls are similar to those found in automobiles. Others are found only in tractor-trailer rigs. The number and function of the secondary controls may vary with the design of the truck or tractor.

Seat Belts and Seat-belt Laws

GO!

Federal Motor Carrier Safety Regulation **392.16 Use of Seat Belts.**

A commercial motor vehicle that has a seat belt assembly installed at the driver's seat shall not be driven unless the driver is properly restrained with it.

All CMV drivers must use a **seat belt** assembly to be properly restrained when driving the vehicle.

According to the National Highway Traffic Safety Administration (NHTSA), death and injury from traffic crashes continue to be among the most serious public health problems facing our country. Motor vehicle injuries constitute 99 percent of nonfatal transportation injuries and 94 percent of transportation deaths. With yearly increases in travel and no improvement over our current safety performance, fatalities and injuries could increase by 50 percent by 2020.

Approximately 5,000 people are killed annually in crashes involving large trucks. Although less than 20 percent of the fatalities in such crashes are occupants of the truck, the truck occupant is often killed in situations that may be preventable had the occupant been wearing a safety belt. In an effort to save lives, individual states across the nation have adopted safety belt laws. As of July 2004, only New Hampshire had no adult safety belt requirements.

All trucks are now equipped with safety belts. Although they will not prevent accidents, safety belts have been found to often be the difference between life and death when accidents occur.

VEHICLE INSTRUMENTS

Scanning the dashboard of a truck or tractor **(see Figure 3–13),** you will immediately notice a number of gauges and meters. These instruments keep you informed about the condition of your rig and its parts. They will also warn you of possible problems and may help avoid major difficulties.

As you learn the skills of a professional driver, you will want to:

- Understand the purpose and function of each instrument

- Understand the information each instrument provides; for example, temperature and pressure gauges can indicate improper or unsafe operating conditions that may damage your rig

- Take action to correct a problem when you notice an improper reading on one or several gauges

- Know when your rig has reached the correct range of operation; for example, a professional driver will know the correct readings necessary for required air pressure, oil pressure, and water temperature

Each vehicle's instruments are divided into two categories:

- **Basic instruments**—to monitor the vehicle's various systems
- **Warning devices**—warning lights or audible signals that indicate when certain systems are malfunctioning or have reached a danger point

Basic Instruments

Speedometer—like that in an automobile, the speedometer in a truck or tractor displays road speed in miles per hour and kilometers per hour **(see Figure 3–14).**

GO!

FMCSR 393.82 requires that every bus, truck, and truck-tractor be equipped with a speedometer indicating vehicle speed in miles per hour, which shall be operative with reasonable accuracy.

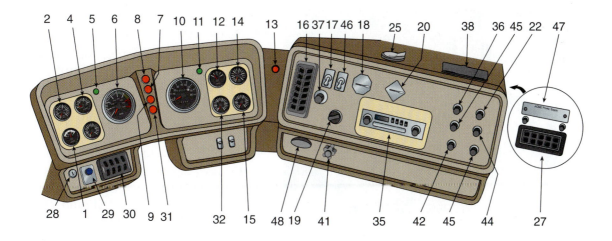

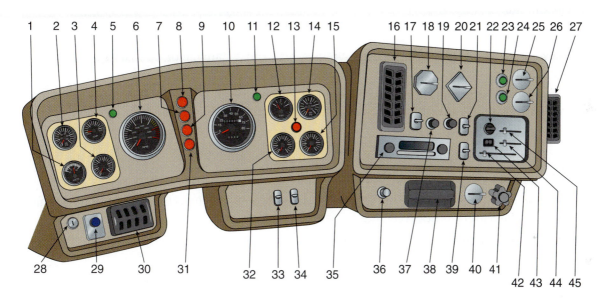

1. Battery voltmeter gauge	17. Headlight switch	33. Cargo lamp switch
2. Engine oil pressure gauge	18. Trailer air supply valve knob	34. Heated mirror switch
3. Optional component gauge	19. Wiper/washer control knob	35. Radio
4. Engine coolant temperature gauge	20. System park brake valve knob	36. Cigar lighter
5. Left-hand turn signal indicator	21. Spot light switch	37. Instrument panel rheostat switch
6. Engine tachometer gauge	22. Heater/AC blower motor knob	38. Ash tray
7. High temperature/low water indicator	23. Interdifferential differential indicator	39. Driving lamp switch
8. Headlight hi-beam indicator	24. Interwheel differential indicator	40. Air slide 5th wheel control lever
9. Low air pressure indicator	25. Interdifferential differential control lever	41. Hand throttle control knob
10. Speedometer gauge	26. Interwheel differential control lever	42. Panel, floor, defroster, control lever
11. Right-hand turn signal indicator	27. Heater/air conditioner diffuser	43. Air conditioner ON/OFF switch
12. Fuel gauge	28. Ignition key switch	44. Fresh/recirculating air control lever
13. Preheater indicator	29. Starter pushbutton	45. Heat/cold control lever
14. Dual air pressure gauge	30. Heater/air conditioner diffuser	46. Marker interrupter switch
15. Optional component gauge	31. Low oil pressure indicator	47. Radio power supply
16. Heater/air conditioner diffuser	32. Optional component gauge	48. Engine stop control knob

▶ Figure 3–13

Vehicle instrument panel.

Figure 3-14

Speedometer.

Odometer—indicates how many miles the rig has been driven.

Tachometer—displays engine speed in revolutions per minute (rpm). The tachometer, or tach, is a guide that indicates when to shift gears. It also assists the driver in using the engine and transmission effectively during acceleration and deceleration.

Fuel gauge—indicates how much fuel is in the fuel tanks. Since the gauge is not always accurate, the driver should check tanks visually before each trip and at all stops.

Voltmeter—measures voltage output of the battery. The meter needle should be between 13.0 and 14.5 volts during normal operation. Higher-than-normal voltage may cause damage or otherwise shorten a battery's life.

Ammeter—measures how much the battery is being charged or discharged. Under normal operating conditions, the ammeter should read as follows:

Engine off—0

Engine starts—needle jumps to the charge side and flutters

Engine warmed—reading drops back to 0 or slightly on the charged side

A consistently high reading indicates the battery may be ready to fail. Continuous discharge means the battery is not receiving a charge from the alternator or generator.

A number of conditions may cause these abnormal readings:

- The voltage regulator is not working properly.
- A bare wire is causing a short circuit.
- The alternator is defective.
- There are loose or worn belts.

Air pressure gauge—the air brake system is activated by air pressure. The air pressure gauge indicates the amount of air pressure in the tanks. Air pressure should start building as soon as the engine starts and continues until the maximum pressure is reached, usually around 120 psi. In normal operation, when the air pressure drops to 90 psi, the air compressor will automatically build back to 120 psi. The air compressor governor controls the operation.

CAUTION!

If the air pressure drops to 60 psi while driving, the low-pressure warning alarm light will turn on. At 20 to 45 psi, the tractor protection valve will close and shut off the air supply to the trailer. Shutting off air supply to the trailer triggers the emergency relay valve, which puts on the trailer's brakes.

Low air pressure can result from air leaks, failure of the compressor or compressor governor control, broken or kinked air lines, or an open air tank petcock.

STOP!

If you have a loss of air pressure, stop your rig at once. Locate the source of the problem and have it repaired immediately. Do not operate your rig without adequate air pressure!

Oil pressure gauge—indicates the oil pressure within the vehicle's lubrication system, in place to keep metal engine parts from overheating while protecting them from wear. If pressure is lost, some trucks have an automatic shutdown mechanism. Lost pressure means there is not enough lubrication in the system. If this continues, the engine can be destroyed within a very short period.

Oil pressure should register within seconds of ignition. It should then rise slowly to the normal operating range. "Normal range" will depend on the type of vehicle and the engine rpm.

CAUTION!

You should stop and check the oil level if pressure does not register or if it fluctuates rapidly at ignition. You should also stop if a loss of pressure occurs. Causes of low oil pressure include lack of oil, oil leaks, and oil pump failure. If the oil level is adequate and there are no leaks, the problem may be the oil pump, a clogged oil line, or a filter.

Other Types of Gauges

The number and types of gauges on a vehicle will vary. The only gauges required by law are the speedometer and the air pressure gauge.

Air brake application gauge—indicates in pounds per square inch (psi) the amount of air pressure used when the brake pedal or the hand brake is applied. This gauge can also indicate the status of the vehicle's brake adjustment.

Coolant temperature gauge—shows the temperature of the coolant in the engine block. The cooling system protects engine parts against destruction from heat produced by the burning of fuel in the combustion chamber, rapid movement, and friction. The normal operating range is between 170 and 195 degrees or the range specified for that particular vehicle.

STOP!

If the coolant temperature gauge registers above the normal range, the engine may be overheating. SHUT DOWN THE ENGINE AT ONCE! Overheating may be caused by (1) not enough engine oil, (2) loose or broken fan belt, (3) malfunctioning fan clutch or control, (4) a blocked radiator, (5) a broken thermostat, coolant pump, or radiator shutter, (6) a severe load—attempting to pull too much or too hard, or (7) the winter front may need to be removed. Remember! Low fluids, oil, or coolant may result in engine shutdown.

Engine oil temperature gauge—indicates the temperature of the engine oil. Normal operating range is between 180 and 225 degrees, about 20 to 60 degrees higher than the coolant temperature. High oil temperature causes the oil to thin, which decreases oil pressure. Engine oil temperatures, however, can run as high as 250 degrees to 265 for a short period without damaging the engine, but NEVER operate the engine above the safe operating range.

Exhaust pyrometer gauge—indicates the temperature of the gases in the exhaust manifold. If these gases become too hot, they can damage the turbocharger. Maximum safe operating temperatures may be indicated on the pyrometer name plate.

Gear box temperature gauge—indicates the temperature of the lubricant in the transmission. Normal readings range from 150 to 200 degrees. A high reading may indicate a low oil level.

Axle temperature gauge—indicates the temperature of the lubricant to the front and rear drive axles. Normal readings range from 150 to 200 degrees. This reading does not vary when the rig is loaded. Higher readings, up to a range between 230 and 250 degrees, are acceptable for short periods. Readings for both drive axles should be within 10 degrees of each other. Generally, the forward rear axle will run hotter than the rear axle.

CAUTION!

Axle temperature gauge readings above the normal range can mean bad bearings or a flat tire.

Warning Devices

Most commercial vehicles are equipped with warning lights and signals to indicate when the rig's fuel, air pressure, or operating temperature has reached a danger point. Some of these warning signals are built into the dash of the tractor. They will signal when there is a problem. When a warning signal occurs, immediately stop the rig **(see Figure 3–15).**

You should become familiar with the following warning devices:

- **Low air pressure warning alarm**—audible or lighted signal when there is low pressure in the air brake system.

- **ABS warning lamp for trucks and tractors**—usually located on the dashboard or instrument cluster, the warning lamp will come on during the bulb check at vehicle ignition and then will turn off if the warning lamp is functioning properly. If the lamp remains on during vehicle operation, this may signal that ABS is not operating. If ABS is not operating, the vehicle will retain normal braking but without the benefits of ABS.

- **ABS warning lamp for trailers**— usually located on the "road side" near the rear of the trailer, the ABS warning lamp is amber.

▶ **Figure 3-15**
Warning lights indicate potential problems.

■ **Automatic traction control (ATC) warning lamp**—will come on at vehicle ignition and will remain on until brake pedal is applied. The lamp will turn off and remain off until a low traction event is encountered. If the vehicle's drive wheels lose traction during acceleration, the ATC lamp will turn on and begin flashing rapidly. The ATC lamp will also flash rapidly when ATC is functioning to assist the driver in accelerating the vehicle.

■ **Coolant level alarm**—lights when the coolant level starts dropping, indicating a possible leak.

■ **Oil level alarm**—lights when the oil level becomes too low for normal, safe operation.

■ **Coolant temperature warning**—lights when the operating temperature is too high for safe operation.

■ **Pyrometer warning**—lights when exhaust temperatures are too high.

■ **Differential warning**—flashes when the interaxle differential is in the locked position.

⚠ **WARNING**

Before starting a vehicle:
- Sit in the driver's seat
- Place shift lever in neutral
- Set the parking brake

⚠ **WARNING**

Before working on a vehicle or leaving the cab with engine running:
- Place the transmission in neutral
- Set the parking brakes
- Block the wheels

⚠ **WARNING**

When parking the vehicle or leaving the cab:
- Always place shift lever in neutral
- Set the parking brakes

⚠ **WARNING**

For safety reasons, always engage the service brakes when moving the shift lever from "N" to one of the other gear positions. (If equipped with auto neutral and parking brake is engaged, transmission remains in neutral.)

⚠ **CAUTION**

To avoid damage to the transmission during towing:
- Place the transmission in neutral
- Lift the drive wheels off of the ground or disconnect the driveline

⚠ **CAUTION**

If engine cranks in any gear other than neutral, service your vehicle neutral safety start circuit immediately.

⚠ **CAUTION**

Do not release the parking brake or attempt to select a gear until the air pressure is at the correct level.

⚠ **CAUTION**

Do not operate the vehicle if alternator lamp is lit or gauges indicate low voltage.

SUMMARY

In this chapter, you have been introduced to the control systems for your rig. You now know what the gauges should read for safe operation. As a professional driver with safety as a personal priority, you understand the importance of using a seat belt at all times. Warning devices were also reviewed in this chapter, as was the need to pay immediate attention to any warning lights or signals from these monitors.

KEY TERMS

Air brake application gauge
Air pressure gauge
Ammeter
Antilock brake system (ABS)
Auxiliary starter button
Axle temperature gauge
Brake controls
Clutch brake
Clutch pedal
Computerized idle timer
Coolant level alarm
Coolant temperature gauge
Coolant temperature warning
Cruise control
Differential warning
Electric retarder
Emergency engine stop
    control

Engine brake
Engine controls
Engine oil temperature gauge
Engine stop control knob
Exhaust brake
Exhaust pyrometer gauge
Foot brake control valve
Fuel gauge
Fuel pedal
Gear box temperature gauge
Hydraulic retarder
Interaxle differential lock
    control
Low air pressure warning
    alarm
Odometer
Oil level alarm

Oil pressure gauge
Parking brake control valve
Primary vehicle controls
Pyrometer warning
Seat belt
Secondary vehicle controls
Speedometer
Splitter valve
Starter button
Steering wheel
Tachometer
Trailer air supply valve
Trailer brake control valve
Trailer emergency relay valve
Transmission control
Voltmeter

REVIEW QUESTIONS

1. Which of the following is not an element of the primary vehicle control system?

    a. clutch pedal   **c.** transmission control

    b. fifth wheel   **d.** steering wheel

2. Which of the following is not a part of the engine control system?

    a. engine control switch   **c.** emergency engine stop control

    b. starter button   **d.** clutch pedal

3. Which of the following is not one of the basic clutch pedal positions?

    a. disengaged   **c.** clutch brake

    b. free play   **d.** engaged

4. Which of the following is not an accurate statement regarding the clutch brake?

    a. It stops or controls the speed of the transmission input shaft and countershaft.

    b. It is used to engage only the first gear or the reverse gear when the vehicle is stopped.

    c. The clutch brake is used in emergency situations to stop the vehicle.

    d. It works when the pedal is within 1 or 2 inches of the floor, depending on its adjustments.

5. For a tractor with a manual transmission, the gear changes are controlled by _____.

    a. the driver

    b. hydraulics

    c. the dispatcher

    d. an onboard computer

6. Which of the following is not a correct statement regarding the trailer supply valve?

    a. In the open position it provides air to the trailer brakes.

    b. In the closed position it shuts off the air supply to the trailer.

    c. It is to be closed when there is no trailer.

    d. It is a safe procedure to use this valve to activate the parking brakes.

7. Which of the following slows the rig by altering the valve timing which turns the engine into an air compressor?

    a. engine brake

    b. exhaust brake

    c. hydraulic retarders

    d. electric retarders

8. When the air supply to the trailer is lost, _____.

    a. the vehicle may safely be driven to a service center

    b. the trailer emergency relay valve is activated

    c. the driver may safely complete the assigned trip without repairs

    d. the driver should make repairs and continue the assigned trip

9. The interaxle differential lock control _____.

    a. is used to equalize power to the axles to help keep the wheels without traction from spinning

    b. is used to lock the rear wheels so an unauthorized person cannot drive the vehicle

    c. should be activated after the wheels start spinning

    d. should only be used at high speeds on interstate highways

10. The trailer brake control valve, also known as the independent trailer brake, _____.

    a. should be used to hold the rig when parked

    b. is to be used when stopping at stop signs and traffic lights

    c. operates the service brakes on the trailer only

    d. is located outside of the cab, near the front of the fifth wheel, and indicates when the trailer brakes are activated

11. Regarding the gauges and meters on a tractor dashboard, which of the following is not a true statement?

   a. It is important for a professional driver to understand the function and purpose of each gauge and instrument.

   b. It is important for a professional driver to understand the information each instrument provides.

   c. It is important for a professional driver to take action to correct a problem when an improper reading is registered on one or several of the gauges.

   d. Since modern tractors have computers to monitor all systems, it is not important for a driver to check the gauges and meters of the vehicle after the trip starts.

12. Which of the following gauges are required by law?

   a. fuel and tachometer

   b. odometer and voltmeter

   c. ammeter and oil pressure

   d. speedometer and air pressure gauge

13. Regarding the basic instrument, the air pressure gauge, which of the following is a correct statement?

   a. It indicates the amount of pressure in the tires of the drive wheels.

   b. It indicates the amount of pressure in the tanks.

   c. It indicates the average of the amount of pressure in the trailer wheels.

   d. It indicates the speed of the wind the rig is heading into.

14. While you are driving, if the air pressure drops to _____ psi, the air pressure warning alarm will activate.

   a. 70

   b. 88

   c. 60

   d. 65

15. If the coolant temperature gauge registers above the normal range, the driver should _____.

   a. shut down the engine at once

   b. reduce the speed of the vehicle and continue the trip

   c. reduce the speed of the vehicle and drive to the nearest repair facility

   d. increase the speed of the vehicle to force more air through the radiator which will cool the engine

Daniel Baez

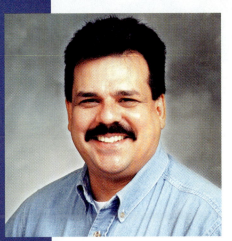

Used with permission of Accent Photography by Terra and Contract Freighters, Inc.

DANIEL BAEZ began his career as a truck driver to earn a better income. "I was working in a food warehouse and wasn't making enough money," he remembers. "A friend told me to go to school with him to learn how to drive a truck. Once I knew how to drive a truck, I learned about the freedom of being out there on the road without the pressure of someone looking over your shoulder all of the time." He attended Tri-State Semi Driver Training and began his career in 1989. In his driving career at CFI, he has driven over 1.3 million miles.

"I like the freedom that the road gives you," he remarks. "You can set your own hours as long as you deliver and pick up in time. I like seeing the country, being in a different place every day." Daniel drove for 12 years as a company driver for CFI before becoming an owner-operator in October 2004, viewing his decision as a chance to build something for retirement.

"I like CFI because they treat me right," Daniel comments. "They don't mess with my pay. Whatever I make, they pay me exactly what I earn." As a company driver, he was impressed with CFI's equipment and maintenance. "They care about the drivers and they care about the equipment," he continues. "It's the best company that I've worked for. I worked for another company for a few years, and I came back [to CFI] because I knew it was a good company. I knew I wouldn't have to worry about other problems, like getting the miles, getting paid on time, and getting what I earned."

Daniel and his wife, Susana, believe patience, mutual support, and constant communication are key to staying connected when Daniel is on the road. "In the beginning I missed my family, but constant communication is the only way you can do it," he advises. "We call our wives and take the frustrations of work out on our families—that's not good communication. I try to separate my work from my family whenever possible. It's very hard not being there, and you need to feel a little sympathy [for your family]. Instead of calling your wife and telling her whatever happens, keep in good communication with your family."

In 1993, Daniel was involved in a head-on collision. Seconds before impact, he saw the face of the man whose vehicle had weaved into his lane. "Thank God it wasn't my fault," he remembers. "Every once in a while that will pop into my mind. I became more aware of my surroundings, even though at that time I did whatever I could to avoid the accident. It made me more aware on two-lane roads—I look farther ahead to the oncoming traffic. You can see from a distance if they're weaving or coming into your lane."

Not all of his memories are so somber. One delivery in California was met with quite a celebration. "They were just opening a store, and they were all waiting for me to get there with furniture from Mexico," Daniel recalls. "They were celebrating that I was getting there, and when I arrived, everybody was cheering. It's a nice memory."

Daniel and Susana reside in El Paso, Texas. Together, they have two children, Danny, Jr. and Alex, and one granddaughter, Hailey. Recently committing to a regional route in Texas, Daniel gets home on a consistent basis. He likes to spend time with his family, work around the house, and cook out as the weather permits.

Used with permission of Contract Freighters, Inc.

Vehicle Systems

OBJECTIVES

When you have completed this chapter, you should be able to:

- Expand your understanding of, and the vocabulary required for, the various vehicle systems.
- Describe and explain the function and relationships between vehicle systems.
- Locate and explain how the frame, axles, wheels and their parts, engine, drivetrain, and brakes operate.
- Understand the relationships of the previously discussed systems.

INTRODUCTION

A tractor-trailer consists of many parts and systems, and while each of these parts and systems perform many specific jobs, they must all work together—much like the organs and systems of the human body work together in healthy people **(see Figure 4–1).**

If a tractor is to work efficiently and effectively, each of its systems must work individually and as a group in order for the tractor to pull its cargo down the road **(see Figure 4–2).**

▶ **Figure 4–1**

A tractor-trailer is made up of many parts and systems.

▶ **Figure 4–2**

The various systems on a tractor-trailer must work together to perform effectively.

This chapter will explore each of these parts and systems and will discuss:

■ The reason for each of the rig's systems

■ The function of the major parts of each system

■ The relationship of the system to safe and economical operation

FRAME, SUSPENSION SYSTEMS, AND AXLES
Frame

The **frame** is the infrastructure around which the rest of the rig is assembled. It is the backbone, so to speak, of the truck tractor and many trailers. Engine mounts are attached to the frame and hold the engine in place. The body of the tractor is connected to and strengthened by the frame. The frame is also the unit through which the axles and wheels are connected to the suspension system.

The frame consists of two steel rails and cross members that run the entire length of the vehicle **(see Figure 4–3).** Lightweight tractors have aluminum rails. Tractors that haul oversized or overweight loads usually have extra-strength steel rails. Cross members connect the two rails

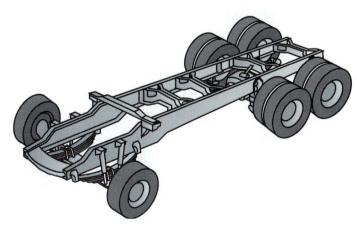

▶ **Figure 4–3**

The frame includes two steel rails that run the length of the vehicle.

and provide strength and support to the frame. Directly or indirectly, the frame is connected to every other system of the tractor.

Figure 4-4

A good suspension system supports the load and transmits full engine and braking power to the chassis frame.

Suspension System

The **suspension system** supports, distributes, and carries the weight of the truck. This system is made up of springs and spring hangers. The front and rear axles are attached to it and the frame rests on it. As the ground changes, this system allows the axles to move up and down, independently, without seriously affecting the cargo. By securing the suspension system at several points along the frame, the stress and shocks from the road can be evenly distributed **(see Figure 4–4).**

A good suspension system should be able to support the load and transmit full engine power or braking power to the chassis frame. It should hold the axles securely to ensure correct driveline alignment and should cushion the ride for the driver and cargo, whether the trailer is empty or loaded.

The two types of suspension systems are **spring leaf suspension** and **air bag suspension** systems. Spring leaf suspension systems consist of narrow metal strips of varying lengths that are bolted together and attached to frame hangers. Heavy-duty systems commonly use the "stack" or "multileaf" spring. Tapered leaf springs are used for lighter weight, tandem axle vehicles. The air bag suspension system uses bags of air placed between the axle and the frame. Widely used on trailers, air bag suspension is also used on truck tractors. Air pressure for the air suspension system comes from the tractor's **air compressor.** Some systems have valves, allowing the driver to adjust air pressure for specific loads. Frame height can also be changed for different loads.

NOTE: Many vehicles use a combination of the spring and air bag suspension systems.

Shock absorbers reduce the motion of the vehicle body as the wheels move over uneven surfaces **(see Figure 4–5).** A shock absorber operates like a piston in a cylinder with a hole in it. Since liquid is almost impossible to compress, liquid is forced through the tiny hole as the shock is compressed. The liquid resists the pressure and smoothes out the ride.

Axles

Axles connect the wheel to the rest of the tractor-trailer. They also support the weight of the vehicle and its cargo. Different axles perform different functions. While all axles support the weight of the vehicle, each type performs a special function:

Front tractor axle—connects the steering mechanism and the brakes.

Rear tractor axle—the power or drive axle. This axle transfers power from the engine and drivetrain to the wheels.

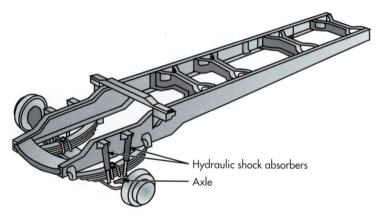

Hydraulic shock absorbers
Axle

Figure 4-5

Shock absorbers reduce the motion of the vehicle as the wheels move over uneven surfaces.

Dead axles

Drop center ▼

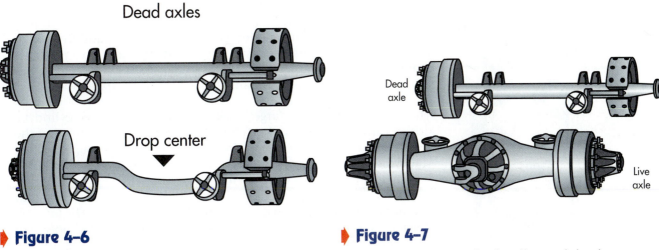

Figure 4–6

The drop-center axle design allows space for the driveshaft.

Figure 4–7

There are two types of axles: live and dead.

Along with trailer axles, the tractor axle also serves as a connecting point for the brakes. All axles fall into two types: dead axles and live axles. A **dead axle** is not powered. It receives or houses the wheel, supports vehicle weight, and provides a place to connect the steering mechanism and brake components. Most dead axles are straight but some have a drop-center design that allows space for the driveshaft **(see Figure 4–6).** Some are I-beam construction, whereas others consist of a hollow tube or box. Examples of dead axles include ordinary trailer axles, converter dolly axles, multiple axle assembly, lift axle, variable-load suspension axles, and sliding tandems.

The **live axle (see Figure 4–7)** is powered and supports the vehicle's weight and sends power to the wheels. The live axle is hollow and, because of this, the gears and axles can transmit through this space to the wheels. Examples of a live axle include **single-drive axles, tandem axles,** and **tri-drive axles.**

ENGINES

The engine provides the tractor's power and there are many different types of engines. Those who want to know in depth about engines and how they work should take a mechanic's training course; however, all professional drivers should know something about how engines operate and the types of engines commonly used in truck transportation **(see Figure 4–8).**

Engines are fueled by diesel fuel or gasoline. Engines used in truck tractors are internal combustion engines, which means the engine burns fuel inside closed chambers. These chambers are called *cylinders* and serve as the "heart" of the engine. These cylinders are where the engine's power is generated to turn the wheels that run the tractor and pull the trailer.

Figure 4–9 shows a four-stroke engine. Key parts of the engine include the **crankshaft,** one or more **camshafts** (magenta and blue), and **valves.** There are one or more **cylinders** (grey and green) and for

Engine Location

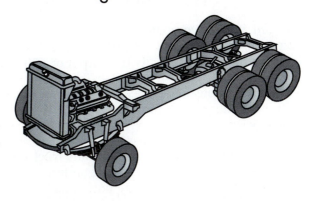

Figure 4–8

Engines come in many types to perform various tasks.

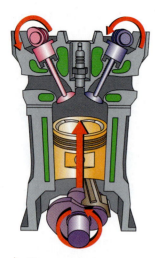

▶ **Figure 4-9**

A typical four-stroke engine.

each cylinder there is a **spark plug** (darker grey), **a piston** (yellow), and a **crank** (purple). A single sweep of the cylinder by the piston in an upward or downward motion is known as a stroke and the downward stroke that occurs directly after the air-fuel mix in the cylinder is ignited is known as a power stroke. The four phases of operation (intake, compression, power, exhaust) take place in separate locations.

The **engine block** is a large block of steel with holes, or cylinders, drilled through it. Think of a cylinder as a coffee can. One end of the can is sealed shut. The other end is open. A piston fits snugly against the cylinder wall, but it can move up and down. When fuel burns within the cylinder **(combustion),** it creates the expansion that forcefully moves the piston. A rod attached to the piston moves with it. Since the rod is connected to a crank, it turns the crank. The up-and-down movement of the piston is converted into the circular motion of the crankshaft. This circular or rotary motion is the force that is applied to move the wheels and, therefore, move the vehicle.

Fuel, alone, will not power an internal combustion engine. In the case of the diesel engine, in place of carburetors, such as those found in automobiles, are fuel injectors that supply fuel to the cylinders and the air that causes combustion is supplied by an air intake system. The extreme compression of the fuel and air mixture in the cylinder by the piston squeezes it so much that the diesel fuel ignites. Once the fuel has burned, it is forced out of the cylinder through exhaust valves and manifolds.

COMPUTER MANAGEMENT SYSTEMS

Today, all new medium- and heavy-duty truck systems are managed by computer. Electronically managed engines cost more than their hydromechanical counterparts but last much longer, make vehicles easier to drive, require less maintenance, and produce much better fuel mileage.

Within a 10-year period (between 1987 and 1997), truck engine management systems sold in North America went from almost 100 percent hydromechanical management to almost 100 percent management by electronics.

The Environmental Protection Agency emission requirements, which triggered the introduction of computerized engine controllers and have also driven their progressive evolution, have brought additional benefits of fuel economy and much greater engine longevity.

Most tractors now use computers to manage engine and other system functions. These functions are cybernetically controlled. Cybernetics is the science of computer control systems.

Onboard vehicle computers are referred to as engine/electronic control modules (ECM) or electronic/engine control units (ECU). These computers normally contain a microprocessor, data retention media, and usually the output or switching apparatus.

With the widespread use of electronics in vehicle systems today, current systems can be read by most electronic service tools in use, which makes diagnostic and servicing procedures much more efficient.

Thanks to computerized electronics, any truck engine management system can be programmed to the preferences of the operator regarding governors, cruise control, road speed limit, critical shutdown sensors, peak braking power, idle speed, and other options.

Management systems for current vehicle systems tend to be classified by the degree of control they have over the fueling pulse. Full authority systems use electronic fuel injectors or electronic unit pumps. The term "full authority" indicates that the electronic engine control unit has full control of the fueling pulse.

Partial authority systems are ECM-managed systems in which an existing hydromechanical fueling apparatus has been adapted for computerized control. These are rapidly becoming obsolete and are not used in current new systems.

FUEL SYSTEM

The **fuel system** sends fuel to the engine. In newer models, fuel management is handled by computerized elements of the system. Computers also regulate the amount of fuel in the system and how much is injected into the cylinders.

The pump moves the fuel from the tank through the filtering system and into the injector. Usually the pump delivers more fuel than is needed, so a pipe returns the extra fuel to the tank.

Just before the fuel reaches the injector, a filter cleans it. Even a small speck of debris or dirt can ruin an injector, so the fuel can never be too clean. Because foreign matter, such as debris or dirt, can cause much damage to the engine and its operation, there is often another filter between the tank and the pump.

The computer figures the right amount of fuel and injects it into the cylinder at exactly the right time and at the right pressure. The amount of fuel needed varies because of power needs. Because most engines are now computerized, their power and the amount of fuel used is optimized and much more efficient than older models.

Fuel Tanks

The **fuel tanks** are containers designed to hold the truck's fuel. Most larger trucks have two fuel tanks, strapped to each side of the frame.

Fuel tanks are vented to maintain equal pressure on the inside and outside. The vent hole is usually in the filter pipe cap or at the top of the tank.

The fuel cap area must be kept clean at all times. The fuel filler cap and the neck of the tank should be completely clean before removing the cap. This will keep dirt and other foreign particulates out of the fuel system.

If the tank is under the chassis, use *great care* when cleaning the cap to keep dirt from getting into the fuel system.

Fuel Filters

Filters in the fuel system clean the fuel as it goes from the entry tube of the tank, through the tank and fuel lines, and into the fuel injectors. A coarse filter is the first dirt block; a finer filter is next; finally, a filter/water separator protects the injector jets and engine from water, rust, and other contaminants.

CAUTION!

This final filter—a filter/water separator—is the most important one to remember in the fuel system, because water can seriously harm the fuel system by encouraging rust and corrosion.

Fuel System Heaters

Trucks driven in cold weather should have **fuel system heaters.** The three types of fuel system heaters available are:

1. Units that heat the fuel in the tank
2. Inline heaters that heat the fuel when it is going from the tank to the injector system
3. Filter heaters that heat the fuel filters which, in turn, heat the fuel as it passes through the injection system

When a truck is driven in severely cold weather, all three types of fuel system heaters may be needed. Chemical additives can also be used to prevent the fuel from gelling and to keep wax crystals from forming. Some chemicals even clean the injectors and improve the fuel.

Diesel Fuel

Diesel fuel offers the following advantages over gasoline. It has a low vaporizing rate and does not create an explosive air–fuel mixture when it is accidentally spilled or leaked. This is an important factor when hauling highly volatile fluids or explosives.

The "cetane number" of diesel fuel indicates the quality of the fuel, showing the amount of time needed for the fuel to ignite the hot air in the combustion chamber of the cylinder. Cetane numbers generally range from 30 to 60. The higher the number, the faster the fuel will ignite.

If the cetane number is too low, the engine will be difficult to start. There may be "knocking" and puffs of white smoke from the exhaust. If it continues, harmful deposits can collect in the cylinders.

A negative characteristic of diesel fuel is that it creates wax crystals in cold weather. These crystals make starting and operating the engine difficult. In the high-tech market of fuel additives, however, new products are now available that provide the following advantages:

- Reduce fuel consumption
- Prevent diesel fuel from gelling in extremely cold temperatures
- Reduce engine maintenance costs and increase the life of a diesel engine
- Reduce fuel emissions, particulates, and exhaust smoke released into the atmosphere from diesel engines

AIR INTAKE AND EXHAUST SYSTEMS

The **air intake** and **exhaust systems** ensure that the engine has enough fresh air to process so that the tractor runs properly. The importance of these systems cannot be overstressed. Fresh air is needed constantly in the engine's air supply system **(see Figure 4–10).**

What Does Each Part of the System Do?

The air intake system delivers fresh air to the cylinders and an air cleaner removes dirt, dust, and water from the fresh air. Clean air flows into the intake manifold (a pipe with an equal number of outlets and cylinders). Each outlet from the manifold is an intake port for a cylinder. Valves regulate the flow of air into the cylinders. Keep the air cleaner clean so it can function at its best. In dusty or rainy weather, check the air cleaners daily.

After combustion occurs in the engine, the exhaust system expels used gases. Exhaust valves open in each cylinder. A stroke of the piston expels the used gases through ports in the exhaust

Air Intake System

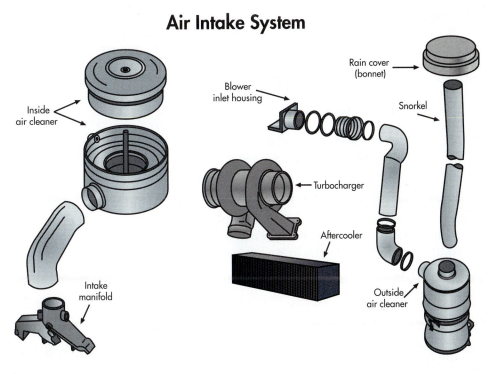

Inside air cleaner

Intake manifold

Blower inlet housing

Turbocharger

Aftercooler

Rain cover (bonnet)

Snorkel

Outside air cleaner

▶ **Figure 4–10**

Fresh air is vital for use in the engine's air supply system.

manifold. The gases pass through the exhaust pipe and a muffler. The muffler quiets the noise and the gases are discharged from the vehicle through a vertical stack or tailpipe.

The **pyrometer,** found on some instrument panels, measures the temperature of the exhaust gases. This temperature may be anywhere from 600 to 1,000 degrees F. The normal operating range varies from truck to truck. It is important that this temperature does not get too high, especially on long grades or mountain roads, because it may damage the engine. If the pyrometer temperature becomes too high, downshift.

The turbocharger converts the power received from the exhaust gases into power that can be used by the engine.

The aftercooler cools the intake air from the turbocharger and returns it to a safe temperature level.

LUBRICATION SYSTEM

The **lubrication system** distributes oil to the parts of the engine. The film of oil between the moving parts keeps them from rubbing together; instead, they ride or slide on the oil. This reduces friction between part surfaces **(see Figure 4–11).** By keeping friction to a minimum, you increase engine efficiency and extend the life of the parts.

Typical Lubricating System

1. Oil pump
2. Oil fill tube
3. Dipstick
4. Rocker and drain
5. Cam pocket drain
6. Oil drain from blower or turbocharger
7. Full-flow oil filter
8. Bypass oil filter
9. Oil cooler
10. Drain to oil pan
11. Oil pickup screen

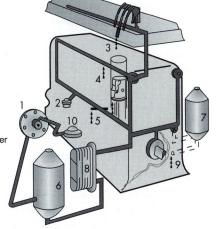

▶ **Figure 4–11**

The lubricating system distributes oil to parts of the engine to reduce the wear and tear caused by friction.

Oil is not pumped directly to the many engine parts that require lubrication. Instead, the "splash method" is used as the bearings and many other rapidly moving engine parts throw off oil. With the constant motion, a fine oily mist reaches those parts not included in the pressure line of the system.

Oil absorbs the heat created from movement of the engine parts and cleans the engine by removing dirt, carbon, and worn metal. The biggest particles settle to the bottom of the **oil pan** while the smaller ones are filtered out.

Another vital function of the lubrication system is to prevent loss of pressure between the pistons and the cylinder wall by forming an oil seal between these parts. Without this seal, when pressure is lost, power is also lost.

Finally, engine oil absorbs shocks by forming a cushion between the surfaces subjected to shocks. For example, each time ignition occurs in the combustion chamber, a sudden force hits the piston. This, in turn, sends the force through a **wrist pin,** connecting rod, and crankshaft. Oil helps absorb the shock of these parts as well as reduce noise and wear and tear.

CAUTION!

Check the oil level in the engine on a daily basis with the dipstick, usually found at the side of the engine.

Oil changes—should be part of the tractor's regular maintenance schedule.

Oil filters—another way to extend the life of an engine is to regularly change oil filters. As the oil circulates through the engine, doing its work of cooling the engine and reducing friction between its parts, it collects dirt, grime, and small bits of metal that must be removed before they cause damage. Oil filters strain out these impurities.

Three types of oil filtering systems are:

1. **Full-flow systems**—in which all oil leaving the oil pump passes through the oil filter. Using the "one-pass" method, all contaminates must be filtered out during this one trip through the filter.

2. **Bypass systems**—or part-flow systems, filter a small amount (about 10 percent) of the oil flow. It is normally used with the full-flow system. It filters excess oil that does not go through the bearings but is normally returned to the oil pan. The flow of oil through the bypass filter is controlled by an opening.

3. **Combination of full-flow and bypass systems**—considered the best type of filtration system, oil from the full-flow filter goes into the bearings and oil from the bypass filter returns to the oil pan.

Centrifugal filter—a type of bypass filter in which the oil entering the permanent housing spins the filter

"This brings back such great memories . . . of the days my older brother called me 'dipstick'!"

at high speed. This forces the dirt and particles out of the oil for more efficient cleaning. It is used in addition to other oil filters.

Dipstick—a device used to indicate the oil level in the engine. The dipstick is marked in increments—"low" or "add"— but this can vary from one manufacturer to the next **(see Figure 4–12)**.

Figure 4–12

The dipstick will tell you if the oil level is low.

To use the dipstick to accurately measure the oil level in the engine, complete the following steps:

1. Turn off the engine.

2. Using gloves, remove dipstick from housing and wipe it thoroughly with a utility rag.

3. Insert the clean dipstick in the shaft where it was housed, withdraw it again, and the level of the oil will be indicated on the dipstick with an oily film.

4. If the oil level is at the "low" or "add" mark, add oil before driving the rig again. Follow manufacturer's recommendations to use proper oil for the truck you are driving.

STOP!

If, when checking the oil levels in the engine, the oil mark is too high on the dipstick or you notice a light foam, check immediately for possible coolant leak.

COOLANT SYSTEM

Heat is the basis of the internal combustion engine. However, intense heat can quickly destroy an engine, so a **coolant system** is needed to keep the temperatures down **(see Figure 4–13)**. As coolant circulates through the engine block and cylinder head, it keeps the engine cool. Remember to think about the engine block as a solid block of steel into which large holes or cylinders have been drilled, although the block is actually a lot more complex than that. In addition to the cylinder holes, the

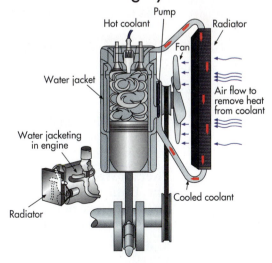

Cooling System

Figure 4–13

The cooling system regulates the heat in an internal combustion engine.

block is honeycombed with a channel that comes very close to all the cylinders. This channel is called the **water jacket.** Here is how it works:

- Coolant flows through the jacket, picking up heat as it goes.
- The channel then takes the coolant to the radiator and in the radiator.
- The coolant flows through small, thin-walled tubes surrounded by air. This cools the coolant before it is pulled into the pump and back into the engine.
- When the coolant enters the water jacket, the process is repeated and the coolant is again cooled.

The filler neck is located in the upper tank of the **radiator.** The **radiator cap** is placed at the top of the filler neck. To the side of the filler neck is an overflow tube that allows excess water or pressure to escape the radiator.

CAUTION!

It is important to keep the radiator filled with the proper amount of coolant.

Too much coolant will flow out when too much pressure builds inside the radiator. If pressure is excessive, it raises the radiator cap from the filler neck and excess coolant and water will boil out and overflow the tube.

When the pressure drops, the cap falls back into place and stops the flow of coolant.

Note: Low fluids may cause engine shutdown or prevent engine from starting.

NOTE: The pressure cap will allow the coolant to reach a higher-than-usual boiling point. For this reason, the cap needs to be tested at each preventive maintenance check.

STOP!

Water should not be used in the cooling system because if it is used alone, it can cause rust or other damage to the system and engine. Commercial antifreeze works better and should be changed annually.

Following are terms related to the coolant system:

Coolant—fluid that circulates within the system, absorbing heat from the engine. It then takes the heat to the radiator for cooling. The coolant then returns to the engine for repeat performance.

Thermostat—a valve in the water jacket located at a point where the coolant leaves the engine. Until the engine runs long enough to heat the coolant, the thermostat is closed. When the engine reaches normal operating temperature, usually 180 degrees F, the thermostat opens and the coolant moves into the radiator.

Radiator—the largest part to be found in the cooling system, the radiator consists of upper and lower tanks, the core, the tube, connections for hoses, and a filler cap. The cap also maintains pressure on the coolant, which is important, because the higher the pressure, the higher the boiling point of the cooler.

Fan belt—a belt from the engine that drives the fan. The belt must be checked for slack, cracks, or worn spots. The fan belt should be tightened or replaced as needed. A shroud or cowling protects the fan belt and directs airflow. Many engines have fan clutches that disengage the fan when it is not needed. The fan can reactivate at any time, which can cause serious injury.

> **CAUTION!**
> A leaking radiator cap can cause the entire coolant system to operate improperly.

ELECTRICAL SYSTEM

The **electrical system** on your tractor is a complex and important system. Without electricity, you could not start your engine, run your lights, or utilize your instruments and gauges. Therefore, it is important to understand this system because it serves many purposes. Following are some basics of the electrical system:

1. An electron is a tiny particle carrying a negative charge of electricity.

2. Electrical flow produces electrical current—and some materials carry this electrical current to its purpose better than others.

3. A good electricity conductor is a material whose electrons can be easily moved. Copper wire is such a conductor and it is used frequently to move electrical charge from its source to its point of use. Because rubber is not a good conductor of electrical current, copper wire is usually surrounded with rubber insulation.

4. Insulated wires bring electrical current where electricity is needed to operate.

5. Terminals are the connecting devices between the electrical wires and the part where electricity is needed. They connect wires to the components.

6. There is also a main terminal where the wires start. This same main terminal contains the system circuit breakers and fuses.

The electrical system consists of four parts:

1. Charging circuit
2. Cranking circuit
3. Ignition circuit
4. Lighting and accessory circuit

Charging Circuit

The five parts of the **charging circuit** are:

- Battery
- Alternator or generator
- Voltage regulator
- Ammeter
- Voltmeter

- Electrical wires
- Battery cable

The charging circuit produces electricity to keep the battery charged and runs the electrical circuits.

Battery

The black boxes called **batteries** work very hard, converting chemical energy into electrical energy **(see Figure 4–14).** Once this occurs, batteries supply power to the rest of the vehicle's electrical system. The parts of the battery include:

- **Case**—to neatly hold all the parts together.

- **Vent caps**—on top of the battery and allow gas buildup to escape. You remove the vent caps to check the battery and you may find them clogged and needing to be cleaned from time to time.

- **Individual cells**—there are dry-charged, wet-charged, and maintenance-free batteries. Dry-charged batteries have no fluids in them when they leave the factory and the dealer adds water to the battery when it is sold. The wet-charged battery has fluid in it when it leaves the factory. These two types must be checked for fluid levels when you do a pretrip inspection.

- **Cell connectors**—these are the transports of the electricity from the cell to the power supply.

- **Terminal posts**—the two posts are located on top of the battery and have a positive post (the larger one) and negative post.

 Figure 4–14

The battery supplies power to all the vehicle's systems.

CAUTION!

Electricity can be dangerous if you do not exercise extreme care when you are working around it. Following are some tips about working around batteries safely:

- Disconnect battery ground strap before you begin any electrical or engine work.

- Connect the ground strap last when you install a new battery.

- Never lay metal tools or other objects on the battery.

- Never hook up the battery backwards—make sure to connect the positive cable to the positive terminal post. Connect the negative cable to the negative post. (The positive cable clamp and terminal are usually larger than the negative cable clamp and terminal.)

- Be careful when handling batteries. Battery acid is corrosive.

- Do not lean too closely to the battery when adding water, as any splash could get into your eyes.

- Keep fires away from batteries. If you are a smoker, save your cigarette until after you have finished working under the hood.

Alternators and Generators

The **alternators and generators** recharge the battery when it loses electricity. The electricity generated can be used by the battery and electrical systems. Most systems today use alternators.

When the engine is running, the alternator is creating electricity. Through computerized control systems, the electricity used for operating—except for starting the engine, which comes from the battery—is provided by the alternator.

Ammeter

The gauge on the instrument panel used to indicate the amount of charge or discharge the battery is receiving from the generator is called the **ammeter.** It should read "zero" when the engine and the electrical system are off. Starting the engine will move the needle from zero to the charge side. Once the engine is on and warm, the needle should drop back to zero. It is also normal for it to read slightly on the charging side.

Voltmeter

The **voltmeter** shows whether the battery is charging properly. This gauge can be identified by the word *volts* on the lower portion of the gauge as well as a picture of the battery. There are three segments of this gauge, each showing a different condition. The far left segment (red) shows undercharging. The middle (green) segment shows normal battery condition. The far righthand (red) segment indicates overcharge. A pointer shows which condition the battery is in at the moment.

CAUTION!

If the voltmeter shows a continuous undercharging or overcharging condition, there is a problem in the charging system.

Voltage Regulator

The **voltage regulator** controls the voltage produced by the alternator. The regulator keeps the battery voltage from getting too high, and thus prevents the battery from overcharging. It also keeps other electrical parts from burning themselves out.

Cranking Circuit

The **cranking circuit** sends electricity from the battery to a small starter motor gear **(see Figure 4–15).** By activating the starter switch, the driver puts the ignition system into motion.

Ignition Circuit

In a gasoline engine, the **ignition circuit** provides sparks for each cylinder to ignite the fuel–air mixture. An ignition circuit is not needed for diesel trucks because the compression of the air ignites the fuel.

Cranking System

Junction block

Cables and wiring

Storage battery

Cranking motor

Cranking switch

▶ **Figure 4–15**

The cranking circuit sends electricity from the battery to a small starter motor.

Lighting and Accessory Circuit

The lighting and accessory circuits send electrical power to:

- Lights (headlights, tail lights, turn signals, running lights)
- Horns
- Instrument lights (speedometer, odometer, gauges, etc.)
- Windshield cleaners (wipers, washers)

GO!

The detachable electrical connection, working between the tractor and the trailer in combination, supplies power from the tractor's power plant to the trailer, where it powers the trailer's lights.

Straight trucks do not have detachable electrical connections.

DRIVETRAIN

The **drivetrain** takes power generated by the engine and applies it to the tractor's drive wheels. As the wheels turn, the rig moves. The drivetrain has five main parts **(see Figure 4–16):**

1. **Clutch**
2. **Transmission**
3. **Driveshaft**
4. **Universal joints**
5. **Differential**

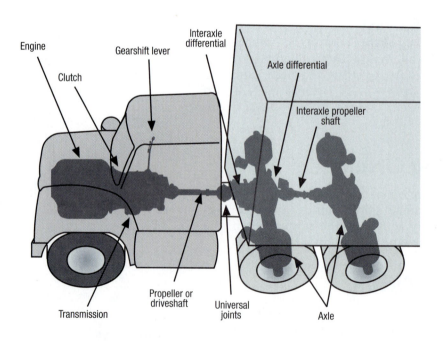

▶ **Figure 4–16**
The main components of the drivetrain.

These five parts perform four basic functions:

1. Connect the engine (source of power) to and disconnect it from the drivetrain.
2. Modify the torque (twist) and engine speed (rpm) produced by the engine to allow the vehicle to operate at its best.
3. Carry the power of the engine to the rear axle and drive wheels.
4. Change the direction of the torque to propel the rear wheels.

The following describes the result of putting various parts of the power train into action. This is an overview, not a complete and detailed explanation.

Clutch

The clutch is used to connect or disconnect the engine from the rest of the power train **(see Figure 4–17).** One of the primary jobs of the clutch is to help the driver easily shift gears. The main parts of the clutch include:

- Clutch housing
- Flywheel
- Clutch disc(s)
- Pressure plate
- Release assembly
- Clutch brake
- Controls

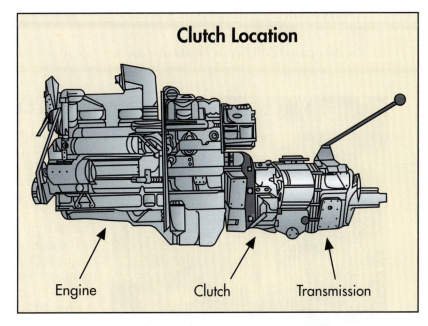

Clutch Location

Engine Clutch Transmission

▶ Figure 4–17

The clutch connects or disconnects the engine from the rest of the power train.

On most trucks, there are three plates that can be pressed together (engaged) or pulled apart (disengaged). The middle plate (called the clutch disc) is the "driven member." It is connected to a shaft leading to the transmission. The other two plates are "driving members" and connect to the engine.

A spring forces the two driving members toward each other, squeezing them against the middle plate until they all turn together as one unit. When the plates are together, the clutch is "engaged." When the plates are apart, the clutch is "disengaged."

The engine flywheel is the first driving member. It has a smooth surface where it squeezes the driven plate. The other driving member is called the pressure place and is made of heavy cast iron that is smooth on one side. It is fastened to the cover, which is bolted to the flywheel so they can all turn together. This disc can slide forward and away from the driven plate.

The driven plate, or clutch disc, is a flat disc of steel with a friction facing on each side. The plate is fastened by grooves or slots called **splines** to a shaft connected to the transmission. The disc fits into the grooves of the shaft so that the plate and shaft turn together and the plate can slide forward and backward on the shaft.

The clutch disc is softer than the other plates and because of this, it will be worn out before damage can occur to other parts of the drivetrain. When a clutch "goes out," it is usually the clutch disc that must be replaced.

CAUTION!

To prevent excessive wear or damage, clutches should be adjusted. Locate the access hole where you can make this adjustment.

There are two types of mechanical clutches:

1. **Direct clutch control**—consists of manually operated assembly made of levers, rods, and springs connecting the pedal to the clutch release mechanism. Conventional tractors often use such a clutch.

2. **Cable-operated clutch control**—uses a cable to replace part of the linkage.

▶ **Figure 4–18**

The transmission is a box of gears usually attached to the clutch housing.

TRANSMISSION

The **transmission** is a box of gears located behind the clutch. The box is usually fastened to the clutch housing **(see Figure 4–18).** The clutch and transmission look like an extension of the engine.

The transmission adjusts the power generated by the engine so it provides the right speed and torque for the job. For example, when a loaded rig moves from a stopped position, a great deal of power is needed. The driver uses the gears in the transmission to provide the needed combination of power, torque, and speed. The transmission then sends, or transmits, the power from its source—the engine—to the drive, or powered axles. This is the power that propels the vehicle.

The gears in the transmission help control the speed and power of the rig. The engine can be kept at a relatively constant speed. The rig, however, can be moved either slowly or rapidly with much the same power output. Once under way, the rig needs less power to keep it going than it needed to start rolling. Gears make this possible.

GO!

There are two basic and related facts to understand when selecting gears:

1. More torque or power means less speed.

2. More speed means less torque.

The higher the gear, the more the speed. The lower the gear, the more the torque.

DRIVESHAFTS AND UNIVERSAL JOINTS

Behind the transmission is a propeller called the **driveshaft.** The driveshaft is a steel shaft that runs from the transmission to the rear of the vehicle. Usually, the driveshaft is hollow.

At each end (front and rear) of the shaft are the **universal joints,** or **U-joints.** They are called universal joints because they can move in almost any direction. They are usually constructed of two U-shaped pieces set at right angles and are fastened together by cross arms of equal length. As the driveshaft spins, it transfers the twisting motion back to the rear axle. The U-joints let the driveshaft change its angle of operation.

The U-shaped pieces (yokes) pivot on the arms of the cross. Since they are two pivots, the shaft can be at an angle and still transmit power. The U-joints do not have to be in a straight line. This is very important, because they become somewhat misaligned with each bump in the road. The rear axle moves up and down with the wheels while the transmission moves very little. The U-joints let the propeller shaft turn, even though its two ends are shifting in relation to one another.

DIFFERENTIAL

The two types of differentials on trucks today are the differential and the interaxle differential. The **differential** divides the drive axle in half, allowing each to spin independently. It performs two specific tasks: (1) It transmits power from the driveshaft to the axles. (2) Because it divides the drive axle into two independent halves, each axle half may turn at a different speed, which allows each wheel to rotate independently. This facilitates cornering.

GO!

When a tractor-trailer rig goes around the corner, the outside wheel must rotate faster than the inside wheel.

There are several types of differentials, but our focus is on the major components of the typical differential. These components include the **drive pinion gear,** the **ring gear,** and four **spider gears.**

The drive pinion gear is connected to the end of the driveshaft and drives the ring gear. Attached to the ring gear are four spider gears, meshing with gears on the ends of the drive axle halves. Each of the spider gears can rotate freely and each axle gear meshes with all four spider gears. This accomplishes the transfer of power from the ring gear through the spider gears and into the drive axle halves.

The pinion and ring gears accomplish two tasks:

1. They turn the torque (force) of the pinion shaft at right angles so the wheels can turn and drive the vehicle.
2. They can reduce speed and increase torque because the pinion gear is much smaller than the ring gear.

If your rig is traveling in a straight line down the highway and both wheels are turning at the same speed, the drive pinions are rotating with the spider gears **(see Figure 4–19).** When the rig maneuvers through a turn, the inside wheels slow and, as one axle half begins spinning at a lower speed, the spider gears begin rotating, allowing the axle halves to spin at different speeds to accommodate the turn without scrubbing the tires.

▶ Figure 4-19

The drive pinions rotate with the spider gears when a tractor-trailer is driving in a straight line and both wheels are turning at the same speed.

The **interaxle differential** divides the two axles, allowing each to turn independently of the other. The interaxle differential is used on tandem rear-drive axle trucks and is sometimes called the "power divider."

CAUTION!

The **interaxle differential** should not be engaged while the vehicle is in motion.

WHEELS

Tires are mounted on wheels and the wheel connects the tire to the axle. The three types of wheels are:

1. Spoke or open
2. Budd or stud piloted
3. Unimount or hub piloted

Spoke wheels are made of two pieces. They are heavy and difficult to align and balance. Spoke wheels clamp onto wheels with wheel clamps; and if these are not installed properly, the wheel will soon be out of round. That means it will wobble when it rolls. Disc or stud-piloted wheels are commonly called Budd wheels and are made of aluminum or high-tensile steel. Alignment is simpler because these wheels can be fastened together with six, eight, or ten wheel studs. Unimount or hub-piloted wheels are often called hub-mount wheels and center on the hub at the center hole or bore of the wheel.

MOUNTING SYSTEMS

The two types of mounting systems are stud piloted and hub piloted. A stud-piloted system uses the studs on the wheel hub to guide and center the wheel. Wheels with the stud-piloted mounting system are often called stud-mount wheels. Stud-piloted wheels are designed to be centered by the nuts on the studs.

Hub-piloted mounting systems use the actual wheel hub to guide and center the wheel. Hub-piloted wheels are used with two-piece flange nuts which contact the disc face around the bolt hole and do not rely on contacting the bolt hole chamfer to function properly. Hub-piloted wheels generally have straight-through bolt holes with no chamfers. This feature provides a visual way of identifying hub-piloted wheels. It is important to use the proper components for each type of mounting and to fit the wheels to the proper hubs.

STOP!

The two types of mounting systems cannot be intermixed.

Wheels are fastened by two methods—ball seat and flange nuts. Ball-seat nuts clamp the wheel on by seating to a tapered part of the stud hole. Flange nuts clamp onto the flat surface and provide more even clamping torque. These two types cannot be intermixed.

TIRES

Although often taken for granted, tires are a critical part of the rig because they provide traction, reduce vibration, and absorb shock. It is important to have good tires—not tires that are good enough, but tires that have good tread, are adequately inflated, and are checked frequently for wear and tear **(see Figure 4–20).** Tires must provide traction in all kinds of weather. They also have to be in shape to transfer braking and driving force to the road.

▶ **Figure 4–20**

Regularly inspect tires for wear and tear.

The three types of tires are:

1. Radial **(see Figure 4–21)**
2. Bias ply **(see Figure 4–22)**
3. Belted bias **(see Figure 4–23)**

Radial
Body cords run perpendicular across the tread, belt piles run circumferentially around the tire under the tread.

▶ **Figure 4–21**

Cross section of a radial tire.

Bias ply
Body cords run diagonally across the tread.

▶ **Figure 4–22**

Cross section of a bias-ply tire.

Belted Bias
Body cords run diagonally across the tread. Belt piles run circumferentially around the tire under the tread.

▶ **Figure 4–23**

Cross section of a belted bias tire.

GO!

All tires have *plies*—separate layers of rubber-cushioned cord. Plies make up the body of the tire and are tied into bundles of wire called bead coils. Plies can be bias, belted bias, or radial.

Bias-ply tires have plies that are placed at a criss-crossed angle. This makes the sidewall and the tread very rigid.

Belted bias tires have plies that cross at an angle with an added layered belt of fabric between the plies and the tread. Belts make the tread more rigid than bias-ply tires and the tread will last longer, because the belts reduce tread motion when the tire is running.

Radial tires have plies that do not cross at an angle but are laid from bead to bead, across the tire. Radial tires have a number of belts and their construction means the sidewalls have less flex and less friction, which requires less horsepower and saves fuel. Plus, radial tires hold the road, resist skidding, and give a smoother ride than the bias types.

STOP!

Never mix radial and bias-ply tires on the same vehicle—or put tires of difference sizes or construction on the same axle.

Other Tire Terms

Bead coils and beads—bead coils form the bead, the part of the tire that fits into the rim. Bead coils provide the hoop strength for the bead sections, so the tire will hold its shape when being mounted on a wheel.

Sidewalls—layers of rubber covering, connecting the bead to the tread. Sidewalls also protect the plies.

Tread—part of the tire that hits the road. Treads are designed for specific jobs such as extra traction and high speed. Tires on steering axles should be able to roll and provide good traction. Drive tires must provide good traction for braking and acceleration. Tires for trailers should roll well. Drive wheel position tires need maximum traction in all conditions.

Inner liner—is the sealing material that keeps air in the tire.

Load rating—refers to the strength of the tire. This can be rated from A to Z—with Z being the strongest. The maximum load rating is shown in pounds. FMCSR 393 does not permit a tire to be used that cannot support the load, and the load rating makes certain you have the right tire.

Hump—pattern of tire wear that has the same appearance as a cupped hand—the hump at the edge or higher part of the cup.

Tie bars and fillets—are design factors, not wear patterns. A *sipe* is a cut across the tread to improve traction.

TREAD DESIGN AND WHEEL POSITION

For highway use, the two truck **tire tread** designs are rib and lug.

Rib tread has grooves in the tire tread that run parallel to the sidewalls. Tires with rib-type tread can be used anywhere on the rig and are designed for highway speeds. They are recommended for the front wheels of tractors and large straight trucks for high-speed, long-haul service. They help the driver maintain control of the vehicle and avoid skids **(see Figure 4–24).**

Lug tread has deep grooves in the tire shoulders that run perpendicular to the sidewalls. These tires are best for the drive wheels. In high-torque road service, they wear better, have greater traction, and have higher rolling resistance than rib types. If you operate in cold weather, it may be wise to use rib tires on the drive wheels for greater fuel efficiency **(see Figure 4–25).**

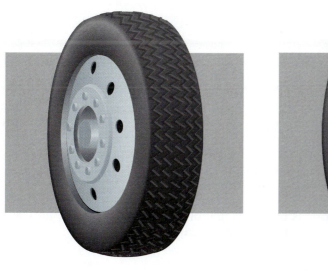

▶ **Figure 4–24**
A tire with rib tread.

▶ **Figure 4–25**
A tire with lug tread.

NORMAL TIRE INFLATION

Tires must be inflated correctly for the rig to perform at its best **(see Figure 4–26).** Maximum pressure is designated in pounds per square inch (psi) on cold tires driven less than 1 mile. This is why you should check tire pressure before you drive—and do not check tire pressure by kicking

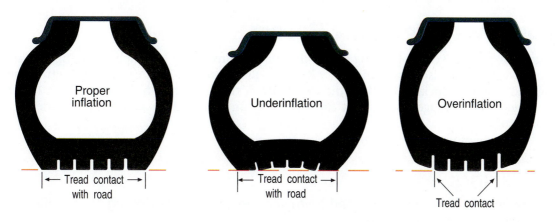

▶ **Figure 4–26**
Properly inflated tires make a rig easier to handle and have a longer road life than under- or overinflated tires.

them! Tires have come a long way since your great-grandpa's day, when kicking actually told you something. Tire pressure should be checked weekly—and more often on long trips. Use a tire gauge and measure tread depth with the proper instrument. Check FMCSR 393.75 for regulations regarding normal tire inflation.

If tire pressure increases more than 10 to 15 psi during normal operation:

- Tires may be underinflated
- Rig may be overloaded
- Tires may not be the right size
- Combination of the above

Whatever the cause, be sure to correct the problem immediately.

Underinflation

Underinflation increases tread wear and reduces tire life. When the temperature increases in an underinflated tire, it can cause the tread to separate from the body or belt ply of the tire.

When a tire is underinflated, it can flex excessively. As this soft tire travels over the road, it builds up heat, which weakens the tire's body cords. If this continues, the body cord deteriorates and may catch fire, due to high internal temperatures.

Underinflated tires also make a rig difficult to control. This is a dangerous situation in and of itself, but it is especially dangerous in extreme conditions or emergencies.

If you are driving on dual tires and one is underinflated or flat, a fire can result; however, the other tire will carry the load until you are able to stop the truck.

New Air Balancing Systems

Newer trucks have air balancing systems—onboard balancing systems for tires and wheels that maximize tire life and smooth your ride. Mounted behind the wheel, they offer permanent solutions for balancing assemblies. Many operate automatically and can adjust instantly for changing conditions.

These balancers extend tire life 25 to 50 percent, prevent cupping, help tires run cooler, solve vibration problems, and automatically balance your tires and wheels while you drive. Most models start working at 20 to 22 mph depending on wheel diameter. This occurs long before vibration due to imbalance, which is at speeds in excess of 35 mph.

How Heat Affects Tire Rubber

A tire can become very hot during a long-distance trip involving high-speed driving. Driving in warm weather can also create unusually high tire temperatures. Heat can affect tire tread bonding and may be associated with an increased rate of tread separation. When tires are hot, they are more easily damaged when they rub against a curb, railroad track, or pit rail guide because rubber softens.

CAUTION!
Remember: If you have just had a tire changed, stop after driving for a while and make sure nuts have not loosened.

Tread Life

Because conditions vary, no one can exactly predict the life of the tire tread. Quality of the tire, how the vehicle is handled, tire inflation, load distribution, and care of the tire will all affect the life of the tread. Average tread life for any tire on the market today has been calculated by each manufacturer. This is good information for the driver because it serves as a guide. If the driver shifts gears smoothly and is generally responsible, he or she may be able to get greater-than-average tread wear. On the other hand, the driver can cut tread life in half by speeding, braking sharply, running over debris, improper air pressure, and running over curbs.

FMCSR 393 provides information about the legal minimum tread depth on a tire. According to this portion of the law, a motor vehicle cannot use tires that:

- Have fabric exposed through tread or sidewalls
- Have less than $\frac{4}{32}$ inch of tread measured at any point in a major tread groove on the front axle
- Have less than $\frac{2}{32}$ inch of tread measured at any point in a major tread groove on all other axles
- Have front tires that have been regrooved, if tires have load capacity equal to or greater than 8.25-20 eight-ply tire

STEERING SYSTEMS

To control your rig, the steering system must be working properly, which is accomplished by checking the parts often to ensure smooth operation **(see Figure 4–27)**.

The steering system allows the driver to make the necessary maneuvers to move the truck from point A to point B. Maneuvers may include turning corners, moving around barriers, and entering and exiting highway ramps—without slipping, sliding, or rolling over.

The steering system begins with the **steering wheel**—the hand control of the wheels connected to the steering axle. Between the steering wheel and the steering axle are the parts that make steering possible:

1. The steering wheel is connected to the steering column and translates the driver's movements to the steering system. When the steering wheel turns, the steering column turns in the same direction.

2. This motion continues through the U-joint to the **steering gear shaft.** From there, the driver's motion continues through another U-joint to the **steering gear box.**

3. The steering gear box is also called "the steering

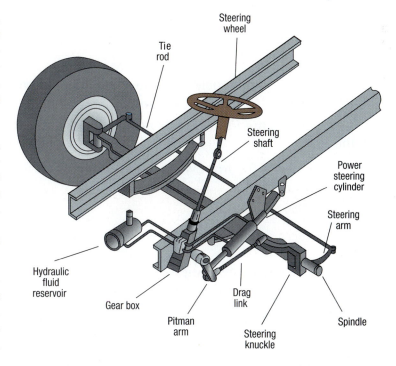

> **Figure 4-27**

The steering system gives the professional driver control of his or her rig.

sector." It changes the rotating motion of the steering column to a back-and-forth motion on the **Pitman arm.**

4. The Pitman arm is a lever attached to the steering gear box and a **drag link** joins the Pitman arm and the steering lever.

5. The steering lever turns the front wheels left and right when the Pitman arm pulls it back and forth. The steering lever connects to the steering knuckle (the moveable connection between the axle and the wheel, which allows the wheels to turn left or right).

6. There is a steering knuckle at the end of each axle. Each contains the seals, bushings, and bearings that support the vehicle's weight. The steering knuckles translate the motion from the driver to the cross-steering lever and the cross-steering tube (the tie rod).

7. Spindles, which are parts of the steering axle knuckles, are inserted through the wheels. Spindles are also called stub axles and are attached to the kingpin.

8. The **tie rod** holds both wheels in the same position. As the left wheel turns, the right wheel follows in the same direction. A kingpin in the steering knuckle gives each wheel its own pivot point.

Wheel Alignment

Manufacturers build in the following alignment features into the front end of the rig. They may be changed as needed.

Caster—the amount of tilt measured in degrees—is the "caster" of an axle. The axle should have a positive caster, meaning it should tilt forward. When set in this manner, the vehicle has a natural tendency to go straight and will also recover from turns more rapidly. Positive caster means easier steering.

Camber—is the degree of tilt at the top of the tires. At its best, the truck's wheels need a positive camber to support the load. When the vehicle is heavily loaded, the tires are straight, relative to the road.

CAUTION!

Other alignment tendencies are often the result of wear and tear. Most noticeable are "toe-in" and "toe-out."

Toe-in means the front wheels are closer together at the front than they are in the rear.

Toe-out means the front wheels are farther apart than the wheels at the rear.

If a vehicle has a **power steering** system, it uses hydraulic pressure or air pressure to assist making the turn, which requires less strength on the part of the driver. Power steering provides greater control of a vehicle with less physical effort. Power steering also reduces driver fatigue because it is less physically demanding. Power steering allows the vehicle to absorb road shocks more and also makes the vehicle easier to maneuver in difficult situations.

When hydraulic pressure assists steering a vehicle, a hydraulic unit replaces the steering gear box and a hydraulic pump is added to the engine to supply the pressure used to help turn the wheels. With hydraulic pressure to help turn the wheels, when the steering wheel is turned to the right, the hydraulic valve senses it, opens, and fluid pressure helps turn the wheels to the right.

COUPLING SYSTEMS

The **coupling system** connects the tractor to the trailer **(see Figure 4–28).** Coupling systems have two main parts—the fifth wheel and the trailer kingpin. Correctly coupling the tractor to the trailer is one of the major responsibilities of every professional driver.

Fifth Wheel

Not really a wheel, the **fifth wheel** is a flat disk on the trailer. The kingpin **(see Figure 4–29)** of the trailer fits into and is held by the fifth wheel. This link allows the tractor to pull the trailer. There are several types of fifth wheels, appropriate for various types of loads:

Fixed-mount type is the most common type. It is secured in a fixed position behind the cab. It has three parts—the top or base plate, the bracket subassemblies, and the frame mounting members. The top plate includes the locking mechanism and bears much of the stress of coupling. The bracket subassemblies hold the top plate in place. The frame mounting members are usually structural steel angles bolted to the fifth wheel.

Sliding (adjustable) type slides backward and forward but can be locked into place to adapt to different loads. The sliding type increases the flexibility of the total rig. The sliding fifth wheel helps the rig conform to state laws regarding vehicle length and distribution of weight over the axles. Sliding fifth wheels may be locked into place in two ways:

1. Pins fit into matching holes in the slider track and hold it in place.

2. A plunger fits into a row of slotted holes in the base to keep it from moving.

The slider can be adjusted automatically or by hand.

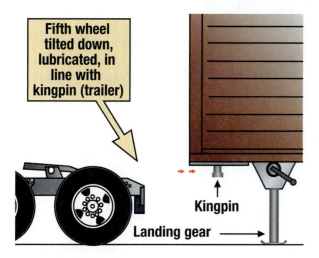

▶ **Figure 4–28**

The coupling system includes the tractor's fifth wheel and the trailer's kingpin.

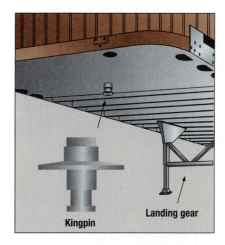

▶ **Figure 4–29**

Close-up of a trailer's kingpin and landing gear. Different kingpin settings affect the hookup.

Fifth Wheel Slack Adjusters

The slack adjuster on a fifth wheel adjusts the kingpin locking mechanism so it will fit snugly around the kingpin. Slack adjusters are used on most mechanical locking mechanisms. Compression locking mechanisms reduce problems with slack.

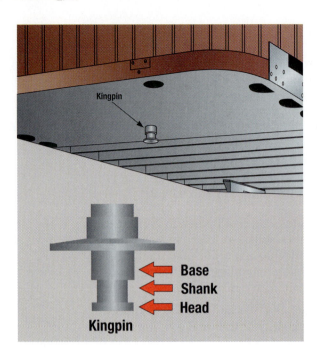

Kingpin

Base
Shank
Head

Kingpin

▶ **Figure 4-30**
The kingpin.

Kingpins

Kingpins are attached to the upper fifth-wheel plate, which is underneath the front of the trailer. The kingpin is usually a 2-inch steel pin that is locked into the jaws of the fifth wheel to couple the tractor to the trailer. It is made of high-strength steel **(see Figure 4–30).**

OTHER COUPLING DEVICES
Converter Dolly

There are two types of **converter dollies:** conventional and jifflox (universal). A **conventional converter dolly** is used to change semitrailers into full trailers when the dolly becomes the front axle of the trailer. A **jifflox converter dolly** is hooked behind the axle of a single axle tractor to convert it to a tandem axle tractor. The tractor can then pull a loaded trailer.

Trailer Landing Gear

When not coupled with a tractor, a trailer needs support for its front end. The landing gear supports the trailer when it is not coupled with a tractor **(see Figure 4–31).** The landing gear is usually hand-cranked and will have skid feet. Landing gears will not resist pressure from the side, front, or rear. They are only a means of stationary support.

▶ **Figure 4-31**
Trailer on its landing gear.

SUMMARY

The major systems you should be familiar with after studying this chapter are the frame, suspension, axles, engine, fuel, exhaust, lubrication, electrical, coolant, brake, steering, and coupling.

KEY TERMS

Air application pressure gauge	Air brake system	Air intake system
Air bag suspension	Air compressor	Air power steering system

Air pressure gauge
Air reservoirs
Ammeter
Antilock brake system
Axles
Battery
Belted bias tires
Bias-ply tires
Bypass system
Cable-operated clutch control
Camber
Carrier bearings
Caster
Centrifugal filter
Charging circuit
Clutch
Combination bypass/full-flow
   system
Combustion
Computer systems
Conclusion
Conventional converter dolly
Converter dollies
Coolant system
Coupling/uncoupling system
Cranking circuit
Crankshaft bearings
Dead axle
Diesel engines
Differential
Dipstick
Direct clutch control
Disk brakes
Disc wheel
Drag link
Drain cocks
Drive pinion gear
Driveshaft
Drivetrain
Drum brakes

Electrical system
Emergency relay valve
Engine block
Engine shutdown systems
Exhaust system
Fan belt
Fifth wheel
Fixed-mount fifth wheel
Frame
Frameless construction
Fuel filters
Fuel system
Fuel system heater
Fuel tank
Full-flow system
Gasoline engine
Generators and alternators
Glad hands/pigtail
Governor
Ignition circuit
Independent trailer brake
Inserts
Interaxle differential
Internal combustion engine
Jifflox converter dolly
Kingpin
Lift axle
Live axle
Low-pressure warning signal
Lubrication system
Lug tread
Multiple axle assembly
Oil filters
Oil pan
One-way check valve
Ordinary trailer axle
Parking brakes
Pitman arm
Power steering
Pusher tandem

Pyrometer
Quick-release valve
Radial tires
Radiator/radiator cap
Relay valve
Rib tread
Ring gear
Safety valves
Shock absorbers
Single-drive axles
Sliding fifth wheel
Sliding tandem
Spider gears
Splines
Spring leaf suspension
Steering arm
Steering gear box
Steering gear shaft
Steering wheel
Supply/emergency brakes
Suspension system
Tag tandem
Tandem axles
Thermostat
Tie rod
Tire tread
Tractor parking valve
Tractor protection system
Tractor steering axle
Transmission
Treadle valve
Tri-drive axles
Twin screws
Universal joints (U-joints)
Variable load suspension
   (VLS) axle
Voltage regulator
Voltmeter
Water jacket
Wrist pins

REVIEW QUESTIONS

1. Regarding the frame of a tractor, which of the following is not a correct statement?

    a. The frame is the backbone of the tractor.

    b. Engine mounts are attached to the frame.

    c. The body is connected to and strengthened by the frame.

    d. Axles are directly connected to the frame.

2. Regarding the suspension system, which of the following is not a true statement?

    a. It distributes the load evenly over the floor of the trailer.

    b. It distributes and carries the weight of the truck.

    c. It is made up of springs and spring hangers.

    d. The front and rear axles are attached to it.

3. Regarding axles, which of the following is not an accurate statement?

    a. They connect the wheels to the rest of the trailer-tractor.

    c. All axles perform the same function.

    b. They support the weight of the vehicle and its cargo.

    d. They support the weight of the vehicle.

4. When a vehicle is loaded and the lift axle is in the lowered position, the axle wear is _____ on the other axles.

    a. increased

    c. reduced

    b. the same

    d. twice as great

5. Regarding live axles, which of the following is not an accurate statement?

    a. It is powered.

    c. It supports the vehicle's weight.

    b. It is not hollow.

    d. It sends power to the wheels.

6. Regarding a pusher tandem, the rear axle is _____.

    a. powered

    c. missing

    b. not powered

    d. powered by an additional engine located at the rear of the tractor

7. A plunger that fits snugly against the cylinder wall and that can move up and down the wall is known as a _____.

    a. crankshaft

    c. connecting rod

    b. carburetor

    d. piston

8. In a diesel engine, the extreme _____ of the fuel–air mixture in the cylinder by the piston squeezes it so much that the diesel fuel ignites.

    a. regression

    c. heat

    b. compression

    d. cold

9. In a gasoline engine, the fuel–air mixture is ignited by_____ from the spark plug.

    a. an electrical spark

    c. heavy gas

    b. compression

    d. none of the above

10. Which of the following is not an accurate statement regarding dirty (fuel with foreign substances) fuel?

    a. A small speck of dirt can ruin an injector.

    c. Since the fuel burns at such a high temperature in the cylinder, dirty fuel is not an issue in the operation of an internal combustion engine.

    b. Dirt in the fuel can damage an engine.

    d. The fuel is filtered to remove dirt.

11. Which of the following is not an accurate statement regarding diesel fuel?

    a. It creates wax crystals in cold weather.

    c. Wax crystals in diesel fuel make starting difficult.

    b. Lower-density fuel is more likely to crystallize or gel in cold weather.

    d. If too many wax crystals collect, the engine will not start.

12. The air cleaner, which is an element of the _____, removes dirt, dust, and water.

    a. exhaust system

    c. fifth wheel

    b. trailer loading system

    d. air intake system

13. The most important function of the lubricating system is to distribute oil to _____ friction between the surfaces of the engine parts.

    a. increase

    b. filter the water in the cooling system to reduce

    c. the cooling system to reduce the

    d. reduce

14. The _____ system distributes oil to parts of the engine to reduce the wear caused by friction.

    a. lubricating

    b. air filter

    c. support

    d. exhaust

15. While the battery provides the energy to start the engine and is used for extra energy when needed, the _____ furnishes all other electrical needs.

    a. exhaust system

    b. fifth wheel

    c. alternator or generator

    d. cranking circuit

16. The _____ takes the power generated by the engine and applies it to the tractor's drive wheels.

    a. freight train

    b. drivetrain

    c. generator

    d. fifth wheel

17. The driver uses the _____ to connect or disconnect the engine from the rest of the drive (power) train.

    a. fifth wheel

    b. lubricating system

    c. clutch

    d. ammeter

18. At each end of the driveshaft are located the _____, which can move in almost any direction.

    a. transmissions

    b. drive pinion gear

    c. universal joints

    d. multiple gear housings

19. When a tractor maneuvers around a corner, the outside wheels rotate faster than the inside wheels, which is made possible because of the _____.

    a. differential

    b. universal joints

    c. driveshaft

    d. fifth wheel

20. The interaxle differential should remain _____ at all times on normal roads in good weather.

    a. locked

    b. unlocked

    c. at the terminal

    d. in the trailer

21. Which of the three elements of a truck's braking system is normally used to slow or stop the vehicle?

    a. parking brakes

    b. service brakes

    c. glad hands

    d. supply emergency brakes

22. In an air brake system, air is _____ to increase the braking force.

    a. frozen

    b. compressed

    c. dried

    d. decompressed

23. If the low-pressure warning signal (a red warning light and or a buzzer) is activated, the driver should _____.

    a. stop at once

    b. disregard the signal as it has to do with atmospheric pressure which is not a concern of the driver

    c. continue driving to the nearest repair shop

    d. continue driving and call the dispatcher for instructions

24. Regarding air pressure in the tires of a rig, which of the following is an accurate statement?

    a. Hitting the tires with a hammer is the best method to check the air pressure.

    b. Checking the air pressure is a function of the shop and is not a concern of the driver.

    c. As the tires heat up from the rig being driven, the air pressure goes down.

    d. Air pressure should be checked with an accurate gauge at least once a week when the tires are cool.

25. The coupling system that connects the tractor to the trailer consists of _____.

    a. the fifth wheel, the trailer kingpin, and the landing gear

    b. the fifth wheel only

    c. the trailer kingpin only

    d. the fifth wheel and the trailer kingpin

5

Basic Control

OBJECTIVES

When you have completed this chapter, you should be able to:

- ■ Explain the routine for starting, warming up, cooling down, and shutting off engines.
- ■ Show how to safety test a trailer hookup.
- ■ Explain the correct way to put a rig in motion.
- ■ Describe the correct way to stop a rig.
- ■ Describe the skills needed to back a rig in a straight line.
- ■ Explain the correct procedures for making right and left turns.
- ■ Define off-tracking.

INTRODUCTION

As you know, professional driving involves more than simply driving a tractor-trailer up and down the highway. As you have already learned—and will continue to learn—professional driving means mastering a number of basic and advanced skills. The first step toward mastering these skills is familiarizing yourself with the correct ways to perform certain tasks and maneuvers by reading about them. The next step is to take what you have learned from this book and classroom discussions to the driving range for practice, practice, practice.

Any professional driver will tell you that driving skills are aspects of the job you will continue to learn as you gain more experience with the tractor-trailer rig and the job of professional driving itself. Professional drivers also will tell you that becoming a professional means spending time polishing each skill you learn.

Getting the feel of basic control from this chapter and then practicing these skills and maneuvers is your next step toward becoming a professional **(see Figure 5–1).**

▶ **Figure 5–1**

Getting a feel for basic control and practicing these skills is the next step toward becoming a professional driver.

START, WARM-UP, AND SHUTDOWN ROUTINES

Starting the Engine

Take the necessary steps to start the engine correctly. Before starting the engine, always check the trailer coupling (described later in the text).

Starting the Four-Cycle Engine

1. Apply the parking brake.

2. Release the throttle (take foot off fuel pedal) and depress the clutch. Make sure the transmission is in neutral.

3. Turn on the ignition/switch key.

4. If the engine does not start in 10 to 15 seconds, then turn the starter off, wait 60 seconds, and try again.

5. Ease your foot off the clutch.

6. Check readings on all gauges and meters.

Engine Warm-up

Engine warm-up is the period of time after starting the engine and before moving your rig that prepares the engine to do its job. During warm-up, gauges in your tractor will indicate when the engine is operating within its specified range.

Always use a low rpm level to warm up the engine, between 800 and 1,000 rpm. By warming up your engine, you:

■ Allow the engine to reach a beginning operating temperature by idling (Remember, however, that excessive idling wastes fuel and can cause unnecessary wear and tear on the engine.)

- Circulate oil and build oil pressure to proper levels
- Reach a favorable clearance between moving parts
- Lubricate all moving parts
- Build up air pressure

Engine warm-up is complete when water temperature reaches anywhere from 120 to 130 degrees F.

New tractor—thousands of dollars. A tank filled with diesel—hundreds of dollars. Engine warm-up—priceless!

CAUTION!

Rapid acceleration or overrevving the engine before it is warmed up causes damage to engine parts over time.

Shutting Down the Engine

Engine shutdown is the period of time after stopping the rig until the engine is turned off. Shutting down the engine requires a cooling-off period to prevent damage to engine parts.

Follow these basic steps for engine shutdown:

1. Depress the clutch and shift into neutral.
2. Release the clutch.
3. Let the engine idle, allowing it to cool down—idling time is determined by cargo being hauled and length of trip.
4. Turn off the key switch/ignition.
5. If engine has stop control, move it to the "off" position to cut off the fuel flow from the injectors.

CAUTION!

Cooling down the engine is as important as the engine warm-up. During the **cool down period,** coolant and oil will flow at reduced temperatures and allow heat built up in the engine to dissipate.

Automatic Shutdown/Startup Systems

All electronic diesel engines are capable of shutting down the engine after a set time period. Cummins Engine Company, for example, manufactures the ICON system. This system automatically controls engine starting and stopping for the purposes of reducing excess idle time and maintaining engine temperatures. It has three modes of operation: engine, cab comfort, and mandatory shutdown. Under engine mode, the system monitors engine oil and battery voltage. If either drops below a set level, the engine automatically starts. Under cab comfort mode, a cab thermostat starts and stops the engine to maintain the desired temperature. Under mandatory shutdown mode, the engine will shut down after 5 or 15 minutes.

PUTTING THE VEHICLE INTO MOTION— AND STOPPING

As you know, moving a tractor-trailer rig is vastly different from moving an automobile. To address this difference, professional drivers learn an array of skills and gain expertise in making it appear that moving a tractor-trailer rig is as easy as moving a personal vehicle.

Three specific steps that should always be followed before moving your rig:

1. Test the tractor-trailer hookup.

2. Put the tractor-trailer smoothly into motion.

3. Stop the tractor-trailer rig smoothly.

Step 1: Test the Hookup

Each time you hook up a trailer you must test the coupling. There are two tests—one for rigs with independent brake control and one for rigs without independent brake control.

To Test Rigs with Independent Trailer Brake Control (Trolley or Hand Valve)

1. Release tractor brakes, depress clutch, and shift into lowest forward gear.

2. Apply the independent trailer brake.

3. Release the clutch to the friction point.

4. Gently pull forward against the locked trailer brakes.

5. Depress clutch.

6. Repeat the entire procedure to ensure proper coupling.

To Test Rigs without Independent Trailer Brake Control (Trolley or Hand Valve)

1. Release tractor brakes, depress clutch, and shift into lowest forward gear.

2. Move trailer protection valve from "normal" to "emergency."

3. Release clutch to friction point.

4. Pull forward gently against the locked trailer brakes.

5. Depress clutch.

6. Repeat the entire procedure.

CAUTION!

Test your rig's hookup at every stop you make—during your shift or during the day.

Step 2: Putting the Tractor-Trailer into Motion

Moving your rig smoothly and with a sense of ease requires much practice and experience in the driver's seat. Remember, there is no substitute for practice **(see Figure 5–2).**

Use the following steps when putting your rig into motion:

1. Release tractor and trailer parking brakes.
2. Push clutch all the way down and shift into lowest gear.
3. Let out clutch slowly as you begin to depress the fuel pedal.
4. When vehicle begins moving, slowly increase engine rpms to increase the rig's speed.
5. Do not rest your foot on the clutch pedal.
6. When the vehicle is in motion with the clutch fully engaged, take your foot off the clutch and prepare to shift into another gear or stop **(see Figure 5–3).**

▶ **Figure 5–2**

There is no substitute for practice when it comes to learning to drive your rig.

▶ **Figure 5–3**

Basic vehicle maneuvers require skill and coordination between the use of the fuel pedal and the clutch.

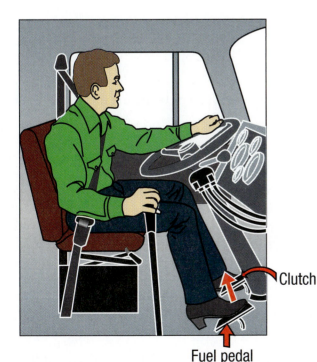

Clutch

Fuel pedal

CAUTION!

With today's electronic engines, extra foot pressure on fuel pedal is not required when releasing the clutch.

Tips for Professional Drivers

■ Always engage clutch slowly to avoid slippage.

■ When starting on an upgrade, shift into the lowest forward gear, slowly release clutch, and as the clutch engages, slowly accelerate and release the parking and trailer brakes.

■ Allow for brake lag.

Step 3: Stopping the Tractor-Trailer

Stopping your rig smoothly is also a skill learned from much practice behind the wheel. To stop a rig smoothly, take the following steps if you are driving a manual transmission. If you are operating a vehicle equipped with an automatic transmission, follow your instructor's recommendations.

1. Push down the brake pedal.

2. Control the pressure so the rig comes to a smooth, safe stop.

3. Downshift as you stop. Do not coast to a stop.

4. If driving a manual transmission, do not push in the clutch until the engine rpm is almost to idle.

5. When you have stopped, select a low gear.

6. If you have stopped properly, there should be no nose rebound or bouncing in the cab.

CAUTION!

Never coast to a stop in neutral or by holding down the clutch. Always downshift to a stop.

BACKING IN A STRAIGHT LINE

Backing maneuvers are covered in detail in a later chapter, but basic information is given here to help you prepare for straight line backing:

1. **Position the vehicle** by moving forward until the tractor and trailer are aligned and the front wheels are straight. Make sure the area is clear.

2. **Shift into reverse gear** and back slowly, using idle speed. Do not ride the clutch or brake pedals.

3. **Use both mirrors constantly** to check behind the rig while backing. Be aware of pedestrians and other vehicles.

4. **Do not oversteer.** The best way to keep your vehicle on course is not to oversteer.

5. **Correct drifting** (when your tractor and your trailer get out of alignment and "drift" in different directions). To correct drift, turn the steering wheel toward the drift as soon as it occurs. If you catch the drift right away, it requires very little movement of your steering wheel to correct it.

6. **Use the push-pull method to keep the trailer in a straight line.** When the trailer gets bigger in the mirror, push the steering wheel toward that mirror. Then, immediately pull the steering wheel back to straighten out the rig. The biggest error in using the push-pull method is not returning the steering wheel to a straight position.

7. **Start again.** If your rig is getting too far out of alignment, it is easier to pull forward and start again. Stop, pull forward, realign your rig, and try it again.

GO!

The key to backing your rig in a straight line is to recognize what direction the trailer is drifting and make the necessary adjustments immediately. **Use both outside mirrors** to help you make these steering adjustments.

TURNING THE VEHICLE

This section describes basic turning maneuvers **(see Figure 5–4)**. Keep the following basics in mind while making turns **(see Figure 5–5)**.

- Know your vehicle.
- Allow for off-tracking.
- Plan ahead.

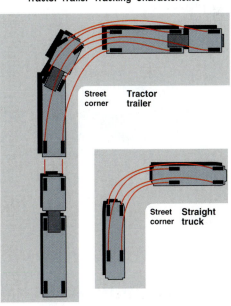

Tractor-Trailer Tracking Characteristics

Street corner   Tractor trailer

Street corner   Straight truck

▶ **Figure 5–4**

Basic turning maneuvers.

▶ **Figure 5–5**

Professional drivers know their rigs and how they will respond to each maneuver.

Off-Tracking in Tractor-Trailer Rigs

Off-tracking is what happens when you turn your rig and the rear wheels do not follow the same path as the front wheels of the rig. The rear wheels follow a shorter path; and the more distance between the front wheels and the rear wheels—and the sharper the turn—the more the rear wheels off-track. Keep off-tracking in mind when making turns or taking curves **(see Figure 5–6).**

Two key factors determine the off-tracking of the trailer:

- **The distance between the kingpin and the rear trailer wheels.** The greater the distance between the kingpin and the rear trailer wheels, the more the off-tracking.

- **The amount of sideways drag of the rear tires.** Sideways drag of the rear tires increases with the number of tires. The more sideways drag, the more off-tracking. Tandem axles have more sideways drag and greater off-tracking than a single rear axle **(see Figure 5–7).**

Off-Tracking Vehicle Path

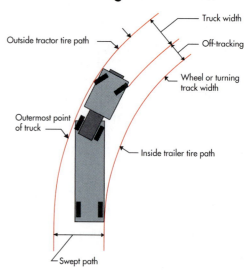

▶ **Figure 5–6**

In off-tracking, the rear wheels of the rig do not follow the same path as the front wheels.

▶ **Figure 5–7**

In low-speed off-tracking, each axle tracks inside the path of the axle in front of it.

Low-Speed Off-Tracking

In low-speed off-tracking, each axle tracks inboard of the axle in front of it. A typical low-speed off-tracking accident involves the trailer sideswiping a car at an intersection.

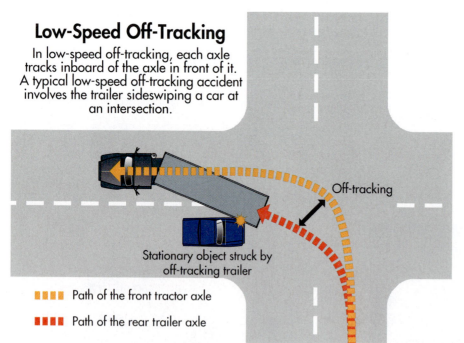

Making Right Turns

Making a successful right turn requires planning, practice, and patience as well as good judgment, driving at the proper speed, and good control of your rig. Most right turns are tighter than the turning radius of your rig **(see Figure 5–8).** To make a turn safely around the corner without hitting a curb or other objects, you will need to use more traffic lanes than you would if you were driving your personal vehicle. At the same time, you do not want to obstruct traffic. If the

▶ **Figure 5-8**

Most right turns require extra room because they are tighter than the turning radius of your rig.

turn is sharp, you should be going slower than usual to make the turn cleanly. If you cannot turn and clear the corner using the space available, then choose an alternate route. Sometimes, by continuing straight ahead for a block or two, you can find space enough to make the turn without hitting the curb or other objects.

CAUTION!

Figure 5-9 shows two options for making turns. One is a good method—the buttonhook—but use caution when using this maneuver. The other method—the jug handle—should be avoided.

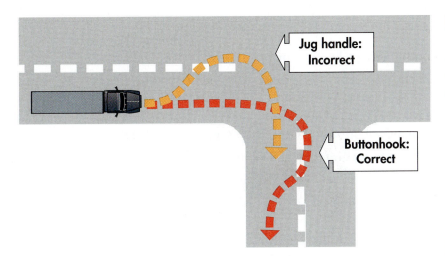

Jug handle: Incorrect

Buttonhook: Correct

▶ **Figure 5-9**

Jug handle turns are sloppy and dangerous ways to make right turns.

Buttonhook

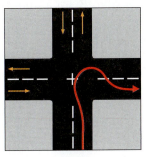

▶ **Figure 5-10**

Buttonhook turns allow safe right-turn maneuvers.

What Is a Buttonhook Turn?

A **buttonhook turn** will allow you to clear the corner without problems, but you should always use caution because you are crossing into another lane when you make the turn **(see Figure 5-10)**. Use the extra space in front of you in this manner:

1. Approach the intersection in the right lane.
2. If the lane width allows, position your rig about 4 to 5 feet from the curb, creating as much space to the right of your rig as possible.

3. Turn on your right turn signal.

4. Scan the intersection, watching for a break in the traffic.

5. Proceed straight ahead until the trailer tires will clear the corner in a hard right turn.

6. Turn hard to the right.

7. Finish the turn in the right lane.

8. Cancel your turn signal.

> ### CAUTION!
> Regardless of the difficulty of the turn, as a professional driver, you must always yield to motorists, cyclists, and pedestrians.

What Is a Jug Handle Turn?

A **jug handle turn** is a sloppy and dangerous way to make a right turn for the following reasons:

1. You gain little if any advantage, because the trailer tires do not have time to move away from the curb.

2. If you signal right but move left, as you must do in a jug handle turn, you confuse traffic and someone behind you may even try to squeeze between the trailer and the curb.

Now, follow these steps to successfully complete a right turn:

1. Signal in advance to let other drivers know your intentions.

2. Adjust your speed as you approach the intersection. This enables you to speed up slightly as you make your turn.

3. Slow down and shift to the proper gear before entering the turn. In this way, you can keep both hands on the steering wheel during the turn itself **(see Figure 5–11)**.

4. Pull your rig farther into the intersection than you would your personal vehicle to avoid running over the curb during the turn, due to off-tracking.

5. Make the turn, turning the steering wheel right and speeding up slightly for a smooth turn.

6. Watch the right mirror for the position of the trailer wheels and to locate other traffic. Then check to the front and left side of your rig.

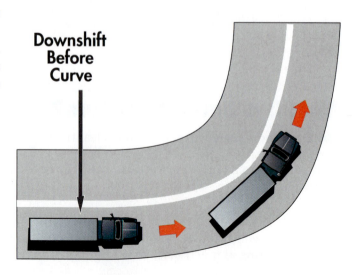

▶ Figure 5–11

Planning ahead means shifting into the proper gear before a turn or curve.

GO! A GOOD RULE OF THUMB WHEN MAKING A RIGHT TURN
Pull about one-half the length of the rig past the corner point of the intersection before beginning the turn. Keep the wheels of your rig straight before turning.

Common Errors in Making Right Turns

Common errors in making right turns include:

- Approaching the intersection too fast
- Not downshifting before the turn
- Shifting gears while turning
- Not allowing for off-tracking of the trailer
- Not getting far enough into the intersection before making the turn

Making Left Turns

Plan ahead before making a left turn just as you would for a right turn. Follow these steps:

1. Slow down as you approach the intersection or prepare to make a left turn.
2. Position your rig in the left turning lane, being as far to the right in the left turn lane as possible and prepare to turn into the left lane.
3. If there are two left turn lanes on the road, use the outside (lane farthest to the right) lane.
4. Put the rig into the correct gear to make the turn.
5. Keep wheels straight.
6. Watch your left mirror during the turn.
7. After turning, turn the steering wheel back to the right to straighten your wheels.

Common Errors in Making Left Turns

Common errors in making left turns include approaching the intersection too fast, shifting gears while turning, and choosing the wrong lane from which to make your turn.

Highway Curves

Position yourself carefully before taking a highway curve **(see Figure 5–12).** To take a right curve, keep the front of your vehicle toward the center of the lane, or the rear of the trailer may run off the road during the curve. To take a left curve, keep the tractor as close to the outer (right) edge of the lane as possible, to prevent the trailer from running over the center line.

RANGE PRACTICE

After you have learned the correct methods for operating and maneuvering your rig, your instructor may take you out for driving range practice **(see Figure 5–13).** You will be expected to:

- Start, warm up, and shut down the engine
- Put the rig into motion and accelerate smoothly

Right and Left Highway Curves

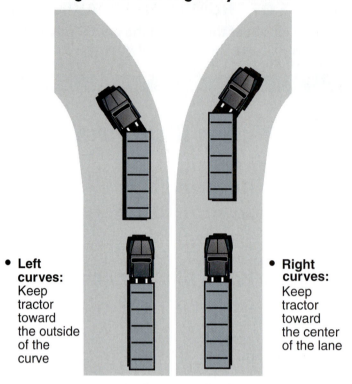

• **Left curves:** Keep tractor toward the outside of the curve

• **Right curves:** Keep tractor toward the center of the lane

▶ **Figure 5–12**

Maneuvering highway curves requires planning and correctly positioning your vehicle in the traffic lane.

▶ **Figure 5–13**

Practice on the driving range will help you master the skills you need to become a successful professional driver.

■ Come to a smooth stop

■ Back in a straight line

■ Make turns correctly from the proper position

To meet these goals, you will need other skills, such as:

■ Coordinated use of the accelerator and clutch

■ Knowing the proper method for putting on air brakes

- Coordinated use of all controls to drive forward or back in a straight line
- Understanding off-tracking, or the path the trailer takes as the entire rig takes curves or makes turns

All of these driving skills can be mastered with driving range practice. As you practice, using care in operating your rig will bring you success as a professional driver and value to your future employers.

SUMMARY

U pon completing this chapter, you are now prepared to explain routines for starting, warming up, and shutting down your tractor. You also know the steps in testing a trailer hookup and can explain how to put your rig in motion smoothly and then stop your rig just as smoothly. You are also familiar with how to back your rig in a straight line, make turns, and take curves while being aware of your off-tracking. Remember, too, learning and mastering all of these skills require practice, guidance from experienced professional drivers, and patience with yourself. Rome was not built in a day—and good professional drivers continue to polish the skills you are now learning. As someone once said, "You'll learn something new every day!"

KEY TERMS

Buttonhook turn
Control routines
Cool down period

Engine shutdown
Engine warm-up
Jug handle turn

Off-tracking
Starting routine

REVIEW QUESTIONS

1. Which of the following is not part of the recommended routine for the startup of a four-cycle diesel engine?

   a. Apply the parking brake.

   b. Operate the starter.

   c. Pump the throttle.

   d. Check the instruments.

2. Which of the following does not happen during engine warm-up?

   a. The air compressor inflates the tires to the correct pressure.

   b. The engine reaches a beginning operating temperature.

   c. The cylinder walls are coated with a film of oil.

   d. The coolant temperature increases.

3. Which of the following is not a recommended practice for fuel efficient warm-up?

   a. Keep the rpm low and the speed under 30 mph.

   b. Check the owner's manual for idling time.

   c. Idle the engine for at least 30 minutes.

   d. Do not idle the engine any more than needed.

4. Which of the following is not a result of inappropriately warming up an engine?

    a. Rapid acceleration before the engine is warm causes crankshaft and bearing damage.

    b. Overrevving the engine causes crankshaft and bearing damage.

    c. Turbocharger bearing damage from lack of lubrications happens.

    d. Engine life is increased.

5. When warming up the engine, which of the following is not one of the instruments checked to see if the readings have reached normal, indicating it is safe to drive the rig at cruising speeds?

    a. coolant temperature

    b. oil pressure

    c. oil temperature

    d. tire air pressure

6. Which of the following does not happen during the cool down of a diesel engine?

    a. The engine idles for up to 5 minutes.

    b. The engine is shut down.

    c. Coolant flows at reduced temperatures.

    d. Oil flows at reduced temperatures.

7. When a trailer is hooked up to a tractor, a test of the coupling must be made _____.

    a. every time

    b. once a week

    c. once a week by a mechanic

    d. annually

8. Regarding putting the tractor-trailer with a manual transmission into motion, when the clutch is slowly engaged (let out), the accelerator is _____.

    a. ignored

    b. fully depressed

    c. slightly depressed

    d. depressed halfway down

9. Which of the following is a correct statement regarding stopping a tractor-trailer with a manual transmission?

    a. Coast to a stop in neutral.

    b. Always downshift to a stop.

    c. Coast to a stop by holding the clutch down.

    d. There should be nose rebound and bouncing of the cab.

10. When attempting to back in a straight line, to correct drifting the driver _____.

    a. turns the steering wheel toward the drift

    b. turns the steering wheel away from the drift

    c. does not turn the steering wheel

    d. neither a, b, nor c

11. Regarding using the push–pull method to keep a trailer in a straight line, when the trailer gets bigger in a mirror, the driver _____.

    a. pushes the steering wheel away from that mirror and immediately pulls the steering wheel back to straighten the rig out

    b. turns the steering wheel two revolutions toward that mirror

    c. turns the steering wheel two revolutions away from that mirror

    d. pushes the steering wheel toward that mirror and immediately pulls the steering wheel back to straighten the rig out

12. During off-tracking, when the rear wheels do not follow the same path as the front wheels, the rear wheels take a _____ path than the front wheels.

    a. longer   **c.** shorter

    b. higher   **d.** lower

13. The greater the distance between the kingpin and the rear trailer wheels, the _____ the off-tracking.

    a. less   **c.** height of

    b. greater   **d.** a and c

14. Since most right turns are tighter than the turning radius of a tractor-trailer rig, in a right turn, to make it safely around a corner without hitting the curb, a driver must use _____ traffic lanes than would be used in a car.

    a. more   **c.** the same

    b. fewer   **d.** it makes no difference

15. When making a left turn in a tractor-trailer rig, a driver should position the rig as far to the _____ in the left turn lane as possible.

    a. left   **c.** position in the lane is not important

    b. middle   **d.** right

6 Shifting

OBJECTIVES

When you have completed this chapter, you should be able to:

- Describe gear-shifting patterns.

- Understand patterns for several types of transmissions.

- Demonstrate methods of shifting through all the gears of conventional transmissions.

- Demonstrate double-clutching and timing the shift for a smooth and fuel-efficient performance.

- Know the proper gears for speed and road conditions.

- Discuss shifting with automatic and semiautomatic transmissions.

- Understand the operation of electronic synchronized and nonsynchronized transmissions.

- Know how to use the instruments and proper controls needed to shift gears properly.

- Be aware of common shifting errors and the results of these errors.

- Demonstrate the use of hands, feet, sight, and hearing for best shifting performance.

- Understand how improper use of clutch and transmission can damage a rig.

INTRODUCTION

Many professional driving students will admit shifting gears looks to be the most difficult of all the new skills they have to learn.

Common sense tells you shifting gears in a commercial motor vehicle could be more difficult than shifting gears in your personal vehicle. Like most professional driving skills, however, shifting can become less intimidating and less difficult with practice and more practice.

This section, like every other chapter of your text, will provide clear definitions and good hands-on knowledge of the skill to help you increase and improve your skills behind the wheel.

This chapter also introduces you to the differences in shifting patterns. It explains clutch and fuel pedal control and how to coordinate hands, eyes, feet, sound, and feel to handle the various transmissions found in today's tractor-trailer rigs.

This information and your time on the driving range or behind the wheel will help you master the skills you need. What you learn from the information provided will serve as a handy reference later. More importantly, however, you will understand that proper gearing evolves from learning, behind-the-wheel practice, and your instructor answering questions you may have.

SHIFT CONTROLS

When you drive a manual transmission **(see Figure 6–1),** the controls used in shifting are as follows:

- Fuel pedal
- Gearshift lever
- Clutch

Fuel pedal—controls the flow of fuel to the engine and governs the speed of the engine. This information is certainly not new, but it is important to remember because engine speed and shifting are closely related.

Gearshift lever—selects a gear and determines how the engine speed is transferred into road speed **(see Figure 6–2).** For example, at a specific engine speed, placing the transmission in a low gear will provide a lot of power to the engine but does not impact road speed, because in a low gear, the power of the engine can be multiplied 10 to 15 times. In a high gear, a high road speed can be attained but actual available power is reduced.

▶ Figure 6–1

Driving a manual transmission requires the use of the fuel pedal, the gearshift lever, and the clutch. Shifting becomes less intimidating with practice.

▶ **Figure 6–2**
Gearshift lever.

NONSYNCHRONIZED TRANSMISSIONS

Nonsynchronized transmissions are those that require "synchronizing" or bringing to the same speed the teeth of the driving gear and the driven gear. When this is done properly, there is no grinding or clashing of the gears.

Double-clutching is a skill used by professional drivers which allows them to control the engine rpm and to shift gears smoothly. Following are the steps to double-clutching and shifting in the simplest form, beginning with **upshifting:**

Upshifting

1. Take foot off fuel pedal.

2. Push clutch pedal down to disengage clutch. Be careful not to engage clutch brake.

3. Move gearshift lever to neutral

4. Release clutch pedal, engaging clutch.

5. When proper rpm for next gear is reached, push clutch down again, being careful not to engage clutch brake.

6. Move gearshift lever to next higher gear.

7. Release clutch pedal, taking foot off clutch and engaging clutch and transmission.

8. Accelerate.

▶ *"40, 50, 60 miles an hour. NASCAR here I come!"*

CAUTION!

The clutch should be pushed down 2 to 3 inches, or just past the free play. It is not necessary to push the clutch all the way to the floor as you would in your personal vehicle—if it has a standard transmission.

Downshifting

1. Take foot off accelerator.
2. Push down clutch.
3. Move gearshift lever to neutral.
4. Release clutch.
5. Accelerate enough to match engine rpm with road speed to avoid clashing gears.
6. Push down clutch.
7. Shift to next lower gear.
8. Release clutch.

Be sure to maintain correct engine speed throughout this procedure **(see Figure 6–3). Downshifting** too early can result in the vehicle having too much speed for the next lower gear. This can cause the engine to rev beyond its operating range and to stress its parts. Downshifting too early may prevent rapid acceleration, if needed.

AIDS TO SHIFTING

The speedometer and the tachometer are necessary tools for shifting gears **(see Figure 6–4).**

Speedometer

Key Elements of Shifting

Fuel pedal: Controls fuel to engine

Clutch: Controls connection between engine and transmission

Gearshift lever: Allows driver to select gears in transmission

- Match engine speed (rpm) to road speed

- Shift smoothly to avoid clashing gears

- Shift by the tachometer
  — Upshift when engine rpm approach top of manufacturer recommended rpm
  — Avoid overspeeding

  — Downshift when engine speed approaches low range of manufacturer recommended rpm

  — Avoid lugging

- Variety of rpm/gearshift patterns

- Learn rpm/shift pattern of vehicle you drive

▶ Figure 6–3

Proper shifting techniques come from behind-the-wheel practice.

While speed ranges often vary with the type of transmission, it is important for you to know the road speeds that correspond to each gear. A professional driver must learn the speed ranges for each specific rig and then upshift or downshift as needed.

▶ Figure 6–4

The speedometer and tachometer are necessary tools for shifting gears.

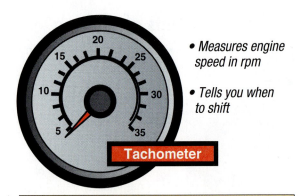

• Measures engine speed in rpm

• Tells you when to shift

Tachometer

Groundspeed and Gear		
Examples of specific gear-to-groundspeed relationships for a nine-speed transmission		
Gear	mph at 1,300 rpm	mph at 1,800 rpm
Low	0	4
1	4	7
2	7	10
3	10	14
4	14	19
5	19	26
6	26	38
7	38	53
8	53	65 *
* Governor set at 1,640 rpm		

▶ **Figure 6–5**

The tachometer indicates engine speed in rpm.

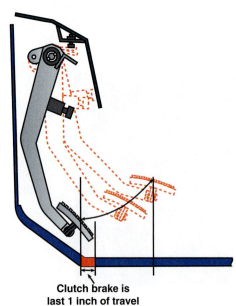

Clutch brake is last 1 inch of travel

▶ **Figure 6–6**

The clutch brake stops gears from turning.

When you reach the top of the speed range for a given gear, it is time to upshift. When you reach the bottom of the speed range for a given gear, downshift.

Tachometer

The **tachometer** displays the engine speed in revolutions per minute (rpm). Just as there is a road speed range for each gear, there is an rpm range for each gear. Upshifting and downshifting are coordinated with rpm ranges the same as they are with roadspeed ranges **(see Figure 6–5).**

Governor

The **governor** prevents the engine from revving too much while downshifting. It also reduces the fuel supply to the engine when the maximum rpm is reached. In electronic engines, this is controlled by a computer chip or module.

Clutch Brake

A clutch has three phases—free play, working, and **clutch brake.** The clutch brake stops the gears from turning. To engage it, push the clutch pedal all the way to the floor. This prevents the gears from clashing when shifting into low or reverse. **Use the clutch brake only when the vehicle is completely stopped (see Figure 6–6).**

Synchronizing Skills

Although depressing/engaging the clutch twice on each shift is a big part of handling a nonsynchronized transmission, it is not the main shifting event. The key skill—the one requiring special shifting—is **synchronizing** (bringing to the same speed) the teeth of the mating gears (driving and driven gears) **(see Figure 6–7).** When gears are synchronized, there is no grinding or clashing of the gears.

The three ways to determine engine speed are by:

■ Reading the tachometer

■ Listening to the rpm

■ Feeling this speed in the tractor

It is true that some drivers think they are using engine rpm to tell them when to shift when, in fact, they are using their actual sense of the rpm. A veteran driver in a nonsynchronized transmission rig uses his or her sense of rpm to know when to shift, and needs three basic skills to properly shift this type of rig:

1. The ability to identify engine rpm

2. Knowing the correct rpm the engine should be turning

3. The ability to bring engine to correct rpm for each task

▶ **Figure 6–7**

Smooth and proper shifting is a sign of a skilled driver.

How does the driver control the tooth speed of the driving gear?

1. After depressing clutch, shift into neutral.

2. Then release the clutch to allow engine rpm to drop on upshift or speed up on downshift.

3. This also adjusts tooth speed of the next driving gear to the speed/rpm of the engine.

How does the driver know how much to increase or decrease engine speed?

1. Always read manufacturer's recommendations first if available.

2. A good rule of thumb is when changing gears, change the rpm by 25 percent, which is about 500 rpm, although some transmissions differ from this rule.

GO!

NOTE: As long as shifts are started at the same rpm, synchronizing rpm will be the same for each shift, which makes shifts a matter of timing and coordination.

What about the synchronizing rpm in more complex shifts?

1. Shifts may be started at various rpm, which means rpm to synchronize the next gear will also vary.

2. On upgrades, rig loses speed during shifts, so start shift a little earlier than you would on flat ground.

3. On downgrades, speed increases.

GO!

NOTE: Any change in vehicle speed occurring during shifting will affect synchronizing rpm. Experience and practice will teach new drivers to deal with each variation.

Another shifting skill required for a nonsynchronized transmission—along with upshifting and downshifting—is called "finding" or "hitting a gear." This occurs when a vehicle is rolling in neutral and the driver must get the transmission into proper gear. This is usually worked out by either mathematics or a sense or feel of matching the mph with the gear or rpm necessary. In general, however, there is only one possible gear for each possible mph. Most drivers use their "sense of feel," where they feel the speed, recall where the stick should be, and then simply put the stick in front of that gear position.

GO! A SUMMARY OF SHIFTING SKILLS

Good shifting technique is the sign of a seasoned professional driver. These skills include:

- Good timing and coordination
- Shifting without forcing, raking, or grinding the gears
- Never riding the clutch pedal
- Always using the clutch to shift
- Selecting the proper gear for the best fuel economy
- Anticipating change in terrain or traffic

A driver needs to know:

- What gear the vehicle is in at any given time
- The top speed and rpm for each gear
- That downshifting at too high a speed causes damage to internal gears
- That automatic transmissions have a longer "coast-down" time than **manual transmissions,** which means you will need to slow down earlier or use the service brakes until the downshift occurs
- The top mph and maximum/minimum rpm for each gear
- About changes in terrain or traffic and what gear will be needed next

What happens if you shift into too low a gear by mistake? You will know immediately because you will hear the engine running too fast (faster than normal). This can damage the clutch, engine, transmission, or drive shaft, and it can cause you to lose control of the vehicle.

What is **lugging** and what can happen if it occurs? Lugging occurs when the driver fails to downshift when the engine speed starts to fall below the normal operating range. In this condition, the tractor produces too little power and begins struggling or lugging. This type of strain can cause engine overheating, damage to the drive train, and stress on most of the rig's systems. It can also shorten the life of all the drive train components.

What is **progressive shifting?** Progressive shifting means shifting before you reach the maximum rpm for the gear your rig is in. Progressive shifting allows you to take the most advantage of the engine's power and save fuel at the same time. It is recommended that all drivers learn this technique, explained in **Figure 6–8.**

Progressive Shifting

Technique used with some engine/transmission combinations

- Shift much like automobile
- Gradually increase
- No need to accelerate to governor unless maximum power required

- Available in some engine/transmission combinations
- Use only if engine and company policy allow

- Advantages
  - Reduces equipment wear
  - Lowers noise level
  - Saves fuel

Example:

rpm requirements for progressive vs. standard techniques
10 speed transmission gear split/1,900 rpm

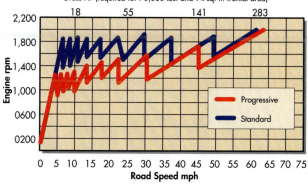

 **Figure 6–8**

Progressive shifting allows the driver to take full advantage of the engine's power.

How is it done? Here are the steps:

1. Think how the engine should feel at that speed and gear.
2. With clutch engaged, throttle up or down until engine feels right.
3. Then push the stick.

It may drop right into gear; but if it does not, generally the best next move is to go to a higher gear.

1. If rpm are too high, grinding noise will be high pitched.
2. If rpm are too low, grinding noise will be deep and hollow.
3. When engine is close to proper rpm, stick vibrations are larger and farther apart.
4. When correct rpm is reached, stick will begin to fall into gear, so disengage the clutch and push stick into place.
5. Then release clutch and speed up.

Finding the synchronizing rpm under all possible shifting conditions is needed to handle a non-synchronized transmission.

CAUTION!

Newer computerized engines are usually set up for progressive shifting. When you accelerate, the engine will "flatten out" at a lower rpm. When you feel this no-power mode, or flattening out, select the next higher gear.

Shifting Procedures

When shifting, shift when the engine reaches cruising rpm instead of the maximum rpm set by the governor or computer. In power gears, shift at the lowest rpm possible without lugging the engine. When downshifting, shift as soon as the rpm reaches peak torque (1,300 rpm on most engines—but check operating manual to make sure). Progressive shifting is advised by many companies because it reduces equipment wear, lowers the noise level, saves fuel, and allows smoother shifts.

SHIFTING PATTERNS AND PROCEDURES

In this section, we will look at the shift patterns of common transmissions: **Spicer Pro-Shift Seven Speed, Eaton Fuller Nine Speed, Eaton Fuller Super Ten, Rockwell Ten Speed,** and **Eaton Fuller Thirteen Speed.**

Spicer Pro-Shift Seven Speed

The Spicer Pro-Shift Seven Speed is a constant mesh (nonsynchronized) twin-countershaft transmission with a single-range operation.

Shift Pattern

The Spicer Pro-Shift Seven Speed transmission uses a simple no-repeat shift pattern, starting at the bottom left and working up through the gears to seventh gear at the bottom right **(see Figure 6–9).** No range selectors or splitters are needed for any of the shifts.

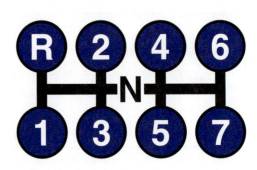

▶ **Figure 6–9**

The Spicer Pro-Shift Seven Speed shift pattern.

Shifting Procedures

Upshifting

- Depress the clutch.

- Move the gear down and the shift lever as far left as possible for first gear.

- To shift to second, double-clutch, move the lever up and slightly to the right.

- Shift up through the next five gears, using normal double-clutching technique and follow the standard "H" pattern.

Downshifting

- Shift from seventh to sixth gear by double-clutching, moving the lever straight forward, and matching the engine speed to the road speed before shifting.

- Use the same procedure for all future downshifts, following the "H" pattern back down to first gear.

Eaton Fuller Nine Speed

The Eaton Fuller Nine Speed is a constant mesh (nonsynchronized) twin-countershaft transmission with high- and low-range operation.

Shift Pattern

Unlike other dual-range transmissions, the Super Ten does not have a range change lever. Instead, there are five gear positions that are split, reducing gear lever movements by half. For example, you start in first gear at the bottom left. Then, preselect the next gear with a splitter button located on the gearshift. To engage the gear, release the throttle to break torque and then accelerate again when you are in gear. You only need to move the gear lever from second to third, fourth to fifth, sixth to seventh, and eighth to ninth.

Shifting Procedures

Upshifting

- Depress the clutch.

- Move the gear lever to first gear.

- To make the splitter shift (first to second, third to fourth, fifth to sixth, seventh to eighth, and ninth to tenth), move the splitter button forward, take your foot off the fuel pedal, wait a few seconds for the gear to engage, and then accelerate.

- To make a lever shift (second to third, fourth to fifth, sixth to seventh, or eighth to ninth), move the splitter button back, double-clutch, and make a normal shift.

Downshifting

- To make a splitter shift down (tenth to ninth, eighth to seventh, sixth to fifth, fourth to third, or second to first), move the splitter button back and when ready, release the throttle, wait a few seconds for the gear to engage, and accelerate again.

- To make a lever shift down one gear, move the splitter button forward, double-clutch, match the engine rpm to road speed, and make the shift.

Rockwell Ten Speed

The Rockwell Ten Speed is a constant mesh (nonsynchronized) twin-countershaft transmission with high- and low-range operation.

Shift Pattern

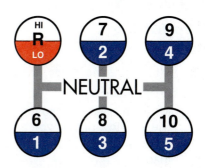

Low range has five forward gears: first through fifth gear. To use high range, lift the range control lever. High range has five more gears: sixth through tenth gear **(see Figure 6–10)**. Begin in first at the bottom left, then up and slightly to the right for second, and through the normal "H" pattern to fifth. To engage sixth, flip up the range lever and move the lever back to the bottom left when you started in first. Then repeat the "H" pattern again for the top four gears.

▶ **Figure 6–10**

The Rockwell Ten Speed shift pattern.

Shifting Procedures

Upshifting

- Depress the clutch.

- Make sure the range lever is down (low range).

- Move gear lever to first gear at the bottom left.

- Shift up through fifth gear, using the double-clutching technique.

- To shift from fifth to sixth, lift the range control lever up before moving the gear lever.

- As the gear lever passes through neutral, the transmission pneumatically (with air assist) shifts to high range.

- Shift from sixth to tenth gears, using the double-clutching technique.

Downshifting

- Shift down from tenth to sixth, using the double-clutching and engine and road speed matching.

- To shift down from sixth to fifth, push the range lever down before moving the gear lever.

- As the gear lever passes through neutral, the transmission pneumatically shifts to low range.

- Shift down from fifth to first using the double-clutching technique and engine and road speed matching.

Eaton Fuller Thirteen Speed

The Eaton Fuller Thirteen Speed is a constant mesh (nonsynchronized) twin-countershaft transmission with high- and low-range operation as well as a splitter on high-range gears.

Shift Pattern

The transmission has five gears in the low range, including a low over low gear. High range has four direct ratios as well as another four overdrive ratios. Overdrive can be engaged in high range with a splitter switch. The shift pattern is a basic double "H." You begin in first gear at the top left **(see Figure 6–11).** Then move through the "H" to fourth. Flip the range lever up, move to fifth and repeat the pattern.

Shifting Procedures

Upshifting

- Depress the clutch.

- Make sure the range lever is down (low range).

- Move the gear lever to first gear (use the low–low only if you are starting from a steep grade with a heavy load).

- Shift up through fourth gear, using the double-clutching technique.

- To shift from fourth to fifth, lift the range control lever up before moving the gear lever.

- As the gear lever passes through neutral, the transmission pneumatically shifts to a higher range.

- Shift from fifth through eighth using normal double-clutching.

- To split a gear in high range (go from direct to overdrive), flip the splitter switch, release the fuel pedal, depress and release the clutch, and accelerate again.

- To shift from overdrive to direct drive in the next higher gear, move the gear level into the next gear and flip the splitter switch just before your foot comes off the clutch.

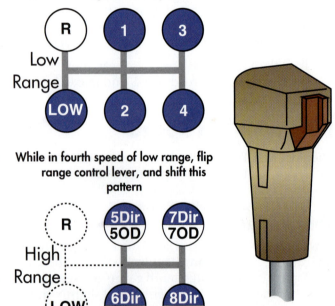

While in low range, shift this pattern

While in fourth speed of low range, flip range control lever, and shift this pattern

Using splitter valve to split the high-range ratios

▶ **Figure 6–11**

Controls and operation of the Eaton Fuller Thirteen Speed.

Downshifting

- To split down from overdrive to direct in the same gear, flip the splitter switch and release the fuel pedal. Then depress and release the clutch and accelerate again.

- To shift down from direct in one gear to overdrive in the next lower gear, flip the splitter switch to overdrive and make a normal downshift.

- To shift from fifth direct to fourth, push the range lever down, double-clutch, and make a normal downshift.

SHIFTING SEMIAUTOMATIC TRANSMISSIONS

Some newer **semiautomatic transmissions** use electronic controls to help the driver shift gears. They are essentially manual transmissions, with a clutch and a similar-looking gear lever, but some of the gears are automated. This section looks at how to operate these transmissions and the shift patterns for three types of transmissions—the **Eaton Fuller Top 2,** the **Spicer AutoMate-2,** and the **Rockwell Engine Synchro Shift (ESS).**

Eaton Fuller Top 2

The Eaton Fuller Top 2 uses the control module of an electronically controlled engine to automatically change the top two gears. It comes in two versions: the Super Ten Top 2 (a 10-speed) and the Super Thirteen Top 2 (a 13-speed). Both are twin-countershaft nonsynchronized transmissions with low-inertia technology that disconnects the back box during compound shifts.

Shift Pattern

The Super Ten Top 2 **(see Figure 6–12)** has the same shift pattern as the standard Super Ten and the Super Thirteen Top 2 has the same change pattern as the Eaton Fuller Thirteen Speed. With both transmissions, the top gear position is marked "A." Once the gear lever is in this position, all upshifts and downshifts between the top two gears are automatic.

Shifting Procedure

- Both transmissions are operated as normal nonsynchronized transmissions in all gears but the top two.

- Automatic mode can only be changed when the vehicle is traveling over 40 mph.

- With the Super Ten Top 2, you change normally to eighth, then double-clutch and move into the "A" position.

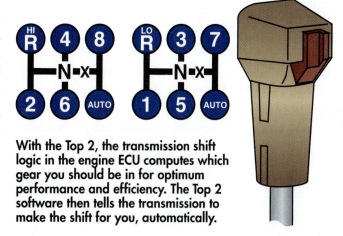

With the Top 2, the transmission shift logic in the engine ECU computes which gear you should be in for optimum performance and efficiency. The Top 2 software then tells the transmission to make the shift for you, automatically.

When starting in first gear, preselect the next gear with the splitter button, release the throttle, and accelerate when you are in gear.

▶ Figure 6–12

Controls and operation of the Eaton Fuller Super Ten Top 2.

- With the Super Thirteen Top 2, you shift normally to eleventh, then double-clutch and move into "A."

- While in the "A" position, the engine and transmission work together to change, up or down, when needed. When a shift point is reached, the engine speed automatically changes to match road speed and the change is made—all without driver input.

■ You can delay an upshift by applying more throttle, or delay a downshift by easing off the throttle.

■ With the engine brake on, the electronic controls automatically extend governed engine speed by 200 rpm to help maintain the lower gear on a downgrade.

Spicer AutoMate-2

The Spicer AutoMate-2 is a 10-speed transmission that uses electronic controls on the transmission to automatically change the top two gears. It is available in direct-drive and overdrive versions.

Shift Pattern

The AutoMate-2 has a familiar 10-speed shifting pattern. First gear is at the bottom left, second is up and to the middle, third is straight down, and so on. When you reach fifth, you flip the range lever up and come back to the bottom left, then up and to the middle for seventh, and straight down for eighth. Once the lever is moved to that position, the transmission automatically senses road and engine speed and changes up to tenth and back down to ninth when necessary.

Shifting Procedure

■ The AutoMate-2 is operated as a normal nonsynchronized transmission in the bottom eight gears. First, use the clutch and then change, up or down, by manually matching the road and engine speeds **(see Figure 6–13)**.

■ Vehicle must be traveling over 38 mph to engage the automatic mode.

■ When reaching eighth gear, double-clutch and move to the "A" mode.

■ No driver input is needed to change gears in ninth and tenth. The transmission automatically senses when a change is needed and then adjusts the engine speed (no matter where the driver has the throttle) and makes the change.

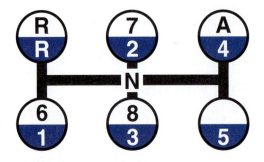

▶ **Figure 6–13**

The Spicer AutoMate-2 shift pattern.

■ Upshifts in the "A" mode can be delayed by applying more throttle, and downshifts can be delayed by easing off the throttle.

Rockwell Engine Synchro Shift

The Rockwell Engine Synchro Shift (ESS) uses engine electronic controls to automatically synchronize the engine speed to the road speed during shifts in all gears. The system reads the input and output speeds of the transmission, the neutral position of the gear lever, and the position of the special shift intent switch on the side of the gear knob. The engine controller processes the information and sends a message to the fuel control system to automatically increase or decrease the engine speed to synchronize with the road speed during shifting. In essence, this turns a nonsynchronized box into a synchronized one. The driver has the option of turning the system off and operating the transmission as a fully manual box.

Shift Pattern

ESS is fitted to either the Rockwell Nine Speed or the Rockwell Ten Speed manual transmissions. It allows the driver to move through the standard shifting pattern. Both transmissions are nonsynchronized boxes with range-change shift patterns **(see Figure 6–14)**.

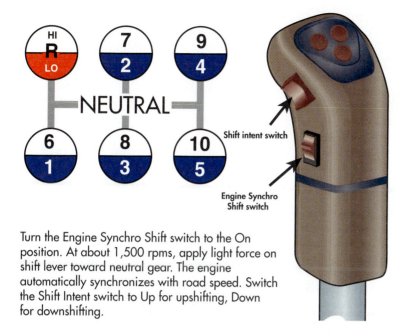

Turn the Engine Synchro Shift switch to the On position. At about 1,500 rpms, apply light force on shift lever toward neutral gear. The engine automatically synchronizes with road speed. Switch the Shift Intent switch to Up for upshifting, Down for downshifting.

▶ **Figure 6–14**

Controls and shift patterns for the Rockwell Engine Synchro Shift.

Shifting Procedure

- To begin, the driver turns the ESS switch on the side of the gear knob to the "on" position.

- The clutch pedal is depressed, first gear is selected, and the clutch is released. Then, the clutch only is used again when bringing the vehicle to a complete stop.

- To shift up, the driver puts the Shift Intent Switch on the side of the gear knob in the "up" position.

- At the appropriate engine speed (around 1,500 rpm) driver applies light force on the shift lever toward neutral while in gear. The transmission should allow a shift to neutral.

- The engine automatically synchronizes with the road speed and allows the driver to move to the next gear without touching the throttle or the clutch.

- Downshifting is similar, except the driver must put the Shift Intent Switch in the "down" position before making the shift. The engine automatically increases its speed to match the road speed for a smooth shift.

- While in the ESS mode, the range control function is automated, so the driver does not have to flip from low to high or high to low.

- Any time the driver uses the clutch while the vehicle is moving or turns the ESS switch off, the transmission reverts back to fully manual operation and the driver must use the clutch and throttle to shift gears.

SHIFTING FULLY AUTOMATIC TRANSMISSIONS

Fully **automatic transmissions** use a torque converter instead of a clutch to transfer power. These converters provide a fluid coupling instead of the hard frictional coupling provided by a clutch. Newer transmission also may have lockup functions that lock the converter when the transmission is in top gear. This provides a solid coupling and improves fuel mileage.

Many automatic transmissions use a lever to change gears **(see Figure 6–15),** but newer models with electronic controls use buttons instead of levers. To select a gear position on these models, simply push a button.

Neutral
　Use when starting, standing, or parking
Reverse
　Vehicle must be completely stopped before using
2-5 or Drive
　All normal driving conditions
2-3 / 2-4
　Lower range for load types and driving conditions
2
　When pulling through mud, snow, or up steep hills
1
　Creeper gear for off-highway use

▶ **Figure 6–15**
Controls and shift procedures for a fully automatic transmission.

Range Selector Positions

Neutral (N)—used for starting, standing still, and parking the vehicle. The parking brake should be set when the vehicle is standing or parked.

CAUTION!
Never coast in neutral, as this will damage the transmission and could cause you to lose control of the vehicle.

▶ **Figure 6–16**
A warning signal sounds when a vehicle is placed in reverse.

Reverse (R)—used to back the rig. There is one gear in the reverse range. The vehicle must come to a complete stop before shifting into reverse. A reverse warning signal sounds when the vehicle is placed in reverse **(see Figure 6–16)**

2-5 or Drive—used for all normal driving conditions, Drive or 2-5 starts in second and shifts up to third, fourth, and fifth as the vehicle accelerates. Downshifting is automatic as your speed slows.

2-3/2-4 Lower range—lower range gears provide greater engine braking and for some road conditions as well as certain cargo and traffic conditions make it desirable to restrict automatic shifting to the lower gear. When the need for this range ends, shift back to high range (Drive or 2-5).

▶ **Figure 6–17**
Low gear is used driving through mud, snow, or up a steep incline.

▶ **Figure 6–18**
Downshifting occurs automatically in an automatic transmission.

2/Low gear—this gear is used for pulling through mud or snow or driving up a steep grade **(see Figure 6–17).** It provides the most engine braking power. The lower range (2-3/2-4) will not upshift above the highest gear unless the engine governor speed for that gear is exceeded.

1/Creeper Gear—this gear is for off-highway use. It provides the greatest traction. Never make a full power shift from creeper gear to a higher range.

Upshifting and Downshifting with an Automatic Transmission

Upshifting Using the Fuel Pedal

■ The pressure of the foot on the fuel pedal influences automatic shifting.

■ When the fuel pedal is fully depressed, the transmission automatically shifts up to the recommended speed for the engine.

■ When the fuel pedal is partially depressed, upshifts occur sooner and at a lesser engine speed.

■ Either method provides the accurate shift spacing and control needed for maximum performance.

Downshifting

■ Occurs automatically **(see Figure 6–18).**

■ The transmission prevents downshifting when engine speed is too high.

SUMMARY

1. Know the shift pattern of the vehicle.
2. Start the rig in the lowest gear.
3. Use the clutch brake properly.
4. Upshift smoothly.
5. Downshift at the precise point and time required.
6. Use double-clutching.
7. Avoid snapping or riding the clutch.
8. Use the tachometer and speedometer to time shifts.
9. Avoid lugging or revving the engine.
10. Do not force the transmission into gear.
11. Avoid overloading the rig.

KEY TERMS

Automatic transmission
Clutch
Clutch brake
Double-clutching
Downshifting
Eaton Fuller Nine Speed
Eaton Fuller Super Ten
Eaton Fuller Thirteen Speed
Eaton Fuller Top 2

Fuel pedal
Gearshift lever
Governor
Lugging
Manual transmission
Nonsynchronized
  transmission
Progressive shifting

Rockwell Engine Synchro
  Shift (ESS)
Rockwell Ten Speed
Semiautomatic transmission
Spicer AutoMate-2
Spicer Pro-Shift Seven Speed
Synchronizing
Tachometer
Upshifting

REVIEW QUESTIONS

1. Which of the following is not a control used in shifting a manual transmission?

   a. clutch

   b. accelerator

   c. fifth wheel

   d. gearshift lever

2. When shifting a manual transmission, engine speed and shifting are _____.

   a. closely related

   b. not related

   c. only done in the shop by a technician

   d. done according to the speed of the fifth wheel

3. In high gear, a higher road speed can be attained, but actual available power is _____.

   a. the same as when in a lower gear

   b. increased

   c. increased by the square of the speed

   d. reduced

4. A standing rig requires _____ power to get it moving than is required to keep it moving once it is underway.

    a. more

    b. the same

    c. double-clutching

    d. less

5. When a driver is slowing down or going down a hill, downshifting acts as a _____.

    a. accelerating force to speed up the vehicle

    b. braking force to slow the vehicle

    c. has no effect on the vehicle speed

    d. b and c

6. The clutch brake _____.

    a. stops the vehicle

    b. stops the clutch from functioning

    c. stops the gears from turning

    d. is used to stop the vehicle only in a clutch (an emergency)

7. A skill used by professional drivers to control the engine rpm and to shift gears smoothly is called _____.

    a. single-clutching

    b. double-clutching

    c. governor

    d. neither a, b, nor c

8. When upshifting a nonsynchronized transmission, simultaneously the foot is taken off the accelerator, _____, and the gearshift lever is moved to neutral.

    a. the clutch is not pushed down

    b. the brakes are applied

    c. a and b

    d. the clutch pedal is pushed down

9. When downshifting, after the gearshift lever has been moved to neutral and the clutch has been released, _____.

    a. apply the brakes

    b. increase the rotation of the fifth wheel

    c. both a and b

    d. accelerate enough to match the engine rpm with the road speed

10. Shifting gears before a rig reaches the maximum rpm for the gear the rig is in, is called _____.

    a. regressive shifting

    b. progressive shifting

    c. lugging

    d. clutch braking

7 Backing

OBJECTIVES

When you have completed this chapter, you should be able to:

- Understand and describe the procedures for backing and parking.
- Prepare for backing maneuvers.
- Explain the principles of reverse steering when backing an articulated vehicle.
- Avoid the hazards of backing.
- Understand the importance of using a helper while backing.
- Explain why drivers should avoid unnecessary backing and blind-side backing.

INTRODUCTION

Backing a 48-foot (or longer) trailer into position without any problems is a satisfying accomplishment. It is also a skill you, as a professional driver, must develop. But, as any experienced driver will suggest: Try not to back your rig any more than necessary, even it if means driving around the block or coming into a dock area from an alternate direction **(see Figure 7–1).**

▶ **Figure 7–1**

Back your rig only if absolutely necessary. If possible, approach the dock area from an alternate direction.

BACKING PRINCIPLES AND RULES

Before getting into the cab to back a vehicle on your own, there are some principles and rules you should know. This chapter contains information you need to know to back a rig safely and efficiently. Studying it will help you master this necessary skill.

Steering Principles

Proper backing technique is necessary for the safe and efficient operation of a tractor-trailer rig in all situations and under all conditions. Unless enough time and attention are devoted to mastering this skill, maneuvering the rig can become very difficult.

Most drivers feel comfortable backing a personal vehicle. A car has two axles. In most cars, the front axle is used for steering and the rear axle has fixed wheels that cannot steer. They simply follow the direction the car is headed.

The technique used to back a tractor-trailer is much different from that used to back a car or pickup truck. Backing a tractor-trailer is more complicated because the rig is made up of two units. The tractor steers both vehicles. The trailer—with its fixed wheels—depends on the tractor for direction. In other words, the tractor steers the trailer **(see Figure 7–2).**

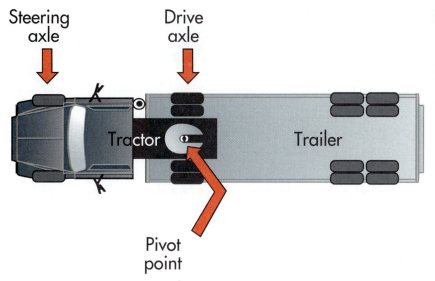

Steering axle

Drive axle

Tractor

Trailer

Pivot point

▶ **Figure 7–2**

To learn backing techniques, new drivers should first be familiar with the parts of their rig involved in backing.

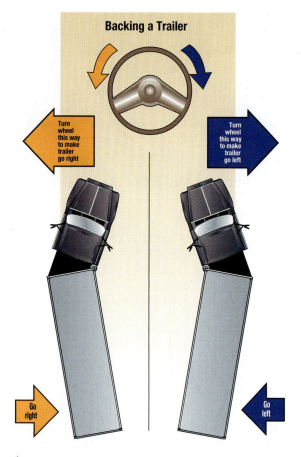

Backing a Trailer

Turn wheel this way to make trailer go right

Turn wheel this way to make trailer go left

Go right

Go left

▶ Figure 7–3

When the tractor moves in one direction when backing, the trailer moves in the opposite direction.

Now the technique starts to get difficult. The rear tractor axle becomes the trailer's steering axle. When you are backing the rig and the tractor moves in one direction, the front of the trailer moves in the same direction, which forces the rear of the trailer in the opposite direction. When you turn the steering wheel to the right, the rear of the trailer goes left. When you turn the steering wheel to the left, the rear of the trailer goes right **(see Figure 7–3).** The amount of turning the trailer does is proportional to the angle created between the trailer and the tractor. As the angle becomes greater, the more the trailer will pivot and the less movement to the rear there will be.

SAFETY RULES WHEN BACKING

Because you cannot see directly behind your vehicle, backing should always be considered a dangerous **maneuver.** Common sense dictates that you should avoid backing when possible. For example, when you park your rig, try to park so you will be able to pull forward when you leave.

Even though you can reduce the need to back your rig by planning ahead, almost everyone who drives professionally will have to back at times. When you do have to back your rig, there are a few rules to remember:

- Avoid backing if possible.
- Inspect your intended path.
- Use a helper to signal your path.
- Back and turn toward the driver's side when possible.
- Use your four-way flashers and horn to assist with safely backing your rig.
- Always watch your mirrors.

Avoid Backing when Possible

Backing up always looks easier in pictures.

On the road, it is sometimes impossible to avoid backing, but when the opportunity arises, always park your rig so you can pull forward when you leave the location.

Inspect Your Intended Path

Whether you will be backing in a straight line or backing and turning, inspect your path before you begin. Get out and walk around your rig. Check the clearance of the path your vehicle will make. Ensure that the road, parking area, or docking areas will be able to support your vehicle. Look for low clearances such as low-hanging wires or debris and roof overhangs. Check for debris in your path, other parked vehicles, or any debris that could move into your path. Is your path sloping down to the dock? Get a mental picture before you begin backing **(see Figure 7–4).**

▶ **Figure 7–4**

Inspect your path before backing. Get out and walk around your rig before backing.

Use a Helper to Signal Your Path

Use a helper or spotter any time you have to back your rig. You cannot see behind your rig and there are blind spots in the mirrors. A helper is always needed for blind-side backing. The helper should stand in front of the truck so the driver can have a clear view of the helper's signals. Hearing the helper's spoken directions is often difficult. Therefore, before you begin the backing maneuver, work out hand signals so you will understand when the helper wants you to stop in order to back your rig safely. Remember that even though you are using a helper, the driver is always responsible for any problems **(see Figure 7–5).**

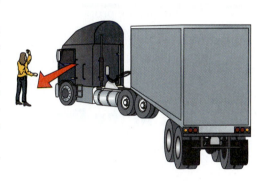

▶ **Figure 7–5**

Whenever possible, use a helper when backing.

Back and Turn toward the Driver's Side when Possible

When you have to back and turn, try to back toward the driver's side of the vehicle. You will have a better view of what you are doing and you will also be able to avoid the dangers of backing to your blind side.

If you back toward the driver's side, you can watch the rear of the vehicle by looking out of the side window and by using your left window and your left mirror. In a tractor with a box trailer, you can only see the side of the trailer in your right mirror during blind-side backing. Do not become focused on one mirror. Always use both mirrors and scan from mirror to mirror several times while backing.

Avoid backing into the street when possible. Back into an alley, instead, so that you can drive out forward. If you must back into the street, driver-side backing allows you to block off the whole street and protect other drivers who might otherwise try to pull around you before you get into position. When possible, try to get a helper to watch your blind side by standing in front of the truck. Other vehicles may try to get around you.

When you know you will have to back your rig, plan ahead so you can use driver-side backing. This may mean going around the block to put your vehicle in the correct position. The added safety and ease of operation is well worth the extra driving.

Use Your Four-Way Flashers and Horn

Once you have inspected your intended driving path, get back into your cab and turn on your four-way flashers. If your truck is not equipped with a backup alarm, blow your horn two or three times before you begin backing. Check both mirrors and the front of your rig constantly.

GENERAL BACKING RULES

The four general rules to remember every time you back your rig. These are:

- Start in the proper position.
- Back slowly.
- Constantly check behind your vehicle.
- Start over when necessary.

Start in the Proper Position

The most important maneuver when you are backing your rig is to begin with the proper setup **(see Figure 7–6)**.

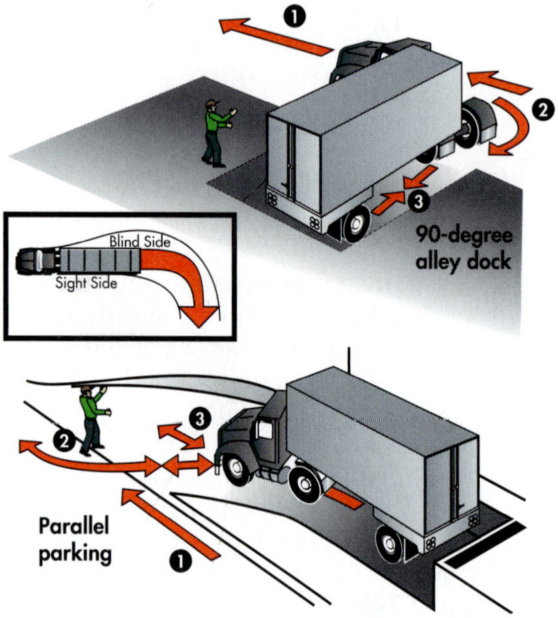

Position your rig properly before beginning to back. Reach the right position by moving forward. When you think the vehicle is in the right position, stop and secure it. Get out and check your position from the front, rear, and both sides. Try to limit the distance of the pull-up. The farther you pull up, the farther you must back up. Use a helper or spotter when possible.

▶ Figure 7–6

Examples of backing maneuvers. 1, set up; 2, back in, pull out; 3, straighten and adjust.

Back Slowly

Use the lowest reverse gear and idle back slowly. Be patient. If possible, stay off the brakes and fuel pedal and avoid riding the clutch.

Constantly Check behind Your Vehicle

Backing a tractor-trailer rig is usually done with mirrors. You should know what the trailer looks like in the mirrors at all times. Use both mirrors and do not become focused on one mirror and use minimal steering correction. It takes 8 to 12 feet for the trailer to react to the driver's direction. Be patient and go slowly.

Start Over when Necessary

If the trailer gets out of position, pull straight forward and start over. It is better to pull forward and try again than continue to back blindly.

BASIC BACKING MANEUVERS

There are four basic backing skills. You should be able to perform all of these safely and efficiently.

- Straight-line backing
- Alley-dock backing
- Straight-line parking
- Parallel parking

Straight-Line Backing

> **CAUTION!**
>
> Before backing, make sure your mirrors are properly adjusted. **G**et **O**ut **a**nd **L**ook! **(GOAL)** to avoid an accident. Once you release the clutch and begin backing, try rolling at a continuous safe, slow speed until you complete the maneuver or need to reposition.

Steps in Straight-Line Backing

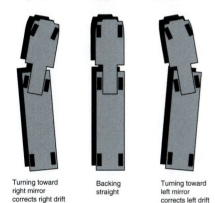

Turning toward right mirror corrects right drift   Backing straight   Turning toward left mirror corrects left drift

1. Position vehicle properly and check path
2. Back as slowly as possible
3. Constantly check behind with mirrors
4. Use push-pull method of steering
   - When the trailer gets bigger in one mirror, turn the steering wheel toward that mirror to correct the drift

▶ **Figure 7–7**

Backing in a straight line is the easiest of all backing maneuvers.

Straight-line backing is the easiest backing maneuver to perform and also serves as a basis for all other backing maneuvers. The point where the tractor and trailer are connected becomes the **pivot point** for your vehicle **(see Figure 7–7).**

A pivot point (or point of **articulation**) is extremely sensitive to movement. If you have the tractor-trailer perfectly aligned and you hold the steering wheel so the wheels are pointing straight ahead, when you begin to move back, rarely will the entire rig move in a straight line. Usually, the trailer will begin to drift either left or right.

The key to backing your rig in a straight line is to recognize what direction the trailer is drifting and make the necessary adjustments immediately. **Use both outside mirrors** to help you make these steering adjustments.

To correct the drift, turn the top of the steering wheel toward the drift. It takes very little movement of the steering wheel to correct the drift, if you adjust early. Do not oversteer and overcorrect **(see Figure 7–8).**

When the trailer begins to respond to your correction, begin turning the wheel in the opposite direction to remove the initial correction. Depending on the length of the trailer, it takes 8 to 12 feet for the trailer to respond. Shorter trailers react faster than longer trailers.

Be patient! Think your moves through carefully. If you find the trailer has gone too far out of line, pull forward and position for another try.

Alley-Dock Backing

Alley-dock backing is required at freight docks when the driver must back in from the street or when the driver must back the rig into a space between two vehicles. The steps include:

1. Pull forward in a straight line near the space at the dock. You should be about 3 to 5 feet out from other parked vehicles. When the front of the trailer is in line with the left side of the parking space, turn hard to the right **(see Figure 7–9).**

2. While continuing to move forward at a speed of about 3 to 5 miles per hour, when the tractor is at the 12-o'clock position, straight away from the parking space, turn to the left.

3. Keep moving this forward position until the trailer is near a 45-degree angle. When the tractor is at a slight angle to the left of the trailer and the parking space can be seen from the driver's window, straighten the steering tires and stop.

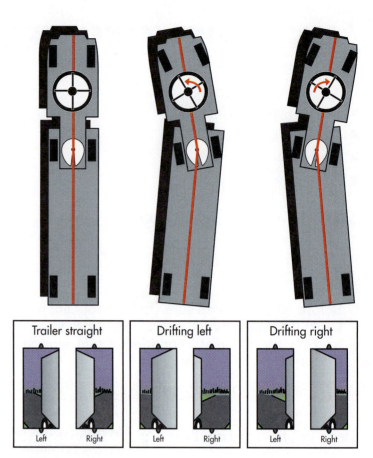

| Trailer straight | Drifting left | Drifting right |
| Left   Right | Left   Right | Left   Right |

▶ **Figure 7–8**

Use your mirrors to watch for and correct trailer drift when backing.

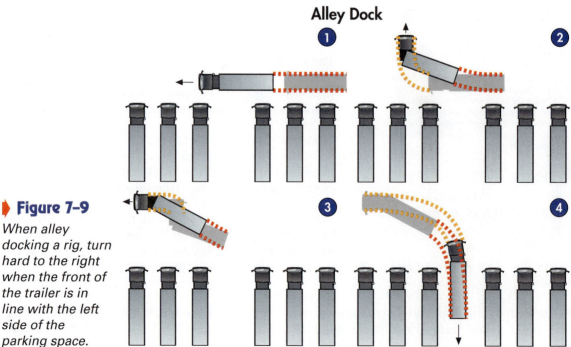

Alley Dock

▶ **Figure 7–9**

When alley docking a rig, turn hard to the right when the front of the trailer is in line with the left side of the parking space.

4. Set your brakes and get out of the cab. Your tractor tandem should be about 12 to 15 feet in front of the left side of the parking space. Be sure the steering tires are straight. Get back into the cab and start backing. Straighten out the rig as you enter the space and watch the direction of the rear tandem. Correct drift as needed. Check for drift using side mirrors and a helper if one is available.

> **CAUTION!**
> Always check both mirrors for room on each side when alley docking. Do not rely on one mirror to guide you.

Straight-Line Parking

Straight-line parking requires the following steps:

1. Pull forward in a straight line near the parking space. You should be about 3 to 5 feet out from the other parked vehicles.

2. Stop when your line of sight is in the middle of the parking space. Look out your right window for a reference point that is within a line of sight and even with the middle of the parking space **(see Figure 7–10).**

3. Continue moving forward. When the front of the trailer is in line with the left side of the parking space, turn hard to the right. Keep turning to the right until the tractor is headed toward the 2-o'clock position.

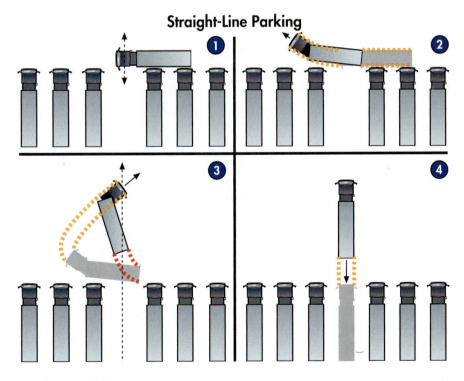

▶ **Figure 7–10**

Before beginning a straight-line parking maneuver, pull the rig forward about 3 to 5 feet from other parked vehicles.

4. Straighten the steering tires and pull forward until the rig is in front of the parking space. Set your brakes and get out of the cab. Be sure the trailer is directly behind the tractor. The rig should be directly in front of the parking space. Get back into the cab and start backing.

Parallel Parking

Parallel parking is required when you need to bring your rig alongside a curb or a dock. The following will help you accomplish this sometimes difficult maneuver:

1. Make certain your rig can fit into the parallel space.

2. You should begin with your rig 2 to 3 feet from other parked vehicles. Pull forward in a straight line near the parking space. Stop when the rear tandem axles of the trailer are about 8 feet in front of the parking space **(see Figure 7–11).**

▶ **Figure 7–11**

When parallel parking, pull the rig 2 to 3 feet from other parked vehicles.

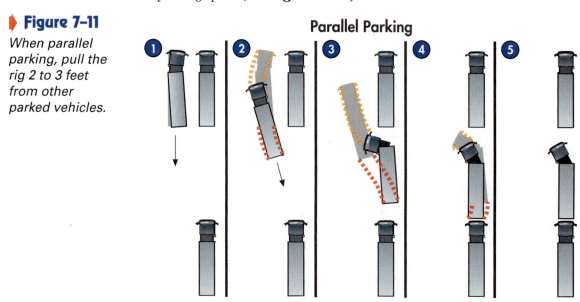

Parallel Parking

3. Set your brakes and get out of the cab. Be sure your rig is in a straight line and is 2 to 3 feet away from other parked vehicles. Check to be sure the rear tandem axles of the rig are 8 feet in front of the parking space.

4. Get back into the cab and begin backing with the steering wheel turned to the left. The angle between the left side of the tractor is about 12 to 15 degrees away from the front of the trailer.

5. Turn hard to the right and continue backing until the tractor and the trailer are in a straight line **(see Figure 7–10, position 2).** Continue backing until the front of the trailer is even with the front of the parking space **(see Figure 7–10, position 3).**

6. Turn hard to the right and continue backing until the trailer is parallel inside the parking space. The tractor should be at an 85- to 90-degree angle to the left. Leave the tractor in this position for an easier exit.

SUMMARY

In this chapter, you have learned the step-by-step procedures for backing a tractor-trailer safely and efficiently. You have also learned that tractor-trailer combinations have different backing characteristics from those of your personal vehicle. How to proceed with alley-dock backing and parallel parking were also explained.

KEY TERMS

Alley-dock backing   Parallel parking   Straight-line backing
Articulation   Pivot point   Straight-line parking
Maneuver

REVIEW QUESTIONS

1. Regarding backing a tractor-trailer, if the rear of the tractor moves to the left, the rear of the trailer _____.

   a. moves to the left   **c.** both a and b

   b. goes in a straight line   **d.** moves to the right

2. When backing, if the tractor and trailer are exactly aligned and the steering wheel is held so the front wheels are pointing straight ahead and parallel to the sides of the rig, the whole unit will _____.

   a. move in a straight line   **c.** always move to the north

   b. rarely, if ever, move in a straight line   **d.** always move to the south

3. When using a helper in backing, the _____ is always responsible for any problems that may arise from the backing maneuver.

   a. driver   **c.** helper

   b. dispatcher   **d.** yard foreman

4. If a driver has to back and turn, it is safer to back and turn toward the _____.

   a. nondriver's side of the vehicle   **c.** a and b

   b. it does not matter which side   **d.** driver's side of the vehicle

5. When preparing to back, if your tractor does not have a backup alarm, you should _____ and then start backing.

   a. turn on your headlights   **c.** sound your horn two or three times

   b. blink your headlights   **d.** turn on you clearance lights

6. The most important maneuver in backing is _____.

   a. starting with the proper setup   **c.** parallel parking

   b. alley docking   **d.** b and c

7. Regarding straight-line backing, before backing the tractor should be _____.

   a. behind the trailer   **c.** at a 45-degree angle with the trailer

   b. directly in front of the trailer **d.** at a 90-degree angle with the trailer

8. When alley docking a rig, the driver turns hard to the right when the _____ is in line with the left side of the parking space.

   a. back of the trailer   **c.** front of the trailer

   b. front of the tractor   **d.** middle of the trailer

9. Regarding straight-line parking, after stopping when the driver's line of sight is even with the middle of the parking space and continuing forward until the trailer is in line with the left side of the parking space and after turning hard to the right, the driver continues to turn hard to the right until the tractor is headed toward the _____ position.

   a. 5 o'clock

   b. 12 o'clock

   c. 3 o'clock

   d. 2 o'clock

10. Regarding parallel parking, when the trailer is parallel inside the parking space, the tractor should be _____.

    a. at an 85- to 90-degree angle to the left

    b. at an 85- to 90-degree angle to the right

    c. parallel to the parking space

    d. neither a, b, nor c

8

Coupling and Uncoupling

OBJECTIVES

When you have completed this chapter, you should be able to:

- Demonstrate the correct way to safely and efficiently couple a tractor with a trailer.
- Demonstrate the correct way to safely and efficiently uncouple a rig.
- Describe the controls used when coupling or uncoupling a rig.
- Explain the hazards of coupling and uncoupling a rig improperly.

INTRODUCTION

A tractor and **trailer** are two separate and independent units until they are brought together and joined—or coupled. This is the driver's responsibility, to couple tractor and trailer or trailers correctly, for the trip **(see Figure 8–1). Coupling** is a basic skill to be mastered by the professional driver operating tractor-trailer rigs. Federal Motor Carrier Safety Regulations require all drivers to be qualified in this operation. The lack of knowledge and skills for coupling and uncoupling tractor-trailer rigs can result in costly damage to the rig, not to mention the dangers that accompany problems related to improper coupling.

The best way to learn coupling is a 15-step approach **(see Figure 8–2)** that protects you and others from injury and your vehicle and cargo from damage. Use this same sequence each time you couple a rig. Follow the 11-step approach in **Figure 8–2** when you uncouple a rig. Trying to couple or uncouple a rig without knowing these sequences can be dangerous.

▶ **Figure 8–1**

It is the driver's responsibility to couple the tractor and trailer before a trip.

COUPLING	UNCOUPLING
Step 1: Inspect fifth wheel and kingpin	Step 1: Position the vehicle
Step 2: Check surrounding area and secure trailer	Step 2: Secure the vehicle
Step 3: Position the tractor	Step 3: Lower landing gear
Step 4: Back slowly into position	Step 4: Disconnect air lines and electrical cord
Step 5: Secure the tractor	Step 5: Release fifth-wheel latch
Step 6: Check the trailer height	Step 6: Lower air suspension
Step 7: Connect the air lines	Step 7: Pull tractor partially clear
Step 8: Supply air to the trailer	Step 8: Secure tractor
Step 9: Start the engine and lock trailer brakes	Step 9: Inspect trailer supports
Step 10: Back under the trailer	Step 10: Pull tractor clear
Step 11: Check the connection	Step 11: Reinflate air suspension
Step 12: Secure the vehicle	
Step 13: Inspect the coupling	
Step 14: Connect electrical cord and check air lines	
Step 15: Raise trailer supports	

▶ **Figure 8–2**

A quick checklist for coupling and uncoupling.

> **CAUTION!**
>
> Typical hazards in coupling or uncoupling a rig include:
>
> 1. When the tractor is not secured, brake lines can be damaged.
>
> 2. When trailer brakes are not functioning, the trailer can be pushed into an obstruction.
>
> 3. When the ground is not firm for uncoupling, the trailer can fall and be damaged.
>
> 4. When trailer wheels are not **chocked,** the trailer may roll or be pushed into an obstruction and be damaged.
>
> 5. When climbing on the tractor during coupling, the driver could fall because of slippery surfaces.
>
> 6. If the driver works under an unsupported trailer (no jackstand or tractor under the trailer's nose) he or she could be injured if the landing gear collapses and the trailer drops to the ground.

THE COUPLING SEQUENCE

The Federal Motor Carrier Safety Administration requires all professional drivers to be qualified in the 15-step coupling operation.

Step 1: Inspect the Fifth Wheel

To make the safest connection possible, inspect the **fifth wheel** and the trailer's kingpin.

- Look for any damaged, loose, or missing parts. Be sure to check the kingpin for bends, breaks, or severe rust.

- **Locking jaws** should be open **(see Figure 8–3).**

- Check to see that the fifth wheel is tilted downward toward the rear of the tractor.

- The fifth wheel should also be greased. Lack of proper lubrication could mean steering problems that result from friction between the tractor and trailer **(see Figure 8–4).**

- Safety release handle should be in the automatic lock position.

Fifth Wheel

1. **Coupler arm**

2. **Release handle and safety latch**

3. **Locking jaws**

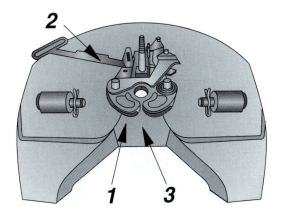

▶ **Figure 8–3**

Major parts of the fifth wheel.

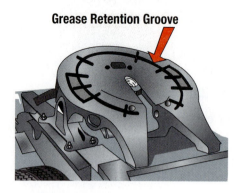

Grease Retention Groove

▶ **Figure 8-4**

The fifth wheel must always have a coating of grease in the retention groove to ensure smooth movement.

■ Slider locks should be in place.

■ The fifth-wheel position should allow coupling without allowing the rear end of the tractor to strike the landing gear.

Step 2: Inspect the Area

Be sure area around the rig is clear of all debris and hazards.

■ There should be enough space in which to maneuver the tractor.

■ Check the cargo to make certain it will not move when the trailer is coupled with the tractor.

■ If the trailer is equipped with spring brakes, make sure these brakes are applied before coupling begins.

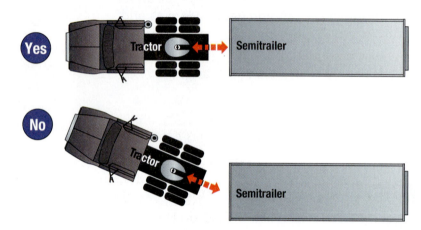

▶ **Figure 8-5**

The tractor should be placed squarely in front of the trailer for coupling—not at an angle.

Step 3: Position the Tractor

The tractor should be placed squarely in front of the trailer. Never back at an angle. The wrong approach by the tractor can push the trailer back, forward or sideways. This could break the **landing gear** and cause the trailer to fall **(see Figure 8–5).**

■ If the situation calls for you to back at an angle, get out of the cab frequently and check the alignment between the fifth wheel and the kingpin.

■ To properly line up your tractor and trailer, use the outside edge of your drive axles and the edge of the trailer or guide points. In doing so, the tractor, outside edge of the drive axle tires, and the edge of the trailer form a straight line, if the trailer is 8 feet (96 inches) wide.

■ If the trailer is 8.5 feet (102 inches) wide, the tractor drive axle tires should be 1-½ to 3 inches inside the outer edge of the trailer **(see Figure 8–6).**

▶ **Figure 8-6**

Proper positioning of the tractor and trailer to begin coupling.

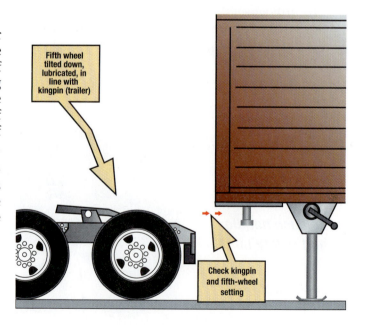

Fifth wheel tilted down, lubricated, in line with kingpin (trailer)

Check kingpin and fifth-wheel setting

GO!

Pulling up directly in front of the trailer is preferred in all cases, but if you have to "angle in," check as often as necessary to make sure the throat of the fifth wheel is aligned with the kingpin.

Step 4: Back Slowly into Position Until the Fifth Wheel Just Touches the Trailer

Back slowly toward the nose of the trailer and stop just before the fifth wheel reaches the trailer.

- If your tractor has air bags, dump the air at this point.
- You should be close enough to compare the fifth-wheel height with the height of the trailer.

CAUTION!

If you are unfamiliar with the tractor and trailer, stop and exit the truck to check the distance from the trailer **(see Figure 8–7).**

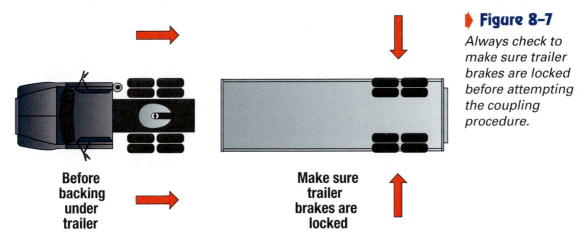

Before backing under trailer

Make sure trailer brakes are locked

▶ **Figure 8–7**

Always check to make sure trailer brakes are locked before attempting the coupling procedure.

Step 5: Secure the Tractor

Shift into neutral, put on the parking brakes, and exit the cab.

Step 6: Check the Trailer Height

Inspect the height of the trailer nose compared to the fifth wheel. The nose should be slightly higher than the back of the fifth wheel. To couple properly, the nose of the trailer should touch the middle of the fifth wheel **(see Figure 8–8).**

You may raise or lower the fifth wheel, using the tractor's adjustable air suspension, if available. The other option is to crank the landing gear, although this may be difficult with a loaded trailer.

- If the trailer is too low, the tractor may collide with it, causing damage.
- If the trailer is too high, it may ride up and over the fifth wheel, colliding with the cab.

Incorrect: Too high

Incorrect: Too low

Correct: Level with fifth wheel

▶ **Figure 8–8**

Inspect the height of the trailer nose compared to the fifth wheel. The nose should be slightly higher than the back of the fifth wheel.

Step 7: Connect the Air Lines

When the height of the trailer is correct, you are ready to connect the tractor's air lines to the trailer. There are two air lines running from the tractor to the trailer, called the "service" and "emergency" lines. **Glad hands** are used to connect the air lines **(see Figure 8–9).**

For the trailer's brakes to work correctly, the air lines must be connected correctly. Match the plug to the connector, but do not force it if it does not fit. Sometimes the tractor's connectors do not match, so use a converter if necessary. Firmly seat the plug in the receptacle. Put on the safety catch or latch to keep them from accidentally separating.

Step 8: Supply Air to the Trailer

After the air lines have been connected and secured, get back into the cab. With the truck engine off, push in the **trailer air supply valve** to supply the trailer brakes with air. Listen for escaping air. If you hear a leak or if the air pressure gauge registers excessive loss of air, correct the problem at once. You will notice air leaking if you connected the air lines incorrectly.

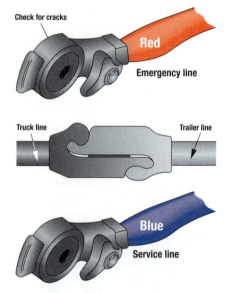

Check for cracks

Red

Emergency line

Truck line

Trailer line

Blue

Service line

▶ **Figure 8–9**

Connect the service and emergency air lines.

Step 9: Release the Tractor's Parking Brake and Put on the Trailer Brake

You are now ready to back the tractor under the trailer, using the following steps:

- Start the truck engine.
- Put the truck into gear.
- Release the tractor's parking brake.
- Apply the trailer brakes.

Step 10: Back under the Trailer

Using the lowest reverse gear, back the tractor slowly under the trailer. You should feel or hear the **kingpin** lock into the fifth wheel **(see Figure 8–10).** Do not hit the kingpin too hard. This could bend the kingpin, buckle the upper plate, jump the pin and cause the trailer to hit the tractor, push the trailer away from the tractor, or damage cargo in the trailer.

▶ **Figure 8–10**

Kingpin locking fifth wheel.

CAUTION!

Do not accelerate while backing under the trailer.

Step 11: Test the Connection

Test the connection by pulling the tractor gently forward in low gear while the trailer handbrake is on **(see Figure 8–11).** As soon as resistance to forward motion is felt, disengage the clutch. Accelerate just enough to keep the engine from stalling. Then test the connection again.

Step 12: Secure the Vehicle

When you are sure of a solid hookup, apply the parking brake. Turn off the engine, put the key in your pocket, and get out of the cab.

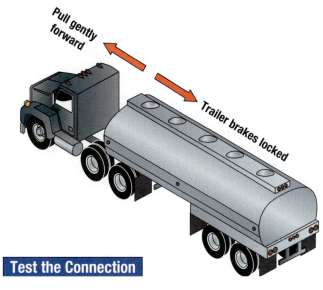

Pull gently forward

Trailer brakes locked

Test the Connection

▶ **Figure 8–11**

Test the hookup by gently pulling the tractor forward in low gear while the trailer hand brake is on.

Step 13: Inspect the Coupling

You will now need to go under the trailer and, by using a flashlight, get a good look at the coupling. Check to see that the following have been done:

- Fifth-wheel jaws have engaged the shank of the kingpin and not the head. If the jaws are closed around the head, the trailer will bounce the kingpin out of the jaws.

- Jaws should be closed and locked. The safety catch should be over the locking lever.

- The upper fifth-wheel plate should be in full contact with the lower trailer plate. There should be no gap between the trailer apron and the fifth-wheel plate. If there is a space between the two, stop and fix the problem before doing anything else. Note: The space may be due to uneven ground surface. If this is the case, move the rig to flat ground and check again.

- Be sure to inspect the coupling each time you stop the truck, once you get on the road, especially when leaving a truck stop or rest area.

STOP!

Never crawl under your rig without putting the ignition keys in your pocket. This will prevent anyone from accidentally moving the rig while you are conducting a coupling inspection.

Step 14: Connect the Electrical Cord and Check Air Lines

Plug the electrical cord into the trailer, then fasten the safety catch. Be sure neither the electrical cord nor the air lines are damaged. These must not hit any moving parts of the rig.

Step 15: Raise the Landing Gear

You are now ready to raise the landing gear **(see Figure 8–12).** Most crank handles have a low speed and a high speed. Use the low speed to start raising the landing gear. Switch to high speed when the trailer weight is off the landing gear. Keep cranking until the landing gear is fully raised—and make sure both legs of the landing gear go up.

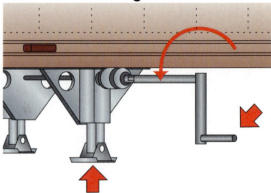

Landing Gear

- Check clearance between rear of tractor frame and/or mudflaps and landing gear.
- Use low range to begin raising landing gear.
- Once free of weight, switch to high gear.
- Crank until fully raised.
- Safely secure crank in holder in low gear.
- Check clearance between top of tractor drive wheels and nose of trailer.

▶ **Figure 8–12**

Raise the landing gear.

 "Hmm . . . wonder if this is what they had in mind when they asked me to hook up the doubles?"

STEP-BY-STEP UNCOUPLING PROCEDURE

Step 1: Position the Vehicle

To prepare to **uncouple** your rig, place the tractor directly in line with the trailer on level ground, to keep from damaging the landing gear when pulling the tractor from under the trailer. Make sure the surface where you plan to uncouple the trailer is level and also will support the weight of the rig.

Step 2: Secure the Vehicle

Place the tractor protection valve in the emergency position. This cuts off the air supply between the tractor and the trailer. Make certain you have backed tightly against the kingpin. If not, it will bind and will not release properly. Put on the tractor's parking brake and exit the cab.

Step 3: Lower the Landing Gear

Inspect landing gear for rust and damage. Then lower the landing gear until both legs touch the ground. **Make sure both legs come down!** If one touches the ground but not the other, find a more level location to drop the trailer. Crank until you see the trailer rise off the fifth wheel.

Step 4: Disconnect and Store the Air Lines and Electrical Cable

Carefully disconnect the air lines and electrical cable. Place the air line glad hands on the dummy couplers behind the cab. Hang the electrical cable down to avoid moisture on the plug and store in its holder. Secure the lines against snagging, scraping, cuts, or other damage.

Step 5: Release the Fifth-Wheel Latch

To release the fifth wheel, raise the release handle lock pin and pull to the open position. On a single axle tractor, this usually is not hard. On tandem axle tractors, however, the release handle is sometimes hard to reach. If it is difficult to reach, use a pull handle or hook.

Step 6: Lower the Air Suspension

If your truck has air suspension, lower the air bags to prevent the end of the tractor from popping up when later pulling clear.

Step 7: Pull the Tractor Partly Clear of the Trailer

Get back into the cab and release the parking brake, leaving the tractor protection valve in the set position. Pull the tractor forward until the fifth wheel begins to clear the trailer apron plate. Stop the tractor while its frame is still under the trailer. This will keep the trailer from falling if the landing gear collapses or sinks.

Step 8: Secure the Tractor

Put on the tractor parking brakes. Exit the cab.

Step 9: Inspect the Trailer Supports

Be sure the landing gear is supporting the trailer and is not damaged.

Step 10: Pull the Tractor Clear of the Trailer

Release the parking brake. Check the area ahead of the tractor and pull the tractor slowly away from the trailer. Uncoupling is now safely completed.

Step 11: Reinflate the Air Suspension System

After pulling the tractor away from the trailer, reinflate the air bags (if this applies to your rig).

GO!

Use the following memory aid (LAPP) to help you remember how to begin the uncoupling procedure:

L = **Lower the landing gear**

A = **Air lines and electrical lines disconnected**

P = **Pull and release arm**

P = **Pin or release pin**

SUMMARY

In this chapter, you have reviewed the steps necessary to couple a trailer to a tractor, uncouple a rig, use the controls needed to couple or uncouple a rig, and how to test the connection.

KEY TERMS

Chock

Coupling

Fifth wheel

Glad hands

Kingpin

Landing gear

Locking jaws

Tractor

Trailer

Trailer air supply valve

Uncoupling

REVIEW QUESTIONS

1. It is the _____ responsibility to couple the tractor and trailer correctly for any trip.

   a. dispatcher's

   b. technician's

   c. foreman's

   d. driver's

2. When positioning the tractor for coupling with a 102-inch (8-½ feet) wide trailer, the tractor drive axle tires should be approximately _____.

   a. 1-½ to 3 inches inside the outside edge of the trailer

   b. 1-½ to 3 inches outside the outside edge of the trailer

   c. in line with the tires of the trailer

   d. 12 inches inside the outside edge of the trailer

3. During the coupling process, when inspecting the height of the trailer nose compared to the height of the fifth wheel, the nose of the trailer should be _____ than the back of the fifth wheel.

   a. lower

   b. slightly higher

   c. 2 feet higher

   d. 3 feet higher

4. During the coupling process, when supplying air to the trailer, if you hear an air leak or the air pressure gauge registers excessive loss of air, then you know you _____.

   a. have not connected the electrical lines correctly

   b. have not connected the air lines correctly

   c. the trailer is not in line with the tractor

   d. the nose of the trailer is too high compared with the fifth wheel

5. During the coupling process, when backing under the trailer, the driver stops when the _____ is felt or heard to lock into the fifth wheel.

   a. nose of the trailer

   b. landing gear

   c. kingpin

   d. driveshaft

6. When inspecting a successful coupling, the driver should see the jaws of the fifth wheel closed and locked around the kingpin with the safety catch _____.

   a. over the locking lever

   b. behind the locking lever

   c. over the rear tires of the trailer

   d. over the rear axle of the tractor

7. To test the tractor and trailer connection (hookup), the driver _____.

   a. drives forward 20 to 30 feet with all brakes off

   b. drives forward 20 to 30 feet with all brakes on

   c. gently pulls the tractor forward in low gear while the trailer hand break is on

   d. lets the mechanic test the connection

8. When preparing for uncoupling, the tractor_____.

   a. can be at any angle with the trailer

   b. should be placed directly in line with the trailer on any kind of ground as the landing gear will support the trailer on any kind of surface

   c. should be placed directly in line with the trailer on level ground

   d. with the trailer attached should be driven to the shop for the mechanic to do the uncoupling

9. Regarding uncoupling, after the fifth-wheel latch has been released and the tractor is being pulled forward, the driver _____.

   a. drives to the technician's shop for the completion of the uncoupling process

   b. drives the tractor at least 15 feet from the trailer to ensure the tractor is clear of the trailer

   c. drives forward at least 3 feet and then backs at least 5 feet to ensure the trailer is on firm ground

   d. drives forward and stops the tractor while the frame is still under the trailer

10. Which of the following is not an element of the memory aid LAPP which helps the driver remember how to start the uncoupling procedure?

    a. lower landing gear

    b. pull forward and then back

    c. air lines and electrical lines disconnected

    d. pull and release arm or release pin

OBJECTIVES

When you have completed this chapter, you should be able to:

- Describe the function of the sliding fifth wheel or trailer tandem axles.

- Explain the concept of shifting weight between the tractor and the trailer.

- Explain the effects of the sliding fifth wheel or trailer tandem action on overall length, maneuverability of the rig, and off-tracking.

- Describe how to lock and unlock a sliding fifth wheel.

- Explain the correct way to slide the fifth wheel of a tractor with a trailer attached.

- Explain the hazards of sliding the fifth wheel or trailer tandem axles improperly.

▶ Figure 9-1

A tractor-trailer can have one or both: a sliding fifth wheel on the tractor and sliding tandem axles on the trailer.

INTRODUCTION

Many tractor-trailers have a **sliding fifth wheel** on the tractor and **sliding tandem axles** on the trailer. Tractor-trailers can have either one or both of them **(see Figure 9–1).**

The sliding fifth wheel can adjust the overall length of the tractor-trailer, adjust the turning radius of the vehicle, and adjust and balance the weight of each of the axles. The sliding tandem axles on the trailer can adjust the off-tracking of the trailer, adjust the turning radius of the vehicle, and adjust and balance the weight on each of the axles of the trailer.

As you can see, wheels and axles have similar effects on both the tractor and the trailer. Their positions are important for the driver to understand if he or she wishes to safely and legally haul a load.

CAUTION!

On every trip and with every load, the driver is responsible for:

- Legal gross vehicle weight
- Overall length of the vehicle
- Amount of weight per axle
- Rig's maneuverability and ability to turn safely
- Knowing all state and local laws/restrictions

The purpose of this chapter is to help you learn how to slide the fifth wheel and the trailer tandem axles. You will also learn some of the basic reasons for making these adjustments to the rig.

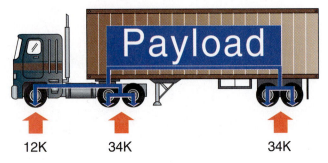

12K   34K   34K

Well-balanced load

▶ Figure 9-2

When a trailer is coupled to a tractor, some of the weight is transferred to the tractor.

SHIFTING WEIGHT

When a trailer is coupled to a tractor, some weight of the trailer is transferred to the tractor through the connection with the fifth wheel **(see Figure 9–2).** If the payload is evenly distributed in the trailer, standard trailer axle and fifth-wheel settings will properly distribute the weight on each axle.

Some trailers have sliding tandem axles to transfer weight to the tractor if the payload in the trailer is not evenly distributed. The amount of the weight transferred to the tractor can be adjusted by sliding the tandem axles on the trailer toward the rear. This will increase the amount of weight on the drive and steering axles of the tractor **(see Figure 9–3).**

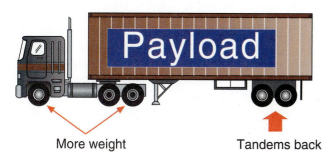

More weight   Tandems back

▶ Figure 9–3

Sliding tandems to the rear increases weight on the drive and steering axles.

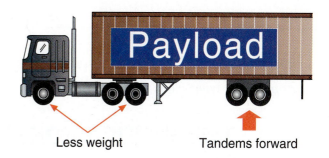

Less weight   Tandems forward

▶ Figure 9–4

Sliding tandems forward shifts weight off the tractor.

By sliding the trailer tandems forward, you can shift weight off the tractor **(see Figure 9–4)**. This causes the weight behind the trailer's tandem axles to actually tip the weight off the tractor. Shifting the weight decreases the amount of weight on the drive and steering axles of the tractor.

Some tractors have a sliding fifth wheel. This can adjust the length of the tractor-trailer and balance, or shift, some of the weight from the trailer to between the steer axle and drive axles of the tractor. By sliding the fifth wheel on the tractor forward, you can transfer weight to the steer axle and also shorten the overall length of the rig.

CAUTION!

If too much weight is shifted to the steer axle, the tractor will be hard to steer. It also may be harder to maneuver **(see Figure 9–5)**. If you shift too much weight, the rig may also be overweight on the steer axle, according to regulations, and at night your lights will not be aimed properly and you will not see as well as usual.

If you slide the fifth wheel on the tractor toward the rear, you can reduce the amount of weight on the steer axle, but you will also increase the total length of the tractor **(see Figure 9–6)**. If too much weight is shifted off the steer axle, the steering will feel light and you will not have as much control over the steering. Shifting too much weight off the steer axle can also make the rig overweight on the drive axles. At night, your headlights will be aimed at the sky instead of the

More weight

▶ Figure 9–5

More weight on the steer axle makes the tractor more difficult to steer and maneuver.

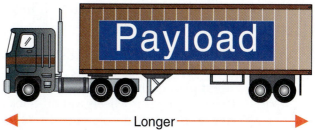

Longer

▶ Figure 9–6

Sliding the fifth wheel toward the rear increases total length of the tractor and reduces weight on the steer axle.

Figure 9-7

Distribution of weight has a teeter-totter effect.

road ahead. As you can see, the positions of the fifth wheel and the trailer tandem axles have a lot to do with the weight per axle and handling of the rig **(see Figure 9–7).**

THE BRIDGE FORMULA

To achieve the maximum legal weight on each axle, you need to know the **Bridge Formula.** The Bridge Gross Weight Formula was developed to prevent stress to highway bridges caused by heavy trucks. All trucks operating on interstate highways and some state highways must comply with the Bridge Formula.

Under the formula rules, tractors must have a minimum **outer spread** (distance between the center of the front axle and the center of the rearmost axle) of 14 feet to scale the maximum 46,000 pounds (12,000 pounds on the steer axle, 34,000 pounds on the tandems). This distance is not affected when you slide the fifth wheel forward or back, but two other distances are affected—the **inner bridge** (between the center of the rearmost axle and the center of the leading trailer axle) and the **outer bridge** (between the center of the forward tractor tandem and the rearmost trailer axle).

Sliding the fifth wheel or a trailer slider will change these distances and may affect your legal load-carrying capacity. For example, a five-axle tractor-trailer must have an outer bridge of at least 51 feet to haul the maximum allowable 80,000 pounds.

MANEUVERABILITY AND OFF-TRACKING

The **maneuverability** and **off-tracking** of the tractor-trailer are affected by the position of the trailer tandems and the position of the fifth wheel. When you slide the fifth wheel to the rear of the tractor, the overall length of the vehicle increases. The distance between the steer axle and the kingpin also increases along with the distance to the trailer tandem axles.

When you turn, the greater the distance between the steer axle and the pivot point (kingpin) of the trailer, the further the trailer will off-track. The swept path of the trailer will increase, so you will need more space to make a turn **(see Figure 9–8).**

The position of the tandem axles of the trailer also affects off-tracking and the space needed to turn. When you slide the tandem axles all the way to the rear, the distance between the kingpin and the real axle wheels increases. The overall length of the vehicle does not change, but the amount of space needed to turn increases **(see Figure 9–9).**

When the tandem axles are all the way back, trailer off-tracking increases, and so does the swept path of the vehicle. The sharper the turn, the more the rear wheels will off-track **(see Figure 9–10).** When you slide the tandem axles forward and the distance between the kingpin and the rear axles decreases, the rig is easier to maneuver. There is also less trailer off-tracking, which is helpful when making deliveries.

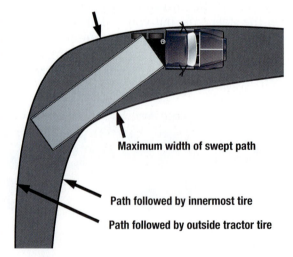

Figure 9-8

Off-tracking in a 90-degree turn.

▶ **Figure 9–9**

The position of the tandem axles of the trailer affect the amount of space needed to turn.

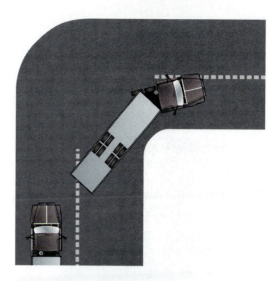

▶ **Figure 9–10**

The sharper the turn, the more the rear wheels will off-track.

CAUTION!

Be careful when the tandem axles are all the way forward because there will be a trailer overhang.

NOTE: The benefits of sliding the tandem axles forward when you drive in heavy (downtown) traffic can be offset by the possible dangers of trailer overhang.

THE FIFTH WHEEL

The two types of fifth wheels are fixed (stationary) fifth wheels and sliding fifth wheels. A **fixed fifth wheel** is usually mounted directly on the **frame rails** of the tractor by a bracket assembly **(see Figure 9–11).** The bracket assembly allows the fifth wheel to rock up and down. The stationary fifth wheel is placed to get the best weight distribution between the tractor's steer axle and the drive axle(s) of a properly loaded trailer.

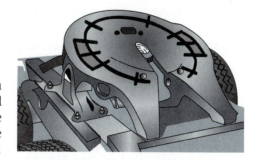

▶ **Figure 9–11**

A fixed, or stationary, fifth wheel.

GO!

Weight adjustments are made by sliding the tandem axles of the trailer.

Sliding fifth wheels are attached to the sliding bracket assembly **(see Figure 9–12).** The sliding bracket assemblies can be attached to a base that has a sliding rail assembly built into it. The base is then attached to the frame rails of the tractor. Then, the fifth wheel and sliding bracket assembly are attached directly to the frame rails.

The fifth wheel has a locking device that holds the sliding assembly in place. The two types of locking assemblies are manual release and air-operated release:

Manual release—allows you to release, or unlock, the sliding mechanism by pushing or pulling a release handle **(see Figure 9–13).** This release handle may be on the driver's side of the fifth wheel or directly in front of the fifth wheel. When the handle is pulled to the unlock position, the locking pins are released from the locking holes or notches on the mounting base or sliding rail assembly.

▶ **Figure 9–12**

A sliding fifth wheel.

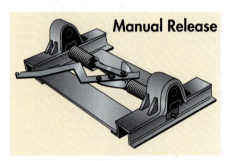

Manual Release

▶ **Figure 9–13**

Manual release allows you to unlock the fifth wheel with a release handle.

CAUTION!

Keep feet out of tire path and use free hand to brace balance.

Air-operated release—lets you release the locking device on the sliding fifth wheel by moving the fifth-wheel release lever in the cab to the "unlocked" position. When the lever is in the unlocked position, air is forced against a piston on the fifth-wheel locking device. The piston forces the locking pins to release from the locking holes or notches on the mounting base or sliding rail assembly **(see Figure 9–14).**

Air Release

SLIDING THE FIFTH WHEEL

▶ **Figure 9–14**

An air-operated release unlocks the fifth wheel by a release lever in the cab.

Sliding the fifth wheel is not a difficult procedure, but it should be done on a level surface, off the road, and away from hazards.

1. Be sure to set the trailer parking brake before getting out of the cab—for any reason. This will keep the tractor from rolling.

2. The trailer must be properly connected to the locked fifth wheel and the kingpin, locked in place.

3. The air and electrical lines should be connected to the trailer.

4. If the trailer has a sliding tandem axle, it should be locked into place.

5. Test the connection to the trailer, gently pulling forward with the trailer brake on. If you have just made the connection to the trailer, look at the connection to be sure the fifth-wheel jaws are locked around the kingpin of the trailer, then crank up the trailer's landing gear.

6. Place the fifth-wheel release handle or lever in the "unlocked" position. Then, put on your trailer brakes, either by pulling down on your trailer brake hand valve (if you have one) or by pulling out the red trailer air supply valve.

7. Release the tractor brake valve. With your tractor brakes released and your trailer brakes engaged, you are ready to slide the fifth wheel.

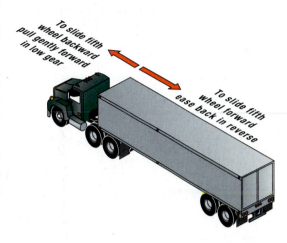

   If you want to slide the fifth wheel forward—put the tractor into reverse.

   If you want to slide the fifth wheel back toward the rear of the tractor— use low gear and ease the tractor forward or backward gently. You may get some resistance from the sliding assembly when you do this **(see Figure 9–15).**

▶ **Figure 9–15**

When sliding the fifth wheel, you may have some resistance from the sliding assembly.

If the fifth wheel has not been moved for quite some time, you may experience what is called **binding.** Look at the fifth-wheel locking pins first to make sure they have unlocked and that the fifth wheel is free to slide. Pressure on the pins may be holding them in place.

If the pins appear to be stuck or binding, you can usually free them by gently rocking the tractor. Corrosion, dirt, or grime may have gotten into the mechanism, causing it to lock. You may have to clean some of the road grime off the mechanism so it can work correctly. You may also want to lower the landing gear. It can help relieve binding and stress, allowing the fifth wheel to move easier.

Once you have moved the fifth wheel to where you want it, place the fifth-wheel release lever or handle in the locked position. With the trailer brakes still on, gently tug or push against the trailer. This will let the fifth-wheel locking pins unseat themselves.

Set the tractor brakes. Look at the fifth-wheel slider to make sure it is properly locked into place—and remember, you have just changed your overall length. This will make a difference in your ride, weight distribution, and maneuverability.

CAUTION! QUICK REVIEW—SLIDING THE FIFTH WHEEL

1. Make sure the tractor is properly coupled to the trailer.

2. Place the fifth-wheel release in the unlocked position.

3. Set the trailer brakes, using the hand valve or by pulling the red trailer air supply valve.

4. Release the tractor brake or parking brake system.

5. Ease the tractor gently in the opposite direction in which you want to move the fifth wheel.

6. Place the fifth-wheel release in the locked position.

7. With the trailer brakes still set, gently tug or push against the trailer to seat the locking pins.

8. Set the tractor brakes and visually check that the fifth-wheel slider is properly locked into place.

9. Remember you have just changed the rig's overall length, and that means the ride, weight distribution, and maneuverability will be different.

TRAILER TANDEM AXLES

Not all trailer axles are tandem axles. A light-duty trailer may have just one axle, and that axle is usually stationary. Trailers with high-rated cargo-carrying-capacity usually have tandem axles. All trailer axles are attached to a suspension system and subframe **(see Figure 9–16).**

One-axle trailer

Tandem-axle trailer

▶ **Figure 9–16**

Light-duty trailers may have only one axle, while trailers with high-rated carrying capacity usually have the tandem axles.

Trailer tandem axles can be grouped into two categories: fixed (stationary) and sliding.

Fixed tandem axle assemblies—include the suspension and subframe. The assembly is usually mounted directly on the frame rails of the trailer. The fixed (stationary) tandem axle assembly is placed to produce the best weight distribution between the tractor and the trailer. Weight adjustments between the tractor and trailer are then made by moving or shifting the load inside the trailer.

Sliding trailer tandem axle assemblies—are also mounted directly on the frame rails of the trailer. The difference is the subframe assembly allows the trailer axles and suspension to **slide,** or move, along the frame rails of the trailer. The part of the subassembly that slides is called the tandem axle slide. There is one slide on each side of the trailer **(see Figure 9–17).**

There are evenly placed holes along the length of the slide. These holes are designed to seat four locking pins that are attached to a locking lever or handle called the **locking lever.** You engage the locking lever manually. There is no in-cab control switch. At the ends of the sliding rails are stops that keep the assembly from coming apart when you slide the axles.

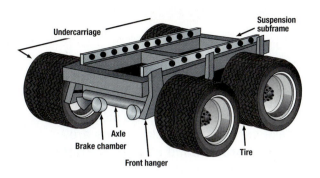

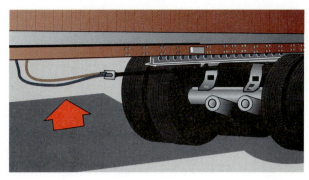

▶ **Figure 9–17**

The part of the subassembly that slides is called the "tandem axle slide."

Sliding the Trailer Tandem Axles

Sliding the trailer tandem axles is similar to sliding the fifth wheel. This also should be done off the road and on a level surface, away from hazards.

1. The trailer should be properly connected to the fifth wheel.

2. The kingpin should be locked into place.

3. The air and electrical lines should be connected to the trailer.

4. The sliding fifth wheel and the trailer's sliding tandem axle assembly must also be locked.

5. If you get out of the cab for any reason, be sure to set the tractor parking brakes. This will keep the tractor from rolling.

6. Now you are ready to test the connection to the trailer by gently pulling forward with the trailer brake in the "on" position.

7. If you have just made the connection to the trailer, look at the connection to make sure the fifth-wheel jaws are locked around the kingpin of the trailer. Then raise the landing gear of the trailer.

8. Locate the locking lever which is usually on the driver's side of the trailer and in front of the trailer's wheels. The lever is usually inside the lever guide that serves as a support. Some units have a safety lock on the locking lever to keep it from bouncing up and down while traveling **(see Figure 9–18).**

▶ **Figure 9–18**

The pin or lug control lever is usually on the driver's side of the trailer, just in front of the trailer wheels.

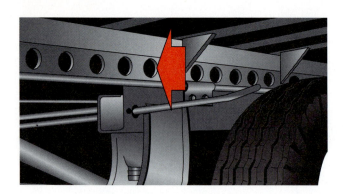

▶ Figure 9-19

Once you have unlocked the slides, make sure all four locking lugs are completely out of the holes in the slides.

9. Get into the cab. Engage the trailer brakes by either pulling down the trailer brake hand valve or pulling out the red trailer air supply valve. You now have your tractor brakes released and your trailer brakes engaged and are ready to slide the tandem axles.

10. If you are going to slide the tandem axles forward, put the tractor into reverse. If you want to slide the tandem axles toward the rear of the trailer, use low gear. With the tractor in gear, ease the tractor forward or backward gently.

11. Once you have moved the sliding tandem axle into position, follow these steps:
    - Put on the parking brakes.
    - Climb out of the truck.
    - Release the locking lever and place it into the locked position.
    - Get back into the tractor.
    - Release the tractor brakes.

12. When you move the sliding tandem axle, you change axle dimensions and will have a difference in your ride, weight distribution, and maneuverability **(see Figure 9–20)**.

13. Decide how you want to set up your rig for loading before it is actually loaded. It is easier to make adjustments on any empty unit than on a loaded one. Even though it may be difficult in the beginning, you need to be skilled in anticipating the needs of each load.

← Tandems back

More off-tracking

→ Tandems forward

Overhang

▶ Figure 9-20

When you move the sliding tandem axle, you change axle dimensions and will have a difference in your ride, weight distribution, and maneuverability.

CAUTION! QUICK REVIEW: MOVING THE SLIDING TANDEM AXLE

1. Make sure the tractor is properly coupled to the trailer.

2. Set the tractor brakes.

3. Lift and pull the locking lever until the grooves slip into the sideways slot on the lever guide. This will disengage the locking pins.

4. Check to make sure all four pins are retracted properly.

5. Set the trailer brakes by pulling out the red trailer air supply valve or pulling down the trailer brake hand valve.

6. Release the tractor brakes by pushing in the yellow parking brake valve.

7. Ease the tractor forward to slide the tandem backward. Ease the tractor backward to slide the tandem forward.

8. Reset the tractor brakes by pulling out the yellow parking brake valve.

9. Release the locking lever. Place it into the locked position.

10. Release the tractor brakes.

11. With the trailer brakes still set, gently tug or push against the trailer to seat the locking pins.

12. Reset the tractor brakes.

13. Look at all four pins to make sure they are firmly seated through the holes of the tandem axle slides. Make sure the locking lever has remained locked and is secured.

14. Inspect the trailer air supply lines and make sure they are not hanging down.

Remember—you have just made changes that will affect the handling of your rig.

How you adjust your fifth wheel and axle depends on a combination of factors, including the following:

- Distribution of weight
- Overall length laws
- Legal axle weight laws
- Bridge weight laws
- Handling stability
- Maneuverability
- Preventing damage to cargo

Driver Tip

A good way to keep track of important information about how to balance loads is to keep a notebook on each customer, describing how you set up your rig for each load as well as directions for getting to the dock, phone numbers, and who to talk to. Also note days and hours of operation, when they ship, and whether an appointment is needed. Then you will be able to set your rig before it is loaded.

CAUTION!

To prevent the trailer from sliding into the cab or the tandems from sliding out from under the trailer, be sure to check the fifth-wheel stop plates and the stop bars, welds, and brackets of the trailer slides to be sure they are intact.

SUMMARY

In this chapter, you have learned the reasons for sliding the fifth wheel or the trailer tandem axles. You have also learned that doing this will change the distribution of weight as well as the overall length of the rig, the ride, maneuverability, and off-tracking of the trailer wheels. Correct ways to slide the fifth wheel and the tandem axle assembly have been explained and illustrated. Finally, you have an understanding of the hazards created when these procedures are not done properly.

KEY TERMS

Air-operated release	Inner bridge	Outer bridge
Binding	Locking lever	Outer spread
Bridge Formula	Maneuverability	Slide
Fixed (stationary) fifth wheel	Manual release	Sliding fifth wheel
Frame rails	Off-tracking	Sliding tandem axle

REVIEW QUESTIONS

1. Which of the following can a sliding fifth wheel not influence?

   a. the overall length of the tractor-trailer

   b. the turning radius of the vehicle

   c. the weight on each of the axles

   d. the center of gravity of the trailer

2. Which of the following can sliding tandem axles on a trailer not influence?

   a. driver reaction time

   b. off-tracking of the trailer

   c. turning radius of the vehicle

   d. the balance of the weight on each of the axles on the trailer

3. Sliding tandem axles to the rear _____ the weight on the drive and steering axles.

   a. decreases

   b. has no effect on

   c. increases

   d. neither a, b, nor c

4. Which of the following is not a result of sliding the fifth wheel of a tractor forward?

   a. Less weight will be transferred to the steer axle.

   b. More weight will be transferred to the steer axle.

   c. The overall length of the vehicle will be shortened.

   d. The turning radius of the vehicle will be shortened.

5. The Bridge Formula is a national formula for _____ designed to protect the country's roads and bridges.

   a. total weight allowed on county bridges

   b. axle spacing

   c. total weight allowed on city bridges

   d. total payload weight allowed on state highways

6. Regarding turning, the greater the distance between the steer axle and the pivot point (kingpin) of the trailer, _____.

   a. the less off-tracking there will be

   b. off-tracking is not affected

   c. neither a, b, nor c

   d. the further the trailer will off-track

7. For a rig with a fixed (stationary) fifth wheel and a properly loaded trailer, weight adjustments are made by _____.

   a. adding additional air pressure to all of the tires

   b. sliding the tandem axles of the trailer

   c. reducing the air pressure in all of the tires

   d. adjusting the center of gravity

8. Regarding sliding the fifth wheel, which of the following characteristics of the rig will not change?

   a. the overall length

   b. weight distribution

   c. maneuverability

   d. the weight on the rear axles

9. Regarding trailers with stationary tandem axles, which of the following is not a correct procedure for adjusting the weight between the tractor and trailer?

   a. moving the load inside the trailer

   b. shifting the load inside the trailer

   c. increasing the air pressure in the trailer tires

   d. a and b

10. If the sliding tandem axles are moved to the rear, which of the following is not correct?

    a. There will be a difference in the ride of the rig.

    b. There will be less off-tracking.

    c. Weight distribution will change.

    d. There will be a difference in maneuverability.

10 Preventive Maintenance and Servicing

OBJECTIVES

When you have completed this chapter, you should be able to:

- Know and understand the different types of maintenance.
- Know how to perform various simple maintenance procedures safely.
- Know your responsibilities in maintaining your rig.
- Know the dangers of certain types of maintenance.
- Understand the inspection, repair, and maintenance requirements as stated in the Federal Motor Carriers Safety Regulations.

Figure 10-1

A well-maintained rig is necessary to do a safe and efficient job.

Figure 10-2

Delivery tanker truck.

INTRODUCTION

Today, more than ever, major motor carriers realize that newer, well-maintained equipment is a necessity for attracting the best professional drivers and conducting business in the most efficient manner. Professional drivers also realize that rigs that are well maintained will do the job much better and more efficiently than those that are neglected **(see Figure 10–1).**

To keep a rig in good shape, a driver must know how to inspect that vehicle and all its parts. A vehicle that is not well maintained may break down, making it difficult to make pickup or delivery appointments **(see Figure 10–2).** Moreover, breakdowns occurring over the road add to the professional driver's stress levels while making it difficult to perform the job in a timely, cost-effective manner.

While some routine servicing tasks can be done by the driver, most service and repair work today should always be done by trained maintenance personnel. When someone who is trained for the job does the servicing and maintenance, the cost is less and it takes less time. If someone who is not trained attempts to work on the rig, it is possible that the work will not be done correctly and, in some cases, if faulty work is done, more damage may be caused. Work not done by professional maintenance personnel may also result in accidents, injuries, or death. In every case, good routine maintenance eliminates downtime, highway breakdowns, and other problems on the road **(see Figure 10–3).**

This chapter is written with three goals in mind:

1. To teach the basic checks and servicing needed for the engine and vehicle

2. To show you how to perform some basic preventive maintenance and simple emergency repairs

3. To emphasize that drivers are not expected to be mechanics. Drivers should not try to do any maintenance or repair work unless they have been taught to do it and have experience repairing it under the guidance of a trained individual.

Figure 10-3

Regular, routine maintenance eliminates downtime and other problems on the road.

PREVENTIVE MAINTENANCE

Preventive maintenance (PM) is the servicing done at regular intervals on a tractor. By servicing the tractor regularly, many costly emergency repairs can be avoided and small problems can be fixed before they develop into larger ones **(see Figure 10–4).**

In many fleets, even the most routine maintenance is performed by a maintenance department, a dealer, an independent garage, or a truck leasing company. Drivers are not permitted to do any maintenance work. Other carriers, however, require the driver to perform certain minor maintenance tasks as part of his or her job. Independent owner-operators generally do more maintenance than those who drive company-owned vehicles.

▶ **Figure 10–4**

Preventive maintenance helps avoid costly emergency repairs

TYPES OF MAINTENANCE

There are three types of maintenance:

- Routine servicing
- Scheduled preventive maintenance
- Unscheduled maintenance and repair

Routine Servicing

Routine servicing can be done by drivers. These tasks include the following:

- Adding fuel
- Adding oil
- Adding coolant
- Draining moisture from fuel and air systems

Scheduled Preventive Maintenance

Scheduled preventive maintenance is servicing based on time or mileage since the last maintenance. Most fleets have a regular preventive maintenance schedule, although it is the driver's responsibility to inform the shop of repairs that are needed or failures that occur between scheduled inspections.

Most preventive maintenance is often set up under four schedules.

Level A—at 15,000 to 25,000 miles—may be combined with level B services.

Includes:

- Grease job
- Oil change

- Filter change
- Checking all fluid levels

Level B—same as level A but more involved. If combined with level A, approximately every 15,000 miles; if not combined, typically every 25,000 miles.

Includes:

- All of level A
- Inspection and maintenance of key components such as lubricating water pump shaft

Level C—conducted every 100,000 to 120,000 miles.

Includes:

- All level A and level B maintenance
- Engine tune-up
- Detailed inspection of all major components
- Road test

Level D—conducted at 500,000 to 750,000 miles.

Includes:

- All of level A, level B, and level C
- Complete overhaul of the engine
- Rebuilding parts
- New fuel pump
- Alternator

Unscheduled Maintenance and Repair

Unscheduled maintenance and repair occurs when unexpected breakdowns or emergencies require immediate maintenance and includes the following:

- Breakdowns on the road
- Repair of accident damage
- Problems found and listed during a driver's pretrip or posttrip inspection report

FEDERAL MOTOR VEHICLE INSPECTION AND MAINTENANCE REQUIREMENTS

All professional drivers must learn what the **Federal Motor Carrier Safety Regulations (FMCSR)** require and then must meet these requirements. Every motor carrier, its officers, drivers, agents, representatives, and employees directly concerned with inspection or maintenance of commercial motor vehicles must comply and be conversant with these rules.

FMCSR Part 396 requires professional drivers to do the following:

Part 396 Inspection, Repair, and Maintenance

1. The report must list any condition that the driver either found or had reported to him that would affect safety of operation or cause a breakdown. If no defect or deficiency is reported or found, the report should state this.
2. The driver must sign the report in all cases.

3. Before dispatching the vehicle again, a carrier shall ensure that a certification has been made as to any defect or deficiency, that they have been corrected, or state those deficiencies that do not require immediate correction. Carriers must keep the original posttrip inspection report and the certification of repairs for at least three months from the date of preparation.

4. Before starting out, the driver must be satisfied that the motor vehicle is in safe operating condition. If the last vehicle inspection report notes any deficiencies, the driver must review and sign to acknowledge that necessary repairs have been completed.

Periodic inspection—Every commercial vehicle, including each segment of a combination vehicle requires periodic inspection that must be performed at least once every 12 months. The original or a copy of the periodic inspection report must be retained by the motor carrier for 14 months from the report date. Documentation (report, sticker, or decal) of the most recent periodic inspection must be kept on the vehicle.

DRIVER VEHICLE CONDITION REPORT (VCR)

Results of the posttrip inspection must be entered on an official driver **vehicle condition report (VCR) (see Figure 10–5)**. The form must be completed even if no defects are found. The driver must make an accurate report of everything found on the posttrip inspection. Then, after accurately and legibly completing the form, the driver must sign and date the document. The report must then be delivered to the supervisor.

Driver's Vehicle Condition Report

Check Any Defective Item and Give Details Under "Remarks."

DATE:_____

TRUCK/TRACTOR NO._____

- ❏ Air Compressor
- ❏ Air Lines
- ❏ Battery
- ❏ Brake Accessories
- ❏ Brakes
- ❏ Carburetor
- ❏ Clutch
- ❏ Defroster
- ❏ Drive Line
- ❏ Engine
- ❏ Fifth Wheel
- ❏ Front Axle
- ❏ Fuel Tanks
- ❏ Heater

- ❏ Horn
- ❏ Lights
  - Head – Stop
  - Tail – Dash
  - Turn Indicators
- ❏ Mirrors
- ❏ Muffler
- ❏ Oil Pressure
- ❏ On-Board Recorder
- ❏ Radiator
- ❏ Rear End
- ❏ Reflectors
- ❏ Safety Equipment
  - Fire Extinguisher
  - Flags-Flares-Fusees
  - Spare Bulbs & Fuses
  - Spare Seal Beam

- ❏ Springs
- ❏ Starter
- ❏ Steering
- ❏ Tachograph
- ❏ Tires
- ❏ Transmission
- ❏ Wheels
- ❏ Windows
- ❏ Windshield Wipers
- ❏ Other

TRAILER(S) NO.(S)_____

- ❏ Brake Connections
- ❏ Brakes
- ❏ Coupling Chains
- ❏ Coupling (King) Pin
- ❏ Doors

- ❏ Hitch
- ❏ Landing Gear
- ❏ Lights – All
- ❏ Roof
- ❏ Springs

- ❏ Tarpaulin
- ❏ Tires
- ❏ Wheels
- ❏ Other

Remarks:_____
_____
_____
_____
_____
_____
_____
_____
_____

❏ CONDITION OF THE ABOVE VEHICLE IS SATISFACTORY

DRIVER'S SIGNATURE_____

❏ ABOVE DEFECTS CORRECTED

❏ ABOVE DEFECTS NEED NOT BE CORRECTED FOR SAFE OPERATION OF VEHICLE

MECHANIC'S SIGNATURE _____ DATE_____

DRIVER'S SIGNATURE _____ DATE_____

Figure 10–5

Vehicle condition report.

> ## CAUTION!
> Completing a thorough driver vehicle condition report is essential for safety and for preventing costly vehicle repairs. It also helps ensure that you do not receive an out-of-service violation on the road when you are pulled over for a roadside inspection.

▶ Figure 10–6

A poorly tuned engine means longer trip time.

Importance of Preventive Maintenance

Failure to perform preventive maintenance can increase the cost of operation. For example, breakdowns on the road may include these extra costs:

- Cargo transfer charge
- Late delivery charge
- Expensive road services such as towing and out-of-town repairs
- Driver expenses while not driving, such as food and lodging

Operating Costs

Vehicles that are poorly maintained cost more to operate; for example, fuel costs are higher. A poorly tuned engine gets fewer miles per gallon and requires longer trip times than a highly tuned engine **(see Figure 10–6).** A breakdown on the road can result in an accident. Of course, this adds to expenses and decreases trip efficiency. The extra costs can include repairing the damage, lost work time, medical expenses, and increased company insurance rates.

BASIC SERVICE AND ROUTINE MAINTENANCE

Drivers should understand and perform basic servicing and routine maintenance, such as:

- Inspect and change engine fluids, certain filters, lights, and fuses
- Drain moisture from air reservoirs and fuel systems

Checking and Changing Engine Fluids, Filters, Lights, and Fuses

This section will discuss the correct maintenance procedures for the following:

- Fuel filter
- Oil level and oil filter
- Coolant level and coolant filter
- Battery fluid level, if applicable

- Power steering fluid level
- Air filter element
- Lights and bulbs
- Fuses and circuit brakers

Checking the Fuel Fluid Level

1. Park the rig on level ground.
2. Open fuel cap.
3. Check the fuel level. Make sure it matches the gauge reading in the cab.

Changing the Fuel Filter Element

1. If you use a filter wrench to remove the old **fuel filter,** be sure to use it at the bottom of the filter so you will not crush the filter shell.
2. Turn the fuel filter element counterclockwise until it comes off the base.
3. Clean the surface of the seal on the filter base. Be sure to always remove the old seal and use a new one.
4. Wipe off any fuel that may have spilled when you took off the filter.
5. Fill the new filter with clean fuel.
6. Screw the filter onto the base until the seal touches the base.
7. Tighten the filter one-half turn.
8. Start the engine. Check for leaks.
9. Discard the old filter element according to EPA standards.

Replacing the Filter

The following method of replacing the filter is general in nature. There are many types of fuel filter systems. To find the correct way to replace your filter, read the manufacturer's instructions.

1. Turn off the fuel supply from the fuel tanks.
2. Place a container under the filter.
3. Open the drain cock in the filter housing base.
4. Drain the filter.
5. Remove the filter body with the element. If you use a filter wrench, be sure to use it at the bottom of the filter so you will not crush the filter shell.
6. Discard the filter element according to EPA guidelines.
7. Clean the housing.
8. Close the drain cock.
9. Install the new filter in the housing.
10. Fill the housing with clean fluid.
11. Install the filter housing containing the new filter element with a gasket. Always use a new seal.
12. Lubricate with fuel or engine oil and tighten.
13. Open the fuel line shut-off valve.
14. Start the engine.
15. Check for leaks.

Draining the Fuel Filter

To drain a fuel filter:

1. Locate the filter and water separator.
2. Remove the drain plug at the bottom of the filter.
3. Allow the water to drain.
4. Replace the drain plug.

Checking the Oil Level

To check the oil level, follow these steps:

1. Park the vehicle on level ground.
2. Shut off the engine.
3. Wait a few minutes for the oil to drain down.
4. Find the dipstick and remove it.
5. Wipe it clean and replace it.
6. Pull it out again.
7. Check the oil level.

The oil level should be between the "full" and the "add" marks. Do not overfill or drive when the oil level is below the "add" mark. Be careful not to overfill when you need to add oil **(see Figure 10–7).**

Changing the Oil Filter

Changing the **oil filter** on a tractor is a messy but important task. It is far harder than changing a car's oil filter. Like fuel systems, what is right for changing the filter on one system may be wrong for another type of system.

 **Figure 10–7**

Be careful not to overfill when adding oil.

Typical Lubricating System

1. Oil from main gallery
2. Oil fill tube
3. Rocker and drain
4. Cam pocket drain
5. Oil drain from blower or turbocharger
6. Full-flow oil filter
7. Bypass oil filter
8. Oil cooler
9. Drain to oil pan
10. Oil pick-up screen

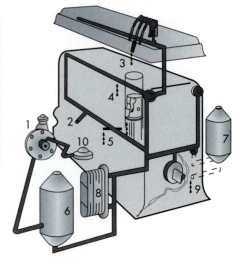

To change an oil filter, follow these steps:

1. Remove the drain plug from the bottom of the filter housing.
2. Drain the oil.
3. Remove the filter housing that contains the filter element. Most filters today are one piece and disposable.
4. Discard the old filter according to EPA standards.
5. Fill the new filter element with clean oil and install it.
6. Secure the housing.
7. Replace the drain plug.
8. Start the engine.

Checking the Coolant Level

To check the **coolant** level, follow these steps:

1. Shut off the engine.
2. Wait until the engine is cool.
3. Put on thick gloves to protect your hands.
4. Remove the radiator cap carefully. Turn the cap slowly to the first stop. Step back while pressure is released from the cooling system.
5. When all of the pressure is released, press down on the cap and remove it.
6. Look at the level of the coolant.
7. Do not add water.
8. Add coolant if needed. Ask maintenance for specific instructions.

GO!
Many tractors now have sight glasses or see-through containers for checking coolant levels. If your rig has one, you will not need to go through the previous routine to check the coolant level. If the coolant level becomes too low, you simply add coolant to the reservoir.

Changing the Coolant Filter

To change the **coolant filter,** follow these steps:

1. Shut off the engine.
2. Wait until the engine is cool.

3. Put on thick gloves. Do not handle a hot filter with your bare hands.

4. Turn the filter element counterclockwise to remove it.

5. Replace it with a new filter element and a new cover gasket.

6. Start the engine.

7. Check for leaks.

Checking the Battery Fluid Level

CAUTION!

Be very careful when checking the level of the **battery fluid.** Follow these safety rules (**see Figure 10–8**):

1. Protect your eyes with safety goggles or glasses.

2. Protect your hands because batteries contain substances that can burn your skin.

3. Do not smoke because batteries give off explosive gases.

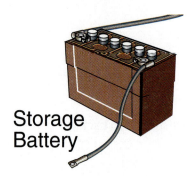

Storage Battery

▶ **Figure 10–8**
Follow the safety rules when checking battery fluid.

Some batteries are maintenance free and do not need to have the level of the fluid checked. Others are not and must have the level of the fluid in the battery checked. Follow these steps to check the battery fluid level:

1. Open battery caps.

2. Check the fluid level.

3. If the battery needs fluid, use distilled water.

4. Fill to the bottom of the split ring in the cell filler well.

Checking the Power Steering Fluid Level

With the engine running at normal operating temperature, turn the steering wheel back and forth several times to stabilize the **power steering fluid** level. To check the fluid level, follow these steps:

1. Turn off the engine.

2. Remove the dipstick.

3. The fluid should be between the bottom of the dipstick and the full mark.

4. If fluid is needed, add enough to raise the level to the full mark but do not overfill.

Changing the Air Filter Element

Dust, dirt, grease, and grime can get into an engine when you change the air filter. Be careful to keep the area as clean as possible. On air cleaners with a restriction indicator, change the element or clean it when the indicator shows "red." On tractors or trucks that have an air filter restriction gauge, consult a mechanic for information on when to change the element.

To change the **air filter element,** follow these steps:

1. Remove the end covering from the housing.
2. Make sure hands are clean.
3. Remove filter element.
4. Inspect the end cover and gasket surfaces for dents or possible air leaks.
5. Check the outlet tube to be sure it is clean and undamaged.
6. Check the filter element for wear.
7. Replace the element if it is damaged.
8. If the filter is not damaged, clean with compressed air. Always blow the air in the opposite direction of the normal cleaner flow. Some filters should not be blown out. If your unit does not have an indicator or air filter restriction gauge, find out how often to replace it.
9. Wipe away any dirt in the filter housing.
10. Install the filter element.
11. Replace the end cover and secure.

CAUTION!

Always handle the filter element carefully to keep dirt from shaking loose onto the clean side of the filter system **(see Figure 10–9).**

Inside Air Cleaner

Outside Air Cleaner

Air Intake System

▶ **Figure 10–9**

Always change the air filter carefully to avoid getting dirt on the clean filter.

Changing a Bulb in a Headlight or Clearance Light

To change a headlight bulb or a clearance light, follow these steps:

1. Park the rig and turn off the engine.
2. Remove the trim ring from the burned-out light.
3. Unfasten the mounting screws.

4. Disconnect and remove the light from the socket. The bulb may be hot, so handle carefully.

5. Clean any dirt or bugs off the socket area.

6. Plug in the new headlight bulb.

7. Test the light to see if it works properly.

8. Fasten the mounting screw.

9. Make sure the new light is clean.

STOP!

Do not touch the headlight adjusting screws when you are changing the bulb!

Changing Fuses and Resetting Circuit Breakers

Fuses—always use a **fuse** that is the right size and has the same amp rating as the fuse it replaces. To change a fuse, follow these steps:

1. Check the fuse and clip holder to be sure they are clean and do not have any burrs.

2. If the holder is dirty, touch up the contact points with a coarse cloth.

3. Gently but firmly snap the new fuse into the clip holder.

4. Make sure there is a good connection between the fuse ends and the fuse holder.

Circuit breaker—To reset the **circuit breaker,** follow these steps:

1. Remove the circuit breaker cover panel.

2. Flip the circuit breaker switch back to reset it.

3. Replace the panel.

Some circuit breakers reset themselves.

CHECKING TIRE AIR PRESSURE

As a professional driver, you should *never* change tires. Allow only qualified mechanics with proper tools and safeguards to change tires because this is extremely dangerous.

To check air pressure:

1. Make sure tires are cool before you check the air pressure.

2. Remove the valve stem cap.

3. Place the air gauge over the valve stem opening.

4. Read the inflation pressure from the gauge.

5. Compare the tire's pressure with the correct pressure listed on the sidewall of the tire.

6. Replace the valve stem cap.

DRAINING THE AIR RESERVOIRS

If your air tanks have drain valves, drain the **air reservoirs** as follows:

1. Park the truck on level ground.
2. Open the draincocks by twisting the valve on the bottom of the tank.
3. Allow all of the air pressure to escape. The air pressure gauge will read 0 psi. This will let the moisture drain out **(see Figure 10–10)**.
4. Close the valve.

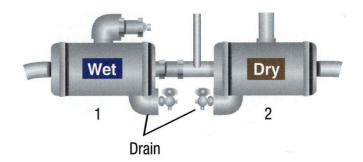

▶ **Figure 10–10**

When air pressure gauge reads "0 psi," moisture will drain from air reservoirs.

ADJUSTING THE TRACTOR-TRAILER BRAKES

Some carriers require their drivers to make minor brake adjustments. Drivers must be certified to adjust brakes and, when asked to do so, must follow company policy. Many tractors and trailers now have automatic slack adjusters, but these also need to be checked regularly for proper adjustment.

Learn what type of braking system your rig has, and know what your employer expects from you as a driver regarding keeping the brakes in proper working order. For your personal safety and the safety of those who share the road, be sure any person who works on your brakes is qualified for the specific braking system on your rig **(see Figure 10–11)**.

WITHIN AN INCH OF YOUR LIFE

IF BRAKE SLACK EXCEEDS ONE INCH, YOU COULD BE DRIVING A "KILLER TRUCK".

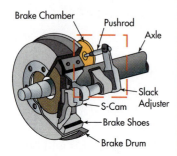

Brake Chamber — Pushrod — Axle — Slack Adjuster — S-Cam — Brake Shoes — Brake Drum

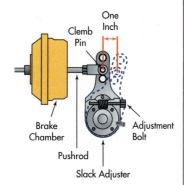

THIS IS THE MOST IMPORTANT INCH OF YOUR LIFE.

One Inch — Clemb Pin — Brake Chamber — Pushrod — Slack Adjuster — Adjustment Bolt

BRAKES SHOULD BE CHECKED BEFORE EACH TRIP AND MORE FREQUENTLY IN HILLY AREAS.

TRUCKERS! Poorly adjusted brakes could cost you time and money with out-of-service violations, jeopardize your safety and that of others due to impaired stopping ability, and even cost you your life. The only way to be sure that your vehicle's brakes are properly adjusted is to physically check each wheel on a regular schedule. It is difficult for you to sense, simply from pedal feel, that your brakes are out of adjustment. Under normal braking conditions, your brakes may respond satisfactorily, but under a hard panic stop you may find that you are unable to stop in time.

HOW TO CHECK
Before checking or making adjustments, be sure that your vehicle is parked on a level surface with the wheels blocked, spring brakes released, and the engine shut off. The following measurements are for *Type 30 air chamber brakes only*. For other types, check with your mechanic, supervisor, or manufacturer.

One-person method: (1) Pull the chamber pushrod to its limit by hand or by prying with a short pry bar. (2) Measure from the clevis pin to the chamber face at both full retraction and at full extension. The difference between the measurements is the pushrod travel or slack. One-half inch is correct, and the *MAXIMUM ALLOWABLE TRAVEL IS ONE INCH* (one-person method).

Two-person method: Make the same measurements described in the one-person method, but with brakes fully applied and with brakes released. Because of the considerable stretching and bending of various parts when using the two-person method, the *MAXIMUM ALLOWABLE TRAVEL IS TWO INCHES* for Type 30 air chamber brakes.

HOW TO ADJUST
Brake adjustment, or "taking up the slack," is done by first making sure the brakes are released, then turning the adjusting bolt on the slack adjuster arm: (1) Depress the spring locking sleeve with a wrench. (2) Tighten the bolt until solid resistance is met. This indicates that the brake linings are touching the drum.

NOTE: Most adjusting bolts require a normal clockwise turn to "set up" the brakes, but some require a counterclockwise turn. Be alert for any outward movement of the chamber pushrod and slack adjuster arm while the adjustment bolt is being turned. This movement means you are turning in the wrong direction.

(3) Restore running clearance by backing off the adjustment between one-quarter and one-half a turn. Re-check the pushrod travel. Proper adjustment leaves one-half an inch. (4) Check each brake drum or rotor for excessive heat soon after the brakes have been adjusted. An extra-hot brake drum means that you have adjusted the brakes too tightly.

For both this type and other types of brake systems, always check with the manufacturer for proper maintenance and adjustment procedures. If you are not comfortable with these procedures, ask your mechanic or supervisor.

Figure 10-11
Have a qualified person regularly inspect your brakes.

SUMMARY

In this chapter, you have learned what types of maintenance are needed for the various systems on your rig. You have learned that preventive maintenance keeps the need for unscheduled or emergency maintenance to a minimum. The types of reports that you, as a professional driver, will be expected to fill out and turn into your carrier's maintenance department have been described. You have also read about how to do certain basic routine maintenance and servicing. You also understand that, under no circumstances, should you ever attempt to change a tire on your rig.

KEY TERMS

Air filter element
Air reservoir
Battery fluid
Circuit breaker
Coolant
Coolant filter

Federal Motor Carrier Safety
   Regulations (FMCSR)
Fuel filter
Fuse
Oil filter
Power steering fluid
Preventive maintenance (PM)

Routine servicing
Scheduled preventive
   maintenance
Unscheduled maintenance
   and repair
Vehicle condition report
   (VCR)

REVIEW QUESTIONS

1. To keep a rig in good shape, a driver must know how to _____.

   a. inspect the vehicle and all its parts

   b. change a tire

   c. change the oil

   d. b and c

2. Preventive maintenance is _____.

   a. repairs to a rig as needed

   b. repairs to the trailer as needed

   c. the inspection done by a driver before the rig is driven

   d. the servicing done at regular intervals

3. Which of the following is not a type of maintenance?

   a. routine servicing

   b. scheduled repairs

   c. the driver's pretrip inspection

   d. unscheduled repairs

4. Regarding federal motor vehicle inspection and maintenance requirements, which of the following is not a Federal Motor Carrier Safety Regulation (FMCSR) that a driver must meet?

   a. Make minor repairs to the engine.

   b. Perform a pretrip inspection before operating a vehicle.

   c. Review the last daily vehicle inspection report

   d. Sign the last daily vehicle inspection report and confirm that a mechanic has completed any needed work on the rig.

5. Which of the following is not a requirement of a driver regarding a daily vehicle condition report (VCR)?

   a. The report must be completed even if no defects are found.

   b. If defects are found in the posttrip inspection, the VCR must be delivered to the head mechanic

   c. The driver must make an accurate report of everything found.

   d. The VCR must be signed and dated by the driver

6. Regarding basic servicing and routine maintenance, which of the following should a driver not do?

   a. Inspect and change engine fluids and certain filters.

   b. Change a tire/wheel.

   c. Drain moisture from air reservoirs.

   d. Inspect and change lights and fuses.

7. Regarding checking the coolant level, which of the following is not a correct statement?

   a. Shut off the engine.

   b. Wait until the engine is cool.

   c. Remove the radiator cap very carefully.

   d. Add water if the coolant level is low.

8. Regarding changing a bulb in a headlight, which of the following is not a correct step?

   a. Turn off the engine.

   b. Clean any dirt or bugs off the socket area.

   c. Fasten the mounting screw.

   d. Always change the headlight adjusting screws because the vibration of the vehicle will cause them to get out of adjustment.

9. Regarding checking the air pressure in the tires of a rig, which of the following is not a correct statement?

   a. Place the air gauge over the valve stem opening.

   b. Compare the reading with the pressure listed on the sidewall.

   c. The tires should be hot to get a true reading.

   d. Replace the valve stem cap.

10. Regarding draining the air reservoirs, which of the following is not a correct statement?

    a. Chock the wheels.

    b. Open the draincocks.

    c. Allow the air pressure to escape.

    d. Park the rig on a hill with the front of the rig pointing downhill so the water will run out of the tanks.

11 Recognizing and Reporting Malfunctions

OBJECTIVES

When you have completed this chapter, you should be able to:

■ Know when vehicle systems and parts are not working correctly.

■ Use the senses of sight, sound, feel, and smell to detect problems.

■ Troubleshoot problems.

■ Discuss the importance of the professional driver being able to completely and accurately describe how the vehicle is functioning to maintenance personnel.

■ Explain to other drivers why they should not try to do any maintenance unless they are qualified.

■ Safely start a vehicle with a dead battery or without air pressure if it has an air starter.

Figure 11–1

As a professional driver you may perform certain simple repairs and adjustments to your vehicle.

INTRODUCTION

Tractor-trailer drivers are not expected to be mechanics.

Most companies have a policy stating clearly what repairs and adjustments may and may not be done by drivers **(see Figure 11–1).** This chapter will help you understand what is generally expected of a driver. You will learn about common mechanical problems, how to identify them, and what to do if they occur. In some cases, the correct action will be to adjust a simple part. In other cases, you will be told to move on to the nearest mechanic or call the company maintenance department for instructions.

You will learn how to use common sense and apply what you know. You also will learn to do only what you are capable of doing, be concerned about safety, and follow company policies **(see Figure 11–2).**

DRIVER RESPONSIBILITY

- Know company maintenance policy
- Identify sources of problems
- Diagnose and fix simple problems when policy permits
- Report symptoms correctly

Figure 11–2

Knowing your exact responsibilities will make you more efficient and effective in your job.

DIAGNOSING AND REPORTING MALFUNCTIONS

Many new trucks have electronic controls that detect problems and sound buzzers or warning lights. From these warnings, drivers can often diagnose a problem. Although you are not expected to become a mechanic, you should be knowledgeable enough of the various systems to find the source of the problem. This section will discuss how to gather information and report it to the mechanic. If this is done correctly, the mechanic can usually pinpoint the problem and come to the site with proper tools and parts.

Driver Awareness

Driver awareness is vital. Drivers can be aware of the rig's problems at all times by using their senses **(see Figure 11–3).**

Seeing

- Look at the instrument gauges and exhaust smoke.
- Look for fluid leaks, damaged tires, and missing wheel lugs.

Hearing

- Listen for any unusual engine noises, air leaks, or other sounds.

DRIVER AWARENESS

■ A driver must be aware of his or her vehicle at all times. Be constantly alert.

Use your senses:

■ Seeing ■ Hearing ■ Feeling ■ Smelling

▶ **Figure 11–3**

Use your senses to detect danger signals given off by the vehicle's different systems.

Feeling

■ Feel for vibrations, thumps, and swaying that is not normal for your truck.

Smelling

■ Be aware when you smell diesel fuel, smoke, or burning rubber.

Report any symptoms or irregularities to your service department. By using your senses, you can notice a defect before it develops into a breakdown, a costly repair, or an accident.

GO!

If you understand the electronic diagnostics on your tractor, you may be able to help the mechanic pinpoint the problem that needs repair.

Early Detection of Malfunctions

By using your senses and noticing symptoms and irregularities early, you can cut repair costs. Problems that are found and fixed in their early stages can prevent major damage from occurring. This means repairs will be minor and the vehicle will spend less time in the shop while operating more efficiently.

If you own the truck, you will be able to work more and spend less for repairs. If you work for a company, your supervisor will be impressed with your efficiency and production **(see Figure 11–4).** When problems are noticed early and corrected, there is not as much chance for equipment failure or accidents. The tractor will probably last longer and, most importantly, your chances of being stranded down the road will be reduced.

EARLY DETECTION OF MALFUNCTIONS

Early detecton of malfunctions results in:

■ Lower maintenance expense
■ Longer vehicle life
■ Minimum downtime
■ Lower operating costs
■ Fewer accidents

▶ **Figure 11–4**

Using your senses and your experience can help head off major problems and damage.

Driver Responsibility

Your company should have a **maintenance policy,** and you should know what they expect from you. You will not have to be an expert, but you should be able to identify the sources of **malfunctions** and diagnose and fix simple problems. How much you are allowed to do and what you do will depend on the company maintenance policy.

STOP!

Do not try to fix any problem unless the maintenance policy permits and you have specific training to do so.

Mechanic Responsibility

The mechanic should:

- Learn about system failures from driver reports
- Diagnose the causes of the problem
- Correct any malfunctions
- Ensure the problem or failure has been fixed before releasing the truck

Driver and Mechanic Joint Responsibility

Drivers and mechanics must work together if the company is to benefit. A driver can be very helpful by knowing the rig and reporting all problems—large or small—as soon as they become obvious. The mechanic can make sure all problems are fixed as soon as possible. When drivers and mechanics work closely together, they can prevent serious damage to the equipment.

Troubleshooting

As a driver you need to know:

- About your vehicle's systems
- Where the systems are located
- The parts of each system
- Where the parts are located
- How each system works
- How all systems work together

Understanding how a system works is the first step to realizing when it is not functioning properly or is in danger of failing. A vehicle will, in most cases, alert you to trouble by warning signals, such as:

- Sharp drop in fuel mileage
- Erratic gauge readings
- A temperature gauge that is too high or too low
- A thump, bump, whine, grind, or rattle

If you know how your vehicle's systems work, you can notice the danger signals more easily. You will be better able to trace a problem to its source, or report your findings to a qualified mechanic.

Detection of Problems

When you notice a symptom, stop the truck as soon as possible (or as soon as the seriousness of the problem dictates). Then think about the problem thoroughly before starting to **troubleshoot.** Start with the most likely cause of the problem, keeping the following points in mind:

■ You are not a mechanic or a mechanical expert.

■ You should not try to do a mechanic's job.

■ If you cannot identify the exact source of the trouble—actually see the part that is broken or malfunctioning—do not try to guess.

■ Carefully describe the problem when you report it. Report what you checked and what you found, observed, smelled, and so on. Include the "what," "when," and "where" and any other information you may have.

Reporting Requirements

The first required step is to report the symptoms of the problem as soon as possible.

Written report—The **Federal Motor Carrier Safety Regulations (FMCSR)** require drivers to submit a **Driver's Vehicle Condition Report (VCR)** for each trip or 24-hour period within a trip. Include any problems in this report. Drivers also must review the previous VCR to verify all problems have been corrected before beginning the next use of the equipment.

 "VCR—Do we have time to watch videos?"

STOP!

A VCR must be submitted for each power unit and each trailer and converter used in a 24-hour period.

Oral report—it often saves time to discuss any problem you have detected with the mechanic, depending on company policy. This gives the mechanic an opportunity to ask questions about your written report and helps in understanding the details of the problem.

Limitations—report only the facts about the symptoms and what your troubleshooting found, but avoid guessing. The mechanic's job is to use the details you supply to solve the problem.

Driver's Vehicle Inspection Report

Each carrier and transportation company has its own DVIR forms. The data the driver supplies should be accurate so that the maintenance department can locate problems quickly and easily **(see Figure 11–5).** If there are no problems, your report should verify that fact. If problems have occurred, you should:

■ Check the appropriate place on the form to show what system or part was involved, if you know

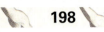

Figure 11-5
Daily VCR form correctly filled out.

Daily Vehicle Condition Report Form Correctly Filled Out

DRIVER'S INSPECTION REPORT
(SEE INSTRUCTIONS ON REVERSE SIDE)
CHECK DEFECTS ONLY. Explain under REMARKS
COMPLETION OF THIS REPORT REQUIRED BY FEDERAL LAW, 49CFR 396.11 & 396.13.
Mileage (No Tenths)

Truck or Tractor No. 1250 | 1 0 1 5 0 6 | Trailer No. 26000

Dolly No. ______ Trailer No. ______ Location: ______

POWER UNIT

GENERAL CONDITION
- ☐ 02 Cab/Doors/Windows
- ☐ 02 Body/Doors
- ☐ ___Oil Leak
- ☐ ___Grease Leak
- ☐ 42 Coolant Leak
- ☐ 44 Fuel Leak
- ☐ ___Other ______ (IDENTIFY)

ENGINE COMPARTMENT
- ☐ 45 Oil Level
- ☐ ___Belts
- ☐ ___Other ______ (IDENTIFY)

IN CAB
- ☐ 03 Gauges/Warning Indicators
- ☐ 02 Windshield Wipers/Washers
- ☐ 54 Horn(s)
- ☐ 01 Heater/Defroster
- ☐ 02 Mirrors
- ☐ 15 Steering
- ☐ 23 Clutch
- ☐ 13 Service Brakes
- ☐ 13 Parking Brakes
- ☐ 13 Emergency Brakes
- ☐ 53 Triangles
- ☐ 53 Fire Extinguishers
- ☐ 53 Other Safety Equipment
- ☐ 34 Spare Fuses
- ☐ 02 Seat Belts
- ☐ ___Other ______ (IDENTIFY)

EXTERIOR
- ☐ 34 Lights
- ☐ 34 Reflectors
- ☐ 16 Suspension
- ☐ 17 Tires
- ☐ 18 Wheels/Rims/Lugs
- ☐ 32 Battery
- ☐ 43 Exhaust
- ☐ 13 Brakes
- ☐ 13 Air Lines
- ☐ 34 Light Line
- ☐ 49 Fifth-Wheel
- ☐ 49 Other Coupling
- ☐ 71 Tie-Downs
- ☐ 14 Real-End Protection
- ☐ ___Other ______ (IDENTIFY)

☐ NO DEFECTS

TOWED UNIT(S)
- ☐ 71 Body/Doors
- ☐ 71 Tie-Downs
- ☐ 34 Lights
- ☐ 34 Reflectors
- ☐ 16 Suspension
- ☐ 17 Tires
- ☐ 18 Wheels/Rims/Lugs
- ☐ 13 Brakes
- ☐ 77 Landing Gear
- ☐ 59 Kingpin Upper Plate
- ☐ 59 Fifth-Wheel (Dolly)
- ☐ 59 Other Coupling Devices
- ☐ 79 Rear End Protection

REMARKS: *Braking response time gradually increased over the course of the day. Vehicle pulled to the right when brakes were applied. This happened each time brakes were applied. Condition gradually kept getting worse. Road conditions were excellent throughout the day. Vehicle was carrying a 65,000 pound payload.*

REPORTING DRIVER: Date *12/10/06*
Name *John Doe* Emp. No. *26*

REVIEWING DRIVER: Date ______
Name ______ Emp No. ______

MAINTENANCE ACTION: Date ______
Repairs Made ☐ No Repairs Needed ☐
R.O.#'s ______
Certified By: ______
Location: ______

SHOP REMARKS: ______

- Describe the symptoms and troubleshooting in as much detail as possible
- Discuss the problem with the mechanic in person or by phone, if company policy permits

Useful Items for the Remarks or Comments Section

- **Symptoms**

  A description of the way the problem appears to the driver.

  How did it start?

  Did it start suddenly or gradually?

  If it came on gradually, over what period of time—several minutes, hours, days?

  When did it appear?

- **Conditions**

  What were the conditions when the symptoms occurred?

  How long had you been driving?

  Was the weather hot or cold?

  What type of cargo and vehicle weight were you carrying?

  How far did your troubleshooting go?

  What did you find?

Example

A driver notices the braking response time is getting slower and the vehicle pulls to the right when the brakes are applied.

It came on gradually during the first morning of the trip.

The weather was moderate.

The cargo was a max load of vegetables.

Troubleshooting consisted of checking tires, suspension, and brakes.

Results

Tire inflation is okay.

There are no broken or bent springs, shock absorbers, and so on.

Problem must be brakes or front-end alignment.

Driver called dispatcher for aid.

Dispatcher told driver to bring truck in at once for servicing.

Troubleshooting Guide

You will find a troubleshooting guide in Appendix A. It is organized by sense; that is, it lists the signals picked up by your senses and the kinds of problems these may indicate.

The following are examples of two signals or symptoms. One is something you can hear, such as a dull thud; the other is something you can see, such as a gauge reading.

Noise: A dull thud—a sound you hear when you turn the wheels of the tractor. What caused the problem?

Possible Systems Involved	Possible Causes
1. Tires	Flat tire
2. Wheels, rims, lugs	Loose wheel or tire lugs
	Rock between duals

Proper Action

1. Stop as soon as you find a safe place.
2. Decide the logical starting point for your troubleshooting. Start with the simplest reason first. In this case, do you have a flat tire? If you do not have a flat tire, you might need to tighten the lugs or remove a rock from between the tires.

> ### STOP!
> Do not—for any reason—try to remove the tire from the rim at any time.

Something you see: Gauge reading—your ammeter shows a continuous maximum charge. Your signals are crossed (**see Figure 11–6**).

Possible Systems Involved	Possible Cause
1. Electrical	Short circuit in wiring

▶ **Figure 11–6**
Gauges often indicate a problem.

Proper Action

1. Disconnect the battery terminals until the short is repaired by a mechanic.

PROBLEM-SOLVING EXERCISES

Following are 12 problems. After your instructor has set the scene, discuss and troubleshoot the following problems. Follow these three steps when solving each problem:

1. **Identify** the systems that may be involved.
2. **Trace** the problem toward its source.
3. **Decide** the best course of action.

Following the problems, the solutions are presented. The systems that may be involved are identified. The possible source of the problem is noted. The best course of action is discussed. Compare these solutions with the class discussion. Was anything important overlooked?

Problem One

Each time you stop, the tractor is bumped or pushed by the trailer.

Problem Two

Your mirrors are adjusted properly but you can see more of one side of the trailer than the other (called trailer dog-tracking).

Problem Three

Your coolant temperature suddenly rises and the oil pressure is falling fast.

Problem Four

The trailer sways too much when you make turns.

Problem Five

The low air warning buzzer keeps sounding for a split second at a time.

Problem Six

The circuit breaker for the trailer's running lights keeps tripping.

Problem Seven

When you make sharp turns on slippery road surfaces, the steering wheel is turned but the tractor continues moving straight ahead. In other words, the tractor does not turn fully in response to the turning of the steering wheel.

Problem Eight

When coupling the tractor to the trailer, the tractor protection valve opens. There is a severe loss of air pressure.

Problem Nine

You hear a loud snap or click when you start the truck from a dead stop.

Problem Ten

You notice exhaust odor in the cab.

Problem Eleven

As you drive, you notice the ammeter registers discharge or there is a low reading on the voltmeter.

Problem Twelve

Excessive smoke is coming from the exhaust pipe.

Solutions

Problem One: Each time you stop, the tractor is bumped or pushed by the trailer.

Possible Systems Involved

- Trailer air brakes
- Coupling

Possible Causes

- Slow timing of the trailer brakes (driver cannot adjust the brake timing between tractor and trailer)
- Air line connections between tractor and trailer
  - Loose glad hand connections
  - Worn or missing O-ring
- Air lines from glad hands to brake chambers
  - Holes or cracks in the line
  - Kinked hose
- Brake chambers
  - Air leaks
  - Slack adjuster
- Fifth-wheel locking mechanism loose
- Fifth-wheel slack adjuster needs adjusting
  - More than one-half inch of horizontal movement between upper and lower halves will cause the unit to be put out of service

Proper Actions

- Stop at first safe place and pull truck off the road.
- Check for causes.
- Call the maintenance department and report problem. Be sure details are correct.

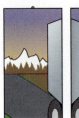

▶ **Figure 11–7**

Although your mirrors are adjusted properly, you can see more of one side of the trailer than the other.

Problem Two: Your mirrors are adjusted properly but you can see more of one side of the trailer than the other **(see Figure 11–7).**

Possible System Involved

- Axles

Probable Causes

- Tractor is not aligned properly
- Sliding tandems
  - Lock pins that hold tandems in place are not in holes
  - Lost pins
  - Pins have jarred loose
- Axles not aligned properly

Proper Actions

- Slow down at once.
- Find a safe place to pull off the road.
- Locate problem areas.
- If you have sliding tandems:
  - Make sure lock pins are in place in holes opposite each other.
  - Replace pins if they are missing.
  - Tighten pins if they are loose.
- If you have fixed tandems:
  - Call maintenance department immediately.

Problem Three: Your coolant temperature suddenly rises and the oil pressure is falling fast **(see Figure 11–8).**

Possible System Involved

- Lubrication

Probable Causes

- Low oil level due to:
  - Lost drain plug
  - Oil filter not properly secured or tightened
  - Broken oil line
  - Blown gasket

▶ **Figure 11–8**

Coolant temperature is rising and oil pressure is falling.

Proper Actions

- Pull off the road at once.
- Stop and turn off engine.
- Check engine oil level. CAUTION: Engine is very hot.
- Check all probable causes.
- Check for oil leaks in the engine compartment and under the truck.
- Call maintenance for assistance—be accurate in details and description of problem.
- Do not restart your engine.

Problem Four: The trailer sways too much when you make turns **(see Figure 11–9).**

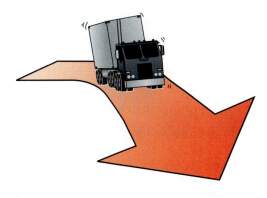

▶ Figure 11–9

Excessive trailer sway may indicate that cargo has shifted.

Possible Systems Involved

- Suspension
- Tires

Probable Causes

- Cargo has shifted
- Broken or loose shock absorbers
- Broken or shifted spring or spring hanger
- Underinflated or flat tires

Proper Actions

- Slow down at once.
- Drive to first safe place and pull off the road.
- Check out possible causes.
- If cargo has shifted, move it back into position and secure it.
- If problem is shock absorber, call your maintenance department.
- If problem is flat tire, call for help.

Problem Five: The low air warning buzzer keeps sounding for a split second at a time **(see Figure 11–10).**

Possible System Involved

- Air brakes

Probable Causes

- Severe air leak
- Loose compressor belt
- Ruptured air line

▶ Figure 11–10

A severe air leak or disconnected air line may cause periodic low air buzzer warnings.

- Disconnected air line
- Petcock open on air reservoirs
- Malfunctioning compressor
- Loose glad hand connections
- Worn or missing O-ring on glad hand
- Blown brake chamber diaphragm

Proper Actions

- Stop at once.
- Park your rig.
- Locate problem.
- Call for assistance.
- Have problem corrected before resuming your trip.

Problem Six: The circuit breaker for the trailer's running lights keeps tripping.

Possible System Involved

- Electrical

Probable Causes

- Exposed or hanging wire (the insulation may have worn off, exposing bare wire)
- Broken ground wire

Proper Actions

- Stop your truck at the first safe spot off the road.
- Turn engine off. Check out the problem.
- Call maintenance or dispatch.
- Tape any bare, exposed wire, if permitted.
- Reset circuit breaker.
- Drive to first truck stop and have electrical system checked by qualified mechanic.

Problem Seven: When you turn sharply on slippery road surfaces, the steering wheel is turned but the tractor continues moving straight ahead **(see Figure 11–11).**

Possible System Involved

- Steering

Probable Causes

- Steering axle too lightly loaded
- Fifth wheel in need of grease
- Fifth wheel iced up

Proper Actions

- Slow down at once and look for a safe place to pull off the road.
- Move the load to get more weight on the fifth wheel.

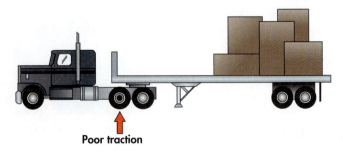

Poor traction

▶ Figure 11–11

Poor traction may be caused by a lightly loaded steering axle.

- If your truck has a sliding fifth wheel, move the fifth wheel forward.

- Grease fifth wheel.

- Remove ice from fifth wheel.

- If rig does not have a sliding fifth wheel but has sliding tandems on the trailer, move the tandems to the rear to put more weight on the fifth wheel by transferring weight to the steering axle.

CAUTION!

This is usually a problem on tandem axle tractors with a short wheelbase. Tandems are a short distance behind the steering wheel and tend to take control of the vehicle, preventing it from moving straight ahead.

Problem Eight: When coupling the tractor to the trailer, the tractor protection valve opens. There is a severe loss of air pressure **(see Figure 11–12).**

Possible System Involved

- Air brakes

Probable Causes

- Glad hands are not seated properly or they have a bad O-ring.

- Air lines are crossed. Service line is connected to the emergency line, and emergency line is connected to service line.

- Trailer air tank petcock is open.

- Broken air lines.

▶ **Figure 11–12**

Crossed air lines may cause a severe loss of air pressure.

Proper Action

- This problem must be found and corrected before you drive from the yard.

Problem Nine: You hear a loud snap or click when you start the truck from a dead stop.

Possible System Involved

- Drive train

Probable Causes

- Loose U-joint

- Excessive wear on U-joint or differential

Proper Actions

- Be very careful when you put the truck into motion.

- Proceed to the nearest mechanic or call dispatch/maintenance.

- Have the drive train checked by a qualified mechanic.

Problem Ten: You notice exhaust odor in the cab.

Possible System Involved

- Exhaust

Probable Causes

- Loose connection in the exhaust system
- Cracked or broken exhaust pipe
- Leaking muffler
- Rusted exhaust system
- Cracked exhaust manifold

Proper Actions

- Open all cab windows.
- Stop at next truck stop/mechanic.
- Have exhaust system checked and repaired by qualified mechanic as soon as possible.

Problem Eleven: As you drive, you notice the ammeter registers discharge or there is a low reading on the voltmeter.

Possible System Involved

- Electrical

Probable Causes

- Loose or broken alternator belt
- Loose wiring connection
- Burned out generator or alternator
- Generator or alternator not adjusted correctly
- Defective voltage regulator

Proper Actions

- Do not shut off the engine.
- Pull off the road at first safe spot.
- Look for any obvious cause:
  - Missing belt (keep hands away from moving belts, pulleys, etc.)
  - Loose connections
  - Bare insulation or a worn wire
  - Short circuit in the wiring
- Go to first available mechanic and get assistance in correcting the problem **(see Figure 11–13).**

Problem Twelve: Excessive smoke is coming from the exhaust pipe.

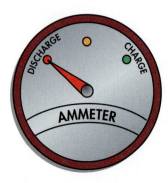

Figure 11–13

When the ammeter registers discharge or there is a low reading on the voltmeter, go to the first available truck stop for a mechanic's assistance.

Possible Systems Involved

- Exhaust
- Fuel
- Turbo malfunction

Probable Causes

- Dirty air cleaner
- Poor grade fuel
- Return fuel line blocked, bent, or squeezed together
- Fuel pump malfunction
- Engine overfueled

NOTE: These are some of the more common problems. There are a number of other possibilities **(see Figure 11–14).**

▶ **Figure 11–14**

Smoke coming from the exhaust pipe may signal a dirty air cleaner, an overfueled engine, or a frozen turbine. Shut down immediately.

Proper Actions

- If you smell oil from the turbo, pull over in a safe spot and shut down immediately.
- Call maintenance department/dispatch for instructions.

Troubleshooting Summary

A good troubleshooter knows his or her vehicle and its systems thoroughly, uses common sense, knows the company maintenance policy, does not attempt to make repairs for which he or she has not been trained, and keeps good records.

EMERGENCY STARTING PROCEDURES

In this section, you will learn the safe way to start a truck that has a dead battery. If a truck has an air starting system and has lost air pressure, it will also have to be manually started. The correct method is explained in this section.

Jump-Starting Dead Batteries

There are three things to remember when you **jump-start** a dead battery:

1. Observe all safety rules.
2. Prepare the truck.
3. Attach jumper cables properly.

Observe All Safety Rules

- Shield your eyes or wear safety goggles.
- Do not smoke.
- Make sure the batteries of both vehicles are negatively grounded and carry the same voltage (use a 12-volt battery to charge a 12-volt battery).
- Keep all battery fluids away from skin and clothing.
- Never jump-start a battery if the battery fluid is frozen.

Prepare the Truck

- Align the vehicles so the jumper cables will reach without strain. Do not allow the vehicles to touch each other.
- Set the parking brake.
- Shift into neutral.
- Add distilled water to dead battery, if needed.

Attach Jumper Cables Properly

- Clamp one cable to the positive (+) pole of the dead battery.
- Clamp the other end of the cable to the positive pole of the booster battery.
- Connect the second cable to the negative (−) pole of the booster battery.
- Attach the other end of the cable to the stalled truck's frame, engine block, or other metal part as a ground.
- Start the booster truck—always start the booster engine first.
- Start the disabled truck.
- Remove the battery cables in reverse order.

STOP!

Do not attempt to jump-start a battery unless you are qualified to do so. Improperly connected cables can result in engine damage.

Starting Trucks That Have Air Starters

To start a truck that has an **air starter** requires fewer safety precautions. It is never a good idea, however, to smoke when inspecting or working on a vehicle **(see Figure 11–15).**

To prepare the vehicle, align the truck with the charged air supply. Hook up the air line properly. When using a compressor, follow these steps:

1. Hook up the air line from the compressor to the glad hand of the disabled truck's air reservoir.
2. Fill the reservoir.
3. Start the disabled tractor's engine.

Safety First

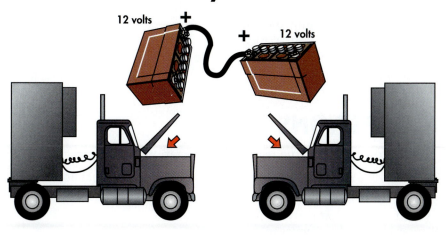

12 volts + + 12 volts

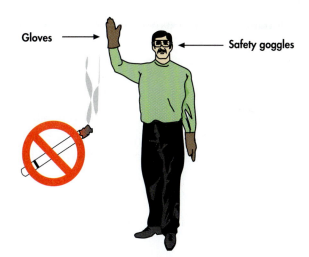

Gloves →   ← Safety goggles

▶ **Figure 11–15**

Safety is your top priority when starting a truck with a dead battery.

When you are using another tractor, supply air in this way:

1. Hook up the air line from one reservoir to the other.
2. Start the booster tractor's engine.
3. Fill the empty air reservoir of the disabled tractor.
4. Start the disabled tractor's engine.

SUMMARY

In this chapter, you have learned the driver's responsibilities in maintaining and servicing his or her vehicle. You also know that a trained mechanic should provide most repairs. This chapter teaches you to troubleshoot and report malfunctions. As a professional driver, you may at some time in your career have a vehicle that will not start. Remember to follow safe and correct emergency starting procedures.

KEY TERMS

Air starter
Driver awareness
Federal Motor Carrier Safety
  Regulations (FMCSR)

Jump-starting
Maintenance policy
Malfunction

Troubleshoot
Vehicle Condition Report
  (VCR)

REVIEW QUESTIONS

1. Which of the following is not true regarding expectations of most tractor-trailer drivers?

   a. They are to follow company policy regarding repairs to the rig.

   b. They are to follow company policy regarding adjustments to the rig.

   c. They are to be mechanics.

   d. a and b

2. Although a professional driver is not expected to become a mechanic, he or she should be _____.

   a. knowledgeable enough of the various systems to find the source of a problem

   b. able to repair a flat tire

   c. able to repair the electrical system

   d. able to repair the fuel system

3. When a driver uses his or her seeing, hearing, feeling, and smelling to collect clues regarding the operation of the rig, the driver is said to be using his or her _____.

   a. reaction time

   b. senses

   c. brake lag time

   d. a and c

4. Which of the following is not a typical result of an early detection of a malfunction of your rig?

   a. lower maintenance expenses

   b. increase in the cost of operating the rig

   c. fewer accidents

   d. longer vehicle life

5. Which of the following is not a driver's responsibility regarding maintenance and/or repairs of a rig?

   a. Know the company expectations.

   b. Identify the sources of malfunctions.

   c. Diagnose and fix simple problems.

   d. Make repairs to the fuel system.

6. Which of the following is not an expectation of a driver regarding troubleshooting the systems of a rig?

   a. Know where the systems are located.

   b. Know the parts of each system.

   c. Make repairs to all the systems.

   d. Know how all systems work together.

7. Regarding a driver's involvement with a rig, if one is searching out the source of a problem and attempting to solve it, one is said to be _____.

   a. troubleshooting

   b. increasing the driver's reaction time

   c. trouble sorting

   d. trouble acting

8. As a professional driver, if your rig experiences a sharp drop in fuel mileage, erratic gauge readings, temperature gauge readings too high or too low, or a thump, bump, whine, grind, or rattle, this should alert you to the fact that _____.

   a. you are driving into a strong wind

   b. you are experiencing a strong crosswind

   c. you have been doing lots of mountain driving

   d. your rig is not working properly or is in danger of failing

9. When reporting the results of your troubleshooting to the company mechanic, which of the following is the least best thing to report?

   a. When I brake, I hear a different kind of noise than I usually hear.

   b. My clearance lights sometime blink when I turn to the right.

   c. I think I hear a rubbing sound coming from the right side of my trailer.

   d. Mary, the cashier at Mell's Diner, told me she thought the brake shoes were going out.

10. If Melissa drives rig A for deliveries from 8 A.M. to 11 A.M. and drives rig B for deliveries from 1 P.M. to 3 P.M., according to FMCSR, how many vehicle condition reports (VCRs) must she fill out for the day?

   a. one for rig A only

   b. one for rig A and one for rig B

   c. one for rig B only

   d. none since Melissa did not drive either rig for 8 hours

12 Communication

OBJECTIVES

When you have completed this chapter, you should be able to:

- Know and understand the importance of using signals to tell other highway users when you plan to change positions in traffic.

- Explain why good communications help avoid collisions and traffic violations.

- Describe how to send and receive communications.

INTRODUCTION

Professional drivers realize if their travel is to be safe and efficient, they must be in constant communication with others on the road.

Does this mean the driver should communicate with everyone, using a cellular telephone or a CB radio? Absolutely not! But it does mean the professional driver must signal his or her next move through traffic, and at the same time, be alert to the messages coming from other drivers, pedestrians, and cyclists.

So, what is good **communication** on the highway, anyway?

It is a skill developed by professionals that uses knowledge, foresight, experience, and understanding of the driver's needs as well as the needs of others on the road **(see Figure 12–1).** In its simplest form, communication on the highway is helping each other get down the road and helping each other get jobs done.

How does good communication occur on the highway?

In addition to using turn signals and emergency flashers when necessary, good communications from your tractor also incorporate the horn and your speed—letting other highway users be aware of your presence, your position, and your intentions.

▶ **Figure 12–1**

Good communication on the highway helps you get down the road and get the job done.

Should drivers of other vehicles automatically know when a big rig pulls behind them, in front of them, or beside them—because the rig is so big?

It may be difficult to believe, but some people do not realize you are there because they are not paying close attention. They may be thinking about dinner tonight, a sore tooth, or a personal problem. They may be talking on the phone or listening intently to the music playing at that moment. Therefore, when you communicate your presence by letting others know where you are, you may be helping everyone avoid an accident down the road.

Another situation occurring on America's highways today is **road rage.** Professional drivers tell of days when they have seen or been involved in a dozen or more of these dangerous incidents. According to psychologist Arnold Nerenberg, road rage occurs in North America as many as 2 billion times every year.

Road rage can be defined as anything from aggressive driving, to criminal behavior, to simply bad driving. One law enforcement officer defines road rage as "an event occurring when drivers are running out of time and running out of options." Another highway veteran calls road rage "a problem of sharing—conflict between the law abiding road user and people who cut in and out, try to beat the traffic."

Because road rage has surpassed epidemic proportions, professional drivers must be constantly aware of how his or her "communication" of their rig's presence or their intentions are perceived. Honking the horn too often, following too closely, or cutting off a driver at a ramp or turnoff may spike the opportunities for road rage.

So, take care in how you communicate with others using the same roadway. Be aware of how important it is to let others know your whereabouts and your intentions, and never overdo signals or flashing lights, speed, or use inappropriate methods to communicate your plans to maneuver your rig.

TELL YOUR INTENT

Even though you know where you are and where you are going at any given time while on the roadways, other highway users do not know. Remember the concern you felt when a bicyclist was in your lane on the highway? The best way to let others know your intent to change lanes, turn, or slow down is to signal before you do it; and there are rules to observe for signaling when driving a rig.

Why do these special rules exist? Because of the size of the rig, your blind spots while driving a rig, and the space you require for turning. The rules help you do everything you can to let others know what you intend to do **(see Figure 12–2).**

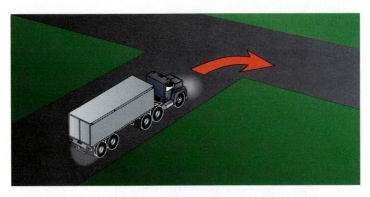

Signal early: Signal for some time before you turn. It is the best way to keep others from trying to pass you when it is not safe to pass.

Signal continuously: Do not cancel the signal until you have completed the turn.

Cancel your signal after you have turned: Turn off your signal if you do not have self-cancelling signals.

▶ **Figure 12–2**

Using signals correctly communicates your next maneuver to others sharing the road.

SIGNALING
Signaling for Turns

The three rules to follow when you signal before making a turn are:

1. Signal early
2. Signal continuously
3. Cancel your signal

   Signal early—as you know, the size of your rig makes it hard for you to see another driver who is about to pass you or who may already be doing so. The best way to keep others from trying to pass when you are ready to make a turn is to give advanced warning. **Put on your turn signal early.**

CAUTION!

The general rule of thumb is to turn on the turn signal one-half block before an intersection or about 500 feet from the intersection on the open highway. According to the FMCSR, you must signal at least 100 feet in advance of your maneuver.

State laws vary from 100 feet to 500 feet. Keep in mind these legal requirements are minimums—100 feet may not be far enough in advance for some traffic or weather conditions.

Signal continuously—you may find that after turning on your signal, you must stop and wait for a safe break in the traffic. Keep your signal on to tell everyone what you are going to do.

Cancel your signal—when you have completed the turn, cancel your signal. Do not cancel the signal until you have completed your maneuver.

GO!

One good way to remember to cancel the signal is to connect it in your mind with the upshift. After completing the turn, speed up, cancel the signal, and upshift. This routine will soon become a habit.

Signaling for Lane Changes

Lane changes require the same early warnings that you signal when making turns. They also need one more signal—the motion of your vehicle. Once you begin your lane change, pause for a few seconds as you enter the new lane. This will catch the attention of those who did not notice your earlier signal and will give them a chance to react **(see Figure 12–3)**.

Slowing Down

Highway users expect vehicles ahead of them to keep moving. Any time you slow suddenly, you should give the drivers behind you some type of warning. *Communicate your intent.* A few light taps on the brake pedal—enough to flash the brake lights without exhausting your air supply—should be enough.

Be prepared to signal a warning in any of the following situations:

> **Trouble ahead**—because of the size of your rig, those behind you will not be able to see any problems on the roadway ahead. Flash brake lights and/or use the horn.
>
> **Tight turns**—few automobile drivers know how difficult it is to make a tight turn in a big rig. Give them a warning signal ahead of time when you plan to make a turn so they will be prepared for you to slow your rig.
>
> **Stopping on the roadway**—unfortunately, some drivers are forced to stop in a traffic lane when others behind them may not expect it. It may be a case of having to unload cargo when there is no space on the curb. Sometimes the reason for stopping may be a railroad crossing. Other times, you have

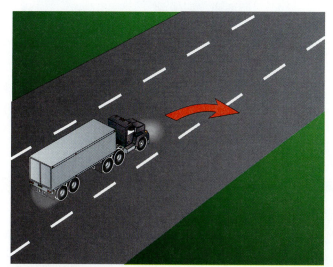

Changing Lanes:
- Check traffic to the front and rear, especially in your blind spot.
- Signal the lane change.
- Do not tailgate while waiting to change lanes.
- Make a smooth lane change, maintain your speed, and allow the correct distance between all vehicles.
- Cancel your signal.

▶ **Figure 12–3**

Following these steps when changing lanes helps maintain roadway safety.

"There's traffic ahead. Danger. Slow down . . . gosh, I love that car."

Avoid Guiding Others

DO NOT SIGNAL OTHERS TO PASS OR CROSS

to stop your rig to back into a driveway, or you may come to a stop because your rig is experiencing mechanical difficulties. Give the drivers following you as much warning as possible.

Driving slowly—sometimes other drivers overtake a slow vehicle more quickly than they realize. If your rig is being slowed by hills or heavy cargo, let other drivers know you are going slowly by turning on your four-way flashers until you are able to resume normal highway speeds.

Do Not Direct Traffic

As a professional driver, your job is to manage your rig, not to tell other drivers what to do. Some drivers mean well as they try to help others by signaling when it is safe to pass, but what they fail to realize is that if their "help" causes an accident, they will be held liable for the damage. Signal only to tell others what *you* plan to do. Leave directing traffic to the police or highway patrol **(see Figure 12–4)**.

Overtaking Other Vehicles

When you overtake other highway users such as an automobile, another rig, a bicyclist, or a pedestrian, it is best to assume that they do not see you; and if they do not see you, there is also a chance they will suddenly move into your path. Before overtaking them, signal that you are there by tapping lightly on the horn. Avoid loud blasts that may startle them, causing them to swerve into your path.

▶ **Figure 12–4**

Remember that your job is to be a professional driver, not to direct traffic.

CAUTION!
Loud blasts on your horn should be used in emergencies only.

Signal any time you overtake and pass pedestrians or cyclists. Obviously you cannot signal every time you overtake another vehicle, but it is a good idea to do it when possible, especially when you approach a driver who is signaling a lane change or starting to pull into your path.

When It Is Hard to See

It is hard to see at dawn or dusk **(see Figure 12–5)**. It is also difficult to see in rain, snow, or during cloudy days, particularly when a driver is fatigued or right after eating a heavy meal.

▶ Figure 12–5

It is often difficult to see or be seen at dawn or dusk.

A rig can be as difficult to see as any other vehicle on the roadway. If you are having trouble spotting oncoming vehicles, assume other drivers are having a tough time seeing you. Turn on your lights and use your headlights to identify your rig as it goes down the highway.

CAUTION!

Use low beams because high beams can be as annoying in the day as at night.

▶ Figure 12–6

Any time you pull your rig off the road, use your emergency flashers.

At the Side of the Road

Anytime you pull off the road and stop, be sure to turn on your four-way flashers **(see Figure 12–6).** This is especially important at night when a driver who has not seen you decides to pull off the road in the same spot.

CAUTION!

Do not trust your tail lights to provide a warning. Many drivers have careened into the rear of a parked truck simply because they were not warned properly. Your four-way flashers are the best signals.

▶ **Figure 12-7**

Reflective triangles.

If you are forced to stop on or near the roadway, use your four-way flashers *and* put out **reflective triangles (see Figure 12–7).** Most rigs are no longer outfitted with flares or fusees, but if you are carrying hazardous materials or have spilled fuel, do not use flares or fusees. Place reflective triangles at the following locations if you are forced to stop on an undivided highway:

- On the traffic side—10 feet (four paces) to the rear of the rig, marking the location of the vehicle

- About 100 feet behind the rig on the shoulder of the lane in which the rig has stopped to give overtaking drivers plenty of warning

- About 100 feet in front of the rig on the shoulder to give oncoming drivers plenty of warning

GO!

According to the law, you must place triangles on the highway within 10 minutes of stopping on or beside the roadway.

Place reflective triangles at the following locations if you are forced to stop on a one-way or divided highway:

- About 10 feet behind the rig—to show approaching traffic your rig's location
- About 100 feet behind the rig
- About 200 feet behind the rig—giving oncoming traffic plenty of warning that there is a stopped vehicle ahead

Always place reflective triangles beyond a hill, curve, or other terrain that keeps drivers of overtaking vehicles from seeing your rig at a distance of 500 feet away.

If you have to double-park on a city street, triangles are not practical. Instead, turn on your four-way flashers so approaching drivers will know your rig is stopped.

USING CELL PHONES SAFELY

Only a few years ago, a **cell phone** was an unheard-of space-age gadget **(see Figure 12–8).** Cell phones are everywhere now and have been recognized as a major distraction for drivers. The evidence linking cell phone use to accidents is so compelling that an increasing number of countries, and U.S. cities, have actually made it illegal to drive while talking on the phone.

Cell phone conversations are dangerous because they distract drivers intellectually. Even if you think you are watching the road during a phone call, you are actually just steering the vehicle by force of habit, and using your logic and reasoning brain for your phone conversation. This means that if you had to make a sudden decision (for instance, if traffic suddenly stopped in front of you on the freeway) you would have to take time to "reengage" your decision-making brain and would not be able to react as quickly as if you had been paying full attention to the road.

Commercial and private drivers have come to depend on the flexibility and convenience cell phones offer, but as a professional driver, your safety is important and it is compromised by a cell phone call. In fact, many carriers have now instituted cell phone use policies. Be sure you know what your employer allows.

While driving, please think carefully whether a call is really necessary before you risk taking your eyes and mind off the road!

▶ **Figure 12–8**

Using a cell phone while driving can be a distraction. Use it only if absolutely necessary.

- ■ After obtaining your cell phone, the first piece of equipment you need to purchase and use is a hands-free feature.

- ■ When possible, avoid phoning and driving at the same time. If you are a team driver, wait until you can get out of the driver's seat before operating a cell phone.

- ■ Be familiar with the phone controls so you do not have to look for buttons.

- ■ Use the memory feature so you do not have to input long numbers when dialing.

- ■ Be aware of your surroundings and keep your eyes moving, scanning, checking mirrors, and so on, at all times. People tend to "look inward" when concentrating on a phone conversation.

- ■ If you are driving in heavy traffic or hazardous conditions, do not answer when the phone rings. Explain to your contacts that this may happen so they know to try again shortly.

- ■ Above all—follow your company's policies regarding the use of cell phones.

SUMMARY

In this chapter, you learned the importance of communicating with other road users. You learned that communication is key to highway safety. The correct ways to signal a turn or lane change, slowing down, and overtaking another road user were explained. You also now know how to place warning devices correctly if you must stop your truck by the side of the road—and, finally, you learned that truck drivers have a responsibility to continually communicate with the driving public—wherever you go.

KEY TERMS

Cell phones   Reflective triangle   Wireless communication
Communication   Road rage

REVIEW QUESTIONS

1. When a professional driver signals his or her next move and at the same time is alert to the messages coming from other drivers, pedestrians, and cyclists, the driver is said to be _____.

   a. driving slow   **c.** needing rest

   b. driving fast   **d.** communicating with others on the road

2. Aggressive driving, criminal behavior, or bad driving can be defined as _____.

   a. good conduct   **c.** good driving

   b. road rage   **d.** safe driving

3. Which of the following is not one of the special rules to use when signaling before making a turn?

   a. signal continuously   **c.** flashing brake light to indicate the rig is slowing for a turn

   b. signal early   **d.** cancel your signal

4. The one additional signal that is needed when making lane changes that is not needed when signaling for turns is _____.

   a. blink the trailer lights   **c.** blink the tail lights

   b. once the lane change is started, pause for a few seconds as the new lane is entered   **d.** sound the horn

5. To communicate an intent to slow suddenly, the professional driver _____.

   a. taps the brake pedal lightly a few times to flash the brake lights   **c.** flashes the head lights

   b. flashes the clearance lights   **d.** turns on the emergency flashers

6. Which of the following is not a good practice when overtaking a pedestrian or a bicyclist?

   a. blast your air horn loud and long to teach them not to use the highway   **c.** a light tap on the electrical horn

   b. a light tap on the air horn   **d.** at night, flash the lights with the dimmer switch

7. Any time a professional driver must pull off and stop at the side of the road, to warn other drivers the _____ should be turned on.

   a. clearance lights   **c.** head lights

   b. left turn signal   **d.** 4-way flashers

8. If a driver is forced to stop on or near the road, reflective triangles must be put out within _____.

   a. 30 minutes   **c.** the first hour

   b. 5 minutes   **d.** 10 minutes

9. If a driver is forced to stop on an undivided highway, to give overtaking drivers plenty of warning, a reflective triangle must be placed _____ behind the rig on the shoulder or in the lane in which the rig is stopped.

   a. 10 feet   **c.** about 100 feet

   b. about 50 feet   **d.** 1 mile

10. If a driver is forced to stop on a one-way divided highway, to give overtaking drivers plenty of warning, a reflective triangle must be placed about _____ behind the rig.

    a. 50 feet   **c.** 75 feet

    b. 200 feet   **d.** 80 feet

13 Space Management

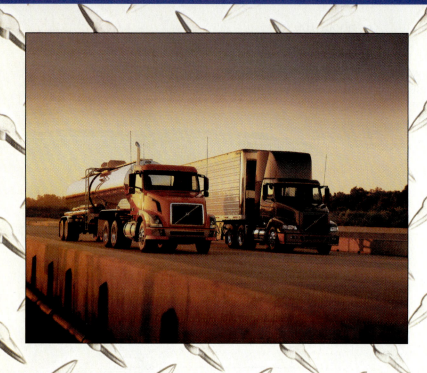

OBJECTIVES

When you have completed this chapter, you should be able to:

- Explain the safest following distance for driving in different conditions.
- Show the importance of maintaining distance between your rig and other vehicles when driving defensively.
- Describe how you, as a professional driver, can control your space on the roadway.
- Prevent the dangers of overhead obstructions.
- Explain the correct procedures for making turns.
- Manage space in intersections.

INTRODUCTION

What does it take to become a professional driver in America's trucking industry? Some would say a citation-free, accident-free record. Others would say vehicles and cargos reaching their destinations without incident or damage. Obviously both of these statements are true, but it takes more than a clean record and a well-handled load. In fact, a professional driver's highest achievement may be managing the space around his or her vehicle at all times **(see Figure 13–1).**

Veterans define **space management** as "maintaining a cushion of air around the vehicle in every environment." For the purposes of this book, we define it as maintaining enough space around your rig to make every trip smooth, comfortable, and above all, uneventful **(see Figure 13–2).**

THE IMPORTANCE OF SPACE MANAGEMENT

When driving a big rig, you need space around your vehicle at all times—in front, to the sides, and to the rear. When emergencies happen on the road, this same space gives you time to adjust.

Other vehicles may stop unexpectedly or turn in front of you. You may need space to change lanes, but you will continually need to check your mirrors and maintain this very important space around your rig. This process takes time, and time requires space.

Professional drivers are concerned with space in all directions—ahead, behind, to the sides, and above and below the rig **(see Figure 13–3).** You also need to be aware of the space necessary for turning, crossing the roadway, and entering traffic.

To have the space you need when something goes wrong, whether it is mechanical problems or problems caused by debris on the roadway or other drivers, you need to continue to manage the

▶ **Figure 13–1**

Managing the space around your vehicle at all times is one sign of a skilled professional driver.

Space Cushion

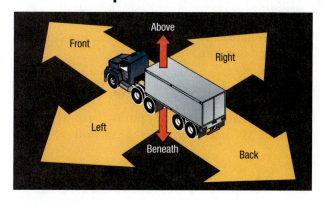

▶ **Figure 13–2**

Maintaining a cushion of air around your vehicle in every environment is good space management.

▶ **Figure 13–3**

You must be concerned with the space in all directions, including below your tractor-trailer.

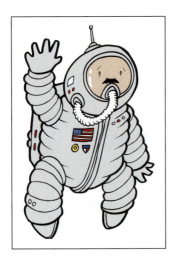

space around your rig at all times. This, of course, is true of all those using the highway, but it is especially important for professional drivers who are driving big rigs, because they take up more space and they need a great deal more space for every maneuver.

SPACE AHEAD

It does not take an experienced driver to realize that the most important space around a rig is the space ahead. This is the amount of space you need to stop your rig in any situation and for any reason. Experience and accident records indicate the vehicle most likely to be hit by a tractor-trailer rig is the one in front of it—the most common cause of these collisions is that the rig has been following too closely.

▶ *"What do you mean, lose the space suit? Don't I need it for this space management thing?"*

If the vehicle ahead is lighter than your rig, it can stop faster and in less space. So, if the small sedan ahead suddenly puts on its brakes, it can stop before you have completed your braking process. If that same small sedan begins to slow down and you—the driver of the rig that is following—fail to notice it, by the time you realize what is happening and decide to put on your brakes, you have used up most or all of the space that separates your rig from that little sedan.

The lesson here is, if you are following too closely, you may not be able to avoid hitting the vehicle in front of you.

How Much Space Do You Need to Be Safe?

How much space should you put between your rig and the vehicle in front of you? A good rule of thumb is that you need 1 second for each 10 feet of your rig's length **(see Figure 13–4)**. That means if you are driving a 40-foot rig, leave at least 4 seconds of time between your front bumper and the vehicle ahead of you. In a 60-foot rig, you will need 6 seconds of space between you and that vehicle traveling in front of yours **(see Figure 13–5).**

Heavy Vehicle Formula
For timed interval following distance

- 1 second required for each 10 feet of vehicle length at speeds under 40 mph
- Above 40 mph use same formula, then add 1 second for the additional speed

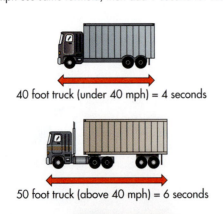

40 foot truck (under 40 mph) = 4 seconds

50 foot truck (above 40 mph) = 6 seconds

60 foot truck (under 40 mph) = 6 seconds

▶ **Figure 13–4**

Determine adequate following distances based on the length of your rig.

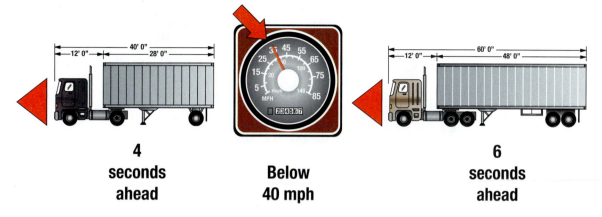

4 seconds ahead

Below 40 mph

6 seconds ahead

▶ **Figure 13–5**

Adequate distance between your rig and the vehicle in front of you is measured in seconds.

GO!

To measure adequate following distance, note when the rear end of the vehicle ahead passes a marking on the road. Then count off the seconds: 1-1000, 2-1000, 3-1000, and so on, until the front of your rig reaches the same spot. Compare your count with the rule of 1 second for every 10 feet of your rig's length.

If you are driving a 40-foot rig and count less than 4 seconds, you are following too closely. Drop back. Then count again. Until you have at least 4 seconds of space between your rig and the vehicle you are following, you are in danger and so are all other road users around you.

For speeds above 40 mph, add 1 second to the basic amount of space needed:

Example: 50-foot rig traveling at 48 mph

- Basic amount of space needed = 5 seconds (50/10 = 5)
- Above 50 mph, add 1 second
- Total following distance needed = 6 seconds (5 rig lengths = 1 speed over 40 mph = 6)

For bad weather, poor visibility, or poor road conditions, you should add at least 1 more second:

Example: 60-foot rig with poor visibility traveling at 55 mph **(see Figure 13–6).**

- Basic amount of space needed = 6 seconds (60/10 = 6)
- Above 40 mph, add 1 second
- Poor visibility, add 1 more second
- Total following distance needed = 8 seconds (6 rig lengths + 1 speed over 40 mph = 1 weather = 8)

NOTE: The times listed here are absolute minimums to ensure seeing time, thinking time, reacting time, and braking time.

▶ **Figure 13-6**

You should have at least four seconds of space between your rig and the vehicle in front of you.

SPACE BEHIND

As you know, you cannot completely control the space behind your rig because you cannot control drivers who approach your rig from behind on the highway. You can, however, do a number of things to have more control over this area:

1. Stay to the right.

1. Be careful when changing lanes.

3. Expect **tailgating** (when another vehicle follows your rig too closely to have adequate time to stop).

4. Respond safely to tailgaters.

■ **Stay to the right**—sometimes going uphill or when a load is very heavy, a rig cannot keep up with other traffic. At these times, it is best to use the special truck lanes or stay as far to the right as possible. In some states, however, driving on the shoulder of the road is illegal. When going uphill, do not try to pass a slower vehicle unless it can be done quickly. Being caught behind two trucks that are side by side is annoying to other drivers and could bring on a case of severe road rage.

■ **Changing lanes**—the length of the tractor-trailer makes it hard to judge whether a lane change can be made safely. Here are a few suggestions to make lane changes safer and easier:

● When in doubt, leave plenty of space between you and other vehicles.

● Wait a little longer before pulling in front of a vehicle you have passed.

● On a multilane road, there is no need to rush your return to the righthand lane (**see Figure 13–7**).

● Do not always trust the signals of other drivers. They may have good intentions, but you really have no idea what they are really going to do.

▶ **Figure 13-7**

When changing lanes, leave plenty of space between your rig and other vehicles.

■ **Anticipate tailgating**—in large vehicles, it is difficult to know when you are being tailgated. A good rule is to expect to be tailgated under the following conditions:

- When you are traveling slowly **(see Figure 13–8)**—drivers trapped behind a slow-moving vehicle tend to edge up too close, even though some states have minimum following distances.

- Bad weather—many drivers follow large vehicles closely in bad weather, especially when visibility is poor or at night.

■ **Respond safely to tailgaters**—if you find yourself being tailgated, these actions may help reduce the chance of an accident:

- Reduce your speed slowly—this may encourage the tailgater to pass you **(see Figure 13–9).**

- Avoid quick changes—if you have to slow down or turn, signal your intentions early and make the change very slowly.

- Increase your following distance—create more space in front of your rig. This will help you avoid the need for making quick changes.

- Do not speed up—tailgaters often tend to stay close, no matter your speed.

- It is better to be tailgated at a low speed than at a high speed.

- Avoid tricks—do not turn on your headlights or flash your brake lights to shake up the tailgater. You could make the situation worse by angering or confusing the driver following you.

▶ **Figure 13–8**

Be aware of being tailgated.

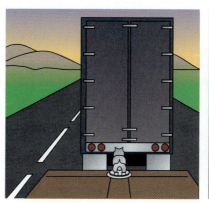

▶ **Figure 13–9**

When being tailgated, the vehicle behind you has a reduced view of the road ahead.

SPACE TO THE SIDES

The wider your vehicle, the less space it has to the sides. To protect yourself on both sides, manage your space with care by keeping your rig centered in your lane. Avoid driving alongside other vehicles. Overtake and pass carefully.

Staying Centered in Your Lane

There is usually little more than a foot between the sides of your trailer and the edges of the lane in which you are driving. Keeping your rig centered is important for safety.

CAUTION!
Keep as much space as possible to the sides of your rig. Keep your rig centered in your lane when meeting, passing, or being passed by other vehicles.

Do not move to the right because of an approaching vehicle. This maneuver may put you too close to the other side of your lane. Also avoid any oncoming vehicles if they move over into your lane.

CAUTION!
Visually scan your mirrors often to be sure your trailer has not drifted out of line. If it has, get in front of it and pull it back into the center of your lane.

Traveling Beside Others

Two dangerous situations can develop any time you travel alongside other vehicles:

1. Another driver may change lanes suddenly and turn directly into your rig.
2. You may need to change lanes and find there is no opening, so you remain trapped in your present lane.

GO!
The best way to avoid potentially dangerous situations is never travel in a pack of vehicles. Maintain space to the side, ahead of, and behind your rig. Find an open spot where you have the road pretty much to yourself. When there are no open spots, stay alert to the traffic around you and be aware of their blind spots. If you have to travel near other vehicles, stay out of their blind spots by dropping back or pulling ahead.

CAUTION!
Stay in one lane. Fewer lane changes equal less opportunity for right lane change crashes.

SPACE OVERHEAD

Hitting overhead objects is a major cause of damage, both to rigs and damage done by them **(see Figure 13–10).** Make sure you have enough clearance overhead at all times.

Most overhead collisions are with low-hanging wires, marquees, signs, and air-conditioning units. Check the heights of any overhead structures before driving under them. If you have any doubt about clearance, slow down and drive very carefully.

▶ **Figure 13–10**

Hitting objects overhead is a major cause of damage to tractor-trailer rigs.

STOP!

If any question remains as you approach the object overhead, stop the rig, get out, and check the clearance before proceeding.

Never rely on posted heights at bridges or overpasses. Repaved roads or packed snow may reduce the clearance space indicated.

The weight of your rig also affects its height. The fact that you were able to drive under a bridge fully loaded does not mean you will clear the same bridge when your trailer is empty or lightly loaded.

Sometimes your rig may tilt to the side of the road because of the road's high crown or different levels of paving. When this occurs, you may not clear signs, trees, or other objects alongside the road. If this is a problem, try to drive a little closer to the center of the road.

STOP!

Backing the rig is often troublesome. Before you back into an area, get out of the cab and check for any overhanging structures because it is often not possible to see these structures or branches while you are backing.

SPACE BELOW

Many drivers overlook the importance of maintaining adequate space beneath their rigs. That space can be "squeezed" when a vehicle is heavily loaded and the springs are compressed, making the vehicle ride lower. When you are driving low-bed equipment, there may not always be enough clearance beneath the rig. The following situations may create a space problem beneath your rig:

Railroad tracks—often extend several inches above the surface of the road. This is often a problem on dirt roads and in unpaved yards where the surface of the track wears away.

STOP!

Do not take a chance on getting hung on a rail. Get out and measure the clearance.

Soft surfaces—make sure any surface will hold the weight of your rig before driving onto that surface. One way to lose clearance is to sink down until the truck frame is resting on the surface.

Shopping center parking lots—many lots are not made for heavy trucks and often erode or holes are created in the pavement as the result of repeated shopper use. If you have a shopping center delivery, check ahead to make sure the surface of the parking lot can handle your loaded rig.

Unpaved surfaces—dirt surfaces will usually support your rig in good weather; however, after a rainstorm, the dirt can quickly become muddy muck. Check before driving onto unpaved surfaces, especially if they are covered with gravel or grass. They may not be as firm as they look.

Excavated areas—can be dangerous, especially for big rigs. They may be covered with planks that cannot bear the weight of your rig. Sometimes they are filled in with loose dirt. Use care when you have to drive near road work or construction.

SPACE FOR TURNS

Having enough room to the sides of your rig when you turn is important **(see Figure 13–11)**. Because your rig has a wide turning radius and needs space for off-tracking, there is a tendency to **sideswipe** other vehicles or turn over objects during turns.

Right Turns

Because most right turns have a tight turning radius, you have to swing wide for a successful turn. Timing is key, so stay to the right as long as possible if you have to swing out to the left to make your turn. Otherwise, the driver of the vehicle following you may not realize you are planning to turn and will try to pass you on your right.

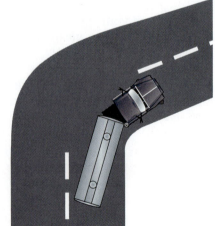

▶ **Figure 13–11**

Having enough space to turn your rig is sometimes difficult.

Here are steps to follow when making a right turn:

- Approach the intersection in the right lane.
- Turn on your right turn signal at least 100 feet before turning.
- Swing left just as you approach the intersection, if you need the room.
- Turn sharply to the right.

If the turn is particularly sharp or difficult, swing out into the street you are about to enter. Watch your off-tracking to avoid running over the curb or grassy areas, which may hide things such as sprinkler heads. Return to the right lane as soon as possible.

GO!

When making a right turn, remember! It is better to travel a few blocks farther and make three right turns to get on a street you want than to endanger others because of a tight turn.

Left Turns

When you make a left turn, be sure you reach the center of the intersection before turning left. If you turn too soon, the side of the trailer, as it off-tracks, may hit an object or a vehicle waiting to enter the intersection.

The choice of lanes is very important in a left turn. If there are two turning lanes, use the right lane. If you begin in the right lane, you will have to swing out in order to make the turn. A driver on your right may not expect you to turn and may drive into the side of your rig.

CAUTION!

When making a left turn, keep traffic in the next lane on the "right side" where you can see it best. A vehicle to your right may be difficult to see.

SPACE TO CROSS OR ENTER TRAFFIC

Drivers new to the profession often do not allow for the size and weight of their rigs when they cross or enter into traffic (see Figure 13–12).

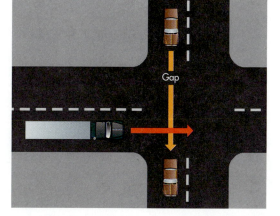

▶ **Figure 13-12**

Keep the size and weight of your rig in mind when crossing an intersection.

CAUTION!

Remember the following when crossing or entering traffic:

■ Because your rig accelerates slowly, it requires more space than a smaller vehicle, so you need a much larger gap to cross or enter traffic than you would need for your personal vehicle.

■ Acceleration varies with the weight of a vehicle. Allow more room and more time to accelerate if you have a heavy load.

■ Before starting to cross a street, think about the length of your rig. Make sure there is enough space for you to clear the intersection completely when you cross.

SUMMARY

In this chapter, you have learned the importance of managing the space around your tractor-trailer. There should always be adequate space in front of it, behind it, to both the right and the left side, and above and below the vehicle.

You also learned the types of hazards you may encounter if you fail to manage these spaces correctly, and you have learned how to convert time into distance, thus being able to decide if you are a safe distance from other road users.

The types of road surfaces that may present a danger were described and you also learned how to make both right and left turns correctly and how to enter or cross traffic safely.

KEY TERMS

Sideswipe
Space management
Tailgating

REVIEW QUESTIONS

1. Maintaining enough space around a rig to make every trip safe, while being considerate of other drivers, is called _____.

   a. distance management
   c. space management
   b. good fuel economy
   d. stomping distance

2. When things go wrong on the road, _____ gives you time to adjust.

   a. space
   c. the mechanic
   b. the dispatcher
   d. the federal regulations

3. Of all the space around a rig, the space _____ is the most important.

   a. behind   **c.** over

   b. under   **d.** ahead

4. Regarding the space needed between your 60-foot rig traveling at 39 mph and a vehicle in front of your rig, you will need _____ of space between the two vehicles.

   a. 60 seconds   **c.** 39 feet

   b. 39 seconds   **d.** 6 seconds

5. Regarding the space between vehicles, if the rig is traveling at a rate of 40 mph or over, how much time is added when figuring space?

   a. 1 second for each 10 mph over 40 mph   **c.** 5 seconds

   b. 1 second   **d.** 1 second for each 10 foot of length of the rig

6. For a 60-foot rig traveling 55 mph in the rain, how many seconds of space will the driver need?

   a. 8 seconds   **c.** 60 seconds

   b. 55 seconds   **d.** 6 seconds

7. If you, as a professional driver, find you are being tailgated, which of the following is not a recommended action?

   a. Slowly reduce the speed of the rig.   **c.** Increase the speed of the rig.

   b. Increase your following distance.   **d.** Avoid quick changes in direction.

8. Regarding space for turns, because of their wide turning radius and _____, rigs frequently sideswipe other vehicles or run over objects during turns.

   a. out-tracking   **c.** over-tracking

   b. off-tracking   **d.** in-tracking

9. Regarding right turns, if the driver has to swing to the left for the turn, the driver should stay to the right as long as possible so _____.

   a. there will not be too much loss of speed by the rig   **c.** other drivers will not attempt to pass on the left side of the rig

   b. other drivers will not try to pass the rig on the right   **d.** federal law requires all right turns by rigs be made out of the left lane so traffic will flow smoothly

10. Regarding crossing or entering traffic, acceleration varies with the weight of the load, therefore _____ if the rig has a heavy load.

   a. more room and more time is needed   **c.** room and time do not increase

   b. less room and less time is needed   **d.** neither a, b, nor c

14

Visual Search

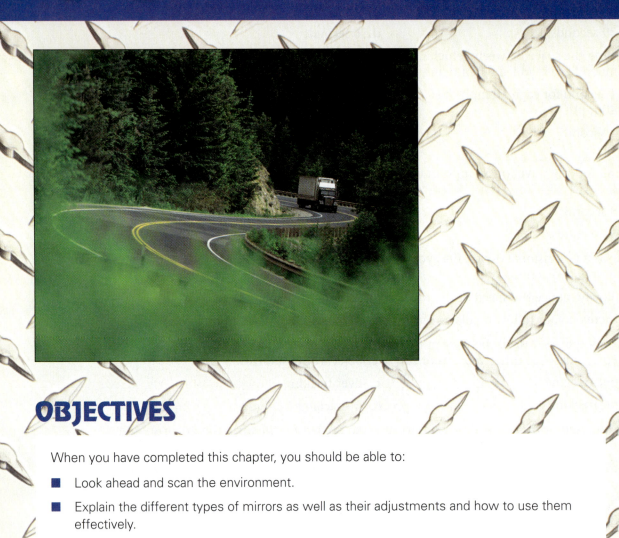

OBJECTIVES

When you have completed this chapter, you should be able to:

- Look ahead and scan the environment.
- Explain the different types of mirrors as well as their adjustments and how to use them effectively.
- Describe the professional driver's responsibility to other drivers.
- Know the importance of using a standard visual search while driving.

INTRODUCTION

To become a safe and efficient driver, it is important to learn how to be constantly aware of the environment—what is going on around your rig at all times **(see Figure 14–1)**. Sound strange? Keep reading!

Imagine having a view of your rig from a few hundred feet above. Notice the space on all sides of the rig—front, back, sides, and top. This is the **external environment**—the environment you will constantly need to see, hear, feel, and sense when driving.

There is also an **internal environment**—the environment in the cab of the tractor—where the driver must be constantly aware of the conditions in which he or she has to work **(see Figure 14–2).**

Why is the interior environment important? Because the cab's environment has a great impact on how the driver feels, how quickly the driver is fatigued, and how well the driver can react to factors on the outside of the cab. Is the temperature too hot or too cold? Are there exhaust fumes filtering into the cab? Does the chatter of the CB distract? Is the music too loud and too chaotic? All of these factors impact how you drive. These environments also change every second your rig is rolling, so you are constantly adjusting your awareness of what is around you.

As you study this chapter, you will learn what you need to know to be constantly aware of your environment and how to respond and drive through each situation.

▶ **Figure 14–1**

Constantly be aware of the environment around your rig.

▶ **Figure 14–2**

The interior environment of the cab also impacts how a driver feels and reacts to outside factors.

THE DRIVER'S VIEW

Think about what you are able to see from behind the wheel of a big rig. The view from the tractor's cab is much different from the view you have when you are behind the wheel of your personal vehicle. Obviously, you can see a greater distance ahead because you are sitting above the traffic. In some cases, you can see over the traffic, which is to your advantage!

On the flip side, you cannot see as well to the sides and rear of your rig as you can when you are driving your personal vehicle. In the cab of a tractor, it is difficult to see the right side of the tractor-trailer and along the drive wheels on both sides. Behind the wheel of a big rig, it is also difficult to see smaller vehicles.

Ultimately, the driver must be able to get a clear, complete, and accurate picture of the outside environment. Of course, there are existing blind spots that cannot be eliminated unless the driver does a vehicle walkaround before getting into the truck and makes the needed adjustments. For example, blind spots exist in the front of the tractor and at the rear of the trailer. To be eliminated, these must be observed and cleared by the driver just as he or she would make sure the direction the truck is going is clear before starting the engine.

▶ **Figure 14–3**

Steering toward an imaginary target in the center of your lane helps keep you in your lane.

FOCUSING ON THE ROAD AHEAD

While most of this discussion may seem obvious, it is important to explore the responsibilities of a professional driver as he or she takes to the road. Without question, looking up the highway as well as watching the road directly ahead and to the back and sides of your rig makes you aware of the environment around the truck **(see Figure 14–3).** Steering toward an imaginary target or a reference point in the center of your lane of travel keeps you in your lane and aware of any possible problems ahead. Having a target will keep you and your vehicle centered in your lane.

Veteran truckers will tell you: A good rule of thumb is to have a target at least the distance you'll travel in the next 12 to 15 seconds. Another name for this is **"eye lead time."** In city driving, 12 seconds equals about one block ahead. On the open highway, 12 seconds ahead is about a quarter mile.

CAUTION!

If you cannot look ahead one block in the city or a quarter mile on the highway, slow down and be extra alert.

Looking as far ahead as possible will give you time to:

- Identify any problems ahead
- Prepare for these problems
- Decide how you can drive defensively around the problem
- Check anything that could keep you from making any changes in speed, direction, lane, etc.
- Take the right action to keep you and others around you safe

Looking ahead 12 to 15 seconds and having enough visual lead time will allow you the ability to react efficiently and safely, save fuel, and save time, because you will have fewer close calls, near misses, or accidents **(see Figure 14–4).**

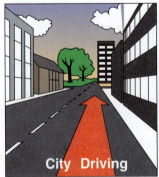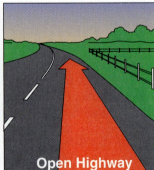

City Driving
12–15 seconds is about 1 block

Open Highway
12–15 seconds is about 1/4 of a mile

▶ **Figure 14–4**

Looking down the road gives the driver time to avoid hazards.

- **Safety**—by looking ahead, you will see hazards early enough to avoid them.

- **Fuel**—by looking 12 to 15 seconds ahead, you can adjust smoothly and avoid quick speed adjustments, which require less fuel.

- **Time**—spotting situations early will help you avoid being trapped behind turning vehicles, getting stuck in the wrong lane, or missing your exit.

SCANNING AND THE VISUAL SEARCH

Although it is important to have 12 to 15 seconds of visual lead time as you drive, be careful not to spend all of your time staring at the roadway ahead. Why? Because it is also important to know what is going on around your rig—to the sides, the back, and even on top of your rig.

Once you have chosen a reference point on the road ahead, make a **visual search** and **scan** around the rest of your rig. The routine looks like this: Look 12 to 15 seconds ahead of the rig and on both sides of the roadway ahead. Now quickly look away from your reference point ahead and scan both sides and in back of the rig before returning to the reference point.

Let us review the routine:

- Pick a reference point 12 to 15 seconds ahead and look at both sides of the road between your rig and that reference point.

- Now quickly look to either side—using your mirrors—and to the back of your rig before picking up the reference point.

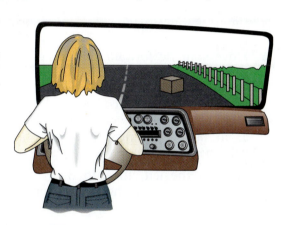

▶ **Figure 14-5**

Visual scanning gives the driver time for defensive action.

When scanning, look for anything that can affect your travel path **(see Figure 14–5)**:

- People—on foot and in cars
- Traffic signs
- Debris on the highway
- Signals
- Slick spots or potholes in the road
- Intersections

- Merging lanes
- Road shoulders
- Construction zones
- School zones
- Stopped vehicles
- Emergency situations

CAUTION!

As you scan, always look for **bail-out areas**—places you can use to avoid a crash.

Once you become accustomed to the visual search and scanning pattern, you will also learn how to pick and choose what you look for, depending on traffic and your driving environment.

Scanning and Driving into Intersections

After stopping at an intersection, know how to look at this environment before moving into and across the traffic lanes. The following guidelines should help:

■ Move your rig forward slowly, giving other drivers a chance to see you and to understand your intentions. The slow, controlled speed will also allow you to stop again before pulling into the path of cross traffic.

■ Look to the left, then to the right, and then straight ahead. Then look left again as you begin to move forward.

▶ "Visual search? I wonder if this is what that instructor meant?"

GO!

The reason for using this order of scanning is:

■ The first lane you cross carries traffic from the left; until this lane is clear, you cannot move forward

■ If the right lane is also clear, you can safely begin to move forward

■ At this point, the second look to the left ensures that there are no changes from that direction

■ You can now go through the intersection, but be aware of blind spots

From your seat in the cab, you can see behind you only in your left and right side-view mirrors. Check these mirrors when you scan and search. It is important to check them before your slow down, stop, or change lanes or direction.

Visual search is one of the most critical components in driver safety and efficiency. A **systematic search** begins with a walkaround of the vehicle every time it is driven, paying close attention to the space in front and at the rear of the vehicle.

The only way to eliminate front and rear blind spots is to first be aware that they are there. The driver sitting behind the steering wheel *always* has a blind spot directly in front of the vehicle that can range a distance of 30 to 50 feet. A blind spot existing directly behind a vehicle can range a distance of 200 feet.

CAUTION!

Imagine an 8-foot-wide trailer, multiplied by the 200-foot distance, could equal 1,600 feet of blind space. So, *always begin a visual search before entering the vehicle.*

Field of View

You have the largest **field of view** in your left side-view mirror. The closer the mirror is to you, the larger the image. The larger the image, the bigger the field of view. Images will appear similar to those in the side-view mirror of your personal vehicle.

MIRRORS

The two types of side-view mirrors are plane (flat) and convex (curved).

■ The **plane mirror** or **West Coast mirror** gives the most accurate view of the rear of the trailer and the roadway behind. It does not give a wide view and it can leave blind spots along the length of the rig **(see Figure 14–6).**

■ **Convex mirrors** are curved to give you a wide-angle view. They are best used for side close-ups because they provide a much wider field of view **(see Figure 14–7).**

Convex mirrors eliminate most, but not all, of the blind area created by the plane mirror. The images you see, however, will be smaller and will appear farther away than they really are. With plane mirrors, the blind areas are too large. Using only the convex mirror creates too much distortion, so it is best to have both plane and convex mirrors on your rig. Many rigs have this combination because it gives drivers the best possible side and rear vision **(see Figure 14–8).**

Field of Vision Using a Plane Mirror

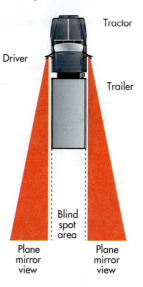

▶ Figure 14-6

The plane mirror gives the driver the best view of the rear of the trailer and roadway behind, but it leaves blind spots.

Field of Vision Using a Convex Mirror

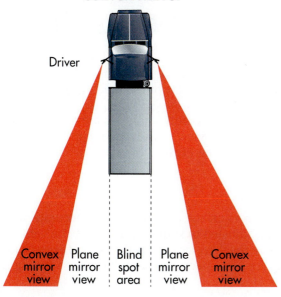

▶ Figure 14-7

Convex mirrors are curved to give a wide-angle view.

Combination of Plane/Convex Mirror

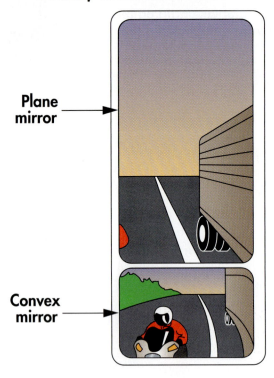

Plane mirror

Convex mirror

▶ **Figure 14–8**
Combination plane/convex mirrors provide the best rear and side vision.

Field of Vision While Making a Right Turn

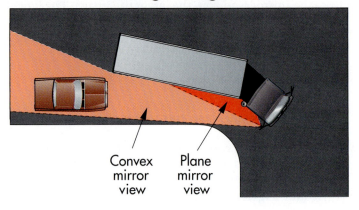

Convex mirror view   Plane mirror view

▶ **Figure 14–9**
The convex mirror gives a wider field of vision when making a right turn.

GO!
Remember that blind spots will still be there, even when using both convex and plane mirrors. Always adjust your mirrors and check both to have the best possible visual of your rig.

A **fender mirror** is mounted on the fender of the tractor. Drivers use the fender mirror because it requires less eye movement and does not interfere with your view of the road ahead.

Wide-angle (convex) fender mirrors let you see a wide field of vision when you are making right turns. This is particularly helpful in making a tight turn. The view of the road is similar to what you see with a convex side mirror but with less distortion **(see Figure 14–9).**

Adjusting Mirrors

Every driver should adjust both the left and right mirrors on the tractor to get an accurate view of the sides and rear of the rig. All mirrors should be adjusted to show some part of the vehicle, such as the trailer body, tires, and so on. This will give the driver a good **point of reference** for judging the position of everything around the rig. For best effect, adjust mirrors when the rig is straight.

GO!

Some rigs have motorized mirrors. These allow adjustment from inside the cab. They can also be used to get a wider view when needed and can then be returned to normal positions.

For left-side mirrors, plane mirrors, the inside vertical edge of the mirror (about ¾ to 1 inch) should show the trailer's body. The remaining part will show what is beside and behind the trailer. The range of view to the side will be about 15 feet. For convex mirrors, the inside vertical edge of the mirror should show part of the trailer. The top horizontal edge should show a view overlapping that of the plane mirror by about 5 feet and going back to the end of the trailer.

For right-side mirrors, plane mirrors, the inside vertical edge of the mirror (about ¾ to 1 inch) should reflect the trailer's body. The rest of the mirror will show what is on the side (for about 15 feet) and behind the trailer. For convex mirrors, the inside vertical edge of the mirror should reflect part of the trailer. The top horizontal edge should show a view overlapping that of the plane mirror by 5 feet and extend to the end of the trailer.

For fender mirrors, the convex fender mirrors on both the right and left side should be adjusted so you can see the trailer's tires, curbs, and other objects when turning **(see Figure 14–10).**

Seeing to the Rear

Checking your rig's mirrors is a part of scanning and searching. Be sure to check the security of your load as well as the tires (looking for blowouts or fire). In addition, your mirror checks can tell you if there are any hazards around your rig as well as what is beside or behind the rig that may be affected by a sudden move.

Using Mirrors When Making Lane Changes

Before making any sudden changes in speed or direction, always check the traffic behind you. **Changing lanes**—always use the plane and convex mirrors when changing your path of travel. Be aware that there are blind spots behind and to each side of your rig.

It is important to make many checks to be sure of the traffic around you and remember it takes longer to check to the rear when driving a rig than it does when you are driving a car. Properly checking the left mirrors takes almost 1 second. Checking mirrors on the right takes approximately 1.5 seconds.

Distortion of Convex Mirrors

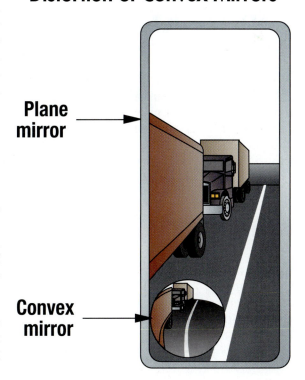

Plane mirror

Convex mirror

▶ **Figure 14–10**

Be aware of the distortion of convex mirrors.

Checking to Sides and Rear

- Check mirrors several times a minute

- Be especially alert at

    — Intersections

    — Shopping centers

    — Construction sites

    — School zones

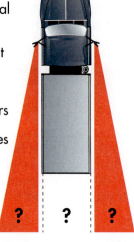

▶ Figure 14–11

Remember, it takes longer to check the rear of the rig than it does to check the rear of your personal vehicle.

Before checking your mirrors, make certain it is safe to look away from the front of the rig. At 55 mph, you travel 80 feet in 1 second. Keep enough space between yourself and the vehicle traveling in front of you. Avoid taking chances. If there is not enough space or time, delay the lane change **(see Figure 14–11)**.

Turning corners—when coming to a corner where you want to turn, check your side-view mirrors before slowing your rig for the turn. Then check them again as you are turning.

CAUTION!

After completing the turn, check the mirrors again to make sure your rig is not entangled with or dragging anything and that your rig has not damaged anything.

SUMMARY

In this chapter, you have learned how to systematically search the driving environment around your rig. You have learned the value of looking ahead and planning for hazards. You now know the correct methods of crossing an intersection and making lane changes using visual search techniques, and you understand the differences between the reflected images in convex and plane mirrors. You are also aware of the importance of adjusting your mirrors before every trip so that you will have maximum visibility when you are on the road.

KEY TERMS

Bail-out areas
Convex mirror
External environment
Eye lead time
Fender mirror

Field of view
Internal environment
Plane mirror or West Coast
    mirror

Point of reference
Scanning
Systematic search
Visual search

REVIEW QUESTIONS

1. Regarding visual search, the space on all sides of the rig a driver constantly needs to see, hear, feel, and sense when driving is called _____.

   a. the internal environment

   b. added space

   c. the external environment

   d. total stopping distance

2. The visual search pattern that helps a driver know what to look at, what to look for, and where to look is called _____.

   a. systematic seeing

   b. blind spot

   c. automatic seeing

   d. visual acuity

3. Looking at a target (point) at least the distance the rig will travel in 12 to 15 seconds is called _____.

   a. go time

   b. eye lead time

   c. following distance

   d. reaction distance

4. The process of looking ahead of the rig 12 to 15 seconds, looking on both sides of the roadway ahead, and scanning both sides and in back of the rig should happen every _____.

   a. 5 miles

   b. 6 to 8 seconds

   c. 30 seconds

   d. mile

5. Regarding scanning and the visual search, the places that a driver can use to avoid a crash are called _____.

   a. safety zones

   b. construction zones

   c. exit ramps

   d. bail-out areas

6. Regarding scanning and driving into intersections, the general guidelines state: look to the left, then to the right, then straight ahead, and then _____ again.

   a. right

   b. straight ahead

   c. left

   d. behind the rig

7. Which of the following provides the driver the most accurate view of the rear of a trailer and the roadway behind it?

   a. plane (flat) mirror

   b. concave mirror

   c. convex mirror

   d. blind spots

8. Which type of mirror is best for side close-up views?

   a. plane mirror

   b. flat mirror

   c. a and b

   d. convex

9. Adjusting the mirrors to show some part of the rig will give the driver a point of reference for _____.

    a. checking the back doors of the trailer

    c. determining the width of the blind spot

    b. determining the speed of other vehicles

    d. judging the position of the other images

10. Properly checking the left and right mirrors when driving a rig takes _____.

    a. about the same time it does when driving a car

    c. about 2-½ seconds

    b. about 1 second

    d. about 1 minute

15

Speed Management

OBJECTIVES

When you have completed this chapter, you should be able to:

- Explain the relationship between speed and stopping distance, hydroplaning, causes of accidents, the driver's ability to control the rig, and the rig's fuel economy.

- Discuss the effect of speed on the rig's weight, its center of gravity, and its stability.

- Show how the driver's available sight distance and the road surface conditions affect choosing a safe speed.

INTRODUCTION

Speed limit laws, which date back to 1901, have traditionally been the responsibility of the states. During the oil shortage of 1973, Congress directed the U.S. Department of Transportation to withhold highway funding from states that did not adopt a maximum speed limit of 55 mph. The National Research Council attributed 4,000 fewer fatalities to the decreased speeds of 1974, compared with 1973, and estimated that returning the speed limit on rural portions of the interstate highway system to pre-1974 levels would result in 500 more fatalities annually, a 20 to 25 percent increase on these highways.

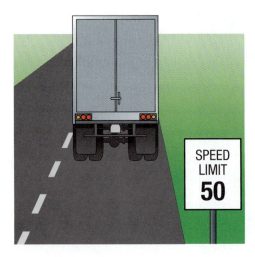

▶ **Figure 15–1**

As a professional driver, it is your job to know the speed limits of the states in which you travel.

As concerns about fuel availability and costs faded, however, speeds began to gradually climb on U.S. highways and by the mid-1980s, a majority of the vehicles across the U.S. highway system were traveling at speeds that exceeded 55 mph. In 1987, Congress allowed states to increase speed levels on rural interstates to 65 mph.

In 1995, the National Highway System Designation Act repealed the maximum speed limit and allowed states to set their own speed limits. Many states quickly raised speed limits on both urban and rural interstates as well as limited access roads. As of June 2000, 20 states had raised speed limits to 70 mph or higher on some roads.

As a professional driver, it is your job to know the speed limits of each of the states in which you travel, but more importantly it is also your job to know the principles of speed management and how to adjust your speed to fit each traffic and road condition you encounter **(see Figure 15–1).**

As the driver of a big rig, you must use not only your knowledge and your skills as a professional driver, but also your best judgment while in traffic. As any veteran driver will tell you, there is no place for individuals who do not look at professional driving as just that—a profession.

SPEED MANAGEMENT TERMINOLOGY

Basic speed rule—requires vehicle operators to drive at a speed that is reasonable and prudent. As a corollary to this rule, state laws usually provide that every person shall drive at a safe and appropriate speed when approaching and crossing an intersection or railroad grade crossing, when approaching and going around a curve, when approaching a hill crest, when traveling upon any narrow or winding roadway, and when special hazards exist with respect to pedestrians or other traffic or by reason of weather or highway conditions.

Minimum speed rule—prohibits a person from operating a motor vehicle at such a slow speed as to impede the normal and reasonable movement of traffic. In order to avoid a possible conflict with the basic speed rule, the law normally provides that a slow speed is permissible when reduced speed is necessary for safe operation or in compliance with law.

Racing on the highway—is usually defined as driving any vehicle in any race, speed competition or contest, drag race or acceleration contest, test of physical endurance, exhibition of speed or acceleration, or for the purpose of making a speed record.

Reckless driving—is normally defined as driving any vehicle in willful or wanton disregard for the safety of persons or property. Note that speed is not necessarily a factor in this offense.

Statutory speed limit—is one specifically provided for under a state's traffic code (rules of the road). Such limits may vary by highway type (e.g., interstate) or by location (e.g., urban district). State laws may require that these limits be posted.

Posted (maximum) speed limit—even though specific speed limits may have been established via legislation, state laws usually allow either state or local authorities to set highway speed limits above or below the statutory ones. Prior to taking such action on any portion of a highway, the law normally requires that governmental authorities conduct a study to determine the safe speed limit for that part of the highway. State laws may also allow such authorities to specify different speed limits on all or selected highways (or portions thereof) either for various times of the day or for various types of vehicles (e.g., trucks).

Work zone speed limits—nighttime roadwork has increased over the last few years and will continue to grow out of necessity. While there are reduced traffic volumes at night, the safety issues relating to traffic control are a major concern. Lower speed limits and extremely high traffic fines for violation of these speed limits are strictly enforced.

SPEED AND STOPPING DISTANCE

Speeding is defined as exceeding, or driving faster than, the legal or posted speed limit. You also speed when you drive too fast for current road, traffic, and weather conditions. The phrase "driving too fast for the conditions" is harder to define specifically, but it is just as important.

The economic cost to society of speeding-related crashes is estimated by the National Highway Transportation Safety Administration to be $27.4 billion per year. In 2000, speeding was a contributing factor in 29 percent of all fatal crashes, and 12,350 lives were lost in speeding-related crashes.

In 2000, 593,000 people received minor injuries in speeding-related crashes. An additional 71,000 people received moderate injuries, and 39,000 received serious to critical injuries in speeding-related crashes.

Speeding reduces a driver's ability to steer safely around curves or objects in the roadway, extends the distance necessary to stop a vehicle, and increases the distance a vehicle travels while the driver tries to react to a dangerous situation.

The physics of speeding involves the concept that the higher the travel speed, the greater the risk of serious injury or death in a crash. Vehicles and their occupants in motion have kinetic energy that is dissipated in a crash. The greater the energy that must be dissipated, the greater the chances of severe injury or death.

When the vehicle you are driving is a tractor-trailer rig, it is important to realize the weight of your load becomes stored energy and adds momentum, particularly when you are attempting to stop or turn your vehicle.

Motor vehicle crashes are complex events with multiple causes, and individuals have a wide range of tolerance to injury, but the amount of energy that must be dissipated, and thus the probability and severity of injury in a crash, is related to a vehicle's speed at impact. The laws of physics tell us that crash severity increases disproportionately with vehicle speed. A frontal impact at 35 mph, for example, is one third more violent than a crash at 30 mph.

Managing speed is a big part of driving safely and a major responsibility for professional drivers. The faster you go, the less time you have to react to what is happening around you, and there is no question that conditions can change in a split second **(see Figure 15–2)**.

▶ **Figure 15–2**

Managing speed is a critical part of driving safely.

CAUTION!

The faster you go, the longer it will take you to stop. It takes more than eight times the distance to stop a vehicle going 50 mph than it does a vehicle going 15 mph.

Table 15–1 provides an explanation of the distance it takes to stop a tractor-trailer on dry pavement. Remember, these distances are not exact. The three distances are:

- **Driver reaction distance**—the distance your rig travels from the time you identify a hazard to the time you apply your brakes.
- **Vehicle braking distance**—the distance your rig travels from the time you apply pressure to the brake pedal until the rig stops.
- **Total stopping distance**—the driver reaction distance plus the vehicle's braking distance.

The weight of the rig, how the brakes are working, and the weight of the load also figure into the braking distance.

Miles per Hour	How Far the Rig Will Travel in 1 Second	Driver Reaction Distance	Vehicle Braking Distance	Total Stopping Distance
15	22 ft.	17 ft.	29 ft.	46 ft.
30	44 ft.	33 ft.	115 ft.	148 ft.
45	66 ft.	50 ft.	260 ft.	310 ft.
50	73 ft.	55 ft.	320 ft.	375 ft.
55	81 ft.	61 ft.	390 ft.	451 ft.

▶ **Table 15–1**

Stopping distances.

There is no speed that will always be a safe speed. Speed must be adjusted to the conditions. Those conditions change often during the trip—even a short trip (**see Figure 15–3**).

▶ Figure 15–3

Empty trucks need greater stopping distances because an empty vehicle has less traction. The brakes, tires, springs, and shock absorbers on heavy vehicles are designed to work best when the vehicle is fully loaded.

DRIVING ON VARIOUS ROAD SURFACES

To steer your rig to a stop, under any conditions, you need **traction.** Traction is created by the friction of tires making contact with the road **(see Figure 15–4).** Sometimes traction is defined as the "grip" of the tires on the road.

Some road surfaces keep tires from having good traction. When this occurs, slow down to maintain control of your rig.

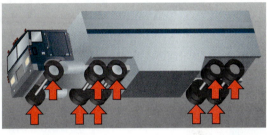

▶ Figure 15–4

The points of friction (traction) between the tires and road are small.

Slippery Surfaces

It takes longer to stop a rig when the road surface is slippery due to rain, ice, or snow. It is also harder to turn your rig in these conditions because the tires lose their grip on the road's surface. If you are to maintain control of your rig, slow down when the road is slippery. This is called managing your speed.

If your rig has antilock brakes, do not expect to stop faster than you would with other brakes. Antilock brakes only allow you to stay in control when braking your rig.

How much you should slow down depends on the conditions and your own confidence about handling your rig. If the surface is wet, you should reduce your speed by at least one fourth. If you are driving 55 mph, slow to at least 40 mph.

STOP!

Professional drivers do not take the risk of driving in snow or icy road conditions.

Identifying Slippery Surfaces

Because it is often hard to know when a road is slippery, get as much information as you can from your dispatcher, Internet road information, or Global Positioning System. You should also look for certain clues to help you identify "bad spots."

Shaded areas—when the sun begins to melt ice and snow, shaded areas of the road stay icy long after open areas are clear. This is especially true around bridges send trees.

"Black ice, eh. Nope . . . never heard of it. 'Course I'm from Florida . . . and about the only ice we ever see is in snowcones during the summer."

Bridges—because air can circulate over and under bridges, these structures tend to freeze more quickly than other parts of the road. Be careful when the temperature is around 32 degrees F. When the ice begins to melt, bridges will be wet and even more slippery.

Black ice—is a thin layer of ice, clear enough to let you see the road beneath. This condition makes the road appear wet. Any time temperatures are below 32 degrees F and the road looks wet, watch out for patches of black ice.

CAUTION!

Another way of detecting black ice is to watch tire spray. If it disappears when the weather is cold enough (32 degrees F or colder), you may be driving on black ice (**see Figure 15–5**).

▶ **Figure 15–5**

Icy, wet roads pose hazards to drivers.

Rainy days—when the temperature is near or below freezing, look for ice beginning to form on your vehicle. An easy way to check for ice is to open the window and feel the front of the mirror. If you feel ice accumulating on the front of the mirror, the road surface is probably getting icy too.

Just after rain begins—when rain begins to fall after a period of dry weather, it mixes with dirt, grease, grit, oil, and other road debris to make the road slippery. For the first 15 minutes of a rain, the road will be very slick. On hot days, this is a problem on asphalt roads because the oil in the asphalt tends to rise to the surface, called **bleeding tar.**

As the rain continues, the mixture is washed away. In heavily forested areas, where there are leaves on the road, the leaves become very slippery even after the rain has stopped because all of the oil and water are trapped between the forest debris and the surface of the road.

Hydroplaning

When water and slush collect on the roadway, your tires may lose contact with the road's surface. This loss of traction is called **hydroplaning.** It is much like waterskiing. A thin film of water separates the tires from the road and your rig simply slides along on top of the water. Under these conditions, you lose much of your ability to steer, brake, or control the rig.

Your rig can hydroplane on even the thinnest layer of water. Usually hydroplaning occurs when you are traveling at higher speeds, but it can also happen at speeds below 30 mph, depending on how much water is on the road and the condition of your tires **(see Figure 15–6).**

TAKING CURVES SAFELY
Center of Gravity

To maintain safety for themselves and those around them, professional drivers learn to adjust their speed to the conditions of the road and the weather at all times. This becomes even more important when you are driving a big rig.

Figure 15–6

When your rig hydroplanes, do not brake but gradually lower speed.

CAUTION!

How the weight of your load is distributed also makes a difference in controlling your rig while driving in extreme conditions.

How high your **center of gravity** is will determine your speed when you drive a curve **(see Figure 15–7).** One layer of crates of equal weight will keep the center of gravity lower than the same number of crates stacked on top of each other in an 8-foot stack. The higher the load is stacked, the higher the center of gravity—and the higher the center of gravity, the more likely the rig will be to tip over during turns **(see Figure 15–8).**

Figure 15–7

Your center of gravity helps determine safe speeds on curves.

Figure 15–8

The higher the center of gravity, the more likely your rig will tip over during turns.

▶ **Figure 15-9**

It is important to properly secure your load. A shifting load can cause serious control problems.

How the load is secured is also important because a shifting load can cause serious control problems for the driver **(see Figure 15-9).**

Adjusting Your Speed

Taking a curve too fast can cause you to lose control of your rig. This happens in one of two ways: (1) The steer tires lose traction and continue straight ahead, called a **skid;** or (2) the tires may keep their traction, but momentum will not allow the rig to turn, which can cause a rollover.

STOP!

Braking as you maneuver through a curve is dangerous because the wheels can lock. Instead of braking in the middle of a curve, slow to a safe speed before entering a curve. Ease off the fuel pedal or downshift.

If you downshift before entering a curve, slow down enough before you shift. This will allow you to speed up when you need to. Then, you can speed up slightly in the curve to help keep your rig stable. Once you are through the curve, bring your rig back up to speed.

NOTE: When approaching a curve, watch your speedometer as you slow to a safe speed. After driving at a high speed for a long period of time, your body may be fooled into thinking you have slowed down enough when, in actuality, you may still be traveling at a rate of speed too high to be safe as you enter the curve.

CAUTION!

The speeds posted for curves are the safe speeds for automobiles driving in good weather. To be safe, drive your truck slower than the posted curve speed.

DRIVING ON HILLS

Gravity affects speed on upgrades and downgrades. On upgrades, your rig is working against gravity. To maintain speed, you must increase pressure on the fuel pedal. Going downhill, your vehicle is working with gravity to increase your speed. Be careful to slow your rig to a safe speed to keep it under control.

WORK ZONE DRIVING SAFETY

While it is desirable to maintain normal speeds, restrictions around highway and roadway construction zones sometimes necessitate reduced speed limits. Lane width reductions, severe alignment changes, workers exposed to high-speed traffic, and other conditions may indicate the need for a reduced speed limit.

Whether or not the speed limit is reduced, adequate enforcement is important to ensure that posted speed limits are obeyed.

CAUTION!

In all cases, drivers should be aware of current conditions in night work zones so that they can seek alternate routes and/or adjust their driving behavior as necessary.

HOW FAR CAN YOU SEE?

When you are driving, you are constantly adjusting your **field of vision,** and in order to do so, you must also adjust your speed to accommodate how far you can see ahead in order to drive safely on various roadway surfaces and in various weather conditions.

Driving at 45 mph, you will need 310 feet to stop your rig. If, because of fog, rain, or snow, you can only see ahead 100 feet, then you are automatically placing yourself in a dangerous situation. Imagine a stalled vehicle on the roadway, just beyond your field of vision.

CAUTION!

A general guideline is that you should always be able to stop within the distance you can see ahead (**see Figure 15–10**).

Effect of Speed on Sight Distance

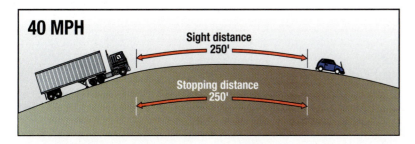

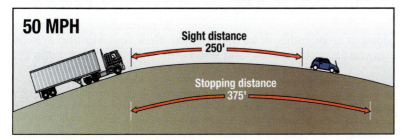

▶ **Figure 15–10**

Your field of vision often requires adjustments in your speed.

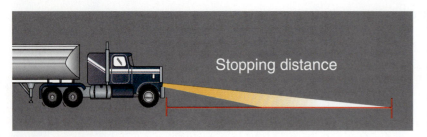

Figure 15-11

Low beams allow you to see about 250 feet ahead.

Night Driving

Apply the same general field-of-vision guidelines to night driving. Low beams let you see about 250 feet ahead. If you drive faster than 40 mph at night with low beams, you will not be able to stop in time to keep from hitting something that suddenly appears on the road in front of you **(see Figure 15–11).**

Bad Weather

Heavy rain, sleet, fog, and smog can greatly reduce your visibility.

CAUTION!

Poor weather conditions also limit what you can see ahead to just a few feet beyond the hood of your rig. To regain better vision of the roadway ahead, slow down as much as necessary to drive safely.

Remember, when it is hard for you to see other vehicles, other drivers also have difficulty seeing you.

Speed and Field of Vision

Your field of vision includes everything you can see in front of you and to the sides while looking straight ahead. The faster you go, the less you can see to the sides.

CAUTION!

As your speed increases, your field of vision decreases. To see something clearly, you must stop your eyes from moving and fix them on the object you want to see.

Remember this when you are looking at cross traffic or at the scene around you. Moving eyes do not see clearly. You cannot react to what you do not see, and you cannot see an object if you are not looking at it.

SPEED AND TRAFFIC

The safest speed in traffic is usually the same speed as other vehicles **(see Figure 15–12).** Accidents happen more often when vehicles are traveling at different rates of speed. As a rule, it is best to blend with other traffic.

Adjust your speed to match that of others while still obeying traffic laws. Some drivers try to save time by speeding, but—of course—this never pays because speeding is risky and often leads to accidents, and when there is other traffic, you usually cannot save more than a couple of minutes in an hour of driving. Bottom line, it is simply not worth the extra risk to speed.

The following may occur if you drive faster than the traffic surrounding you:

▶ **Figure 15–12**

Go with the flow. The safest speed in traffic is the same speed as the other vehicles.

- You will have to pass many other vehicles and each time you change lanes to pass, there is a risk of an accident.

- You tire faster from driving faster.

- You will be more likely to attract the attention of law enforcement personnel in the area.

- You will waste fuel and increase the wear and tear on your brakes (going with the flow is not only safer but also easier and cheaper).

SUMMARY

Now that you have completed this chapter, you have learned the critical importance of speed management and heeding speed limits. You understand and can explain the relationship of speed to stopping distance, hydroplaning, fuel economy, and accidents. You also have learned how speed affects your ability to control the rig; and, because you have completed this chapter, you can now discuss the effect of speed on the rig's weight and center of gravity as well as a rig's loss of stability. Finally, you also can show how the driver's available sight distance and road surface conditions affect choosing a safe speed.

KEY TERMS

Black ice	Gravity	Speeding
Bleeding tar	Hydroplaning	Total stopping distance
Center of gravity	Managing speed	Traction
Driver reaction distance	Skid	Vehicle braking distance
Field of vision		

REVIEW QUESTIONS

1. Regarding speeding, which of the following is the most complete answer: A driver is said to be speeding when the driver is driving too fast for current _____.

   a. road conditions   **c.** a, b, and d

   b. traffic conditions   **d.** weather conditions

2. Which of the following is not an element of total stopping distance?

   a. time of the day
   b. perception distance
   c. brake lag distance
   d. driver reaction distance

3. The distance a rig travels from the time a driver identifies a hazard until the brakes are applied is known as the _____.

   a. vehicle braking distance
   b. perception distance
   c. brake lag distance
   d. driver reaction time

4. _____ , sometimes called "grip," is created by the friction of tires making contact with the road.

   a. Reaction time
   b. Speed
   c. Traction
   d. Stopping distance

5. When the road surface is slippery, it takes longer to stop as well as being harder to turn a rig because _____.

   a. of more traction
   b. the tires lose their grip on the road
   c. of reaction time
   d. of brake lag time

6. After snow and/or ice collects on a roadway or bridge and it begins to melt, bridges and shaded areas _____.

   a. may be more slippery than other areas
   b. will be dry before the other areas of the roadway
   c. will be best for speeding
   d. will provide more traction than dry areas

7. A thin layer of ice that looks wet and is clear enough to let the driver see the road beneath is called _____.

   a. ice cakes
   b. black ice
   c. ice pack
   d. stopping distance

8. The higher the center of gravity, _____ during turns.

   a. the more stable the rig will be
   b. the more a driver may speed
   c. the more likely a rig will tip over
   d. a and b

9. If a driver takes a curve too fast, with the tires keeping their traction, and momentum will not allow the rig to turn, the result will be _____.

   a. a skid
   b. a safe turn
   c. a and b
   d. a rollover

10. In traffic, the safest speed is usually _____.

    a. faster than other vehicles
    b. the same speed as other vehicles
    c. slower than other vehicles
    d. two times the speed of the slowest vehicle

16 Night Driving

OBJECTIVES

When you have completed this chapter, you should be able to:

- Show how varying amounts of light affect your ability to see.
- Describe how and when to use high-beam headlights.
- Know the three factors that most affect night driving—the driver, the road, and the rig.
- Get your rig ready for night driving.
- Explain how headlight glare interferes with the vision of other drivers.
- Understand the importance of adequate sleep for safe night driving.

INTRODUCTION

Think about the last time you drove between the hours of dusk and dawn. You probably stopped around 6 P.M. or later and had a good meal. Then you climbed into your personal vehicle and hit the road.

Unfortunately, the first several hours after a meal are the ones where you will find yourself less alert and more fatigued than any other time . . . but there you were—after a meal, driving down the highway (probably going 60 to 70 mph) and drowsy. FYI—drowsiness makes driving more difficult because it dulls concentration and slows reaction time.

That evening meal—that one factor alone—makes driving at night more difficult and dangerous than any other time of the day. Why? Because eating a heavy meal makes you drowsy.

Why else is night driving so dangerous? One obvious answer is darkness. Ninety percent of a driver's reaction depends on vision, and vision is severely limited at night. Depth perception, color recognition, and peripheral vision are compromised after sundown.

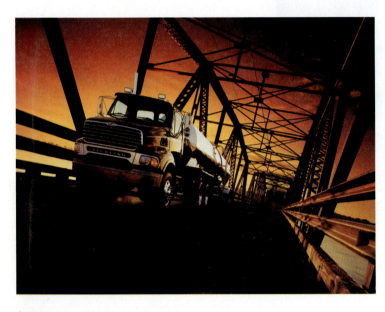

▶ Figure 16–1

Pay special attention when driving at night.

Traffic death rates are three times greater at night than during the day, according to the National Safety Council. Yet many of us are unaware of night driving's special hazards or the effective ways to deal with them.

Night driving problems require special attention from the professional driver in the form of changes for the following:

- Inspection routines
- Scan and visual search
- Communication
- Speed control
- Space management

This chapter discusses how to meet the special demands of driving safely at night **(see Figure 16–1).**

NIGHT DRIVING FACTORS

Why is night driving demanding?

First and foremost, because of the lack of daylight, it is more difficult to see at night. This isn't rocket science, but it is a factor you must always consider when you drive at night. Bottom line, your field of vision is limited at night.

Because there is less light and your vision is decreased, in order to see possible road hazards, you must be closer to them—which means less time to react and less space to maneuver defensively.

Not being aware of this simple fact causes more than one-half of all traffic accidents occurring between the hours of dusk and daylight **(see Figure 16–2).**

▶ Figure 16–2

Your field of vision is limited when there is less light.

CAUTION!

The following are quick reference rules for driving at night.

Beyond using courtesy and common sense, remember the following:

- Never overdrive your headlights. Always keep them clean and aimed properly. Use them at dusk and dawn. Bright lights must be dimmed 500 feet before meeting an oncoming vehicle or 300 feet before passing a vehicle.

- If street or freeway lights cause glare, dim your dashboard lights and use your sun visor. Avoid using any other light inside your vehicle.

- Roadway signs are more difficult to see at night.

- Use edge lines and center lines of the roadway as guides.

- Do not stop on the roadway. If you must stop, carry and use your four-way flashes and place your safety triangles on the roadway.

The four main factors that contribute to night driving problems are:

1. Driver
2. Road
3. Vehicle
4. Weather

The Driver

As a professional driver, you should be aware of the factors that affect your driving at night. These factors include vision, glare, fatigue, inadequate sleep, and lack of experience.

Vision—becomes more difficult at night. Your eyes need time to adjust to the change between daylight and darkness, but even after they adjust, your eyes cannot see as well at night as they can during the day. Objects are harder to identify, you cannot see as well to the sides of the rig, and your field of vision is severely limited at night.

Glare—often causes temporary blindness from oncoming headlights and other lights. As you may also realize, recovering from glare takes time. Unfortunately, while your eyes recover, you and your rig continue moving down the highway.

Fatigue—is always a concern when you drive, but it is more of a concern at night. Why? Because you do not see as clearly when you are tired and cannot react as quickly to what you see. As you become less alert, you are slower to see hazards and react even more slowly to avoid them.

Fatigue on the road can be a killer. It happens frequently on long drives, especially long night drives. You may have recognized some warning signs of fatigue, such as back tension, burning eyes, shallow breathing, inattentiveness, and any kind of erratic driving such as drifting, abnormal speed, tailgating, or failure to obey traffic signs.

Relieve fatigue by stopping and walking around your rig. If you still feel fatigued, stop and take a nap.

Inadequate sleep—often figures as a major problem with night driving. Consider this familiar scenario: You have been on the road a while. The highway seems endless. The cab's interior is warm and you are tired. You stare straight ahead, at miles and miles of road, as you start to feel your shoulders sag and your eyes slowly close.

Abruptly, you open your eyes, jerk up in your seat. You have started to drift out of your lane, or maybe even off the road. You steer back into the lane, take a few deep breaths, and realize, fearfully, what just happened. You were asleep.

- Thirty-seven percent of drivers have nodded off for at least a moment or fallen asleep while driving at least once in their driving career.

- Eight percent have done so in the past 6 months.

An obvious cause of fatigue is lack of sleep. Without 7 or 8 hours of sleep the night before a trip, you are courting fatigue. Get enough rest, and do not start a trip late in the day. Long-distance driving is hard work, and you need to be fresh and alert.

The only solution to inadequate sleep is *sleep*. Find a safe, guarded rest area, truck stop, or service station. Even a 20-minute nap may refresh you enough to get to a hotel or motel. (This is an emergency maneuver. Do not try it as a common driving technique.)

Safe driving demands your full attention. If you feel your eyelids getting heavy, then your next actions may not simply determine whether you will stay awake, but whether you will stay alive.

Lack of experience—as a professional driver and the problems of reduced vision, glare, and fatigue add up to the fact that new drivers have higher nighttime accident rates than more experienced drivers. In view of these statistics, learn to adjust your speed, space management, and driving techniques to match the demands of driving at night.

Road Conditions Affecting Night Driving

Several conditions affect night driving:

1. Weather
2. Low-level light at night
3. Changes in levels of light
4. Knowledge of the road
5. Other road users and their actions
6. Drivers under the influence of alcohol or drugs

Weather—whether it's a humid, sultry night where no position is comfortable or you're in the middle of a blizzard, weather is always a major factor in night driving. Fog, for example, is probably the least expected and the most frequent "surprise" road condition. Remember to use low beams and to reduce your speed in these conditions.

Driving in wet weather can also be equally demanding, not only because you are at a much higher risk of skidding or being unable to stop quickly, but you must also contend with the glare that comes from wet, rainy roads. Be prepared by lowering your speed and being alert for hazards in the road or erratic drivers around you.

Low-level light at night—usually comes from the headlights of vehicles on the road. Headlights are useful for a short and narrow path directly ahead of your vehicle. However, it is useful to remember that headlight beams do not bend around corners.

Changes in levels of light—causes you to continually adjust your eyes to different types and degrees of light. Flashing lights (and especially flashing neon lights) distract as much as they illuminate. Traffic signals are often hard to see against a background of other lights in towns and cities. Going through a business district in the rain, for example, can be difficult because of the extra glare created by the wet road surfaces. Your rig also may need extra stopping distance in this situation.

▶ **Figure 16–3**

Be alert for obstacles when working in darkened delivery areas and loading docks.

Poorly lit work areas—even if your driving skills at night are top notch, you must constantly be alert for obstacles in your work area if you have to deliver a load at night. Be aware of every step you take on a dark dock or a poorly lit delivery area. Safety should always be your first concern when working at night **(see Figure 16–3).**

Knowledge of the road—be extra alert on roads you have never driven before. Do not take even familiar roads for granted, however. Your view of the road will not be the same at night, so situations on the same road will also change.

Other road users—pedestrians, joggers, bicyclists, and animals, cannot see better than you can at night. They also cannot be seen as well at night as they can during the day. All are hazards you need to be aware of and should be looking for when you drive at night.

Drivers under the influence of alcohol or drugs—are always out there. Despite the efforts of Mothers Against Drunk Drivers and law enforcement agencies, there are always people driving under the influence. Your chance of meeting one of these folks increases after sundown. Keep this in mind when driving past roadside taverns and businesses such as liquor stores, strip clubs, or ballrooms and dance halls.

Driving Your Vehicle at Night

As a professional driver, it is your responsibility to make sure your rig is safe for night driving **(see Figure 16–4).** Be sure to check the following:

- Headlights
- Auxiliary lights
- Turn signals
- Windshield
- Side mirrors
- Rearview mirrors

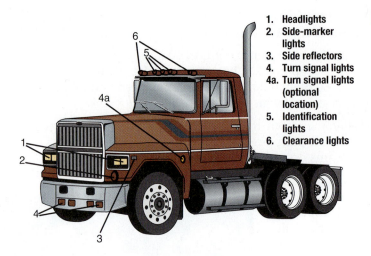

1. Headlights
2. Side-marker lights
3. Side reflectors
4. Turn signal lights
4a. Turn signal lights (optional location)
5. Identification lights
6. Clearance lights

▶ **Figure 16-4**

Your rig should be equipped with the proper tools to make driving at night less difficult.

Headlights

Your tractor's headlights are your first and best source of light on the road after sundown. They are also your rig's main signal of its location to other road users. Be sure your headlights are clean and properly adjusted at all times.

It goes without saying—the distance you can see ahead at night is much less than it is during the day. Low-beam headlights light a path of about 250 feet ahead of your rig (less than the length of a football field). High beams light 350 to 500 feet ahead.

Your **sight distance** is limited to the range your headlights provide. You must drive at a speed that allows you to stop within your sight distance. If your speed is greater than this, you are **overdriving** your headlights **(see Figure 16–5).** Driving within your headlights or sight distance is your best bet for avoiding accidents with objects or other road users **(see Figure 16–6).**

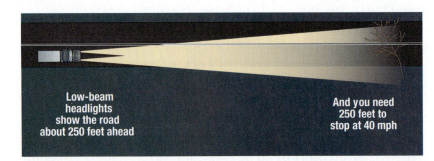

Low-beam headlights show the road about 250 feet ahead

And you need 250 feet to stop at 40 mph

▶ **Figure 16-5**

Never overdrive your headlights or sight distance.

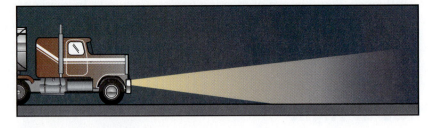

▶ **Figure 16-6**

Slow down so you can stop in the distance you can see ahead.

Auxiliary Lights

When all lights are working, big rigs are easily visible and can be seen by other road users **(see Figure 16–7).** The following **auxiliary lights** must be cleaned regularly and kept in working order:

- Auxiliary lights
- Reflectors
- Clearance lights
- Identification (ID) lights
- Tail lights
- Brake lights

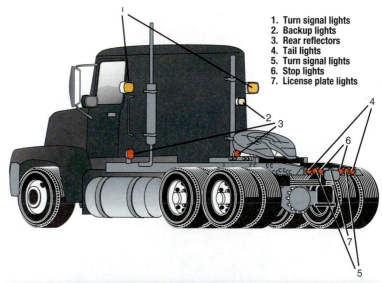

Figure 16-7

Auxiliary lights on your rig make it easier for others to see you at night.

1. Turn signal lights
2. Backup lights
3. Rear reflectors
4. Tail lights
5. Turn signal lights
6. Stop lights
7. License plate lights

Turn Signals

Turn signal lights are key signals to other drivers of your intentions. How well you communicate with other drivers depends on your turn signals **(see Figure 16–8).** Turn signals that are not working or dirty do not allow you to signal your intent on the highway, and will increase your risk for accidents.

Windshield

A clean windshield is a must for safe driving during the day or night **(see Figure 16–9).** If a clean windshield shuts out 5 percent of the available light, think about how much light is blocked by a dirty windshield, plus it can cut your ability to see and relate to traffic. Clean the outside and inside of your windshield before each trip so that you can see as well as possible.

Mirrors

Mirrors help you see what is going on around you. Unless you can see the other vehicles, you cannot relate to them. Be sure to keep your mirrors clean and properly adjust them before each trip and after each stop.

NIGHT DRIVING PROCEDURES

Before attempting to drive at night, the first step is to prepare yourself and your rig.

If you wear glasses, make certain you have regular, annual checkups and testing to keep your lens prescription up to date. Also make certain your glasses are clean. Dirty or scratched lenses increase the effects of glare.

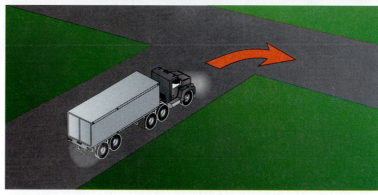

Figure 16-8

Turn signals assist in communicating with other roadway users at night.

Figure 16-9

A clean windshield and wipers that function are a must for safe driving at night.

▶ *"They told me to never drive at night without a flashlight, but this is ridiculous!"*

The next step of your preparation for driving at night is to plan your route. Know where the rest stops are located. Think ahead about any known hazards or construction areas along your route. Know the locations for unlighted areas of the road, exit ramps, and construction areas. Then, always expect changes—and keep your eyes open for these.

Check all lights on your rig during your pretrip inspection. Clean all lights and mirrors, and replace lights that are not working. Never go on the road with a malfunctioning light.

Avoid Blinding Other Drivers

Headlight glare from oncoming and following vehicles can be a problem for every driver on the highway.

The FMCSR state that a driver must dim his headlights 500 feet before encountering an oncoming vehicle. This regulation not only meets all state laws, but it also makes sense to be considerate on the highway. If your headlights make it hard for an oncoming driver to see, then you and your rig are also in danger.

Dim your headlights before they impair the vision of other drivers. Although not required by the FMCSR, you should also dim your headlights 200 feet before overtaking another vehicle. In addition to eliminating a road rage situation, this action also complies with most state laws.

Avoid Blinding Yourself

To facilitate night driving, keep your cab as dark as possible. Adjust your instrument panel lights to a low level, yet make sure they are bright enough to read easily.

Use high-beam headlights only when it is safe and legal to do so. Many drivers make it a habit to always drive with low beams at night, but this can seriously cut down their vision. Always try to give yourself the best night vision **(see Figure 16–10).** Take advantage of headlights from the vehicles ahead to spot hazards, and let road signs and reflectors act as visual guides.

NIGHT DRIVING ADJUSTMENTS

To drive safely at night, the driver must modify some basic daytime driving techniques.

Communicating—make sure you signal to reduce speed, stop, or turn in plenty of time. It is wise to signal earlier than you would during daylight conditions. Check to make sure your tail lights, backup lights, and turn signals are in working order before each trip and before leaving each stop.

Signal your presence because eye contact is not possible at night. Light use of the horn can be helpful. Never hurt the vision of others by using your headlights to signal a lane change or other maneuver.

Space—because you cannot see as well or as far at night, you need more time to react to events around your rig. Get the needed time by increasing the space around your rig **(see Figure 16–11).** Increase your following distance at night by at least 1 second more than the normal daytime following distance.

Speed—adjust your rig's speed to keep the stopping distance within your sight distance. Do not overdrive your headlights. A lower speed is needed to keep from hitting objects when they suddenly come into view. If you do not adjust your speed to nighttime conditions, you will have too little time and too little space to safely react to hazards **(see Figure 16–12).**

Use high beams when safe and legal to do so

▶ **Figure 16–10**

Use high beams when they will not impact visual fields of oncoming drivers.

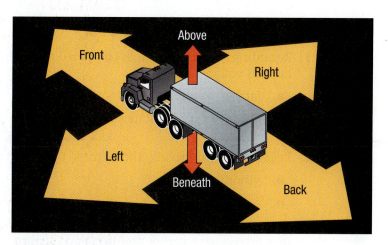

▶ **Figure 16–11**

Managing the space around your rig is more crucial at night.

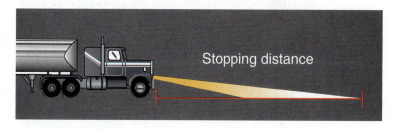

Stopping distance

▶ **Figure 16–12**

Appropriate speeds keep your rig's stopping distance within your sight distance.

SUMMARY

In this chapter, you have learned the many differences between driving during daylight hours and driving from dusk to dawn. You have learned that inspection routines must be altered and that communication with other drivers must be done by signaling because you do not have eye contact with them at night.

You have also learned that you must slow down so that you will be able to stop within the distance you can clearly see ahead. The reasons for allowing more space around your rig and between you and other highway users were explained.

Finally, you learned that adequate sleep is immensely important for safe night driving and that changes while driving at night are made for safety reasons. As a responsible professional, you will want to create the safest road conditions possible for yourself and for other drivers.

KEY TERMS

Auxiliary lights   Overdriving   Turn signal lights
Fatigue   Sight distance   Vision
Glare

REVIEW QUESTIONS

1. Regarding seeing at night, as compared to seeing in daylight, in order to see possible hazards you must be_____.

   a. farther from them   **c.** not a, b, or d

   b. about the same distance as in daylight   **d.** closer to them

2. Regarding night driving, the factor(s) that affect(s) night driving is(are) _____.

   a. vision   **c.** glare

   b. a, c, and d   **d.** fatigue

3. Lack of experience driving a rig and the problem(s) of _____ add(s) up to the fact that new drivers have higher nighttime accident rates than more experienced drivers.

   a. vision, glare, and fatigue   **c.** brake lag time

   b. stopping distance   **d.** center of gravity

4. After sundown, when driving past taverns, liquor stores, or similar businesses, the chances of _____ increases.

   a. stopping distance   **c.** reaction time

   b. meeting a driver under the influence of drugs or alcohol   **d.** brake lag time

5. The range of vision your headlights provide is your _____ distance.

   a. stomping   **c.** sight

   b. reaction   **d.** brake lag

6. At night if one is driving at such a speed that the rig cannot be stopped within the driver's sight distance, then the driver is said to be overdriving _____.

    a. the brake lag time

    b. the driver's reaction time

    c. his headlights

    d. the center of gravity of the trailer

7. Auxiliary lights, such as marker and clearance lights on a rig, _____.

    a. make it easier for others to see your rig at night

    b. because of the glare they produce make it more difficult for others to see your rig at night

    c. increase reaction distance

    d. increase brake lag time

8. The FMCSR state that a driver must dim his or her headlights _____ before encountering an oncoming vehicle.

    a. 500 yards

    b. 1,000 feet

    c. 1,000 yards

    d. 500 feet

9. Regarding lights inside the cab of a rig at night, the _____ the inside of a cab, the harder it is to see outside.

    a. darker

    b. brake lag time increases if it is darker inside the cab

    c. brighter

    d. a and b

10. Regarding space around your rig, at night a driver should increase his or her following distance by at least _____ more than normal daytime following distance.

    a. 10 seconds

    b. 1 second

    c. 1 minute

    d. 15 seconds

17

Extreme Driving Conditions

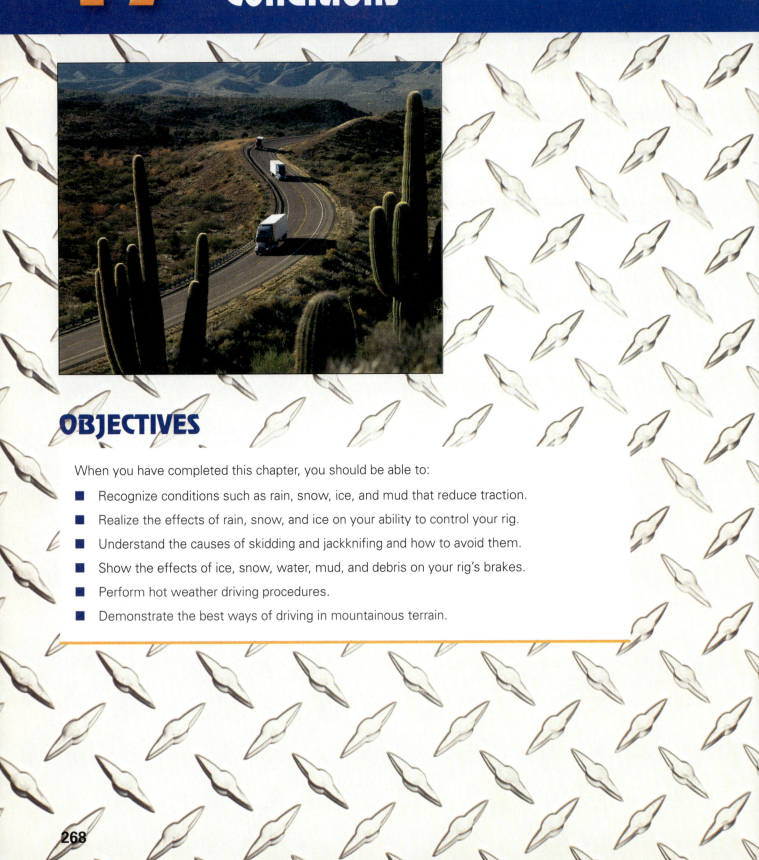

OBJECTIVES

When you have completed this chapter, you should be able to:

- Recognize conditions such as rain, snow, ice, and mud that reduce traction.
- Realize the effects of rain, snow, and ice on your ability to control your rig.
- Understand the causes of skidding and jackknifing and how to avoid them.
- Show the effects of ice, snow, water, mud, and debris on your rig's brakes.
- Perform hot weather driving procedures.
- Demonstrate the best ways of driving in mountainous terrain.

INTRODUCTION

The words **extreme driving conditions** are familiar to every driver, and you have probably heard them many times, but what do they really mean?

Figure 17–1

Extreme driving conditions mean driving in the most difficult of circumstances—cold, wet, icy, hot, foggy, etc.

"Extreme" means the worst. The term *"extreme"* refers to the most difficult of anything—extreme sports, extreme poverty, extreme—the worst you can find in any category. So, what are the worst driving conditions? That means driving when it is cold, wet, icy, dry, hot, snowing, high winds or foggy conditions. Driving in mountain ranges and across the desert is also considered extreme driving conditions.

Be aware you cannot learn how to drive in all of these extreme conditions by reading a book or sitting in a classroom. On the other hand, before you encounter extreme driving conditions of any type, it may be good to have some tips and other information under your belt **(see Figure 17–1).** You never know when it will come in handy, so keep reading, and read carefully.

EXTREME WEATHER

Knowing your way around your rig, including its parts and its systems, is the first step in preparing yourself for driving in extreme conditions. Reduced **traction** and poor **visibility** are two major safety hazards that occur in extreme conditions. Less traction increases the stopping distance and decreases the driver's ability to control the rig. Reduced visibility means you will not see hazards as quickly and you will have less time to respond to anything up ahead.

Vehicle Checks

Be sure both you and your rig are ready and equipped to drive into extreme weather conditions. If you are not ready or are unsure, then stay put. Make a thorough pretrip inspection **(see Figure 17–2).** Your pretrip inspection should include a check of the following:

Coolant level and antifreeze concentration—make sure the coolant system is full because a low coolant level affects operation of the heater and defroster as well as engine performance.

Heating equipment—a poorly heated cab can reduce your performance efficiency. Check the heater hose for wear as well as the controls and fans. Also check window defrosters.

Wipers/washers—check for cracks, collapsed areas, and loose clamps. Make sure reservoir is full and fluid is not frozen. In cold weather, add antifreeze and make sure wipers are in top shape and working order.

Tires—check mountings and look for flaws on sidewalls or treads. Check air pressure with tire pressure gauge. Make sure tires are properly inflated and tread depth is safe. Tires must have enough traction to easily push the rig over wet pavement or through snow.

SPECIAL EXTREME WEATHER CHECKLIST FOR PRETRIP INSPECTION

- Coolant and antifreeze
- Heater/defroster
- Wipers/washers
- Tires
- Chains
- Brakes
- Lights and reflectors
- Windows and mirrors
- Hand and toe holds

- Radiator shutters and winter fronts
- Exposed wiring and air lines
- Fuel tank
- Engine and exhaust systems
- Coupling devices
- Interaxle differential lock
- Emergency equipment
- Weather reports and road conditions

▶ **Figure 17–2**

Extreme weather conditions will change your pretrip inspection priorities.

Chains—some states require chains during certain periods of the year. Know these states and their chain laws. Carry the correct number of chains and make certain they are in working order. Watch for broken hooks, worn or broken cross links, and bent or broken side chains.

Brakes—they should apply pressure equally and at the same time. If one wheel stops turning before the others, it may cause a skid or other handling problem. Check brake linings for ice, which can cut the braking power. Finally, drain the moisture from tractor and trailer air tanks, because water in the lines can cause the brakes to freeze.

Lights and reflectors—make sure the lights and reflectors are free of mud or dirt, not broken or bent. How well you see and how well others see you depends on the lights and reflectors being in top shape.

Radiator, shutter, and winter front—remove any ice from the winter front which can keep shutters from opening and cause the engine to overheat. If the engine overheats, then you may need to adjust the shutters on your winter front. Close them if the engine is too cold.

Wiring and air lines—be sure all wiring and lines are properly supported and remove any ice or snow before and during the trip. Buildup can cause lines to sag and eventually snap.

Fuel tank—be sure the fuel tank is full before you begin a trip. If extreme weather is expected, top off your tank frequently. Beware of low-quality fuel that can gel in cold weather. It is wise to fill the tank at the end of the trip to reduce moisture buildup. Drain water from the bottom of the fuel tank. Ice buildup on a crossover line can freeze or break the line between fuel tanks.

Engine and exhaust system—keep exhaust connections tight to prevent carbon monoxide from leaking into the rig.

Coupling devices—make sure the fifth wheel is coated with a winter grade lubricant to prevent binding. This also will help steering on icy or wet slippery roads.

Interaxle differential lock—do not lock or unlock while wheels are spinning (see Figure 17–3).

Emergency equipment—have proper clothing, extra food, water, gloves, an extra blanket or two, and a new battery in your cell phone when driving into extreme weather. You should also have a scraper, snow brush, small folding shovel, triangles, and a fire extinguisher.

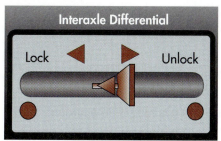

Interaxle Differential

Lock ◄ ► Unlock

Lock
Wheels have to be locked before driving on a slippery surface and before they start to spin.

Unlock
Normal position.

▶ **Figure 17-3**

If your rig has an interaxle differential lock, operate it according to directions in the owner's manual.

▶ *"I knew I forgot something when I left the terminal."*

Weather reports and road conditions—through your dispatcher you can receive The Weather Channel, NOAA weather radio, 5-1-1 phone, and Internet services offered by local radio and television stations. These are reliable sources for current weather information. Mountain passes have additional information sources, and truck stops on either side of major passes have pass boards at the fuel desk. Local authorities fax current conditions for posting on the board. Some states such as Oregon have live road cams of the passes showing at the truck stops. Idaho broadcasts pass conditions on CB channel 19.

Tire Chains

Tire chains are a must for driving in snow, ice, or extreme winter conditions, mainly because they prevent skidding and increase your rig's pulling and braking power. Chains can increase traction by as much as 500 percent. Mount tire chains at the first sign of snow—you will probably need reinforced chains for long periods of extreme driving.

When to Use Chains

Many states have specific rules about when to use chains. Some states require chains be carried in the truck during certain months. Other states have laws that indicate where chains must be installed on the rig. In some western states, the locations of tire chains on the rig will vary from region to region. It is the professional driver's job to know these regulations.

A chain control area is a highway area where it is illegal to drive without chains. Checkpoints are usually set up ahead of these areas, where trucks are stopped to see that the proper number of chains are on board. If not, the inspector will not allow the rig into the chain control area. This could mean costly downtime.

When you see the warning, "Chains advised," you have the choice of whether to drive using tire chains. Be extremely careful in these areas. There can be large fines if you spin out, jackknife, or block the highway because you did not have snow chains.

States with Chain Laws

Chain laws vary from state to state. Some states have outlawed the use of tire chains because of the wear and tear they cause on their highways. Heavy-snow states, however, have strict laws regarding carrying and using tire chains and impose penalties on truckers who are not equipped with the right number and right-sized tire chains. The following is a partial listing of general laws regarding tire chains:

California—does not require CMV drivers to carry chains, but if you do not have them in a tire chain control zone, you will be stopped until it is determined it is safe to travel.

Colorado—CMV drivers who fail to carry tire chains are fined $100. If an accident occurs that blocks the highway, another $500 fine is levied as well as a $60 surcharge.

Montana—use chains when indicated by highway signs. The minimum required are chains on the drive wheel of one axle.

Nevada—CMV drivers are required to carry tire chains for two wheels of the drive axle and two braking wheels of the trailer.

Oregon—chains are required for all vehicles in bad weather. This "conditional road closure" covers all Oregon highways and the chain law goes into effect when icy conditions exist. The fine for not having tire chains in these conditions is $165 and is classified as a Class C traffic infraction.

South Dakota—will post travel restrictions, allowing only vehicles with chains to move on state highways.

Utah—has no chain laws but suggests CMV drivers carry chains for their own safety between November 1 and March 31.

Washington—CMV drivers must carry chains at all times between November 1 and March 31. If you do not have chains, you will be fined $100. If you fail to put on the chains, a mandatory court appearance is required.

Wyoming—in icy weather, travel may be restricted to all-wheel-drive vehicles or motor vehicles equipped with tire chains.

Idaho, Iowa, Minnesota, North Dakota, and Wisconsin—no chain laws are currently on the books. Law enforcement officials in Wisconsin, however, prefer CMV drivers to use chains in icy conditions.

Safety When Installing Chains

Never forget your personal safety, the safety of your rig, and the safety of others when putting on tire chains. In many states, "chain-up" areas are provided for this task and some have Department of Transportation officers on site to make certain your chains have been installed properly.

When you are installing your chains, make certain you are in a safe and secure place, away from highway traffic. Note the following when preparing to put on snow chains:

- Pull well off the road.
- Park on a level, solid surface.
- Be careful because walking can be difficult on a snowy or icy surface.
- Be sure to put the chains on, right side out.
- Be sure to put a chain on the left rear trailer tire to help hold the trailer on the highway.

How to Install Chains

Many professional drivers prefer to have an experienced installer put on tire chains. However, the following steps provide a general guideline:

1. Put on your vehicle's emergency brake to make sure it does not roll or slide.
2. Wear heavy gloves.
3. The tighter the chains are installed, the longer they and the tires will last.

4. Check inflation pressure before installing chains.

5. Lay the chains flat on the ground so that each side is parallel. Make sure there are no twists in the chain links and the wire locks are on the outside.

6. Drape the chains up and over the top of each tire, keeping the J-hook on the inside. Make sure the smooth side of the cross-member hook ends are facing away from the tire.

7. Release the emergency brake and move rig forward slowly until the wire lock is roughly axle high.

8. Apply the emergency brake.

9. Hook up the outer side chains by tugging firmly on both ends of the outer side chain to remove slack.

10. Thread the wire lock through a link.

11. Fasten the J-hook by inserting it through the side cross link from the other end of the side chain. Pull the slack toward the outside edge of the tire.

12. Drive one-quarter mile and retighten as necessary to remove slack.

STARTING YOUR ENGINE IN COLD WEATHER

In the winter, all engines are more difficult to start. The lower the temperature, the more difficult it is. Big rigs are no exception. There are, however, certain devices that can be helpful in getting an engine started, even in the coldest weather:

- Special starting substances, like ether or ether-based fluid
- Glow plugs
- Preheaters

Ether

Ether has a very low flash point. It ignites easily, even in subzero temperatures. Since it is such a high energy fuel, using ether has a few drawbacks. If not used properly or used too often, ether can damage the engine by cracking cylinder heads, breaking pistons, or snapping connecting rods.

NOTE: Most motor carriers do not recommend or allow ether on their units because it causes over-revs and blown engines when not used correctly.

CAUTION!

Ether is highly flammable. If you spill any on your clothing, change immediately. Stay away from open flames, matches, cigarettes, or hot exhaust pipes and heaters. They could cause your clothing to ignite.

Ether is packaged in aerosol cans, pressurized cylinders, driver-controlled injection systems, or capsules. These can be applied manually and automatically.

Aerosol spray cans, capsules, and pressurized cylinders are used manually. The capsules can be placed in a special holder attached to the air cleaner. Each capsule is good for one start. They also require only one person to start the engine.

Aerosol spray cans and pressurized cylinders require two people to start the engine. One person sprays ether into a rag in front of the air cleaner while the other person starts the engine. Be cautious, however, because too much spray may cause flashback fire or engine damage.

Automatic injection systems need only the driver to start the engine. Ether is put into the engine in one of two ways. The driver turns on a switch in the cab and ether is injected into the engine, or ether is injected automatically when the engine is started.

The automatic injection system should not be used with aerosol ether.

Glow Plugs

Glow plugs are simply electric heating elements that warm the air coming into the engine from the air intake. They can be mounted in the intake manifold or in each combustion chamber. On diesel engines, they are sometimes located in the precombustion chamber. They raise the temperature in the chamber and it is the hot, compressed air that ignites the fuel. This usually takes about 60 seconds.

STOP!

Never use ether and glow plugs at the same time!

Preheaters

Preheaters keep the engine warm while parked for the night. Of the two types, in-block and immersion, most of the preheaters used are the in-block type. They fit into the freeze plug holes in the lower water jacket. The other end of the preheaters heats the coolant to approximately 160 degrees F, which is near normal operating temperature. The coolant circulates through the engine and keeps it warm. The immersion type of preheater is used on off-highway construction vehicles and mining equipment.

AN ENGINE THAT WILL NOT START

If your engine will not start when you use starting aids, check to be sure the engine is getting fuel. To do this, check your rear-view mirror to see if vapor or smoke is visible from the exhaust stack. Check the fuel tanks and the fuel lines to be sure they are not blocked by ice or gelled fuel, and check the fuel tank vent.

STOP!

Do not crank the engine if it is not getting fuel. This will only run down the battery.

Never crank the engine more than 15 seconds at a time. If the engine is getting fuel and still will not start, check the electrical system. If the rig has an electrical starter, remember the battery does not operate at full capacity in cold weather. The battery must be in the best possible condition. Check for the following:

- Corrosion on the terminals
- Loose connections
- Cracks in the cables
- Moisture in the cables

If the rig has an air starter, the engine will not start unless there is an air supply. If there is no air, the air supply can be restored from another tractor or an air compressor.

BAD WEATHER OPERATING HAZARDS

The two major hazards when driving in bad weather are reduced visibility and reduced traction **(see Figure 17–4).**

PRIMARY HAZARDS

Reduced visibility

Reduced traction

- Road surface
    — Different surfaces, different degrees of traction
    — Be aware of changing conditions
- Speed
    — Speed magnifies mistakes
    — Determine the speed at which the wheels roll without spinning
    — Adjust speed to changing road surfaces and conditions

▶ **Figure 17-4**

The two major driving hazards in bad weather are lower visibility and less traction.

Reduced Visibility

When ice and snow build up on windows and mirrors, your visibility is reduced and you cannot see the driving environment around you as well. When this happens, you must stop and clean windows and mirrors. Do not drive with your side or rear-view mirrors blocked. All lights and reflectors should also be free of ice, snow, mud, and dirt. Stop and clean them when needed. Some states will issue a citation for a dirty windshield. Even when your windows, lights, and reflectors are clean, your visibility is sometimes limited by rain, snow, or fog. Slow down and drive carefully.

STOP!

Sometimes visibility can be almost zero. This happens at night in heavy snow, a downpour, or dense fog. Driving is not safe under these conditions. Stop and wait until your visibility improves before continuing.

Reduced Traction

As you will recall, the definition for *traction* is the grip or friction created between your rig's tires and the pavement. Different surfaces offer different amounts of traction. Some states use asphalt for roads that reduce spray and hydroplaning when wet. If there is ice or packed snow, about 80 percent of your traction is lost.

Slippery roads due to rain, sleet, ice, or snow will cause drive wheels to spin easily. This often results in less traction and, therefore, less control of the rig. As you drive, be aware of changing conditions. To check traction, periodically put on your brakes.

Proper tire inflation, tread, and weight on the drive wheels provides better traction and better control of your rig.

Speed is another factor in the traction equation. As the rig's speed increases, traction decreases. When traction is poor—for any reason—slow down until you have the rig well under control.

If the road is wet, reduce your speed by one fourth. If you are driving 55 mph, slow to 40 mph. On packed snow and icy surfaces, stop your vehicle. Do not attempt to drive on these extremely dangerous surfaces. If you are forced to drive on snow or ice, cut your speed to about one third the normal speed, or around 18 mph.

Remember—these are only general guidelines. Your exact speed should be determined by how much control you have of your rig. If that requires going slower than the general guidelines, go slower.

The following are also factors for determining a safe speed:

- Weight of rig
- Type of rig
- Condition of tires
- Type of road surface
- Temperature
- Type of precipitation

It is important to mention black ice in this section. Black ice is so clear you can see the road surface beneath it. It usually is difficult to spot but is often found on bridges, in dips in the road, beneath overpasses, in shaded areas, and on the lower sides of banked curves.

Black ice is also hard to spot at night. If a driver is not aware of black ice, it can be very dangerous.

When driving in sleet, check the front of your mirror for ice. If there is buildup of ice on the front of your mirror, then there is probably ice on the road and the safest option is to park your truck.

Skidding

The four basic causes for **skidding,** when tires lose traction on the road, are:

1. Driving too fast
2. Overacceleration
3. Overbraking
4. Oversteering

Driving too fast for road conditions causes most of the serious skids. Drivers who adjust their driving to the conditions do not overaccelerate and do not have to overbrake or oversteer because of too much speed.

Overbraking means braking too hard for the surface conditions. Excessive use of the service brakes is one cause of overbraking. Suddenly releasing the fuel pedal can also cause a braking effect that throws the rig into a skid. Skids also can be caused by using the engine brake incorrectly or downshifting to a gear lower than the speed requires. Drivers tend to overbrake when they drive too fast for the conditions, do not look far enough ahead, or do not leave enough following distance.

Oversteering occurs when a driver tries to round a turn too fast and turn the steering wheel too quickly. The drive wheels naturally want to continue to move straight ahead. Then, there is too little grip between the tires and the road. The result is a skidding trailer and a tractor-trailer jackknife.

Jackknifing

When the drive wheels lose traction, they cause the tractor-trailer to skid. This skid can result in a **jackknife.** Be careful not to make things worse by putting on the brakes or adding power in a skid **(see Figure 17–5).**

SKIDDING AND JACKKNIFING	
Causes	
■ Overacceleration	■ Oversteering
■ Overbraking	■ Speed too fast for conditions

▶ **Figure 17–5**

Four primary causes of skidding and jackknifing.

DRIVING IN BAD WEATHER

Professional drivers soon learn that trips in bad weather take longer than driving the same distance under good weather and road conditions. This section focuses on driving on slippery surfaces and the problem with wet brakes.

Driving on Slippery Surfaces

Take the following precautions on slippery surfaces:

■ Start slowly. At the beginning of your trip, take your time so you can get a feel for the road. Do not hurry.

■ Adjust your turning and braking to the conditions. Make turns as gradually as possible. Avoid braking any harder than necessary. Do not use the engine brake, if possible **(see Figure 17–6).**

■ Check your mirrors for the trailer when you brake, to be sure it is not drifting to one side. You can prevent a jackknife by acting when there is still time to recover.

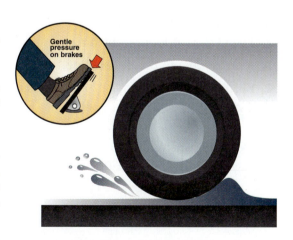

Gentle pressure on brakes

▶ **Figure 17–6**

If your rig has antilock brakes, apply them and hold for safest stop.

■ At night, if your trailer's lights begin to show in your mirror, it may mean the trailer is jackknifing.

■ Adjust speed to the conditions. Do not overtake and pass other vehicles unless you have to, and slow to a safe speed.

■ Watch far enough ahead to flow with the traffic, to help you avoid the need to change speeds rapidly.

■ Take curves and turns at slower speeds than usual. Brake before curves. Be sure you are in the right gear before you enter a curve. Speed up slightly in the curve.

■ As it gets warmer, ice melts and becomes more slippery. Slow down even more, if necessary.

■ Avoid driving beside other vehicles, and stay out of packs and caravans.

■ Maintain longer following distance.

■ When traffic ahead looks congested, fall back. Stop, if necessary, and wait for traffic to thin out.

■ Plan ahead for stops. Avoid panic stopping.

■ Do not pump antilock brakes. Apply them and hold to provide the safest stop.

Wet Brakes

When you drive in heavy rain or deep standing water, the brakes will get wet. Then the linings may slip on the drum or disc and cause uneven braking. The final result can be loss of brakes, wheel lockup, veering from one side of the lane to another, or a jackknife.

Avoid standing water when possible; however, if you must drive through water, follow these steps:

1. Slow down.
2. Shift to a lower gear.
3. Place your left foot lightly on the brake.
4. Increase engine speed (rpm).
5. Accelerate through the water.

After you are out of the water, do the following:

1. Stay in low gear.
2. Keep your left foot on the brake.
3. Increase rpm to prevent stalling.
4. Keep light pressure on the brakes for a short distance to dry them out.
5. Release the brakes.

Check the rear of your rig to make sure no one is following too closely. Then, make a test stop to be certain your brakes are working properly.

Summary: Bad Weather Operation

All drivers and rigs have limits. As a professional driver, one of your duties is to know these limits and adjust your driving to the changing conditions. The best way to avoid accidents in bad weather is to adjust your speed, braking, steering, and space cushion. When it is too dangerous to drive, stop and wait until conditions improve and are safe for driving.

A Vehicle That Becomes Stuck

The best advice concerning a stuck vehicle is—DON'T GET STUCK! You can sometimes keep from getting stuck by smarter driving.

STOP!

Stay away from situations that can cause a rig to get stuck, such as soft dirt on the roadside, deep snow, mud, ice, and slippery highways.

When in doubt, avoid any unknown or suspicious surfaces. Be alert when you leave the main road to make a delivery or when you pull off the road for rest, repair, or a vehicle check.

Freeing a Stuck Rig

To free a stuck rig, follow these steps:

1. Do not spin the drive tires or rock back and forth. These actions will dig the vehicle in more. On ice, spinning the wheels will cause heat. This will warm the ice under the tires and reduce traction by about 50 percent.

2. Use traction aids—dig under the front of the drive wheels and scatter sand or gravel in their path.

3. Lock the interaxle differential (if your rig has one).

4. Use a low gear, such as second or third gear. This will keep the wheels from spinning by reducing the force and applying it smoothly.

5. Start with the steering wheels straight ahead. If you have to start with the wheels turned, accelerate gently. Turn the steering wheel back and forth gently (less than an inch) to prepare a path for the wheels.

6. As you begin to move, accelerate gently and smoothly. Ease off the accelerator if you start to slide.

GO!

Avoid:
- Soft berms
- Deep snow
- Muddy roads

When stuck:
- Do not spin wheels
- Use traction aids
- Lock interaxle differential
- Place in higher gear
- Accelerate gradually

When using a tow truck, remember:
- You are responsible for your vehicle and your cargo
- Maintain control of the operation
- Stay informed during all steps of the towing operation

Towing

If your efforts to free your rig fail, call a tow truck. Remember that you are responsible for the equipment and the cargo, so you should be available to help supervise the towing operation.

Agree on a procedure before the operation is underway. Ask questions before the operation begins to free your rig, such as:

- In what direction will the tow truck pull the rig?
- In what direction should you steer, if this is needed?
- When is the tow truck to stop?

If Your Rig Breaks Down in a Remote Area

If your rig breaks down in a remote area or you are stranded in a remote area because of bad weather conditions, stay in your cab. Being out in the wind and cold can be dangerous. Put on extra clothing to stay warm. Do not try to hike for help. You may not make it or may become disoriented in heavy snow or rain. Stay with your rig so you can move it if it needs to be towed out of deep snow or mud.

If you must leave your rig for any reason, attach a note to the steering wheel stating the time you left the rig and which direction you went.

CAUTION!

If your rig is stuck but the engine is operational, do not allow exhaust fumes to collect in the cab. Keep a window open slightly.

Smart professionals are always prepared for emergencies when bad weather is expected by carrying a supply of drinking water, candy bars, fruit, blankets, extra clothing, and toilet paper.

DRIVING IN HOT WEATHER

In hot weather, it is particularly important for your rig to be in top condition and you to be prepared for the worst conditions. Watch the following areas carefully while driving in hot summer weather:

Vehicle inspection—an important driver preparation task. You are the one who will be out on the highway with your rig, so make sure you know how to deal with severe heat. Also make certain your rig, its systems, and all its equipment can stand the heat.

Tires—check mounting and inflation (see **Figure 17–7**). If you are hauling hazmat, inspect tires every 2 hours or 100 miles; if

▶ **Figure 17–7**

In hot weather, check tires, mounting, and inflation to guard against blowouts or fire.

you are not hauling hazmat, inspect tires every 3 hours or 150 miles. An increase of 10 to 15 psi is common. Check the heat of the tire with the back of your hand. If the tire pressure increases more than 15 psi or the tire becomes extremely hot when you test it, stop driving. The tire could blow out or catch fire. Let the tires cool off.

STOP!

Never bleed air from tires when they are hot. Let them cool and then recheck the pressure.

Engine lubrication—oil helps cool the engine. Keeping the oil at the proper level is mandatory at all times, but particularly in hot weather. Check the oil level before you start each trip and often while en route. Check the oil temperature gauge regularly.

Engine coolant system—although big and powerful, engines are also quite delicate. They need heat to run, but too much heat can damage them quickly. The engine coolant system is vital to proper engine operation and should be kept full and clean. Also watch your water temperature gauge **(see Figure 17–8).**

Some types of engines tend to run warmer than others, so always carry extra coolant. If you must add coolant, allow the engine to cool first. Then run the engine at high enough rpm to circulate the fluid. Very carefully remove the coolant reservoir cap with a heavy rag. Keep your face and body clear because the coolant may spray. Add new coolant slowly.

Engine belts—check belt tension. Then check for fraying, cracking, or wear. Slipping belts can cause the fan or water pump to stop operating, which will result in an overheated engine.

▶ **Figure 17–8**

In warm weather, check your water temperature gauge often.

Hoses—check for cracks, fraying, and kinks. Be sure hoses do not collapse when the engine accelerates. Coolant must circulate freely to keep the engine operating at peak performance and the right temperature.

DRIVING IN THE DESERT

To some people, the desert contains a unique beauty. To others, it is a vast expanse of sand and rock. Regardless, the desert does have certain characteristics all professional drivers should know and understand.

Washes—these are secondary roads often built through dry riverbeds. During heavy rains, these roads, or washes, can flood quickly. When it looks like rain, get to the main road as soon as possible.

Bleeding tar—tar used to pave roads comes to the surface in hot weather. Spots where tar is bleeding can become very slippery. Watch for these areas and avoid them when possible.

High speeds—often happen unintentionally after driving over long, flat desert roads for long periods of time. Keep an eye on your speedometer.

Vehicle breakdown—when breakdowns occur in remote areas, do not leave your vehicle. Use your dispatcher or your cell phone to communicate your position and your situation. Sit under the trailer, out of the sun, while awaiting help to arrive. Drink plenty of fluids if they are available to avoid dehydration.

MOUNTAIN DRIVING

Mountain driving is different from other driving conditions, and there are a number of considerations to keep in mind when driving through mountainous terrain. First, you and your rig must deal with gravity—the force that pulls objects toward the center of the earth. Gravity also changes normal driving patterns. No matter whether you are going uphill or down a grade, the pull of gravity is so severe you must adjust your driving.

CAUTION!

Failing to make adjustments in your driving style while driving in the mountains can make your trip more difficult and more tiring. You also may damage your rig.

When you climb a grade, gravity adds to the weight of the load. This pulls the rig down and takes more horsepower to move the rig. It is also difficult to pass other vehicles when climbing a hill.

When you go downhill, gravity pulls the rig forward **(see Figure 17–9)**. This increases forward momentum. If the grade is steep, gravity can pull the vehicle off the road on curves, bumps, or loose gravel.

Inspections

Before driving in the mountains, it is important to inspect the following to maintain a high level of safety:

- Check the air brake system carefully.
- Make sure the compressor can maintain full reservoir pressure.
- Be sure the pressure drop when brakes are fully applied is within normal limits.
- Look for ice buildup on service brakes.
- Check for correct adjustments on slack adjusters.
- Listen for air leaks—check when brakes are both on and off.
- Make sure glad hands and air lines are secure.
- Check brake drums for overheating, but do not touch the drum. Hold the back of your hand close to the drum. Some heat is normal, but high heat is not.
- Be sure the trailer supply valve is working.

Figure 17-9

In mountain driving, gravity requires adjustments to normal driving patterns.

TRUCKS
GEAR
DOWN

FOR
NEXT
5
MILES

ALLOW ENGINE COMPRESSION
AND FRICTION TO HELP
SLOW YOUR VEHICLE

When Driving on Upgrades

Shifting—when rpm falls, downshift to the next lower gear. Gravity cuts your speed during the downshift. Complete the shift quickly before the rpm reaches the bottom of the range. Downshift until you reach the gear necessary to maintain the rpm.

Position—drive upgrades with patience. Move your rig to the far right truck lane. Stay in this lane and do not try to pass if you cannot do so quickly and safely.

CAUTION!

Remember, a slow uphill truck creates a negative reaction about the entire transportation industry in the minds of other road users. Other drivers may lose patience and make reckless moves. Don't be tempted to follow their lead.

STOP!

Most states require vehicles to use four-way flashers when driving at speeds under 40 mph.

Watch your gauges—pulling a heavy load on a long grade can cause overheating. Check the coolant and water temperature gauges often. Shift a few hundred rpm earlier than the lowest rpm for that gear to help compensate.

When Driving on Downgrades

When driving on a downgrade, watch for signs showing the angle and length of the grade. These will help you decide on the correct speed while going downhill. Never go faster than the posted minimum speed. Talk with other drivers who have made the same downhill runs before because they often have helpful suggestions.

Because gravity plays such a big role in mountain driving, allow for the pull of gravity on your rig when going downhill. Make sure your brakes are properly adjusted. Check the traffic pattern in your mirrors, especially to the left and to the rear.

STOP!

Downshift before you start down the hill. NEVER downshift while going downhill because you will not be able to get into a lower gear while traveling at a high speed. You may not be able to shift at all; and if that happens, you will lose all braking effect from the engine.

If you try to force an automatic transmission into a lower gear at a high speed, you can damage the transmission; and if you damage the transmission, you will lose all engine braking.

When you are in the right gear, your engine will not race. Be sure your speed is not too fast for the total weight of your vehicle and its cargo, length of the grade, steepness of the grade, road conditions, and weather.

Use your engine as the primary way to control your speed. The braking effect of the engine is greatest when it is near the governed rpm and the transmission is in a lower gear. Save your brakes until you really need them.

STOP!

Never shift into neutral and coast because it is both illegal and unsafe.

If you use your brakes too often, then they may get hot and fade. You will have to apply them harder to get a braking effect. If you keep using them, then they may fail completely and you will be without brakes.

The American Association of Motor Vehicle Administrators makes the following recommendation:

"Once the vehicle is in the proper low gear, the following braking technique is suggested:

1. Apply the brakes just hard enough to feel a definite slowdown.
2. When speed has been reduced approximately 5 mph below your safe speed, release the brakes. Brake application should last about 3 seconds.
3. When your speed has increased to your safe speed, repeat steps 2 and 3."

For example, if your safe speed is 40 mph, do not put on the brakes until you reach 40 mph. Then brake hard enough to reduce your speed to 35 mph. Release the brakes and repeat as often as you need to until you reach the end of the downgrade.

GO!

Upgrades:

- Downshift until you find a gear that will maintain rpm.
- Position vehicle in the right lane.
- Do not pass.
- Turn on four-way flashers if speed drops to 40 mph.

Downgrades:

- Never downshift while descending.
- Use a low gear.
- Go slowly.
- Use close-to-rated engine speed to maximize drag.
- Use snubbing method when braking.
- Turn on your four-way flashers.

AUXILIARY BRAKES AND SPEED RETARDERS

Auxiliary brakes and **speed retarders** reduce the rig's speed without using the service brakes. This saves wear and tear on the brakes. The retarders help control the rig on long grades. They can often keep the rpm within a safe range. If not, the service brakes will have to be used to keep the rig under control.

Types of Auxiliary Brakes and Speed Retarders

The four basic types of auxiliary brakes and speed retarders are as follows:

- Engine brakes
- Exhaust brakes
- Hydraulic retarders
- Electric retarders

Engine brakes—eliminate the engine's power stroke and convert the engine to an air compressor for braking purposes. Compressed air is expelled and slows the piston movement.

Exhaust brakes—back exhaust gases into the engine to create 40 to 50 psi of pressure to slow piston movement. Exhaust brakes may be controlled by an on-off switch in the cab. Other types operate with an automatic switch that is turned on by releasing the fuel pedal and turned off by depressing the clutch pedal.

Hydraulic retarders—are mounted between the engine and the transmission. They can be adjusted manually to different levels of operation. The higher the setting, the more effective their performance. They have a treadle valve and may have a clutch switch.

Electric retarders—are mounted in the drive line and slow the driveshaft rotation with an electromagnet that can be turned on or off. There is no in-between setting.

Operation and Control

Because these devices can be noisy, be sure you know whether they are permitted in the area where you are driving. You will also need to know which gears they may be used with, as well as the proper rpm for their use and what kinds of weather you may use them in. Speed retarders are useful any time the service brakes are used continuously, usually in the mountains or on long downhill grades.

ESCAPE RAMPS

Escape ramps are designed to stop a vehicle safely without injuring people or damaging cargo **(see Figure 17–10).** They are built to stop a 50,000-pound GVW tractor-trailer traveling at 55 mph about 450 feet into the ramp. Stopping feels like a hard lock wheel stop on dry pavement.

Gravity Ramp

TRUCK ESCAPE RAMP

▶ **Figure 17–10**

Escape ramps are available on mountain roads or continuous grades.

Ramps either sink the rig in loose gravel or sand or send it up an incline. The grade may be as much as 43 percent. Either way, damage to the rig and cargo is limited to minor scratches, nicks, lost battery covers, and other minor problems.

The four basic types of ramps are:

- **Gravity ramps**—have a loose material surface, such as pea gravel. The grade is usually from 5 to 43 percent.
- **Sand piles**—are mounds or ridges built high enough to drag the undercarriage of the rig. Sand piles are from 85 to 200 feet long.
- **Arrester beds**—are masses of loose materials (usually pea gravel) arranged in flat beds from 300 to 700 feet long.
- **Combination ramp and arrester bed**—rely on the loose surface material to stop the rig. They have a grade of 1.5 to 6.7 percent and are from 500 to 2,200 feet long.

CAUTION!

If you find yourself having braking problems on a grade, remember the following:

- First tighten your seat belt.
- You can use an escape ramp.
- Try to enter the ramp squarely and not at an angle.
- Escape ramps save lives and cargos.
- You probably will have to pay to have your rig towed back to the highway.
- When in doubt, use the ramp.

SUMMARY

In this chapter, you learned that driving in adverse conditions differs greatly from driving in good weather and on good roads. You also learned that rig inspection procedures in extreme driving differ from normal inspection routines.

You learned how to become aware of possible bad weather conditions and what you should do when you encounter or anticipate them. You also learned several methods for starting an engine in cold weather and what to do if your tractor will not start.

You learned how to avoid skids and how to dry out the truck's brakes should they become wet. You also learned your responsibility should your rig become stuck and require towing. The hazards of driving in hot weather and in the desert were explained.

Finally, you learned that driving in the mountains takes special skills and you learned about auxiliary braking systems, the best way to drive on downgrades, and the use of escape ramps.

KEY TERMS

Arrester beds	Engine brakes	Sand pile
Auxiliary brakes	Escape ramp	Skidding
Bleeding tar	Exhaust brakes	Speed retarders
Combination ramp and arrester bed	Extreme driving conditions	Tire chains
Electric retarders	Gravity ramp	Traction
Emergency equipment	Hydraulic retarders	Visibility
	Jackknife	

REVIEW QUESTIONS

1. Conditions such as cold, wet, heat, wind, snow, fog, or mountain ranges are _____.

   a. excellent driving conditions
   b. extreme driving conditions
   c. good driving conditions
   d. a and c

2. One of the two major safety hazards caused by driving in extreme weather that increases stopping distance and decreases the driver's ability to control a rig is _____.

   a. less traction
   b. increased traction
   c. brake lag time
   d. increased center of gravity

3. A low coolant level in the cooling system affects the _____.

   a. brake lag time
   b. operation of the heater and defroster
   c. center of gravity
   d. efficiency of the brakes

4. Regarding the vehicle check for extreme weather driving, the tread depth of the front (steering) tires should have at least _____ tread on every major groove.

   a. 1 inch
   b. ½ inch
   c. 4⁄32 inch
   d. 3 inches

5. When checking the brake balance as part of the extreme weather checklist, the brakes should _____.

   a. apply more pressure on the front wheels
   b. apply more pressure on the drive wheels
   c. apply more pressure on the trailer wheels
   d. all apply pressure equally and at the same time

6. Regarding fuel selection in extreme weather (cold), a driver should beware of low-quality fuel because it _____.

   a. gets poor mileage per gallon
   b. has a tendency to explode
   c. causes longer brake lag time
   d. can freeze (gel) in the fuel lines and filters

7. Broadcasting on 162.40 to 162.55 MHz, the _____ broadcasts constant, updated forecasts from many locations around the country.

   a. National Public Radio
   b. National Weather Radio Service
   c. FMCSR Radio
   d. American Trucking Associations

8. When a rig is going up hill in heavy wet snow, tire chains increase the pulling power of the drive wheels by _____.

   a. increasing the traction of the drive wheels
   b. increasing the traction of the trailer wheels
   c. decreasing the traction of the drive wheels
   d. increasing the reaction time of the driver

9. Single chains, made for single tires, are to be used on _____.

   a. the left front tire of the tractor only
   b. the right front tire of the tractor only
   c. the outside tire of dual wheels
   d. the right inside tires of the trailer

10. Regarding starting your engine in cold weather, the lower the temperature _____.

    a. the harder engines are to get started   **c.** the greater the traction

    b. the easier engines are to get started   **d.** the more quarts of ether should be poured into the air cleaner

11. When attempting to start an engine, never crank the engine more than _____ at a time.

    a. 1 minute   **c.** 2 minutes

    b. 30 seconds   **d.** 15 seconds

12. Which of the following is not a major hazard when driving in bad weather?

    a. less visibility   **c.** a and b

    b. less traction   **d.** lower center of gravity

13. Proper tire inflation, tread depth, and weight on the drive wheels provide _____ and better control of a rig.

    a. a higher center of gravity   **c.** a and d

    b. better traction   **d.** less traction

14. Regarding driving on curves and turns on slippery surfaces, which of the following is not a recommended practice?

    a. speed up slightly in the turn or curve   **c.** reduce speed during a curve or turn

    b. shift to the correct gear before entering a curve or turn   **d.** brake before a turn or curve

15. The best advice regarding stuck vehicles is _____.

    a. do not spin the wheels   **c.** do not get stuck

    b. place in higher gear   **d.** use traction aids

16. If a tow is needed, who is responsible for the rig?

    a. driver of the tow truck   **c.** service technician

    b. dispatcher   **d.** driver of the rig

17. Regarding mountain driving, the force that pulls objects toward the center of the earth and affects a rig going up hill as well as down hill is called _____.

    a. gravity   **c.** friction

    b. traction   **d.** center of gravity

18. Regarding driving on downgrades, which of the following is the correct procedure for shifting?

    a. upshift before starting down the hill   **c.** downshift before starting down the hill

    b. downshift once you are on the downgrade   **d.** upshift once you are on the downgrade

19. Regarding driving on downgrades, according to the American Association of Motor Vehicle Administrators' Model CDL Manual, once a vehicle is in the proper low gear and the brakes have been applied hard enough to feel a definite slowdown, _____.

    a. when the speed has reduced to approximately 5 mph below the safe speed, release the brakes until the speed increases to the safe speed, then repeat for the remainder of the hill

    b. shift to a lower gear until the rig reaches an unsafe speed, then shift again to a lower gear, repeat for the remainder of the hill

    c. shift to a higher gear and then apply the brakes until a safe speed is reached then shift to a higher gear again, repeat for the remainder of the hill

    d. continue to apply the brakes down the remainder of the hill

20. Auxiliary brakes and speed retarders _____.

    a. reduce a rig's speed without using the service brakes

    b. reduce the rpm of the engine and increase power to the drive wheels

    c. are used in emergencies only

    d. along with electric retarders reduce the amount of electricity needed to operate the rig

18

Skid Control

OBJECTIVES

When you have completed this chapter, you should be able to:

- Show how skid control can prevent accidents.
- Explain vehicle control factors including traction, wheel load, and force of motion.
- Understand the causes of skidding.
- Illustrate a tractor-trailer jackknife, front-wheel skid, and an all-wheel skid.
- Explain recovery techniques.
- Show why most skids can be prevented and can occur at any speed.
- Describe the ways to recover from a skid if it is detected early enough.

INTRODUCTION

When any vehicle skids, the operator loses control. Skids occur when tires lose their grip on the road. What many people do not know is that drivers can prevent most skids, and, in fact, it is much easier to prevent a skid than to correct one.

Skids can occur because of one of the following four driver mistakes. The most common is trying to quickly change speed (overacceleration). The next most common cause of a skid is trying to change direction too quickly (oversteering). The other two reasons skids occur are overbraking (braking too hard and locking up the wheels or using the speed retarder when the road is slick) and driving too fast, which results in the most serious skids.

▶ **Figure 18–1**

Most skids happen when the road is slippery.

Most skids happen when the road is slippery due to rain, snow, and ice **(see Figure 18–1).** Loose material on the pavement—like gravel or wet leaves—can also make the road slippery and interfere with traction. Because most skids are caused by a sudden change in speed or direction, professional drivers must always be aware of the weather conditions and the road's surface and adjust their speeds based on these factors.

In this chapter, you will learn about skids, how skids happen, how they can be prevented, and how to make corrections and recover control, once the vehicle begins to skid. Hands-on experience should be practiced only on a special driving range or skid pad, never on the open road.

VEHICLE CONTROL FACTORS

When the vehicle control factors are not in balance, a skid will occur. Factors that affect control of the vehicle include **traction, wheel load,** and **force of motion.**

Traction

The two types of traction are as follows:

- **Rolling traction**—the friction of one surface rolling over another, for example, the friction of a rolling tire moving over the road in the same direction the rig is moving.

- **Sliding traction**—the friction of one surface sliding across another. This occurs when other forces acting upon surfaces are greater than the traction between them. This can happen whether the wheels are locked or turning.

Tires may slide in any direction when they lock up from too much braking. Too much **centrifugal force** (outward force) also may cause tires to slide sideways, even though they are turning.

Wheel Load

Wheel load is the downward force of weight on a tire. The greater the load on the tire, the better the traction. Wheel load is determined by the weight of the vehicle plus the weight and distribution of the load.

Notably, while wheel load may increase the downward force and the amount of tread touching the pavement, wheel load may not actually improve the traction. For example, if there is ice or snow on the road surface, there is still a lack of adequate traction and skidding can occur.

Some tractor-trailer drivers have the misconception that a heavier wheel load will guarantee better traction on slippery surfaces, but this is not true.

Force of Motion

The force of motion of the rig is determined by its weight and speed. The heavier the rig and its load and the faster it travels, the greater the force that moves that rig. To keep the rig under control, the professional driver must avoid skids.

CAUSES OF SKIDS

There are several reasons a truck will begin to skid, but the two basic causes are changes in speed and changes in direction **(see Figure 18–2).**

Change in Speed

A sudden change in speed can result from either too much braking or speeding up too fast. If the forces of motion are greater than the traction of the tire against the pavement when you brake, instead of stopping, the rig will skid. Make a conscious effort to periodically check your speed—do not trust your instincts.

Skids involving speed may be from braking or acceleration. Braking skids can result in:

- Wheel lockup
- Tire slides

Both of these conditions increase the rig's stopping distance and cause the driver to lose control **(see Figure 18–3).**

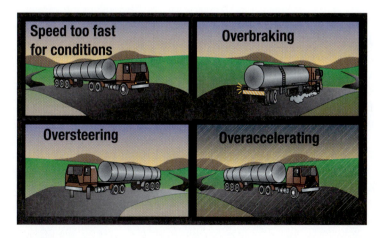

▶ **Figure 18-2**

All professional drivers need to understand the most common causes of skids.

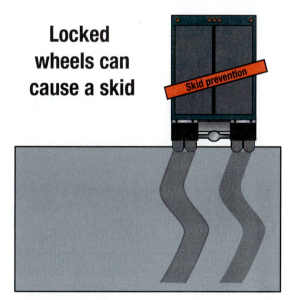

▶ **Figure 18-3**

Wheels can lock when you apply brakes too hard, downshift too much, or suddenly slow down.

Wheel Lockup

Wheel lockup happens because you:

- Put on the service brakes, exhaust brakes, or speed retarder too hard
- Downshift too much
- Slow suddenly

You lose control when the locked wheels slide and the rig skids out of control. The skid may be straight ahead, sideways, or a jackknife. The unit will be out of control until you, the driver, correct the problem, or a collision occurs.

Tire Slides

Tire slides occur when the forces from weight and acceleration of the rig are greater than the ability of the tires to maintain traction. Wheel lockups and tire slides increase the rig's stopping distance. And remember—sliding tires do not slow a vehicle as well as rolling tires.

Spinning tires occur when the force from acceleration on the drive wheels is greater than the ability of the tires to provide traction. The wheels spin, but the vehicle does not move. The spinning continues until the driver stops accelerating. The rear of the tractor may also move in a sideways spin, called a **power skid.**

Slowing too fast may also cause a skid. If the rig has moved onto ice and the driver suddenly recognizes the problem, he or she may quickly react by removing their foot from the accelerator. This reaction may reduce the wheel speed too fast and cause a skid; so if possible, slow before reaching any icy spots on the road.

CAUTION!

Remember the major cause of skidding is a sudden change in either speed or direction.

Change of Direction

Changing the direction of your steering too quickly can cause the rolling tires to lose their friction with the road surface. When this happens, the rig continues in the direction it has been moving instead of changing to follow the direction of the steering wheels.

When a vehicle makes a turn, centrifugal force makes it keep going in the same direction. As a result, the vehicle tends to slide outward in a turn.

If the rate of speed or the sharpness of the turn is too great, centrifugal force exceeds traction. This causes the tires to skid sideways. A new driver may put on the brakes suddenly, which causes the tires to lock up and makes the skid worse because the driver has even less control.

> **CAUTION!**
> When you brake your rig too hard, you will cause a skid. You also need to know that when you speed up too quickly, you can also cause a skid because you increase the wheel speed to a point where the tires cannot provide traction. The result is a **jackknife**.

PREVENTING SKIDS

In any situation, it is always better to prevent a skid than to try to recover once a skid occurs. Safe driving practices can help prevent skids. The following tips may help you avoid skid situations:

- Adjust your speed on curves to reduce your chances of a cornering skid.
- Drive within your sight distance to reduce the need for sudden stops and the possibility of a braking skid.
- Maintain enough following distance so you will not have to make a quick stop.
- Do not drive too fast on slick surfaces.
- Adjust your speed to the surface and weather conditions and to the curvature of the road.
- Do not overbrake.
- Do not suddenly downshift.
- Use the brake limiting valve correctly.
- Inspect the air and brake systems before and during each trip. All wheels should start stopping at the same time. If they do not, a skid can result when you brake your vehicle.
- Inspect tires, front wheel alignment, and suspension system.
- Load cargo properly.

TRACTOR-TRAILER SKIDS

Tractor-trailer skids are grouped according to what happens to the rig as a result of the skid. The four major types of skids are:

1. Trailer jackknife
2. Tractor jackknife
3. Front-wheel skid
4. All-wheel skid

"What is it they say? Oh yeah . . . you'll never skid if you stay in a rut . . . but they weren't talking about driving a big rig."

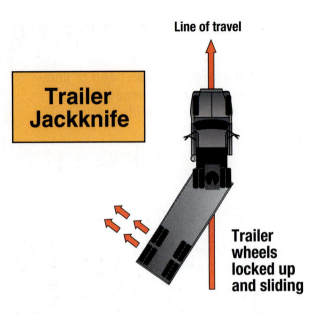

Line of travel

Trailer Jackknife

Trailer wheels locked up and sliding

▶ **Figure 18–4**

A trailer jackknife is caused by excessive braking or sharp cornering.

Trailer Jackknife

A trailer jackknife is caused by too much braking or cornering. In either case, the trailer tires skid because they become locked. The force that locks them overcomes the traction with the surface of the road **(see Figure 18–4).**

Overbraking—caused by putting on the footbrake too hard or not using the trailer brake correctly. The trailer brake should not be used for stopping the entire rig. Sometimes the driver is forced to use the brakes excessively because of a mechanical problem, such as:

- A faulty air system that sends too much pressure to the trailer wheels

- Not adjusting the brakes on the trailer equally, called cam-over

- Worn trailer brake linings that cause a brake seizure

Excessive cornering—if a rig enters a curve too fast for the surface conditions, the tires may lose traction, causing the rig to jackknife or skid out of control.

CAUTION!

Always adjust your speed—to the road conditions and to the curve—before you enter a curve. This will help you avoid a jackknife.

When entering curves, ease off the fuel pedal and then accelerate through the curve. This is done so the tractor pulls the trailer through the curve rather than allowing the trailer to push the tractor through the curve **(see Figure 18–5).**

▶ **Figure 18–5**

Rounding a curve.

STOP!

Be sure to always inspect the air system and brakes before and during every trip.

Tractor Jackknife

A tractor jackknife (also called a **drive-wheel skid**) occurs when the tractor drive wheels lose traction **(see Figure 18–6).** This happens because of:

- Wheel lockup
- Overacceleration
- Trailer override

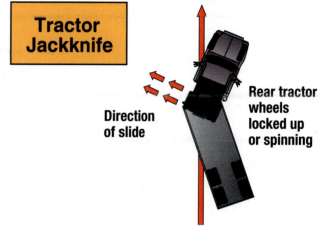

When any of these three conditions occur, the drive wheels have less traction than the front wheels, so they try to overtake the front wheels. As a result, the rear of the tractor tends to swing out—and as it does, the tractor pulls the trailer outward. Then, the trailer pushes the tractor outward and a jackknife results.

▶ **Figure 18–6**

A tractor jackknife occurs when the tractor drive wheels lose traction.

If a drive-wheel skid occurs on ice or snow, it can be easily managed by taking your foot off the accelerator. (If road conditions are very slippery, push in the clutch.) Otherwise, the engine will keep the wheels from rolling freely and regaining traction.

Wheel lockup—occurs for the following reasons:
- Putting on the brakes too hard
- Downshifting on a slippery road surface
- Sudden release of fuel pedal on a slippery surface with retarder on
- Load imbalance (drive wheels too lightly loaded)
- Faulty brakes
- Poor tread on the drive tires

Overacceleration—occurs when too much pressure for the gear and vehicle speed is placed on the fuel pedal, which causes a power skid. Most power skids occur while driving on a slippery surface, the rig has an engine with high horsepower (high torque), or the trailer is heavily or improperly loaded.

Trailer override—when you brake, the cargo may push the trailer against the tractor. This forces the tractor out of line and creates a jackknife. Trailer override most likely will occur if the pavement is slippery, the trailer is not loaded properly, or the cargo is not distributed correctly or secured properly. It can also occur if the rig is taking a curve or making a rapid lane change.

The best way to prevent a tractor jackknife is to avoid the following:

- Overbraking
- Overaccelerating

- Sudden downshifts
- Sudden turns
- Incorrect loading

Front-Wheel Skid

Front-wheel skids happen when you lose front-wheel traction **(see Figure 18–7)**. The rig continues to move forward but you cannot steer it. The rig also may move sideways or fail to round a curve. Front-wheel skids are usually caused by:

- Too big a load on the fifth wheel (this happens when cargo is not properly loaded and it shifts forward when you brake your rig)
- Too much speed
- Not enough front tire tread
- Hydroplaning
- Oversteering in combination with any of the above mentioned reasons
- Malfunction of the brake system
- Worn brake linings or other brake defects
- A dry fifth wheel

Front wheel skids can be prevented by:

- Slowing your speed when driving on slippery pavement (caused by rain, snow, sleet, ice, or fog)
- Loading cargo correctly
- Inspecting tires, front-wheel alignment, and suspension system—and having any problems you find corrected
- Using good braking techniques

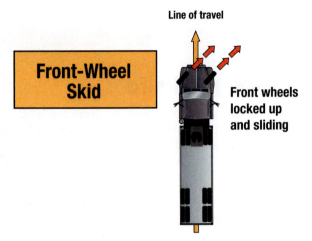

▶ **Figure 18–7**

Front-wheel skids occur when your front wheels lose traction.

All-Wheel Skid

When all wheels lock and do not roll, your rig will lose traction. It stops rolling and starts to slide. The rig often continues in a straight line without traction; and, without traction, the driver loses control **(see Figure 18–8).**

The major causes of this kind of skid are excessive speed and overbraking on a slippery surface. In cases of overbraking, one set of wheels generally locks up before the others. In some cases, even light brake pressure causes the wheels to lock up.

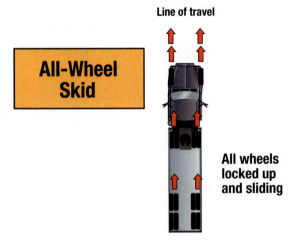

▶ **Figure 18–8**

The major causes of all-wheel skids are excessive speed or overbraking on slick roads.

To prevent all-wheel skids:

- Allow plenty of stopping distance
- Control your speed
- Do not brake too much on slippery surfaces

CAUTION!

If you must brake on a slippery surface, use light, steady braking to maintain control of your rig.

Summary of Skid Prevention

As discussed earlier in this chapter, preventing skids is a priority task for professional drivers. You learned that controlling your rig comes from managing your speed; and the space around your rig is also a priority, especially when driving in extreme conditions.

Most skids result from sudden changes in speed or direction. Overbraking and oversteering as well as fast acceleration or deceleration cause the sudden changes that often result in skids.

Skidding usually occurs on slippery surfaces. To prevent skidding:

- Avoid quick braking and quick turns on slippery pavement
- If you must turn or brake your rig, do no more than is absolutely necessary

ANTIJACKKNIFE DEVICES

Antijackknife devices are made to restrict trailer swing and prevent damage to the rig; however, these devices do not prevent skidding. There are two basic types of antijackknife devices:

- Fifth-wheel devices
- Cable devices

    Fifth-wheel antijackknife devices—are automatic and restrict the rotation of the king-pin. This prevents a collision between the trailer and the cab. They are mounted on the tractor and can be used with any type of trailer.

    Cable antijackknife devices—are mounted to the trailer and connected to the tractor. They are activated by hard braking and keep the trailer and tractor in line.

CAUTION!

The disadvantage to using the cable antijackknife devices is that they conflict with skid recovery. Hard braking prevents the use of controlled braking and, in some situations, cable devices may actually make a skid worse.

ANTILOCK BRAKES

Due to federal government mandates, antilock brakes are now required equipment on all tractors manufactured after March 1, 1997, and all trailers built after March 1, 1998.

When used properly, an **antilock brake system (ABS)** is a safe and effective braking system. ABS allows the driver to maintain directional stability, control over steering, and in some situations, to reduce stopping distances during emergency braking situations, particularly on wet and slippery road surfaces. To gain this safety advantage, drivers must learn how to operate their ABS correctly.

An antilock braking system works with the regular or foundation brakes on your vehicle. ABS simply keeps your base brakes from locking up. In vehicles not equipped with ABS, the driver can manually pump the brakes to prevent wheel lockup. In vehicles equipped with ABS, the driver's foot remains firmly on the brake pedal, allowing the system to automatically pump the brakes.

When your brakes lock up on wet and slippery roads or during a panic stop, you lose steering control and your vehicle can spin. Rear wheel ABS prevents wheel lockup so that your car stays in a straight line.

Antilock systems use electronic controls to read wheel speed and prevent the brakes from locking up the wheels under hard braking. This feature increases driver control during braking but does not necessarily shorten stopping distances. Antilock brakes are most effective when you hit the brake pedal and hold it down.

NOTE: Since antilock brake systems lose their effectiveness with "pumping" the brakes, stab braking may not be the skid-recovery technique of choice, because it actually reduces the effectiveness of the tractor brakes and increases the braking power coming from the trailer. This situation sets up your rig for a trailer skid or the inability to come to a stop as soon as necessary. Controlled braking is the correct technique in this type of skid.

SKID RECOVERY

Almost all tractor skids are corrected by the same techniques:

1. Disengage the clutch
2. Get off the brakes
3. Countersteer

Most skids happen when you try to change speed too quickly for the conditions. Remove your foot from the brake pedal to reduce skidding. Then you can more easily gain control of the direction the rig is going. Do not put on the independent trailer brake.

STOP!
If the trailer has started to jackknife, putting on the trailer brake will only make the situation worse!

If overbraking resulted from downshifting, depress the clutch quickly and then use the ABS. If overacceleration has caused the skid, you should ease off the fuel pedal. Then depress the clutch pedal to remove engine power from the drive wheels.

Corrective Steering

In a tractor jackknife, corrective steering is needed to put the tractor back on course **(see Figure 18–9).** Steer toward the direction the rig is moving. Steer in the line of travel.

Oversteering—on a slippery surface, when you lose control of your steering and traction, you must oversteer (turn beyond the intended path of travel). Unless you oversteer, you will not be able to regain control of your rig.

Countersteering—when you try to correct a skid, little traction makes the rig slow to respond. As the rig resumes the correct course, the driver must countersteer early. Do this to avoid a new skid **(see Figure 18–10).** Continue countersteering until the rig is on a straighter path. Each countersteering movement should get smaller until the rig is going straight again. If a new skid happens because you countersteered too late, the rig may turn beyond the intended path and spin out. Although it may not spin out the first time you countersteered too late, each correction may make the situation worse until a spinout occurs.

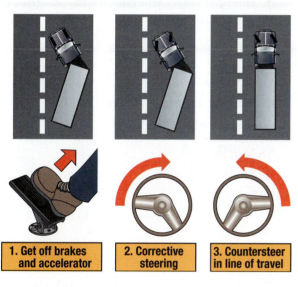

1. Get off brakes and accelerator
2. Corrective steering
3. Countersteer in line of travel

Corrective steering   Countersteer

▶ **Figure 18–9**

When a tractor jackknife occurs, corrective steering can often put the tractor back on course.

▶ **Figure 18–10**

Countersteering will help you avoid a new skid.

Braking to a Stop

Once a vehicle is on a straight path, you can brake to a stop. It is best to brake lightly and steadily. If the vehicle is equipped with antilock brakes, a light, steady application of the brake is best.

SUMMARY

In this chapter, you learned the types of skids and what can be done to prevent them. You also learned there are ways to recover from each type of skid in order to prevent damage to your rig and injury to yourself or others. The conditions that cause skids were also discussed.

KEY TERMS

Antilock brake system (ABS)
Cable antijackknife devices
Centrifugal force
Countersteering
Drive-wheel skid

Fifth-wheel antijackknife
    devices
Force of motion
Jackknife
Oversteering
Power skid

Rolling traction
Sliding traction
Tire slides
Traction
Wheel load
Wheel lockup

REVIEW QUESTIONS

1. When the vehicle control factors are not in balance, _____.

   a. the vehicle will be overweight

   b. the brakes control the vehicle more efficiently

   c. a skid will occur

   d. the fifth wheel will balance the weight of the tractor and the trailer

2. Regarding vehicle control factors, which of the following is not a factor that controls the vehicle?

   a. traction

   b. wheel load

   c. time of day

   d. force of motion

3. The "grip" between the tires and the road surface is known as _____.

   a. friction

   b. traction

   c. center of gravity

   d. centrifugal force

4. Wheel load is determined by the weight of the vehicle and _____.

   a. the weight and distribution of the load

   b. the weight of the load

   c. the center of gravity of the load

   d. b and c

5. The force of motion of the rig is determined by _____.

   a. traction

   b. the weight and speed of the rig

   c. friction

   d. brake reaction time

6. Which of the following is *not* a condition that can produce a skid?

   a. overbraking

   b. oversteering

   c. overaccelerating

   d. increased traction

7. When the force from acceleration on the drive wheels is more than the tire's ability to provide traction, _____ occurs.

   a. a power skid

   b. a gravity skid occurs

   c. a trailer jackknife

   d. an antigravity skid occurs

8. Regarding changes of direction, if the rate of speed or sharpness of a turn is too great and the rig slides outward, centrifugal force of the rig exceeds _____.

   a. the braking force of the rig

   b. the traction of the tires

   c. oversteering

   d. countersteering

9. In any situation it is always better to _____ than to try to recover once a skid occurs.

   a. drive faster to increase centrifugal force

   b. countersteer

   c. increase the center of gravity

   d. prevent skids

10. In a trailer jackknife, which is caused by excessive braking or sharp cornering , the trailer wheels _____.

    a. increase traction   **c.** a and b

    b. increase friction   **d.** lose traction

11. A tractor jackknife (drive-wheel skid) occurs when the tractor drive wheels _____.

    a. increase traction   **c.** lose traction

    b. increase friction   **d.** a and b

12. Which of the following is not a cause of front-wheel skids?

    a. loss of front wheel traction   **c.** too big a load on the fifth wheel

    b. increased traction   **d.** too much speed

13. Which of the following is *not* one of the best ways to prevent all-wheel skids?

    a. reduce the time on slippery areas by driving faster   **c.** do not brake too much on slippery surfaces

    b. allow plenty of stopping distance   **d.** control your speed

14. Most skids result from _____.

    a. sudden changes in speed   **c.** sudden changes in direction

    b. a and c   **d.** sudden changes in the fifth-wheel alignment

15. Regarding skid recovery, which of the following is not one of the techniques used to recover from a skid?

    a. increase the speed of the rig   **c.** get off the brakes

    b. disengage the clutch   **d.** countersteer

19 Hazard Awareness

OBJECTIVES

When you have completed this chapter, you should be able to:

- Recognize possible hazards.

- Determine when the road or the surroundings may pose a danger.

- Describe why a driver must always be alert to the changing scene.

- Explain the various dangerous road conditions, such as slippery surfaces, uneven surfaces, curves, soft surfaces, and sloping roads.

- Describe common highway threats to safety, such as debris, obstructions to visibility, and crosswinds.

- Recognize clues that tell you when other road users may be a possible safety hazard.

- Explain the importance of recognizing hazards early.

INTRODUCTION

As a professional driver, you must have skills in a number of areas, but the majority of your skills are focused in two areas: (1) your vehicle and (2) dealing with the driving environment.

The driving environment includes the roadway and its condition, weather, buildings, people, signs, trees and animals **(see Figure 19–1)**. To operate safely at all times, you must be familiar with this environment and the possible changes that may occur as you drive from one area to another.

Some of what you will see along the roadway will be friendly, such as wide shoulders, emergency ramps, and climbing lanes. Some elements of the environment will be neutral, such as signs, stores, and homes along the roadway. Other elements, however, will be dangerous, such as drunken or ill drivers in other vehicles, crosswinds on a mountain pass, heavy sleet or snow, high winds, low bridges, wires, and trees.

The purpose of this chapter is to assist you in becoming aware of the driving environment and the clues it offers to help you drive safely. As a professional driver, part of your job is to recognize and interpret these clues so that you can adjust your driving and continue your trip in a safe, economical manner.

▶ **Figure 19–1**

You must be familiar with your driving environment in order to operate safely.

WHAT IS A HAZARD?

As you probably know, a **hazard** is any condition or road user (another vehicle and driver, cyclist, pedestrian, or animal) that could create a possible danger to you, your cargo, and your rig. *Possible* is the key word, because these elements may or may not become a hazard and a danger on the road. Either way, you should be aware of the possibilities. For example, the brake lights of the vehicle ahead as it approaches an exit ramp could signal a possible danger **(see Figure 19–2)**. You do not know what that driver intends to do. When a driver's brake lights go on, this may signal that the driver is unsure about his or her exit. At the last minute, the driver of that vehicle could change his or her mind and veer back into your lane. If this happens, that vehicle is no longer a hazard. It is now a danger, because you will have to react by either clearing the lane or using your brakes. What if there is not enough room in the next lane for you? What about the "slosh factor" if you are driving a tanker **(see Figure 19–3)?**

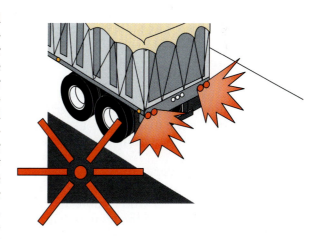

▶ **Figure 19–2**

Seeing a vehicle's brake lights is a clue indicating a possible hazard.

This example brings a laser focus on the whole idea of recognizing hazards. A driver who did not understand the vehicle was a hazard would not respond until it started to change lanes, and then his or her response might have been to brake suddenly or to rapidly change lanes. Both maneuvers could easily cause an accident.

Tanker drivers must be aware of the "slosh factor" when stopping abruptly.

Commentary driving helps you become more aware of your environment and the activities of the other drivers on the highways.

COMMENTARY DRIVING AND HAZARD PERCEPTION

Before continuing our discussion about hazards and how to recognize them along the highway, it is important for you to understand the skill of "commentary driving."

Commentary driving is making comments about what you see as you drive. During the on-street part of your instruction, you may be asked to try this exercise. It will help you identify hazards and will let your instructor know what you are seeing and how you react to what you see.

In commentary driving, you do not discuss what you see at length. Your job is to see and identify any possible hazard, using brief statements such as "truck in front of me . . . could stop quickly without warning." Such statements make you aware of a possible hazard **(see Figure 19-4).**

This simple example makes commentary driving sound really easy. Depending on the situation, however, commentary driving may not be as easy at it sounds. Seeing and talking about a car beside the road sounds like an easy thing to do, but when you add the tasks of professional driving, commenting can become very demanding.

Commentary driving has its boosters and its naysayers. Some people like the procedure, some do not. Even though it may seem difficult at first, you will find that it helps you become a professional driver who is more aware of the surrounding environment and the activities of those vehicles sharing the highway with you.

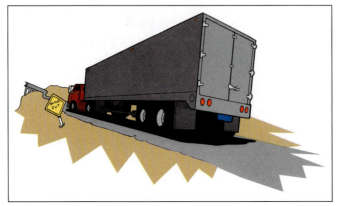

▶ *Commentary driving: "Hauling down the highway, full speed ahead . . . uh, oh 'Bridge Out' . . . 'Like a bridge over troubled waters.' . . ."*

Guidelines for Commentary Driving

The following steps are required for commentary driving:

1. Identify in your mind any hazard—object, road condition, or road user—that is a possible threat to your safety. Identify and describe only those hazards to which you are prepared to respond.

2. Describe the hazard as concisely as possible—what and where it is.

    Example: Child in the street on the left

    Pavement in the shade of that bridge

3. Use only a few words to describe what makes it a hazard.

    Example: Child is looking the other way

    Pavement might be slippery

4. In a conflict situation (where a crash is possible), describe only the vehicle or object in conflict with your rig.

    Example: Car in my lane

    Bicyclist with back toward me in my lane

    Wind blowing debris across the road

5. When the object, road condition, or person is not a hazard, say nothing.

LEARNING TO RECOGNIZE HAZARDS

Learning to recognize hazards is much like learning to read—we first see how letters look and sound, and then we begin to pick out whole words. The words soon fit together into sentences and those single letters we learned in the beginning now have meaning.

You learn to recognize hazards much the same way. When driving, it is difficult to see every detail in the environment that surrounds you. As a professional driver, however, you must train yourself to become acutely aware of everything going on around you. Often, you only see **clues** about what is happening, then you begin fitting these clues together as you go down the highway.

Hazards—when clues are seen—are usually fairly easy to figure out and then you can decide your response. Unfortunately, professional drivers learn to recognize these clues because of close calls, near misses, other drivers' stories, or accidents.

In the previous situation, for example, the car's brake lights were a clue. The car ahead was slowing down or stopping. The driver sees the brake lights and either responds or prepares to respond. Seeing and knowing what the brake lights mean is recognizing a hazard. Though the vehicle slowing down is not a direct threat to your safety, you must be aware that it remains a possible hazard.

SOURCES OF CLUES

Clues to hazards can be found around your rig in every driving environment. There are three types of clues:

- Road conditions
- Appearance of other road users
- Activities of other road users

Road Conditions

Road conditions are a major factor in tractor-trailer accidents because of the following:

1. Big rigs travel more miles and in more bad weather than most other vehicles.

2. Big rigs are less stable because of a higher center of gravity, their size, and their weight. These factors make them tip over more easily than most other vehicles on the highway.

3. Big rigs require longer stopping distances than most other vehicles on the highway.

Road characteristics that can be hazardous to tractor-trailer rigs include surface conditions, shape, and contour. Road surfaces can also be hazardous if they are slippery, soft, sloping, and uneven or littered with debris.

Slippery Surfaces

Sometimes it is difficult to tell if a road is going to be slippery. The following sections describe some of these conditions **(see Figure 19–5).**

Road Hazards

▶ **Figure 19–5**

Road conditions signal possible hazards.

Wet weather—in wet conditions, many surfaces may be more slippery than they look. Patches of oil dripped from passing vehicles is very slippery just after it starts to rain. Painted or paint-striped areas, railroad tracks, and construction plates also can be slippery **(see Figure 19–6).**

Cold weather—in cold weather conditions look out for black ice, shaded areas, and bridges. Black ice is a thin, clear coating of ice that makes the road appear wet. Shaded areas on the highway can freeze in wet weather when the rest of the roadway is dry. Bridges, both the traveled surface and the roadway below a bridge, tend to freeze more quickly than the rest of the roadway.

▶ **Figure 19–6**

In wet weather, many surfaces become slick and dangerous.

Hot weather—in hot weather conditions, oil may come to the surface of an asphalt road and make it slippery. When driving on an asphalt road, be very careful when it starts to rain. The water mixes with this surface oil and reduces traction, causing the surface to become very slippery until the oil is washed away **(see Figure 19–7).**

Figure 19–7

A slippery roadway requires more stopping distance for a big rig.

Soft Surfaces

Some surfaces such as asphalt, construction areas, and soft shoulders will not bear the weight of a fully loaded rig. On very hot days, some asphalt roadways may become soft, and your rig may sink into it. In construction zones, surfaces that cover filled-in sewer trenches and septic tanks are seldom strong enough to hold the weight of a truck. Graded shoulders also may become very soft after a heavy rain or when the snow thaws. In these conditions, there is a danger your rig may sink or turn over.

Sloping Surfaces

A curve that is not properly banked is a hazard. The wheels of your rig are more likely to slide on the curve, so you must take these curves at a slower speed. Learn to recognize when a curve is not properly banked. Roads that are high in the middle and low on each side (sometimes called "high crown" roads) are worse than flat roads. On curves, a wrong-way slope can cause severe front-end dip, front wheel lockup, or loss of control.

Debris

No matter the size of your vehicle, debris on the road is always a hazard. A small box may contain heavy material that can cause control problems or damage to your tires or the rig itself. If a box does not move with the wind, think of it as a hazard. A pile of rags and paper or cloth sacks can also be hazards because they may contain cement or another hard substance. If you hit them, you can damage tires, wheel rims, air lines, electrical lines, or fuel crossover lines.

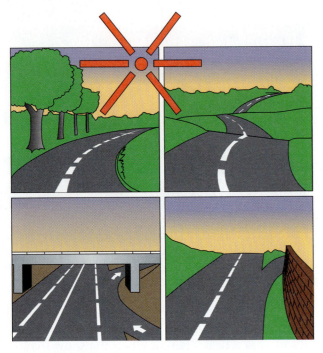

▶ Figure 19–8

The shape or contour of the road can create a driving hazard.

Uneven Surfaces

Bumps in the road can hang up a low trailer and damage the undercarriage or tear off the dolly wheels. Try to avoid driving through puddles. Often seemingly small puddles can disguise deep potholes that can make you lose control of your rig and cause damage to your equipment.

Contour of the Road

The shape or contour of the road can create hazards. The most common problems result from curves that restrict visibility. Another common problem is the crosswinds that occur around curving terrain **(see Figure 19–8).**

Curvature—is the amount of curving the earth does in your line of sight. Trees, power lines, or buildings can be clues to a curving road before you reach the actual curves. Are they in a straight line? Do they go up and down toward the horizon?

The **curvature** of expressway ramps can be dangerous for all drivers, but they are even more difficult and dangerous for tractor-trailer drivers. Curving, downhill ramps are especially difficult because the weight and high center of gravity of a rig work with the **centrifugal force** that automatically pulls your rig to the outside of the curve to make holding onto the road more difficult **(see Figure 19–9).**

▶ Figure 19–9

The force that attempts to push a vehicle off the road in a curve is centrifugal force.

Restrictions to visibility—many road characteristics restrict the driver's vision. Be prepared for these situations:

■ At sunrise or sunset, you can be faced with extreme glare at the crest of a hill. It may help to lower your visor and put on your sunglasses.

■ At night, as you approach a hilltop, lights from the other side of the highway warn of ongoing traffic. Be ready for headlight glare and protect yourself by looking to the right edge of the road.

■ When approaching a tunnel in daylight, remember your eyes adjust slowly to changes in light. Take off your sunglasses before entering the tunnel. Put them back on as you leave the tunnel. Do the same when you enter a warehouse or dark alley on a sunny day **(see Figure 19–10).**

Crosswind areas—on windy days, you can be hit with a violent **crosswind** when moving from a protected area into an open area. A sudden crosswind can cause you to lose control of your rig, so look for the absence of trees, hills, or other protection when you come out into the open after driving in protected terrain.

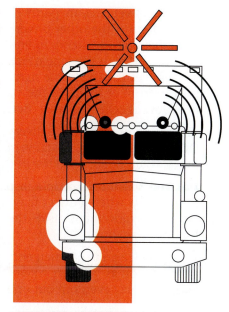

▶ **Figure 19–10**

When approaching a tunnel during the day, take off your sunglasses and turn on your low beams.

Appearance of Other Road Users

Drive defensively! While no driver can watch every move of every other road user, he or she can drive so that if the other driver makes a dumb or dangerous move, an accident can be avoided.

CAUTION!

Other drivers are really not bad drivers, but they are not educated in the hazards of operating near a CMV and are sometimes careless. Anytime you share the roadway, be alert to other users. It makes good sense!

It also makes sense to watch for clues that tell you other road users may be ready to do something unexpected. For example, you must be ready to deal with another driver's sudden change of speed or direction. Among the clues to watch for are obstructed vision, distraction, confusion, slow travel, impatience, and impairment.

Obstructed Vision

People who cannot see the road well are a serious hazard to other drivers. This section discusses clues that identify drivers who may have obstructed vision.

Vehicles with limited visibility—include vans, loaded SUVs, and cars with obstructed rear windows. These drivers may have limited ability to see the road around them. Drivers of rental trucks are often not familiar with their limited vision. Be alert for these drivers.

Sometimes vehicles are partly hidden by a blind intersection. You can see the other vehicle, but you know the other driver cannot see you. This is a defensive driving situation; and a good example is when you enter an intersection with the intention of turning left. If oncoming traffic in the lane nearest to you is stopped to let you turn, you may not be able to see vehicles passing to the right of the stopped vehicles. They, of course, are a hazard if you turn in front of them. In these situations, the height of your cab can be helpful but it does not prevent other roadway users from being hidden from your view.

The vision of drivers of delivery trucks is sometimes blocked by packages or vehicle doors. Drivers of step vans, postal vehicles, and local delivery trucks may leave their vehicles in a hurry, often double-parking in the roadway. Watch out for these drivers.

Parked vehicles—people in parked vehicles should always be considered a hazard. You never know when a driver may open the door and climb out of the vehicle in front of you. Watch for movement inside the vehicle. Parked vehicles may also move out into your lane without signaling.

When police units or emergency units are along the side of the road, move as far left as possible as soon as you can. Slow down if you can do it safely because anything can happen. Someone may even run out or be pushed into traffic lanes.

CAUTION!

States such as Kansas issue citations for not moving to the far left for emergency or law enforcement vehicles stopped by the side of the road.

Distraction

If a driver is looking at, thinking about, or reacting to anything else, he or she may not see your rig. This is a distracted driver **(see Figure 19–11).** A driver can attend to only those parts of the driving environment he or she can see, hear, or sense. Therefore, help other drivers see and pay attention to you and your rig. The following are some common clues that signal a distracted driver.

▶ **Figure 19–11**

Cell phones, crying children, and driving an unfamiliar road can distract drivers.

Distracted Drivers

Lack of eye contact—road users looking elsewhere—at children, at a roadmap, or other distractions—may not be aware of your rig and may pull into your path. Always try to make eye contact with others, although positive eye contact is no guarantee they are aware of you. Pedestrians and cyclists may often assume you will yield or give them room.

Talkers—people talking to others in their vehicle have already taken their full attention away from the driving environment. They may not be aware of your rig, so stay alert!

Workers—highway construction, road repair, and utility workers often are not concerned about traffic. They may think someone else is directing traffic. Delivery people may be distracted by their work or their schedules, especially if they are loading and unloading. The presence of road repair equipment or delivery trucks is a clue for the professional driver to remain on high alert **(see Figure 19–12)**.

Vendors—a vendor's vehicle, such as an ice cream van or taco wagon, is a clue to a hazard. People seem to forget there is traffic when they deal with a neighborhood street vendor. They walk or run across streets and roads without paying attention. Ice cream trucks and small children are also a dangerous combination.

Objects appearing from the side—a baseball, basketball, or other object appearing in the street usually means a child is following, so be prepared to stop.

▶ **Figure 19–12**

Highway construction sites and workers around those sites often present a hazard.

Disabled vehicle—a vehicle being worked on beside a road or street is always a hazard. Drivers changing a tire or looking under the hood are usually not thinking about traffic—so always be on the alert when passing a breakdown on the highway.

People talking on cell phones—do not always have their minds or attention on their driving or what is happening around them. Be particularly careful around these drivers. They are often driving on autopilot.

School bus—slowing or stopping school buses almost always mean children are on the move. They may come out from in front of or behind the bus. From either side of the road, expect the unexpected and know state laws concerning school buses.

Toll booths—always check ahead as well as in your rear-view mirrors for pedestrians at toll booths. These may be drivers who have gotten out of their cars or toll booth employees who fail to realize the danger of walking near tractor-trailers.

Confused Drivers

Confused drivers are those driving more slowly than the rest of the traffic. They may be visiting the area or just driving through, but they tend to stop or change direction without warning **(see Figure 19–13)**. Clues that a driver may do something unexpected include:

- Cars topped with luggage
- Cars pulling a camping trailer

Hazards

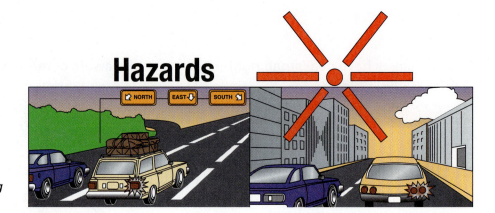

▶ Figure 19–13
Confused drivers present big hazards. Look for clues.

- An RV, with or without a tow vehicle
- Cars with out-of-state license plates
- Unexplainable actions such as stopping in mid block, changing their minds about taking a certain exit at the last minute, changing lanes for no apparent reason, or backup lights suddenly going on
- Slow driving, frequent braking, or stopping in the middle of an intersection
- Obvious looking for street signs, looking at maps, or searching for house numbers

Slow Travel

Motorists who do not travel at the normal speed are a hazard. Sometimes it is difficult to judge how fast you are closing in on or overtaking a vehicle. Following it too closely can create a problem. Identifying a slow driver early can prevent an accident. Clues that help identify slow-moving vehicles include:

- Underpowered vehicles such as a subcompact, extremely old vehicle, recreational vehicle, or any vehicle towing a house trailer or other heavy load
- Farm or construction equipment, such as tractors or bulldozers
- Mopeds or other smaller motorcycles
- Vehicles with the slow-moving vehicle symbol—an orange triangle with red sides. At night this symbol may look like an orange blob.
- Vehicles signaling a turn into an alley, driveway, shopping center, or those turning left that pause for oncoming traffic.

Impatience

Impatient drivers often view all trucks as slow moving. Because they do not want to be caught behind a tractor-trailer, they may recklessly try to get in front of you—at all costs. Watch for impatient drivers who overtake and pass you and then cut back into your lane too quickly. They may even slow down after making the pass.

At intersections, be alert for drivers who pull out before it is safe. They are trying to avoid waiting until you and your rig pass through.

A commercial vehicle driver whose income depends on speed sometimes becomes impatient. They see you and your rig as getting in the way of the job they are trying to do. A taxi driver, messenger, delivery driver, or any other worker behind schedule can be a hazard. Keep your eyes open for these drivers.

Impaired Drivers

While you may meet an impaired driver at any time, you are more likely to meet one late at night **(see Figure 19–14).** Two common forms of impairment are being **under the influence** of alcohol or drugs and fatigue.

Clues to a driver being under the influence are:

- Weaving across the lanes
- Running off the right side of the road
- Going over the curb while turning
- Stopping at a green light or sitting too long at a stop sign with no crossing traffic in the vicinity
- Driving with the window open in cold weather
- Erratic speed—too fast or too slow or changing speeds often
- Driver talking to self
- Throwing materials out of the window
- Acting unusually happy or extremely depressed

Impairment Clues

Weaving

Wrong stopping/delay

Speed errors

Open window in cold weather

▶ **Figure 19–14**

You are more likely to meet an impaired driver late at night.

These clues may not mean that a driver is impaired, but your job is to be alert for such clues and to stay out of the way of impaired drivers. If the clues you see are strong enough, you may want to contact authorities. Remember, though, you are only reporting unusual or strange behavior. Do not suggest that the other driver may be impaired, because that is for the authorities to decide. Sometimes strange, erratic driving is the result of other conditions.

Drivers who are drowsy or suffering from fatigue often provide a number of clues, including:

- Weaving across lanes
- Running off the right side of the road or crossing the center stripe
- Erratic speeds—slowing down and then speeding up

Be aware that these clues could mean more than fatigue or drowsiness. Stay out of the way of these drivers.

CAUTION!

Anytime you see another highway driver driving recklessly, weaving across lanes, driving erratically, or speeding up and then slowing down, drive defensively. Stay out of this driver's way, a safe distance behind or pull off the road if it is possible to do so.

Activities of Other Road Users

Any road user can be a hazard. Clues to these hazards can often be seen in their activities. Examples include:

- Movement by the driver
- Movement of the vehicle

- Buttonhook turns by other rigs and other drivers
- Activities around buses and taxis
- Pedestrians and cyclists
- Conflicts

Movement by the Driver

Before making an erratic move or doing something dangerous, a driver will often make some sudden movement. Watch the heads, bodies, and vehicles of other drivers.

Head movement—looking to the side means the driver plans to change direction. Drivers usually look in the direction they are going to turn. A turn of the head, therefore, may warn of a possible turn of the vehicle. A driver looking in the rear-view mirror may also signal they are planning to make a lane change.

Body movement—drivers often straighten up just before turning to brace themselves for the turn and to get better control of the steering wheel.

Vehicle movement—drivers often edge across a lane in the direction of an intended turn. This sideways or lateral movement may be a clue for an impending lane change.

Buttonhook—big-rig drivers, because of the length of their rigs, often make a buttonhook turn when they need to make a tight, right turn. They often swing wide to the left to gain turning space before they make a right turn. Other drivers do this too. Be on the lookout for buttonhook maneuvers and do not try to pass a vehicle on the right that has swung out to the left just before coming to an intersection.

Buses and Taxis

Passengers leaving buses may cross the highway from the front or the back of the bus. In some cases, they may not be able to see your rig as they make a decision to cross the road. Therefore, it is up to you to be aware of the hazards.

A taxi that is reducing speed is a clue to a possible hazard. Another possible hazard is a taxi driver looking for passengers or following a passenger's directions. These drivers often act in ways that create hazards. Slow driving, U-turns, quick stops, and changes in direction are common. Pass taxis carefully because passengers may leave a taxi from either side as soon as the taxi stops. Also be on the alert for pedestrians running to catch a taxi.

CAUTION!
Always be prepared to stop quickly on city streets with bus and taxi traffic.

Pedestrians and Cyclists

Pedestrians and cyclists can be a hazard for many reasons **(see Figure 19–15).** Watch for people on the sidewalk, shoulder of the road, or on the road itself.

- They may travel with their backs to traffic.
- They are sometimes careless.
- Their vision may be limited by their clothing or something they are carrying, such as a hat pulled too low or an umbrella.
- They may not realize they have moved directly in your path.

Pedestrian Hazards

▶ **Figure 19–15**
Closely watch pedestrian traffic.

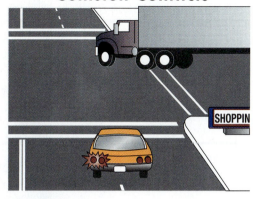

Collision Conflicts

▶ **Figure 19–16**
A conflict occurs when one vehicle is on a collision course with another vehicle or object.

Be aware that children are easily distracted. They tend to act without thinking or looking around them. When kids are playing, they often do not think about the traffic.

Emergency Areas

Accident **scenes** and hospital emergency areas are dangerous for all drivers because of curious lookie lou's and rubberneckers. This is also true in slow-moving traffic. People become stressed because they have been slowed down and are trying to see the reason for the traffic delay, which distracts them from watching the road. Beware of cell phone users in emergency areas and on the highway in general. Without question, you cannot pay attention to a phone conversation and watch the road carefully at the same time.

Conflicts

A **conflict** occurs when a vehicle is on a collision course with an object or another road user. Other road users become a problem for the professional driver when you have to make a sudden change in direction or make a sudden stop. Such actions can damage your rig or cargo. Being able to see and understand conflicts early is an advantage **(see Figure 19–16).** You can then plan what you will do and can often avoid the conflict.

Obstructions

A few common obstructions are:

■ The end of a lane

■ A barricade

■ Slow-moving or stalled traffic

■ A disabled vehicle

■ An accident on the roadway

Obstructions may be in your lane or another lane. If the obstruction is in your lane, you must see the hazard in time to avoid conflict with it. If the obstruction is in a lane going the same direction as yours or is in an opposing lane, you must watch for other road users who may move into your path **(see Figure 19–17).**

▶ **Figure 19–17**
Whether on the open road or on a winding mountain road, alway be alert for obstructions.

Merging

Certain merge situations may force another vehicle into your path. Examples would include a car entering a freeway, pulling out of a driveway or side street, or a vehicle moving out of a parallel parking space.

Intersections

When streets or roads come together, conflicts can develop. Other road users may not stop or yield the right of way. They may be in your blind spot or hidden by shrubbery, signs, or buildings. Road users in conflict with you and your rig may come from the right, left, or the opposite direction. At times, you may even find yourself in conflict with more than one road user. The bottom line is be aware, be alert, and be ready to react.

SUMMARY

Your ability to blend with other highway users depends on how well you can see and understand your surrounding environment and the clues provided by other highway users. The road environment includes the roadway, the curvature of the road, the surface condition, and the immediate area around the road.

As a professional driver, you must watch for and interpret the intentions and actions of the drivers around you. Watch for clues to guide you and to help pinpoint possible hazards.

You should understand that driving is a social act because it involves you, other drivers, and every object in your immediate environment. Your success as a professional driver depends on how well you identify and interpret potential hazards and how quickly you can react by adjusting your driving or your position on the road.

KEY TERMS

Buttonhook	Conflict	Hazard
Centrifugal force	Crosswind	Scene
Clue	Curvature	Under the influence

REVIEW QUESTIONS

1. Any condition or road user that could create a "possible" danger to you, your cargo, and/or your rig is known as a _____.

   a. centrifugal force   **c.** hazard

   b. center of gravity   **d.** safety feature

2. Regarding clues, drivers learn to recognize clues to possible hazards, interpret the clues, and _____.

   a. react in a safe and responsible manner

   c. always slow the rig

   b. always increase the speed of the rig to avoid the hazard

   d. increase the traction of the tires by increasing the speed

3. The force that pushes a vehicle off the road in a curve is called _____.

   a. traction   **c.** friction

   b. centrifugal force   **d.** center of gravity

4. Curving expressway ramps that are downhill are especially bad for rigs because the weight and the _____ of the rig work with centrifugal force to pull the rig to the outside of the curve.

   a. friction   **c.** high center of gravity

   b. traction   **d.** a and b

5. If another driver is looking at, thinking about, or reacting to anything else, _____.

   a. this driver would be of no danger to you as these are characteristic of safe drivers

   c. the center of gravity of their vehicle will increase

   b. their brake lag time will increase

   d. he or she may not see your rig

6. When a driver sees a slowing or stopped school bus, which of the following cannot be expected?

   a. children are on the move

   c. children may come out from in front of the bus

   b. children may come out from behind the bus

   d. children will exit the bus and yield to all oncoming traffic

7. As a professional driver, when are you most likely to meet an impaired driver?

   a. at high noon   **c.** on Sunday in front of a church

   b. late at night   **d.** 3 o'clock in the afternoon

8. Regarding activities of other road users, before doing something hazardous a driver often _____.

   a. makes some sudden movement of his or her body

   c. increases the friction of the tires

   b. increases the traction of his or her rig   **d.** b and c

9. When a vehicle is on a collision course with an object or another road user, a (an) _____ is said to occur.

   a. conflict   **c.** increased amount of friction

   b. increased amount of traction   **d.** increased brake lag time

10. If an obstruction is in a lane going the same direction as you or in an opposing lane, then you _____.

   a. must speed up to avoid the obstruction

   c. decrease your traction

   b. increase your center of gravity

   d. must watch for other road users who may move into your path

20 Railroad Crossings

OBJECTIVES

When you have completed this chapter, you should be able to:

- Identify active and passive railroad crossings.
- Understand the dangers of active and passive railroad crossings.
- Know how physical characteristics of crossings affect a driver's visibility.
- Know and explain the illusion created by a train's speed.
- Identify behavior factors inhibiting a driver's field of vision.
- Identify common driver distractions affecting safety at crossings.
- Know and explain "best practices" for drivers at railroad crossings.
- Know the rules and procedures associated with various loads and railroad crossings.

INTRODUCTION

Most professional drivers are well versed on the nation's highway systems—where to expect construction and where to be ready to avoid other hazards. As a professional driver, however, you must also think about how much rail traffic travels the nation's railways every day of the year.

Train traffic means hazardous railroad crossings and there are literally thousands criss-crossing the country.

America's landscape is currently dotted with more than 280,000 public and private highway–rail grade crossings. In recent years, roughly 300 to 400 deaths have occurred annually at the nation's grade crossings, a statistic that has received significant attention from transportation agencies.

According to available statistics, when motorists disregard signs, lights, bells, and gates at railroad crossings, a collision involving a vehicle and a train is forty times more likely to result in a fatality than a collision involving another vehicle.

New Ruling to Prevent Crossing Collisions

New guidelines for professional drivers and motor carriers are in place in an effort to decrease railroad crossing accidents. With these new guidelines, reckless truckers who tempt fate at railroad crossings by trying to beat oncoming trains stand to lose their commercial driver's license, and their employers could face fines up to $10,000.

The new guidelines cover convictions of federal, state, or local laws dealing with five types of offenses:

- Failing to make a required stop before railroad tracks
- Failing to slow down and check for a train
- Getting caught on the track for lack of sufficient space to clear the crossing
- Failing to obey a railroad signal or the directions of an official at a crossing
- Getting hung up on the tracks because of insufficient ground clearance

Drivers convicted of violating one of these offenses will lose their CDL for at least 60 days for the first offense. Subsequent convictions written within a 3-year period would result in a 120-day suspension for the second offense and a 1-year suspension for a third offense.

Motor carriers whose drivers break crossing laws are subject to the fines if it can be proven that they authorized or encouraged the drivers to ignore the regulations. Carriers may also be fined if they fail to take actions to prevent further offenses.

In the year 2000, according to the Federal Railroad Administration, there were 3,500 collisions at **highway–rail grade crossings** in the United States. These collisions resulted in 425 deaths and 1,219 injuries. An additional 463 pedestrians died in 1999, walking on or along tracks.

Today, more than nine times a week, a truck with a trailer and a train collide. There are many more near-hits in addition to these collisions. Nearly half of all collisions occur at railroad crossings equipped with properly functioning automatic warning devices (flashing lights with bells or gates with lights and bells).

When you think about railroad crossings, also think about this: An 18-wheeler going 50 miles an hour needs the length of a football field to stop. It takes a train, traveling at the same speed, more than a mile and a half to come to a halt, which is why professional drivers pay particular attention to railroad crossings, both marked and unmarked. Understand, too, that a train is at least 3 feet wider than the tracks—and that your view of an oncoming train is going to be distorted because you are looking down the tracks.

More recently, it has been noted that most collisions involving vehicles and trains occurred when the vehicle ran into the side of the train as it crossed the intersection. Studies show that these collisions occur because of the driver's inattention, overdriving his or her headlights, or driving while stressed or fatigued and thus being too distracted to notice the train.

According to the Federal Motor Carrier Safety Administration regulations:

> Every motor vehicle shall, upon approaching any railroad grade crossing, make a full stop not more than 50 feet, nor less than 156 feet from the nearest rail of such railroad crossing, and shall not proceed until due caution has been taken to ascertain that the course is clear; except that a full stop need not be made at:
>
> - A street car crossing within a business or residence district of a municipality.
>
> - A railroad grade crossing where a police officer or a traffic control signal (not a railroad flashing signal) directs traffic to proceed.
>
> - An abandoned or exempted grade crossing which is clearly marked, as such by or with the consent of the proper state authority, when such marking can be read from the driver's position.
>
> All such motor vehicles shall display a sign on the rear reading, "This Vehicle Stops at Railroad Crossings."

Operation Lifesaver

In Idaho, in 1972, Operation Lifesaver came into being when the national average of collisions at highway–rail grade crossings exceeded 12,000 annually. A nonprofit, nationwide public education program dedicated to ending crashes, injuries, and fatalities at intersections where roadways meet railways, Operation Lifesaver was originally a 6-week public awareness campaign launched by Idaho Governor Cecil Andrus, the Idaho Peace officers, and Union Pacific Railroad as a one-time, one-state initiative.

During the campaign's first year, Idaho's crossing-related fatalities dropped by 43 percent and, when the Operation Lifesaver campaign was adopted by Nebraska the next year, that state's collision rate was reduced by 26 percent. Today Operation Lifesaver programs are active in 49 states nationwide and are credited with helping save 10,000 lives and preventing 40,000 injuries through its national outreach program.

ACTIVE VERSUS PASSIVE RAILROAD CROSSINGS

An **active railroad crossing** usually attracts high traffic and is marked with the familiar white crossbuck with flashing lights or the crossbuck with flashing lights and a gate. These active warning devices activate only when a train is approaching the crossing, or intersection.

Almost two thirds of all railroad crossings in the United States, however, are **passive railroad crossings,** which means they are marked with advance warning signs, pavement markings, and crossbucks, but there are no gates and no flashing lights. It is, therefore, up to you—the professional driver—to look both ways and to make certain no train is coming before you proceed.

Table 20–1 shows highway–rail grade crossing information from 1981 to 2000.

Year	Collisions	Fatalities	Injuries
2000	3,502	425	1,219
1999	3,489	402	1,396
1998	3,508	431	1,303
1997	3,865	461	1,540
1996	4,257	488	1,610
1995	4,633	579	1,894
1994	4,979	615	1,961
1993	4,892	626	1,837
1992	4,910	579	1,969
1991	5,386	608	2,094
1990	5,713	698	2,407
1989	6,525	801	2,868
1988	6,615	689	2,589
1987	6,391	624	2,429
1986	6,396	616	2,458
1985	6,919	582	2,687
1984	7,281	649	2,910
1983	7,616	575	2,623
1982	7,748	607	2,637
1981	9,295	728	3,293

▶ **Table 20–1**

Highway–rail grade crossing collisions and casualties at public and private crossings for all highway users.

DRIVER BEHAVIOR AT PASSIVE RAILROAD CROSSINGS

On any day at any time in your driving career, you will fit one of three driver profiles: (1) the content driver, (2) the sad driver, or (3) the conflicted driver.

Content Driver

In this scenario, the content driver is satisfied with his life. There is more happiness than sadness, there are few problems, and life is balanced and seems good.

How does this state of mind translate into driving behavior?

You are rested and ready to do a good job behind the wheel. You drive with skill and confidence. You know and obey the laws, you maintain your rig in top shape, and your skill level is higher than average, not only in handling your rig on the highway but also in your relationships with coworkers, shippers, and consignees. You are proud of the job you do, you take care of yourself, and you are achieving your career and life goals at a solid clip.

Sad Driver

When you are performing within the sad driver scenario, your outlook on life is shaded. You may not be sad to the point of depression, but you fail to see much of the good that life has to offer. Your relationships may not be on the best footing, you may have financial problems, or you may be at a point in life where nothing seems to be going right.

You may have some health concerns, you do not have time to do what you need to do and you always seem to be behind schedule. Because of nagging problems you do not always sleep well at night and spend much of your rest tossing and turning in your sleeper.

Your rig has had a string of mechanical problems, your relationship with your foreman or supervisor has not been going well and, bottom line, you are just not happy with yourself, others, or life in general.

When you drive, although your knowledge and skill level are high, you are sometimes careless on the highway. You become angry with other drivers, you do not like the way the eggs were prepared at breakfast, and you think the truckstop overcharged you the last time you fueled your rig.

You like driving but may not like your employer. Your appearance has changed from its usual professional standard and you have gained weight. You have several goals to pursue at this moment, but you lack motivation to obtain the goals.

You may see what is in front of you, but you are not fully aware of your total environment. You may tend to tailgate the vehicle in front of you, not because you are being malicious, but because you are just not paying attention like you usually do.

Conflicted Driver

In the conflicted driver scenario, you are unhappy to the point of depression. Your relationships with others are terrible. You have just broken up with your partner, you have money problems, and you may be drinking when off duty.

You dislike your job, you think your rig is falling apart, and you get angry with the way other people drive. Because of your level of seniority, you think you get the worst runs, have to unload more often than your fellow drivers, and, physically, you feel terrible most of the time because you cannot sleep as well in the sleeper as you once did.

You feel badly about yourself and others. When you drive, you are more aggressive and less considerate than usual. You take unnecessary chances on the road, try to beat the odds when possible, and push the limits when you have the opportunity.

Your appearance is as sloppy as your driving. You have withdrawn from most of your relationships. You lack goals and motivation to achieve.

When you drive, your mind wanders. You feel sorry for yourself and you think about other people in other places. More than once, you have had to maneuver quickly to avoid a collision. You are doing your job but your appearance is more like that of a zombie than a human being.

Truthfully, any driver who is conflicted for more than a week should seek special help in sorting out his or her problems. This driver may have just experienced a personal loss such as the death of a family member or a divorce. This driver could have recently filed for bankruptcy or have problems with alcohol or other substance abuse.

Even if the driver seeks professional help, he or she will continue to drive and make unsafe decisions—at least for a while. If this person is you, get help as soon as possible. Similarly, if you see a fellow driver having a difficult time, encourage him or her to seek help as soon as possible. You could be saving lives.

DRIVER DISTRACTIONS AND PASSIVE RAIL CROSSINGS

Because your life outside your work has a direct impact on how you perform each day, your attitude—happy, sad, or conflicted—does a lot to distract you from what you do as a driver. For example, if you feel happy, you will see the warning signals at an active rail crossing and be alert for trains at passive rail crossings, If you feel sad, you may not automatically stop at a highway–rail grade crossing; and if you are in a conflicted state, you may not even notice you are rolling over a railroad crossing.

WARNINGS TO HEED

The following warnings are important to recognize:

Crossbuck sign—is one of the oldest warning devices. It is a white regulatory, X-shaped sign with the words "Railroad Crossing" in black lettering. They are usually positioned alongside the highway prior to a railroad crossing, on the right-hand side of a public roadway on each approach to the highway–rail grade crossing, when possible. The crossbuck sign signals all vehicles approaching the crossing to yield and is required at all public highway–rail grade crossings **(see Figure 20–1).**

Advance warning sign—is a round yellow warning sign (minimum of 36 inches in diameter) with a black "X" and "R-R" located alongside the highway in advance of the crossing. It serves to alert the motorist that a crossing is ahead. The advance warning sign is usually the first sign you see when approaching a highway–rail grade crossing.

▶ **Figure 20–1**

Crossbuck signs are one of the oldest railroad warning devices.

The distance of the sign from the track is dependent on the posted highway speed, but should not be less than 100 feet in advance of the nearest rail. This distance will allow the vehicle's driver ample time to comprehend and react to the sign's message by slowing down, looking, listening, and being prepared to stop if a train is approaching.

Cantilevers—are structures sometimes used to locate the flashing light signals over one or more lanes of vehicular traffic. Some states require the signals to be placed over the center of each lane. Other states mandate the signals be located to the right of the lane. Cantilevers are being used in increasing numbers because several states have required roadside installation to be set back farther from the roadway surface.

Flashing light signals—are regulatory devices installed on a standard mast or cantilever which, when activated, display red lights flashing alternately. The number of flashes per minute for each incandescent lamp is between 35 and 55. Each lamp is illuminated the same length of time. Flashing light signals indicate the approach of a train and require a complete stop by the professional driver **(see Figure 20–2).** When a train is approaching the highway–rail grade, the flashing light signals are activated. These flashing signals are mandatory

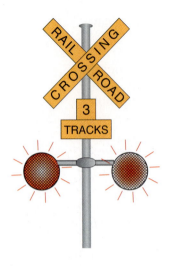

▶ **Figure 20-2**

Flashing light signals.

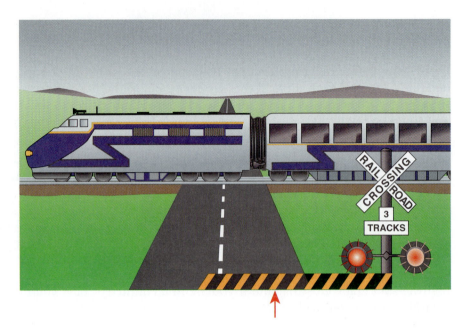

▶ **Figure 20-3**

Standard warning gate.

when gates are used to stop traffic at a highway–rail grade crossing. When both the gate and the flashing light signals are activated, the gate arm light nearest the tip is illuminated continuously and the other two lights flash alternately in unison with the flashing light signals. These signals are found at all types of public highway–rail grade crossings. They normally are placed to the right of the approaching highway traffic on all roadway approaches to a crossing.

Standard bell—a device, which, when activated, provides an audible warning which may be used with flashing light signals and gates. A standard bell is most effective as a warning to pedestrians and bicyclists. The bell is usually activated when the flashing light signals are operating. In some cases, the bell stops ringing when the lead end of the train reaches the crossing or when gate arms descend to within 10 degrees of the horizontal position. A new technology being used by most railroads is the electronic bell, with a volume that can be adjusted to various levels, depending on the location.

Standard warning gate—a device that was first introduced in 1936, the standard gate assembly is an active traffic control device used with flashing lights **(see Figure 20–3).** The device consists of a drive mechanism and a fully reflectorized red and white striped gate arm with lights. In the "down" position, these gates extend across the approaching lanes of highway traffic about 4 feet above the top of the pavement. In its normal upright position—when no train is approaching or occupying the crossing—the gate arm should be either vertical or almost vertical. A standard warning gate is normally accompanied by a crossbuck sign, flashing light signals, and other passive warning signs.

Four-quadrant gate—compared to a standard gate assembly, these have an additional pair of dual gate arms. These gate arms are lowered on each side of a bidirectional crossing. Potential gate violators are prevented from driving around the gates because the intersection is entirely sealed off. Operating like the standard gate and the long arm gate, the four-quadrant gate restricts motorists from entering a highway–rail grade crossing by lowering the gate arm when the presence of a train is detected.

Barrier Gates—a fairly new warning gate technology that locks into a post when in the down position. This feature disallows vehicles from driving around them at a crossing. When a vehicle attempts to drive through the gate, the cables grab it like a net to prevent it from attempting to cross. These cables are designed to catch a pickup truck traveling up to 50 miles an hour and stop it with a soft landing, causing no harm to the driver or passengers. There are currently only a few locations where a barrier gate is being used.

Surfacing—the highway–rail grade crossing surface usually consists of pavement or other highway and rail surface materials on the approaches and crossover points with the railroad track. As the vehicle moves across the highway–rail grade crossing, the material on which its tires roll is commonly referred to as a crossing surface. This surface must carry the train or highway vehicle and transmit the wheel loads to the foundation structure. The surface of the roadway at the crossing is an important aspect of the highway–rail grade crossing. If the crossing surface is uneven, rough, or littered with exposed and protruding spikes, attention is on the surface rather than the warning signals **(see Figure 20–4).**

▶ Figure 20-4

Crossing surfaces provide an even surface for vehicles to pass over the railway tracks.

Median barriers—consist of a prefabricated mountable island. The island is placed in the center of the roadway leading up to the highway–rail grade crossing. Used at several crossings around the country, a key advantage to median barriers is they are a proven low-cost investment with a high rate of safety return.

Intelligent Transportation Systems (ITS)—these are applications of electronics, communications, and information processing products and services used to solve surface transportation problems such as safety issues at grade crossings. ITS projects are developed with the following goals: increased safety, increased efficiency, improved mobility, increased productivity, and conserving energy while improving the environment.

ITS projects have been implemented across the country in several metropolitan areas. Five of these demonstration projects are grade crossing safety projects:

■ In Maryland's Timonium Road project, an active warning sign to alert motorists that a second train is approaching while they are stopped at a light rail grade crossing is being tested.

■ In San Antonio, the Advanced Warning to Avoid Railroad Delays (AWARD) system was designed to help motorists avoid delays due to railroads that cross freeway frontage roads. Radar and sensors at three grade crossings detect the presence of a train. The data are transmitted to San Antonio's area-wide database and flow into traveler information services and the Transguide Traffic Management Center, in vehicle navigation units, kiosks, a web page, and variable message signs. This information on blockages allows drivers to select a different route to reach their destination.

■ At Mystic, Connecticut's School Street crossing, which is part of the Amtrak high-speed rail corridor, four-quadrant gates, loop detectors, train control systems, video monitoring systems, and operational test and prototype systems have been placed to improve safety.

■ The Illinois Department of Transportation is conducting a pilot study of advisory on-board vehicle warning systems at grade crossings. In the study, the driver's perception of these systems is being evaluated. Five crossings on Metro's Milwaukee North Line are being studied. Three hundred vehicles, including school buses, transit vehicles, municipal vehicles, and commercial vehicles have been equipped with the warning system, which is a receiver activated by a transmitter at the crossing to provide advance warning to the driver of a train at the crossing.

- In Minnesota, a project similar to that in Illinois is being tested—the viability of in-vehicle signing in school buses at grade crossings and the impact on driver behavior. Special crossbucks at five signalized crossings in Minnesota transmit signals, which are received by "smart" license plates, which, in turn, activate in-vehicle displays to warn of approaching trains at the crossings.

OTHER DEVICES

Following are additional signals, signs, and warnings:

Yield sign—this sign assigns right of way. Vehicles controlled by a yield sign need to avoid interference with other vehicles, including trains, which are given the right of way.

"Do Not Stop on Tracks" sign—a black and white regulatory sign placed at a crossing when an engineering study or experience determines there is a high potential for vehicles stopping on the tracks.

Stop sign—a red regulatory stop sign with lettering intended for use where motor vehicle traffic is required to stop. This sign can be added to the crossing, requiring all vehicles to come to a complete stop before crossing the railroad tracks.

"Tracks Out of Service" sign—this sign is for use at a crossing in lieu of the crossbuck when a railroad track has been abandoned or its use discontinued.

Parallel track signs—diamond-shaped yellow advance warning signs located in roadways to the railroad tracks indicate the road ahead will cross tracks. These signs are intended to warn motorists making a turn that there is a highway–rail grade crossing immediately after the turn.

"Low Ground Clearance" warning sign—a new advance symbol sign for railroad grade crossings is a warning where conditions are sufficiently abrupt to create hang-ups of long wheelbase vehicles or trailers with low ground clearance. Based on research conducted by the Federal Highway Administration, which tested the new sign with New York's professional driver population, this sign may be used at these special locations **(see Figure 20–5).**

Multiple track crossing signs—these signs indicate the number of tracks crossing the highway–rail grade crossing and will be placed on the post below the crossbuck.

RR lettering—these white **pavement markings** are set into the surface of or applied to the pavement in advance of the crossing, which is for the purpose of advising, warning, and guiding traffic **(see Figure 20–6).**

WHAT EVERY DRIVER NEEDS TO KNOW ABOUT RAILROAD CROSSINGS

Drivers should stay alert at places where the roadway crosses railroad tracks. These highway–rail grade crossings are a special kind of intersection—a highway–rail intersection. If possible, plan your route to avoid crossing railroad tracks.

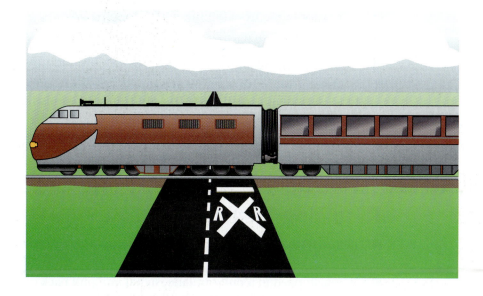

▶ **Figure 20-6**
RR lettering.

Be aware that local and state laws may be more restrictive than the following reminders:

- As a professional driver, you should expect a train to come through a highway–rail grade crossing at any time.

- You should be aware that a train's size and weight, combined with other factors, create an optical illusion. This makes it virtually impossible for you to judge the speed and distance of an oncoming train from the crossing, so never try.

Approaching the Crossing

- Never ignore flashing lights, bells, closing gates, or stop signs.
- Look up and down the track and test your brakes.
- Be certain to check for a train. Roll down your windows; turn off fans and radios; listen for warning signals.

Stopping Safely at Highway–Rail Intersections

At 80,000 pounds, pulling a 53-foot trailer, a typical rig on a level road with good surface conditions requires at least 14 seconds to clear a single track and more than 15 seconds to clear a double track **(see Figure 20–7).**

Keeping this in mind, the following precautions are suggested when coming to a highway–rail intersection:

▶ **Figure 20-7**

Take the proper precautions—allow sufficient time for your rig to safely cross railway tracks.

- Stop no closer than 15 feet and no farther than 50 feet from the nearest rail.

- Never stop on the tracks, and never enter a crossing unless you have enough space to fully clear the tracks.

- Never try to drive around lowered gates. If you suspect a signal malfunction, call local law enforcement, the railroad, 911, or the 1-800 number posted on the warning device.

- If there is a line of traffic at a traffic light and you may have to stop on a railroad track, a good rule of thumb is never stop, even if you do not see a train coming.

- Check for traffic from behind while stopping gradually. Use a pull-out lane, if available.

- Turn on four-way flashers; leave on until following traffic has stopped safely.

- To better hear the train, roll down the window and turn off the stereo, CB, and fans.

- While stopped, look carefully in each direction for approaching trains, moving head and eyes to see around obstructions such as mirrors and windshield pillars.

- Never race a train to a crossing.

- If a train is stopped nearby, do not cross the tracks for any reason. It is illegal and also dangerous. Many railroad crossings have multiple tracks and you may not see another train—because of the stopped train—about to cross the intersection.

Resuming Travel

- Before resuming, make sure there is enough room on the other side of the tracks for the entire rig to clear the tracks, including any trailer overhang.

- If you stopped in a pull-out lane, signal and pull back onto the road when there is a safe gap in traffic. Expect traffic in other lanes to pass you.

- Use the highest gear which will let you cross the tracks without shifting.

- If the red lights begin to flash after starting over tracks, KEEP GOING. Lights should begin flashing at least 20 seconds before the train arrives at crossing.

Special Situations

All professional drivers, no matter what their cargo, should be aware that certain rigs can get stuck on raised railroad crossings:

- Low slung units, such as lowboys, car carriers, moving vans, and possum-belly livestock trailers

- Single-axle tractors pulling a long trailer with its landing gear set to accommodate a tandem-axle tractor

If You Get Stuck or Hung on Tracks

If you are crossing raised railroad tracks and your rig gets caught on the tracks, first get out of the truck and away from the tracks. Check signposts or signal housing at the crossing for emergency notification information. Then call 911 as soon as possible, giving the location of the crossing. To give emergency teams the best possible location, use all identifiable landmarks, especially the DOT number if one is posted.

SUMMARY

In this chapter, you have gained insight into the dangers of railroad crossings as well as the number of accidents involving tractor-trailers and trains every year. You have also learned about "smart streets and road" projects and what they offer in the way of safety for drivers. Finally, you now understand the importance of practicing safety at all times when you cross railroad tracks, the hazards of getting stuck or hung on the tracks, and how to maintain the safety and security of your rig and your cargo when crossing railroad tracks.

KEY TERMS

Active railroad crossings
Advance warning sign
Crossbuck sign
Highway–rail grade crossing

Low Ground Clearance
  warning sign
Passive railroad crossings
Pavement markings

Tracks Out of Service sign
Yellow diamond-shaped
  parallel track sign

REVIEW QUESTIONS

1. A railroad crossing that is marked with the familiar white crossbuck sign with flashing lights or a crossbuck with flashing lights and a crossing gate is known as a(n) _____ railroad crossing.

   a. passive

   b. active

   c. inactive

   d. impassive

2. A railroad crossing that is typically marked with advance warning signs, pavement markings, and crossbucks, but with no gates or flashing lights, is known as a(n) _____ crossing.

   a. passive railroad

   b. active railroad

   c. inactive railroad

   d. low priority railroad

3. A low ground clearance sign warns drivers that _____.

   a. camels may be crossing the road ahead

   b. a railroad crossing is at the top of a hill

   c. the road approach to the railroad crossing is very bumpy

   d. their trucks may get hung up on the track

4. A railroad crossing where the crossbuck lights are flashing requires _____.

   a. that the driver speed up to avoid a long delay for a train

   b. a complete stop by the rig

   c. that the driver turn around and find another route to the destination

   d. that the driver slows for tracks under construction

5. Yellow diamond-shaped parallel track signs located in roadways close to railroad tracks indicate _____.

   a. two or more railroad tracks ahead which are parallel

   b. the tracks ahead are parallel to an adjacent interstate highway

   c. the road ahead will cross tracks

   d. that after a right or left turn, the rig will be on a road that is parallel to an adjacent railroad

6. As a professional driver, you should expect a train to come through a highway–rail grade crossing _____.

   a. on a regular schedule

   b. only at night

   c. at any time

   d. only in the mornings

7. At 80,000 pounds and pulling a 53-foot trailer, a typical rig on a level road with good surface conditions requires _____ to clear a single track.

   a. at least 14 seconds

   b. 5 seconds

   c. at least 1 minute

   d. 44 seconds

8. Regarding resuming travel after stopping at a railroad crossing, a professional driver will make sure there is enough room on the other side of the tracks for the entire rig to clear the tracks, including the train's overhang, which is _____ wider than the rails on both sides.

   a. 6 feet

   b. 1 foot

   c. at least 3 feet

   d. 10 feet

9. If you are transporting chlorine or any placarded hazardous materials, or driving a cargo tank used for hazardous materials, whether loaded or empty, you are required to _____ .

   a. stop at highway rail intersections

   b. stop only at crossings with a signal

   c. stop only at rail crossings within cities

   d. b and c

10. When you are stopped at a railroad crossing and look down the track at an approaching train, you will experience an optical illusion which makes a train appear _____.

    a. nearer than it really is

    b. to be going faster than it really is

    c. a and b

    d. father away and traveling more slowly than it really is

OBJECTIVES

When you have completed this chapter, you should be able to:

- Think ahead to avoid possible driving emergencies.
- Show how driving past an emergency may be better than trying to stop.
- Describe safest ways to make quick stops and quick turns off the road.
- Describe the safest way to return to the highway.
- Explain the safest ways of dealing with brake failure and blowouts.

Figure 21–1

In an ideal road environment, vehicles of all types should allow adequate space between themselves and others on the road.

INTRODUCTION

In an ideal road environment, vehicles of all types—cars, vans, trucks, motorcycles, buses, and bicycles—should maintain adequate space between themselves and other road users **(see Figure 21–1).** This would not only be a safe environment for everyone, but it also would help each user avoid any problems. The cold, hard reality, however, is that this does not always happen.

When we slide behind the wheel of any vehicle, we can make mistakes and, unknowingly, create an emergency. In fact, anything can happen at any time in traffic. The professional driver is aware of this possibility and can, in most cases, avert accidents. However, sometimes the driver has no ability to control the situation.

This chapter should help you prepare for, recognize, and respond to possible emergency situations on the roadway. Before we get into the specifics, however, the following tips may assist for the professional driver when making emergency maneuvers:

1. If you see an obstacle in your path, often the best maneuver is to steer around it to try to miss it. Stopping is not always the best option because (1) you may not have enough room to stop, and (2) sometimes a quick stop may cause the tractor-trailer rig to flip or jackknife.

2. Once you have steered around whatever was in your path, you will turn the wheel back in the other direction. This is called **countersteering** and you must be prepared to steer in the opposite direction. A speedy reaction time is important in this maneuver.

3. When turning to miss an obstacle, do it quickly and do not apply your brakes, as you could skid out of control.

4. In most situations, steering to the right will move you and your rig out of harm's way. If you are blocked on both sides, moving to the right is the best choice, because you will avoid moving into the oncoming traffic or causing anyone to move into the opposite lane.

5. If you have to leave the paved roadway to avoid an accident, try to keep one set of wheels on the pavement for better traction.

6. If your brakes fail, downshift to the lowest gear possible and try to pump the brakes. With hydraulic brakes, you can often build enough pressure to stop the vehicle. The emergency brake is another option, but be sure to press the release button or pull the release lever at the same time you pull the emergency brake. If nothing works, find an escape ramp or turn uphill. This will sometimes slow your vehicle.

7. If your tires fail (thumping, vibration, or if steering feels tight), stop as soon as possible. To maintain control of your vehicle, hold the steering wheel firmly and stay off the brake until the vehicle has slowed. Then pull off the road and stop.

8. Professional drivers always allow themselves more space to stop than the average driver. This precaution is especially important in an emergency situation when the CMV must stop unexpectedly or swerve to miss an obstacle.

AVOIDING EMERGENCIES

The best way to handle an emergency is to avoid it in the first place. This may sound simple, but most emergencies happen when drivers make mistakes. These mistakes often create unsafe situations, which brings us to the first rule of the road: If we do not practice **defensive driving**, then accidents will occur.

Professional drivers reduce the chance of accidents by using their knowledge and the skills gleaned from this book, and learning to recognize possible emergencies and react to them in order to avoid a problem.

There are a number of practices professional drivers can use to reduce the chances of an emergency **(see Figure 21–2):**

- Vehicle inspection
- Visual search
- Recognizing hazards
- Communication
- Speed management
- Space management
- Night driving skills and tactics
- Skills in driving during extreme operating conditions
- Maintaining good health
- Observing safety practices

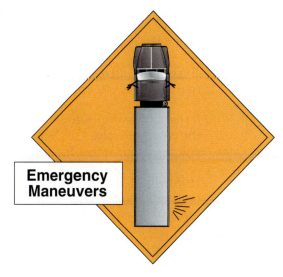

▶ Figure 21-2

There are a number of skills that can help you reduce the chances of an emergency.

An Indiana University study found that one third of all vehicle accidents could have been avoided with the proper driving techniques. Though an escape route or "out" was usually available, most drivers hit their brakes and let their vehicles skid out of control, according to the study. Panic braking is a result of habit. Drivers tend to put on the brakes any time there is an emergency or difficult situation.

EMERGENCY MANEUVERS

Six types of emergency maneuvers are reviewed in this section:

1. **What to do when skidding occurs**—regaining control of your vehicle
2. **Evasive steering**—steering out of an emergency situation
3. **Off-road recovery**—using the roadside as an escape path and then safely returning to the highway
4. **Emergency stopping**—stopping quickly while keeping the vehicle under control
5. **Handling brake failure**—stopping the truck when you lose your brakes
6. **Blowout**—maintaining control when a front tire blows

What to Do When Skidding Occurs

Whenever your tires lose traction, a skid can result. The obvious move is applying the brakes, but braking often causes other problems.

Oversteering can also cause skidding, so avoid turning the wheels more than the vehicle itself can turn.

Driving too fast is one of the most common reasons a vehicle goes into a skid. Manage your speed, matching it with road and weather conditions.

Another common reason a rig will skid is when the rear wheels lose traction from overbraking or overaccelerating.

When you skid because of ice or snow, simply take your foot off the accelerator and push in the clutch.

When the rear wheels skid, it is usually a result of overbraking and the wheels locking.

To correct a drive wheel braking skid, take your foot off the brake, allow the wheels on the rear to roll, and if you are on icy roads push in the clutch to let the wheels turn freely.

If the vehicle begins to slide sideways, steer in the direction you want the vehicle to go—and turn the wheel quickly. As a vehicle corrects its course, the tendency is to keep on turning. So, unless you turn your wheel the other way quickly, you may start skidding again.

Front wheel skids occur, usually when driving too fast, because of worn front tires or overweight on the front axle. In a front wheel skid, the best maneuver is to let the vehicle slow down. Stop turning or hard braking. Slow as quickly as possible without skidding.

Evasive Steering

Evasive steering is a safe way to get out of or avoid an emergency situation **(see Figure 21–3).** It reduces the chances of an accident, reduces the severity of the accident, and allows the use of possible escape routes. *Reducing the chance of an accident* by turning your truck is the faster evasive maneuver. Turning can be accomplished more quickly than stopping your rig. Often you can turn far enough to avoid the emergency. *Reducing the severity of the accident* occurs when you use evasive steering because you will, in almost all cases, avoid a head-on collision. With the size, weight, and height of a truck, a head-on or rear-end collision is likely to be fatal. *Using possible escape routes* should always be an option, whether it is a formal escape route, another lane, or the road's shoulder. If a lane is available, a quick lane change is often the best escape route. If there is not a lane available, the shoulder of the road is sometimes a suitable escape.

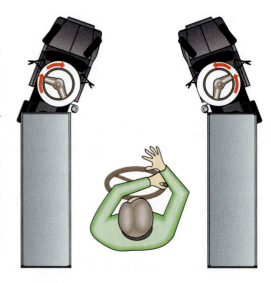

▶ **Figure 21–3**

Evasive steering is a safe way to avoid an emergency situation.

If there is a choice between a collision and trying an evasive action, trying to evade the collision is usually safer, but a sharp turn of the steering wheel can often cause a rollover. Using other evasive actions is usually safer.

If you are hauling a stable load and your rig has a low center of gravity, you have the best chance of avoiding an accident when using an evasive action. Firm traction on the road or shoulder offers added safety.

General Procedures for Evasive Steering

■ When using evasive steering, turn the steering wheel as little as possible to avoid the emergency. Turn quickly. Be sure to use correct braking while turning. Countersteer once you have passed the emergency.

Steering to the left is usually a bad move because the other driver may try to correct by pulling back into their lane, and you will still be on a collision course.

Stopped Vehicle. Problems from this occur in two ways:

■ You may be following the car ahead too closely and then suddenly the car stops.

■ You come over the top of a hill to find a stopped vehicle in your lane.

When these situations occur, there are three possible evasive actions:

▶ Figure 21–5

The height of the cab lets you see the oncoming lane when maneuvering out of an emergency situation.

1. If the lane to your left is clear, you can turn into that lane and avoid the obstacle. This move is usually better than a swerve to the right because it prevents sideswiping a vehicle on your right. The height of the cab allows you to see if the oncoming lane is clear **(see Figure 21–5)**. This is one emergency situation in which it can be safe to turn left into an oncoming lane.

2. If you are driving along a clear shoulder with a good surface, you can swerve to the right. Sideswiping another vehicle on a shoulder is rare.

3. If you are in one of the middle lanes of a multilane road, move into whichever lane is clear. Otherwise, evade to the right. If there is a vehicle in the right lane, it is better to force it over than to force another vehicle into an oncoming lane.

Merging Vehicle. A merging vehicle can create an emergency situation in the following ways **(see Figure 21–6)**.

■ Another vehicle may try to change lanes and move into your lane.

■ Another vehicle may try to merge onto the highway without yielding to you.

■ A vehicle may pull out from a side street, driveway, or parking space.

■ Another road user—such as pedestrian or cyclist—may enter the highway.

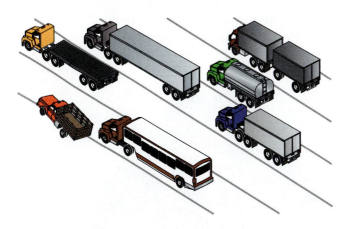

▶ Figure 21–6

An accident waiting to happen: A merging vehicle in your lane.

Common sense tells you that blasting your air horn can and usually does startle the other driver or individual. Sometimes, a blast on your horn will frighten the other driver to the point that he or she will veer into your lane or make a sudden stop. If this happens, you may be required to do more evasive steering to avoid the problem.

Some drivers think using the horn will annoy other drivers, and formal studies about driver behavior find this to be exactly the case. In an emergency situation, however, annoying other drivers by using your horn is better than a collision.

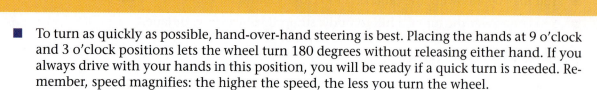

- To turn as quickly as possible, hand-over-hand steering is best. Placing the hands at 9 o'clock and 3 o'clock positions lets the wheel turn 180 degrees without releasing either hand. If you always drive with your hands in this position, you will be ready if a quick turn is needed. Remember, speed magnifies: the higher the speed, the less you turn the wheel.

- Brake before turning. If possible, avoid braking in a turn. By braking before the turn, you can make a sharper turn and decrease the chance of a rollover or a jackknife.

- After making an evasive turn, be ready to countersteer immediately. Do it smoothly to keep your rig from going out of the escape path or off the road. Timing is very important. Begin to countersteer as soon as the front of the trailer clears the obstacle.

Every state has seat-belt laws, so you should always drive with them locked in place. When you turn the steering wheel of a rig quickly, you can slide out from under the wheel and lose control, which is another reason for wearing your seat belt at all times.

Evasive Driving in Specific Situations

Different evasive techniques are needed in different situations. Common situations involve an oncoming vehicle, a stopped vehicle, or a merging vehicle.

Oncoming Vehicle. Probably the most common of the emergencies you will encounter, an oncoming vehicle is also one of the most frightening **(see Figure 21–4).** Another vehicle comes toward you from the opposite direction usually due to driver error, because the driver is impaired or experiencing a health emergency. In any event, you must try to prevent a collision. The best move is usually to try and move to your right. A blast of your horn may startle the oncoming driver into corrective action.

▶ **Figure 21–4**

An oncoming vehicle in your lane is one of the most frightening and potentially most dangerous emergencies.

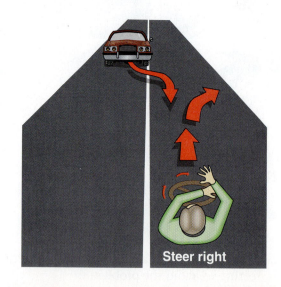

Steer right

Stopping Instead of Evasive Steering

A quick stop is always safer than an evasive turn because there is no risk of a collision with a vehicle you did not see—if you have room to make a quick stop. Such a stop also is not likely to cause a jackknife or a rollover.

When evasive steering is not possible, braking is your only option. Even if you cannot bring your rig to a full stop, the impact of the collision will not be as hard, and both vehicles may have less damage. There will also be less chance for injury or death. Activate your four-way flashers to warn traffic behind you.

Your ABS makes it possible to brake and make an evasive turn at the same time without losing control of your rig.

Off-Road Recovery

When the area beside the road provides the best escape path, it may be either the right shoulder of the road or the shoulder of the median strip. Most drivers try to avoid leaving the road **(see Figure 21–7)** because staying on the road is a well-ingrained habit. Some drivers fear the shoulder will not support the rig, or they may have heard stories of a crash when the roadside is used for evasive action. The truth, however, is that most roadside crashes occur because drivers are distracted or fall asleep. Keep in mind that many evasive actions are successful and do help avoid accidents. Unfortunately, these successes are never reported.

Sometimes drivers wait too long to leave the road. Successful **off-road recovery** means the driver must leave the road at once when the problem occurs. Most accidents that result from using the roadside are caused by the driver's poor technique. Generally, off-road recovery is safe when the roadside is wide enough and firm enough to handle the rig and the driver uses good judgment and strong technique in controlling the vehicle.

Off-Road Recovery

- Reduce speed
- Avoid braking within the turn
- Minimize turning
- Point of return decisions
- Return to roadway techniques

▶ **Figure 21–7**

Most drivers try to avoid steering their rigs off the road.

> **Off-road recovery procedure**—as soon as you see a need to leave the road to avoid a collision, remember to brake before turning and avoid braking in the turn unless your rig has **antilock brakes.** Also, turn as little as possible.
>
> Is the roadside clear? Decide when and how to countersteer, and how to handle the wheel drop that happens when wheels leave the road **(see Figure 21–8).**
>
> **Brake before turning**—when you plan to leave the road, slow down as much as possible. Brake to control your rig.
>
> **Turn as little as possible**—keep one set of tires on the pavement, if possible, because you will be able to maintain control of your steering. Traction is also better on the pavement because gravel and dirt reduce traction. Reduced traction causes skids. Turn as little as possible on the roadside and maintain as straight a course as possible.

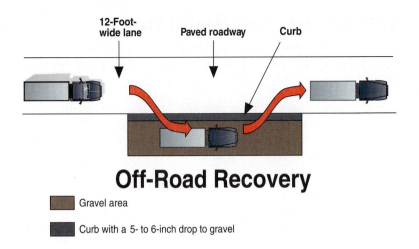

Using good techniques and skills can help avoid accidents in emergencies.

12-Foot-wide lane   Paved roadway   Curb

Off-Road Recovery

Gravel area

Curb with a 5- to 6-inch drop to gravel

CAUTION!
Remember—each turn creates another possibility for a skid!

Returning to the highway—when your rig leaves the road, do not try to return to the highway too quickly. Grasp the wheel firmly and think about steering straight ahead. Stay on the roadside and allow the engine compression to stop the rig. Put on the brakes only when you have slowed enough to stop safely. Signal and check your mirrors before returning to the highway.

If there is a telephone pole, sign, parked vehicle, or other obstacle in your path, stay off the road until your view is clear. Then turn back sharply onto the road. Attempting a gradual return to the roadway may cause you to lose control of your rig and go into a skid. The skid may make your rig cross over into an oncoming lane, jackknife, or roll over. Turning sharply lets you countersteer and decide the point where you will return to the road.

Countersteering—means when you return to the road, turning quickly as soon as your right front wheel rides up onto the surface of the road. Both turning back on the road and countersteering should be done as a single steering move.

When wheels drop off the road—do not try to return the wheel to the road at once. Instead, come to a complete stop before attempting to return to the road. Follow the same procedure as you do for an off-road recovery. If the path ahead is clear, let the vehicle slow to a complete stop and then return to the road when it is safe.

Emergency Stopping

By using your brakes properly, you can maintain control of the rig and shorten the distance required in emergency stopping. By hitting your rig's antilock brakes hard and holding down the brake pedal, the system's electronic controls will ensure the wheels do not lock.

If a vehicle pulls in front of you and you are going to overtake it quickly at your present speed, you can steer to the left or right (evasive steering) and brake quickly.

If oncoming traffic and vehicles on the right prevent evasive steering, you have no choice but to brake quickly.

Handling Brake Failure

Well-maintained brake systems rarely fail completely. Several devices are designed for **handling brake failure** and preventing accidents. Keep your cool and you can usually bring your rig under control and to a safe stop.

Brakes usually fail because of lack of air pressure, air blockage, brake fade, or mechanical failure **(see Figure 21–9).**

> **Loss of air pressure**—when a leak occurs in the system, a warning buzzer sounds when air pressure gets too low. When this happens, stop at once.

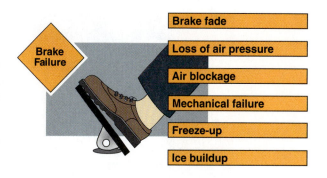

Brake Failure

| Brake fade |
| Loss of air pressure |
| Air blockage |
| Mechanical failure |
| Freeze-up |
| Ice buildup |

▶ **Figure 21–9**

Well-maintained brake systems rarely fail. Those that do fail do so for these reasons.

STOP!

If you do not stop when you hear the low pressure warning sound, you may lose more air from the system and your brakes will fail so that you cannot stop your rig.

A built-in safety system automatically puts on the brakes when the air loss reaches a critical level. This happens while there is still enough air in the system to stop the rig. However, if the air loss is too fast, the air supply may be used up before the rig is stopped.

The independent trailer brake valve will not put on the trailer brakes because they also depend on the air system. If the rig has spring-loaded parking brakes, the brakes will come on automatically when the air pressure fails. They will generally stop the truck unless it is on a steep downgrade.

CAUTION!

Independent trailer brakes can fade to a point where they are ineffective in stopping your rig.

Air blockage—occurs when air is kept from reaching the brakes. A common cause is water freezing in the air system.

Brake fade—occurs when the brakes overheat and lose their ability to stop the truck on a downgrade **(see Figure 21–10).**

Mechanical failure—occurs when some part of the braking system does not work. Usually, this will not affect all the brakes at the same time, and the rig can be stopped.

Figure 21-10
When driving a long, steep downhill stretch, professional drivers should always be prepared for brake failure.

What To Do When Brake Failure Occurs

If your brakes fail, you must reduce speed as much as possible and find an escape path and follow it.

Reduce speed—if your brakes fail and your rig is on a level surface, try to downshift to allow the engine to serve as a brake to slow the rig. It also raises the revolutions per minute (rpm) and increases the air pressure. Keep downshifting until your rig is moving slowly enough so you can stop it with the spring-loaded parking brake.

STOP!

Do not downshift on a downgrade!

Find an escape path—by looking for an escape route at once. Do not wait to see if the rig can be stopped. If you do so, you may go past the only available escape path. Safe escape paths include:

- Side road (particularly one that runs uphill)
- Open field (even though you may damage the undercarriage of your tractor)
- Runaway vehicle escape ramp

Other Things You Can Do

Create drag—to slow down, rubbing tires along the curb or sliding your truck down a guardrail may help. In open country, you may be able to drive into heavy brush or small bushes. Remember that the main idea is to prevent serious damage to your rig and serious injury to you and others by avoiding a collision with other vehicles. Firm steering control is essential using this technique.

Inspect the brakes—after escaping an emergency. Pull over to the side of the road and do not return to the highway until your brakes are working properly. This may require road service. Some drivers foolishly try to nurse their rigs to the closest technician, but this is not recommended because of the danger and risk involved.

Blowout

A **blowout** occurs when a tire suddenly loses air. This can happen because the tire may be worn to the point that it is too thin to hold air, have a crack in the tire casing, or be damaged from debris, potholes, curbs, nails, and so on. Blowouts can often be prevented by thorough pretrip inspections and proper braking.

What Happens When a Tire Blows Out?

Steering problems are your first concern because the rig may veer to the side. A blowout to the rear tractor tires may produce a vibration in the cab. This can cause the rear of the tractor to pull in the direction of the air loss. Trailer tire blowouts can generally be identified by handling difficulties or by the sound of the tire blowing out. If it is an outside tire, you may be able to see it in your mirrors.

Front Tire Blowout

The front tire blowout usually occurs with a loud bang. Remember, however, a tire can also deflate without a sound. Grasp the wheel tightly so it will not be jerked from your hands. You may have steering problems **(see Figure 21–11).** You want to keep the rig from veering off to the side. Speed up to stop the side force and regain control. Then bring the vehicle to a gradual and controlled stop.

Having to grasp the wheel tightly in an emergency is one reason to hold the steering wheel at the 9 o'clock and 3 o'clock positions at all times. When holding the wheel at these positions, the thumbs should be facing up. The force of a blowout can break a thumb wrapped around the wheel or under a wheel spoke. When the blowout occurs, by speeding up at once, you can keep the rig moving in a straight line. Slow down gradually when you have the rig under control.

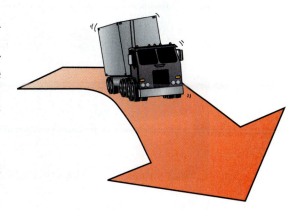

Figure 21–11

A front tire blowout will cause steering problems.

CAUTION!

Braking after a front tire blowout is dangerous because it shifts weight to the front of the vehicle and makes steering more difficult **(see Figure 21–12).** After the engine has slowed down the rig, it is then safe to gently apply the brakes and pull off the road.

Rear Tire Blowout

A rear tire blowout is not as dangerous as a blowout of a front tire. You usually will not feel any pull on the steering wheel but the truck may pull to the side of the flat. When this occurs, do not brake at once. Let the rig slow down gradually. Then brake slowly and pull off the road before gently braking the rig to a stop. Be sure to check inside and adjacent tires for damage.

When a blowout occurs, have the tire changed as soon as possible. Check for any damage the blown tire may have caused, including the following:

■ Air lines and other adjacent parts
■ Wheel rim
■ Fire
■ Damage to other vehicles

► **Figure 21-12**

Braking after a front tire blowout is dangerous because it shifts weight to the front of the vehicle, making it difficult to steer.

SUMMARY

In this chapter you learned how to avoid some of the common driving emergencies. You were shown how to steer evasively, how to recover when the rig goes off the road, and how best to stop in an emergency. You also learned the reasons for brake failure and what to do when that occurs. Tire blowouts were described and techniques for dealing with them were provided.

KEY TERMS

Air blockage	Brake fade	Evasive steering
Antilock braking system	Countersteering	Handling brake failure
Blowout	Defensive driving	Off-road recovery

REVIEW QUESTIONS

1. When one drives in such a manner as to avoid or get out of problems that may be created by other drivers, one is said to be using _____.

   a. offensive driving

   b. negative driving

   c. defensive driving

   d. the center of gravity of the rig

2. Evasive steering, off-road recovery, emergency stopping, and handling brake failure are types of _____.

   a. emergency maneuvers

   b. nonemergency maneuvers

   c. center of gravity utilization

   d. b and c

3. Regarding emergency maneuvers, after making an evasive turn and the front of the trailer clears the obstacle that caused the evasive turn, the driver should _____.

   a. counterattack

   b. countersteer

   c. utilize counter gravity

   d. utilize counter traction

4. Regarding a stopped vehicle in your lane, if you are driving in the middle lane of a multilane road and none of the adjacent lanes are clear and a stopped vehicle is too close to avoid a collision, you should _____.

   a. evade to the left

   b. hit your brakes

   c. evade to the right

   d. speed up

5. Regarding off-road recovery procedures, if a driver brakes in the turn when leaving the roadway, the brakes could lock and may cause a _____.

   a. brake lag

   b. center of gravity

   c. reaction time

   d. skid

6. Regarding emergency stopping, the act of putting on the brakes with a steady pressure just short of wheel lockup is called _____.

   a. stab braking

   b. controlled braking

   c. counter braking

   d. reaction time braking

7. Regarding a loss of air pressure in the air system, if a leak occurs in the air system and a warning buzzer sounds, the driver should _____.

   a. drive to the next truck stop

   b. continue driving and call the dispatcher

   c. continue driving and call the company mechanic

   d. stop at once

8. Which of the following is not a procedure to utilize if the brakes fail?

   a. reduce the speed of the rig

   b. downshift if on a downgrade

   c. find an escape path

   d. create drag

9. Braking immediately after a front tire blowout is dangerous because it _____, making it difficult to steer.

   a. shifts weight to the front of the vehicle

   b. shifts weight to the rear of the vehicle

   c. shifts weight to the rear of the trailer

   d. shifts weight to the front of the trailer

10. When there is a rear tire blowout, the truck may _____.

    a. pull to the side opposite the flat

    b. increase the friction of the front tires

    c. pull to the side of the flat

    d. a and b

22 Accident Procedures

OBJECTIVES

When you have completed this chapter, you should be able to:

- Explain the correct procedures a professional driver should follow at the scene of an accident.

- Detail the information required for an accident report.

- Know which subjects the professional driver should never discuss after an accident.

- Outline the driver's responsibility in an emergency.

- Know how to protect an accident scene.

- Describe types of fires and how to extinguish them.

- Explain the special skills needed to handle a hazardous materials spill.

- Know what special reports are needed when hazardous materials are involved in an incident.

INTRODUCTION

Like any major industry, accidents sometimes occur in the transport of cargo from point of origin to point of delivery. When an accident does occur—whatever the severity—the professional driver should know his or her responsibilities, including what to do immediately and what not to do **(see Figure 22–1).**

This chapter will explain the professional driver's responsibilities at the scene of the accident and in protecting equipment, cargo, and human life. This discussion will include what to do about your rig, how to report an accident, how to protect yourself and others, and how to prevent a fire or control a fire if one ignites. It will also cover what equipment to use, how to act safely, what you must do to stay within the law, and how to report an accident.

▶ **Figure 22–1**

When an accident occurs, the professional driver should know his or her responsibilities. Courtesy of Colorado State Police.

WHEN AN ACCIDENT OCCURS

When an accident occurs, there are federal laws and company policies to guide the professional driver, both at the scene and in reporting the incident.

Steps to Take at the Scene of an Accident

Drivers should:

1. Stop immediately.
2. Compose yourself.
3. Follow company procedures to the letter.
4. Protect the scene to prevent further accidents.
5. Notify proper authorities.
6. Remember diesel fuel makes the road slippery if spilled.
7. Provide reasonable assistance to injured persons.
8. Protect injured persons, not moving them unless they are in danger of additional injury (trained medical emergency personnel should move them, reducing the chance for further injury).

Get the following information from others involved in the accident:

■ Name and address of drivers

■ Name and address of motor carrier, if any other commercial vehicles were involved

■ Vehicle registration or license place number

■ Driver's license number and state issuing it

■ Name and address of insurance companies and policy numbers

Give the following information to the other persons involved in the accident:

- Your name and address
- Name and address of your carrier
- Your vehicle registration or license plate number
- Your driver's license number and state issuing it
- Name and address of the company insuring your rig and the policy number

Report the accident to your company as soon as possible.

You can expect to be tested for drugs or alcohol in your system after the accident. It is the carrier's responsibility to ensure the driver is tested for drugs or alcohol if someone dies as the result of the accident, if someone is injured and must receive treatment away from the scene, or the vehicle is damaged so much it must be towed from the scene and the driver of the commercial vehicle receives a citation for a moving violation. Carriers must make sure their drivers know the rules for drug testing.

Common sense, the company's policy, and the law provide a guide for all drivers after an accident has occurred. Companies often provide guidelines for drivers after an accident **(see Figure 22–2).** These guidelines include:

1. Shut off engine and turn on four-way flashers.
2. Call for help—police and ambulance, if needed—and protect injured from further injury.
3. Protect the scene to prevent further accidents.
4. Stay calm and courteous at all times.
5. Notify the company.
6. Remain on the scene until the company releases you to leave.
7. Provide required identification when requested.
8. Collect facts (e.g., required ID of those involved, names/phone numbers of witnesses).
9. Say nothing about who is at fault. Do not offer to pay damages, and do not accept payment from anyone involved.
10. Make sure any spilled cargo has been cleared before leaving the scene.
11. Check your rig to make sure it is in a condition to be driven again.

12. File a complete accident report.
13. Expect a drug test if accident is DOT reportable.

▶ **Figure 22-2**

The driver is responsible for the safety of others and for protecting the scene.

Colliding with an Unattended Vehicle

If a commercial motor vehicle hits an unattended vehicle, the driver should stop and make a reasonable effort to locate the driver of the other vehicle. If he or she cannot be located, the CMV driver must leave a note on the other vehicle where it will be easily seen. The note should contain the driver's name and address as well as the name and address of the carrier. The note should be attached in such a way it will not blow away or fall off. It should be placed where the driver can see it easily, because if it appears there was no note, you could be charged with a hit-and-run offense.

GO!

Some drivers carry disposable cameras with them so they can take photographs if they are in an accident. The photos a driver takes at the scene are not just for showing damage to his or her rig. These photos may also become important guidelines if the accident is reconstructed for insurance purposes.

NOTE: When taking photographs, focus on the vehicles, skid marks, damage to vehicles, and position of the vehicles. It is not your job to take photos that include accident victims.

CAUTION!

Only take photos after making sure the scene—and any victims—are protected and assisted, law enforcement has been notified, and you have reported the accident to the company.

Accidents while Transporting Hazardous Materials

A professional driver with a cargo of hazardous materials should be aware that any accident can be dangerous. Always check shipping papers prior to beginning the trip to know what class of hazardous material and the approximate amount you are hauling.

The driver must make sure shipping papers for hazardous materials are within easy reach throughout the trip and are readable. Placards must show the product's name or be empty. In 2001, placards with slogans, such as "Have a nice day!" or "Drive safely," were outlawed.

If you are hauling hazardous materials and have an accident, you should:

- Check for any leaks or if any cargo has been spilled and assume it is hazardous material. Do not allow anyone to walk or drive through the spills.
- Keep onlookers away **(see Figure 22–3).**
- Stay upwind of any spills. Do not allow anyone to eat, drink, or smoke in the area.
- Advise emergency responders about hazardous materials involved and allow them to check the shipping papers. Always check to be sure papers are legible when you accept a shipment.

Keep people far away and upwind

▶ **Figure 22–3**

Keep onlookers away and stay upwind of any spills.

- Set out warning devices to protect the scene.

- Notify local authorities. Be sure they understand the truck is transporting hazardous materials. Tell them the classes and quantities on board.

- Contact the motor carrier. Make sure the carrier understands hazardous materials are involved and whether there has been a spill. If the accident is near water, inform the carrier of this situation as well.

- Follow the company's policy regarding the driver's responsibilities at the scene of the accident.

ACCIDENT REPORTING WHEN HAZARDOUS MATERIALS ARE INVOLVED

When a vehicle transporting hazardous materials is involved in an accident, additional reports must be made. Usually the carrier handles these reports, based on the information given by the driver. The driver should not handle any of this reporting except in the following circumstances:

- The driver is an owner and operator.

- The driver cannot contact the motor carrier for whom he or she is driving.

- The shipper's instructions require reporting by the driver.

- The authorities at the scene request the driver make a report.

Emergency Procedures

Because the laws are constantly changing, always check with your employer before you begin a trip in which you are hauling hazardous materials. Learn what you must do if there is an accident or spill **(see Figure 22–4).** You may need to notify some of the following agencies:

> **U.S. Coast Guard National Response Center**—helps coordinate emergency forces in response to chemical hazards. Their number is 1-800-424-8802.

> **Chemical Transportation Emergency Center (CHEMTREC)**—tells emergency responders what they need to know to make the proper notifications **(see Figure 22–5).** Their 24-hour number is 1-800-424-9300 (emergency calls only). You can call 1-800-226-8200 for information.

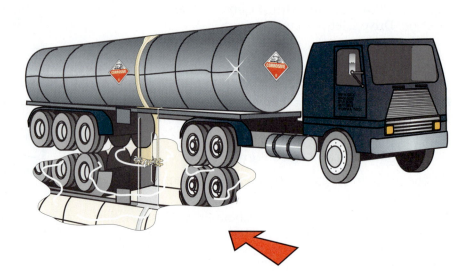

▶ **Figure 22–4**

The driver is responsible for preventing further accidents or injury.

your company supplies an accident packet, use the witness cards to get names and addresses. If no one volunteers as a witness, record the license plate numbers of possible witnesses. Note addresses of nearby buildings from which someone may have seen the accident.

Remain at the scene—do not leave the scene until your carrier instructs you to do so. Be sure you have given all the required information to authorities and others involved in the accident.

If there is a cargo spill, remove the unbroken packages as safely as possible. Clean up contents of broken packages as soon as possible. If you are hauling hazardous material, you will need specialized cleanup. Do not handle the product unless you have been trained to do so and have the necessary special equipment.

Give your rig a pretrip type of inspection to see if it is safe to drive **(see Figure 22–12).** If it is unsafe, call a mechanic to make repairs or a tow truck to remove the rig from the scene.

By law, every accident must be reported, regardless of how bad it is. Leaving the scene of an accident is a major traffic violation. A conviction for leaving the scene of an accident while driving a commercial motor vehicle will result in losing your CDL for one year in addition to any other penalties imposed.

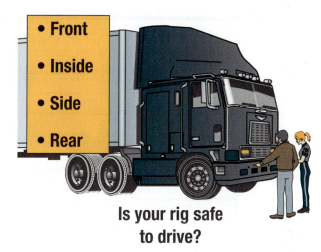

Figure 22–12

Before leaving the accident scene, inspect your rig to ensure that it is safe to drive.

STOP!

Failure of a driver to report an accident to the motor carrier will almost always result in the driver losing his or her job. The driver will also be subject to prosecution.

Importance of driver's information—be very careful when you get information at the scene of an accident **(see Figure 22–13).** This information will affect everything that occurs as a result of the accident. Your information is needed by the company to prepare the required reports for the carrier's insurance company, state agencies, and the U.S. DOT, if required.

The driver's information helps the company determine legal obligations. The company also needs to update the driver's record and to reach an equitable settlement if there are claims.

What the driver tells the company may also be used to find measures that can be taken to prevent similar accidents in the future. Additionally, this information may be used to assess the company's overall experience and trends in accidents.

Sample Supervisor's Investigation Report

COMPANY Safe Company Trucking	TERMINAL OR DIVISION Tenth Street Terminal
DRIVER M. Peachy	TYPE OF VEHICLE IDENTIFYING NO. Single Truck
LOCATION OF ACCIDENT *(Street, town, state)* Tenth Street Terminal Yard	DATE AND TIME OF ACCIDENT February 6, 200X 8AM

NO. OF PERSONS INJURED AND EXTENT OF PROPERTY DAMAGE *(Company and other)*
No injuries.

Left rear fender (apx. $50.00 damage)

No damage to truck, bumper contacted car.

DESCRIPTION OF ACCIDENT   *(State in detail what occurred just before, and at the time of the accident)*
Truck rolled away from loading dock, no chocks were placed at rear

wheels. Truck was not in gear, parking brake was not securely set.

(Truck brakes were out of adjustment.) Truck rolled apx. 10 feet and

struck rear fender of parked car in yard. Car was parked illegally

in yard.

UNSAFE CONDITION   *(Describe unsafe conditions such as faulty brake, light, etc. contributing to accident)*

No chock blocks on truck.

Brakes out of adjustment.

UNSAFE ACT   *(Describe the unsafe action of driver as turning from wrong lane, speeding, failing to signal, etc.)*

Brakes not secured when parked. Truck not in gear.

Car parked in truck area.

REMEDY   *(As a supervisor, what action have you taken or do you propose taking to prevent a repeat accident)*

Check truck dock for chocks. Require chocks at loading dock and stops.

Driver issued warning. Keep private vehicles out of loading area.

SUPERVISOR *R.Ray*	REVIEWED AND APPROVED BY	DATE REPORT PREPARED February 8, 200X

(Use reverse side for sketch and additional detail)

▶ **Figure 22-13**

The driver's information affects everything that occurs as a result of the accident.

Summary of Accident Reporting Requirements

Unless the professional driver is an owner-operator, he or she does not prepare the reports for the insurance company or the state or federal agencies; however, the driver should understand the state and federal reporting requirements, as follows:

State reporting requirements—every accident resulting in a fatality or personal injury must be reported to state authorities. Each state has its own limit for reporting property damage accidents. The limit amounts range from $50 to $2,000. The driver involved in a property damage accident should be sure to check with the police about reporting requirements.

Federal reporting requirements—a motor carrier operating in interstate or foreign commerce must report accidents to local authorities if they result in:

- Fatalities
- Injury requiring treatment away from the scene
- Disabling damage to one or more vehicles requiring the vehicles to be towed from the scene

Local authorities are responsible for notifying the U.S. DOT. An accident does not have to be reported to the DOT if it only involves getting on or off a vehicle or loading or unloading cargo, unless the incident releases hazardous material, and then it *must* be reported.

Accidents and the Professional Driver

A professional driver works hard to maintain an accident-free driving record. Carriers also place a high priority on accident-free miles—in commercial vehicles and their own personal vehicles—often awarding drivers who have clean driving records.

The FMCSR requires interstate motor carriers to annually review the record of each driver. This includes an evaluation of each driver's accident record and number of traffic violations.

Every accident costs the carrier money, even though the driver may not be to blame. If the driver is at fault in any way, the cost to the company is much greater.

Usually, the transportation industry decides whether an accident could have been prevented **(see Figure 22–14).** This is more than just a question of whether the truck driver was issued a citation. They decide if the driver failed to take any action that could have prevented the accident.

Under the trucking industry's standards, an accident is considered preventable if the driver did anything that contributed to it or if the driver did not try to avoid it.

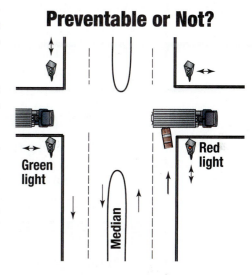

Preventable or Not?

Figure 22–14

The trucking company usually decides whether the accident could have been prevented.

GIVING FIRST AID

First aid is immediate and temporary care given to an accident victim until professional help arrives. To administer first aid, you should have training, such as that offered by the American Red Cross course, "Essential First Aid and CPR," so you can be of help if needed in an emergency **(see Figure 22–15).**

As a professional driver, if an accident occurs and you are one of the first on the scene, then offer help. If help is already on the scene, you do not need to stop. If your help is not needed, your stopping will only add to the congestion at the scene of the accident.

Limitations

A person's ability to help is limited by company policy and the state's laws for limits they place on you. Learn

Figure 22–15

To administer first aid, you need proper training. Courtesy of Colorado State Police.

about each state's "Good Samaritan" laws, which protect a person giving reasonable first aid. Learn also about each state's requirements for persons who are trained in first aid and cardiopulmonary resuscitation (CPR).

Basic Principles of First Aid

It is important to stay calm in an accident situation. Do not move anyone who is injured unless there is danger to that person from fire, heavy traffic, or other serious threat. Take the following steps:

■ Get help by calling police and ambulance

■ Keep onlookers back

■ Make the victims comfortable

■ Keep the injured warm

■ Never give water or other liquids to an unconscious or partially conscious person

■ Talk calmly to the victim and get the victim's permission to help

■ Never discuss the extent of a victim's injuries

First Aid Summary

It is best to get training from the American Red Cross or other agency before you need to give first aid. If you have to give first aid, know your limits, know the state and federal laws for treating victims, and follow company policy.

FIRES AND FIREFIGHTING

It is always better to prevent a fire than to have to extinguish one. Ways to prevent fires and methods for putting them out will be discussed in this section.

While fires occur in only a small percentage of truck incidents, such incidents usually cause property damage, severe injuries, and fatalities.

All professional drivers have the responsibility of putting out a vehicle fire. The first priority, in this situation, is protecting your life and the lives of others **(see Figure 22–16).** Then try to save the vehicle and its cargo.

▶ **Figure 22–16**

Fires occur in only a small percentage of truck accidents.

What Causes Fires?

Fires can start after accidents, as a result of a fuel spill, or the improper use of flares. There is also the possibility of a tire fire.

Underinflated tires and dual tires that touch create friction enough to cause fires. On some trucks, there is also a strong possibility of electrical fires, usually coming from short circuits caused by damaged insulation or loose wires.

Carelessness is one of the major causes of vehicle fires, with behaviors such as smoking around the fuel pump, improper fueling, and loose fuel connections. There is also the possibility of flammable cargo and cargo not being properly sealed, ventilated, or loaded, which can cause a fire.

> **CAUTION!**
>
> All of these reasons make it very important to make a complete pretrip inspection of electrical, fuel, and exhaust systems, plus tires and cargo.

To burn, a fire needs fuel, a source of heat, oxygen, and a chemical chain reaction **(see Figure 22–17)**. If you remove one of these elements, there will be no fire. You can put out a fire by cooling it to the point that it will not burn; and you can usually do this by putting water on the fire or smothering it, which cuts off the supply of oxygen. You can also put out a fire by using a gas or powder. The powder releases a gas that, when heated, smothers the flames. Certain agents such as Halon and some dry chemicals extinguish fires by interrupting the chain reaction.

Remove Any Side of the Tetrahedron

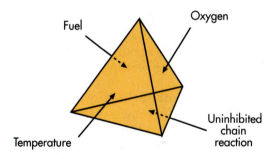

And There Is No Fire

▶ **Figure 22–17**

If you remove one of the required elements, a fire will not burn.

Different Types of Fires

The four different types or classes of fires are **(Figure 22–18)**:

Class A—a fire involving ordinary combustibles such as wood, paper, and cloth

Class B—a fire involving flammable (or combustible) liquids and gases such as gasoline, diesel fuel, alcohol, paint, acetylene, and hydrogen

Classes of Fires

A. Wood, paper, ordinary combustibles
Extinguish by cooling and quenching
Use: water or dry chemicals

B. Gasoline, oil, grease, other greasy liquids
Extinguish by smothering, cooling, or heat-shielding
Use: carbon dioxide or dry chemicals

C. Electrical equipment fires
Extinguish with nonconducting agents:
Carbon dioxide or dry chemicals
Do not use water

▶ **Figure 22–18**

Different types of fires require different fire extinguishers to be brought under control.

D. Fire in combustible metals
Extinguish by using specialized extinguishing powders

Fire Extinguisher Type	For	Class of Fire
Regular dry chemical		B,C
Multipurpose dry chemical		A,B,C, or B,C
Purple-K dry chemical		D
KCL dry chemical		B,C
Dry powder special compound		D
Carbon dioxide (gas)		B,C
Halogenated agent (gas)		B,C
Water		A
Water with antifreeze		A
Water, loaded stream style		A,B
Foam		B, some use on A

Class C—a fire in live electrical equipment. You must put these fires out with something that does not conduct electricity. After the electricity source has been cut off, extinguishers suitable for Class A or Class B fires may be used.

Class D—a fire in combustible metals, such as magnesium and sodium. These fires can only be extinguished with special chemicals or powder.

Putting Out Different Types of Fires

Different fires must be put out using different methods. For example, using a stream of water on a burning liquid or a water-reactive hazardous material will make the situation worse. On other types of fires, such as a burning tire, water is needed to cool the burning material even though smothering may temporarily control visible flames.

FIRE EXTINGUISHERS

FMCSR Part 393.95 requires that professional drivers always carry a fire extinguisher. Part 393.95 also requires the fire extinguisher in your truck be inspected every 2 years **(see Figure 22–19).**

When fighting fires, know the type of fire you are fighting. Fires involving wood, paper, cloth, or trash and other ordinary material are Class A fires. When the fire is fueled by gasoline, grease, oil, paint, or other flammable liquids, the fire is a Class B fire. Electrical fires are Class C fires.

Most **fire extinguishers** are marked by a letter or a symbol to indicate the classes of fires for which they can be used. Every tractor or truck with a gross vehicle weight rating (GVWR) of 10,001 pounds or more must have a fire extinguisher. The extinguisher must be checked as part of the pretrip inspection.

Most trucks carry a 5-pound fire extinguisher—it's the law. These can put out Class B and C fires. If the vehicle is hauling hazardous materials that are placarded, then a 10-pound B:C fire extinguisher filled with a dry chemical is required. When squeezing the handle on this kind of extinguisher, a needle punctures an air pressure cartridge inside the tank and released air pressure forces the powder out of the tank. This powder travels through the hose and nozzle and onto the fire, thus extinguishing the fire by smothering it.

To use the extinguisher, aim it at the base of the fire. The base of the fire is the problem, not the flames themselves **(see Figure 22–20).**

▶ Figure 22–19

If a vehicle transports hazardous material, the fire extinguishers must have a UL rating of 10B:C or more.

• Aim at Base of Flames

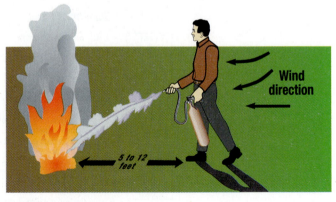

▶ Figure 22–20

To put out a fire, aim the extinguisher at the base of the flames and spray back and forth.

Know how to use the fire extinguisher in your truck. When using the extinguisher, stay as far from the fire/flames as possible. Position yourself with your back to the wind. Continue dousing the fire until whatever is burning has cooled. The presence of smoke or flames is not important. Make sure the fire is completely out so it will not start again.

CAUTION!

Keeping in mind that caution is most important, it may also be helpful to know that fires have been made worse by drivers who do not know what to do. Follow these steps for successful and safe firefighting:

1. Get the vehicle off the road and stop in the nearest safe place. Park in an open area, away from buildings, trees, brush, and other vehicles. DO NOT PULL INTO A SERVICE STATION!

2. Use your CB or cell phone to notify police, highway patrol, or 911. Be sure to give your location.

3. Keep the fire from spreading, so before trying to put out the fire, do what you can to keep it from traveling elsewhere.

4. For engine fires, turn off the engine. Avoid opening the hood. Aim the fire extinguisher through the radiator louvers or from beneath the vehicle.

5. Keep the doors shut if the cargo is on fire. Opening the doors will feed the fire with air from outside.

6. Use water on burning wood, paper, or cloth, but not on electrical fires because you could get shocked. Do not use water on a gasoline fire, because it will feed and spread the flames.

7. A burning tire should be cooled, so you will need to bathe it with a lot of water. If no water is in the area, throw sand or dirt on the flames.

8. Use the right kind of fire extinguisher.

ADDITIONAL INFORMATION ABOUT TRUCK FIRES

If your tractor-trailer should catch fire, immediately drive it to the nearest, safest place and stop. Stay as far away from buildings as possible. Get help, and if the tractor can be unhooked from the trailer safely then do so to help stop the spread of the fire.

Tire Fires

Tire fires usually occur because the air pressure in the tire is too low. Tires that are low or flat flex too much, which causes heat to build up inside the tire. When it gets hot enough, the surface will burst into flame. You can control the flames with a fire extinguisher, but large quantities of water must be poured on the tire to cool it down. Then the fire can finally be put out. Tires can easily reignite because heat builds up between the plies **(see Figure 22–21)**.

Tire fires can be prevented by checking to be sure the tires are properly inflated. Tires can be checked best by using a truck tire gauge. It is the only way to be sure the air pressure is balanced for dual tires. Because of the nature of their cargo, drivers transporting hazardous materials are required to check the tires every 2 hours or after each 100 miles of travel.

▶ **Figure 22–21**

Tire fires can be extinguished with a fire extinguisher and a large quantity of water.

Cargo Fires

Cargo fires often become unmanageable, especially if they ignite in a closed van. You may not know there is a fire until smoke seeps out around the cargo doors. To keep the fire smoldering instead of burning, keep the doors closed. This will limit the oxygen reaching the fire.

Stop in a safe location and get help. Let the fire department open the cargo doors to lessen flare-up. If you can safely do so, remove the undamaged cargo before firefighters put water on the fire. Better yet, check your carrier's safety policy for what they require in case of a fire.

Fuel Fires

Any truck crash creates a great risk for fire, particularly if the fuel tank is ruptured or a fuel line breaks. The leaking fuel may be ignited by sparks from the accident or other source **(see Figure 22–22).** The truck's fire extinguisher may not control a fire from a large fuel spill. Although diesel fuel does not burn as easily as gasoline, it will burn if it gets hot enough.

▶ **Figure 22–22**

In an accident, leaking fuel may be ignited by sparks from another source.

If you find any fuel leaks during a pretrip inspection, correct them before starting your trip. Be sure the caps are secure on the fuel tanks. When you refuel, do not smoke or allow others to smoke around you. Metal-to-metal contact must be maintained between the nozzle and the fill pipe.

Federal law states it is unlawful to fill any fuel tank to more than 95 percent of its capacity. This prevents spills when the fuel expands as it warms. If the cargo is hazardous material, a person must control the flow of fuel when the truck is being refueled.

Electrical Fires

Electrical fires can happen when the insulation on wiring is worn or frayed. If the bare wires touch each other or other metal parts of the truck, a fire can result. In an accident, damaged wiring can short circuit and cause a fire. If you can safely disconnect the battery when there is an electrical fire, this will remove a source of heat.

Making Safety a Habit

Always check your rig and your cargo, pretrip and en route, including the tires, wheels, and truck body, for signs of heat. Always fuel the vehicle safely and be careful with any part of the vehicle that usually creates heat or flame. While driving, check gauges and other instruments often. Use mirrors to look for signs of smoke; and if any system is overheating, fix it before you have a bigger problem.

SUMMARY

In this chapter, you learned how a driver should react in case of an accident: what information to obtain, what information to give others involved in the accident, and what subjects not to discuss. The requirements for hazardous material spills were outlined. The types of fires and ways of fighting them were also discussed. You also learned there are different types of fire extinguishers and how they are used in different types of fires.

KEY TERMS

Accident packet
Centers for Disease Control
  and Prevention
Chemical Transportation
  Emergency Center
  (CHEMTREC)

Class A fire
Class B fire
Class C fire
Class D fire
Emergency triangles
Fire extinguisher

First aid
Hazardous Materials Incident
  Report
National Response Center
U.S. Coast Guard National
  Response Center

REVIEW QUESTIONS

1. If you are involved in an accident, which of the following is not a correct action?

a. Stop immediately.

b. Leave the scene of the accident within 15 minutes because you have a schedule to keep.

c. Protect the scene to prevent further accidents.

d. Notify proper authorities.

2. If a driver of a rig hauling hazardous materials has an accident, which of the following is not a correct action?

a. If oil, diesel, fuel, or any other flammable substance spills on the highway, burn it off so the highway will not be slick.

b. Do not allow anyone to walk or drive through any spill.

c. Keep onlookers away.

d. Stay upwind of any spills.

3. If a driver is involved in an accident that results in a fatality, the _____ must be notified.

   a. U.S. Coast Guard National Response Center

   b. Chemical Transportation Emergency Center

   c. a, b, and d

   d. National Response Center

4. What type of warning device must be carried on all commercial vehicles?

   a. emergency triangles

   b. fuses

   c. handheld flashlight

   d. a, b, and c

5. When setting up warning devices (triangles), so you can be seen by oncoming traffic, the triangles should be carried _____.

   a. behind you

   b. at your side in your right hand

   c. in front of you

   d. at your side in your left hand

6. Regarding placement of warning devices, on a hill or curve the rearmost triangle should be placed _____.

   a. 500 feet from the rear of your rig

   b. 1,000 feet from the rear of your rig

   c. one-half mile from your rig

   d. where oncoming motorists will receive adequate warning before coming upon your rig

7. Regarding handling an accident scene, after stopping and protecting the scene, a professional driver's first priority is to _____.

   a. call a lawyer

   b. call the dispatcher

   c. being aware of your limitations, help anyone who is injured

   d. regardless of your knowledge of first aid, administer first aid to all injured persons

8. Since every accident must be reported regardless of how bad it is, a conviction for leaving the scene of an accident while driving a commercial motor vehicle will result in losing your CDL for _____.

   a. six months

   b. six months if you are at fault

   c. no time if not your fault

   d. one year in addition to any other penalties imposed by state law

9. Regarding federal requirements for motor carriers operating in interstate or foreign commerce, which of the following is not an incident that must be reported to local authorities?

   a. a fatality

   b. an injury requiring only treatment at the scene of the accident

   c. an injury requiring treatment away from the scene of the accident

   d. disabling damage to one or more vehicles requiring the vehicle to be towed from the scene

10. As a professional driver, if your tractor-trailer should catch fire, you should _____.

    a. stop immediately

    b. drive to the nearest truck stop and report the fire

    c. drive to the nearest fire station

    d. immediately drive it to the nearest safe place and stop

23 Special Rigs

OBJECTIVES

When you have completed this chapter, you should be able to:

- Identify common special rigs.
- Understand the function, operating characteristics, size, special features, and hazards of special rigs.
- Know the special skills and training needed to operate some rigs.
- Know the hazards of operating a rig when not qualified.
- Be aware of various types of cargos that are hauled.

INTRODUCTION

A **special rig** is any combination vehicle differing from the standard tractor and 48-foot to 53-foot dry freight trailer van with five axles and 18 wheels **(see Figure 23–1).** In this section, we will describe many of the common special rigs and the special skills needed to drive them **(see Figure 23–2).**

▶ **Figure 23–1**

Special rigs are any combination vehicle differing from the standard tractor and forty-eight to fifty-three foot dry freight trailer with five axles and eighteen wheels.

Special Purpose Vehicles

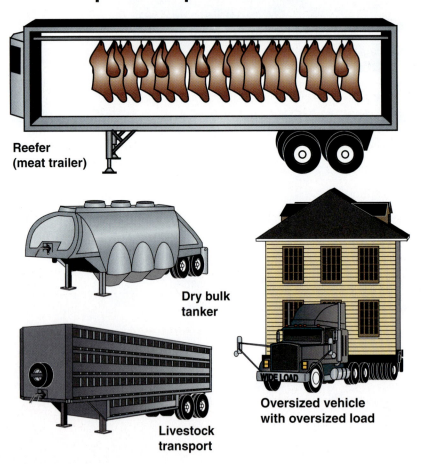

Reefer
(meat trailer)

Dry bulk
tanker

Livestock
transport

Oversized vehicle
with oversized load

▶ **Figure 23–2**

Special rigs are designed to haul specialized loads and require special driving skills.

CAUTION!
Because special rigs require special handling skills, professional drivers who drive them should be specially trained, either in school or by the employer.

The following information is intended only to familiarize you with the unusual nature and driving requirements associated with some of the more common special rigs.

Among special rigs used commonly today are those:

- With more than one point of **articulation,** or **multiarticulation (see Figure 23–3)**

- That are **overlength, overheight, overwidth,** or **oversize**

- With a low ground clearance

- With a high center of gravity, when loaded

- With load stability problems

- That are used for special cargos

- That require special handling

"We talked about special rigs in school, but I never expected to see this!"

The word *articulate* means "consisting of segments separated by joints." A multiple-articulation rig is one with several parts connected by joints. A typical tractor-trailer has just one joint—the connection at the kingpin and the fifth wheel between the tractor and the trailer.

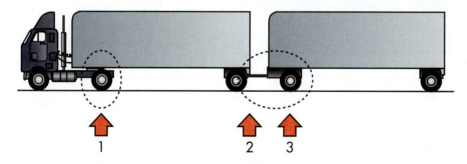

The three articulation points of a twin trailer combination
1. Tractor fifth wheel and lead trailer kingpin connection
2. Lead trailer pintle hook connection with dolly tow bar
3. Dolly fifth wheel and rear trailer kingpin connection

▶ **Figure 23–3**
A typical tractor-trailer rig has one joint. Twin trailers have three articulation joints.

> ### CAUTION!
> Steering a special rig can be affected by dry (lacking lubrication) fifth wheels on the tractor and dolly.

LONG COMBINATION VEHICLES

Rigs with more than one trailer are known as long combination vehicles. They include:

- Twin trailers
- Rocky Mountain doubles
- B-trains
- Triple trailers

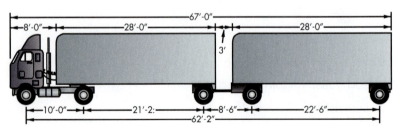

▶ **Figure 23–4**
A double trailer.

Twin Trailers

These rigs are also known as double bottoms, doubles, or sets **(see Figure 23–4).** The two basic types of twin trailers are **standard doubles** and **turnpike doubles.**

Standard Doubles

Standard doubles use two semitrailers. The second trailer is converted into a full trailer by using a **converter dolly** (a set of wheels with a fifth wheel). The second semi couples with the fifth wheel at the converter. Most converters have a draw bar with one eye that connects to the pintle hook on the back of the first trailer.

These are known as **A-dollies.** Some converters have a set of two parallel eyes that hook into two pintle hooks on the back of the first trailer. These are known as **B-dollies.** A rig with an A-dolly is also known as an **A-train** and a rig with B-dollies can be called a **C-train (see Figure 23–5).**

Identifying Characteristics. Doubles have three points of articulation:

- First trailer kingpin and the fifth wheel
- Pintle hook and eye
- Converter dolly fifth wheel and the kingpin of the second trailer

Typical dimensions of a tractor-semitrailer with a 48-foot semitrailer

Typical dimensions of a twin trailer truck (Note: Use of conventional tractor adds 3 to 7 feet to total length.)

▶ **Figure 23–5**
Trailer lengths vary and each combination requires special techniques in handling.

Other Major Characteristics. Trailer lengths for doubles vary from 26 to 28 feet with overall lengths from 65 to 75 feet. Trailers may be vans, flatbeds, tankers, cargo, or others.

Special Handling Skills. Driving doubles requires some special handling techniques:

- Always hook the heavy trailer as the lead trailer.

- Always avoid backing. This vehicle is not designed for the backing maneuver.

- Steering must be smooth. Jerking or whipping the steering wheel may cause the second trailer to overreact **(see Figure 23–6).**

- Do not brake while negotiating a curve. This will cause the second trailer to dip.

- Be aware of the rig's greater length when passing other vehicles, changing lanes, or crossing intersections and railroad tracks.

- You cannot make tight turns with these closely coupled vehicles.

- Try to avoid bumps, potholes, and other road hazards. These can cause the tops of the trailers to bump each other.

- Be aware where your wheels are tracking. It is harder to stay in your lane when making turns with doubles.

▶ **Figure 23–6**

Steering a set of trailers should be smooth because jerking or whipping the steering wheel may cause the second trailer to overreact.

Special Requirements. A professional driver must have a doubles/triples CDL endorsement. A driver must also have specialized knowledge and skills to safely drive double rigs. These rigs may be used in many states but are prohibited in others. Check the regulations for each state in which you will be driving doubles for the maximum allowed lengths and weights.

GO!

Check each state's regulations to make sure you have the required permits before driving doubles in those states.

During pretrip and en route inspections, the driver must inspect the following:

- The drawbar and pintle hook articulation
- Safety chains
- Light cords
- Air line hookup
- Valve positions

More difficult coupling and uncoupling procedures must also be mastered.

Turnpike Doubles

Commonly used on turnpikes in eastern states, turnpike doubles typically have nine axles.

Identifying Characteristics.
- Trailer lengths of 40 to 48 feet

- Overall rig length of 100 feet or more
- Usually equipped with high-powered engines and multiple-gear transmissions

Other Major Characteristics and Handling. Turnpike doubles have the same handling characteristics as standard doubles. The longer trailers, for example, require more room for maneuvering.

Trailers are 26 to 28 feet long, and the overall length of the rig is 100 feet or more (as allowed in some states). These trailers may be vans, flatbeds, tankers (used mostly in the western states), or various types of cargo trailers.

Special Requirements. A doubles/ triples endorsement is required on the CDL for these rigs. Professional drivers are required to have more skill and more knowledge when driving turnpike doubles **(see Figure 23–7)**. If a special permit is held, turnpike doubles can be used on certain toll roads. For more information, see individual state regulations. Inspection procedures are basically the same as those used for standard doubles. Toll road authorities sometimes require special, more demanding inspection routines.

▶ **Figure 23–7**

Turnpike double: A three-axle tractor pulling two tandem axle semitrailers—nine axles in all.

Rocky Mountain Doubles

Rocky Mountain doubles are larger than standard doubles but smaller than turnpike doubles. The lead trailer is typically longer than the second trailer.

Identifying Characteristics

Semitrailers are 40 to 50 feet long. Full trailers are 26 to 29 feet long. The rig's overall length is 80 to 100 feet.

Other Major Characteristics and Handling

Rocky Mountain doubles have the same handling characteristics and require the same driving skills as standard doubles, but the long lead trailer requires extra space for maneuvering. Trailers may be vans, flatbeds, or tankers.

Special Requirements

Professionals driving Rocky Mountain doubles must have a Doubles/Triples Endorsement on their CDL. More knowledge and driving skills are also required.

Special permits are needed to operate Rocky Mountain doubles, and they are most commonly permitted on limited access roads in the western U.S. and western Canada.

B-Trains

A **B-train** is a rig with two semitrailers pulled by a tractor. The first trailer has two or three axles on the rear of the trailer body. The second or third axle extends beyond the rear of the trailer body and under the nose of the second semitrailer. A fifth wheel is mounted above the second axle, which removes the need for a converter. The second semitrailer couples to the first semi, using the fifth wheel. This arrangement eliminates one point of articulation **(see Figure 23–8).**

Identifying Characteristics

Combinations with one tractor and one semitrailer have one point of articulation. Doubles have three; B-trains have two.

When a semitrailer has tandem axles, they are usually located all the way under the trailer. In B-trains, the second axle extends beyond the rear of the first semitrailer.

Other Characteristics

The trailers and overall length vary depending on the state or province in which they are driven. For example, there may be two 40-foot trailers or one 40-foot trailer and one 27-foot trailer. The trailers may be vans, tankers, flatbeds, dumps, and so on.

▶ Figure 23–8

A B-train is composed of a tractor towing two semitrailers. The trailers have an extended frame with a fifth wheel for attaching the next trailer made of a B-dolly and semitrailer.

B-trains have been used in Canada for many years but they are now being seen more frequently in the U.S. They carry many types of cargos.

In a C-train **(see Figure 23–9),** the rig includes a tractor, semitrailer, B-dolly, and second semitrailer.

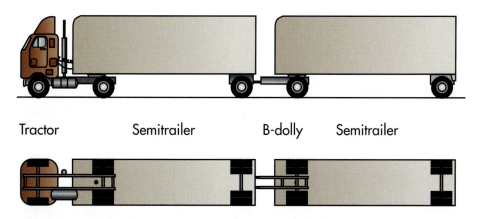

▶ Figure 23–9

A C-train is composed of a tractor-trailer semitrailer towing one or more full trailers made of a B-dolly and semitrailer.

Special Handling

In addition to the safe driving practices for regular combinations are a number of special handling points for B-trains:

- Backing is difficult and should be avoided; however, B-trains are easier to back than regular doubles.

- Steer smoothly—jerking or whipping the steering wheel causes the second trailer to overreact.

- Driver must be aware of the rig's greater length when overtaking and passing other vehicles, changing lanes, and crossing intersections and railroad crossings.

- Driver must remain aware of tracking to be able to stay in the proper lane when driving curves.

Special Requirements

Driving a B-train requires special training, skills, and knowledge. A doubles/triples endorsement is needed on the CDL. With special permits, these rigs may be driven on certain roadways only. For more information, see each state's requirements.

Triple Trailers

Other names for **triple trailer** rigs are triples, triple headers, triple bottoms, or triple sets.

Description

Triple trailers are combination rigs with three semitrailers pulled by a tractor. The second and third semis are converted to full trailers by converters. They are connected by drawbars and pintle hooks **(see Figure 23–10).**

▶ **Figure 23–10**

Triples—or triple trailers.

Identifying Characteristics

Similar to doubles, triples have a number of connection points—five to be exact. There are three kingpin and fifth-wheel connections and two eye and pintle hook connections. The length of each trailer is 26 to 28 feet.

Other Major Characteristics

Characteristics are about the same as they are for doubles. Trailer lengths are 26 to 28 feet, and overall length of the rig varies, up to 100 feet, depending on state regulations. Trailers may be flatbeds, tankers, boxes (used mostly in the western U.S.), or any type of cargo trailers.

Special Requirements

Professionals who drive triples must have the doubles/triples endorsement on their CDL and are required to have different skills from those who drive doubles. The drivers must also have more driving skills. Special permits are needed when using certain highways. Check each state's requirements and regulations before driving triples in those states.

SPECIAL TRAILER TYPES

These trailers are used for oversized loads, and include lowboys, drop frames, flatbeds, and open-top vans. They have multiple wheels and axles, depending on the vehicle, cargo weight, and state laws.

Many of these special trailers have **outriggers** to support oversized loads. Converter dollies may be attached in the usual way or to the cargo itself to distribute the weight over more axles and to support larger loads.

These rigs are used for hauling various types of large, overweight loads including:

- Equipment for power plants
- Nuclear reactors
- Industrial dryers
- Generators
- Oil field equipment
- Heavy construction equipment

Special Requirements

Special training, additional skills, and specialized knowledge are needed by the professional driver who drives rigs using special trailer types. A doubles/triples endorsement is required on the CDL. With special permits, these rigs may be operated on certain highways, often at designated times of the day. For more information, see each state's laws and regulations.

Examples of Special Trailer Types

Two-axle double drop low bed with outriggers—this rig has a double-top frame and two rear axles. Outriggers are attached to each side of the trailer. When they are extended, they support wider loads **(see Figure 23–11).**

▶ Figure 23–11

Two-axle double drop deck low beds often use outriggers to support oversize loads.

Five-axle removable gooseneck low bed with detachable two-axle dolly—this low-bed frame has three rear trailer axles. A two-axle dolly is attached to the rear of the trailer. The detachable **gooseneck** lets the trailer rest on the ground when loading heavy equipment such as bulldozers, front loaders, and backhoes **(see Figure 23–12).**

▶ Figure 23–12

Five-axle removable gooseneck, low bed with detachable two-axle dolly.

Custom trailer and dolly for hauling large diameter and long items—this rig has a drop frame and two rear axles **(see Figure 23–13).**

▶ **Figure 23–13**

Custom trailer and dolly for hauling large-diameter and long commodities.

Two-axle float—this rig has a flatbed frame with two rear axles and no landing gear. It is used mainly in the oil fields for hauling drilling equipment **(see Figure 23–14).**

▶ **Figure 23–14**

Two-axle float.

Four-axle removable gooseneck low bed with outriggers—this rig has a low-bed frame, four rear trailer axles, and a detachable gooseneck. This allows the trailer to rest on the ground for loading heavy equipment such as bulldozers and cranes. For wide loads, outriggers may be attached **(see Figure 23–15).**

▶ **Figure 23–15**

Four-axle removable gooseneck low bed with outriggers.

Multiwheel low-bed trailer with jeep dolly—this rig has a low-bed frame and two rear trailer axles **(see Figure 23–16).** A two-axle dolly is attached to the trailer using the actual cargo. One end of the cargo rests on the dolly; the other end rests on the trailer. A two-axle jeep dolly can be attached to the fifth wheel. The fifth wheel is between the tractor and the trailer.

▶ **Figure 23–16**
Multiwheel low-bed trailer with jeep dolly.

LOW-CLEARANCE VEHICLES

The two types of low-clearance vehicles are drop deck and double drop deck **(see Figure 23–17).**

The **double drop deck** drops close to the ground. The **single drop deck** drops about half that distance. Both drop far enough behind the kingpin plate to keep the tractor hookup from hitting the trailer drop. Be sure the fifth wheel is not too far forward. The tractor frame must not hit the trailer drop and the rear wheel must not hit the trailer on sharp turns.

Drop decks haul heavy, oversized cargos or larger, space-demanding loads **(see Figure 23–18).**

Special Requirements

Low-clearance vehicles are similar to other special rigs in their requirements for special training, added skills, and knowledge needed by drivers. With special permits, these rigs may be operated on certain highways. For specific guidelines and other information, check individual state regulations and requirements.

Double Drop Low Bed

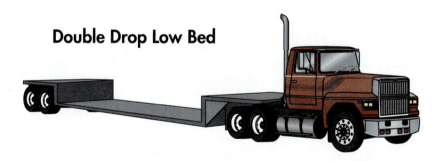

Double Drop Furniture Van

▶ **Figure 23–17**
Low-clearance vehicles.

▶ **Figure 23–18**

Drop deck or double deck vehicle.

▶ **Figure 23–19**

Flatbed rig.

Double Drop Deck

Low beds are also known as flatbeds or lowboys. They haul heavy equipment such as bulldozers, cranes, or earth movers **(see Figure 23–19).** They also haul oversized items such as equipment for power plants, boilers, and generating stations. They may have as many as four axles and 24 wheels. These trailers can have bottom clearance problems at railroad crossings, curbs, and large potholes and require special skills for driving and maneuvering.

Warehouse or furniture vans are the most commonly used vans in the household goods moving industry. The drop-in frame provides a greater load capacity. For instance, a drop of 27 inches gives an additional 3,000 cubic feet of cargo space. Generally, these vehicles are easy to load by hand because of the drop; however, the wheel housing can be a problem if a forklift is used.

Electronics vans are designed to handle delicate electronic equipment. They have air ride or soft ride suspension to protect fragile loads. Now they are also used to haul high-bulk, low-weight items such as clothing, potato chips, and plastics; but these vans have a smaller drop (21 inches) than a warehouse van. They also have smaller (15-inch) wheels, which make room for a flat floor with no wheel wells. The drawback is these vans provide less space for cargo and cause more heat buildup in the brake drums and tires.

Single Drop Deck

This low-bed design is also known as the flatbed. These can haul higher loads without going over the legal height limits. Bottom clearance problems are not as bad as those of the double drop frames **(see Figure 23–20).** These trailers can have many axles and wheels, depending on type and weight of load.

Warehouse, furniture, or electronics vans can have either a single drop frame or double drop frame design.

HIGH CENTER OF GRAVITY IN VEHICLES

As the name suggests, the bulk of the weight of the cargo in these rigs is high in the load. The **center of gravity,** therefore, is farther from the road. This makes the trailer more likely to roll over when taking a curve **(see Figure 23–21).**

Single Drop Warehouse Van

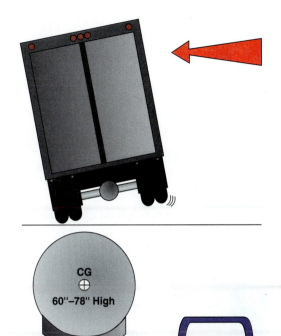

Single Drop Low Bed

▶ **Figure 23–20**

Low beds are designed to carry higher loads, and bottom clearance problems are not as frequent.

▶ **Figure 23–21**

Trailers with high centers of gravity are more likely to roll over on a curve.

Dry Bulk Tankers

The shape of the semitrailer varies but is usually cylindrical. It may be high at each end and slope to a center bottom discharge gate. Trailer lengths vary. The high center of gravity requires careful speed control, particularly on curves.

Dry bulk tankers haul such items as flour, sugar, powdered milk, ground limestone, cement, fly ash, and plastic pellets. These rigs are usually loaded through openings in the top. They are unloaded by a blower from the tractor or through the bottom of the tanker.

Liquid Cargo Tankers

Milk tankers are rarely used for other cargos. These **smoothbore tanks** do not have **baffles** or **bulkheads.** Their smooth linings must be kept very clean. These rigs can be difficult to handle because they must be driven with partial loads. As deliveries are made and the cargo is reduced, handling characteristics change **(see Figure 23–22).**

The smooth interior of the tanks and partial loads make driving challenging **(see Figure 23–23).** Drivers should accelerate slowly, avoid braking turns and turn only at safe speeds.

▶ **Figure 23–22**

Liquid cargo tanker.

▶ **Figure 23-23**

When driving tankers, accelerate slowly, avoid braking turns, and turn at safe speeds.

CAUTION!

The greater the speed, the greater the force of the load.

UNSTABLE LOADS

The two common types of unstable loads are:

- Liquid in tankers
- Livestock or carcasses, sometimes called "swinging meat"

It usually takes the first 100 to 200 miles of a trip for swinging meat to interlock and stabilize.

Liquid Tanker

Liquid tankers are used to transport liquid cargo such as gasoline, asphalt, milk, orange juice, or liquefied gases **(see Figure 23–24)**. The tanker itself may be hot, cold, or pressurized. The type of tanker used will depend on the cargo it carries.

▶ *"Hmmm . . . should have double-checked the lock on those doors before I left the last truck stop. Looks like I'm gonna be a few head short."*

The semitrailers of these liquid tanker rigs are usually oval, circular, or square. The load/unload mechanism may or may not be connected to the tractor **(see Figure 23–25)**.

The number and lengths of compartments vary. There may be one compartment or many. Some contain **baffles** (walls with holes to reduce surge) or **bulkheads** to prevent liquid from surging, front to back. Handling these vehicles can be very difficult. **Surging loads** create an unstable vehicle.

Petroleum or chemical tankers have one to five compartments and may or may not have baffles. Their capacity can be as high as 9,500 gallons.

▶ Figure 23–24
Liquid tanker.

Examples of Tankers

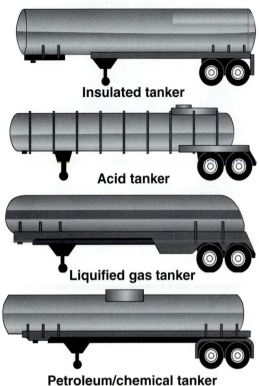

Insulated tanker

Acid tanker

Liquified gas tanker

Petroleum/chemical tanker

▶ Figure 23–25
Tankers transport various types of liquid cargo, hot, cold, and pressurized.

Acid tank rigs have a small-diameter tank with outside stiffener rigs and a variety of linings or baffles. They are sometimes insulated and carry up to 6,000 gallons of liquid.

Liquid gas tankers are designed for high pressure and carry butane, propane, oxygen, hydrogen, and other gases in a liquefied state.

Insulated tankers carry heated material Steel tankers can carry materials as hot as 500 degrees F (260 degrees C). Aluminum ones carry loads up to 400 degrees F (204 degrees C).

Special Requirements for Driving Liquid Cargo Tankers

There are special requirements for liquid cargo tanker drivers. They:

■ Must be familiar with the characteristics and handling requirements of their vehicles

Refrigerated Trailer

The two types of reefers:

■ Nose mount
■ Belly mount

Nose mount trailers have the refrigeration unit at the upper front of the trailer **(see Figure 23–26).** In **belly mount** trailers, the unit is under the trailer.

Both are box-type semitrailers. Some have racks or rails suspended from the roof. Beef, pork, and lamb are hung from these racks or rails. Others

▶ Figure 23–26
Refrigerated trailer—"reefer"

Refrigerated Semitrailer

▶ **Figure 23-27**

"Reefers" carry loads requiring controlled, cooler temperatures.

▶ **Figure 23-28**

Refrigerated haulers have their own engine and fuel tanks separate from the tractor.

have separate compartments. Some cargo can be kept frozen while other cargo is only cooled. These units have slotted floors and canvas ducts in the ceiling to let air or gas circulate **(see Figure 23–27)**.

Refrigeration units have their own engines and may be powered by gasoline, diesel fuel, or liquefied petroleum gas. They also have their own fuel tanks. Generally, the floors, sides, and roofs are thickly insulated **(see Figure 23–28)**.

Refrigerated trailers, or reefers, that have rails attached to the trailer roof from which to hang meat present a special problem because the high-hanging meat raises the vehicle's center of gravity.

GO!

It takes 100 to 200 miles for hanging meat to stabilize. Stepping on the brakes a few times will help slide the hooks forward. Do this before adjusting sliders for weight distribution.

Loosely packed, swinging meat loads create dangerous stability problems. Swinging meat is more of a handling problem than sloshing liquid in a tanker. Safe handling procedures are vital.

Special Requirements for Driving Reefers

Special training, additional skills, knowledge, and experience are all needed by the professional driver before driving special rigs. A doubles/triples endorsement on the driver's CDL is also needed. With special permits, these rigs may be operated on certain highways. For information, check each state's laws.

Before driving a reefer, carefully inspect each trailer for holes in the walls, ceiling and ducts, doors, and door gussets. Also check the fuel level, the reefer's engine coolant, and oil and refrigerant levels **(see Figure 23–29)**. En route, the driver should monitor the operation of the reefer unit.

▶ Figure 23-29

Before a trip, a driver must inspect the refrigeration unit for holes in the walls, ceilings, and doors and check the fuel, coolant, oil, and refrigerant levels of the reefer unit.

SPECIAL CARGO VEHICLES

Any rig designed to haul one certain type of cargo is special. For example, a tanker designed to transport edible cargo should not carry any loads that cannot be eaten.

Pole Trailer

A **pole trailer** carries long, narrow cargo. It may be telescoped—made longer or shorter—to fit the load. Cargo may be poles, timbers, logs, steel girders, or concrete beams **(see Figure 23–30).**

The load-carrying bed consists of two U-shaped cradles (bunks) connected by a steel pole (reach). The reach is the part that can be lengthened or shortened. Some rigs do not have a reach. If this is the case, the load becomes the body. Sometimes a straight truck is used as the tractor and the front bunk of the trailer is mounted on the flatbed of the truck body.

Autotransport Trailer

The autotransport trailer hauls cars, SUVs, and pickup trucks. It can carry six full-size cars or up to 10 subcompacts. Sometimes another car is mounted on the rack above the tractor. A rear ramp can be raised or lowered to allow cars to be driven on and off the transport **(see Figure 23–31).**

SPECIAL HANDLING VEHICLES

These rigs have special handling problems because of visibility, location of the steering axle, and so on.

Pole Trailer

▶ Figure 23-30

Pole trailers carry long narrow loads, such as logs, poles, timbers, girders, or concrete beams.

▶ Figure 23-31

Auto transporter.

Low Cab Forward

The cab is in front of the engine on this small diesel used for city pickup and delivery. A heavy-duty diesel may be used as a combination city and short distance haul rig.

Snub Nose Tractor

The engine extends back into the cab of the snub nose tractor, which is otherwise a conventional tractor. It is often used for close-clearance city work **(see Figure 23–32).**

▶ **Figure 23–32**

City pickup and delivery truck.

Yard Tractors

Sometimes known as a cab-beside-engine, the yard tractor is a heavy-duty diesel most frequently used as a yard horse. Its job is to shuttle, or transfer, trailers from one part of the yard to another **(see Figure 23–33).**

▶ **Figure 23–33**

One model of a yard tractor.

Dromedary Tractor

The dromedary tractor has a cargo body mounted just behind the cab and ahead of the fifth wheel. Its cargo space—or drom box—may be loaded from the rear or through side doors.

SUMMARY

Many of the special rigs described in this section are dangerous in the hands of an untrained driver. All require special instruction and training. Most special rigs also require special permits and endorsements.

KEY TERMS

A-dolly	Gooseneck	Refrigerated trailer (reefer)
Articulation	Liquid tankers	Rocky Mountain double
A-train	Livestock transport	Single drop deck
Baffle	Multiarticulation	Smoothbore tank
B-dolly	Multiwheel low-bed trailer	Special rig
Belly mount	Nose mount	Standard double
B-train	Outriggers	Surging loads
Bulkhead	Overheight load	Triple trailer
Center of gravity	Overlength load	Turnpike doubles
Converter dolly	Oversize load	Two-axle double drop low
C-train	Overwidth load	bed with outriggers
Double drop deck	Pole trailer	Two-axle float
Dry bulk tankers		

REVIEW QUESTIONS

1. Any combination vehicle that differs from the standard tractor and 48- to 53-foot dry freight trailer with five axles and 18 wheels is known as a(n) _____.

    a. ordinary rig   **c.** special rig

    b. B-train   **d.** turnpike double

2. A multiple-articulation rig is one that has _____.

    a. a high center of gravity   **c.** poor traction

    b. several parts connected by joints   **d.** multiple driver trains

3. Which of the following is not one of the special handling techniques required for driving rigs with more than one trailer?

    a. When slowing for a curve, it is better to brake in the curve because it makes the following trailer(s) follow the path of the first trailer.

    c. The driver must avoid backing.

    b. Always hook the heavy trailer as the lead trailer.

    d. The driver must avoid jerking or whipping the steering wheel because this act may cause the following trailer(s) to overreact.

4. Which of the following is not a true statement regarding the special requirements for driving doubles or triples?

    a. Special skills are needed.

    b. Special knowledge is needed.

    c. All states have the same rules and regulations regarding doubles and triples.

    d. Special permits may be needed.

5. Regarding special trailer types used for oversized loads, which of the following is not a correct statement about the use of converter dollies?

    a. The converter dollies may be attached to the load itself.

    b. The dollies distribute the weight over more axles.

    c. They support longer loads.

    d. Reduced air pressure in the tires of the dollies increase the stability of the load.

6. Regarding low-clearance vehicles such as double drop frame and single drop frame trailers, which of the following is not a correct statement if the fifth wheel of the tractor is in the most forward position?

    a. The tractor frame may hit the trailer drop.

    b. The stability of the trailer will be increased.

    c. The rear wheels may hit the trailer on sharp turns.

    d. a and b

7. Which of the following is not a characteristic of high-center-of-gravity vehicles?

    a. The bulk of the weight of the cargo is low in the load.

    b. The bulk of the weight of the cargo is high in the load.

    c. The center of gravity is farther from the road than in a vehicle with a low center of gravity.

    d. The trailer is more likely (than a lower center of gravity vehicle) to roll over when taking a curve.

8. Which of the following is not a correct statement regarding pulling a trailer transporting livestock?

    a. The cargo shifts.

    b. These type rigs have a permit to drive at least 10 mph above the speed limit to keep the animals cool.

    c. The balance and stability change when slowing.

    d. When preparing to stop, the driver should tap the brakes lightly to set the animals.

9. The load of a liquid tanker may surge when stopping, starting, and/or changing directions which creates a(n) _____.

    a. stable vehicle

    b. situation that does not affect the vehicle

    c. unstable vehicle

    d. a and b

10. Refrigerated trailers (reefers) that have rails attached to the trailer roof from which meat is hung _____.

    a. raise the center of gravity of the trailer

    b. lower the center of gravity of the trailer

    c. make the trailer more stable on turns

    d. make the trailer more stable when stopping

24 Handling Cargo

OBJECTIVES

When you have completed this chapter, you should be able to:

- Know the importance of handling cargo safely.
- Specify the professional driver's responsibility for handling cargo.
- Outline the carrier's responsibility for handling cargo.
- Describe the methods of containing and securing cargo.
- Identify state and federal regulations that control how cargo is shipped.
- Explain the distribution of weight when loading cargo.
- Describe special handling that certain materials require.

▶ **Figure 24–1**

Professional drivers must know how to properly handle and load cargo to avoid shifting or damage in transit.

INTRODUCTION

Professional truck drivers have more skills than simply driving a truck down a highway. To call yourself a "professional," you must also have the ability and the knowledge to properly handle and load cargo that will avoid damage in transit **(see Figure 24–1).**

Professional drivers also realize that properly loaded cargo will add to the operating efficiency of any rig. Freight that is improperly loaded not only presents the possibility of being damaged in transit but also is a danger to the driver and to other highway users. An overloaded truck or a load that is improperly secured presents an enormous threat to safety, on or off the highway, and because of this the FMCSR set specific methods for securing cargo and specific vehicle weight limits for rigs.

NEW CARGO SECUREMENT REGULATIONS

On September 27, 2002, FMCSA revised its regulations concerning protection against shifting and falling cargo for commercial motor vehicles (CMVs) engaged in interstate commerce. These rules became effective January 1, 2004.

The new cargo securement standards are based on the North American Cargo Securement Standard Model Regulations. They reflect the results of a multiyear comprehensive research program to evaluate current U.S. and Canadian cargo securement regulations; the motor carrier industry's best practices; and recommendations presented during a series of public meetings.

The new regulations require motor carriers to change the way they use cargo securement devices to prevent articles from shifting on or within, or falling from, CMVs. In some instances, the changes may require motor carriers to increase the number of tiedowns used to secure certain types of cargos. However, the rule generally does not prohibit the use of tiedowns or cargo securement devices currently in use. Therefore, motor carriers were not required to purchase new cargo securement equipment to comply with the rule.

▶ **Figure 24–2**

New cargo securement rules apply to cargo-carrying commercial vehicles operated in interstate commerce, such as hauling grain.

The intent of the new regulations is to reduce the number of crashes caused by cargo shifting on or within, or falling from, CMVs operating in interstate commerce, and to harmonize to the greatest extent practicable U.S., Canadian, and Mexican cargo securement regulations.

The new cargo securement rules apply to all cargo-carrying CMVs (as defined in 49CFR 390.5) operated in interstate commerce **(see Figure 24–2).** This includes all types of articles of cargo, except commodities in bulk that lack structure or fixed shape (e.g., liquids, gases, grain, liquid concrete, sand, gravel, aggregates) and are transported in a tank, hopper, box, or similar device that forms part of the structure of a commercial motor vehicle.

Requirements for Securement Devices

The new rules require that all devices and systems used to secure cargo to or within a vehicle must be capable of meeting the performance criteria. All vehicle structures, systems, parts, and components used to secure cargo must be in proper working order when used to perform that function with no damaged or weakened components that could adversely affect their performance. The cargo securement rules incorporate by reference manufacturing standards for certain types of **tiedowns** including steel strapping, chain, synthetic webbing, wire rope, and cordage.

FMCSA has updated the rules to reference the November 15, 1999, version of the National Association of Chain Manufacturers (NACM) Welded Steel Chain Specifications. The agency notes that some of the working load limit values in the 1999 version differ slightly from the previous edition of this publication. The 1999 version also includes working load limits for a new grade of alloy chain, grade 100. Generally, the working load limits are the same as those in the 1991 publication.

Changes in the references do not necessarily mean the older securement devices need to be replaced. Motor carriers are not required to replace tiedown devices purchased prior to January 1, 2004. If the tiedowns satisfied the old rules, the devices should also satisfy the new rules.

"What do you mean I can't secure cargo with duct tape anymore?"

Proper Use of Tiedowns

The new regulations require each tiedown to be attached and secured in a manner that prevents it from becoming loose, unfastening, opening, or releasing while the vehicle is in transit **(see Figure 24–3).** All tiedowns and other components of a cargo securement system used to secure loads on a trailer equipped with rub rails must be located inboard of the rub rails when practicable. Edge protection also must be used when a tiedown would be subject to abrasion or cutting at the point where it touches an article of cargo. The edge protection must resist abrasion, cutting, and crushing.

Figure 24–3

As a professional driver you are responsible for properly tying down your cargo.

Front End Structures on CMVs

FMCSA revised its rules concerning front end structures or headerboards by changing the applicability of the requirements to cover CMVs transporting cargo that is in contact with the front end structure of the vehicle. By contrast, the old rules required certain vehicles to be equipped with front end structures regardless of whether the devices were used as part of a cargo securement system.

General Rule

Cargo must be firmly immobilized or secured on or within a vehicle by structures of adequate strength, **dunnage** (loose materials used to support and protect cargo) or dunnage bags (inflatable

OUT-OF-SERVICE CRITERIA FOR LOAD MANAGEMENT

The following are points covered by roadside inspectors regarding how cargos are loaded and those loading errors that could cause a rig to be put out of service:

- Spare tire or portion of load/dunnage could fall from vehicle.

- Fitting for securing container to container chassis solely via corner fittings (for intermodal freight) is improperly latched.

- 25 percent or more of type/number of tie-downs required by FMCSR 393.102 are loose or missing.

- 25 percent or more of required type or number of tie-downs are defective.

- Chain is defective if working portion contains knot or damaged, deformed, or worn links. Clevis-type repair link, if as strong as original link, is okay.

- Wire rope is defective if working portion contains kinked, birdcaged, or pitted section; over three broken wires in any strand; over two broken wires at fitting; over 11 broken wires in any length measuring six times its diameter (e.g., with 0.5 inch thick rope, more than 11 broken wires in any 3-inch section); repairs other than back or eye splice; or discoloration from heat or electric arc.

- Fiber rope is defective if working portion contains burned or melted fibers, except on heat-sealed ends; excessive wear, reducing diameter 20 percent; any repair (properly spliced lengths are not considered a repair); or ineffective (easily loosened) knot used for connection or repair.

- Synthetic webbing is defective if working portion contains a knot; more than 25 percent of stitches separated; broken or damaged hardware; any repair or splice; overt damage; severe abrasion; cumulative for entire working length of one strap, cuts, burns, or holes exceeding width of ¾ inch for 4-inch-wide webbing, exceeding width of ⅝ inch for 3-inch-wide webbing, or exceeding width of ⅜ inch for 1 ¾-inch-wide or 2-inch-wide webbing. Multiple defects confined to one strand of a strap are not cumulative (just measure largest single defect in that strand).

- Load binders or fittings that obviously are cracked, worn, corroded, distorted, or discolored from heat or electric arc.

- Evidence of wire rope slipping through cable clamp.

- Anchor point on vehicle displays: distorted or cracked rails or supports, cracked weld, or damaged or worn floor rings.

bags intended to fill space between articles of cargo or between cargo and the wall of the vehicle), shoring bars, tiedowns or a combination of these.

Cargo Placement and Restraint

Articles of cargo that are likely to roll must be restrained by **chocks,** wedges, a cradle, or other equivalent means to prevent rolling. The means of preventing rolling must not be capable of becoming unintentionally unfastened or loose while the vehicle is in transit. Articles of cargo placed beside each other and secured by transverse tiedowns must be:

1. Placed in direct contact with each other
2. Prevented from shifting toward each other while in transit

Minimum Working Load Limit for Cargo Securement Devices and Systems

The total working load limit of any securement system used to secure an article or group of articles against movement must be at least one half the weight of the article or group of articles. The total working load limit is the sum of one half the working load limit of each tiedown that goes from an anchor point on the vehicle to an attachment point on an article of cargo; and the working load limit for each tiedown that goes from an anchor point on the vehicle through, over, or around the cargo and then attaches to another anchor point on the vehicle.

Minimum Number of Tiedowns

The cargo securement system used to restrain articles against movement must meet the minimum tiedown requirement **(see Figure 24-4).** This requirement is in addition to complying with rules concerning the minimum working load limit. When an article of cargo is not blocked or positioned to prevent movement in the forward direction, the number of tiedowns needed depends on the length and weight of the articles. There must be one tiedown for articles 5 feet or less in length, and 1,100 pounds or less in weight; two tiedowns if the article is one of the following:

1. At or less than 5 feet in length and more than 1,100 pounds in weight
2. Greater than 5 feet but less than 10 feet, regardless of weight

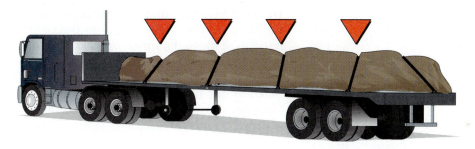

▶ **Figure 24-4**

Cargo should have at least one tiedown for each 10 feet of cargo. Make sure you have enough tiedowns to meet this need. No matter how small the cargo is, there should be at least two tiedowns holding it.

When an article of cargo is not blocked or positioned to prevent movement in the forward direction, and the item is longer than 10 feet in length, then it must be secured by two tiedowns for the first 10 feet of length, and one additional tiedown for every 10 feet of length, or fraction thereof, beyond the first 10 feet. For example, if an article is blocked, braced, or immobilized to prevent movement in the forward direction by a headerboard, bulkhead, other articles that are adequately secured, or other appropriate means, then it must be secured by at least one tiedown for every 10 feet of article length, or fraction thereof.

Special Rule for Special-Purpose Vehicles

Generally, the basic rules concerning the minimum number of tiedowns do not apply to a vehicle transporting one or more articles of cargo such as machinery or fabricated structural items (e.g., steel or concrete beams, crane booms, girders, and trusses, etc.) which, because of their design, size, shape, or weight, must be fastened by special methods. However, any article of cargo carried on that vehicle must be secured adequately to the vehicle by devices that are capable of meeting the performance requirements and the working load limit requirements.

Commodity-Specific Securement Requirements

FMCSA has adopted detailed requirements for the securement of logs, dressed lumber, metal coils, paper rolls, concrete pipe, intermodal containers, automobiles, light trucks and vans, heavy vehicles, equipment and machinery, flattened or crushed vehicles, roll-on/roll-off containers, and large boulders.

Pole Trailer

▶ **Figure 24-5**

Pole trailers carry long narrow loads, such as logs, poles, timbers, girders, or concrete beams.

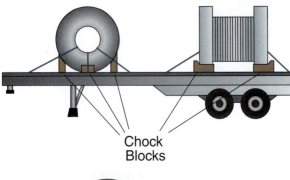

Chock
Blocks

Coil Tie-Down

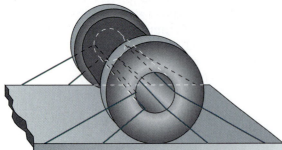

▶ **Figure 24-6**

Cargo must be secured to prevent shifting or falling during transit.

Logs—the rules for the transportation of logs are applicable to the transportation of almost all logs **(see Figure 24–5)** with the following exceptions:

1. Logs that are unitized by banding or other comparable means may be transported in accordance with the general cargo securement rules.

2. Loads that consist of no more than four processed logs may be transported in accordance with the general cargo securement rules.

3. Firewood, stumps, log debris, and other such short logs must be transported in a vehicle or container enclosed on both sides, front, and rear and be of adequate strength to contain them. Longer logs may also be transported in an enclosed vehicle or container.

Dressed lumber and similar building products—the rules in this section apply to the transportation of bundles of dressed lumber, packaged lumber, and building products such as plywood, gypsum board, or other materials of similar shape. Lumber or building products that are not bundled or packaged must be treated as loose items and transported in accordance with the general cargo securement rules. The term *bundle* refers to packages of lumber, building materials, or similar products which are unitized for securement as a single article of cargo.

Metal coils—the rules in this section apply to the transportation of one or more metal coils which, individually or grouped together, weigh 5,000 lbs (2,268 kg) or more **(see Figure 24–6).** Shipments of metal coils that weigh less than 5,000 lbs (2,268 kg) may be secured in accordance with the general cargo securement rules.

Paper rolls—the rules for securing paper rolls are applicable to shipments of paper rolls which, individually or together, weigh 5,000 lbs (2,268 kg) or more. Shipments of paper rolls that weigh less than 5,000 lbs (2,268 kg), and paper rolls that are unitized on a pallet, may either be secured in accordance with the rules in this section or the general cargo securement rules.

Concrete pipe—the rules in this section apply to the transportation of concrete pipe on flatbed trailers and vehicles and lowboy trailers. Concrete pipe that is bundled tightly together into a single rigid article with no tendency to roll, and concrete pipe loaded in a sided vehicle or container, must be secured in accordance with the general rules.

Intermodal containers—the requirements for intermodal containers cover the transportation of these containers on container chassis and other types of vehicles. Intermodal containers are freight containers designed and constructed to permit them to be used interchangeably in two or more modes of transportation **(see Figure 24–7).** Cargo contained within intermodal containers must be secured in accordance with the general cargo securement rules or, if applicable, the commodity-specific rules.

Automobiles, light trucks, and vans—this portion of the new standards applies to the transportation of automobiles, light trucks, and vans which individually weight 10,000 lbs (4,536 kg) or less. Vehicles which individually are heavier than 10,000 lbs (4,536 kg) must be secured in the same manner as heavy vehicles, equipment, and machinery **(see Figure 24–8).**

Heavy vehicles, equipment, and machinery—these requirements are applicable to the transportation of heavy vehicles, equipment, and machinery which operate on wheels or tracks, such as front-end loaders, bulldozers, tractors, and power shovels and which individually weigh 10,000 lbs (4,536 kg) or more. Vehicles, equipment, and machinery lighter than 10,000 lbs (4,536 kg) may be secured in accordance with these rules; the rules for automobiles, light trucks, and vans; or the general freight requirements **(see Figure 24–9).**

Flattened or crushed vehicles—the transportation of vehicles such as automobiles, light trucks, and vans that have been flattened or crushed is covered by these requirements. The transportation of automobiles that are flattened or crushed in a crash or accident, as opposed to being intentionally flattened or crushed in preparation for transportation to recycling facilities, is not subject to these requirements. However, vehicles damaged in a crash or accident are subject to the general cargo securement requirements.

Roll-on/roll-off or hook-lift containers—these rules apply to the transportation of roll-on/roll-off or hook-lift containers. A hook-lift container is a specialized container, primarily used to contain and transport materials in the waste, recycling, construction/demolition, and scrap industries, which is used in conjunction with specialized vehicles in which the container is loaded and unloaded onto a tilt frame body by an articulating hook arm. Hoist-type equipment should be considered separate and distinct from roll-on/roll-off equipment. Containers transported on hoist-type equipment must be secured in accordance with the general securement rules.

Figure 24-7
Intermodal container.

Figure 24-8
Auto carrier.

Figure 24-9
Trucks are used to haul heavy equipment such as bulldozers and front-end loaders.

Large boulders—the rules in this section are applicable to the transportation of any large piece of natural, irregularly shaped rock weighing in excess of 11,000 lbs (5,000 kg) or with a volume in excess of 2 cubic meters on an open vehicle, or in a vehicle whose sides are not designed and rated to contain such cargo. Pieces of rock weighing more than 220 lbs (100 kg), but less than 11,000 lbs (5,000 kg) must be secured, either in accordance with this section or in accordance with the general cargo securement rules, including (1) rock contained within a vehicle which is designed to carry such cargo; or (2) secured individually by tiedowns, provided each piece can be stabilized and adequately secured. Rock which has been formed or cut to a shape and which provides a stable base for securement must also be secured, either in accordance with the provisions of this section or in accordance with the general securement rules.

IMPORTANCE OF HANDLING CARGO PROPERLY

Without a doubt, carrying goods safely and efficiently is the backbone of this nation's trucking industry. Americans rely on trucks to carry goods from manufacturers to the retail outlet in the shortest time possible. This reliance also includes delivering the merchandise safely and in the best condition.

Today's tractor-trailer rigs are designed to safely carry maximum payloads built of strong, lightweight materials. To make good use of this equipment, professional drivers know how to protect their vehicles—and their cargo—from costly damage.

FMCSR 393 states that no person shall drive a commercial motor vehicle unless the vehicle's cargo is properly distributed and adequately secured. No company, by law, should ever allow you to drive your vehicle unless the cargo is properly distributed and adequately secured.

GO!
The professional driver's responsibility for that cargo begins at the point of loading and continues until it has been delivered. In the interim, you should take all precautions to prevent any claims for loss, theft, or damage to this cargo.

The only protection you and your company have against liability for cargo claims is your professionalism and your skill as a professional driver. All too often most preventable cargo claims result from inadequate concern or effort on the part of the driver.

ACCEPTING AND LOADING FREIGHT

When you accept freight for your trailer, you become responsible for safely delivering the load in good condition **(see Figure 24–10)**. Always inspect cargo for:

- The condition of the packages
- Any leaky contents
- Broken pallets or turn shrinkwrap
- The proper container for the material
- Proper quantities as listed on the shipping documents
- Compatibility with the other freight

- Identification marks and addresses
- Weight: will the rig be overweight?
- Identification of any hazardous materials
- Any packages marked glass or fragile

Bring any damage or inaccurate counts to the shipper's attention at once. Usually there is a company policy on accepting such shipments. Contact your supervisor when in doubt about accepting any shipment.

Loading Cargo

Always put the tractor in gear and put on the parking brake when loading or unloading. Never attempt to load freight on your trailer without the proper tools. Some common tools for loading cargo are described in the sections that follow.

Forklifts—are used for loading pallets or heavy objects **(see Figure 24–11)**. Occupational Safety and Health Administration (OSHA) laws require that forklift operators become certified on the individual type of forklift they operate. Never operate a forklift for which you are not certified.

Pallet jacks—are used for loading palletized cargo. They are similar to the forklift, only smaller. Use the same safety rules as when operating a forklift:

- Do not operate unless you are qualified to do so
- Make sure the equipment is rated to handle the load
- Check your overhead clearance
- Operate the equipment carefully
- Use dockboards to bridge between the loading dock and the trailer
- Do not damage the freight with the equipment
- Do not raise freight higher than necessary
- Avoid tilting the load. You might drop the freight
- Do not damage the trailer

Cranes and hoists—are often used to load cargo. Watch for the following details to avoid injury or cargo damage:

- Check the load rating of winches, cables, chains, and so on
- Never exceed the rated load
- Do not stand under raised cargo
- Provide protection in case the chain or cable breaks and whips around
- Never drop freight on your trailer

▶ **Figure 24-10**

The driver is responsible for delivering his or her load in good condition.

▶ **Figure 24-11**

Operate only forklifts on which you have been personally trained and certified. It is an OSHA (Occupational Safety and Health Administration) regulation.

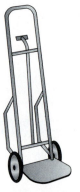

Carton truck   **Utility truck**

Drum truck   **Barrel-lift truck**

 Figure 24-12

Hand trucks make carrying small loads easier.

▶ **Figure 24-13**

Use a drum truck to move a drum too heavy to lift.

Hand trucks—are often used to carry small loads from the trailer to a storage area **(see Figure 24–12).** There are certain safety rules to follow when using them:

■ Never stack boxes so high they obstruct your vision when using a hand truck

■ Never stack boxes so high they topple over

■ Use ramps or dockboards between the trailer and the dock

■ Never load an object that is too big for the hand truck

Drum trucks—are used to load drums. Secure the locking strap and do not try to move a drum that is too heavy to handle **(see Figure 24–13).**

Hand tools or hooks—do not damage the outside packaging when using these tools. Learn to identify fragile cargo. Use tools only for the purpose for which they were designed.

FUNDAMENTALS IN HANDLING CARGO

The following steps should be used in handling cargo:

Step One: Inspecting and Securing Cargo

1. The inspection process begins while cargo is being loaded.

2. It continues as part of your pretrip inspection—checking for overloads, poorly distributed and balanced weight, and cargo that is not properly secured.

3. Check again after you have driven 25 miles from the originating dock or terminal, which is a federal regulation, so adjustments are needed.

4. Check again every 3 hours or every 150 miles that you drive.

5. Check every time you take a break during your trip.

Step Two: Loading Cargo

Before loading, look at the floor of the trailer and make certain there are no nails, splinters, or other obstacles that could damage the cargo. In vans, make certain floor and walls are clean and dry.

As any cargo is loaded onto a trailer, the weight of the total cargo must be evenly distributed between all the axles.

It is the driver's responsibility not to overload the vehicle. Check the legal weight limit where you are, because all states have maximum gross vehicle and axle weights. As you review legal cargo weights, it is important to know the following terms:

Gross vehicle weight (GVW)—is the total weight of a single vehicle and its load.

Gross combination weight (GCW)—is the total weight of a powered unit, its trailer, and its load, such as a loaded tractor-trailer.

Gross combination vehicle weight rating (GCVWR)—is the maximum specified by the manufacturer for a specific combination of vehicles and their loads.

Center of gravity—is the point where weight acts as a force; it affects the vehicle's stability.

Axle weight—weight transmitted to the ground by one axle or one set of axles. Axle weight is not how much axles themselves weigh; axles support the vehicle and its load.

Tire load—maximum weight a tire can carry safely at a certain tire pressure. This information is stamped on the side of the tire. If tires are overinflated or underinflated, this rating may no longer apply and, thus, an underinflated or overinflated tire may not carry the same load safely that it could with the right inflation pressure.

Suspension systems—all have a manufacturer's weight/capacity rating. The manufacturer states how much weight these parts can carry safely.

Coupling device capacity—all coupling devices are rated by the manufacturer for the weight they can safely carry.

Bridge weight—because bridges can handle only so much weight at any one point, some states have bridge laws—a formula used to determine how much weight is put on any point of the bridge by any group of axles, like one set of tandems. If the vehicle has more than one set of tandems, the formula takes into account how close the sets of axles are to each other. The resulting maximum axle weight for axles that are closer together may be lower for each axle in the group.

Balancing the Load

Some people in the trucking business have a sixth sense about how to achieve a balanced load. Others learn from experience.

Distribute the weight of the cargo over all axles and remember the center of gravity factor. You should put the load's center of gravity where it has the most support.

The height of the vehicle's center of gravity is important for safe handling of that vehicle. If cargo is piled high on or in the trailer or if heavy cargo is on top, this high center of gravity will cause the rig to tip over. This is especially true on curves or if you have to suddenly swerve to avoid an accident or a hazard.

It is best if distribute the weight of the load over all axles and keep the center of gravity as low as possible. Load the heaviest parts of the cargo under the lightest parts **(see Figure 24–14).**

Picture your empty vehicle sitting on level ground. Remember that the weight should be distributed over all the axles, including the front axles under the cab. Draw a line from wheel to wheel. When the center of gravity is over the center of this rectangle, the vehicle will be most stable.

▶ Figure 24–14

Heavy load.

Importance of Balanced Weight

- A poorly balanced load will make the vehicle tough to handle and unsafe.

- Too much weight on the steering axle makes the vehicle difficult to steer and can damage the steering axle and tires.

- Underloaded front axles can make the steering axle weight too light, creating problems in steering safely.

- Too little weight on the driving axles indicates poor traction (in bad weather it will be difficult for the truck to keep going).

- If the center of gravity is too high, the possibility of rollover increases.

- If the center of gravity is too high on a flatbed load, it will shift to the side and may fall off.

STOP!

Oversized loads usually require special permits, may be allowed on certain roads only at certain times, and may be asked to take "irregular" routes rather than usual interstate routes. Some oversized loads are required to have escorts, either those provided by the carrier (a pilot car) or the police.

Step Three: Securing Cargo

Proper loading is an important part of moving freight safely and efficiently from one point to another. Securing the cargo is equally important for the same reasons: safety and efficiency.

Following are step-by-step guidelines for properly securing all types of loads:

Action Load Locking Bars for Vans

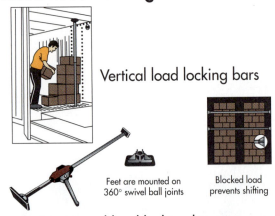

Vertical load locking bars

Feet are mounted on 360° swivel ball joints

Blocked load prevents shifting

Horizontal load locking bars

Horizontal load locking hoops
(Slip over the ends of lock bars above)

In the Cargo Compartment

- **Bracing** is a method that prevents movement of the cargo in the trailer or any other cargo compartment. When you brace a load, you use various elements to steady the load, from the upper part of the cargo to the floor. You also place braces on the walls of the compartment to minimize movement **(see Figure 24–15).**

- **Blocking** is another method, used in front, in back and/or on the sides of a piece of cargo to keep it from sliding in the trailer. Blocking is usually shaped to fit tightly against and around the cargo and then is secured to the deck of the trailer to prevent the cargo from moving **(see Figure 24–16).**

- **Load locks** are long poles that stretch from wall to wall in a trailer. These should be at the rear of the load to prevent cargo from falling. Place one at the top and another halfway down.

▶ **Figure 24–15**

Federal regulations set standards for securing cargo with various devices.

Material blocked and braced in a van trailer

Right

Wrong

▶ **Figure 24–16**

Time taken to correctly block and brace cargo prior to departure will save valuable time later.

CAUTION!

When loading pallets, make certain the pallets do not lean. Each should be placed tightly against the one ahead or in front of it. Leave space between rows of pallets and between pallets and the walls of the trailer.

On the Flatbed Trailer

■ Tiedowns are used to keep cargo from moving in closed trailers and flatbed trailers without sides. This secures the cargo, preventing it from shifting and/or eventually falling off the trailer. To use tiedowns to secure cargo, they must be of the right type and the right strength. Tying down a mammoth turbine with kite string will not secure the cargo.

CAUTION!

As a rule, the combined strength of all cargo tiedowns must be strong enough to lift one and one-half times the weight of the cargo that is to be tied down.

■ Proper tiedown equipment includes ropes, straps, and chains.

■ Tension devices used in tiedowns include winches, ratchets, and cinching components.

■ All tiedowns regardless of material should be attached correctly to the vehicle, using hooks, bolts, rails, and rings **(see Figure 24–17).**

■ According to the new securement standards, the following applies to all tiedowns:

1. Tiedowns and securing devices must not contain knots.

2. If a tiedown is repaired, it must be repaired in accordance with the applicable standards or the manufacturer's instructions.

3. Each tiedown must be attached and secured in a manner that prevents it from becoming loose, unfastening, opening, or releasing while the vehicle is in transit.

TYPE	ADVANTAGES	DISADVANTAGES
Nylon rope	Easily installed and adjusted	Stretches and becomes loose
Wire rope	Very strong	Difficult to handle
Web (nylon) straps	Strong, lightweight, easily adjusted	May become frayed or cut by sharp edges
	May be used with ratchet or winch assemblies	Sunlight rots nylon fiber
	Inexpensive and easy to store	May not be used to secure steel machinery or certain metal products
Steel straps	Good for securing boxes on pallets or wooden crates on vehicle	No means of adjustment during transport
		Vibration can cause failure
		Straps over 1 inch wide need two pairs of crimps
		May cut into cargo and become loose
Hooks and chains	Strong and durable	May damage cargo if too tight
	Readily available	Not of equal strength for rated load
	Hooks may be replaced and easily checked	
	Easily adjusted during transport	

▶ **Figure 24–17**

Evaluation of tiedown devices.

4. All tiedowns and other components of a cargo securement system used to secure loads on a trailer equipped with rub rails, must be located inboard of the rub rails whenever practicable.

5. Edge protection must be used when a tiedown would be subject to abrasion or cutting at the point where it touches an article of cargo. The edge protection must resist abrasion, cutting, and crushing.

CAUTION!

Each tiedown, or its associated connectors or attachment mechanisms, must be designed, constructed, and maintained so the driver of an intransit commercial motor vehicle can tighten them. However, this requirement does not apply to the use of steel strapping.

MANUFACTURING STANDARDS FOR TIEDOWN ASSEMBLIES

An Assembly Component of	Must Conform to
Steel strapping[1,2]	Standard Specification for Strapping, Flat Steel and Seals, American Society for Testing and Materials (ASTM) D3953-97, February 1998[4]
Chain	National Association of Chain Manufacturers' Welded Steel Chain Specifications, November 15, 1999 [4]
Webbing	Web Sling and Tiedown Association's Recommended Standard Specification for Synthetic Web Tiedowns, WSTDA-T1, 1998 [4]
Wire rope [3]	Wire Rope Technical Board's *Wire Rope Users Manual,* 2nd edition, November 1985 [4]
Cordage	Cordage Institute rope standard: 1. PETRS-2, Polyester Fiber Rope, 3-Strand and 8-Strand Constructions, January 1993 [4] 2. PPRS-2, Polypropylene Fiber Rope, 3-Strand and 8-Strand Constructions, August 1992 [4] 3. CRS-1, Polyester/Polypropylene Composite Rope Specifications, 3-Strand and 8-Strand Standard Construction, May 1979 [4] 4. NRS-1, Nylon Rope Specifications, 3-Strand and 8-Strand Standard Construction, May 1979 [4] 5. C-1, Double Braided Nylon Rope Specifications DBN, January 1984 [4]

[1]Steel strapping not marked by the manufacturer with a working load limit will be considered to have a working load limit equal to one fourth of the breaking strength listed in ASTM D3953-97.

[2]Steel strapping 1 inch (25.4 mm) or wider must have at least two pairs of crimps in each seal and, when an end-over-end lap joint is formed, must be sealed with at least two seals.

[3]Wire rope which is not marked by the manufacturer with a working load limit shall be considered to have a working load limit equal to one fourth of the nominal strength listed in the manual.

[4]See 393.7 for information on the incorporation by reference and availability of this document.

■ The new law also specifies:

1. The minimum number of tiedowns required to secure an article or group of articles against movement depends on the length of the article(s) being secured.

2. When an article is not blocked or positioned to prevent movement in the forward direction by a headerboard, bulkhead, other cargo that is positioned to prevent movement, or other appropriate blocking devices, it must be secured by at least:

   ■ One tiedown for articles 5 feet (1.52 meters) or less in length, and 1,100 lbs (500 kg) or less in weight.

   ■ Two tiedowns if the article is 5 feet (1.52 meters) or less in length and more than 1,100 lbs (500 kg) in weight or longer than 5 feet (1.52 meters) but less than or equal to 10 feet (3.04 meters) in length, irrespective of the weight.

   ■ Two tiedowns if the article is longer than 10 feet (3.04 meters), and one additional tiedown for every 10 feet (3.04 meters) of article length, or fraction thereof, beyond the first 10 feet (3.04 meters) of length.

If an individual article is required to be blocked, braced, or immobilized to prevent movement in the forward direction by a headerboard, bulkhead, other articles which are adequately secured, or an appropriate blocking or immobilization method, it must be secured by at least one tiedown for every 10 feet (3.04 meters) or article length, or fraction thereof.

3. **Special rule for special-purpose vehicles.** The rules in this section do not apply to a vehicle transporting one or more articles of cargo such as, but not limited to, machinery or fabricated structural items (e.g., steel or concrete beams, crane booms, girders, and trusses) which, because of their design, size, shape, or weight, must be fastened by special methods. However, any article of cargo carried on that vehicle must be securely and adequately fastened to the vehicle.

Fundamentals of Cargo Securement

The new cargo securement rules are applicable to the transportation of all types of articles of cargo, except commodities in bulk that lack structure or fixed shape (e.g., liquids, gases, grain, liquid concrete, sand, gravel, aggregates) and are transported in a tank, hopper, box, or similar device that forms part of the structure of a commercial motor vehicle. The commodity-specific rules take precedence over the general requirements of this section when additional requirements are given for a commodity listed in those sections.

General—cargo must be firmly immobilized or secured on or within a vehicle by structures of adequate strength, dunnage or dunnage bags, shoring bars, tiedowns, or a combination of these.

Cargo placement and restraint—cargo likely to roll must be restrained by chocks, wedges, a cradle, or other equivalent means to prevent rolling. The means of preventing rolling must not be capable of becoming unintentionally unfastened or loose while the vehicle is in transit.

Articles or cargo placed beside each other and secured by transverse tiedowns must either be placed in direct contact with each other or be prevented from shifting toward each other while in transit.

Minimum strength of cargo securement devices and systems—the total working load limit of any securement system used to secure an article or group of articles against movement must be at least one half times the weight of the article or group of articles. The total working load limit is the sum of:

- One half of the working load limit of each associated connector or attachment mechanism used to secure a part of the article of cargo to the vehicle, and

- One half of the working load limit for each end section of a tiedown that is attached to an anchor point.

WORKING LOAD LIMITS (WLL), CHAIN

	WLL in kg (lbs)				
Size mm (inches)	Grade 30 Proof	Grade 43 High Test	Grade 70 Transport	Grade 80 Alloy	Grade 100 Alloy
7 (1/4)	580 (1,300)	1,180 (2,600)	1,430 (3,150)	1,570 (3,500)	1,950 (4,300)
8 (5/16)	860 (1,900)	1,770 (3,900)	2,130 (4,700)	2,000 (4,500)	2,600 (5,700)
10 (3/8)	1,200 (2,650)	2,450 (5,400)	2,990 (6,600)	3,200 (7,100)	4,000 (8,800)
11 (7/16)	1,680 (3,700)	3,270 (7,200)	3,970 (8,750)		
13 (1/2)	2,030 (4,500)	4,170 (9,200)	5,130 (11,300)	5,400 (12,000)	6,800 (15,000)
16 (5/8)	3,130 (6,900)	5,910 (13,000)	7,170 (15,800)	8,200 (18,100)	10,300 (22,600)

Chain Mark Examples

Example 1	3	4	7	8	10
Example 2	30	43	70	80	100
Example 3	300	430	700	800	1000

Synthetic Webbing

Width mm (in)	WLL kg (lbs)
45 (1-3/4)	790 (1,750)
50 (2)	910 (2,000)
75 (3)	1,360 (3,000)
100 (4)	1,810 (4,000)

Wire Rope (6 × 37, Fiber Core)

Diameter mm (in)	WLL kg (lbs)
7 (1/4)	640 (1,400)
8 (5/16)	950 (2,100)
10 (3/8)	1,360 (3,000)
11 (7/16)	1,860 (4,100)
13 (1/2)	2,400 (5,300)
16 (5/8)	3,770 (8,300)
20 (3/4)	4,940 (10,900)
22 (7/8)	7,300 (16,100)
25 (1)	9,480 (20,900)

Manila Rope WLL

Diameter mm (in)	WLL kg (lbs)
10 (3/8)	90 (205)
11 (7/16)	120 (265)
13 (1/2)	150 (315)
16 (5/8)	210 (465)
20 (3/4)	290 (640)
25 (1)	480 (1,050)

Nylon Rope WLL

Diameter mm (in)	WLL kg (lbs)
10 (3/8)	130 (278)
11 (7/16)	190 (410)
13 (1/2)	240 (525)
16 (5/8)	420 (935)
20 (3/4)	640 (1,420)
25 (1)	1,140 (2,520)

Polypropylene Fiber Rope WLL (3-Strand and 8-Strand Constructions)

Diameter mm (in)	WLL kg (lbs)
10 (3/8)	180 (400)
11 (7/16)	240 (525)
13 (1/2)	280 (625)
16 (5/8)	420 (925)
20 (3/4)	580 (1,275)
25 (1)	950 (2,100)

Double Braided Nylon Rope WLL

Diameter mm (in)	WLL kg (lbs)
10 (3/8)	150 (336)
11 (7/16)	230 (502)
13 (1/2)	300 (655)
16 (5/8)	510 (1,130)
20 (3/4)	830 (1,840)
25 (1)	1,470 (3,250)

Polyester Fiber Rope WLL (3-Strand and 8-Strand Constructions)

Diameter mm (in)	WLL kg (lbs)
10 (3/8)	250 (555)
11 (7/16)	340 (750)
13 (1/2)	440 (960)
16 (5/8)	680 (1,500)
20 (3/4)	850 (1,880)
25 (1)	1,500 (3,300)

Steel Strapping WLL

Width × thickness mm (in)	WLL kg (lbs)
31.7 × 0.74 (1-1/4 × 0.029)	540 (1,190)
31.7 × 0.79 (1-1/4 × 0.031)	540 (1,190)
31.7 × 0.89 (1-1/4 × 0.035)	540 (1,190)
31.7 × 1.12 (1-1/4 × 0.044)	770 (1,690)
31.7 × 1.27 (1-1/4 × 0.05)	770 (1,690)
31.7 × 1.5 (1-1/4 × 0.057)	870 (1,925)
50.8 × 1.12 (2 × 0.044)	1,200 (2,650)
50.8 × 1.27 (2 × 0.05)	1,200 (2,650)

Headerboards—located at the front end of the load, are also called headache racks and protect the driver from the freight shifting or crushing in an accident or a sudden stop. Front-end headerboards protect the driver who is carrying these kinds of loads.

Covered Cargo: What You Should Know

In the past, when you have seen an 18-wheeler pulling big cargo pieces on a flatbed trailer, you probably thought it was covered to keep it clean. According to regulations, cargo is covered for two reasons: (1) to protect people from spilled cargo, and (2) to protect the cargo from the weather. In some states, the cargo must be covered to prevent spills. Find out what the covering rules are in the states where you will be running.

Tarps

Tarps (tarpaulins) are used to protect cargo **(see Figure 24–18)**. Tarps are used to cover most freight and are tied down with rope, webbing or elastic hooks. Be sure to have enough tarps to cover a load measuring 8 × 14 × 42 feet.

Spill Protection
• To protect public
• To meet state law requirements

Cargo Protection
• To prevent corrosion or other weather damage
• Company can be liable for ruined cargo
• Use tarp when needed
• Make sure tarp does not leak
• Make sure tarp is tied properly so it will not tear or leak

 **Figure 24–18**

Cargo covers.

STOP!

Remember, it is always better to buy protection with tarping than to pay a damage claim.

Worn tarps or tarps with holes offer little or no protection. Make sure to inspect your tarps regularly to ensure they will be functional when needed. If you do not have enough tarps to protect your load, contact your supervisor.

In some states, the cargo must be covered to prevent spills. Find out what the covering rules are in the states where you will be running.

To tarp a load—lift the rolled up tarp to the top of the front racks; then, unroll it over the bars to the back of the truck bed. Pull it tight. Tie it to cross bars on the rack. If the tarp is placed over the cargo tightly and evenly, it will not flap **(see Figure 24–19).**

To tarp a load that is uneven or of irregular shape—place the tarp on the cargo after the tiedown assemblies are tight. Then tie down the tarp to prevent wind and weather damage. Longer ropes may be needed to tiedown irregular configurations. Overlapping the front will help keep wind and weather out.

To "smoke tarp" a load on a flatbed—cover the front part of the load to keep exhaust from smokestacks from discoloring the load.

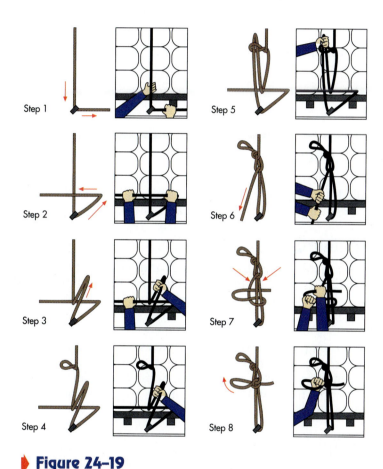

▶ **Figure 24–19**
Trucker's draw hitch.

While on the road, professional drivers check the covering on a load every 150 miles of driving or more frequently. When a cover pulls free, uncovers the cargo, and is flapping in the wind as your trailer pulls down the highway, you should stop and reattach it immediately so that the cover will not fly off and block your vision or someone else's.

GO!

Remember: You cannot inspect a sealed load, but you should check to see that you are not exceeding the gross weight or axle weight limits.

Never secure tarp edges to the outside of the trailer rub rail. This allows grime and moisture to seep under the tarp.

CAUTION!

Winds can be dangerous when installing tarps, so always:

1. Consider the wind direction.

2. Consider the strength of the wind or expected gusts.

3. Secure tarps in a sequence that minimizes risks.

4. Get help and avoid injury.

Loading Flatbed Loads

If a crane or forklift is to be used in placing or unloading a heavy piece of freight, place loose packing material (called dunnage) under the load. This will allow the forklift at the receiving dock or destination to get under the load without a problem.

Sealed and Containerized Loads

Container traffic—cargo that is placed in a container and sealed to be carried as part of its journey by rail or ship—is a fast-growing component of the U.S. freight business. Some shippers prefer containerized shipments because they are often easier to handle and more secure, especially if the cargo is traveling by ship or rail.

Containers, once they reach port, are loaded onto trucks and are on their way to the end user. Containers may also be transported from manufacturer or shipper from the shipper's location to the loading dock for rail or transocean movement. Some containers have their own tiedowns that attach to a special frame for container loads. Others are loaded onto flatbed trailers and are secured with tiedowns every 2 feet, just like any other cargo.

Cargo Requiring Special Handling

Dry bulk tanks—like liquid tankers, dry bulk tankers have a high center of gravity, which means the driver will use special care, particularly when rounding curves and entering or existing a freeway by using a freeway ramp. With the dry bulk tanker or any tanker, always drive at a speed well under that posted on curves, ramps, and in any kind of weather.

Swinging meat—a side of beef or any other meat can be extremely unstable, hanging in a refrigerated trailer (reefer). It also has a high center of gravity **(see Figure 24–20).** Drive under the speed limit and use care on curves, turns, ramps and in bad weather.

▶ Figure 24-20

Cargo, such as meat hanging in a refrigerated trailer, requires special handling.

Livestock—hauling live animals such as beef, hogs, horses, sheep, and goats creates the same problems as liquid loads, and adds a few additional challenges. Livestock trailers always have a high center of gravity. Live animals also have a tendency to lean while going around a curve; and this creates a problem similar to the liquid surge found in liquid tanks.

If you do not have a full load, use portable bulkheads to keep the animals from moving around. The tighter the animals are packed, the less movement.

Remember the 'nose factor.' When parked in a truckstop or roadside rest area, remember to park downwind or, because of the odor, you will accumulate many enemies.

Step Four: Driving with a Load

The high center of gravity associated with some trailers and the way cargo is loaded has already been covered. Remember when you are loaded and have a high center of gravity to give yourself plenty of time and room to stop, plus drive slowly on curves, entrance ramps, exit ramps, and turns.

When You Are Loaded

A heavy load gives you better traction, which means you can stop better.

A light load does not give good traction. You may be able to move faster but it also takes more distance to stop this type of vehicle.

Poor distribution of cargo weight makes axles too light, which makes it easier to skid.

When You Are Turning

A loaded trailer puts more weight on the axles, including the steering axle. The heavier the weight on the steering axle, the more difficult the rig will be to steer.

Too much weight on the rear axles means not enough weight on the steering axle. This decreases steering control.

Driving Banks and Curves

A load with a high center of gravity will make driving banks and curves more hazardous. If the cargo is loaded incorrectly with a high CG, the vehicle will tip on a steep bank or curve. The same will happen if cargo is unbalanced when it is loaded.

If you are driving a flatbed on a bank or curve and your cargo is not secure, it may shift or fall off on a curve or steep bank.

If you are hauling hanging sides of meat, suspended from rails in the trailer, the swinging caused by the motion of the trailer may cause a problem. As the meat swings more and more, the sides of meat build momentum, which can make the vehicle very unstable, especially on curves and ramps.

If you are hauling dry bulk, then you will be driving a tanker which has a high CG because of its design. Sometimes on curves and sharp turns or ramps, the load will shift, creating a dangerous situation.

Driving Upgrades and Downgrades

A properly secured load will not cause problems, but any time a vehicle is loaded, it will perform differently on upgrades and downgrades **(see Figure 24–21).**

If the truck is overloaded, it will navigate a hill very slowly. If possible, use a climbing lane. Otherwise, be aware of traffic behind you and other drivers who may be apt to tailgate your vehicle.

On a downgrade, the vehicle that is loaded will pick up momentum at a greater rate than the same, unloaded vehicle. If your speed on the downgrade becomes excessive, use your brakes; but remember that trying to slow or stop a loaded vehicle going at a high speed on a downgrade may cause brake failure, a common accident and one that is easily prevented.

▶ **Figure 24–21**

A fully loaded vehicle will perform differently on upgrades or downgrades than on a level highway.

Dunnage—this softer packing material is often used to secure cargo and keeps water-sensitive cargo from making contact with the trailer floor. When using dunnage, place it in such a manner to support the total weight of the cargo you are securing.

Friction mats—placed on the deck or between cargo these must provide resistance against forward movement equal to 50 percent of the weight of the cargo resting on it.

Wooden restraints—ash, beech, elm, hickory, hard sugar maple, and oak are used as blocks, braces, chocks, cradles, dunnages, and wedges to prevent rolling or as high-pressure restraints. The wood must be strong enough to withstand being split or crushed by the cargo or tie-down. Their working load limit is required to be 50 percent or greater than the weight of the material to stop it from moving forward.

Step 5: Cargo Responsibilities

The Shipper's Responsibility

Whether the shipper is the originator or the pass-through for a shipment, the shipper is responsible for packing and loading the cargo in a manner that will ensure safe transportation. The shipper is also responsible for determining whether any protective devices are required to ensure safe transport of the shipment.

Once the driver has had an opportunity to size up the load—and if the driver sees the packaging or protective devices for any shipment as inadequate—the driver should call the driver manager or dispatcher for help in resolving the problem. Under no circumstances should the driver argue with the shipper about how they have packaged or loaded the merchandise.

The Driver's Responsibility

Although many drivers do not load or supervise the loading of the trailers they pull, they are still responsible for checking to see that all cargos are properly secured **(see Figure 24–22).**

When loading cargo, the driver is responsible for:

■ Preparing the bill of lading if one has not been provided by the shipper

■ Counting the cargo—and making sure the count matches the shipper's count (Never assume the count is correct until you have counted the cargo yourself.)

▶ **Figure 24–22**

When you accept freight, you become responsible for the safe delivery of that shipment.

- Inspecting the cargo (Do not assume preloaded cargo is undamaged. If inspection is not possible, notify the safety department or the dispatcher where you work.)

- Recording the condition of the cargo (If the cargo is in perfect condition or is less than perfect, record it on the bill of lading and notify your dispatcher. When necessary, take photos of the shipment. An accurate description and photos of preexisting damage helps reduce your liability in the event of a claim.)

It is fairly easy to make a visual check if cargo is loaded on a flatbed or open trailer. If an enclosed van has locking security seals, a more creative method for checking the load is required. When you check your cargo, include:

- A visual check of the springs and tires of your tractor and trailer for signs of overloading

- Checking for any sagging or bowing of the trailer which is also a sign of overload

- Awareness of whether you have enough power to move the rig

- General handling characteristics of the rig

- Checking for any leaks that could indicate damaged cargo

- Figuring the weight of the load by adding all weights shown on shipping papers

If the trailer is an open type or a van without seals or restricted access, the driver is responsible for checking the load for:

- Weight distribution—heavy items loaded close together

- Heavy freight loaded high in the trailer or positioned where it could fall on other cargo during transport

- Fragile or hazardous material

- Loose freight not properly secured by holding devices or dunnage

- Materials not compatible

- Regulated or restricted materials

The driver is also responsible for checking all parts necessary for hauling, containing, and protecting cargo. These may include:

- Tailgates
- Tailboards
- Doors
- Headerboards
- Tarps

The Consignee's Responsibility

The consignee (or receiver) of the freight is responsible for unloading, counting, and inspecting cargo. They are then responsible for noting any overages, shortages, or damages on the delivery receipt. To signify they have received the shipment, consignees must also sign your delivery receipt. Do not refuse to allow them to note any cargo damages, shortages, or overages on the delivery receipt.

VEHICLE WEIGHT

Limits on the weight and size of vehicles vary from state to state, and some have lower limits than others. Check the size and weight regulations for each state you will drive through. (Thomson Delmar Learning publishes a handy reference, *Trucking Rules and Regulations*, that lists size and weight regulations by state.)

Violations for your rig's being overweight are often expensive and can reflect on your driving record **(see Figure 24–23).**

States set legal
weight limits

▶ **Figure 24–23**

Each state sets its own weight and length load limits.

Officials are permitted to detain an overweight vehicle and may make the driver off-load the cargo or redistribute the weight, in addition to charging the driver with a fine.

STOP!

A rig that is detained for an overload results in great expense for the trucking company. It also means a late delivery to the customer.

Weights are usually checked in the following ways:

Individual wheel weight—usually checked by state or local officials with a portable scale that measures the load on each wheel. Wheel weights are then checked against the permitted load for each tire.

Axle weight—also checked with a portable scale. The weight of each wheel on an axle is recorded. The weights are then added to find the axle weight. At weigh stations, drive each set of axles onto the scale to measure the axle weight.

Combined axle weight—tandem or triple axles can have a different weight per axle as compared to a single axle. To find the total combined axle weight, add the weights of all the axles. You can also find the total weight by driving the entire rig onto the scale platform.

Gross vehicle weight (GVW)—is the total weight of a straight truck and its load.

Gross combination vehicle weight rating (GCVWR)—is the total weight of a tractor, trailer, and load. Local or state officials may check the GCVWR by weighing each wheel or axle individually and adding the total or by having you drive the entire rig onto the platform scale to be weighted as a unit.

More restrictions are placed on short, heavy rigs for wheel, axle, and gross weights, because the total load is distributed over a shorter surface. This increases the stress placed on bridges and other highway structures.

STOP!

If you pull a heavy cargo in an intermodal container on a short trailer or chassis, you may exceed the weight limit for some bridges. Always know your gross vehicle weight.

Some states are testing "smart" weigh stations that electronically weigh trucks that pass over a set of specially designed sensors.

Manufacturers' warranties and liabilities may be affected if you exceed the rated weight for each of your rig's components. Limits include the following:

- Tires—maximum load at specified inflation
- Suspension system—maximum for spring assembly
- Axle weight—rated weight for single or combination
- Fifth wheel—maximum pull weight
- GCVWR—recommended gross weight

DISTRIBUTION OF WEIGHT

If cargo weight is not distributed properly, the rig will be harder to handle. Distribution of weight on a tractor depends on the location of the fifth wheel:

- With a single rear axle, the fifth wheel should be slightly in front of the axle.
- With a tandem rear axle and a stationary fifth wheel, weight should be slightly in front of the tandem center line.
- With a tandem rear axle and a sliding fifth wheel, the last notch of the slider adjustment should be just ahead of the tandem center line.

With a movable fifth wheel, move it forward and the load shifts more to the steering axle(s). Move it back and the load shifts to the tractor drive axle(s).

The rig will handle differently, depending on the way you distribute the weight. When the load is moved forward, the rig will handle more easily and will allow for better cornering. If too much weight is shifted forward, you can lose traction on the rear axles and steering will be difficult.

> **CAUTION!**
> When you move a load forward, be careful not to exceed the legal weight limits for the front axle.

Weight shifted too far back causes light steering with poor control. It can also overload the drive axles **(see Figure 24–24).**

Distribution of weight in a trailer is just as important. Distribute the weight of the cargo as evenly as possible between the trailer's rear axle(s) and the tractor's drive axle(s) **(see Figure 24–25).** If you are pulling double trailers, center the weight on the converter dolly.

When you load the trailer, be sure to:

- Find out the total weight of the load.
- Load half in front and half in the rear, if possible.
- Spread the load evenly over the floor from side to side to prevent shifting.
- Keep heavy freight as low as possible to help keep the rig's center of gravity low.

Weight Distribution on Tractor and Trailer

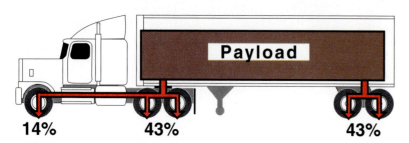

Payload

14%   43%   43%

Example of a Well-Balanced Load

Tractor
- Distribute weight properly over axles
- Weight distribution depends on position of fifth wheel
  - Single axle - slightly forward of center line
  - Tandem axle
    - Stationary - just ahead of center line
    - Sliding - last notch of slider adjustment
    - Fifth wheel moved forward
      - More of load shifted to front axle

Trailer
- Divide load evenly between front and rear
- Adjust load to meet axle weight limitations
  - Heavy freight on bottom
  - Properly distributed

▶ **Figure 24–24**

It is the driver's responsibility to see that each load is balanced and weight is distributed evenly over all axles.

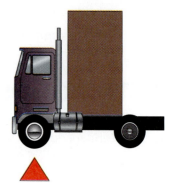

▶ **Figure 24–25**

Too much weight on the steering axle can damage the axle and tires and cause hard steering.

■ Spread out any heavy cargo to prevent concentrated stress on the trailer's floor **(see Figure 24–26).**

■ Do not load heavy objects where they can fall on other freight.

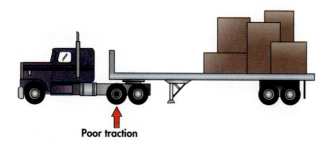

Poor traction

▶ **Figure 24–26**

How cargo is loaded will impact the rig's overall traction.

■ Move the heavy freight as needed to keep the weight evenly distributed after part of the cargo has been unloaded **(see Figure 24–27).**

■ The weight can be adjusted in trailers with sliding rear axles by moving the axle.

■ Slide the axle forward to shift more weight to the trailer axle and off of the tractor drive axle.

■ Slide to the rear position to shift the most weight to the tractor drive axle.

With sliding axles or fifth wheels, be aware of the bridge formula laws that dictate axle spacing. On interstate highways and some state routes, you are required to have certain axle spacing to haul maximum allowable weights.

High Center of Gravity

Some vehicles have a high **center of gravity (see Figure 24–28).** This means the weight is carried high off the road. Such rigs are top-heavy because they carry hanging loads, such as meat

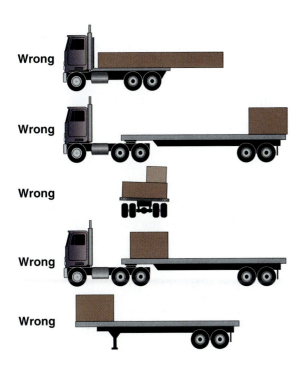

Wrong

Wrong

Wrong

Wrong

Wrong

> **Figure 24–27**
Examples of improper weight distribution.

> **Figure 24–28**
Tankers have a higher center of gravity.

or they carry tiered loads such as livestock or liquid loads in bulk, such as milk or gasoline. These high-center-of-gravity rigs require special skills in handling, loading, and unloading.

SUMMARY

In this chapter, you learned why it is important to handle cargo properly. You have also learned the professional driver's responsibilities for handling various cargos. You discovered there are laws regarding the way cargo is shipped and how it must be secured. You also know the importance of weight limits and distribution of weight when handling cargo.

KEY TERMS

49 CFR Part 166
Axle weight
Blocking
Bracing
Bulkhead
Cargo retainer bars
Center of gravity
Chocks
Combined axle weight

Drum truck
Dunnage
FMCSR Section 392.9
Forklift
Gross combination vehicle
   weight rating (GCVWR)
Gross vehicle weight (GVW)
Hand truck
Headerboard

Individual wheel weight
Pallet jacks
Placards
Tanker endorsement
Tarps
Tiedowns
Weight distribution

REVIEW QUESTIONS

1. Properly handling and loading cargo that will avoid damage in transit and add to the operating efficiency of the rig is the responsibility of the _____.

   a. dispatcher

   b. professional driver

   c. shipper

   d. receiver

2. Regarding cargo distribution and securement, FMCSR Section 392.9 states in part that if the vehicle's cargo is not properly distributed and adequately secured _____.

   a. the driver cannot be required to drive the load

   b. the driver can decide if he or she drives the load

   c. if the dispatcher says the load is okay the driver must drive

   d. if the shipper says the load is okay the driver must drive

3. FMCSR require drivers of tiedown loads to inspect the load _____.

   a. within the first 25 miles

   b. only at the beginning of the trip

   c. each 100 miles of the trip

   d. within the first 50 miles

4. Regarding tiedown components and their anchor points in cargo securement, the working load limit is the lowest load limit for tiedown components or their anchor points _____.

   a. multiplied by four

   b. whichever is greater

   c. divided by six

   d. whichever is least

5. A device that protects the driver from the freight shifting or crushing him or her during a sudden stop and/or accident is called a _____.

   a. high center of gravity

   b. backboard

   c. headboard

   d. friction board

6. A friction mat placed on the deck or between cargo must provide resistance against forward movement equal to _____ percent of the weight of the cargo resting on it.

   a. 50

   b. 30

   c. 20

   d. at least 20

7. The one responsible for packing and loading cargo in a manner that will ensure safe transportation is the _____.

   a. driver

   b. receiver

   c. shipper

   d. dispatcher

8. Once a driver has an opportunity to evaluate a load, and if the driver sees that packaging or protective devices for the shipment are inadequate, the driver should _____.

   a. have the customer make corrections

   b. call the driver manager or dispatcher

   c. accept the load as the customer presents it

   d. call the federal transportation agency as inadequate packaging or protective devices is a violation of federal law

9. The one responsible for seeing that all cargos are properly secured and that the cargo's weight is evenly distributed over all axles is the _____.

   a. shipper

   b. loader of the cargo

   c. dispatcher

   d. driver

10. If your tractor is attached to an enclosed van with locking security seals, which of the following is not a recommended method to check the enclosed cargo?

    a. Conduct a visual check of the springs and tires of the rig for signs of overloading.

    b. Quiz the shipper regarding the weight and securing methods of the cargo.

    c. Know the general handling characteristics of the rig.

    d. Figure the weight of the load by adding all the weights shown on the shipping papers.

11. If your tractor is attached to an open-type trailer or van without seals or restricted access, which of the following is the driver not responsible for?

    a. waterproof packing of the freight

    b. weight distribution

    c. heavy freight loaded high in the trailer

    d. regulated or restricted materials

12. When hauling cargo, you must stop within the first 50 miles of your trip and then _____ to check your load and all securing devices.

    a. once daily

    b. 30 minutes before delivery

    c. every 3 hours or 150 miles thereafter

    d. every 5 hours or 200 miles thereafter

13. Drivers should be alert for hazardous materials packaged in small quantities such as paints, hair spray, drain cleaners, cleaning products, and all aerosols that may be shipped as _____.

    a. household goods

    b. drugstore goods

    c. grocery goods

    d. consumer commodity ORM-D

14. The gross combination vehicle weight rating (GCVWR) is the _____.

    a. total weight of the tractor and trailer

    b. total weight of the tractor, trailer, and load

    c. amount of weight allowed on any interstate highway

    d. amount of weight allowed on most bridges

15. Regarding weight distribution on the tractor and trailer, which of the following is an example of a well-balanced load?

    a. The rear axles of the tractor will have two times the weight of the axles of the trailer.

    b. All axles, including the steering, will have the same weight on them.

    c. The rear axles of the tractor and the axles of the trailer will have the same amount of weight on them.

    d. The steering axle will have the most weight on it.

25 Cargo Documentation

OBJECTIVES

When you have completed this chapter, you should be able to:

- Check the shipping documents to verify the cargo and quantity to be shipped.
- Check documents for compliance with the law.
- Understand the legal terms of a shipping contract.
- Explain how drivers can protect themselves and their companies from loss claims.
- Specify how shipping document copies are distributed.
- Explain what possession of the papers means.

INTRODUCTION

The **documentation** that accompanies shipments serves many purposes. Its most important use is to provide an accurate record of the cargo **(see Figure 25–1).** In some cases, it also serves as a contract for transportation services. As a professional driver, you must be able to understand the terms and content of the shipping documents and your legal responsibilities.

> **Figure 25–1**
>
> *Documentation must be accurate because it often serves as a record of the cargo.*

How important is your understanding of cargo documentation?

If you do not understand how to properly prepare and handle the papers that document the freight you haul, you may:

- Be liable for civil or criminal penalties if there is a cargo loss or shortages
- Suffer damage to your reputation as a professional driver
- Be fired from your job
- Endanger the health and safety of many by not communicating the dangers of a hazardous materials load

DEFINITION OF TERMS

To better understand certain words used by the shipper, carrier, or the person to whom delivery is made, you will need to know specific terms and exactly what they mean. The following terms have specific meanings when referring to the trucking industry:

Shipper (consignor)—person or company offering the goods for shipment

Receiver (consignee)—person or company to whom goods are being shipped or consigned

Motor carrier—the person or company in the business of transporting goods; in this chapter, *carrier* may mean:

- ■ **Private carrier**
- ■ **For-hire carrier**
  - ● **Common carrier**
  - ● **Contract carrier**
  - ● **Exempt commodity carrier**

Freight forwarder—a person or company that arranges for the transport of freight.

Originating (pick up) carrier—the carrier that first accepts the shipment from the shipper.

Connecting carrier—any carrier that transports freight to an interchange location and then transfers the cargo to another company to continue transport of the shipment.

Delivery (terminal) carrier—the carrier that delivers the shipment to the consignee.

Bill of lading (BL)—written contract between the shipper and the carrier for transporting a shipment. This paper identifies all freight in the shipment as well as the consignee, the delivery location, and the terms of the agreement.

Straight bill of lading—contract providing for delivery of a shipment to the consignee. The driver does not need to get a copy from the consignee when the goods are delivered.

Order notify bill of lading—a bill of lading that permits the shipper to collect payment before shipping reaches its destination. A driver must pick up the consignee's copy of the BL before delivering the shipment.

Through bill of lading—a bill of lading used with shipments transported by more than one carrier that has a fixed rate for the services of all carriers.

Manifest—a list describing the entire shipment on a vehicle.

Packing slip—a detailed list of packed goods prepared by the shipper.

Freight bill—a bill submitted by a common carrier for transport services. The freight bill contains much of the same information as the bill of lading. A copy usually serves as a receipt for services when signed by the consignee.

Delivery receipt—a paper signed by the consignee or an agent of the consignee, accepting the shipment from the driver. The driver keeps the receipt as proof of delivery.

Warehouse receipt—a paper signed by the driver to prove the shipment was unloaded at a warehouse.

Agent—a person or company acting as the official representative of another, such as a consignee's agent.

Hazardous materials shipping paper—a bill of lading describing hazardous materials by proper shipping name, hazard class, identification number, and the quantity being shipped. This form must be legible.

Hazardous waste manifest—a form describing hazardous waste and identifies the shipper, carrier, and destination by name and by identification numbers assigned by the Environmental Protection Agency. The shipper prepares, dates, and signs the manifest. All carriers of the shipment must sign the paper. It also must be signed by the consignee and the driver keeps a copy.

"Need to keep these hazmat shipping papers with me at all times . . . does that mean I have to take them to bed?"

TRANSPORTATION CHARGES AND SERVICES

Transportation charges are the fees for transportation services. They may include payment for the goods shipped (COD shipments). It is important to understand the terminology used about the charges and payments for services. This helps protect you from liability and personal expense.

Usually, the cost for goods in the shipment is agreed upon by the shipper and the customer before the shipment is offered for transport. Sometimes the carrier will also have to collect the payment for the goods being shipped from the receiver and return this payment to the shipper. The shipper and carrier usually agree on the transportation charges before the freight is loaded.

Types of Payment

Prepaid shipments—transportation charges are paid at the shipping point.

Collect-on-delivery (COD) shipments—the driver must collect payment before the cargo can be unloaded **(see Figure 25–2).** The payment may be for the transportation charges only or also include the cost of the goods. The driver must know the company's policy for the types of payment that can be accepted, such as certified check, money order, or cash.

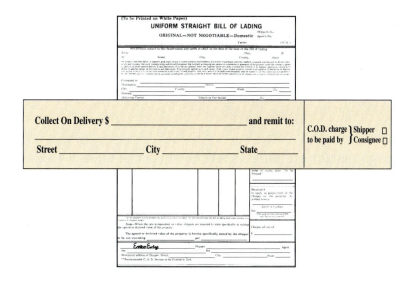

▶ **Figure 25–2**

On COD shipments, the driver must collect payment before the cargo is unloaded.

NOTE: You will see very few COD shipments.

Order notify shipment—payment for the goods is made when the driver gets a copy of the order notify bill of lading from the consignee. At that point, the driver must get the bill from the consignee before delivering the shipment. In both prepaid and COD shipments, the bill must be signed and sent back to the carrier.

Transportation Rates

Charges for transportation are figured by multiplying the rate by the weight of the cargo and distance the load will be shipped **(see Figure 25–3).** Rates are based on the value of the cargo and services performed by the carrier.

▶ **Figure 25–3**

Transportation rates are calculated by multiplying the rate by the weight of the cargo and the distance the load will be shipped.

STOP!

It is important to understand that weights appearing on the freight bill may be true weights or estimated weights. If the weight is estimated, there could be a significant difference between the true and estimated weights—sometimes by as much as 1,000 pounds.

The value of the cargo used for rate purposes is either the actual value of goods shipped as shown on the bill of lading or the value shown on the BL is set by the shipper as the limits of carrier liability **(see Figure 25–4).**

Services to be performed by the carrier are based on special handling requirements and **tariffs.** Tariffs are lists of services common carriers perform for the public and the rates charged for them.

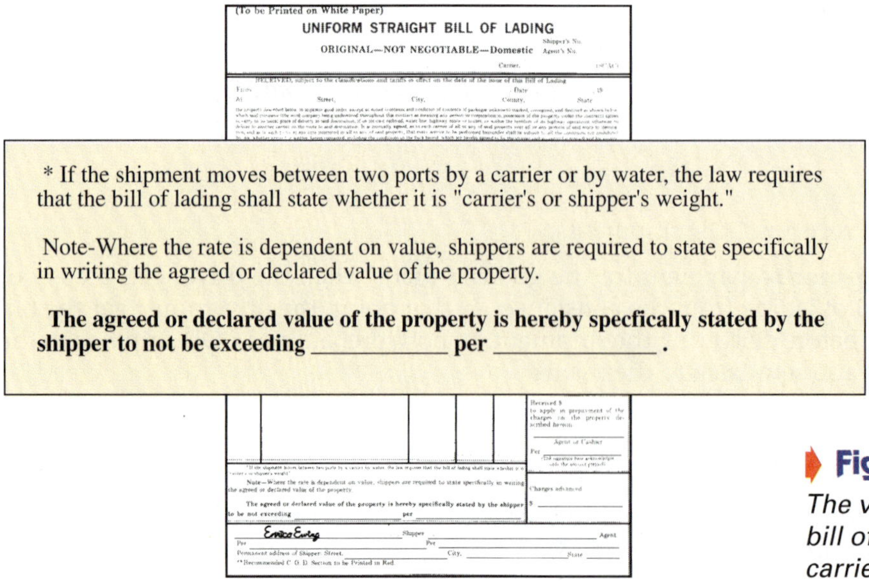

(To be Printed on White Paper)

UNIFORM STRAIGHT BILL OF LADING

Shipper's No.

ORIGINAL—NOT NEGOTIABLE—Domestic   Agent's No.

Carrier

RECEIVED, subject to the classifications and tariffs in effect on the date of the issue of this Bill of Lading

* If the shipment moves between two ports by a carrier or by water, the law requires that the bill of lading shall state whether it is "carrier's or shipper's weight."

Note-Where the rate is dependent on value, shippers are required to state specifically in writing the agreed or declared value of the property.

The agreed or declared value of the property is hereby specfically stated by the shipper to not be exceeding _____ per _____ .

▶ **Figure 25–4**

The value shown on the bill of lading limits the carrier's liability.

Services and Surcharges

Rates for services and surcharges, or additional charges, are negotiated between the shipper and the carrier before the carrier accepts the shipment. Surcharges may include those charges for special services to be performed by the driver when delivery is made, such as inside delivery, storage, or other charges.

> **GO!**
>
> It is important for the driver to know the meanings of the terms describing certain services. The services should be clearly stated in the bill of lading.

Inside delivery—indicates freight is to be delivered inside the building rather than unloaded at the curb.

Tailgate delivery—the freight is unloaded and delivered at the tailgate (back) of the truck.

Helper service—a helper is to be provided for loading or unloading freight. The bill of lading specifies who will pay for the helper.

Residential delivery—the BL will specify the address and method for collecting payment if the shipment is going to a residence.

Dunnage and return (DR) charges—when the weight of the dunnage is listed on the bill of lading. If shipper wishes it to be returned, this will be stated on the bill of lading.

Storage and delay (S&D) charges—an additional amount to be paid to the carrier if delivery is postponed by the consignee or shipper, or if a shipment must be stored before it can be delivered. These terms are stated on the bill of lading.

Detention time or demurrage—detaining a vehicle beyond a given time. Payment is made to the carrier when the delivery is delayed.

BASIC SHIPPING DOCUMENTS

A bill of lading is a contract between a shipper and a carrier. It lists all the goods in the shipment and any special handling requirements or conditions for transportation. It is a legally binding document that is regulated by federal law.

There are several different types of bills of lading that serve the following purposes:

- Identifies the type and quantity of freight being shipped
- Shows the ownership of the goods
- States the value of the freight in case of loss or damage
- Establishes the rates and freight charges
- Serves as a legal contract
- Identifies the point of origin of the shipment and where it is being shipped
- States the methods of payment for all charges
- Serves as a permanent record of the transactions

Uniform Straight Bill of Lading

The most common type of bill of lading is the **uniform straight bill of lading.** It is a contract that the parties cannot change. The goods must be delivered to the consignee or an authorized representative **(see Figure 25–5).** There are usually three copies:

(To be Printed on White Paper)

UNIFORM STRAIGHT BILL OF LADING
ORIGINAL-NOT NEGOTIABLE-Domestic

Shipper's No. _____
Agent's No. _____

_____ Carrier _____ (SCAC)

RECEIVED, subject to the classifications and tariffs in effect on the date of the issue of this Bill of Lading.

From _____ Date _____ , 20 _____

At _____ Street, _____ City, _____ County, _____ State _____

The property described below, in apparent good order, except as noted (contents and condition of contents of packages unknown) marked, consigned, and destined as shown below, which said company (the word company being understood throughout this contract as meaning any person or corporation in possession of the property under the contract) agrees to carry to its usual place of delivery at said destination, if on it's own railroad, water line, highway route or routes, or within the territory of its highway operations, otherwise to deliver to another carrier on the route to said destination. It is mutually agreed, as to each carrier of all or any of said property over all or any portion of said route to destination and as to each party at any time interested in all or any of said property, that every service to be performed hereunder shall be subject to all the conditions not prohibited by law, whether printed or written, herein contained, including the conditions on the back hereof, which are hereby agreed to by the shipper and accepted for himself and his assigns.

Consigned to _____
Destination _____ Street _____
City _____ County, _____ State _____ Zip _____
Routing _____
Delivering Carrier _____ Vehicle or Car Initial _____ No. _____

Collect On Delivery _____ and remit to: | C.O.D. charge to be paid by } Shipper ☐ Consignee ☐
_____ Street _____ City _____ State _____

No. Packages	Kind of Packages, Description of Articles, Special Marks, and Exceptions	*Weight (Subject to Correction)	Class or Rate	Check Column	Subject to Section 7 of conditions, if this shipment is to be delivered to the consignee without recourse on the consignor, the consignor shall sign the following statement: The carrier shall not make delivery of the shipment without payment of freight and all other lawful charges.
					(Signature of consignor)
					If charges are to be prepaid write or stamp here "To be Prepaid."
					Received $ _____ to apply in prepayment of the charges on the property described hereon.
					Agent or Cashier

*If the shipment moves between two ports by a carrier or by water, the law requires that the bill of lading shall state whether it is "Carrier's or shipper's weight."

Note -Where the rate is dependent on value, shippers are required to state specifically in writing the agreed or declared value of the property.

The agreed or declared value of the property is hereby specifically stated by the shipper to not be exceeding _____ per _____

Charges advanced:
$ _____

_____ Shipper _____ Agent
Per _____ Per _____
Permanent address of Shipper: Street, _____ City, _____ State _____

► Figure 25–5
Uniform straight bill of lading.

- Copy 1—original copy sent to the consignee
- Copy 2—shipping order copy is carrier copy
- Copy 3—memorandum copy is shipper copy

A uniform straight bill of lading **(see Figure 25–6)** will have the:

1. Carrier's name
2. Shipper's name
3. Date goods were accepted by the carrier
4. Number of items in the shipment and a description of each
5. Condition of the packages or goods in the shipment
6. Space for the driver to note damage, shortages, or improper packing
7. Name of the consignee
8. Address to which the shipment can be delivered
9. Routing, if more than one carrier will transport cargo
10. Identification of connecting carriers, if any are necessary
11. Freight charges and method of payment, such as COD or prepaid

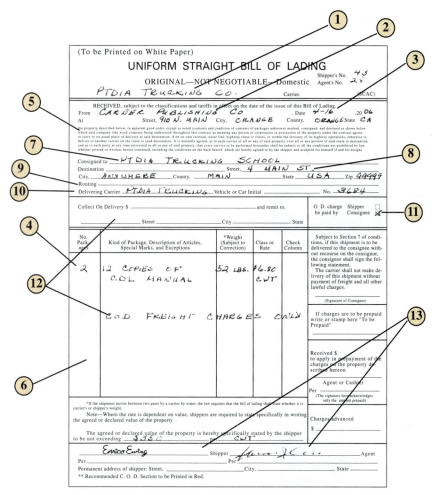

Figure 25–6

The uniform straight bill of lading must contain specific information about the shipment.

12. Special handling services

13. Signatures of the shipper and the driver as agents for the carrier (the bill is not valid without signatures)

Contract information will be detailed on the back of copy 2 in case the driver must check for specific duties on delivery.

Order Notify Bill of Lading

An order notify bill of lading is a special type of BL. Ownership of the shipment can be transferred by the valid sale of this document. There will be three copies:

- Copy 1—original copy (yellow)
- Copy 2—shipping copy (blue)
- Copy 3—memo copy (white)

The information describing the freight in the shipment will be the same as that needed for the uniform bill of lading.

The driver must check the back of the yellow page (original) to make sure it is signed by the shipper and any bank or financial institution that has paid the shipper. If there is any question about the validity or proper preparation of the order notify bill of lading, contact the financial department or billing agent for your company.

The driver must not deliver any part of the shipment unless he or she has the original copy (copy 1) of the bill. After delivery, the original copy of the bill is given to that consignee. The holder of the order notify bill of lading is the legal owner of the freight.

Household Goods Bill of Lading

A **household goods bill of lading** is used by moving companies for their shipments. This bill serves as a legal contract between the shipper and the carrier. The household goods bill of lading lists the carrier and the customer and is a combined bill of lading, freight bill, and a record of the items in the shipment. It also states their appearance, their condition, and how they are packaged.

Legal requirements for weighing a load with a household goods bill of lading differ from those of ordinary freight.

Freight bills are prepared by the carrier from the bill of lading **(see Figure 25–7)**. Drivers are mainly concerned with copy 1 of the BL, which serves as the delivery receipt copy. The driver must have the consignee sign the bill, showing he or she accepts the shipment—before it is unloaded.

The freight bill will tell the driver if the carrier charges are prepaid or if there is a COD charge due on delivery. Freight bills are usually preprinted with **pro numbers** (progressive numbers). These numbers are in front of the freight bill numbers. Often the driver will have

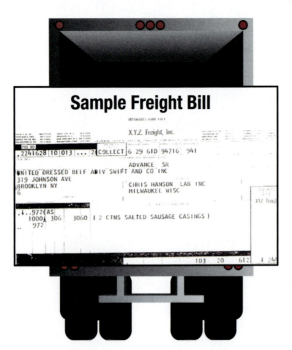

▶ **Figure 25–7**

Freight bills are prepared by the carrier from the bill of lading.

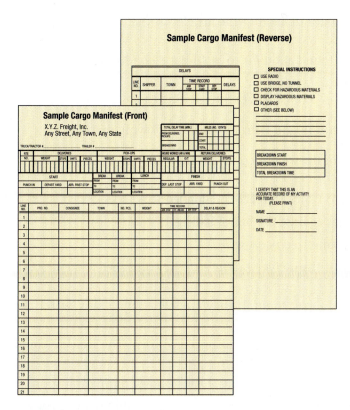

Figure 25–8

Drivers refer to cargo manifests as "pro bills" or "pro sheets" because the manifests list all freight bills.

Figure 25–9

Never sign a shipping document unless you completely understand the terms and conditions.

to identify the bill by its pro number. Sometimes drivers refer to cargo manifests as "pro bills" or "pro sheets" because the manifest lists all freight bills **(see Figure 25–8).**

Other Documents

Invoice—a bill from the shipper listing the goods, prices, and total due. This may be mailed to the consignee, or the driver may have to give it to the consignee if the freight comes as a COD shipment.

Packing slip—a list of the total parts packaged in a shipment. The responsibility of opening packages and checking the contents against the packing slip belongs to the consignee.

DRIVER'S SIGNATURE AND RESPONSIBILITY

The driver's signature on a shipping document puts that driver and his or her company on the line **(see Figure 25–9).** NEVER sign a shipping document unless you completely understand all the terms and conditions. Be sure you compare all descriptions with the freight offered for loading.

The driver's signature on a bill of lading means:

- You and your company are legally responsible for fulfilling all the terms and conditions of the contract.

- You and your company agree to the methods and rates of payment for the services you stated.

■ You and your company are responsible for delivering the articles in the quantities listed in good condition to the consignee.

■ You have inspected the shipment and found all items to be in good condition. The count is also correct.

■ You have noted any shortages, damages, or mistakes before signing the bill.

As a professional driver, protect your reputation and your job in the following manner:

■ Never take the word of someone else for the freight count or the condition of the shipment. Always count the cargo yourself.

■ Always observe the loading of cargo to ensure all pieces are loaded.

■ Check the descriptions on the packages against the bill of lading.

■ Learn to quickly and correctly count palletized packages.

■ Check the address on the freight against the delivery address of the consignee to avoid loading the wrong cargo.

■ Handle fragile goods properly when you load them. If they are loaded by others, watch for any rough handling and breakage.

■ Never load or permit someone else to load leaking packages or drums. The leakage could damage other freight.

■ Note freight that is poorly packaged and could come out of the package during transport.

■ Know the policies of your company for refusing damaged or incomplete shipment. If you accept these for shipment, it could result in freight claims.

PREVIOUSLY LOADED TRAILERS

Before signing a bill of lading for a shipment not loaded in your presence, inspect the load, if possible. Check the bill of lading for incompatible freight, overweight shipments, and so on. Also check the general appearance of the load for proper blocking and bracing.

If the trailer is sealed with a security seal or you cannot visually inspect the load, make a note on the bill of lading that reads "shipper's weight, load, and count." This releases you and your company from responsibility for any shortage or damage unless it is caused by an accident.

▶ **Figure 25–10**

For trailers with security seals, record the serial number of the seal on all copies of the bill of lading.

Security Seals

For trailers that are equipped with **security seals** by the shipper:

■ Record the serial number of the seal on all copies of the bill of lading **(see Figure 25–10).**

■ Note on the bill of lading "shipper's weight, load, and count."

■ Check the seal to be sure it is properly locked. The serial number must match the number noted on the bill of lading.

■ Have the consignee sign for the shipment on delivery BEFORE breaking the seal.

■ If the seal is broken en route—for inspection by law enforcement officials—obtain their signature(s), badge number(s), and department(s) and get a replacement seal.

■ If the seal is broken en route by someone other than an enforcement official, notify your dispatcher or supervisor at once.

DELIVERY OF FREIGHT

When you deliver freight, remember—you are responsible for the shipment until it is accepted by the consignee:

■ Make sure delivery is to the proper consignee.

■ Obtain the correct signature on freight bills, bills of lading, receipts, or other documents before unloading the shipment.

■ Collect COD payments before unloading cargo.

■ Obtain the properly signed order notify bill of lading before you unload the shipment.

■ Check to be sure the entire consignment is delivered.

■ Any differences, shortages, or changes in the method of payment should be reported to your dispatcher or supervisor before you release the shipment to the consignee.

■ Know your company policy on freight delivery problems.

INTERLINE FREIGHT

Pick up freight from an **interline carrier** in the same way you would from a shipper. Deliver freight to an interline carrier as if it were a consignee:

■ Always inspect the shipment for damage or shortages.

■ Compare the bill of lading with the freight.

■ Do not sign freight bills, bills of lading, or receipts until you note any shortages or damages and they are signed by an interline carrier.

■ Make sure you thoroughly understand any special services and the method of payment.

■ Get signatures and receipts before you release the shipment to the connecting carrier.

■ If there is an equipment interchange with the connecting carrier, know the policy of your company. Always follow the established procedures.

Remember, you are responsible not only for the freight but also for making sure the trailer is within legal limits. Check the weight of the shipment on the papers so you will not accept an overloaded trailer.

HAZARDOUS MATERIALS AND WASTE

Hazardous materials shipments must be specially labeled, prepared, handled, documented, and placarded.

Communication of hazards in transportation is vital to public health and safety **(see Figure 25–11).** If there is an accident or spill, police, fire, and emergency crews must be able to quickly recognize the presence of these materials.

As a professional driver, you must know how to recognize hazardous materials shipments and be aware of the dangers of each hazard class.

▶ **Figure 25–11**

All hazmat shipments must be specially labeled, prepared, handled, documented, and placarded.

The Shipper's Responsibilities

By federal law, the shipper is required to:

- Train all employees involved in hazmat functions
- Identify all hazardous materials by hazard class
- Properly pack the material in the correct packaging
- Prepare the shipping papers, listing—in this order—the proper shipping name, hazard class, identification number, and packing group
- State the total quality or volume of the material
- Properly label each package with the correct hazard class label if one is required
- Mark each package with the proper shipping name and identification number for the contents
- Provide placards for the carrier
- Provide the emergency response telephone number

The Driver's Responsibilities

By federal law, drivers are required to:

- Check the bill of lading for hazardous material cargo
- Make sure the shipping papers are complete and accurate
- Check the shipping papers to make sure the shipper's certification form is signed **(see Figure 25–12)**
- Check the packages for proper labeling and marking
- Check compatibility and segregation requirements for the materials
- Observe the special handling and loading requirements
- Properly placard vehicle as required on all four sides **(see Figure 25–13)**
- Make certain shipping papers are within driver's reach or on the driver's seat if the driver has left the truck **(see Figure 25–14)**
- Comply with FMCSR

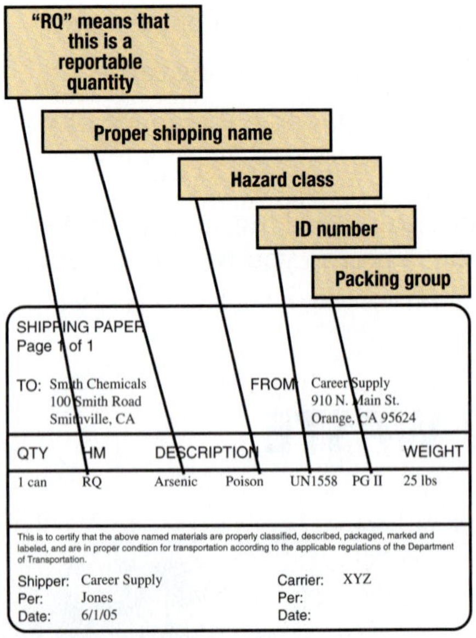

Figure 25–12

Hazmat shipping papers itemize the contents of a hazmat cargo and serve to inform drivers of any special handling requirements.

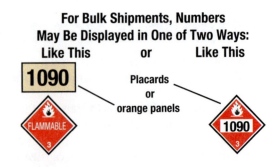

Figure 25–13

There are two ways of displaying numbers on bulk shipments.

HAZARDOUS MATERIALS SHIPPING PAPERS

KEEP THIS ENVELOPE VISIBLE AND ACCESSIBLE

- While Drving - papers must be within driver's reach with seat belt fastened.
- In Driver's Absence From Unit - Papers must be on driver's seat or in pouch on driver's door.

Date	Vehicle No.	Dispatched By	Classification of Hazardous Materials on Vehicle	Weight	Type of Placard	Applied By

IN CASE OF SPILL OR OTHER EMERGENCY CALL _____

Mark the location of each class of Hazardous Materials loaded onto the vehicle on the Diagram below.
BEFORE GIVING TO DRIVER

DRIVER'S INSTRUCTIONS ON REVERSE SIDE OF ENVELOPE

▶ **Figure 25–14**

Hazmat shipping papers must be within the driver's reach or on the driver's seat if the driver has left the truck.

SUMMARY

In this chapter, you have learned the importance of cargo documentation: bills of lading, freight bills, cargo manifest, invoices, packing slips, and hazardous materials shipping papers. The responsibility of the shipper and the driver were explained. How to accept a load for shipment and the correct way to deliver it were described.

KEY TERMS

Agent
Bill of lading (BL)
Collect-on-delivery (COD) shipments
Common carrier
Connecting carrier
Contract carrier
Delivery (terminal) carrier
Delivery receipt
Detention time or demurrage
Documentation
Dunnage and return (DR) charges
Exempt commodity carrier
For-hire carrier

Freight bill
Freight forwarder
Helper service
Household goods bill of lading
Inside delivery
Interline carrier
Invoice
Manifest
Order notify bill of lading
Order notify shipment
Originating carrier
Packing slip
Prepaid shipments
Private carrier

Pro numbers
Receiver (consignee)
Residential delivery
Security seals
Shipper (consignor)
Storage and delay (S&D) charges
Straight bill of lading
Tailgate delivery
Tariff
Through bill of lading
Transportation charges
Uniform straight bill of lading
Warehouse receipt

REVIEW QUESTIONS

1. The most important use of the documentation that accompanies shipments is to
_____.

   a. determine the route the driver should take to deliver the cargo

   b. determine the center of gravity of the cargo

   c. determine the air pressure for the trailer's tires

   d. provide an accurate record of the cargo

2. The consignee is _____.

   a. the person or company that offers the goods for shipment

   b. the person or company that is transporting the goods

   c. the person or company to whom the goods are being shipped

   d. the person or company that checks the load for hazmat items

3. A bill of lading is _____.

   a. a written contract between the shipper and the carrier for transporting a shipment

   b. a verbal contract between the shipper and the carrier for transporting a shipment

   c. a detailed list of packed goods that is prepared by the shipper

   d. a paper signed by the consignee or an agent of the consignee accepting the shipment from the driver

4. The most common type of bill of lading, which is a contract that the parties cannot change and requires that the goods must be delivered to the consignees or an authorized representative, is a (an) _____.

   a. original bill of lading

   b. nonuniform bill of lading

   c. order notify bill of lading

   d. uniform straight bill of lading

5. The responsibility for opening packages and checking the contents against the packing slip belongs to the _____.

   a. driver

   b. consignee

   c. person packing the trailer

   d. dispatcher

6. If you are asked to tow a trailer that is sealed with a security seal or you cannot visually inspect the contents, what should you do to release you and your company from responsibility for any damage unless the damages are caused by accident?

   a. Insist the shipper make the contents of the trailer available to you for a visual inspection.

   b. Make a note on the bill of lading: "shipper's weight, load and count."

   c. Accept the load but notify the Federal Transportation Commission that the shipper is in violation of federal regulations.

   d. Take the trailer as if you had inspected the contents.

7. Which of the following is not a shipper's responsibility regarding hazardous material and waste?

   a. Determine the route the rig should take to make the delivery.

   b. Train all employees involved in hazmat functions.

   c. Identify all hazardous materials by hazard class.

   d. Provide the emergency response telephone numbers.

8. Which of the following is not a responsibility of the driver regarding transporting hazardous material and/or waste?

   a. Check the bill of lading for hazardous material cargo.

   b. Check the packages for proper labeling and marking.

   c. Check FMCSR for route to take to make the delivery.

   d. Observe the special handling and loading requirements.

9. Placards are diamond-shaped signs that _____.

   a. indicate the increase in total stopping distance because of the characteristics of the load

   b. indicate the center of gravity of the load

   c. tell the hazard class of the shipment

   d. tell the driver the location of the delivery site

10. Which of the following is not a method of distinguishing hazardous materials listed on bills of lading that also have nonhazardous materials listed?

    a. listing the hazardous materials last on the bill of lading

    b. listing the hazardous materials first on the bill of lading

    c. highlighting the entry

    d. printing the entry in contrasting color

26 Trip Planning

OBJECTIVES

When you have completed this chapter, you should be able to:

- Explain how to locate the starting point and destination of a trip on a map.
- Plan trip routes using maps.
- Discuss how software has streamlined the trip-planning function.
- Choose alternate routes.
- Estimate mileage and travel time.
- Know how to obtain necessary permits.
- Describe types of vehicles and cargos most likely to have routing restrictions or special requirements.
- Explain how to get information about special requirements.
- Describe how to plan for personal needs and expenses on a trip.
- Describe the various types of enforcement procedures.

INTRODUCTION

As well as driving a rig safely, the professional driver must be able to read and understand maps, know the general size and weight laws of the various states, and understand registration and fuel tax requirements **(see Figure 26–1).** Along with trip-planning skills, the professional driver also must be aware of special regulations to be followed when planning a trip.

Part of the professional driver's job is to keep accurate records to show compliance with the hours of service regulations as well as cargo, fuel tax payments, and registration fees **(see Figure 26–2).**

As a professional driver, you should be able to estimate:

- Mileage from point of origin to destination
- Trip time
- Fuel requirements
- Personal financial needs

Depending on the carrier, the driver may be involved with these aspects of trip planning. Companies differ in how routes are planned. In many cases, the carrier will use routing software, which considers fuel purchase sites, rest stops, road conditions, and other elements.

TYPES OF DRIVING RUNS AND ASSIGNMENTS

Various types of runs are made in the trucking industry. Some carriers operate only a single type of run. Others operate a variety. As a professional driver, you may have a choice in the type of run you are assigned.

Many times, the driver will be given specific instructions about which routes to use. These instructions must be followed. In other cases, company management specifies the use of a specific route because it may be the safest or the best highway conditions. Going off an assigned route without a good reason is a serious violation of company policy and may result in disciplinary measures or termination.

Local Operations

Local pickup and delivery (P&D)—driver operates in and around certain cities, delivering freight to its final destination and picking up freight from shippers. Local P&D may also move freight between nearby points of origin and destinations. Local drivers must know the street system well so that pickups and deliveries can be made in the safest, quickest way. The local P&D driver also must know the local traffic patterns in order to avoid areas of congestion and delay when possible.

Peddle run—a type of local P&D operation. Usually freight is hauled from the terminal to separate destinations in the nearby area. Peddle run drivers also pick up freight along the route and

Figure 26–1

Professional drivers must have trip-planning skills and knowledge of state laws and regulations affecting drivers.

Figure 26–2

Professional drivers are responsible for keeping accurate records of their trips.

bring it back to the terminal. Because of frequent changes in points to be served, drivers of this type of service may be asked to select their routes because they will know the quickest and safest routes.

Shuttle operations—drivers move empty or loaded trailers between nearby points, such as terminals to customer, drop yards to customer, railheads to customer, and vice versa. The number of trailers a driver can move during a single driving period will depend on the distances involved.

▶ **Figure 26-3**

Long-distance operations are used for cross-country runs.

Long-Distance Transport

Long-distance transport involves moving cargo from point of origin to one or more distant destinations **(see Figure 26–3)**. Several types of operations fall into the general classification, including one in which the long-distance driver will return to the home terminal at the end of 10 hours of driving. In other cases, the driver may be on the road for 2 days or more at a time. Brief descriptions of several types of long-distance operations follow:

Regular run—the driver operates between the same points on each trip and may not have a regular starting and finishing time for each period of driving.

Open dispatch—the driver goes from point of origin to a distant point. Depending on the driving time and the need to comply with hours-of-service limits, the driver may take another unit to an additional destination. After resting in compliance with the Hours-of-Service ruling, the driver may be given a run heading toward the home terminal or may be dispatched to another point. This cycle may be repeated for several days before the driver returns home.

Regular route—refers to line-haul transport between given origins and destinations using assigned highways. Most less-than-truckload (LTL) fleets are regular route operations **(see Figure 26–4).**

▶ **Figure 26-4**

A regular route is line-haul transport between origin and destination using assigned highways.

Irregular route—long-distance transport between a combination of origin and destination points using any suitable route. This type of run is also called **over-the-road trucking.** In this type of operation, the professional driver is most likely to be asked to select a route, although management may set the route to be used and the driver must comply with this route.

Relay run—refers to a trip in which a driver drives for the maximum allowable hours and then goes off duty as prescribed by the hours-of-service laws. Another driver takes the unit on to the next point. This cycle may be repeated several times as the truck is driven from origin to final destination by several different drivers.

Meet and turn—a relay run in which two drivers start driving toward each other from different points and meet at a chosen midpoint. At the meeting place, the drivers exchange complete units or only trailers. Then, each driver goes back to his starting point.

Turnaround run—a driver travels for about 5 hours to a destination and then returns to the home terminal. At the turnaround point, the driver may switch units or trailers for the return trip.

Sleeper operations—the driver of a rig with a sleeper berth can accumulate the required off-duty time as long as he or she meets the hours-of-service standard. The sleeper operation may use a single driver or a two-driver team **(see Figure 26–5)**.

▶ **Figure 26-5**

Drivers with sleeper rigs can save lodging costs on the road.

ROUTE SELECTION

There are many types of highways and each type is coded on a map. If you understand this code, you will be able to know which roads are interstate highways, which are state highways, and which highways are country roads. The various types of highways are described in the following section. They are listed in order of preference to use:

- Interstate routes
- Toll roads
- U.S. numbered routes
- State primary roads
- Other streets and highways

Interstate routes—usually preferred because they separate opposing traffic, have limited access, and bypass many small towns. Although they are considered the safest highways, drivers must be aware that these popular and much used highways can sometimes be snarled by bad weather or traffic congestion, especially in the urban areas. Drivers should be aware of the growing number of "trucks only" lanes on interstate routes.

Toll roads—similar to interstates, these roads require users to pay a toll. In many states, toll roads are part of the interstate system. The decision to use a toll road must be based on many factors in addition to cost. Drivers should also consider:

- Differences in time and distance over alternate routes
- Terrain and traffic
- Road conditions
- The need to go through built-up areas
- The amount of stop-and-go driving
- Wear and tear on the equipment
- Fuel usage

U.S. numbered routes—make up the major through routes. Those that parallel interstates may be good alternatives in case of delays on interstates because of traffic or weather.

State primary routes—are major routes that may be as good as, or even better than, a nearby U.S. numbered highway.

Other streets and highways—are often used to reach loading or unloading points. Generally, drivers choose county roads or other routes designated by number or letter. These are the through routes set by the local authorities and are generally better than other local streets to safely handle truck traffic.

Special Situations

Because it is not possible to foresee every problem, professional drivers must learn to approach new situations carefully and to use common sense. Some of the special situations you may find are: **local truck routes, posted bridges,** and **restricted routes.**

Local truck routes—many cities and towns have designated routes for trucks. Although they are not always well marked, the driver must stay on these truck routes to avoid a ticket.

Posted bridges—many bridges have special weight restrictions. Do not cross a bridge if your rig's weight is more than the weight posted. Some fines are as much as $10,000 **(see Figure 26–6).**

Restricted routes—one reason to prohibit trucks from using some roads is a long past history of accidents. Always heed posted prohibitions. If you drive on restricted road, you may be cited by local law enforcement, be faced with a hazardous condition, or be unable to avoid an accident.

▶ **Figure 26–6**

Never use a bridge if your rig is heavier than the posted weight.

There are other ways to get information about certain routes or get the help you need when planning a trip. Suggested ways include:

■ Talking to other truck drivers or local residents about road conditions

■ Using local Internet Web sites for route information, traffic conditions, and suggested alternate routes

■ If you are near a destination, stopping and calling the shipper or consignee for directions

■ Making inquiries about local conditions at truck stops, firehouses, police stations, or other locations where people may know the information you need

■ Looking in a road atlas—many have information on restricted routes, low clearances, etc.

■ Using your CB to ask questions about the route

MAP READING

Being able to read maps is an important skill for the professional driver. However, because of continually improving software, trip planning can also be done through the use of computer programs with a great deal more information and accuracy.

Part of the professional driver's job is to locate unfamiliar pickup and delivery points. Maps continue to be a good investment because they provide a good backup for the driver who relies on computerized trip planning. You may want to purchase an **atlas,** a collection of maps from all U.S. states, Canadian provinces, and Mexican states. These may be purchased in bookstores or truck stops.

Local or area map—useful for the local driver because it will detail local streets. Plan to buy a new local map every year, particularly in fast-growing areas.

State map—free state maps are available at many border information centers and along interstate highways.

Atlas—a driver expecting to travel extensively throughout the country should consider investing in an atlas. In addition to state, city, and area maps, certain atlases may include the following information:

■ Location of permanent scales

■ Low underpasses

■ Size and weight limits

■ Fuel taxes

■ Designated routes for operation of twin trailers and 53/103 foot semitrailers or other specialized equipment

■ State laws for access to the Designated Highway System

■ Driving distances

Pointers for Reading Maps

■ In most cases, North is at the top of the map. It is often indicated by an arrow symbol with the letter N or a symbol showing all four points of the compass. In some cases, a map of a small area may be printed with North to one side. North will almost always be shown by some symbol.

■ Read the key or legend that explains the symbols and colors used to show the interstates, federal, state and local routes, rest areas, interchanges, distances, and other important features.

■ Learn to figure the distance between points by adding the mileage figures shown along the route. Black numbers often refer to short distances between two black dots. Red numbers refer to longer distances between two red dots.

Some maps have mileage charts showing approximate distances between principal cities and towns. Driving times are usually for automobiles, so allow more time for trucks. Computerized trip planning software also provides this information automatically.

Learn to use the grid coordinates of a map to locate specific cities or towns. Numbers are printed across the top and bottom of the map. Letters are printed down each side. Most maps have an index and will list the names of cities and their grid coordinates, such as A-10. To find the location, look down from 10 and across from A to find that particular city where the two coordinates intersect.

CALCULATING TRAVEL TIME AND FUEL USAGE

Knowing how to figure the distance, your average speed, and trip time are required for trip planning. The driver who wants to track the average speed and fuel usage may want to invest in a laptop computer, trip planning software, or at the very least a calculator. The following formulas are often used by truck drivers for these calculations:

> **Distance** = Speed multiplied by time
>
> 50 mph × 9 hours = 450 miles
>
> **Average speed** = Distance divided by time
>
> 450 miles divided by 9 hours = 50 mph
>
> **Trip time** = Distance divided by average speed
>
> 450 miles divided by 50 mph = 9 hours

KEEPING RECORDS

A driver must carry all up-to-date papers while on duty. Each carrier has its own way of keeping records to meet the information needs of that carrier and to help drivers remain within the law. You must use the record-keeping method your company specifies.

If a driver does not keep the records the company requires, both the driver and the company can be penalized. Not carrying the right papers or keeping necessary records may also cause delays in being paid.

"Well, no. I never learned to calculate mileage and fuel, so I need to know if I can make it to Phoenix on fumes."

The driver must carry the following documents at all times because law enforcement officers have the right to examine them:

- Driver's license
- Medical certificate
- Driver's daily log
- Driver's Vehicle Condition Report

Driver's license—a valid commercial driver's license with all required endorsements

Medical certificate—current and valid health record for the driver; and the driver must be in compliance with any special requirements such as glasses or hearing aids

Driver's daily log—correctly completed and available for the last 7 days as well as the current day

Driver's Vehicle Condition Report—prepare at the end of the trip or tour of duty

Shipping papers—to describe the contents of the freight being hauled

Trip reports—generally include the following data:

- Name of driver
- Terminal
- Vehicle identification
- Departure time from terminal
- Routing instructions
- Address of each stop to deliver or pick up freight
- Times of arrival and departure from each stop
- Quantity of freight handled
- Time of return to terminal
- Space for remarks

CAUTION!

The driver must always comply with company policies when preparing trip reports.

Onboard Recorder

More carriers are now using onboard recording equipment. Some carriers use this equipment to show compliance with hours-of-service rules. If the company for which you work uses such devices, they will train you in how to use them properly so you can maintain your Driver's Daily Log.

Some trucks have recorders installed to control how the truck is operated. Basic information recorded includes:

- Time engine is running
- Whether the truck is stopped or moving
- Speed
- Miles driven

Calculating Personal Needs

When planning any trip, drivers should consider their personal needs. These needs include expenses to be met while on the trip, how they will be reimbursed—or if they qualify to be reimbursed by the carrier, and what paperwork must be kept to prove expenses and how forms should be completed. These expenses and who is usually responsible are as follows:

Meals	Driver expense
Lodging	Driver expense
Fuel	Company expense

En route repairs	Company expense
Tolls	Company expense, if authorized
Permits	Company expense
Special fees	Company expense

Each company handles expense reimbursement according to set policy. Find out how your company handles expenses before you begin a trip. Keep copies of all receipts for your personal records. Retain logbooks to document your daily expenses for tax purposes.

Be Aware of Weather Conditions

Drivers should know the kind of weather to expect during each trip. They should know when they might encounter extreme weather conditions and carry the right kinds of clothing for any situation. Clothing for working outside the truck during bad weather should also be included. Many drivers also carry blankets, a sleeping bag, and extra food and water in case they are stranded.

TRIP PLANNING SOFTWARE

The market for trip planning software contains scores of choices for today's professional driver. This routing software contains common capabilities, including:

- Geocoding addresses, that is, locating the latitude and longitude by matching the address against data contained in a digital map database

- Determining the best paths through street networks between pairs of geocoded points

- Solving vehicle routing problems, assigning stops to routes and terminals, sequencing stops, and routing vehicles between pairs of stops

- Displaying the results in such a way that dispatchers can communicate results to drivers, loaders, and other personnel

The following trip planning software was chosen at random to illustrate some of the available applications for trip planning purposes.

CoPilot Truck®

ALK Technologies' CoPilot Truck software combines truck routing, mileage, and mapping capabilities with in-vehicle GPS navigation and route guidance to create the first onboard laptop computer navigation system specifically designed for owner-operators, leased-operators, and company drivers.

Data in the newly released CoPilot Truck | Laptop 4 solution include over 7 million miles of U.S. roadways, 31,000 exit numbers, and more than 100 million addresses. Canadian map data cover 830,000 road miles and more than 10 million addresses. Also incorporated are over 3 million points of interest, including truck stops, truck washes, and weigh stations.

ProMiles®

ProMiles, by the ProMiles Software Development Corporation, offers door-to-door addressing along with truck attributes such as designated truck routes, hazardous restrictions, and weight and height restrictions. By combining this functionality with Tele Atlas' detailed routing and addressing content, the new version of ProMiles offers even more solutions to trip planning, incorporating Tele Atlas' turn-by-turn data into its routing and logistics products for street-level routing applications.

PC*Miler®

PC*Miler, also by ALK Technologies, is a point-to-point routing, mileage, and mapping software application which generates detailed reports, routes, mileages, and maps over the entire U.S., Canadian, and Mexican truck-usable highway network. It features the largest and most accurate North American highway database on the market. PC*Miler includes point-to-point distance calculations, including rate determination, driver pay, and instant customer quotes. It also offers routing and optimization, including dispatch and routing, route optimization, trip time and cost estimates, load planning, truck stop routing, and instant rate quotes, and gives detailed driving instructions including trip time and cost reports as well as map quality graphics.

VEHICLE LICENSING AND PERMITS

Every vehicle must have a registration (license) in order to operate. Fees are paid each year and registration plates are issued. The majority of trucks or truck-tractor combinations weighing more than 26,000 pounds will be registered under the **International Registration Plan (IRP).**

The IRP is a registration agreement among the states and Canadian provinces based on the percentage of miles driven by that rig in each state or province. License fees are paid to each state or province in which the vehicle operates. A cab card is issued to the vehicle, stating the IRP areas in which the vehicle is allowed to operate.

Usually the company obtains the registration plate, but the driver is responsible for keeping mileage records. The percentage of fees paid to each state depends on the number of miles driven in that state compared to the miles driven in all states and provinces.

If a truck that has IRP plates plans to operate in a state not shown on the IRP cab card, a trip permit must be obtained. The company is responsible for telling the driver how to obtain these permits, which are usually issued for a given period of time, ranging most often from 24 to 72 hours. Federal laws require all states to be members of IRP.

Fuel Tax Law

To legally operate in any state, a truck must be registered for **fuel use tax** purposes. When it is registered, a fuel tax decal is issued and placed on the door of the tractor. The decal is evidence the vehicle is registered for fuel use tax purposes. The price of the decal varies from state to state. The fuel use tax itself is paid quarterly by the company. The fuel tax registration law is usually enforced by the state revenue or taxation department.

The carrier pays the fuel tax in each state, based on the number of miles driven in that state. If the carrier buys more fuel in a state than is needed to cover its fuel tax obligation, the carrier gets a tax credit. On the other hand, if not enough fuel is bought in a state, the carrier must pay more tax.

The driver must be sure he or she gets receipts for all fuel purchases, although many companies now use computerized tracking of their fuel purchases and drivers are directed to buy from certain fuel companies that provide this tracking information as part of their service.

Weight Distance Taxes

Some states charge a **weight distance tax**—sometimes called a mileage tax, ton-mile tax, or axle tax. These taxes are paid by the carrier and are based on the annual ton mileage **(see Figure 26–7).** The carrier must also file a quarterly report. States often require trucks to be registered for the weight distance tax. Once taxes are paid, the carrier usually obtains a decal or

Mileage Control (Speedometer Mileage Readings)

Destination _____

Date _____ Unit Nos. _____

Driver _____

New Jersey
Beginning _____
State Line OUT _____
State Line IN _____
Ending _____

New York
State Line IN _____
State Line OUT _____

Connecticut
State Line IN _____
State Line OUT _____

Pennsylvania
State Line IN _____
State Line OUT _____

▶ **Figure 26-7**

The mileage control sheet is used by the carrier to track its mileage taxes.

number for the tractor. These taxes are enforced by the state's highway department or transportation department.

FEDERAL LENGTH AND WEIGHT LIMITS

A driver is responsible for staying within federal and state weight and length laws. All states must allow truck combinations of certain weights and lengths to operate on roadways that are part of the **National System of Interstate Highways,** a system also known as the **Designated System** or **National Network.** Most of these highways are identified with the letter I and the number of the highway, such as I-80 or I-45. Many multilane, divided highways, such as the U.S. routes and turnpikes, are also part of this system.

Many state highways have requirements similar to the following federal weight and size limits, so it is always wise to check the applicable maps or computer data for actual dimensions and weights.

Vehicle Weight

A maximum of 20,000 pounds may be carried on any one axle (except steer axles, which are allowed only 12,000 pounds) and 34,000 pounds on the tandem axle. An overall gross weight of

80,000 pounds is allowed on a typical five-axle tractor-trailer. The way the axles are spaced and the number of axles may lower the single and tandem axle limits. Rigs must stay within weight-to-length limits based on the weight of groups of two or more adjacent (following) axles.

The **Federal Bridge Formula** is used to calculate permissible gross loads. Ideally, a typical 80,000-pound fix-axle highway rig should carry 12,000 pounds on the front axle and 34,000 pounds on each of the tandems. The tractor must have an outer spread (distance between the middle of the front axle and the middle of the rearmost axle) of at least 14 feet. The formula also requires minimum distances between the tractor and the trailer axles (**inner** and **outer bridge**).

Vehicle Length

There is no limit on the overall length of a tractor-trailer on the interstates and other designated highways, but some states do limit lengths. These are typically measured from the center of the trailer tandems. Pay special attention if the trailer is over 48 feet long. Some states require a permit for this length.

No state can prohibit doubles on the interstate. Longer doubles—more than 28 feet per trailer—and triple trailer combinations usually operate under special permits.

STATE LIMITS

Unless they are controlled by federal interstate law, weight and size limits vary from state to state. If a driver is not certain about the state's limits, he or she should find out about the limits before entering the state. Dispatchers usually have this information or it can be found in Thomson Delmar Learning's *Trucking Rules and Regulations*. The state police, highway patrol, departments of transportation, and state trucking associations can also provide accurate information.

When deciding whether a tractor-trailer is within limits, the four key factors to be considered are vehicle weight, the number of axles, vehicle length, and vehicle height and load.

Vehicle weight—many state agencies provide color-coded maps (red, green, purple) that identify load maximums to be carried on various roads. These maps are based on the condition of the road and the weight that can be supported by the bridges. You can weigh your rig at fleet or shipper terminals or on public scales at truck stops. Some public scales will certify weight and even pay overweight if they are wrong.

Number of axles—state bridge laws limit the maximum weight that may be carried. The laws are determined by the number of axles and the distance between them on a rig. While most states have adopted the Federal Bridge Formula to determine axle weight limits and gross weight limits, some states use other means for figuring these limits.

Vehicle length—is regulated by both state and local governments. They also set the maximum load, length, and overhang (the distance beyond support of the load bed) permitted. The legal length may be set in terms of either overall length (from bumper to bumper) or trailer length.

Vehicle height and load—while some states permit vehicle heights of 14½ feet, most restrict heights to 13½ feet. This limit includes the load. Overpasses on most interstates have clearances of 16½ feet but some are only 13½ feet. Always check on these height limits before starting your trip.

Special Permit Hauling

Loads that are larger than either state or local laws allow will require special permits. You can get these permits from state agencies and police departments. Typical loads requiring these permits include machinery, buildings, and bridge construction girders.

Some permits limit hours of operation, such as before sundown, after sunrise, or during rush hours. They will also specify the routes to be used **(see Figure 26–8).** Permits may:

- Be limited to specific vehicles
- Require the use of special signs, such as "Oversize Load"
- Require the use of escort vehicles in front of and behind the load
- Require using special lights, such as rotating amber lights
- Specify the route to be followed

Drivers may have to submit their planned route before they can get a permit. If a detour or delay occurs, the driver should call the state or local agency that issued the permit to request a change in time or route.

Hauling this load requires a special permit

▶ Figure 26–8
Special permits often limit hours of operation and routes used.

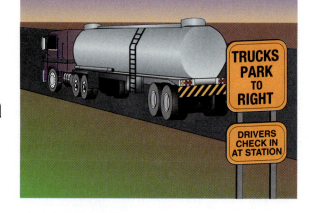

▶ Figure 26–9
Be sure to obey all instructions at scales and ports of entry and during roadside inspections.

ROADSIDE ENFORCEMENT

As well as the normal enforcement of traffic laws, there are three other types of controlling activities routinely carried on by the states. Drivers need to be aware of scales, ports of entry, and roadside safety inspections **(see Figure 26–9).** In many cases, these functions are carried out at a single location.

Ports of Entry

Ports of entry are locations where the driver must stop and prove the carrier has authority to operate in the state. In some cases, the driver may have to buy permits or pay fees **(see Figure 26–10).** Weighing may also be done at a port of entry. Do not pull onto the scales. Instead, park near the scales and walk up to get your permit. Some states fine drivers if they pull onto the scales without a permit, and sometimes the Driver's Daily Log will be checked for hours-of-service violations and then time-stamped by the person on duty.

Roadside Safety Inspections

Roadside safety inspections are done at scales, ports of entry, or special safety inspection facilities, or a suitably safe area. The driver must show his or her license, medical certificate, driver's

▶ **Figure 26–10**
Observe all signs, follow instructions, and have all paperwork ready for inspection at a port of entry.

logs, and the shipping papers for the load. Inspectors have the authority to inspect cargo, even if it is sealed. If a sealed load is inspected, a new seal will be put on by the inspector and the driver should record the identification numbers, both of the old seal and the new seal. The driver may be put out of service at once for the following:

■ Hours-of-service violation

■ A vehicle so unsafe it is likely to be involved in an accident or a breakdown

■ Leaking hazardous materials

At the end of the roadside inspection, the driver will be given a copy of the form filled out by the inspector. This form must be turned in to the carrier. If the driver will reach a company facility within 24 hours, the form may be turned in at that time. If not, the driver should mail the form to the carrier.

SUMMARY

This chapter presents the different types of trucking operations and how to plan a trip. You learned about the different types of roads and various trip-planning software. The permits that may be required were explained and methods of reading maps and calculating travel time and fuel consumption were also discussed. Legal weight and length limits were described and planning for personal needs during a trip was also emphasized.

KEY TERMS

Atlas	Fuel use tax	Irregular route
Average speed formula	Inner bridge	Local pickup and delivery
Designated System	International Registration	(P&D)
Distance formula	Plan (IRP)	Local truck routes
Federal Bridge Formula	Interstate routes	Long-distance transport

Meet and turn	Port of entry	Shuttle operations
National Network	Posted bridges	Sleeper operations
National System of Interstate Highways	Regular route	State primary routes
	Regular run	Toll roads
Open dispatch	Relay run	Trip time formula
Outer bridge	Restricted routes	Turnaround run
Over-the-road trucking	Roll and rest	U.S. numbered routes
Peddle run	Safe Haven	Weight distance tax

REVIEW QUESTIONS

1. Who is responsible for knowing the various state rig size and weight laws and understanding registration and fuel tax requirements?

   a. dispatcher

   b. professional driver

   c. shipper

   d. receiver

2. Moving cargo from a point of origin to one or more distant destinations is known as _____.

   a. long-distance transporting

   b. local pickup and delivery

   c. a peddle run

   d. shuttle operations

3. The usually preferred nontoll roads that separate opposing traffic, have limited access, and bypass many small communities are known as _____.

   a. U.S. numbered routes

   b. state primary routes

   c. interstate routes

   d. local streets

4. To determine the time needed (trip time) to drive a specific distance, the professional driver _____.

   a. multiplies gallons used by distance of the trip

   b. divides gallons used by distance traveled

   c. divides distance traveled by time

   d. divides trip distance by average speed

5. Regarding the up-to-date documents that a professional driver is required to have while on duty, which of the following is not required?

   a. driver's license

   b. a complete record of all repairs to the tractor

   c. medical certificate

   d. driver's inspection report

6. The International Registration Plan (IRP) is a registration agreement among the states and Canadian provinces _____.

   a. offering discount lottery tickets to drivers of big rigs

   b. offering fuel discounts for professional drivers

   c. offering discounts at national quick food chains

   d. based on the percentage of miles driven in each state or province

7. The Federal Bridge Formula is used to calculate the _____.

   a. permissible gross loads

   b. weight of the freight load allowed on federal bridges

   c. minimum weight on the steering axle

   d. weight of the freight load allowed on state and local bridges

8. Which of the following is not one of the key factors in deciding whether a tractor-trailer is within state length and weight limits?

   a. vehicle weight

   b. the total stopping distance of the rig at 30 mph

   c. the number of axles

   d. vehicle length, height, and width

9. Regarding special permit hauling for loads that are larger than either the state or local laws allow, which of the following is typically not one of the restrictions for this type of operation?

   a. limited to specific vehicles

   b. requires using special lights

   c. movement of the load should be at night

   d. requires a specific route

10. During a roadside safety inspection, which of the following is not typically an element of the inspection?

    a. brake lag time

    b. driver's log

    c. driver's license

    d. driver's medical certificate

27

Hours of Service

OBJECTIVES

When you have completed this chapter, you should be able to:

■ Understand the reasons behind the federal hours-of-service laws.

■ Know the new hours-of-service laws.

■ Record your time and activities while on the road.

■ Make entries in a logbook and know what information must be included.

■ Compute on-duty hours and required rest stops while on the road.

INTRODUCTION

Sixty years ago, federal laws were developed to regulate the number of hours a driver could spend on the clock and behind the wheel. As a professional driver, you have a daily responsibility of maneuvering up to 40 tons of loaded equipment in all types of demanding weather, traffic, and road conditions **(see Figure 27–1)**. The hours-of-service laws were designed to help keep you at your best and safest level of performance.

Aside from the fact that drivers and trucks continue to move freight from point A to point B, the motor carrier industry has drastically changed since 1939 when the original **hours-of-service (HOS) regulations** were mandated for truck drivers. Roads are better designed, constructed, and maintained in a nationwide network to provide greater mobility, accessibility, and safety for all highway users. Vehicles have been dramatically improved in terms of design, construction, safety, comfort, efficiency, emissions, technology, and ergonomics.

Proposed changes for the HOS regulations were under consideration by the Federal Motor Carrier Safety Administration (FMCSA) for several years before a final rule was announced in 2003. Because it was concerned about the effect of fatigue as a contributing factor in commercial motor vehicle crashes, Congress directed the FMCSA to begin to research a rule change designed to increase driver alertness and reduce fatigue-related incidents in 1995.

In response to this congressional directive, FMCSA analyzed the scientific research, convened expert panels, held hearings and round-table discussions, and reviewed over 53,000 sets of individual comments submitted during the rulemaking process. The new regulations, as written, were designed to provide an increased opportunity for drivers to obtain necessary rest and restorative sleep, and, at the same time, support the realities of modern motor carrier transportation.

More information about these hours-of-service changes can be found on the Federal Motor Carriers Safety Administration website at http://www.fmcsa.dot.gov.

▶ **Figure 27–1**

Federal laws regulate the number of hours a driver can spend on the road.

NEW HOURS-OF-SERVICE RULING—THE BASICS

The hours-of-service ruling, published in the April 28, 2003, *Federal Register* and effective June 27, 2003, was formally enforced beginning on January 4, 2004. In 2005, additional changes were made and went into effect in October 2005. The new Hours-of-Service ruling applies to all "property-carrying drivers" and motor carriers operating in interstate commerce.

The new rules allow drivers to drive for up to 11 straight hours, 1 more hour than they had been allowed; but drivers are also required to take at least 10 hours off between shifts, two more than before **(see Figure 27–2)**. The "new" HOS do not apply to passenger-carrying drivers such as motor coach operators and do not change the rules for the driver's daily logbook.

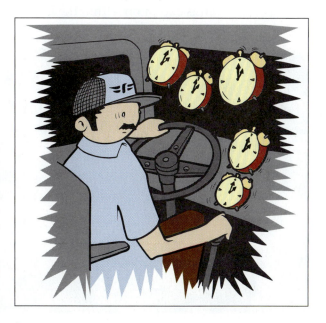

▶ *"Driving through the time zones gets a little tricky—and don't forget about daylight savings!"*

▶ **Figure 27–2**

In adverse driving conditions, drivers may exceed hours-of-service rules to reach a safe place.

What the New HOS Ruling Actually Changed

According to the new HOS ruling, drivers now have a 14-hour work cycle and are allowed 11 hours of **drive time;** but the biggest difference is that the loading/unloading time is folded into the 14-hour cycle.

FMCSA believes these rules will reduce deaths associated with driver fatigue by 25 percent, and prevent over 1,300 fatigue-related injuries per year. Additionally, the new HOS rules state:

- A driver may not exceed 11 hours drive time after 10 consecutive hours off duty.

- A driver may not drive beyond 14 hours after coming on duty (after 10 consecutive hours off duty).

- A driver may not drive following 60 hours on duty in any 7 consecutive days.

- A driver may not drive following 70 hours on duty in any 8 consecutive days.

- Any period of 7 consecutive days may end with the beginning of any off-duty period of 24 or more consecutive hours.

- Any period of 8 consecutive days may end with the beginning of any off-duty period of 34 or more consecutive hours.

  16-Hour exception for property-carrying drivers (short-haul exception)—drivers may extend the 14-hour on-duty period by 2 hours if they (1) are released from duty at the normal work reporting location for the previous five duty tours, (2) return to the normal work reporting location and are released from work within 16 hours, and (3) have not used this exception within the last 6 days, except following a 34-hour restart of a 7/8 day period.

  Sleeper berth exception—to use any of the HOS provisions regarding sleeper berths, a driver must do one of the following:

  1. *Continuous Sleeper Berth Provision:* Spend at least 10 consecutive and uninterrupted hours in the sleeper berth. **(see Figure 27–3).** *Sleeper Berth Provision:* The equivalent of at least 10 consecutive hours off-duty (equivalent means at least 8 hours but less than 10 consecutive hours in a sleeper berth and a separate period of at least 2 hours but less than 10 consecutive hours either in the sleeper berth or off-duty, and any combination of both).

  2. *Continuous Off-Duty and Sleeper Berth Provision:* Spend at least 10

▶ **Figure 27–3**

Sleeper cab.

consecutive hours sleeper berth and off-duty time combined and uninterrupted. Further details are available at www.fmcsa.dot.gov/

Industry exceptions—oil field operations, groundwater well-drilling operations, construction materials and equipment operations, and utility service vehicle operations must comply with the new 11-hour driving, 10 consecutive hours off-duty, and 14-hours on-duty requirements of the new rule. However, the 24-hour restart provisions in these operations remain in effect.

Agricultural exemption—agricultural operations retain their current exemption from driving time requirements for transportation occurring within a 100 air-mile radius of a farm or distribution point during planting or harvesting season within each state, as determined by the state.

Operators of property-carrying commercial motor vehicles not requiring a commercial driver's license—Drivers of non-commercial driver's license (CDL) vehicles (those vehicles not requiring a CDL to operate) who are operating within a 150 air-mile radius of their normal work reporting location and return to their normal work reporting location at the end of their duty tour are now covered by a separate HOS provision. Drivers meeting these conditions are not eligible for the existing 100 air-mile radius provision in § 395.1(e) or the current 16-hour exception in § 395.1(o), since those conflict with this new "Non-CDL, 150 Air-Mile Radius" provision. These drivers are required to comply with the following:

    a. The 11 hours driving, minimum 10 hours off-duty, 14 consecutive hour duty period, 60/70 hours in 7/8 days, and 34-hour restart all apply.

    b. On any 2 days of every 7 consecutive days, the driver may extend the 14-hour duty period to 16 hours.

    c. There is no requirement that the driver be released from duty at the end of the 14- or 16-hour duty periods. The driver may continue to perform non-driving duties, which would be counted against the 60/70 hour weekly limitation.

    d. Time records may be used in lieu of records of duty status (RODS).

34-Hour Restart—Previously, a driver was required to be in compliance with the "60/70 on-duty hours in 7/8 days" limitation before the driver could start counting a 34-hour restart period. Now the 34-hour restart period may begin at the start of any consecutive 34-hour off-duty period.

Fatigue Prevention

One of the major reasons for changing the HOS rule was to prevent CMV drivers from becoming fatigued due to their hours of service. For more than a decade, studies have examined driver fatigue, its causes, and ways to prevent it.

Each year, according to the National Highway Traffic Safety Administration (NHTSA), 100,000 police-reported crashes are the direct result of driver fatigue. These drowsy driving-related accidents cause an estimated 1,500 deaths and 71,000 injuries each year. In some states, such as New Jersey, new laws have been passed, making "driving while drowsy" a criminal offense; and experts say drowsiness and driver fatigue are increasingly viewed as a criminal offense in courtrooms across the country under existing reckless driving and vehicular homicide laws.

Obviously, when you are behind the wheel and begin feeling sleepy, you are in a dangerous situation. That feeling of sleepiness, or fatigue, slows reaction times, decreases awareness, increases aggressiveness (tired, cranky drivers often react differently to other drivers and may be more prone to road rage and speeding), and impairs judgment enough to cause a crash.

A recent survey from the National Sleep Foundation shows that about 50 percent of adult drivers say they have driven a vehicle while feeling drowsy in the past year.

Figure 27-4

Your biological clock tells your body when it's hungry, when it's energetic, and when it's time to sleep.

When you think of the term "biological clock," you probably think it is all about women and their childbearing years. However, each individual has a biological clock that tells the body when it is hungry, when it has energy, and when it is tired **(see Figure 27–4).** The biological clock causes changes in the body's temperature and causes the person to feel wide awake or sleepy.

Twice a day—once in early afternoon (between 2 and 5 P.M.) and once in the early morning (between 2 and 6 A.M.)—your biological clock may make you feel sleepy, too sleepy to operate a vehicle safely.

Research by FMCSA determined that driver alertness and performance were more consistently related to time of day than time on task. Drowsiness episodes were eight times more likely between midnight and 6 A.M. than at other times during the day.

To avoid driver fatigue, drivers should be aware of their own biological clock and to know which times of the day they are most alert. In addition, drivers should take the responsibility to get enough sleep during off-duty hours.

In many cases, drivers try to battle fatigue with a variety of methods, such as coffee or cola (caffeine), or drugs (No-Doz). However, studies have found when a driver is sleep deprived, taking these stimulants only causes drivers to experience "micro-sleeps," or brief, four- to five-second lapses; these are even more dangerous than fatigue because four to five seconds is plenty of time and gives a driver plenty of room to become involved in a crash.

How To Know If You Are Sleep Deprived

Another study by FMCSA found that during their main daily sleep period, drivers slept only about 5 hours, which was 2 hours less sleep than their "ideal" requirement of slightly over 7 hours. The bottom line is that getting enough sleep is essential to a driver's performance behind the wheel.

But, here's the caveat—most drivers don't realize that they haven't had enough sleep until they start dozing off behind the wheel. A few danger signals leading up to feelings of heavy fatigue include:

- Eyes close by themselves or go out of focus.
- You have trouble keeping your head up.
- You cannot stop yawning.
- Thoughts are wandering and disconnected.
- You suddenly do not remember driving the last several miles.
- You miss an exit.
- You tend to speed up or slow down.
- You start drifting in and out of your lane.

Most people do not realize that getting less than 7 or 8 hours of sleep in a 24-hour period can lead to chronic sleepiness and can also cause irritability, crankiness, and depression. It also makes

451

it more likely that the driver will fall asleep while driving, and the only way to correct this situation is to get more or better sleep.

The following suggestions may help to avoid driving tired, although the best way to avoid problems with fatigue is to get plenty of good, healthy sleep:

- Before starting your run, get enough sleep—even take a short nap before going on duty.
- If driving alone, try to keep alert by talking on the CB radio. If team driving, talk to your co-driver. If you are both too sleepy to drive, pull over and take a nap.
- Be aware of any feelings of drowsiness and if you are too drowsy to drive, stop and take a nap.
- Schedule breaks to get out of your seat every 100 miles or every 2 hours.
- Get fresh air into the cab.

New HOS Rules Overturned by Court

On July 16, 2004, a federal court threw out new government rules extending the amount of time that commercial truckers can drive between breaks.

The U.S. Court of Appeals for the District of Columbia, a three-judge panel, said the Federal Motor Carrier Safety Administration failed to consider "drivers' health in the slightest," as required by law.

The court, in a 3-0 ruling, was acting on a suit brought by Public Citizen and highway safety groups. The American Trucking Association joined the FMCSA in arguing for maintaining the new rules.

The government had argued that the new rules would make the roads safer because truckers would have to rest for 2 more hours between driving shifts. The Transportation Department estimated the change would reduce deaths resulting from truck driver fatigue from 440 to 335 a year. But safety groups and the International Brotherhood of Teamsters said that allowing a trucker an extra hour behind the wheel would cause more accidents, not fewer.

FMCSA has 45 days to file for a rehearing of the issue, and because that time limit could be extended to 52 days (or until an official opinion is issued), the decision does not go into effect. FMCSA may also seek a delay in the effective date for the decision, which could add 90 days or more to the time frame. In the interim, the current HOS rules remain in effect.

GO!

Adverse driving conditions, such as snow, sleet, fog, icy pavement, and other unusual road or traffic conditions, may prevent the driver from completing a scheduled run in the time allowed by the Hours-of-Service law. In such cases, the driver is legally allowed to reach the original destination or a safe place to park the rig and wait for safer driving conditions. Adverse driving conditions must be noted in the "Remarks" section of the Daily Log.

NEW HOS RULES IN A NUTSHELL

These regulations apply only to property carriers and drivers. Passenger carriers and drivers will continue operating under the existing rules while fatigue issues specific to the passenger carrier industry are assessed.

Old Hours-of-Service Rules

All CMV drivers may not drive:

- More than 10 hours, following 8 hours off duty

- After 15 hours on duty, following 8 hours off duty

- After 60/70 hours on duty in 7/8 consecutive days

New Hours-of-Service Rules

Property-carrying CMV drivers may not drive:

- More than 11 hours, following 10 hours off duty

- Beyond 14 hours after coming on duty, following 10 hours off duty

- After 60/70 hours on duty in 7/8 consecutive days, a driver may restart a 7/8 consecutive day period after taking 34 or more consecutive hours off duty

Simply stated, this means:

Drivers may drive up to 11 hours instead of 10 hours, but are limited to 14 hours in a duty period.

The 14-hour duty period may not be extended with off-duty time for meal and fuel stops, and so forth. Only the use of a sleeper berth can extend the 14-hour on-duty period.

Each duty period must begin with at least 10 hours off duty, rather than 8 hours.

The 60 hours on duty in 7 consecutive days, or 70 hours on duty in 8 consecutive days, remains the same, but drivers can restart the 7/8-day period by taking at least 34 consecutive hours off duty.

16-Hour Exception for Property-Carrying Drivers

Drivers may extend the 14-hour on-duty period by 2 hours if they:

- Are released from duty at the normal work reporting location for the previous five duty tours

- Return to the normal work reporting location and are released from work within 16 hours

- Have not used this exception within the last 6 days, except following a 34-hour restart of a 7/8-day period

Sleeper berth exception—to use any of the HOS provisions regarding sleeper berths, a driver must do one of the following:

1. *Continuous Sleeper Berth Provision:* Spend at least 10 consecutive and uninterrupted hours in the sleeper berth. *Sleeper Berth Provision:* The equivalent of at least 10 consecutive hours off-duty (equivalent means at least 8 hours but less than 10 consecutive hours in a sleeper berth and a separate period of at least 2 hours but less than 10 consecutive hours either in the sleeper berth or off-duty, and any combination of both).

2. *Continuous Off-Duty and Sleeper Berth Provision:* Spend at least 10 consecutive hours sleeper berth and off-duty time combined and uninterrupted. Further details are available at www.fmcsa.dot. gov/

Industry exceptions—oil field operations, groundwater well-drilling operations, construction materials and equipment operations, and utility service vehicle operations must comply with the new 11-hour driving, 10 consecutive hours off-duty, and 14-hour on-duty requirements of the new rule. However, the 24-hour restart provisions applicable to these operations remains in effect.

Agricultural exemption—agricultural operations retain their current statutory exemption from driving time requirements for transportation occurring within a 100 air-mile radius of a farm or distribution point during planting or harvesting season within each state, as determined by the state.

RECORD OF DUTY STATUS

There are only two ways permitted by federal law to record a driver's duty status. The status must be noted in the **Driver's Daily Log** or the **carrier's time record.** The carrier's time record may be used only when:

- The driver operates within a 100-mile radius of his or her home terminal.

- The driver reports back to her home terminal and was not on duty more than 12 hours.

- The driver has at least 8 hours off duty after each 12 hours on duty.

- The driver does not drive more than 10 hours following 8 hours off.

- For 6 months, the carrier prepares and maintains records showing the time drivers go on duty and go off duty, the total hours per day, and the preceding 7-day record for new or part-time drivers.

The form shown in **Figure 27–5** is used for first-time or part-time drivers. The Driver's Daily Log **(see Figure 27–6)** is the most commonly used record of duty status for drivers. Other than pickup and delivery (P&D) drivers, most tractor-trailers are driven over 100 miles from their home terminals.

Federal laws require every carrier to make certain each driver records, in duplicate, or on an on-board recorder (OBR), his or her duty status for each 24-hour period. This information must be recorded in a specific way on a specific form.

The Driver's Daily Log form in **Figure 27–6** shows the entries the driver must make on the daily log. The correct blanks in which entries must be made are identified by the number of the duty status or other information that is required.

Duty status must be recorded as:

1. Off duty or OFF

2. Sleeper berth or SB (if a sleeper berth is used)

3. Driving or D

4. On-duty, not driving, or ON

5. Each change of duty status must show the name of the nearest city, town, or village, and the state abbreviation in the "Remarks" section.

The form must also show the following:

6. Date by month, day, and year

7. Number of miles driven each day

8. Tractor and trailer numbers and license plate number

HOURS OF SERVICE RECORD FOR FIRST TIME OR INTERMITTENT DRIVERS

Name (Print) _____
First   Middle   Last

DAY	TOTAL TIME ON DUTY
1	_____
2	_____
3	_____
4	_____
5	_____
6	_____
7	_____

TOTAL _____

I hereby certify that the information contained heron is true to the best of my knowledge and belief, and that my last period of release from duty was from

_____ to _____
(Hour/Date)   (Hour/Date)

Signature _____ Date _____

▶ **Figure 27-5**

Typical hours-of-service form for first-time or intermittent drivers.

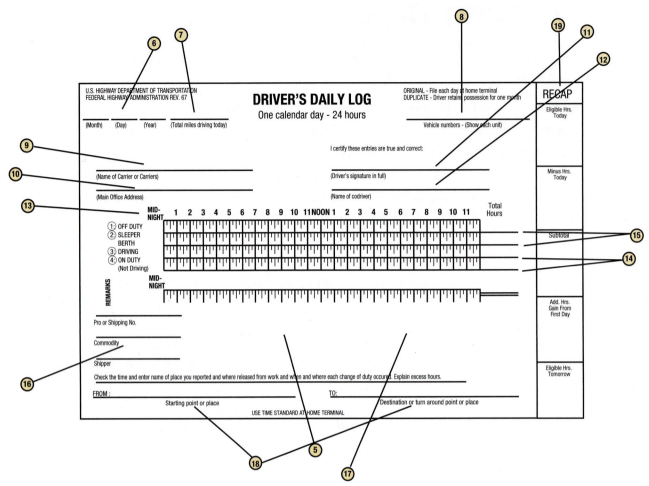

▶ Figure 27-6

Typical page from a Driver's Daily Log. There are many types of Driver's Daily Log forms. Ask your carrier which type they prefer you to use.

9. Name of the carrier or carriers (When you drive for more than one carrier in a 24-hour period, you must show the names of all carriers and the time you started and finished work at each.)

10. Address of the carrier's main office

11. Driver's signature on certification

12. Name of the co-driver, if there is one

13. Starting time for the 24-hour period

14. Total hours in each on-duty status

15. Total hours of duty status for the day (line 14 plus line 15 must equal 24)

16. Shipping document number or the name of the shipper and the product

17. City and state where the change of duty status took place, including such information as adverse weather or emergency conditions in the "Remarks" section

18. On some Driver's Daily Log forms, the starting point and final delivery (If the run is a turnaround back to the original terminal, enter the name of the most distant point and then the words "and return.")

19. Although it is not required by law, it is a good idea—and often a company policy—for the driver to complete the Recap section of the Driver's Daily Log. List the number of hours remaining on duty and state whether you will be driving **(see Figure 27–7).**

Recap

1	2	3	4	5	RECORD OF TIME WORKED	1	2	3	4	5
DAILY TOTAL DUTY & DR. HRS.							DAILY TOTAL DUTY & DR. HRS.			
LAST SEVEN CONSECUTIVE DAYS IN PRECEDING MONTH		8 DAYS – 70 HOURS			DRIVER:	LAST SIX CONSECUTIVE DAYS IN PRECEDING MONTH		7 DAYS – 60 HOURS		
		TOTAL ON-DUTY HOURS LAST 8 DAYS	TOTAL ON-DUTY HOURS LAST 7 DAYS	HOURS AVAILABLE FOR ON-DUTY TIME NEXT DAY (70 MINUS) (COL. 4) ▼	MONTH:		10	TOTAL ON-DUTY HOURS LAST 7 DAYS	TOTAL ON-DUTY HOURS LAST 6 DAYS	HOURS AVAILABLE FOR ON-DUTY TIME NEXT DAY (60 MINUS) (COL. 4) ▼
							15			
					BOOK NUMBER:		4			
							15			
							0			
1					INSTRUCTIONS	1	0	54	44	16
2					This form is designed for use in maintaining a running record of a driver's time on-duty each day. It may be used equally well for drivers working on a midnight-to-midnight or noon-to-noon basis and, by using the proper chart, for drivers eligible to work 60 hours in 7 consecutive days or 70 hours in 8 consecutive days. The person using the chart can also determine the time that a driver has available for work the next day in compliance with the Hours of Service Regulations of the Department of Transportation.	2	10 1/2	54 1/2	44 1/2	15 1/2
3						3	10 3/4	45 1/4	40 1/4	19 3/4
4						4	10 1/2	50 3/4	46 3/4	13 1/4
5						5	10	56 3/4	41 3/4	18 1/4
6						6	3 1/4	45	45	15
7					In keeping the record, be sure to use the proper chart. For a driver working 70 hours in 8 consecutive days, use the chart on the left. For a driver working 60 hours in 7 consecutive days, use the chart on the right.	7				
8						8				
9					Column 1 of each section lists days of the month, 1-31 inclusive, plus the last days of the preceding month that must be counted.	9				
10						10				
11					In column 2 of the proper section enter the time on-duty for the day, (the total of Line 3, Driving, and Line 4, On-Duty Not Driving of the Drivers Daily Log). If the driver does not work on any day, enter a "0" for that day and compute other figures in accordance with the instructions below, as though he had worked.	11				
12						12				
13						13				
14						14				

▶ **Figure 27–7**

A form used to recap a week of driver activity. Be sure to follow the instructions on the form because different logbook designs may present the recap in a slightly different manner.

Driver's Daily Log Entries

The Driver's Daily Log is the professional driver's personal record of duty status and the time worked for each employer **(see Figure 27–8).** If the driver was paid for work for a noncarrier, this time must also be recorded as on-duty time.

All entries must:

- Be made only by the driver.
- Be legible (readable).
- Be current to the last change-of-duty status.
- Be made using the time zone of the driver's home terminal. For example, a driver on a run from the home terminal in California to New York City must use Pacific Standard Time when making entries in the Driver's Daily Log.
- Be certified as correct by the driver's signature.
- Be made on the correct section of the grid. A solid line will divide every 24-hour period.
- Be readable on the duplicate copy.

According to the FMCSA, it is now acceptable to use OBRs as a Driver's Daily Log to record duty status as long as the computer-generated

▶ **Figure 27–8**

A Driver's Daily Log is a personal record of time worked for each employer.

printout includes the minimum information required by Part 395.8 of the FMCSR and must be formatted in accordance with the rules. In addition, the driver must adhere to the following:

- Print the log at the completion of each day and sign it. Note that the driver's signature cannot be electronic. The driver must physically sign the log after printing it.
- Be able to print the log for the current 24-hour period on demand.
- Maintain a copy of printed and signed log printouts for the previous 7 consecutive days and have it available for inspection at the request of an enforcement officer.

Recording Your Duty Status

Each page of the Driver's Daily Log represents a 24-hour period. **Sleeper berth time** is only the time spent resting in an approved type of sleeper berth. Time spent sleeping on the seat or while sitting in the cab cannot be counted as sleeper berth time. All the time spent at the controls of the rig must be counted as driving time. Changes in duty status must be recorded to the nearest quarter hour. The driver must have daily logs for the previous 7 days.

All daily logs must be kept by the driver for 7 days, and turned into the carrier within 13 days, either in person or by mail. The daily logs may be kept temporarily at the home terminal by the carrier; then kept at the carrier's main office for at least 6 months from the date on the log.

Schedule

The Driver's Daily Log shown in **Figure 27–9** shows entries made by a driver on a midnight-to-midnight run from Richmond to Newark. Notice how the 24-hour period contains a solid line made by the entries.

6:00 A.M.–7:25 A.M.: Driver reported to work at his home terminal in Richmond and helped load his trailer.

7:15 A.M.–7:30 A.M.: Picked up the shipping documents and did the pretrip inspection.

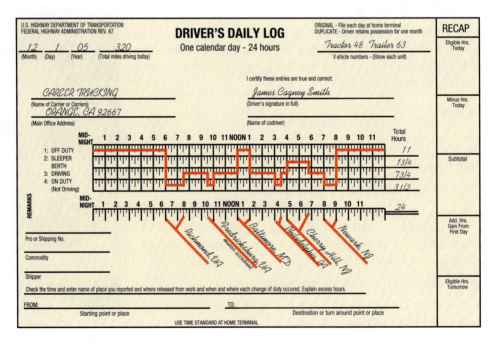

▶ **Figure 27–9**

Daily log showing entries for a midnight-to-midnight run.

7:30 A.M.: Driver got behind the wheel and began driving.

9:30 A.M.–10:00 A.M.: Driver was in minor accident near Fredericksburg. He filed a police report.

12:00 Noon: Driver arrived at company's terminal in Baltimore. Was relieved from duty to go to lunch while repairs were made to his tractor. The driver returned to the terminal at 1:00 P.M. and resumed trip.

3:00 P.M.–3:30 P.M.: Made deliveries at two locations in Philadelphia.

4:00 P.M.: Stopped at rest area in Cherry Hill.

4:00 P.M.–5:45 P.M.: Slept in sleeper berth.

5:45 P.M.: Resumed driving.

7:00 P.M.: Arrived in Newark terminal. Parked rig and went to driver's lounge to complete paperwork.

7:00 P.M.–8:00 P.M.: Driver completed daily log, vehicle condition report, and insurance report on the accident.

8:00 P.M.: Driver went off duty.

DRIVER DECLARED OUT OF SERVICE

A driver may be declared out of service **(see Figure 27–10)** by any agent of the Department of Transportation for either of the following reasons:

- The driver has been on duty too many hours.
- The driver does not have daily logs for the previous 7 days.

Out of Service

▶ **Figure 27–10**

A driver declared out of service loses time, money, and often a job.

STOP!

A driver who has not completed the log for the current day and the day before, but has logs for the previous 6 days, may be given a chance to bring logs up to date without being declared out of service.

If a driver is declared out of service because of too many hours on duty, he or she cannot drive until they have been off duty long enough to be eligible to legally drive again.

If the driver is declared out of service for not having daily logs, he or she may not drive until they have been off duty for 8 hours in a row and can legally drive again.

PENALTIES

Drivers who make false entries on their daily logs, do not prepare a daily log, or drive more than the allowable hours are subject to serious penalties. These laws are enforced by the Department of Transportation and penalties may include:

- Drivers placed out of service (shut down) at roadside until the driver has accumulated enough off-duty time to be back in compliance
- State and local enforcement officials assessing fines
- FMCSA levying civil penalties on driver or carrier, ranging from $550 to $11,000 per violation depending on severity
- Carrier's safety rating downgraded for a pattern of violations
- Federal criminal penalties being brought against carriers who knowingly and willfully allow or require HOS violations

Carriers who do not keep proper records on all drivers are also subject to heavy fines and civil liability if there is an accident, because the driver has violated the regulations.

SUMMARY

In this chapter, you have learned about the changes made in the federal hours-of-service laws. You have also learned the importance of keeping an accurate daily log. The details of the on-duty and off-duty time requirements were explained. The penalties for both drivers and carriers if they fail to abide by these rulings in their operations were outlined. Finally, you have learned a neat and readable log is the result of a driver's professional responsibility and is the product of a positive and professional attitude.

KEY TERMS

Carrier's time record
Driver's Daily Log
Drive time

Hours-of-service (HOS)
   regulations
Off-duty time
On-duty time

Principal place of business
Sleeper berth
Sleeper berth time

REVIEW QUESTIONS

1. The hours-of-service laws were designed to _____.

    a. make as much money as the rig can

    b. make the dispatcher's job easier

    c. help keep you at your best and safest level of performance

    d. move cargo from point A to point B as fast as possible

2. In 1995, Congress directed the FMCSA to research a change in the hours-of-service rule, because it was concerned about _____.

    a. freight not moving fast enough

    b. about the effect of fatigue as a contributing factor in commercial motor vehicle crashes

    c. stopping distance of rigs

    d. center of gravity of loads

3. The hours-of-service ruling, published in the April 28, 2003, *Federal Register* and effective June 27, 2003, formally enforced January 4, 2004, allows drivers to drive for up to _____ straight hours.

    a. 13

    b. 10

    c. 15

    d. 11

4. The same hours-of-service ruling as mentioned in the previous question requires drivers to take at least _____ hours off between shifts.

    a. 11

    b. 10

    c. 9

    d. 12

5. According to the new hours-of-service ruling, drive time and _____ of loading/unloading time is included in a 14-hour cycle.

    a. all

    b. ½

    c. ⅓

    d. ¾

6. When does your "biological clock" make you too sleepy to operate a vehicle safely?

    a. three times per day—two times in the afternoon and one time in the early morning

    b. one time per day at about 1:00 P.M.

    c. one time per day at about 10:00 A.M.

    d. twice a day—once in the early afternoon and once in the early morning

7. The best way to avoid driving tired and having problems with fatigue is to _____.

    a. get plenty of good, healthy sleep

    b. drink coffee or cola (caffeine)

    c. use drugs (No-Doz)

    d. talk on the CB

8. Which of the following activities can extend the 14-hour on-duty period?

    a. off-duty time for meals

    b. the use of a sleeper berth

    c. off-duty time for fuel stops

    d. a and c

9. Driver's Daily Log entries regarding time entries must be made using the time zone _____.

    a. the rig is currently in

    b. of Central Standard Time

    c. of the driver's home terminal

    d. of Eastern Standard Time

10. Which of the following is not one of the penalties that may be assessed for false entries by a driver on the daily log?

    a. driver placed out of service at roadside until the driver has accumulated enough off-duty time to be back in compliance

    b. state and local enforcement officials may assess fines

    c. driver placed out of service, but permitted to drive to the nearest motel for rest until the driver has accumulated enough off-duty time to be back in compliance

    d. the carrier's safety rating can be downgraded for a pattern of violations

28 Driving International Routes

OBJECTIVES

When you have completed this chapter, you should be able to:

- Drive with some knowledge about safety and security when entering Canada or Mexico from the United States.

- Describe FAST and the role it plays at the U.S./Canadian border.

- Understand the basics of NAFTA.

- Understand the laws that affect driving in Canada.

- Understand the laws that affect driving in Mexico.

- Report an emergency in either Mexico or Canada.

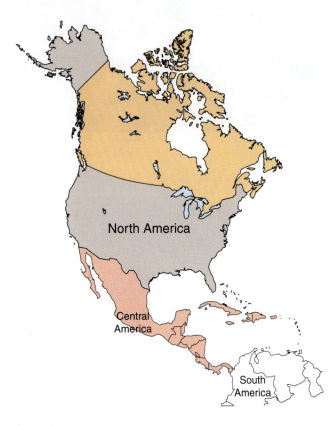

▶ Figure 28-1

The North American Free Trade Agreement (NAFTA) was designed to improve all facets of doing business between the United States, Canada, and Mexico.

INTRODUCTION

When implemented in January 1994, the originators of the **North American Free Trade Agreement (NAFTA)** intended to improve all facets of doing business among the participating countries—Canada, the U.S., and Mexico **(see Figure 28-1).** Their goal was to eliminate almost all tariffs and also targeted barriers to trade, such as import licenses.

At this writing, trucks from Mexico continue to be held at the border into the U.S. Talks continue to move forward but no trucks from Mexico can exceed the 20-mile limit. The same applies to U.S. trucks going into Mexico.

If you are driving international routes, it is important to know that all motor carriers operating in NAFTA countries must follow the same federal and state/provincial regulations and procedures that apply to all carriers originating in that country **(see Figure 28-2).**

All safety regulations, insurance requirements, tariff requirements, and payments of taxes and fees apply to anyone operating a truck in that country. Foreign carriers and drivers also must follow Customs, immigration laws, and regulations of the countries in which they are driving.

▶ Figure 28-2

Carriers operating in NAFTA countries must follow the federal and state/provincial regulations of the country in which they are driving.

SUGGESTIONS FOR SECURITY WHEN DRIVING INTERNATIONALLY

Regardless if you drive international routes, one of your first priorities should be to assure your personal security and the security of your vehicle and cargo. Following are suggestions for safe trips in any country, at any time:

1. Never leave your vehicle unlocked, even when your engine is idling.

2. Do not leave valuables unattended. Lock them in the motel or truck stop safe.

3. If you spend the night at a motel, make certain the door to your room is locked at all times. For added security, use the night chain or other secondary locking devices.

4. Report all suspicious persons and activities in hallways or parking areas to management.

5. Keep all valuables in your vehicle out of sight.

6. Do not carry large amounts of cash. Use travelers checks and credit cards as much as possible. If needed, carry cash in a money belt under your clothing.

7. While out walking, remain in well-lighted and traveled areas. Do not take shortcuts through darkened areas.

CROSSING INTO CANADA

When NAFTA was passed, it provided a continuity in the efforts by the U.S. and Canada to improve the movement of freight and people over the border. With an average flow of more than $1.9 billion worth of goods across the border into both countries each day, both governments continue to have a huge interest in seeing their neighboring nations continue to enjoy economic stability.

Four months after the terrorist attacks on New York and Washington, D.C., in 2001, Canada's foreign minister, Pierre Pettigrew, and Tom Ridge, Director of Homeland Security for the United States of America, co-signed the U.S.–Canada Smart Border Declaration, outlining an action plan to identify and address existing security risks at the border. The plan also attempted to expedite traffic into both countries with new processes at the border into each country.

One year later, a status report on the implementation of this effort showed progress. Specifically, it was reported that the efforts on both sides of the border were steadily improving the smooth flow of traffic crossing the border each day.

Facts About Canada

- The population of Canada is 31,485,623 people, approximately one-tenth the population of the United States.

- Quebec has the highest annual snowfall with 337 centimeters.

- The highest point in Canada is Mt. Logan (in the Yukon) at 5,959 meters.

- In Canada, the infant death rate is lower and the life expectancy is longer than in the U.S.

- Every product in Canada is labeled in English and French.

- Canadians use the metric system as the preferred unit of measure.

- Canada contains almost 10 million square kilometers of land and 891,163 square kilometers of water.

- The good news is Canada has more donut shops per capita than the U.S.

- Sports fans in Canada favor hockey and lacrosse.

- St. John's, Nova Scotia is the wettest area of Canada, receiving 1,482 millimeters of rain each year.

- Canadian stamps must be used when mail is sent from Canada. Rates are 47 cents within Canada, 60 cents to the U.S., and $1.05 to countries overseas.

- There are $1 and $2 coins—and prices appear to be higher than in the U.S. because of the Canadian monetary system. For exchange rates, visit www.bankofcanada.ca

- The Trans-Canada Highway is usually two lanes wide. Highway 401 north of Toronto is 16 lanes wide in places.

Figure 28-3

Commercial Vehicle Safety Alliance (CVSA) rules and guidelines are used on roads in Canada and the United States.

The Commercial Vehicle Safety Alliance

The rules and guidelines of the **Commercial Vehicle Safety Alliance (CVSA)** are used on all roads across Canada just like they are across the United States **(see Figure 28–3).** Similar to those in the United States, CVSA guidelines are used by inspectors performing roadside inspections of commercial vehicles. If you, your paperwork, or your vehicle do not conform to CVSA guidelines—in the U.S. or Canada—you risk being placed out of service or given a restricted service condition. Both entail hassle, paperwork, fines, and jail time, depending on the severity of your infraction(s).

In Canada, you can be put out of service if you are not of legal age to drive; if you do not have proper license to drive; if you do not pass physical requirements; if you are sick, fatigued, or otherwise impaired; or if you are driving under the influence of drugs or alcohol.

You can also be put out of service if you have exceeded the legal number of hours of service, have an incomplete log or no driving log, or if your vehicle does not pass inspection.

Mechanical problems can include defective brakes, defective coupling devices, defective or missing safety devices, defective exhaust system, defective or missing lighting devices, unsafe loading standards, defective steering mechanisms, defective or inadequate suspension, defective frame, defective or inappropriate tires, wheels, and rims, or insufficient welds, glazing of the windshield, or defective windshield wipers **(see Figure 28–4).**

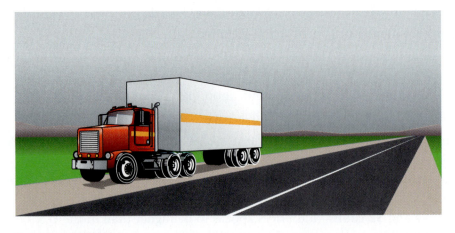

Figure 28-4

You can be put out of service if your vehicle does not pass inspection.

If your vehicle passes a roadside inspection, a CVSA sticker, which is good for 3 months, will be placed on your vehicle.

Crossing the Border into Canada

Any international driver hauling freight into Canada will need the following items and documentation:

1. Valid commercial driver's license (CDL)

2. Proof of citizenship—birth certificate, passport, proof of Canadian landed immigrant status (form IMM 1000)

3. Vehicle license and permits, including valid International Fuel Tax (IFT) and International Registration Plan (IRP) permits

4. Operating license (also called an operating authority or safety certificate) recognized by each jurisdiction in which you will be traveling

5. Required number of copies of paper work for Canadian Customs

How to Report an Emergency in Canada

- To report an emergency, dial 9-1-1 and give your complete number (mobile phone and area code).

- Tell the operator your exact location as precisely as possible. Look for street signs, highway markers, and other landmarks.

- Stay on the phone as long as you are needed for information. Do not hang up until the emergency operator tells you to do so.

- Keep your mobile phone on in case the operator needs to call you back.

Canadian Speed Limits

The speed limits in Canada are posted in kilometers per hour as opposed to miles per hour. The speed limit on most city streets is 50 km/hr (30 mi/hr). On most highways, the speed limit is posted as 100 km/hr (60 mi/hr). Speed limits may vary among the provinces, so keep an eye on the posted speed limit signs. A rule of thumb is to multiply the posted speed limit by 6 and then divide by 10 to convert the posted kilometers per hour to miles per hour.

Canadian Monetary System

The **monetary exchange rate** varies from establishment to establishment. As there are no laws enforcing the rate of exchange on foreign currency, it is wise to change your money at a bank or a reputable currency exchange. Banks are generally open 10:00 A.M. to 4:00 P.M., Monday through Friday. An increasing number are open evenings and Saturday mornings.

Because of the fluidity of the exchange rate, check with the bank of your choice once you cross the border.

Trucking Across the Border

To save waiting time and to maintain your projected schedule, know the hours of operations of the **border crossing** you wish to use as well as the hours of operation for the destination where you want to clear Customs.

Nonresident drivers crossing into Canada will need to know when Canadian border crossings are open. For specific information about a particular crossing, call 800-461-9999 or visit the website http://www.ccra-adrc.gc.ca and find "Customs" by using the A–Z index.

The following provincial border crossings are open 24 hours a day, 365 days a year. All other border crossings provide service from 8:00 A.M. to 5:00 P.M., Monday through Friday.

Alberta	Coutts Crossing
British Columbia	Pacific Highway, Osoyoos and Kingsgate
Manitoba	Emerson
New Brunswick	Woodstock, St. Stephen
Ontario	Pigeon River, Ft. Francis, Sault Ste. Marie, Sarnia, Prescott, Lansdowne, Ft. Erie, Niagara Falls, Windsor
Quebec	Lacolle, St. Armand-Phillipsburg, Stanhope, Rock Island
Saskatchewan	North Portal

Wait times are usually less than 5 minutes at most crossings, Mondays through Thursdays. On weekends, wait times may be as much as 20 minutes. Periodically, wait times at the Port Huron, Michigan, bridge can be as long as 45 minutes.

Clearing Customs

1. The first advice to heed in getting through **Customs** at any border is to take your time. Relax, smile, and always be ready for an inspection, and this means having your trailer loaded so it can be inspected easily. To accomplish this, let the shipper know that the shipment needs to be packed to avoid delay at the border.

   If you have waiting time, practice patience, be cordial, and be helpful with inspectors. Remember that it is a serious offense under the Customs Act to leave the border and/or to not report to the compound when requested.

2. Know what your cargo contains so you can answer any questions the Customs inspector may have.

3. Declare all of your personal goods, including prescription drugs, firearms, or pets. Be prepared to pay duty and taxes, depending on your personal declaration of goods.

4. It is unlawful to carry firearms in the cab of your vehicle. Additional weapons such as switchblades, butterfly knives, or mace are either restricted or prohibited. If you have this contraband in your cab, it will be seized and shipped back to your home address at your expense.

CAUTION!
An inspection of your cargo does not carry a cost; if an inspection fee is charged, report this immediately.

One other point to remember is if you attempt to deliver cargo that has not been released by Customs, your truck and cargo may be seized and you will be additionally punished with a sizable fine.

The FAST Program

The **Free and Secure Trade (FAST) program** is a joint Canada–U.S. initiative involving the Canada Customs and Revenue Agency, Citizenship and Immigration Canada, the United States Customs Service, and the United States Immigration and Naturalization Service. FAST supports moving preapproved eligible goods across the border quickly and verifying trade compliance away from the border.

It is a harmonized commercial process offered to preapproved importers and carriers, and registered drivers. Shipments for approved companies, transported by approved carriers using registered drivers, will be cleared into either country with greater speed and certainty, and at reduced cost of compliance.

FAST focuses on greater speed and certainty at the border and reduces the cost of compliance by:

- Reducing the information requirements for Customs clearance
- Eliminating the need for importers to transmit data for each transaction
- Dedicating lanes for FAST clearances
- Reducing the rate of border examinations
- Verifying trade compliance away from the border
- Streamlining accounting and payment processes for all goods imported by approved importers (Canada only)

What You Can Bring into Canada

Pets

You can bring pet dogs or cats that are 3 months old or older into Canada from the U.S. if you have a certificate from a licensed veterinarian identifying the animal by breed, age, sex, coloring, and distinguishing marks. The certificate must also show the animal has been vaccinated against rabies during the last 3 years. Animal tags are not acceptable and cannot be used as a substitute for this certificate **(see Figure 28–5).**

Firearms

Canada has strict laws about **firearms.** If you plan to bring one into the country, you must declare them at Customs when you enter. If you fail to register them, Customs officials have the right to seize your firearms and you will face criminal charges. For more information regarding a specific firearm or any applicable fees, call the Canadian Firearms Center at 1-800-731-4000.

▶ **Figure 28-5**
You can bring your pet cat or dog into Canada if it is three months or older and you have the proper documentation.

Alcohol

The FMCSA specifically addresses the use of alcohol and illegal drugs for commercial drivers. In Canada, many of the same rules apply. No open containers of beer, wine, or other alcoholic beverages are allowed in the truck. You cannot carry alcohol or illegal drugs in your cab or drive while under the influence of alcohol or illegal drugs.

Canadian officials have the right to test you if they suspect you are driving under the influence of alcohol or illegal drugs. If you test positively, you will be fined and subject to criminal conviction as well as seizure of your vehicle and its cargo.

Driving Time in Canada

Commercial drivers in Canada are allowed to drive 13 hours. Maximum time on duty, including driving time, stands at 15 hours. This requires at least 8 hours off duty before you can return to driving or duty. In any 7-day period in Canada, drivers may be on duty for only 60 hours. During an 8-day period, drivers can be on duty a maximum of 70 hours.

Necessary Records in Canada

Like the U.S., all commercial drivers in Canada are required to maintain up-to-date logbooks. If a driver fails to keep his or her log current, he or she can lose his or her license to drive, be fined, taken out of service, or face a combination of these penalties. Like the U.S., it is unlawful to maintain more than one daily log or to falsify the daily log.

If you want to use electronic or other mechanical devices to maintain your daily log, this is permissible as long as the device records all required information and you have signed copies of each log generated for the current trip. Required information includes (1) the number of hours spent driving each day, (2) the on-duty hours each day, (3) the total on-duty hours accumulated for the current periods of 7, 8, or 14 days, and (4) the changes of your duty status and when these changes occurred each day.

What Other Documents are Needed to Cross into Canada? All drivers must also have a current commercial driver's license plus current registrations and licenses for the vehicle. If your trip will involve travel to several provinces, states, or countries, you are also required to have an International Fuel Tax Agreement (IFTA) sticker.

The required registration for the area in which you plan to travel must also be available if you are asked for this documentation. This ensures that your International Registration Plan (IRP) card is current for all areas in which you will be traveling and will prevent you from paying additional registration fees.

CROSSING THE BORDER INTO MEXICO

A professional commercial driver who drives in Mexico should remember that he or she is in a foreign country with different laws, customs, poverty levels, education levels, and safety standards. The driver also needs to realize that laws and customs are changing in Mexico because of the changing political climate of all of North America, security concerns, and changing NAFTA rules **(see Figure 28–6).**

Because of these changes, the Mexican customs broker hired for your shipment will be your best source of current information. The Mexican customs broker will have the most up-to-date information about the best route to your destination along with the best fuel stops, hotels/motels, and restaurants.

▶ **Figure 28-6**

Check with the Mexican customs broker for your shipment to find out the most up-to-date laws and regulations for driving in Mexico.

Facts About Mexico

- **Official name:** The United Mexican States (or Estados Unidos Mexicanos in Spanish)

- **Geography:** Covers approximately 761,600 square miles

- **Population:** 103,400,165 (July 2002 estimation)

- **Capital city:** Mexico City (or Distrito Federal in Spanish)

- **Number of states:** Thirty-one and one federal district. Each state is headed by an elected governor

- **Major transportation centers:** Border cities: with connections to major interior cities—Tijuana to Baja California, Nogales to the Pacific Coast, Ciudad Juarez to Chihuahua, Torreon, Monterrey, San Luis Potosi, Mexico City and Guadalajara, Nuevo Laredo to Monterrey, San Luis Potosi, Mexico City and Guadalajara, Reynosa and Matamoros to Monterrey, San Luis Potosi, Mexico City and Guadalajara

  Interior cities: Chihuahua, Monterrey, San Luis Potosi, Guadalajara, Mexico City

- **Miles of highways (paved):** Total 60,000 miles of which 4,000 miles are expressways (estimated 1997)

- **Climate:** Varies from tropical to desert with high rugged mountains, low coastal plains, and high plateaus. Mexico's climate is generally more closely related to altitude and rainfall than to latitude.

- **Economy:** An estimated 40 percent of all Mexican citizens live below the poverty line. Main crops are corn, wheat, soybeans, rice, beans, cotton, fruit, coffee, tomatoes, beef, poultry, dairy products, and wood products.

  Industries include food and beverages, tobacco, chemical, iron and steel, petroleum, mining, textiles, clothing, motor vehicles, and consumer durables.

  Export commodities include manufactured goods, oil and oil products, silver, fruits, vegetables, coffee, and cotton.

  Export-partners: USA 88.4 percent, Canada 2 percent. Import-partners: USA 68.4 percent, Canada 2.5 percent.

  Currency is the Mexican **peso** (MXN). Exchange rate: Mexican pesos per U.S. dollar—9.1614 (January 2002)

Mexico's Telephone System

Domestic telephone service offers twelve main lines per 100 persons. Adequate service is available for business and government. The use of cellular telephones is common for much of the domestic service. Internationally numerous satellite earth stations are giving Mexico improved access to South America, Central America, and much of the United States. Check with your communications provider to determine the availability of cellular telephone service in Mexico.

Reporting an Emergency in Mexico

If you have an emergency while driving, the equivalent of "9-1-1" in Mexico is "0-6-0", but this number is not always answered. If you are driving on a toll highway or **cuota,** or any major highway, contact the **Green Angels,** a fleet of trucks with bilingual crews that operate daily. The Green Angels may be reached directly at (01) 55 5250-8221. If you are unable to call them, pull off the road and lift the hood of your truck. Chances are they will find you.

Buying Diesel Fuel in Mexico

Gasoline prices in Mexico are government controlled. Prices fluctuate with the economy. There is only one grade of diesel fuel in Mexico and it is sold in liter measures **(see Figure 28–7).** One liter is close to one quart. Four liters equal about 1 gallon. To convert liters to gallons, divide the number of liters purchased by 4 to calculate the number of gallons purchased. Look for the black sign that signals diesel fuel is sold at that location.

▶ **Figure 28–7**

Gas prices in Mexico are controlled by the government and fluctuate with the economy.

The Language

Of the population over age 15, almost 90 percent can read. The principal language of the country is Spanish, with various regional dialects spoken. English is also spoken, particularly in larger communities.

Holidays in Mexico

Mexico celebrates many holidays. Independence Day is September 16. The Day of the Dead is November 1. If you are driving in Mexico, it is important to know about their national holidays because, in many cases, the holidays signal business closings and thus delivery of freight may be difficult.

Hours of Service in Mexico

To date, there is no governmental limit to the number of hours driven per shift in Mexico.

Traveling Safely in Mexico

(Information provided by the U.S. Bureau of Consular Affairs)

Personal identification needed to enter Mexico—the government of Mexico requires that all U.S. citizens present proof of citizenship and photo identification for entry into Mexico. A U.S. passport is recommended, but other U.S. citizenship documents such as a certified copy of a U.S. birth certificate, a Naturalization Certificate, a Consular Report of Birth Abroad, or a Certificate of Citizenship are acceptable. Driver's permits, voter registration cards, affidavits, and similar documents are not sufficient to prove citizenship for readmission into the United States.

What to avoid in Mexico—visitors should avoid demonstrations and other activities that might be deemed political by the Mexican authorities. Mexican constitutional provisions prohibit political activities by foreigners, and such actions may result in detention and/or deportation.

Safety and Security When Visiting Mexico

To obtain security information before traveling in Mexico, please visit the following Web site: http://www.state.gov

The following recommendations may be helpful:

- Visitors should be aware of their surroundings at all times, even when in areas generally considered to be safe.

- Exercise caution when traveling on all highways in Mexico and use toll (*cuota*) roads, rather than the less secure free (*libre*) highways, when possible. Never hitchhike or accept rides.

- Be wary of persons representing themselves as Mexican police or other local officials.

- Do not hike alone in backcountry areas, or walk alone on lightly frequented beaches, ruins, or trails.

Driving Safety

While in any foreign country, U.S. citizens may encounter road conditions that differ significantly from those in the United States. In Mexico City, in order to cut down on air pollution, authorities restrict traffic. Vehicles not registered in Mexico are not allowed to drive one day of the week, as follows: The restriction is based on the last digit of the license plate. On Mondays, license plates with the last digit of 5 or 6 cannot drive. On Tuesdays, those with the last digit of

7 or 8 cannot drive. On Wednesdays, vehicles with license plates ending in 3 or 4 are not allowed. On Thursday, no driving for vehicles with license plates ending in 1 or 2. On Fridays, no driving of vehicles with a final digit of 9 or 0 as well as vehicles with temporary license plates. On Saturdays and Sundays, all vehicles may drive. Failure to abide by this schedule may result in a vehicle being impounded as well as fines.

In Mexico, the condition of urban roads is considered good **(see Figure 28–8).** Rural road conditions and maintenance are ranked as fair, and the availability of roadside assistance such as the Green Angels, government agents authorized to provide roadside assistance, is fair.

▶ **Figure 28-8**

Urban road conditions in Mexico are rated "good," rural roads are rated "fair."

Avoid excessive speed and, if possible, do not drive at night. Loose livestock can appear on roads at any time. Construction sites, abandoned vehicles, or other obstacles are often unmarked or poorly marked. Be prepared for sudden stops.

Driving Licenses

U.S. driver's licenses are valid in Mexico. Mexican insurance is required for all vehicles, including rental vehicles.

The government of Mexico strictly regulates the entry of vehicles into Mexico. Mexican Customs laws require that vehicles must be driven by the owner or the owner must be inside the vehicle. If not, the vehicle may be seized by Mexican customs and will not be returned under any circumstances.

Motorists should be aware that within Mexico City, vehicular traffic is restricted in order to reduce air pollution. The restriction is based on the last digit of the vehicle license plate. This applies equally to permanent, temporary, and foreign (U.S.) plates.

Legal Problems While in Mexico

In Mexico, U.S. citizens are subject to Mexico's laws and regulations, which sometimes differ significantly from those in the United States and may not afford the protections available to the individual under U.S. law. Americans who commit illegal acts have no special privileges and are subject to full prosecution under the Mexican judicial system. Penalties for breaking the law can be more severe than in the United States for similar offenses. Persons violating Mexico's laws, even unknowingly, may be expelled, arrested, or imprisoned.

Prison conditions in Mexico can be extremely poor. In many facilities, food is insufficient in both quantity and quality, and prisoners must pay for adequate nutrition from their own funds.

Penalties for Drug Offenses in Mexico

Penalties for drug offenses are strict and convicted offenders can expect large fines and jail sentences up to 25 years. As in the United States, the purchase of controlled medication requires a doctor's prescription. The Mexican list of controlled medication differs from that of the United States, and Mexican public health laws concerning controlled medication are unclear and often enforced selectively.

Further information on bringing prescription drugs into the United States is available from the U.S. Customs Service at the following Web site: http://www.customs.ustreas.gov

The **U.S. Embassy** cautions that possession of any amount of prescription medicine brought from the United States, including medications to treat HIV and psychotropic drugs, such as Valium, can result in arrest if Mexican authorities suspect abuse or if the quantity of the prescription medicine exceeds the amount required for several days' use.

Penalties for Firearms Violations

Do not take any type of firearm or ammunition into Mexico without prior written authorization from the Mexican authorities **(see Figure 28–9).** Entering Mexico with a firearm, certain kinds of knives, or even a single round of ammunition is illegal, even if the firearm or ammunition is taken into Mexico unintentionally. Firearms and ammunition of a caliber higher than .22 are considered for the exclusive use of the military and their importation carries penalties of up to 30 years in prison. The Mexican government strictly enforces its laws restricting the entry of firearms and ammunition along all land borders and at airports and seaports.

▶ **Figure 28–9**

Do not take firearms into Mexico without prior written permission from the Mexican authorities.

SUMMARY

In this chapter, you received information about driving safely and securely when entering Canada or Mexico from the U.S. You also learned something about each of these neighboring countries, the requirements to cross the border into Canada, and the documentation required. You learned some of the basics regarding the North American Free Trade Agreement, using the FAST system to clear customs in Canada, and the laws affecting driving in Canada and Mexico. You also learned something about reporting emergencies in both countries; about laws regarding pets, firearms, drugs, and alcohol; and penalties for taking such items into other countries.

KEY TERMS

Border crossing
Commercial Vehicle Safety
   Alliance (CVSA)
Cuota
Customs

Free and Secure Trade (FAST)
   program
Firearms
Green Angels
Monetary exchange rate

North American Free Trade
   Agreement (NAFTA)
Peso
U.S. Embassy

REVIEW QUESTIONS

1. Regarding suggestions for safe trips in any country, which of the following is not a correct statement?

   a. Never leave your vehicle unlocked, even when your engine is idling.

   b. Do not leave valuables unattended; lock them in the motel or truck stop safe.

   c. It is safe to walk or go anywhere you like because local police always look out for foreigners.

   d. Keep all valuables in your vehicle out of sight.

2. When NAFTA was passed, it _____.

   a. provided a continuity in the efforts by the United States and Canada to improve the movement of freight and people over the border

   b. focused on restricting trade in Europe

   c. focused on improving trade in South America

   d. focused on improving world trade

3. Canadians use the _____ system to measure speed and fuel.

   a. imperial

   b. U.S.

   c. modified imperial

   d. metric

4. The rules and guidelines of the Commercial Vehicle Safety Alliance are used on all roads across Canada just like they are across _____.

   a. all of South America

   b. all of Central America

   c. all of Europe

   d. the United States

5. The Free and Secure Trade (FAST) supports moving _____ across the border quickly and verifying trade compliance away from the border.

   a. race cars only

   b. preapproved eligible goods

   c. all items manufactured in Europe

   d. any items from South America

6. Which of the following is not a good practice regarding getting through Canadian customs?

   a. Have your trailer loaded so it can be inspected easily.

   b. Be cordial and helpful with inspectors.

   c. Do not declare personal goods such as prescription drugs, firearms, pets.

   d. Know what your cargo contains so you can answer any questions the authorities may have.

7. Regarding commercial drivers in Canada, which of the following is not a correct statement?

   a. Maximum time on duty is 15 hours including driving time.

   b. Drivers are allowed to drive 10 hours in a 24-hour period.

   c. The driver is required to have 8 hours off duty before driving again.

   d. In any 7-day period, drivers may be on duty for only 60 hours.

8. Because of changes in Mexico brought about by such things as changing political climates, security concerns, and changing NAFTA rules, _____ is (are) the best source of information concerning the best route to your destination, best fuel stops, hotels/motels, and so forth.

   a. the Mexican customs broker hired for your shipment

   b. other drivers

   c. newspapers, magazines, etc.

   d. television news

9. Since fuel in Mexico is sold in liter measures, to convert liters to gallons divide the number of liters purchased by _____.

    a. 6   **c.** 4

    b. 10   **d.** 2

10. Regarding hours of service in Mexico, which of the following is correct?

    a. Mexican law is the same as U.S. law.

    b. Drivers may drive 15 hours with 9 hours off duty.

    c. Drivers may be on duty 15 hours with 13 hours of driving and 9 hours off duty.

    d. There is no governmental limit to the number of hours driven per shift.

29 Transportation Security

OBJECTIVES

When you have completed this chapter, you should be able to:

- Understand the reasons for increased security measures within the transportation industry.
- Be able to discuss the professional driver's responsibilities for maintaining security during each trip.
- Be able to identify governmental agencies involved in transportation security.
- Identify ways in which you can personally increase the security of your rig and your cargo.

INTRODUCTION

Security has always been a major part of a professional driver's job. Every year, millions of dollars in cargo and equipment are stolen, and while much is recovered, much more disappears. This type of theft, pilferage, and loss is costly to consumers, carriers, and you, the driver.

Prior to **September 11, 2001,** and the destruction of the World Trade Center towers, most Americans thought **terrorist activities** happened in some other country, certainly not in their own.

It is now obvious that terrorism is a very real danger in this hemisphere, and will continue to be a concern for years to come.

Historically, motor vehicles of all kinds, particularly trucks—because of their larger capacities—have been used as means of delivery for terrorist activities, and there is every reason to believe that terrorist activities using a truck as a delivery system will continue to be real threats to the safety of people everywhere. Recall in 1983, a ¾-ton pickup truck loaded with explosives was used to attack the U.S. Embassy in Beirut, Lebanon, killing 83 people. In the horrendous aftermath of the Oklahoma City bombing, it was found the delivery device for the explosives was a rented straight truck. Car bombs are used all over the world today, taking down buildings and destroying lives in their wake.

Trucks as **weapons of mass destruction** are indeed a threat **(see Figure 29–1).** A B-52 bomber can deliver 2,000 pounds of precision munitions per bomb within 10 meters of its target. A tractor-trailer rig has the capacity to deliver 40,000 pounds of precision munitions within 10 meters of its target. It is therefore the responsibility of all professional drivers to be aware of the possibilities of their rigs being used to perpetrate a terrorist's mission and to prevent the use of their rig and those of their fellow drivers as weapons of mass destruction.

▶ **Figure 29–1**

Security has always been a major part of a professional driver's job.

THE DEPARTMENT OF HOMELAND SECURITY

Because the threat of terrorism became a reality in 2001 in this country, the following year the Homeland Security Act established the Department of Homeland Security as an executive department of the United States. Its mission is threefold:

- Prevent terrorist attacks within the U.S.
- Reduce the vulnerability of the U.S. to terrorism
- Minimize the damage and assist in the recovery from terrorist attacks occurring in the U.S.

In a speech delivered in March 2005, to the Security Policy Institute, Secretary of Homeland Security Michael Chertoff explained:

Risk management is fundamental to managing the threat, while retaining our quality of life and living in freedom. Risk management must guide our decision-making as we examine how we can best organize to prevent, respond and recover from an attack. We all live with a certain amount of risk. That means that we tolerate that something bad can happen; we adjust our lives based on probability; and we take reasonable precautions.

TRANSPORTATION SECURITY ADMINISTRATION

On November 19, 2001, President George W. Bush signed into law the **Aviation and Transportation Security Act (ATSA),** which among other things established a new **Transportation Security Administration (TSA)** within the Department of Transportation. This act established a series of challenging but critically important milestones toward achieving a secure air travel system.

The Transportation Security Administration was formed to protect the nation's transportation systems, to ensure freedom of movement for people and commerce. In its capacity as a federal agency, the TSA will continuously set the standard for excellence in transportation security through its people, processes. and technologies.

TRUCKING SECURITY GROWS INTO LARGER ISSUE

Since the events of September 11, 2001, the area of security has gained much additional attention, from every level of government. Today's terrorists not only want to topple buildings and kill people, but also cripple entire countries. Experts in terrorism warn that the trucking industry is a ripe target for the next round of terrorist activities.

During an address to the Truckload Carriers Association in 2002, Ken Allard—a retired army officer and security and information intelligence analyst for MSNBC cable network—made this assessment: "The goal of terrorists is not to destroy our buildings and kill our citizens. They want to destroy our economy and our way of life. Terrorism is a threat to everything we do and to everything we stand for."

James Hall, former chairman of the U.S. National Transportation Safety Board, addressing the same group, said this:

> The challenge for trucking is to build security into operations in the same way that safety has been promoted. With narrow profit margins and increasing insurance premiums, many executives will question how to pay for increases in security. For instance, federal, state, and local officials have called for new and redundant background checks and identification procedures for transportation employees. If enacted, some of these proposals could bankrupt many trucking companies.
>
> Trucking is vulnerable to terrorists. Added expense along with increased paperwork will do little to relieve that vulnerability, so the first step toward defeating terrorists is to understand the nature of the threat.
>
> Understanding the threat shows that vulnerability is not limited to the security of company facilities, employees or loads. Attacks on customers or suppliers can harm truck lines just as badly as an attack on the company. An attack on infrastructure, such as power supplies or water sources, could severely damage a local economy.

Hall added that no one could afford to adopt security measures that do not work or that ruin the transportation economy in the process. He encouraged carriers and professional drivers to:

■ Make plans for alternate communication systems in case of primary telephone or radio network damage

▶ **Figure 29-2**

Drivers and their communications systems can be the "eyes" and "ears" of America.

■ Test these plans to ensure the backup systems are working at all times

■ Use the company safety program to build security awareness throughout the entire company, not just drivers

■ Identify key emergency management officials in areas where the carrier operates (Contact these officials and set a procedure for getting in touch with them at any time.)

■ Drivers and their satellite tracking and communications systems can become the eyes and ears of America **(see Figure 29–2).**

SUGGESTED PROTECTIVE MEASURES

Terrorists continue to select soft targets for attack, particularly those that will yield a high casualty count. Examples include residences, recreational and shopping venues, and business buildings and complexes. All available antiterrorism measures should be rigorously reexamined to include physical security perimeters and set-back distances between security fences, key buildings, and barricades.

In 2004, the Department of Homeland Security submitted the following guidelines for trucking transportation general awareness:

General Awareness Procedures

■ Review current contingency plans and, if not already in place, develop and implement procedures for:

  ● Receiving and acting on threat information

  ● Alert notification

  ● Terrorist incident response

  ● Evacuation

  ● Bomb threat

  ● Hostage and barricade

  ● Chemical, biological, radiological, and nuclear (CBRN)

  ● Incident management procedures, accountability

■ After implementing plans and procedures, conduct internal training exercises and invite local emergency responders (fire, rescue, medical, and bomb squads) to participate in joint exercises.

■ Coordinate and establish partnerships with local authorities and other business/facility owners to develop intelligence and information-sharing relationships.

Security Personnel Procedures

■ Arrange for law enforcement vehicles to be parked randomly near entrances and exits.

■ Increase the number of visible security personnel where possible.

- Institute/increase vehicle, foot, and roving security patrols varying in size, timing, and routes.

- Implement random security guard shift changes.

- Approach all illegally parked vehicles in and around facilities, question drivers and direct them to move immediately; if the owner cannot be identified, have the vehicle towed by law enforcement.

- Institute a robust vehicle inspection program to include checking under the undercarriage of vehicles, under the hood, and in the trunk. Provide vehicle inspection training to security personnel.

The Carrier Should

- Ensure all levels of personnel are notified via briefings, email, voice mail, and signage of any changes in threat conditions and protective measures.

- Encourage personnel to be alert and immediately report any situation that appears to constitute a threat or suspicious activity.

- Encourage personnel to take notice and report suspicious vehicles.

- Encourage personnel to know emergency exits and stairwells and the locations of rally points to ensure the safe egress of all employees.

The DHS also invited commercial carriers and others to report information concerning suspicious or criminal activity to local law enforcement, the local FBI Joint Terrorism Task Force, or the Homeland Security Operations Center (HSOC). The HSOC may be contacted via telephone at (202) 282-8101 or email at HSCenter@dhs.gov.

INCREASING YOUR RIG'S SECURITY

One lesson learned from September 11 is to never underestimate the enemy or the potential danger of any situation. If something does not seem right, call the police, the FBI, or your company/dispatcher immediately **(see Figure 29–3).**

Security on the Road

- Be alert when leaving a location. Criminal surveillance often begins at or near your origin.

- Do not discuss your cargo, destination, or trip specifics on the CB or near strangers.

- If you believe you are being followed, call 911 and your dispatcher immediately.

- Avoid being boxed in on the road. Where possible, leave room in front and behind your rig.

- Look for vehicles following you, especially if there are three or more people in the following vehicle.

- If you believe there is a threat of hijacking, notify your dispatcher and try to keep your rig moving.

▶ **Figure 29–3**

Call the proper authorities if you suspect a dangerous situation.

▶ Figure 29–4

If you stop, leave your rig in a secure parking lot or truck stop. Do not leave it idling.

When You Stop Your Rig

- If you stop for a meal, try to stop where you can meet a buddy or make sure someone in the parking area knows you, your rig, and how long you will be parked.

- Leave your rig in a secure parking lot or truck stop. If not possible, be certain someone you trust can watch your rig **(see Figure 29–4)**.

- If team driving, always leave one person with the rig.

- Never leave your rig running with the keys in it. Instead, shut off the engine and lock the doors.

- If at all possible, do not stop in unsafe or high crime areas. If you are in a strange destination, ask about the safest place to park your rig.

- Always lock the cargo door(s) with padlocks.

- Use trailer door seals to prevent and identify tampering.

Tractor-Trailer Security

The following steps will help increase the security for your tractor-trailer rig when you have to stop, before going on the road, and while it is being loaded:

- Use an engine kill switch.

- Use tractor and trailer locking devices.

- Guard electronic tracking systems.

- Check your system often and notify the dispatcher if there is any type of malfunction in your system.

- If you drop a trailer, use a fifth-wheel lock when possible.

WHAT SECURITY IS IMPORTANT?

Security expert Jeff Beatty believes an interruption in America's commercial transportation system could do untold—if not irreparable—damage to the U.S. economy as well as take a tremendous toll on human life.

Beatty suggests food riots could break out if regular shipments were not able to move into grocery stores within several hours after an attack. "This would happen not because the shelves were bare but because the public would be insecure about what was going to happen next," he said, "and, therefore, the cost of a single large truck bomb incident could reach $5 billion—with government response driving the cost up by 10 times."

In devising a security plan, the American Trucking Associations (ATA) want to deter terrorists and, most importantly, reduce vulnerability and ward off attacks. One of the most important parts of a security plan, according to the ATA, is putting the right person behind the wheel, which can be done with the proper **background checks (see Figure 29–5).**

Other aspects of a security plan include load tracking, cargo security, and employee training—to do their jobs correctly while staying alert to terrorist threats or any unusual activity.

The centerpiece of the ATA security plan is training to:

- Know what to look for and where to be alert

- Look at what is "vulnerable" and what is to be a "likely target"

Figure 29–5

One of the most important parts of a security plan is to know who is behind the wheel.

- Detect operational acts—what terrorists do during their rehearsals—for example, in Oklahoma City, there were 140 "acts" of observing the building, observing traffic patterns, observing likely parking spots, and so forth

- Know your fellow drivers

- Know your neighbors in a parking lot

- Know who is driving what rig

WHAT ELSE CAN BE DONE?

Technical Innovation

Make yourself aware of technical innovations that assist in security:

- Invest in a **cellular telephone,** satellite tracking, and surveillance systems.

- Look at state-of-the-art seals and locks.

- Ask if access control systems are appropriate.

- Consider tamper-proof locking features for fifth wheels.

- Consider use of blanket-type alarms that signal when blanket is moved.

- Consider installing **electronic engine controls** that require a code, in addition to a key, to start the vehicle.

Communications

Consider communications as a big piece of any security plan:

- Develop a communications network to share information with others in the industry.

- Develop a means of communication from office to vehicle.

Emergencies

While driving in the United States, call 911 for the following emergencies:

- Life-threatening road conditions
- DWI and erratic driving
- Criminal activities such as assaults, drug activity
- Vehicle accidents, including instances of hit and run
- Medical emergencies
- Unsafe equipment and insecure loads, which may endanger other drivers
- Life-threatening instances of road rage
- HazMat spills/accidents involving HazMat loads
- Any other life-threatening emergency witnessed by an observant driver

For nonemergencies, dial 1-855-TRUCKIN (878-2546) when you see:

- Hazardous road conditions—in all weather
- Closed roads/highways
- Abandoned vehicles
- Stolen vehicles
- Broken traffic signals
- Reckless or aggressive driving
- Excessive speed
- Stranded motorist
- Nonthreatening debris on the highway, such as dead animals, wayward orange cones, car parts, and tire treads
- Congestion

Understand that terrorist activities tend to happen in groups, and if one attack occurs then heighten security immediately. Always increase security measures if the United States is engaged in military activity in a foreign country.

▶ **Figure 29-6**

Using a cell phone while driving can be unsafe.

Wireless Telephones

Wireless phones give professional drivers the ability to communicate by voice almost anywhere, anytime, and with anyone. Each year, billions of cell phone calls are made, and these numbers are rapidly increasing.

The following tips will help make your cell phone calls safer and less distracting if you must use your cell phone while you drive **(see Figure 29–6).** It is important to note, however, that while most professional drivers carry cell phones, rarely do they use these phones while they drive because of safety factors.

- Get to know your phone and its timesaving features, such as speed dial and redial. If you can, memorize the phone's keypad so you can use the speed dial function without taking your eyes off the road.

- Install a hands-free device if you can, and use a speaker phone when possible.

- Position your phone within easy reach and make sure you can grab it without taking your eyes off the road. If you get an incoming call at an inconvenient time, let your voice mail answer it for you.

- Stop any conversations during hazardous driving conditions or high traffic situations. As a professional driver, your first responsibility is to pay attention to the road.

- Do not take notes or directions or look up phone numbers or addresses while driving. Avoid a dangerous situation because you are reading or writing and not paying attention to the road or other vehicles.

- Place as many calls as possible when you are not moving or before pulling into traffic. If you do need to make a call, dial a few numbers, check back on traffic, and then complete dialing the number.

- Never get into a stressful or emotional conversation while driving. These kinds of conversations can be distracting and dangerous.

En Route Security for Yourself and Your Rig

The following suggestions may help drivers maintain security for themselves, their rigs, and their cargos when on the road.

- Avoid high population areas, including downtown or metropolitan areas, tunnels, and bridges (see 49 CFR 397.67 at http://www.fmcsa.dot.gov).
- Ensure all hazardous materials are delivered as soon as possible.
- Drivers should always lock vehicles when in transit or when vehicles are left unattended.
- Drivers must be aware if a vehicle or vehicles are following their trucks.
- Drivers should also beware of strangers asking inappropriate questions about their rigs or their cargos or destinations.
- Drivers should be suspicious of individuals asking them to stop as a result of an alleged traffic accident. If unsure whether an accident has occurred, drive to a police station or well-lit, busy location before stopping.
- Be cautious about stopping to help stranded motorists or at accident scenes. The better route would be to call the state police and report the stranded motorists or the accident.
- Do not pick up hitchhikers.
- Do not discuss the nature of your cargo over the CB radio, at coffee shops, truck stops, or elsewhere.
- Be aware of your surroundings at all times.
- Have the means to maintain communication with your company or dispatcher at all times. These means would include cell phones, two-way radios, CBs, and satellite communications systems.
- Be aware of the technology that could help you increase and improve your personal security and the security of your rig and your cargos, such as cell phones, satellite tracking and surveillance systems.
- Look for state-of-the-art locks and seals.
- Consider tamper-proof locking features for fifth wheels, so trailer loads cannot be stolen.
- Consider installing electronic engine controls that require a code in addition to a key to start the vehicle.
- Consider theft-prevention devices, steering locks, fuel cutoff switches, electrical cutoff switches, and other high-security ignition devices.

As a professional driver, be aware that terrorist activities tend to occur in a series. If new attacks begin, tighten your security because of the possibilities of increased efforts on the part of terrorists.

It is also important to increase security measures when your nation or a neighboring nation is involved in military activities in foreign countries. U.S. military involvement in a foreign land only invites retaliation from the terrorists bred in that country. It also gives terrorists, in general, a reason to heighten their efforts to attack your nation in as many ways as possible.

Finally, those suspicious activities you would have ignored a couple of years ago now are good reasons to remain vigilant and report what you have observed. Not reporting suspicious activities that may lead to violence and death is more of a problem than reporting activities that may not lead to violence. Law enforcement does not mind following a lead that does not pan out, and it is much worse to miss warning signs that are costly in lives and property.

Remember that terrorism costs more than buildings. It costs lives, national confidence, and our ability to grow as a free nation. Protect yourself at all costs. Protect your rig and your cargo. It is a big part of the job!

SUMMARY

Without a doubt, as a professional driver, your first responsibility remains your personal safety as well as the safety of your rig and its cargo.

In this chapter, you learned the reasons for an increased emphasis in security during loading, over the road, and during unloading. You also learned about certain things to watch for and what to do/who to notify if suspicious activities or situations arise. Finally—and most importantly—you learned the importance of protecting yourself at all costs.

KEY TERMS

Aviation and Transportation
   Security Act (ATSA)
Background checks
Bioterrorism
Cellular telephone

Electronic engine controls
Hazardous materials
Homeland Security
   Administration
Safe Explosives Act

September 11, 2001
Transportation Security
   Administration (TSA)
Terrorist activities
Weapons of mass destruction

REVIEW QUESTIONS

1. Security _____.

    a. is only the responsibility of the dispatcher

    b. is only the responsibility of the shipper

    c. has always been a major part of a professional driver's job

    d. is only the responsibility of the receiver of the goods

2. Regarding the Department of Homeland Security, which of the following is not one of its stated missions?

   a. reduce the total stopping distance of rigs

   b. prevent terrorist attacks within the U.S.

   c. reduce the vulnerability of the U.S. to terrorism

   d. minimize the damage and assist in the recovery from terrorist attacks that do occur within the U.S.

3. Which of the following is not one of the recommended procedures for increasing security on the road?

   a. Be alert when leaving a location.

   b. Do not discuss your cargo or destination near strangers.

   c. Avoid being boxed in on the road.

   d. If you believe there is a threat of hijacking, stop your rig and lock the doors.

4. If you stop your rig for food, rest, etc., which of the following should you not do?

   a. Leave your rig running with the key in it.

   b. Stop where you can meet a buddy or make sure someone in the parking area knows you, your rig, and how long you will be parked.

   c. Leave your rig in a secure parking lot or truck stop.

   d. If team driving, always leave one person with the rig.

5. According to the American Trucking Associations (ATA), one of the most important parts of a security plan is _____.

   a. having all professional drivers armed

   b. putting the right person behind the wheel, which can be done with the proper background checks

   c. to lock the rig, if the engine is left running, when the driver is away from the rig

   d. to not take the same route to a destination so hijackers will not know where a rig will be traveling

6. Which of the following is not a centerpiece of the ATA security plan?

   a. know what to look for and where to be alert

   b. look at what is "vulnerable" and what is to be a "likely target"

   c. know who is driving what rig

   d. when a driver leaves the rig with the engine running, the doors should be locked

7. One of the technical innovations that assists in security is installing electronic controls that require a _____, in addition to a key to start the engine.

   a. a second key

   b. honk of the horn

   c. code

   d. a and b

8. Regarding wireless telephone safety, a professional driver's first responsibility is to _____.

   a. pay attention to the road

   b. respond immediately to calls from the dispatcher

   c. respond immediately to calls from the shipper

   d. respond immediately to calls from the receiver of the items shipped

9. Which of the following is not a suggestion made to help drivers maintain security for themselves, their rigs, and their cargos when they are over the road?

    a. Always stop and help at accident scenes.

    c. Do not pick up hitchhikers.

    b. Consider installing electronic controls required to start the engine.

    d. Avoid high population areas, including downtown or metropolitan areas, tunnels, and bridges.

10. As a professional driver, your first responsibility is _____.

    a. to the dispatcher

    c. to the receiver of the goods shipped

    b. to the shipper

    d. your personal safety as well as the safety of your rig and its cargo

OBJECTIVES

When you have completed this chapter, you should be able to:

- Understand the importance of presenting a good image to the public.

- Explain the results of presenting a poor public image.

- Describe what professional drivers can do to present a good public image for the industry.

- Explain the importance of good relations with customers.

- Describe the proper procedures for applying for a job as a professional driver.

- Understand reasons a driver candidate can be disqualified from job consideration.

INTRODUCTION

Public relations can be defined as how the general public thinks about or views a subject, an issue, or an industry.

Much of what the general public thinks about the trucking industry comes from how they see drivers behave on the road **(see Figure 30–1)**. Thoughtful and courteous tractor-trailer drivers create a positive impact on how the public views the entire industry. On the other hand, one careless or rude truck driver on the highway, in a truck stop, or in a roadside park can immediately create a poor image for the entire industry.

If you think about it, tractor-trailer drivers are the front-line public relations team for the carrier they represent and for all the people who work in the transportation industry. Professional drivers are the part of the industry the public sees most often and the image they create is the image the general public remembers.

▶ **Figure 30–1**

The public's perception of the trucking industry comes from the driver behavior they see on the road.

It is human nature for the memory of the public to be a short one. A four-wheeler driver may have seen a trucker risk his or her life to keep other highway users safe and may have had positive interactions with professional drivers on the highway for years. Then, they may see a truck driver taking chances—perhaps repeatedly changing lanes in heavy traffic or cutting off other drivers on a freeway—and suddenly the positive image becomes a negative.

If the public does not like what they see, they will remember. Some may even complain to a lawmaker and, bottom line, the industry will hear about it in ways that will hurt business and ways that will affect earnings and jobs.

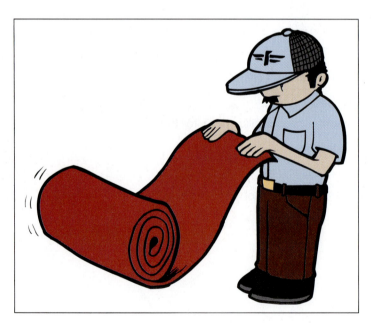

▶ *"When it comes to good PR, there's nothing too good for my fellow highway users."*

In this chapter, we will discuss not only how professional drivers can create positive public relations but also the importance of good **employee–employer relations**. At the end of the chapter, we discuss the professional driver's job search, qualifications, and recommendations for handling the job interview.

PUBLIC RELATIONS

How well do you think the general public perceives the trucking transportation industry? How does the general public see the professional driver? In most cases, the relationship between the general public and the trucking industry is determined by how well professional drivers obey the laws and regulations meant to protect road users. Professional drivers can improve the image of the trucking transportation industry by obeying the laws, being courteous, and using everyday common sense on the road, at roadside parks, and at truck stops.

Image of the Trucking Industry

The trucking industry operates under many state and federal laws and regulations. Most of the laws have been made to protect the public. Some pose challenges to the transportation industry:

- High road use taxes
- Laws restricting vehicles from using certain roads
- Lower speed limits for heavy vehicles
- Hours-of-service rules that make it difficult for drivers to get the rest they need

The public's image of the trucking industry heavily influences laws made that affect the industry. This image of the trucking industry and professional drivers—whether accurate or not—often results in legislation that is unfavorable to the industry and decreases profits **(see Figure 30–2).** These difficulties sometimes mean loss of jobs within the industry.

One driver's thoughtlessness can have a dramatic impact on the entire industry. Therefore, the industry—particularly the American Trucking Associations—but other industry groups as well, has taken steps through programs, such as the America's Team, to introduce the public to the industry and to the importance of the jobs being done every day by professional drivers.

Courteous drivers who know and practice safe driving at all times can truly be seen as "knights of the road" by the general public **(see Figure 30–3).**

 **Figure 30-2**

The public image of the trucking industry influences the laws that affect it.

Figure 30-3

It is important to present a positive image to the public.

Contact with the Public

Professional drivers have numerous opportunities for public contact, which can be either cooperative or abrasive. Drivers must take great care that their conduct and actions create a positive picture of the industry.

STOP!

All of us have stress in our lives—but THERE IS NO EXCUSE FOR ROAD RAGE from a professional driver.

▶ **Figure 30-4**

A neat appearance will gain more respect for the industry.

Every professional driver is responsible for maintaining a positive image while driving—and you do this by obeying the law, making a clean and neat appearance, and sharing the road courteously.

Obeying the law—is first and foremost. Laws are meant to protect every citizen and visitor to this country, and should be obeyed at all times. When professional drivers obey the law, they project the image of true professionals. Obeying the law also cuts down on incidents that make life harder for your fellow drivers, the industry, and yourself.

Making a good appearance—a clean, neat, professional appearance gains respect for drivers and for the industry they represent. Professional drivers should also make it a priority to stay in top physical, mental, and emotional shape **(see Figure 30–4).**

Professional drivers must be sure rigs are in top condition, as well. A good pretrip inspection may prevent an accident or breakdown. A clean, well-maintained vehicle makes the industry look good. Flapping tarps, spilling cargo, and dragging chains or ropes say we belong to a shoddy industry.

Sharing the road—because professional drivers must share roads with the public, conflicts can occur. A few of the actions that create public resentment toward the transportation industry are:

- **Space related**—following too closely or driving in packs that prevent other drivers from passing

- **Speed related**—speeding and cutting in and out of traffic

- **Going uphill**—attempting to pass another vehicle without enough speed results in two trucks blocking the flow of traffic. You could block an unmarked emergency or police vehicle. The same situation can occur when trucks do not keep to the right and pull over to allow other vehicles to pass. Be careful, and do not pull onto a soft shoulder because your rig could sink, turn over, or throw gravel at vehicles behind you

- **Passing**—when the truck cuts off other drivers or does not signal his or her intention to pass

- **At intersections**—never try to bluff your way through intersections. Trucks are large and can frighten some drivers to react in a way that causes an accident. Other drivers do not always leave enough room for a tractor-trailer to make a turn. Keep cool and be aware that many of today's drivers do not always heed red lights. Look both ways after the light turns green, and be sure there are no emergency vehicles approaching.

- **Use of headlights**—not dimming lights when meeting or following other vehicles can be dangerous. Shining high beams into vehicles ahead can confuse the driver and possibly cause an accident. Remember—the posted speed is the maximum you should drive. Remember, too, you are always creating an image.

- **Noise**—using your horn when it is not needed is irritating and often frightening. Mufflers that are damaged or not the right type create unnecessary and irritating—noise.

- **Parking incorrectly**—when you block traffic unnecessarily, people may think it is deliberate, which reflects negatively on you, your carrier, and your industry.

Improper behavior on the streets and highways can also give the trucking transportation industry a black eye. Yelling, foul language, and obscene gestures accomplish nothing and, if reported, may cause you to lose your job.

You are the professional! The best policy is to act like a professional at all times **(see Figure 30–5)**. Remember, many trucks on the road today have a phone number painted on them that people may call to report both good and bad driving habits.

Make a habit of being clean, neatly groomed, and neatly dressed when on duty. If your carrier prefers uniforms, be sure yours is neat, clean, and pressed. Be courteous and polite and avoid arguments. You represent an entire industry.

Figure 30-5

A professional manner on and off the road is the best policy.

CUSTOMER RELATIONS

As far as the general public is concerned, professional drivers ARE the company. As a driver, how you act can lose or gain business for your company. The extra effort it takes to do a good job and present a positive image is well worth the effort, both short-term and long-term. Both you and the company will benefit from good **customer relations.**

CAUTION!

Remember: How you and your equipment look are important, too—and first impressions count!

Factors that affect your image as seen by the public mean more when the public is a customer. The image you project is the customer's closest view of the company **(see Figure 30–6).**

Company policies and procedures were set up to attract and grow the business. Follow the company policy for cargo and freight documentation and handling, dealing with customers, and dealing with problems.

Drivers who do not follow company policy give the company a bad reputation. Moreover, neglecting company policy can result in the loss of your job. If you have a problem at a customer location or on the road, call the dispatcher. It is the company's job to help you.

A positive attitude is extremely important. What does a positive attitude look like? Check out the following:

- Promptness when picking up or delivering cargo
- Courtesy—to everyone
- Politeness, helpfulness, and honesty at all times

Tips for Good Customer Relations

• Follow company procedures
• Do not argue or lose your temper
• Be courteous
• Be polite, honest, and helpful
• Always thank the customer

If you give that extra care,
you may get more business!

Remember... the driver has more
contact with customers than
any other person in the company

▶ **Figure 30–6**

Good customer relations begin with drivers who conduct themselves professionally at all times.

- A sincere interest in doing a good job
- An easy manner—not arguing or allowing yourself to become provoked

EMPLOYER–EMPLOYEE RELATIONS

Before you read further, ask yourself this question: If you were running a trucking company, what kind of employees would you want to work for your firm?

Your answer, of course, is that you would want people who work hard, are reliable, responsible, dependable, and will help your company make money.

In this section, we discuss the requirements of a good employee, attitudes and conduct, and required skills.

Basic Job Requirements

A good attitude is a must for success in finding and holding any job. The general qualifications expected of a professional tractor-trailer driver mandate that a driver must:

- Meet the requirements of federal law, including the medical qualifications and having the correct CDL
- Meet the employer's needs and qualifications as stated in company policy
- Know about the trucking industry and have the attitudes and interests suited to its environment **(see Figure 30–7).**

Do You Want To Drive A Tractor-Trailer?

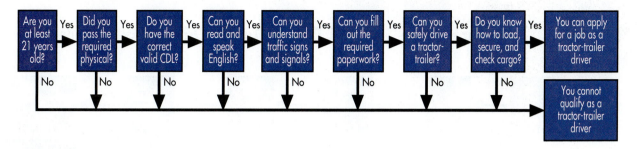

▶ **Figure 30–7**

Basic job requirements for professional drivers.

Requirements of Federal Law

People who apply for professional tractor-trailer driving jobs must meet the U.S. Department of Transportation (DOT) qualifications as stated below:

▶ **Figure 30–8**

Professional drivers need to pass certain tests.

- Be at least 21 years old (although 18 year olds are allowed to drive intrastate)

- Be physically qualified, according to FMCSR 341.91

- Have a valid CDL

- Be able to read and speak English (in some states, tests are administered by interpreters if a candidate's English is not strong enough)

- Understand traffic signs and signals

- Be able to fill out required paperwork

- Be able to safely drive a tractor-trailer

- Know and use the correct methods of securing cargo

- Be able to determine if cargo is properly loaded and secured

Professional tractor-trailer drivers must also pass certain tests and be able to fill out the applications that are required **(see Figure 30–8).**

- Fill out a job application that meets DOT requirement FMCSR 391.21 (carrier will supply application).

- Take a written test and a road test given by the company (the DOT requires the company to keep the results on file).

- Have passed all the tests needed to earn the CDL:
  - General Knowledge Test
  - Air Brakes Test
  - Combination Vehicles Test
  - Pretrip Inspection Test
  - Basic Control Skills Test and Road Test

Drivers who operate double or triple trailer combinations or tankers or haul hazardous materials must pass additional tests before they can drive these vehicles **(see Figure 30–9).**

Do You Want To Get A CDL That Will Let You Drive A Tractor-Trailer?

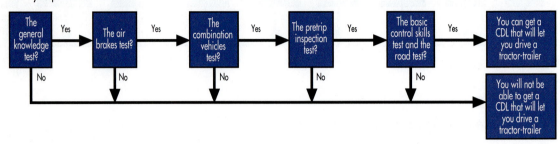

Figure 30–9
Requirements to earn a CDL.

Disqualifications

Under FMCSR 391.15, an applicant for a CDL that will allow him or her to drive a tractor-trailer must be disqualified for any of the following reasons:

- Medical reasons
- Loss of license
- Operating a commercial motor vehicle (CMV) while under the influence of alcohol, illegal drugs, or other stimulants
- Transportation, possession, or unlawful use of a Schedule I drug
- Being in an accident that results in injury or death and leaving the scene
- Conviction of a felony involving the use of a commercial motor vehicle

CAUTION!

As the holder of a CDL, you are subject to employment, random, and postaccident drug testing.

General Qualifications

Professional driver applicants should know something about the various types of vehicles used in the transportation industry **(see Figure 30–10).** They should also be informed about the systems and components of the various vehicles. Applicants should be able to speak the language of the industry and know how to fill out the required paperwork.

A knowledge of state and local traffic regulations and laws must be demonstrated. This includes the basic hazardous materials requirements.

Being able to drive safely and learning to drive the employer's vehicles safely are vital skills. The professional driver also must know how to handle cargo using the correct methods at all times.

To qualify, an applicant must have a positive attitude toward the trucking industry, the employer, and the job itself. One of the biggest reasons new drivers have difficulty is because they have unrealistic expectations about the job and its requirements.

Every applicant must be willing to follow company policies regarding hours of work, safety rules, and public relations.

Finally, the candidate must have a personality that suits the job. This includes a high level of interest in the job, maturity, safety awareness, enthusiasm, and a responsible work ethic.

▶ Figure 30-10

Professional driver applicants should know about the various vehicles used in the transportation industry.

Company Policy

Each company has its own policies. Company policy must be followed, even if it differs from what you have learned in school or elsewhere. Find out what is expected during your job interview, and then meet those expectations.

Most carriers have company policies that cover:

- Hours of work and benefits
- Basic work rules
  - Types of supervision
  - Requirements for advancement
  - Discipline, including rules for dismissal
- Safety rules
  - Safety training
  - Safety meetings
  - Safe driving and cargo handling rules
- Vehicle inspection and maintenance requirements
  - Instructions
  - What is expected of the driver
  - Forms to be filled out
- Rules for trips
  - Driving rules for fuel economy
  - Where and when drivers can make fuel and rest stops
  - Reimbursement policy for drivers
  - Use of credit cards
  - Cash advances
- Relations with customers and the public
  - Dress code
  - Conduct expected

What Companies Cannot Require of a Driver

No driver can be required to work in violation of state, federal, or local regulations. Drivers must be provided with a safe place to work and a safe vehicle. No driver is allowed to violate the hours-of-service regulations or safety regulations.

Whistleblower Protection Program

The Whistleblower Protection Program provides protection from discrimination for air carrier industry employees who report information related to air carrier safety or participate in other protected activities.

Employees of air carriers, their contractors, and their subcontractors are protected from retaliation, discharge, or otherwise being discriminated against for providing information relating to air carrier safety violations to their employer or to the federal government, or filed, testified, or assisted in a proceeding against the employer relating to any violation or alleged violation of any order, regulation, or standard of the Federal Aviation Administration or any other federal law relating to air carrier safety, or because they are about to engage in any of these actions.

To qualify for protection under the Whistleblower Protection Program, you must:

1. Be or have been an employee as mentioned
2. Be or have been engaged in an activity as mentioned
3. Believe you are being or have been discriminated against by your employer for engaging in an activity as mentioned

For more information, you may call the FAA Whistleblower Hotline at 1-800-255-1111 (press 1 for main menu, then press 5).

Drivers and Company Policy

The more a driver applicant knows about a company, the easier it is to get a job interview and do well during the interview. The internet may be a good source of information about a prospective employer. If possible, know the answers to the following questions in advance:

- Do you have the abilities the employer needs?
- If additional training is available, are you willing to learn?
- Is this a place where you want to work?
- Are the hours, pay, and working conditions going to meet your needs?

Obviously, the greatest chance for a good match is when the company and the applicant agree that their needs will be met through the job.

Finally, an applicant's attitude is as important as their knowledge of the company requirements. The key attitudes to have for a successful job search are:

- Loyalty
- Dependability
- Safety mindedness
- Honesty
- Enthusiasm
- Team player
- Good representative for the company

APPLYING FOR A JOB

Generally, when you apply for a job as a professional tractor-trailer driver, you must fill out an application, give references for the prospective employer to check, and provide employment history for the past 10 years. The next step is attending a job interview and being tested.

The application form is the first impression you make on the potential employer. If your application is completed neatly and is accurate and honest, you will usually make a good impression on the employer. However, whether you meet their requirements is not always easy to tell from the application without also having an interview.

CAUTION!

Avoid leaving blank spaces on the application. Some carriers receive numerous applications per day and do not have time to check incomplete applications.

References Are Important

When the potential employer asks for references, you should supply a list of the names and addresses of previous employers. If there are "holes" in your work record, be prepared for questions about what you were doing during those periods, employment-wise. It is important that you give an accurate account of your previous driving record. Always be honest and truthful.

Next to the road test, the interview is the most important of finding a job, and you have a chance to sell yourself. The four key rules for a good job interview are:

- Be prepared
- Know how to act during the interview
- End the interview on a positive note and thank the person for the time and consideration
- Do not overstay your appointed time for the interview

Preparing for the Interview

To prepare for the interview, do the following:

- Learn all you can about the company. Ask current and former employees and visit the corporate website.
- Be ready to ask intelligent questions, such as the following:
  - What are the company policies?
  - What are the chances for training?
  - Is there opportunity for advancement?
- Know your own abilities and limitations. Be realistic.
- Know whether you can drive the kind of vehicle used in this job and handle the cargo.
- Know whether you need extra training.
- Tell the truth—even if it is not always pretty.

Make sure you have all the necessary paperwork with you, including the correct license, endorsement, certifications, and letters of reference.

Be ready for the interview. Be on time or even a bit early. Visit the location a day or so before the interview so you will not get lost or delayed. Dress neatly but ready to drive if you are asked to take a road test.

How to Act During the Interview

The interview is your chance to sell yourself. Be on time, be polite and courteous, and if you are a smoker, refrain from smoking even if you are invited to do so. When you are asked about your qualifications and experience, present them clearly and honestly. Do not stretch the truth. Be sure the interviewer knows what you have done in the past. Show how your experience and qualifications fit with what the company needs **(see Figure 30–11)**.

Most people are a little nervous before and during interviews. Do not let this bother you. Just try and be as relaxed as you can be—and be yourself. Keep a positive attitude about the job. If possible, do a little research on the Internet and find out something about the company's history and mission.

▶ **Figure 30–11**

Be prepared and be yourself at an interview.

GO!

A good attitude is often what makes the difference in who gets the job! Never be negative about a previous employer.

Remember, the interviewer's job is to learn about you—to find out who you are and what you are like. Try to answer questions clearly but do not volunteer unnecessary information. Try to keep your conversation focused on the job and why you are the best candidate for that job.

Ask questions. Find out about the company.

End the Interview Well

Thank the interviewer for his or her time and interest. If you are interested in the job, show your interest in the company and the job and repeat how you believe you can meet the company's needs. Ask how and when you will be informed of the company's decision **(see Figure 30–12)**.

Remember, you may not get the job. If you do not—and you think the company is a place where you want to work—you may choose to accept a job as a helper or dock worker as a place to begin. By proving your strong work ethic and your interest in becoming a professional driver for the company, you may be considered for the next open position.

▶ Figure 30–12

After the interview, thank the interviewer for his or her time.

▶ Figure 30–13

The road test is the most important part of applying for a job.

Tests

Be prepared and well rested before sitting for any written tests or before taking road performance tests. To prepare for the written tests, study the regulations regarding safe driving practices and review the state-prepared handbook and the FMCSRs available on the Internet at www.fmcsa.dot.gov.

Review safe driving information and procedures learned during your classes and it is also a good idea to purchase the review book, *Pass the CDL,* published by Thomson Delmar Learning.

It is also helpful to study the tests at the end of each chapter in this book as a practice review.

The road test is the most important part of applying for a job **(see Figure 30–13).** The test will probably include a pretrip inspection, coupling and uncoupling, backing, parking, and driving in traffic.

Be comfortably dressed and ready for the test. Bring gloves, rags, and driving equipment. Ask about unfamiliar parts or accessories. If you feel you are not yet qualified to drive the rig, do not drive. Never take the risk of driving an unfamiliar vehicle for testing purposes.

Physical Examination

You must have a current and valid doctor's certificate, stating you have passed a physical examination and meet the minimum qualifications for the DOT physical exam. If you have not had a physical examination, you will need to get one. The carrier may refer you to a specific physician or you may get a physical from your family physician.

SUMMARY

In this chapter, you have learned that how a professional driver acts has much to do with how the public views the trucking industry as a whole. You have also learned how to present a positive image, both on the highway and in other public places. Ways to maintain good public relations have been explained in this chapter as well as how to become a professional driver, finding a job, and handling the job interview.

KEY TERMS

Customer relations   Employer–employee relations   Public relations

REVIEW QUESTIONS

1. Regarding public relations, who are the front-line public relations persons for the trucking industry?

   a. the owners of the trucking companies

   b. the professional drivers

   c. the shippers

   d. the receivers of the freight shipped

2. Courteous drivers who know and practice safe driving at all times can truly be seen by the public as the _____.

   a. "knights of the night"

   b. "knights of the day"

   c. "king of public relations"

   d. "knights of the road"

3. Regarding contact with the public, most conflicts occur _____.

   a. while sharing the road

   b. because of improperly loaded trailers

   c. because of a high center of gravity

   d. because of state regulations

4. Regarding good customer relations, the _____ has more contact with customers than any other person in the company.

   a. dispatcher

   b. professional driver

   c. company owner

   d. office manager

5. Which of the following is not a basic job requirement for a professional driver?

   a. meet the requirements of federal law, including the medical qualifications and having the correct CDL

   b. meet the employer's needs and qualifications as stated in the company policy

   c. know all the federal laws regarding the trucking industry

   d. know about the trucking industry and have the attitudes and interests suited to its environment

6. According to FMCSR, which of the following will not disqualify an operator of a tractor-trailer rig from driving?

  a. operating a CMV while under the influence of alcohol, amphetamines, or narcotics

  b. being in an accident that results in injury or death and leaving the scene

  c. speeding

  d. conviction of a felony involving the use of a CMV

7. Regarding state, federal, or local regulations, a driver can _____.

  a. not be required to violate these regulations

  b. violate these regulations if told to do so by the dispatcher

  c. violate these regulations if told to do so by the shipper

  d. violate these regulations if told to do so by the receiver of the freight shipped

8. Which of the following is not a key attitude that a professional driver should have to be successful on the job?

  a. loyalty

  b. dependability

  c. enthusiasm

  d. independence, doing things on your own

9. Regarding opportunities for advancement in the trucking industry, advancements usually come from _____.

  a. the beginning drivers

  b. other industries

  c. within the industry

  d. driver training schools

10. When being interviewed for a job, if you have questions it is best to _____.

  a. ask questions

  b. wait until you get the job and then ask questions

  c. wait until after the interview and look for the answer on the Internet

  d. ask other drivers

Bill Compton

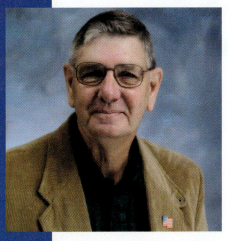

Used with permission of Accent Photography by Terra and Contract Freighters, Inc.

"IF YOU'RE GOING to start driving, pick a good company; make sure they're solid and they're going to stand behind you," advises Bill Compton. "There are a lot of companies that mislead you. They stretch the truth and make things sound better than they really are. CFI is not one of those companies."

Bill Compton grew up on a farm near Lockwood, Missouri, and actually started his driving career hauling grain and cattle. He started driving professionally back when diesel fuel was around $0.09 per gallon. "In 1956, I had the chance to go to college," Bill remembers. "But back then, I didn't want to go to college, didn't want to get an education." His first truck was a 1948 model White. "It might do 50 miles an hour if you dropped it out of an airplane," he continues. "It was pretty crude compared to today's standard. There was no air conditioning, no comfort for the driver. Heaters were not that great and the defrosters didn't work well. I remember having to scrape the frost off of the inside of the windshield. It was miserable driving with coat and gloves on inside the cab."

Bill first joined CFI in 1980. He was an owner-operator for 17 years, and over the course of that time, he had a total of five trucks that he owned and drove himself. He decided in 1997 to become a company driver, to receive better benefits for his family.

"CFI is a good solid company," he states. "You don't have to worry about the paycheck being good or not when you go to the bank, and they have good benefits. I've known CFI since the early 1960s, back before deregulation."

Bill lives in Carthage, Missouri, with his wife Joan of almost 23 years. Together, they have four daughters and three grandchildren. "[Being gone] is harder on the kids than anything," he asserts. "My wife was dad and mom to the kids, and we talked on the phone every night. Phone bills used to be very high—it's a lot better now with cell phones. We always talk every night—sometimes two or three times a night if I get lonesome or she has a problem. Some couples can handle it and some can't. It really takes two special people to make it work." When he gets home, Bill tackles his honey-do list and hunts quail and turkeys.

"Take your time and do your best," Bill advises. "Don't let anything crowd you. You're the one that's in charge of that vehicle and you have to remember that. Plan your trips and plan your time so that you're not crowded. Check your equipment and make sure it's safe."

Bill has driven over 3 million miles with CFI, only the third person to accomplish this feat since CFI's founding in 1951.

"I like the freedom of not having somebody looking over your shoulder," Bill remarks. "You can stop when you want to and eat when you want to eat. You know what work you've got to do, and if you figure out your time schedule, you can do what you want to do. When I started, it was the money. There were a lot of times back in the 60s and 70s when we made as much as lawyers were making. It was partly the money and partly the freedom that has kept me driving."

In his 24-year driving career, Bill has had many good times and seen many things. "We see things the average person will never see—both terrible accidents and wonderful things," he observes. "I've seen places I would never have seen if I wasn't driving a truck."

Used with permission of Contract Freighters, Inc.

31 Professional Driver Health, Safety, and Security

OBJECTIVES

When you have completed this chapter, you should be able to:

- Understand the demands of professional driving and why it demands good health and good health habits.

- Describe the causes and cures of fatigue.

- Explain the FMCSR regarding drug and alcohol use.

- Know the benefits of a healthy diet, regular exercise, and plenty of rest.

- Understand the causes of stress on the job.

- Describe how to lift heavy objects safely.

Figure 31-1

Being flexible and willing to do whatever the job takes helps establish you as a true professional.

INTRODUCTION

A number of large carriers report the greatest lack of information among new drivers is about the job itself. In many cases, new drivers have no idea what the job entails, other than driving a truck.

As a professional driver, one of your greatest challenges is to remain flexible in your outlook and willing to do whatever the job takes until you have established yourself as a professional and a valuable addition to the company's driver roster.

Initially, your schedule may not be what you want it to be. Your routes may not be your choice; however, with experience and as you gain seniority, you can make your job what you want it to be **(see Figure 31–1).**

Another challenge for every professional driver is that of staying healthy, which is more than eating the right diet, getting enough rest, getting exercise a few times a week, and avoiding stress. Staying healthy means doing all of these and anything else you can do to maintain good health, a positive outlook, and time for a satisfying career **(see Figure 31–2).**

PHYSICAL REQUIREMENTS FOR INTERSTATE TRUCKERS

- Vision

  20/40 vision

  Peripheral vision—at least 70 degrees in each eye

  Distinguish red and green

  Eye check every 24 months

- Hearing

  Hear forced whisper at 5 feet

- Stamina

  To meet job requirements (e.g., loading and unloading)

- Disqualifications

  Loss of limb(s) or disease that limits limbs

  Chronic illness that seriously affects driving

  Examples:

  - Diabetes
  - Heart disease
  - Alcoholism

- Required physical examination

  Every 2 years

  At carrier's discretion

  After serious injury or illness

- Certification by physician

  Must be carried at all times

  As important as driver's license

Figure 31-2

Professional drivers are required to pass the DOT physical examination every 2 years.

Today's drivers also need to avoid fatigue . . . and, although it goes without saying, it is worth mentioning that professional drivers should avoid alcohol and drugs at all costs.

The Federal Motor Carrier Safety Regulations address alcohol, drugs, and fatigue. Know what these laws say in order to keep your license and maintain your career and your paycheck.

The purpose of this chapter is to explain these laws and to give you information to help you "be the best you can be" behind the wheel, at home, and in all parts of your life.

OVERVIEW

In the year 2000, the estimated life expectancy of a U.S. citizen was close to 74 years. That number, of course, depends on the health habits of the individual.

To determine how professional drivers compared to the U.S. population in general, researchers asked drivers about their lifestyles and their health habits.

What is the health condition of the current driving population compared to the U.S. population? The following data gathered from 3,000 drivers at an industry trade show tell us about driver lifestyles.

HEALTH OF U.S. AND PROFESSIONAL DRIVERS		
Activity	**U.S. Population**	**Professional Drivers**
Smoking	27%	49%
Obesity (heavyset)	33%	73%
High blood pressure (hypertension)	26%	33%
Poor eating habits	80%	80%
Exercise regularly	25%	8%

Traditionally, health habits of U.S. professional drivers have not been very good **(see Figure 31–3).** In fact, older drivers in the current driver population may be headed, at breakneck speed, toward a collision with serious and possibly career-ending health problems.

How to Change the Current Health Trends

A professional driver knows what has to be done to keep a truck running smoothly and to ensure a safe trip **(see Figure 31–4).** Each part and each system contributes to keeping the vehicle operating safely.

The same principle is true for the body. To keep the body healthy and running smoothly, the driver must have—or develop—good eating habits, regular exercise, the proper amount of sleep, and a plan to manage stress.

▶ **Figure 31–3**

Health habits make a difference in how you feel and how well you do your job.

▶ **Figure 31–4**

A professional driver must keep his or her truck in good condition so it runs smoothly and ensures a safe trip. The same applies to your body.

▶ *"Only 16 more jumping jacks and then five times around the rig . . . that'll get my heart pumping."*

DRIVER NUTRITION

Poor Eating Habits Common Among Professional Drivers

Long hours behind the wheel, varying work cycles, and being away from home are factors that contribute to poor eating habits for professional drivers; however, these habits can be changed with a little effort **(see Figure 31–5).** Otherwise, you will fall into the same habits as those

To qualify, an applicant must have a positive attitude toward the trucking industry, the employer, and the job itself. One of the biggest reasons new drivers have difficulty is because they have unrealistic expectations about the job and its requirements.

Every applicant must be willing to follow company policies regarding hours of work, safety rules, and public relations.

Finally, the candidate must have a personality that suits the job. This includes a high level of interest in the job, maturity, safety awareness, enthusiasm, and a responsible work ethic.

▶ **Figure 30-10**

Professional driver applicants should know about the various vehicles used in the transportation industry.

Company Policy

Each company has its own policies. Company policy must be followed, even if it differs from what you have learned in school or elsewhere. Find out what is expected during your job interview, and then meet those expectations.

Most carriers have company policies that cover:

- Hours of work and benefits
- Basic work rules
  - Types of supervision
  - Requirements for advancement
  - Discipline, including rules for dismissal
- Safety rules
  - Safety training
  - Safety meetings
  - Safe driving and cargo handling rules
- Vehicle inspection and maintenance requirements
  - Instructions
  - What is expected of the driver
  - Forms to be filled out
- Rules for trips
  - Driving rules for fuel economy
  - Where and when drivers can make fuel and rest stops
  - Reimbursement policy for drivers
  - Use of credit cards
  - Cash advances
- Relations with customers and the public
  - Dress code
  - Conduct expected

What Companies Cannot Require of a Driver

No driver can be required to work in violation of state, federal, or local regulations. Drivers must be provided with a safe place to work and a safe vehicle. No driver is allowed to violate the hours-of-service regulations or safety regulations.

Whistleblower Protection Program

The Whistleblower Protection Program provides protection from discrimination for air carrier industry employees who report information related to air carrier safety or participate in other protected activities.

Employees of air carriers, their contractors, and their subcontractors are protected from retaliation, discharge, or otherwise being discriminated against for providing information relating to air carrier safety violations to their employer or to the federal government, or filed, testified, or assisted in a proceeding against the employer relating to any violation or alleged violation of any order, regulation, or standard of the Federal Aviation Administration or any other federal law relating to air carrier safety, or because they are about to engage in any of these actions.

To qualify for protection under the Whistleblower Protection Program, you must:

1. Be or have been an employee as mentioned
2. Be or have been engaged in an activity as mentioned
3. Believe you are being or have been discriminated against by your employer for engaging in an activity as mentioned

For more information, you may call the FAA Whistleblower Hotline at 1-800-255-1111 (press 1 for main menu, then press 5).

Drivers and Company Policy

The more a driver applicant knows about a company, the easier it is to get a job interview and do well during the interview. The internet may be a good source of information about a prospective employer. If possible, know the answers to the following questions in advance:

- Do you have the abilities the employer needs?
- If additional training is available, are you willing to learn?
- Is this a place where you want to work?
- Are the hours, pay, and working conditions going to meet your needs?

Obviously, the greatest chance for a good match is when the company and the applicant agree that their needs will be met through the job.

Finally, an applicant's attitude is as important as their knowledge of the company requirements. The key attitudes to have for a successful job search are:

- Loyalty
- Dependability
- Safety mindedness
- Honesty
- Enthusiasm
- Team player
- Good representative for the company

INTRODUCTION

Public **relations** can be defined as how the general public thinks about or views a subject, an issue, or an industry.

Much of what the general public thinks about the trucking industry comes from how they see drivers behave on the road (**see Figure 30–1**). Thoughtful and courteous tractor-trailer drivers create a positive impact on how the public views the entire industry. On the other hand, one careless or rude truck driver on the highway, in a truck stop, or in a roadside park can immediately create a poor image for the entire industry.

If you think about it, tractor-trailer drivers are the front-line public relations team for the carrier they represent and for all the people who work in the transportation industry. Professional drivers are the part of the industry the public sees most often and the image they create is the image the general public remembers.

It is human nature for the memory of the public to be a short one. A four-wheeler driver may have seen a trucker risk his or her life to keep other highway users safe and may have had positive interactions with professional drivers on the highway for years. Then, they may see a truck driver taking chances—perhaps repeatedly changing lanes in heavy traffic or cutting off other drivers on a freeway—and suddenly the positive image becomes a negative.

If the public does not like what they see, they will remember. Some may even complain to a lawmaker and, bottom line, the industry will hear about it in ways that will hurt business and ways that will affect earnings and jobs.

▶ **Figure 30-1**
The public's perception of the trucking industry comes from the driver behavior they see on the road.

In this chapter, we will discuss not only how professional drivers can create positive public relations but also the importance of good **employee–employer relations.** At the end of the chapter, we discuss the professional driver's job search, qualifications, and recommendations for handling the job interview.

PUBLIC RELATIONS

How well do you think the general public perceives the trucking transportation industry? How does the general public see the professional driver? In most cases, the relationship between the general public and the trucking industry is determined by how well professional drivers obey the laws and regulations meant to protect road users. Professional drivers can improve the image of the trucking transportation industry by obeying the laws, being courteous, and using everyday common sense on the road, at roadside parks, and at truck stops.

 "When it comes to good PR, there's nothing too good for my fellow highway users."

30 Public Relations and Job Search

OBJECTIVES

When you have completed this chapter, you should be able to:

- Understand the importance of presenting a good image to the public.
- Explain the results of presenting a poor public image.
- Describe what professional drivers can do to present a good public image for the industry.
- Explain the importance of good relations with customers.
- Describe the proper procedures for applying for a job as a professional driver.
- Understand reasons a driver candidate can be disqualified from job consideration.

drivers who now are dealing with health problems such as obesity, diabetes, heart disease, and sleep apnea. Try to avoid:

- Eating foods high in fat content (1 ounce of fat contains 2 ½ times the calories of 1 ounce of protein or carbohydrates)

- Eating fried foods

- Eating breaded fried foods such as fried fish and chicken-fried steak

- Eating gravies and sauces, as most have high fat content

- Eating too much salt

- Not eating enough vegetables and fruits

- Not eating enough foods high in fiber content

- Not drinking enough water

- Snacking on cookies and doughnuts

▶ **Figure 31–5**

Driver preparing for the road.

Helpful Hints for Good Nutrition

To increase your opportunities to look good, feel good, and handle your job efficiently, try to:

- Reduce amount of fast foods

- Avoid fried foods

- Eat roasted or baked meats

- Remove the skin from chicken

- Use nonfat spreads on breads and potatoes

- Take a portable cooler or refrigerator on the road (more economical than restaurants)

- Eat breakfast from your cooler (yogurt, banana, apple, fruit juice)

- Carry snacks in your cooler (fruits, such as apples, bananas, peaches, plums, grapes, raisins; raw vegetables such as celery, carrots, green or yellow squash, bell peppers)

- Drink diet drinks or water

- Choose a salad bar for one of your daily meals and use nonfat dressings

- Avoid desserts, as many are high in fat content

The Four Best Eating Habits

When you are out on the road dealing with heavy traffic, careless four-wheelers, construction, and tight schedules, it is sometimes difficult to remember all this information about a good diet

Figure 31–6

The foods and beverages you consume each day contribute to fatigue.

(see Figure 31–6). Try to follow these four good eating habits and you will make a positive impact on your health.

- No fast foods—too much fat and salt
- No fried foods
- Breakfast and snacks from your cooler
- Salad bar for one meal each day

WHAT ABOUT EXERCISE?

To keep your body running as smoothly as your rig, you must have a total exercise program. A total exercise program consists of movement, strength training, and development of flexibility.

Movement can be any activity that is done briskly, including walking, swimming, playing basketball, rope jumping, mowing the grass, hiking, playing golf, riding a stationary bike, or any number of other activities.

Walking will be stressed here because it requires no special facilities or equipment—only a pair of shoes, an open space, and a professional driver with a desire to stay healthy.

Effects of Physical Activity on Health and Disease

With a minimum of 30 minutes of exercise per day, you can do much to stay healthy and feel good while on the road. Always get clearance from a physician before beginning an exercise program.

The following is what you can achieve by adding physical activity to your daily routine:

- *Overall mortality:* high to moderate levels of regular physical activity is associated with lower mortality rates.
- *Cardiovascular diseases:* regular physical activity decreases the risk of cardiovascular diseases and prevents or delays the development of high blood pressure and reduces blood pressure in persons with hypertension.
- *Cancer:* regular physical activity is associated with a decreased risk of colon cancer.
- *Diabetes:* regular physical activity lowers the risk of developing diabetes.
- *Osteoporosis:* physical activity is essential for maintaining peak bone mass in adults.
- *Falling:* reduces the risk of falling due to increased strength and balance.
- *Obesity:* reduces obesity by increasing the amount of calories used.
- *Mental health:* reduces and relieves the symptoms of stress, makes you look better, and feel better.
- *Low-back pain decreases:* research has shown that strong low-back muscles are less prone to injury.

JOB STRESS

Being a professional driver can be very stressful. Tight schedules, heavy traffic, higher costs of fuel, construction zones, crabby shippers, and aggressive four-wheelers all lead to driver stress. Many drivers also report experiencing a high level of stress involving their families because of the complexities of today's society.

Definition of Job Stress

The National Institute for Occupational Safety and Health (NIOSH), the federal agency responsible for conducting research and making recommendations for prevention of work-related illness and injury, define **job stress** as:

> The harmful physical and emotional responses that occur when the requirements of a job do not match the capabilities, resources or needs of the worker.

Causes of Job Stress

Nearly all experts agree that job stress results from the interaction of the worker and the conditions of work. The exposure of stressful working conditions can have a direct influence on workers' safety and health. The following job conditions may lead to stress:

- *The design of the task:* heavy workloads, infrequent rest breaks, long hours, and hectic and routine tasks.

- *Comments:* most professional drivers would agree that they have heavy workloads, infrequent rest breaks, long hours, and hectic tasks.

- *Management styles:* lack of participation by workers in decision making, poor communications in the organization, lack of family-friendly policies.

- *Interpersonal relations:* poor social environment and lack of support or help from coworkers and supervisors. If a driver is a "people person," this could be a real problem. Some companies are addressing this problem by letting family members accompany the driver.

- *Career concerns:* job insecurity and lack of opportunities for growth, advancement or promotion. Many drivers feel there is little room for advancement or promotion in the industry. Some prefer to work for themselves, buy a rig, and become a contract driver.

- *Environmental conditions:* unpleasant or dangerous physical conditions such as crowding, noise, air pollution, or ergonomic problems. Such factors as aggressive drivers, poor sleeping conditions, heavy traffic, bad weather, miles and miles of construction, diets high in fat content, and lack of exercise lead to stress for the professional driver.

After looking at any of these working conditions, it is obvious that being a professional driver is a very stressful job.

Job Stress and Its Toll on Your Health

Medical authorities tell us there is a relationship between job stress and health and report the following:

> *Cardiovascular disease:* psychologically demanding jobs that allow employees little control over the work process increases the risk of cardiovascular diseases.

> *Musculoskeletal disorders:* it is believed that job stress increases the risk of development of back and upper-extremity disorders.

> *Psychological disorders:* several studies suggest that job stress leads to job burnout.

Workplace injury: there is some indication that stressful working conditions interfere with safe working practices and set the stage for injuries at work.

Cancer, ulcer, and impaired immune functions: some studies indicate a relationship between stressful working conditions and these health problems.

Where Family Stress Begins

Not only does a professional driver have stress caused by the job, but many also have family situations that cause additional stress. Because the driver is gone from home so much, situations arise that cause both the driver and family members stress.

CAUTION!

When the driver is gone for long periods of time, relationships with his or her children will probably change and the significant other that remains at home will have to assume family duties that the driver may have performed.

The driver probably will miss many of the children's important events such as birthdays, school activities, and athletic events. The driver may not be at home to help in the event of illnesses or accidents. Missing the important events in a child's life may cause anger in the child and cause the driver to feel guilty. This then causes stress in the family.

The significant other who remains at home may experience major changes in the family role. With the driver gone, the partner must perform all the child rearing duties such as attending school and athletic events and taking care of the children in the event of illness or accidents. In addition to caring for the children, the partner often has to deal with household emergencies such as stopped-up sewer lines and car repair. Dealing with these issues sometimes makes the stay-at-home partner frustrated and angry. The driver may feel guilty not being at home to help with such emergencies. This causes more stress in the family.

So the driver who has a very stressful job is now experiencing additional stress about his or her family life. Many family therapists say the best thing a family can do to reduce stress is to make a greater effort to communicate.

The driver and his or her family could have a family meeting and talk about the situation. The driver could explain to the family why he or she is gone so much. The stay-at-home partner could talk about the problems of running a one-parent household. The children should have their say about the driver being gone so much. Each family member should express his or her view.

The meeting should conclude with the driver restating his or her position about driving and assuring each family member that he or she loves them.

That is an example of how communications in the family can reduce the driver's stress. There are other methods the driver can use to communicate with the family. Some drivers use cell phones and call home each day. Many drivers send email messages daily to the family. Some companies allow significant others and/or children to go on the road with the driver.

GO!

These activities allow the family to communicate. When family members communicate and assure each other of their love, the stress level of the family will go down.

What You Can Do About Job Stress

Fortunately there is something that can be done about job stress. The activities necessary to reduce job stress can be divided into two parts—organizational change and **stress management.**

Organizational Changes

Since professional drivers spend most of their time alone on the road, organizational changes will not make a significant change in a driver's level of stress. Some organizational activities, such as award banquets for safe drivers, company health newsletters, gyms at terminals, supplying phone cards to the driver so he or she can call home, and allowing family members to accompany the driver, obviously help reduce a driver's stress. If nothing else, just because of the time the driver spends alone on the road, the job of reducing stress falls on the shoulders of the driver.

Managing Stress

Most medical experts agree that the following activities help reduce stress:

- Have a balance between work and family or personal life. There is not much a professional driver can do in this area. Try to stay in contact with friends and family members by telephone or email. Some companies allow family members to accompany the driver on the road, and this adds to the balance a driver needs between work and personal life.

- Develop a supportive network of friends and coworkers. This is another area that is not very helpful to the professional driver, since the driver is on the road so much that there is little time to interact with friends and coworkers. A special warning to drivers: With the increase of AIDS and other sexually transmitted diseases, it would be to a driver's advantage to avoid any "special friends" while on or off the road.

- Eat a low-fat diet mostly of green vegetables, beans, legumes, fruit, rice, pasta, cereals, and low-fat milk and yogurt. This is one area where a professional driver has control. As previously stated, eat breakfast and snacks from foods in your cooler or refrigerator, avoid fast and fried foods. Have one meal per day from a salad bar. Use the Food Guide Pyramid to help make wise food choices.

- Walk 30 minutes a day, five days per week. This is another area where the driver has control. Walking 30 minutes per day will drain stress and make the driver feel better. Some drivers report that their walk done in the morning helps to jump-start their day. Be safety conscious while walking just as you are when you are driving.

- Have a positive outlook and take time to relax. This is another area where the professional driver has control. Many medical authorities think taking time out to relax and having a positive attitude is the most effective way to reduce stress.

GO!

The areas a professional driver needs to focus on to manage stress are diet, walking, having a positive outlook, and creating relaxation times. Since diet and exercise are covered in other areas of this book, having a positive outlook and using the relaxation response will be examined here.

ALCOHOLISM AND DRUG ABUSE

It is not rocket science to understand that drinking, drugs, and driving do not mix. According to the rules and regulations governing professional drivers, those who use alcohol and drugs—particularly while or before they are scheduled to drive—will lose their licenses and their ability to drive professionally **(see Figure 31–7).**

MYTHS AND TRUTHS ABOUT ALCOHOL

Myth	Truth
Alcohol increases mental and physical ability.	Nonsense. It decreases both. A person under the influence of alcohol usually thinks he or she is doing better than they really are.
Some people can drink without being affected.	Not true. Any person who drinks is affected by alcohol. Some persons may be slower to show the effects because of greater body weight or experience.
If you eat a lot before drinking, you will not get drunk.	Not true. Food will slow down the absorption of alcohol, but it will not prevent it.
Coffee and fresh air will help a drinker sober up.	Not true. Only time will help a drinker sober up. Other methods just do not work.
Stick with beer—it is not as strong as wine or whiskey.	False. There is the same amount of alcohol in a 12-ounce glass of 5% beer, 5-ounce glass of 12% wine, or 1 ½-ounce shot of 80-proof liquor.

▶ **Figure 31–7**

Drinking and driving do not mix.

Besides loss of income or a career, the use of alcohol and drugs also costs users the health of their bodies.

More than 100,000 Americans die each year as a result of alcohol abuse, and alcohol is a factor in more than half of the country's traffic accidents, homicides, and suicides **(see Figure 31–8).** Alcohol abuse also plays a role in many social and domestic problems, from job absenteeism and crimes against property to spousal and child abuse. In addition, drinking increases the risk of

▶ **Figure 31–8**

All forms of alcohol have the same effect and can cause you to lose your CDL if you drink and drive.

death from automobile crashes as well as recreational and on-the-job injuries. Both homicides and suicides are more likely to be committed by persons who have been drinking. In purely economic terms, alcohol-related problems cost society approximately $185 billion per year. In human terms, the costs cannot be calculated.

Moderate alcohol use—up to two drinks per day for men and one drink per day for women and older people—is not usually harmful for most adults. (A standard drink is one 12-ounce bottle or can of either beer or wine cooler, one 5-ounce glass of wine, or 1.5 ounces of 80-proof distilled spirits.) Nonetheless, a large number of people get into serious trouble because of their drinking. Currently, nearly 14 million Americans—one in every thirteen adults—abuse alcohol or are an alcoholic **(see Figure 31–9).**

BAC	EFFECTS
.01–.04	Judgment and inhibitions are slightly affected. Drinker is more relaxed, sociable, and talkative. Some risk if drinker drives.
.05–.09	Judgment, vision, and coordination are affected. Behavior changes. Drinker has false sense of security. Serious risk if drinker drives.
.10 and over (legal level of intoxication in most states)	Judgment, vision, and coordination are seriously affected. Drinker is not able to drive safely because of dangerously lessened abilities.

▶ **Figure 31–9**

Effects of alcohol and blood alcohol concentration increases.

Several million more adults engage in risky drinking that could lead to alcohol problems. These patterns include binge drinking and heavy drinking on a regular basis. In addition, 53 percent of men and women in the United States report that one or more of their close relatives have a drinking problem.

The toll of alcohol on physical health can range from mild mood changes to complete loss of coordination, vision, balance, and speech. Any of these can signal a temporary poisoning of the system called "acute alcohol intoxication or drunkenness."

For most people, these effects usually wear off in several hours after the person has stopped drinking; however, a .08 percentage of alcohol in the bloodstream is considered by many law enforcement agencies as evidence of intoxication.

Larger amounts of blood alcohol can impair brain function and eventually cause unconsciousness, and as more than a few newspaper articles have reported (particularly on college campuses), an extreme overdose can be fatal.

Most people fail to realize that continued alcoholism becomes a progressive and potentially fatal disease. **Alcoholism** is characterized by an overwhelming craving for, increased tolerance of, physical dependence upon, and loss of control over drinking alcohol.

Alcohol abuse is defined as a pattern of drinking that results in one or more of the following situations within a 12-month period:

■ Failure to fulfill major work, school, or home responsibilities

■ Drinking in situations that are physically dangerous, such as while driving a car or operating machinery

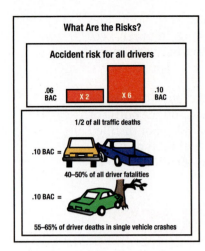

What Are the Risks?

Accident risk for all drivers

.06 BAC   X 2   X 6   .10 BAC

1/2 of all traffic deaths

.10 BAC =

40–50% of all driver fatalities

.10 BAC =

55–65% of driver deaths in single vehicle crashes

▶ **Figure 31–10**

Alcohol risks for drivers.

■ Having recurring alcohol-related legal problems such as being arrested for driving under the influence of alcohol or for physically hurting someone while drunk **(see Figure 31–10).**

■ Continued drinking despite having ongoing relationship problems that are caused or worsened by the drinking

Although alcohol abuse is basically different from alcoholism, many effects of alcohol abuse are also experienced by alcoholics.

The physical dependence on alcohol may or may not be obvious to other people. While some chronic alcoholics get very drunk, others exercise enough control to give the appearance of coping with everyday affairs in a near-normal way. However, alcoholism can lead to a number of physical ailments, including hypoglycemia, brain and heart damage, enlarged blood vessels in the skin, chronic stomach inflammation, and the more damaging inflammation of the pancreas.

Alcoholism often causes impotence in men, damage to the unborn child in a pregnant mother, and an increased risk of cancer of the voice box, esophagus, stomach, pancreas, and upper gastrointestinal tract.

Because alcoholics seldom have adequate diets, they are likely to have nutrtional deficiencies. Heavy drinkers typically have impaired liver function, and at least one in five develops cirrhosis of the liver, a fatal disease.

CAUTION!

The alcoholic's continual craving for alcohol makes halting the use of alcohol extremely difficult. The alcoholic's condition is also complicated by denying that she/he has a serious problem.

Although alcoholism can be treated, a cure is not yet available. In other words, even if an alcoholic has been sober for a long time and has regained good health, he or she remains susceptible to relapse and must continue to avoid all alcoholic beverages. "Cutting down" on drinking does not work. Cutting out alcohol is necessary for a successful recovery.

If your health care provider determines that you are not alcohol dependent but are nonetheless involved in a pattern of alcohol abuse, he or she can help you to:

■ Examine the benefits of stopping an unhealthy drinking pattern

■ Set a drinking goal for yourself (Some people choose to abstain from alcohol; others prefer to limit the amount they drink.)

■ Examine the situations that trigger the unhealthy drinking patterns, and develop new ways of handling those situations to maintain the drinking goal

Some individuals who have stopped drinking after experiencing alcohol-related problems choose to attend AA meetings for information and support, even though they have not been diagnosed as alcoholic.

Drug Abuse

In the year 2000, illegal drug use cost America close to $161 billion, including $110 billion in lost productivity, $12.9 billion in health care costs, and $35 billion in other costs, such as efforts to stem the flow of drugs.

Beyond the raw numbers are other costs to society:

- Spread of infectious diseases such as HIV/AIDS and hepatitis C either through sharing of drug paraphernalia or unprotected sex
- Deaths due to overdose or other complications from drug use
- Effects on unborn children of pregnant drug users
- Other effects such as crime and homelessness

Drug addiction is a complex brain disease. It is characterized by drug craving, seeking, and using drugs that persist even in the face of extremely negative consequences. Drug seeking becomes compulsive, in large part, as a result of the effects of prolonged drug use on brain functioning and, thus, on behavior. For many people, drug addiction becomes chronic, with relapses possible even after long periods of abstinence.

The physical signs of abuse or addiction can vary depending on the person and the drug being abused. For example, someone who abuses marijuana may have a chronic cough or worsening of asthmatic conditions. THC, the chemical in marijuana responsible for producing its effects, is associated with weakening the immune system, which makes the user more vulnerable to infections such as pneumonia. Each drug has short-term and long-term physical effects; stimulants such as cocaine increase heart rate and blood pressure, whereas opioids such as heroin may slow the heart rate and reduce respiration.

Commonly abused drugs include alcohol, cocaine, club drugs, heroine, inhalants, LSD, marijuana, methamphetamine, ecstasy, nicotine, PCP, prescription drugs, and steroids.

Many people view drug abuse and addiction as strictly a social problem. Parents, teens, older adults, and other members of the community tend to characterize people who take drugs as morally weak or as having criminal tendencies. They believe that drug abusers and addicts should be able to stop taking drugs if they are willing to change their behavior.

Addiction begins with drug abuse when an individual makes a conscious choice to use drugs, but addiction is not just "a lot of drug use." Recent scientific research provides overwhelming evidence that not only do drugs interfere with normal brain functioning creating powerful feelings of pleasure, but they also have long-term effects on brain metabolism and activity. At some point, changes occur in the brain that can turn drug abuse into addiction, a chronic relapsing illness. Those addicted to drugs suffer from a compulsive drug craving and usage and cannot quit by themselves. Treatment is necessary to end this compulsive behavior.

A variety of approaches are used in treatment programs to help patients deal with these cravings and possibly avoid drug relapse. The National Institute on Drug Abuse—a part of the National Institutes of Health—has reported that addiction is clearly treatable.

Like people with diabetes or heart disease, people in treatment for drug addiction learn behavioral changes and often take medications as part of their treatment regimen.

Behavioral therapies can include counseling, psychotherapy, support groups, or family therapy. Treatment medications offer help in suppressing the withdrawal syndrome and drug craving and in blocking the effects of drugs. In addition, studies show that treatment for heroin addiction using methadone at an adequate dosage level combined with behavioral therapy reduces death rates and many health problems associated with heroin abuse.

▶ **Figure 31-11**

The Federal Motor Carrier Safety Regulations provide guidelines for establishing programs to help prevent substance abuse-related accidents.

NOTE: Employed drug abusers cost employers about twice as much in medical and worker compensation claims as their drug-free coworkers (information provided by the National Institute on Drug Abuse).

Random Drug Testing

FMCSR 382 outlines the purpose and procedure for carriers to establish programs designed to help prevent accidents and injuries resulting from the misuse of alcohol or use of controlled substances by drivers of commercial motor vehicles **(see Figure 31–11).**

According to this ruling, no driver shall report for duty or remain on duty requiring the performance of safety-sensitive functions while having an alcohol concentration of .04 or greater. No employer having actual knowledge that a driver has an alcohol concentration of .04 or greater shall permit the driver to perform or continue to perform safety-sensitive functions.

No driver shall use alcohol while performing safety-sensitive functions. No employer having actual knowledge that a driver is using alcohol while performing safety-sensitive functions shall permit the driver to perform or continue to perform safety-sensitive functions.

No driver shall perform safety-sensitive functions within 4 hours after using alcohol. No employer having actual knowledge that a driver has used alcohol within 4 hours shall permit a driver to perform or continue to perform safety-sensitive functions.

No driver required to take a postaccident alcohol test shall use alcohol for 8 hours following the accident, or until he/she undergoes a postaccident alcohol test, whichever occurs first.

No driver shall refuse to submit to a postaccident alcohol or controlled substances test , a random alcohol or controlled substances test, a reasonable suspicion alcohol or controlled substances test, or a follow-up alcohol or controlled substances test. No employer shall permit a driver who refuses to submit to such tests to perform or continue to perform safety-sensitive functions.

No driver shall report for duty or remain on duty requiring the performance of safety-sensitive functions when the driver uses any controlled substance, except when the use is pursuant to the instructions of a licensed medical practitioner who has advised the driver that the substance will not adversely affect the driver's ability to safely operate a commercial motor vehicle.

No driver shall report for duty, remain on duty, or perform a safety-sensitive function, if the driver tests positive or has adulterated or substituted a test specimen for controlled substances. No employer having actual knowledge that a driver has tested positive or has adulterated or substituted a test specimen for controlled substances shall permit the driver to perform or continue to perform safety-sensitive functions.

Testing Requirements

Preemployment Testing

Prior to the first time a driver performs safety-sensitive functions for an employer, the driver shall undergo testing for controlled substances as a condition prior to being used. No employer shall allow a driver, who the employer intends to hire or use, to perform safety-sensitive functions unless the employer has received a controlled substances test result indicating a verified negative test result for that driver.

Postaccident Testing

As soon as practicable following an accident involving a commercial motor vehicle operating on a public road in commerce, each employer shall test each of its surviving drivers for alcohol.

Random Alcohol and Drug Testing

Every driver shall submit to random alcohol and controlled substance testing. The selection of drivers for random alcohol and controlled substances testing shall be made by a scientifically valid method, such as a random number table or a computer-based random number generator that is matched with drivers' Social Security numbers, payroll identification numbers, or other comparable identifying numbers. These tests will be unannounced.

Reasonable Suspicion Testing

An employer shall require a driver to submit to an alcohol test when the employer has reasonable suspicion to believe that the driver has violated the FMCSR. The employer's determination that reasonable suspicion exists to require the driver to undergo an alcohol test must be based on specific, contemporaneous, articulable observations concerning the appearance, behavior, speech, or body odors of the driver.

An employer shall require a driver to submit to a controlled substances test when the employer has reasonable suspicion to believe that the driver has violated the prohibitions of the FMCSR concerning controlled substances. The employer's determination that reasonable suspicion exists to require the driver to undergo a controlled substances test must be based on specific, contemporaneous, articulable observations concerning the appearance, behavior, speech, or body odors of the driver. The observations may include indications of the chronic and withdrawal effects of controlled substances.

ANNUAL OR BIANNUAL DOT PHYSICAL

Regulation 391.43 of the Federal Motor Carrier Safety Administration's regulations outlines the medical examination for professional drivers that must be done every 2 years.

The purpose of the history taken by the examiner and the physical examination conducted by the examiner is to detect the presence of any physical and mental defects. A history of certain defects may be cause for rejection or may indicate the need for making certain lab tests or a closer examination.

Defects may be recorded which do not, because of their character or degree, indicate that certification of physical fitness should be denied. However, these defects should be discussed with the driver and he or she advised to take the necessary steps to ensure correction, particularly in the case of neglect could lead to a condition that could affect his/her ability to drive safely.

The following parts should be completed by the medical examiner performing the physical:

Appearance: the examiner is directed to note any overweight, any posture defect, perceptible limp, tremor, or other defects that could be caused by alcoholism, thyroid intoxication, or other illness.

The FMCSR provides that no driver shall use a narcotic or other habit-forming drugs.

Head-eyes: if the applicant wears corrective lenses, these should be used during the visual testing. If the driver habitually wears contact lenses while driving, there should be sufficient evidence to indicate that he or she has good tolerance and is well adapted to their use. The use of contacts should be noted on the record.

Drivers who have lost one eye are not qualified to operate commercial vehicles under existing FMCSRs.

Ears: note any evidence of middle ear disease, symptoms of dizziness, or Meniere's syndrome. When recording hearing, record distance from patient at which a force whispered voice can first be heard. If audiometer is used to test hearing, record decibel loss at 500 Hz, 1,000 Hz, and 2,000 Hz.

Throat: note any evidence of disease, deformities of the throat likely to interfere with eating or breathing or any condition of the larynx that could interfere with the safe operation of a CMV.

Chest and heart: stethoscopic examination is required. Note murmurs and arrythmias and any past or present history of cardiovascular disease of a variety known to be accompanied by syncope, dypsnea, collapse, enlarged heart, or congestive heart failures. EKG is required when stethoscopic findings so indicate.

Blood pressure: record using a blood pressure cuff. If the blood pressure is consistently above 160/90 mm Hg, further tests may be necessary to determine whether driver is qualified to operate CMV.

Lungs: if lung disease is detected, state whether active or arrested. If arrested, you must give your opinion as to how long it has been arrested.

Gastrointestinal system: note any diseases of the esophagus, stomach, small or large intestine.

Abdomen: note any wounds, scars, injuries, or weakness of muscles of abdominal walls sufficient to interfere with normal function. Any hernia should be noted, including how long it has been present and if adequately contained by truss.

Abnormal masses: if present, note location and if tender, whether applicant knows how long they have been present. If diagnosis suggests the condition may interfere with control and safe operation of CMV, more tests should be made before applicant can be certified.

Tenderness: when tenderness is noted, state where it is most pronounced and the suspected cause. If diagnosis suggests condition may interfere with control and safe operation of CMV, more tests should be made.

Genitourinary: a urinalysis is required. Acute infections of the genitourinary tract noted and indications from urinalysis of uncontrolled diabetes, symptomatic albumin urea in the urine, or other findings indicating health conditions that may interfere with control and safe operation of CMV will disqualify applicant from operating a CMV.

Neurological: pupillary reflexes should be reported for both light and accommodation. Knee jerks are to be reported absent only when not obtainable upon reinforcement and as increased when foot is actually lifted from the floor, following a light blow to the patella. Sensory vibratory and positional abnormalities should be noted.

Extremities: care should be taken to examine upper and lower extremities. Record the loss or impairment of a leg, foot, toe, arm, hand, or finger. Note all deformities, the presence of atrophy, semiparalysis, or paralysis or varicose veins. If a hand or finger deformity exists, determine whether sufficient grasp is present to enable driver to secure and maintain a grip on the steering wheel. If a leg deformity exists, determine whether there is sufficient mobility and strength present to enable the driver to operate pedals properly.

Particular attention should be given to, and a record should be made of, any impairment or structural defect which may interfere with the driver's ability to operate a CMV safely.

Spine: note deformities, limitation of motion, or history of pain, injuries, or disease in cervical or lumbar spine region. If findings dictate, x-ray or other examination should be used to diagnose congenital or acquired defects.

Rectogenital studies: diseases or conditions causing discomfort should be evaluated carefully to determine the extent to which the condition might be handicapping while lifting, pulling, or during periods of prolonged driving that might be necessary as part of the driver's duties.

Laboratory and other special findings: urinalysis is required as well as other tests as medical history and physical findings may indicate as necessary. A serological test is required if applicant has a history of luetic infection or findings indicating the possibility of latent syphilis. Other studies deemed necessary by the examiner may also be ordered.

Diabetes: if insulin is necessary to control a diabetic condition, the driver is not qualified to operate a CMV. If mild diabetes is noted and stabilized by use of a hypoglycemic drug and a diet that can be obtained while the driver is on duty, it should not be disqualifying; however, the driver must remain under adequate medical supervision.

The examiner will ask the driver if there is any history of head or spinal injuries, seizures or convulsions or fainting, extensive confinement by illness or injury, heart disease, tuberculosis, syphilis, gonorrhea, diabetes, stomach ulcer, nervous stomach, rheumatic fever, asthma, kidney disease, muscular disease, any other diseases or permanent defect from illness or injury, psychiatric disorder, and any other nervous disorder.

Once the examination and the medical history is complete, the examiner will sign a certificate, stating that the driver has met all requirements and is certified to safely control and operate a CMV.

DRIVER SAFETY

The need for **safety equipment** and safe practices while performing nondriving tasks cannot be stressed enough. Many accidents and injuries happen while the professional driver is working around the vehicle or with cargo. These nondriving accidents can be costly in a number of ways. They can even cause a driver to miss paychecks or be out of work for a long period of time.

> **STOP!**
> YOU CAN NEVER BE TOO SAFE. SAFETY SHOULD BE A HABIT, ON OR OFF DUTY!

Safety Dress and Proper Equipment

Dressing properly for the job requires the arms, legs, and feet to be covered. Shorts, flipflops, and tee-shirts are not enough. Heavy denims offer the best protection. In cold weather, wear warm clothing and dress in layers. In warm weather, wear light colors and protect your skin and eyes from the sun's rays.

Protect your hands. Many professional drivers are the victims of hand injuries each year. Typical hazards include sharp steel bands used to tie boxes and crates, nails, broken glass, pointed wire, and irritating or corrosive chemicals.

Avoid wearing jewelry because it can get snagged and cause serious injuries. Always wear gloves when handling cargo or inspecting your rig. Selecting the right gloves is important. Gloves should have a good gripping surface. Hazardous materials or wastes usually require special gloves. Ordinary gloves may trap corrosives. Rubber or latex gloves do not **(see Figure 31–12).**

Protect your eyes. If you require prescription lenses and wear glasses, make sure they are shatterproof. Wear sunglasses to protect your eyes from glare and make certain they are high quality so they will filter

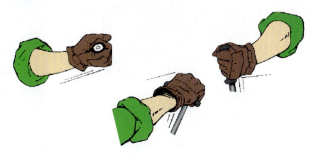

▶ **Figure 31–12**
Protect your hands.

out infrared rays. Protective goggles or a face shield may be needed with some cargo; for example, goggles will protect your eyes when dealing with dust, flour, or cinders.

Protect your feet. Safety shoes protect your feet from falling objects. Steel-toed shoes or work boots are best and are required by some trucking companies. Do not wear sandals or flipflops on the job.

Special Protection Equipment

Circumstances may require special equipment for protection:

- Hard hat protects your head from chains or falling cargo at construction and delivery sites.
- Respirator prevents being overcome by fumes when handling chemical loads and liquefied chemicals. Some chemical loads require a self-contained breather (air supply). Find out what is needed. Take nothing for granted.
- Splash aprons prevent liquids from splashing on your skin and causing burns.
- Goggles or a face shield prevents severe eye damage from flying particles.
- When handling chemicals, do not wear contact lenses. Fumes can become trapped under them and cause blindness.
- Dust masks prevent respiratory problems when handling dry chemicals or similar loads. Some companies require drivers to be clean shaven with no facial hair so dust masks and face shields will fit tightly.
- Shin guards with heavy metal plates protect the front of the leg and tips of the shoes from rolling steel bars.
- Special coveralls protect the body from corrosives and other hazardous materials.
- Gas masks protect from poisonous gases and other hazardous materials **(see Figure 31–13).**

Danger Zones

There are many hazards when you work around a tractor-trailer or with cargo **(see Figure 31–14).** A driver can be seriously injured if he or she falls, trips, or gets bumped. A driver must use care when exiting the cab or trailer. Most accidents in the vehicle and cargo **danger zones** can be avoided if the driver makes safety a habit and is aware of these dangers.

▶ **Figure 31–13**

Special cargos require special protective equipment.

▶ **Figure 31–14**

There are many hazards working around tractor-trailers. Take care getting out of your cab or trailer.

Use great care when you are in the following areas:

- Cab
- Coupling and uncoupling area
- Rear end of the trailer
- Cargo area
- Around the vehicle
- Truck stops
- Loading areas

Cab—the height of the cab presents a great danger to the driver. Handholds or steps can become greasy or otherwise slippery. When getting into or out of the cab, look at the surfaces and always use the three-point stance when getting into the cab. Always enter and exit facing the inside of the cab area. Other injuries that are possible in the cab area include:

- Injury from a falling hood if you are looking at or working on the engine
- Thumb injuries from the steering wheel if the proper grip is not used
- Falls from the cab or missteps when entering or exiting

Coupling and uncoupling area—the coupling/uncoupling area can be dangerous because of grease and oil **(see Figure 31–15).** If you have to stand on the vehicle to connect the air lines or electric cables, be careful of slippery surfaces, such as the fuel tank or battery box, because these are especially dangerous when wet or covered with ice, oil, or grease. If possible, use surfaces that have been treated with a rout material or that have a ribbed grid plate. Without proper precautions, pulling the release latch handle during coupling or uncoupling is dangerous because you may be thrown off balance and injure your back.

Figure 31–15

The coupling and uncoupling area can be dangerous.

Rear of the trailer—open and close the swinging cargo door with great care to avoid injury or damaging the freight. When you open the door, remember the cargo may have moved and be resting against it. If it is, the door will pop open from the force of the cargo as soon as the latch is released. If that happens, you could be knocked down and have cargo fall on your back. Be careful when it is windy. The cargo doors can break your fingers and hands or knock you down.

Some drivers have been hurt closing the door because they stood on the trailer dock, grabbed the strap, and jumped to the ground. If the strap breaks or the driver loses grip, he or she can fall to the ground.

Use common sense when using a power lift or tailgate to load or unload heavy cargo. Keep your hands and feet as well as your cargo away from areas of shearing or pinching. Be sure the cargo is secure and will not fall off.

Other problems include:

- Slippery surfaces
- No handhold
- Nails or splinters from the trailer floor

Always used the proper handholds and steps when available, and wear gloves when possible.

Cargo area—various types of trailers and cargos present different types of hazards. For instance, working with a tanker sometimes requires climbing to the top to hook or unhook dome covers. Flatbeds have no sides so there is a danger of falling off while tying down cargo. Open-top vans mean you have to climb up the side to tie down the tarp cover. Working inside a van is dangerous for many reasons:

- You may have to climb in, over, and around cargo to find a piece that is to be unloaded.
- You can be bruised or cut by nails or broken glass.
- You can bump into the sharp edges of cargo.
- Cargo can fall on you when you are climbing around.

Around the vehicle—there are many aspects that can cause injuries. Damaged rigs can cause injury. Tears in the trailer's skin and unrepaired damage to fenders, bumpers, or hood can cut if you rub against or bump into them.

CAUTION!

When working at night, a flashlight is a must. You cannot couple or uncouple a rig or do a pretrip inspection without light.

Working under a rig is always dangerous. Make sure the vehicle is in the right gear and the auxiliary brake is on. Be sure, too, that the keys are in your pocket so no one can hop into the rig and move it while you are working underneath.

Cleaning the windshield—if possible, use an extension handle on a squeegee when cleaning the windshield of your rig. Then you can stand on the ground rather than having to climb on the tractor. If you must climb to clean it, be careful of slippery surfaces. Keep both feet and one hand securely on the vehicle at all times.

Lifting—because many injuries occur when lifting heavy objects, the following eight steps are recommended (**see Figure 31–16**).

1. Feet should be shoulder's length apart—one alongside and one behind the object.
2. Turn your forward foot in the direction of the movement.
3. Keep back straight.
4. Tuck in your chin.
5. Grip object with your palm and fingers.
6. Tuck in your elbows and arms.
7. Put your body weight directly over your feet.
8. Avoid twisting—a common cause of back injuries.

▶ **Figure 31-16**

Use the correct techniques when lifting anything.

CAUTION!

Always wear gloves—they will help your grip and will protect your fingers while guarding against pinching your hands when lifting.

ROADSIDE EMERGENCIES

When you must stop in an emergency, be careful. How, when, where, and under what conditions you stop your rig make a difference between safety and serious problems.

If you park on the shoulder of the road, there is a great chance you could be rear ended. Pull off the road as far as possible. Look for a truck stop or rest area. Be alert when there is no breakdown lane or adequate area to stop your rig. Rural roads and city streets do not have breakdown lanes.

Check before stopping. Be particularly careful in the dark because you cannot tell what surface is available for stopping your rig. During heavy rain or snow, a road shoulder may be too soft to support the weight of your rig. It could get stuck or could even roll over on a soft surface.

STOP!

Many drivers have been injured while checking a vehicle stuck on an icy or slippery hill. A rig can slide downhill and roll over the driver.

Get out of the cab safely. Many drivers who have stopped properly in an emergency get hurt while leaving the cab. Never jump from the cab. Use the three-point mount and dismount. Do not get out on the driver's side into the path of oncoming traffic. Remember to turn on the four-way emergency flashers. After you safely get out of the cab, put out emergency triangles to warn other drivers of a problem.

More safety reminders—you can never be too careful or too safe. Be especially alert in extreme weather.

- **Cold metal**—in cold weather, always wear gloves. In freezing weather, your hands can stick to cold metal and you can ruin your skin trying to remove them from the cold objects.

- **Hot tires**—you can receive serious burns checking hot tires. Never touch a tire—always place the back of your hand near the tire's surface.

- **Live wires**—if electrical wires land on your rig in a storm, do not move around in the cab or touch anything you are not already in contact with. If you have a cell phone or CB, call for help.

In addition to driving hazards, professional drivers should be aware of the security of themselves, their rigs, and their cargos at all times. Among other hazards are hijacking and robbery. These can usually be avoided best by following company policies. Be aware of high crime areas and know which types of cargos are more likely to be targets. Always keep your cargo doors locked, even when the trailer is empty. It is illegal (per FMCSR) to pick up hitchhikers. Do not carry a gun. It is illegal without a permit and a permit is generally only valid in the state in which it is issued.

CAUTION!

Do not set yourself up for crime. Do not carry a lot of cash. Stay away from dangerous areas. If something looks suspicious, call for help on your cell phone or CB. Stay away from dark, unlighted areas.

CAUSES OF ACCIDENTS

Most over-the-road accidents are preventable. The three main causes of traffic accidents are:

- Vehicle defects
- Road or weather conditions
- Driver error

Of the three, driver error is the main cause of most highway accidents.

Vehicle defects—mechanical defects, poor maintenance, and poor inspections are common causes of accidents. Parts that are falling or are in danger of falling often do so while the rig is on the road. Overloaded or improperly loaded rigs also lead to accidents.

Road or weather conditions—slippery roads, poor visibility, lack of light (especially at dusk or dawn), and headlight glare can lead to accidents. Accidents are also caused by poorly maintained roads and signals. Some examples of this are potholes, stop signs hidden by branches, and exit ramps that are too sharp for heavy-duty vehicles.

Driver error—as a major cause of accidents, driver error can be caused by stress, both on and off duty, lack of good physical condition, and fatigue. By being aware of what is going on around the rig, thinking ahead, and using good judgment, many times a driver can make adjustments before a problem or opportunity for an accident occurs **(see Figure 31–17)**. A driver's errors are usually caused by one or more underlying causes:

- Not being alert or lacking concentration on what is happening around the rig
- Letting your mind wander to other things, such as a cell phone conversation while driving
- Driving while impaired—with impairment caused by illness, alcohol, substance abuse, or prescribed medication that makes you drowsy or interferes with concentration or fatigue **(see Figure 31–18)**

Drive Safely

▶ **Figure 31–17**

Following too closely is one of many invitations to trouble.

▶ **Figure 31–18**

Use of alcohol or drugs can lead to traffic accidents, resulting in injury, death or property damage. It can also lead to arrest, fines, jail sentences, and the end of a driving career.

- Trying to make up for lost time
- Showing off or being too aggressive
- Lack of technical knowledge of the vehicle
- Poor driving skills
- Failing to recognize personal limitations

Driving a tractor-trailer rig is a full-time job, just like piloting an airplane or monitoring delicate equipment. It takes all of your attention at all times. Nobody can drive a problem and a rig at the same time. It is up to you—the professional driver—to park either the problem or the rig **(see Figure 31–19).**

 **Figure 31–19**

Operating a tractor-trailer requires your full attention at all times. If you are distracted by a problem, pull over and park your rig.

DRIVER FATIGUE

Driver fatigue has been a safety issue of special concern to the transportation industry for more than a decade. Many commercial vehicles run at night, and drivers sometimes have irregular and unpredictable work schedules. Most of their mileage is compiled during long trips on interstate and other limited-access highways. Because of the CMV's high annual mileage exposure (often five to ten times that of passenger vehicles) and other factors, commercial drivers' risk of being involved in a fatigue-related crash is far greater than that of noncommercial drivers, even though CMV drivers represent a relatively small proportion of all drivers involved in fatigue-related crashes.

In addition, many other crash causation factors, such as alcohol use, speeding, and other unsafe driving acts, are generally less common in crashes involving commercial drivers. Thus, fatigue is a relatively larger concern for these CMV drivers and their employers.

To learn more about driver fatigue, FMCSA Driver Alertness and Fatigue Research and Technology (R&T) focused on this topic in 1998. The study involved real revenue runs, four different driving schedules, eighty drivers, and more than 200,000 miles of highway driving. The numerous measures included the drivers' alertness and performance during driving and their physiology during off-duty sleep periods.

The study indicated that drivers are not very good at assessing their own levels of alertness. In fact, there was a tendency for drivers to rate themselves as more alert than the performance tests indicated. Researchers in the study reported that drowsiness on the job was highly variable; for example, 36 percent of the drivers were judged to have never experienced drowsiness on the job.

The following quiz was developed to assess what individuals know about sleep, fatigue, and sleep deprivation. See how you do.

This is a quiz to determine how much people know about sleep and sleep debt.

1. Coffee overcomes the effects of drowsiness while driving. (T or F)

2. I can tell when I'm going to go to sleep. (T or F)

3. Rolling down my window or singing along with the radio will keep me awake. (T or F)

4. I'm a safe driver so it doesn't matter if I'm sleepy. (T or F)

5. You can stockpile sleep on the weekends. (T or F)

6. Most adults need at least 7 hours of sleep each night. (T or F)

7. Being sleepy makes you misperceive things. (T or F)

8. Young people need less sleep. (T or F)

9. Wandering, disconnected thoughts are a warning sign of driver fatigue. (T or F)

10. Little green men in the middle of the road may mean the driver is too tired to drive. (T or F)

11. On a long trip, the driver should never take a break but try to arrive at the destination as quickly as possible. (T or F)

12. A microsleep lasts 4 or 5 seconds. (T or F)

Driver fatigue quiz answers

1. FALSE. Stimulants are no substitute for sleep. Drinks containing caffeine, such as coffee or cola, can help you feel more alert, but the effects last only for a short time.

2. FALSE. Sleep is not voluntary. If drowsy, you can fall asleep and never even know it. You cannot tell how long you have been asleep.

3. FALSE. An open window or the radio has no lasting effect on a person's ability to stay awake.

4. FALSE. The only safe driver is an alert driver. Even the safest drivers become confused and use poor judgment when sleepy.

5. FALSE. Sleep is not money. You cannot save it up ahead of time and you cannot borrow it. As with money, however, you can go into debt.

6. TRUE. The average person needs 7 or 8 hours of sleep a night. If you go to bed late and wake up early to an alarm clock, you probably are building a sleep debt.

7. TRUE. One warning sign of a drowsy driver is misjudging surroundings.

8. FALSE. Young people need more sleep than adults. Males under 25 are at the greatest risk of falling asleep. Half of the victims of fatigue-related crashes are under 25.

9. TRUE. If you are driving and your thoughts begin to wander, it is time to pull over and take a break.

10. TRUE. Seeing things that are not there is a good indication it is time to stop driving and take a rest.

11. FALSE. Driving, especially for long distances, reveals a driver's true level of sleepiness. To be safe, drivers should take a break every 3 hours.

12. TRUE. During a microsleep of 4 or 5 seconds, a car can travel 100 yards, plenty of time to cause a serious crash.

Some drivers believe they experience more drowsiness, depending on when they drive, but researchers found no difference in the amount of drowsiness during variously scheduled trip segments. What was apparent was a surprising number of drivers suffered from a condition called **sleep apnea,** a condition caused by automatic cessation of breathing while the driver is asleep. Because this cessation awakens the individual, their sleep is interrupted several times during the night and this often causes fatigue while driving.

Researchers also have reported no significant relationships between driver age and fatigue. There were no consistent differences between older and younger drivers in terms of observed drowsiness, frequency of naps, self-ratings, or driving performance.

Changes in driving performance, measured by increasing variable steering and lane tracking, were found as a result of fatigue. This correlation between drowsiness and degraded driving performance supports the concept of continuous monitoring of driver performance to detect fatigue.

The DOT and other agencies and organizations have performed and continue to sponsor a wide range of research on technological fatigue-detection and prevention countermeasures. Their study also identified methods used by drivers to ward off fatigue, and napping was found to be the most effective, not only in countering fatigue and drowsiness but also in operating performance. Some drivers appeared much better than others at maintaining alertness in the long-haul CMV environment, especially at night.

As a result of the research, it was recommended that drivers need to be educated about how to obtain more sleep, especially if they will drive at night. Further study findings showed that drivers were generally poor judges of their own levels of fatigue/alertness. This finding indicates a need to train drivers to better assess their current levels of fatigue while driving, perhaps by learning to become more conscious of changes in their physical state and subtle changes in their driving performance.

PROGRESS IN FATIGUE MANAGEMENT

There is no quick fix and no single solution to the fatigue problem. Sleep is the principal countermeasure to fatigue. All drivers require adequate sleep. Drivers must also be afforded the opportunity to obtain adequate sleep on their off hours and encouraged to do so.

Bottom line, when drivers feel fatigued, the best, safest and only solution is sleep **(see Figure 31–20)**. Pull off the road in a safe and legal place to sleep. Secure your vehicle and get comfortable. Most company policies require calling the dispatcher to let them know you are taking a break because of fatigue.

There are many myths about how to cure fatigue, but none work. Sleep is the only cure when fatigued or feeling drowsy behind the wheel. Never push your own personal limits. Take a break and nap before trying to continue your trip.

▶ **Figure 31–20**

If you are fatigued, pull off in a safe spot and get some sleep.

In this chapter, you learned about stresses confronting the professional driver as well as suggestions for maintaining balance between work and family. You also learned about the DOT physical and what is expected. You read about the importance of refraining from the use of drugs and alcohol and the penalties for use while on the job. You also learned about the drug testing requirements for professional drivers, including preemployment, random, and postincident testing. Finally, you learned more about driver fatigue, its impact on the transportation industry, and recent findings on sleep deprivation, sleep apnea, and driver fatigue.

KEY TERMS

Alcoholism	Drug testing	Safety awareness
Cold metal	Fatigue management	Safety equipment
Danger zones	High blood pressure	Sleep apnea
Diet and exercise	Job stress	Stress management
DOT physical examination	Lifting safety	Substance abuse
Driver error	Nonslippery surfaces	Vehicle defects
Driver fatigue	Random drug testing	

REVIEW QUESTIONS

1. A survey of 3,000 professional drivers at a trade show indicates that the driver's health habits were _____ the U.S. population.

   a. worse than

   b. better than

   c. about the same as

   d. ranged from about the same as, to better than

2. Regarding keeping the body healthy and running smoothly, which of the following is not recommended?

   a. good eating habits

   b. use of caffeine to stay alert when fatigued and sleepy

   c. regular exercise

   d. good eating habits

3. Which of the following is not one of the four "best" eating habits?

   a. breakfast and snacks from your cooler

   b. no fried foods

   c. salad bar for one meal each day

   d. fast foods one time per day

4. Regarding the effects of physical activity on health and disease, with a minimum of _____ minutes of exercise per day, you can do much to stay healthy and feel good while on the road.

   a. 15

   b. 45

   c. 60

   d. 30

5. Regarding the definition of *job stress*, complete the following statement: "The harmful physical and emotional responses that occur when the requirements of a job do not match the capabilities, resources or needs of the _____."

   a. dispatcher

   b. shipper

   c. worker

   d. owner

6. Regarding an attempt to reduce any family stress caused by a professional driver's job, many family therapists say _____.

   a. the driver should tell the family how hard his or her job is

   b. the family should make a greater effort to communicate

   c. the family should ignore the situation

   d. a and c

7. Because of the time the driver spends alone on the road, the job of reducing stress falls on the shoulders of the _____.

   a. driver

   b. dispatcher

   c. driver's family

   d. owner

8. Which of the following is not recommended by medical experts to help reduce stress?

    a. Have a balance between work and family or personal life.

    c. Consume alcohol beverages.

    b. Walk 30 minutes a day, 5 days per week.

    d. Have a positive outlook and take time to relax.

9. Alcohol is a factor in more than _____ of the country's traffic accidents, homicides, and suicides.

    a. ½

    c. ⅚

    b. ¾

    d. ⅓

10. What percent of men and women in the U.S. report that one or more of their close relatives have a drinking problem?

    a. 25

    c. 53

    b. 35

    d. 73

11. Which of the following is not a characteristic of alcoholism?

    a. an overwhelming craving for alcohol

    c. increased tolerance of alcohol

    b. a gain in body weight

    d. physical dependence upon and loss of control over drinking alcohol

12. Alcoholism can _____.

    a. not be treated

    c. be treated and cured

    b. be treated but there is no cure

    d. not be treated or cured

13. Which of the following is not a characteristic of drug addiction?

    a. drug craving

    c. it is not a treatable disorder

    b. drug seeking becomes compulsive

    d. drug use is persistent even in the face of extremely negative consequences

14. The procedures designed to help prevent accidents and injuries resulting from the misuse of alcohol and controlled substances by drivers of commercial motor vehicles states, in part, that no driver shall perform safety-sensitive functions within _____ hours after using alcohol.

    a. 12

    c. 8

    b. 24

    d. 4

15. According to federal rulings (FMCSR 382), no driver, while having an alcohol concentration of .04 or greater shall _____.

    a. report for duty or remain on duty requiring the performance of safety-sensitive functions

    c. not drive, but may load trailers

    b. not drive over 50 mph

    d. not drive over 35 mph

16. Federal Motor Carrier Safety Administration regulations (391.43) require that professional drivers must have a medical examination every _____.

    a. year

    c. 3 years

    b. 6 months

    d. 2 years

17. Regarding safety dress, which of the following is not proper dress for a professional driver?

    a. heavy denims

    c. warm clothing and layers in cold weather

    b. shorts, flipflops, and tee-shirts

    d. light colors and protection for your skin and eyes in warm weather

18. Regarding exiting the cab of the tractor, which of the following is not a safe practice?

    a. Exit the cab with your back to the cab so you can see oncoming traffic.

    c. Look at the surfaces.

    b. Always use the three-point stance.

    d. Be alert for grease or ice on surfaces during winter.

19. Which of the following is the main cause of most highway accidents?

    a. vehicle defects

    c. road conditions

    b. weather conditions

    d. driver error

20. Which of the following is the principal countermeasure to fatigue?

    a. exercise

    c. diet

    b. sleep

    d. caffeine

32 Hazardous Materials

OBJECTIVES

When you have completed this chapter, you should be able to:

- Understand the various classes of hazardous materials and the rules that apply to handling and hauling HazMat.

- Respond safety if an incident or spill involving hazardous materials occurs.

- Carry out the driver's responsibilities when hauling hazardous materials.

- Protect yourself and others while loading hazardous materials or if an incident involving hazardous materials occurs.

- Understand and correctly handle shipping papers involving hazardous materials.

- Maintain security when hauling a HazMat load.

INTRODUCTION

As of April 2003, new HazMat rules required shippers registered as HazMat shippers with the Department of Transportation and shippers of certain highly hazardous materials to develop and implement written security plans. In addition, all shippers (registered or not) and carriers of **hazardous materials** must ensure that their employee training includes a security component. General awareness HazMat training also is required within 90 days of new hires or at next recurrent training for existing employees.

Effective January 31, 2005, the Transportation Security Administration (TSA) requires background information and fingerprints from applicants trying to obtain HazMat Endorsement on their CDL.

In compliance with the U.S. Patriot Act, the **HazMat Threat Assessment Program** establishes the risk of an individual seeking to transport hazardous materials as being a potential terrorist threat. Under the rules governing the HazMat Threat Assessment Program, an applicant will be disqualified from holding a HazMat Endorsement (HME) if he or she:

- Has been convicted or found guilty by reason of insanity in a military or civilian court for any of the permanently disqualifying crimes

- Has been convicted or found not guilty by reason of insanity in a military or civilian court within the past 7 years for a felony on the list of disqualifying crimes

- Has been released from prison within the past 5 years for any of the disqualifying crimes

Any current HazMat driver who has a disqualifying offense prohibiting the holding of a HazMat Endorsement must immediately surrender the HME to the State Department of Motor Vehicles.

To learn more about the HazMat Threat Assessment Program, visit the Transportation Security Administration's website at www.hazprints.com

THE HAZMAT CDL ENDORSEMENT

If you plan to transport hazardous materials in quantities that require hazardous materials placards on your vehicle, you must read this chapter carefully because you will need to pass the **HazMat Endorsement** for your CDL **(see Figure 32–1).**

The Commercial Motor Vehicle Safety Act of 1986 made it a requirement that all persons with a HazMat Endorsement on their CDL will have to retake the HazMat Endorsement test each time they renew their CDL.

▶ **Figure 32–1**

To transport hazardous materials, you will have to pass the Hazardous Materials Endorsement for the CDL.

> **CAUTION!**
> If you are hauling HazMat and you don't have the Hazardous Materials Endorsement on your CDL, you will be fined and possibly jailed for noncompliance. So, the word is DON'T BREAK THE RULES. These rules are here for your safety and the safety of others.

Focus on Hazardous Materials

Hazardous materials are becoming more and more frequent cargo. Because of the incidents in Oklahoma City and the terrorist attacks of September 11, there have been changes in how Haz-Mat is handled and changes in how it should be hauled. If you regularly haul HazMat cargos, you must know and practice the latest and safest way to handle these kinds of loads.

Some states now ask drivers to retake the HazMat Endorsement every two years. Others do not, so check with your local department of motor vehicles to find out.

HM-181 and 126-F Training Guidelines

HM-126-F requires HazMat training (covering HM-181) be provided for all drivers who transport HazMat. This regulation further requires that a record of the driver's training in HazMat be kept on file while that driver is employed with the company and for 90 days after the driver leaves employment.

The record must have (1) the driver's name, (2) most recent training date, (3) description of the training materials used to meet the requirements of the section, (4) name and address of person providing training, and (5) certification that the employee was trained and tested according to regulations.

HM-126-F also requires that all drivers involved in transporting HazMat be trained by the carrier in (1) general awareness, (2) function specific, (3) safety training, and (4) driver training.

To certify that training and testing was conducted, the trainer must teach the general awareness portion of the training from the Hazardous Material chapter. The Hazardous Material Regulations (HMR) can be found in parts 171–180 of Title 49 of the Code of Federal Regulations (49 CFR 171-180).

HazMat Training and Testing

All drivers involved in transporting hazardous materials, according to regulations, receive training and testing. The employer is required to provide this training and to keep a log (record) of this training as long as that employee works for the company and for 90 days after he or she leaves. Regulations also require that employees receive updated HazMat training every two years.

Drivers who haul flammable cryogenic liquids and certain route-controlled quantities of radioactive material are required to receive training every two years. These drivers must also, at all times, carry a dated certificate showing the date of training.

If you haul quantities requiring placards in cargo tanks and portable tanks, you must also have training in HazMat every two years.

HazMat and Special Routing

Sometimes drivers with loads of HazMat are required to take certain routes, and some states require a special permit before certain HazMat is moved. Make sure you know about any special rules regarding HazMat from your state and in the areas in which you will be driving. You can find out from your company's safety official or the local DMV to make certain you comply with all federal and state HazMat regulations.

Why Special HazMat Regulations Are Needed

Although it is handled and hauled like other cargo, some hazardous materials can injure or kill people if allowed into the environment. So the reason for the regulations is to lessen the danger.

HazMat rules exist for drivers as well as for shippers. These rules—called **containment rules**—are very clear about how a material is packaged, loaded, hauled, and unloaded. These procedures assure HazMat is contained and handled properly and guard against problems of leaking and spillage.

Anyone dealing with HazMat—shippers and carriers—are required to tell drivers and others about the hazardous qualities of the cargo they are carrying. In case of an accident, drivers hauling HazMat must warn motorists and others about the risks in case of an accident or spill.

The Importance of Placarding

If you are hauling a HazMat load, you are required to use **placards** on all four sides of your vehicle, letting other drivers know the risk. As a professional driver, is it also your job to make sure shipping papers are in the proper place and can be easily found when HazMat is being moved **(see Figure 32–2).**

▶ **Figure 32–2**

Placards help fire and emergency personnel identify dangerous cargo in the event of an accident or spill.

CAUTION!
The responsibility for the proper and lawful handling of hazardous materials is shared among the shipper, the carrier, and the driver.

THE SHIPPER'S ROLE IN HAZARDOUS MATERIAL HANDLING

Anyone sending the HazMat from Point A to Point B must understand and use HazMat regulations in order to decide the following for each HazMat product:

- Proper shipping name
- Hazardous class
- Identification numbers
- Correct type of packing
- Correct label and marking on the package
- Correct placard(s)

The shipper is also responsible for packing the HazMat properly, labeling it properly, and identifying it properly on the package. The shipper must use the diamond-shaped labels indicating the HazMat within the package **(see Figure 32–3).** If the label cannot be placed on the package, the shipper must attach a tag or decal, indicating the hazard involved. The shipper must also certify on the shipping papers that the shipment has been prepared according to regulations. (The only exception is when the shipper is a private carrier, transporting its own products.)

▶ **Figure 32–3**

The shipper is also responsible for properly packaging and labeling HazMat packages.

THE CARRIER'S RESPONSIBILITY IN HANDLING HAZARDOUS MATERIALS

The carrier plays a smaller but equally important role. The carrier must:

- Transport the shipment to the proper destination
- Ensure that the shipper has correctly named, labeled, and marked the HazMat shipment
- Report any accident or incident involving HazMat to the proper government agency
- Always park in a safe place **(see Figure 32–4)**

▶ **Figure 32–4**

When carrying hazardous materials, always park in a safe place.

THE DRIVER'S RESPONSIBILITY IN HANDLING HAZARDOUS MATERIALS

The professional driver's first duty in handling a HazMat load is to double-check the shipper and the carrier, making sure the load is properly identified, marked, and labeled if it is hazardous material.

- Verify that shipping papers are properly completed.
- The driver must REFUSE to haul any leaking cartons or shipments.
- The driver must communicate the risk by attaching proper placards to the vehicle.
- The driver must deliver products as safely and quickly as possible, following federal and state HazMat regulations.
- The driver is required to keep all HazMat shipping papers in proper place.
- Verify or apply proper placards.

This is important information, so a review will be helpful. As a driver:

1. You need to be able to recognize you are loading and will be hauling hazardous materials. How do you do that? First look at the shipping papers. Then determine if hazardous materials are being shipped.

2. If HazMat is part or all of the cargo, look to make sure the shipping papers are properly filled out with the shipping name, hazard class, and ID number, listed in that exact order.

3. The driver must also look for highlighted products or the letters X or RQ in the HM column.

4. When accepting a delivery for shipment, the driver must be 100 percent sure the shipping papers are correct, packages are properly labeled, and vehicle is loaded properly and displaying the appropriate placards.

STOP!

If you are not 100% certain that the process has been followed TO THE LETTER, you should contact the terminal dispatcher and make certain . . . AND NEVER ACCEPT DAMAGED OR LEAKING HAZMAT SHIPMENTS.

The driver can protect himself by being knowledgeable of the three main Hazardous Material Lists that shippers, carriers, and drivers are to use. The following lists determine the proper handling of any HazMat load:

- Hazardous Material Table
- List of Hazardous Substances and Reportable Quantities
- List of Marine Pollutants

STOP!

Remember! Before transporting any unfamiliar products or items, look for its name on the three lists. Each list will have the proper shipping name, hazardous class, identification number, and proper labeling required.

If you have questions about the load, call your dispatcher.

Explosive Classes of Hazardous Materials

An **explosive** is any material, substance, or item (such as an explosive device) designed to operate through an explosive action or through a chemical reaction; or, this material may function in a similar manner, even though it was not designed to explode.

Class 1—Explosives

Division 1.1   Explosives that are a mass explosion hazard—if one goes, they all go—which makes for a bad situation. This type is dangerous, to say the least.

Division 1.2   Explosives that are not a mass explosion hazard but are a projection hazard.

Division 1.3   Explosives that have a fire or minor blast or minor projection hazard, or both, but not a mass explosion hazard.

Division 1.4   Explosive devices with a minor explosion hazard (can contain more than 25 grams of detonating material).

Division 1.5   Insensitive explosives that usually carry a mass explosion hazard but chances are remote. Under normal conditions, this type would make the transition of being on fire and then exploding.

Division 1.6   Explosives without mass explosion hazard. This type has only very insensitive detonating substances and demonstrates little chance of accidental fire or explosion.

Class 2—Gases

Division 2.1   Any material that, at 20 degrees C or 68 degrees F and 14.7 psi pressure, will ignite when in a mixture of 13 percent or less by volume with air or has a flammable range with air of at least 12 percent, regardless of the lower limit.

Division 2.2   Nonflammable and nonpoisonous compressed gases. This includes compressed gas, liquefied gas, pressurized cryonic gas, and compressed gas, which is in solution. In other words, any material or mixture which exerts an absolute pressure on the packaging of 40 Asia at 2 degrees C (68 degrees F). Any material in this division does not meet the definition of Division 2.1 or 2.4.

Division 2.3   Known to be poisonous and toxic enough to be a hazard to human health, even if adequate data do not currently exist, but have been toxic to lab animals. Scientifically, this type has an LC value not more than 5,000 PPM.

Class 3—Flammable Liquids

Class 3 has no divisions. A flammable liquid is one with a flash point of not more than 140 degrees F, except for materials meeting the definition of any Class 2 material. This class also includes a mixture having components that have a flash point greater than 141 degrees F or higher—if it makes up at least 99 percent of the total volume of the mix. Or it could also be a distilled spirit of 140 proof or lower, considered to have a flash point of lower than 73 degrees F.

Class 4—Flammable Solids

Division 4.1   Flammable solids of three types: (1) wetted explosives that when dry are explosives of Class 1, except those of compatibility group A; (2) self-reactive materials that may undergo—at normal or elevated temperatures—a decomposition that could make them ignite. (This can happen in high transport temperatures or through contamination.) Any solids that are readily combustible can create fire through friction. This material shows a burning rate faster than 2.2 mm per second); and (3) metal powder, which can ignite and react over the test area in 10 minutes or less.

Division 4.2	These liquid or solid materials, even in small quantities, ignite within 5 minutes of exposure to air under certain test procedures.
Division 4.3	These materials that can become spontaneously flammable on contact with water. This division also contains material that can emit (give off) flammable or toxic gases at a rate of 1 liter per kilogram per hour or greater.

Class 5—Oxidizing Substances

Division 5.1	Because they emit oxygen these materials can cause or increase the combustion of other materials.
Division 5.2	This class includes organic peroxide, a derivative of hydrogen peroxide.

Class 6—Poisons

Division 6.1	This class includes materials that are toxic to humans or so toxic they pose a health hazard during transportation. The class also includes materials presumed hazardous to humans because of laboratory tests; and it includes irritants such as tear gas.
Division 6.2	Infectious substances which may cause disease or death in animals or humans. This includes human or animal excretion, secretion, blood tissue, and tissue components.

Class 7—Radioactive Material

This class includes any radioactive material, which has a specific activity greater than 0.002 microcopies per gram.

Class 8—Corrosive Material

Includes materials that cause destruction/irreversible damage to human skin tissue on contact—either liquid or solid; also has high corrosion rate on steel and/or aluminum.

Class 9—Other Regulated Material

Any material, which presents a hazard during transport but is not included in any of the other classes and is subject to HazMat regulations.

WHAT DRIVERS SHOULD KNOW ABOUT SHIPPING PAPERS

The **shipping paper** is a document describing the HazMat the driver will be carrying **(see Figure 32–5)**. Every item listed on the shipping paper must show the hazard class. Shipping papers include bills of lading and manifests. Having incorrect or incomplete shipping papers is the most frequent violation found during roadside inspections of HazMat loads.

What Should be Shown on the Shipping Paper

Each copy of the shipping paper should have numbered pages with the first page indicating the total number of papers for the shipment. The shipping paper should have the proper description of any hazardous material, and the shipper's certificate—signed by the shipper's representative—must also be included. This certificate verifies that the shipment has been prepared according to all applicable regulations.

TENNESSEE EXPRESS
www.tcwonline.com

615-255-1122
FAX 615-780-3246
22 Stanley Street
Nashville, Tennessee 37210

TNXP 11/1/04

Date: **STRAIGHT BILL OF LADING – SHORT FORM – Original – Not Negotiable**

SHIP FROM

Name: Pace Chemical Co., Inc.
Address: 810 Atlanta Rd.
City/State/Zip: Atlanta, GA 30010

SHIP TO

Name: ABC Warehouse Co., Inc.
Address: 411 Pine St.
City/State/Zip: Nashville, TN 37210

THIRD PARTY FREIGHT CHARGES BILL TO:

Name:
Address:
City/State/Zip:

SPECIAL INSTRUCTIONS:

Bill of Lading Number: 123654
CARRIER NAME: TENNESSEE EXPRESS, INC.
Trader number: 5342
Seal number(s): 2465

SCACL TNXP
Pro number:

Freight Charge Terms:
(freight charges are prepaid unless marked otherwise)
Prepaid X Collect ____ 3rd Party ____

____ (check) Master Bill of Lading: with attached underlying Bills of Lading

COD Amount: $ ____
Fee Terms: Collect: ____ Prepaid: ____
Customer check acceptable: ____

Trailer Loaded:
X By Shipper
____ By Driver

Freight Counted:
X By Shipper
____ By Driver/pallets said to contain
____ By Driver/Places

CARRIER INFORMATION

QTY	TYPE	COMMODITY DESCRIPTION Commodities requirign special or additional care or attention in handling or showing must be marked and packaged as to assure safe transportation with ordinary care.	WEIGHT	H.M. (X)
800	cases	Pesticide, Liquid, Toxic, n.o.s.	40000#	X
		class 6.1, un2902, IL		
		(contains pyrethrin)		
		seal #2465 SL+C		
		In case of emergency, call		
		CHEMTREC (24 hours)		
		1-800-424-9300 TOTAL		

NOTE Liability Limitation for loss or damage in this shipment may be applicable. See 49 U.S.C. § 14706(c)(1)(A) and (B).

RECEIVED, subject to individually determined rates or contracts that have been agreed upon in writing between the carrier and shipper, if applicable, otherwise to the rates, classifications and rules that have been established by the carrier and are available to the shipper, on request, and to the terms and conditions set forth on the reverse side heron as well as to all applicable state and federal regulations.

Shipper Signature — Date 11/01/04
This is to certify that the above named materials are property classified, packaged, marked and labeled, and are in proper condition for transportation according to the applicable regulations of the DOT.

Carrier Signature — Pickup Date 11/01/04
Carrier asknowledges receipt of packages and required placards. Carrier certifies emergency response information was made available and/or carrier has the DOT emergency response guidebook or equivalent documentation in the vehicle.
Property described above is received in apparant good order, except as noted.

Shipper Signature
The carrier shall not make delivery of this shipment without payment of freight and all other lawful charges.

Where the rate is depandant on value, shippers are required to state specifically in writing the agreed or desclared value of the property as follows: "The agreed or declared value of the property is specifically stated by the shipper to be not exceeding ____ per ____

Figure 32-5

Example of HazMat shipping paper.

The Important Uses of Shipping Papers

The shipping paper is used for several purposes, the primary one being to communicate what is being shipped and if there is risk involved. If, for some reason, the driver is injured or taken ill and unable to speak, the shipping paper would inform the authorities if hazardous materials are included in the cargo.

After the attending officials obtain information regarding the shipment, they can take appropriate action to protect the safety of everyone. This makes the shipping paper a vital part of the shipment and emphasizes why it should be filled out correctly. Lives may be at stake and fast action may be required—there is no time to decipher what the cargo holds.

GO!

There are exceptions about how shipping papers are handled. A private shipper carrying its own freight does not need to sign a shipper's certificate.

MIXED SHIPMENTS OF NON-HAZMAT AND HAZMAT CARGOS

In the case where you are hauling nonhazardous and hazardous materials, and the shipping papers show a mix of hazardous materials and nonhazardous materials, those items that are hazardous must be marked by:

- Describing the item first
- Highlighting or printing in a different color
- Placing an X before the shipping name in the column marked HM
- Using the letters RQ if the shipment is a reportable quantity

CAUTION!

The description of the hazardous product must include (1) the proper shipping name, (2) the HazMat class or division, and (3) the ID number in that order. Do not use abbreviations. The only abbreviation permitted is for the packaging type and the unit of measure which can appear on the shipping paper before or after the description.

If the shipment is hazardous waste, the word *waste* must appear before the name of the material being shipped.

Also included must be the total quality and unit of measure (e.g., drums, cylinders, cartons). If the HazMat shipment is a reportable quantity, the letters RQ must be on the shipping paper under HM.

WHEN HAZMAT IS INVOLVED IN AN ACCIDENT

It may be necessary for law enforcement officials to obtain information quickly, so the following also applies to the shipping papers:

- The shipping papers must be tagged or tabbed and placed on top of all other shipping papers. This is the responsibility of the carrier and the driver.
- When the driver is out of the truck, shipping papers must be placed on the driver's seat or in a pouch in the driver's door.
- While driving, the driver must place shipping papers in a pouch in the driver's door or in clear view of the driver when the seat belt is being used.

STOP!

Once the HazMat has been unloaded, it is the driver's responsibility to remove the placards!

HAZMAT EMERGENCIES

The *Emergency Response Guidebook* (*ERG*, for short) is used by firefighters, police officers, and industry safety personnel and others in the event of an emergency involving HazMat. This book is available from the DOT.

When an emergency occurs, police and fire personnel must determine what type of HazMat is involved; and this is accomplished by looking at shipping papers, looking at placards, and getting information from the driver. In some accidents, however, there may be no time to locate shipping papers or talk to the driver. The only thing left is to look at the placards.

Once the type of HazMat is determined, personnel can then take steps to protect life and property, which is one more reason why the right placards are used, the shipping papers should always be accurate, and the driver must be aware of what is being hauled.

Driver's Responsibility in Case of an Accident Involving HazMat

The following is your responsibility at the scene of an accident involving HazMat:

- Warn people of danger and keep them away.
- If you can do so safely, contain the spill.
- Contact the appropriate emergency response personnel (police, fire, or other emergency responders) and tell them what has happened.

Be prepared to provide the following information to emergency responders:

- HazMat product's shipping name, hazard class, and ID number
- Extent of the spill
- Location
- When accident/incident happened
- Phone number where you can be reached

Let them hang up first; make sure they have all the information they need. Then contact your dispatcher and follow your instructions.

If a Fire Occurs

Never attempt to fight a HazMat fire unless you have specific training on how to do it. The power unit of a vehicle with placards must have a fire extinguisher with a UL rating of at least 10 BC.

If a Leak or Spill Occurs

First of all, do not touch the material, because certain HazMat can kill you, just by touching it or breathing its fumes. Determine what the HazMat is by looking at shipping papers but do not go near the spill or allow anyone else to go near it. Contact the local authorities and your dispatcher as quickly as possible.

STOP!

If a leak or spill occurs, do not attempt to move the vehicle unless you have to because of safety concerns.

If you are driving and notice something leaking from the vehicle, pull as far off the road as you can, get the shipping papers, and get away from the vehicle. Then send someone for help. Stay away from the truck, but keep it in sight so you can keep others away.

Do not drive to a phone if you spot a leak.

When sending someone for help, write down your location, description of emergency, your name, your carrier's name and phone number, and the shipping name, hazard class, and ID number.

Never smoke or allow smoking around the vehicle.

If you see leakage or damage to a HazMat package while unloading, get away from the vehicle as quickly as possible and contact your dispatcher immediately. Do not touch or inhale the material!

If certain types of hazardous materials leak or spill, the Department of Transportation and the Environmental Protection Agency must be notified. The Hazardous Substances and Reportable Quantities List will tell you if the cargo is a reportable quantity. The product and the amount spilled decides whether it is reportable.

An asterisk (*) next to the name indicates the product also appears on the **hazardous materials table.**

If there is any size spill of any HazMat, the driver must report the spill to the carrier.

The carrier reports it to the National Response Center, and they have the ability to contact the proper law enforcement agency and the proper containment or cleanup personnel.

The carrier is required to call the National Response Center (800-424-8802) if an incident of leakage or spill occurs and:

- Someone is killed
- Someone is injured and requires hospitalization
- Estimated property damage exceeds $50,000
- One or more major roadways is closed for 1 hour or more
- Fire, breakage, spillage, or suspected radioactive contamination occurs
- Fire, breakage, spillage, or suspected contamination of etiologic agents occurs

When calling the NRC, give the following information:

- Name
- Name/address of carrier
- Phone number where carrier can be reached

- Date, time, and location of event

- Extent of injuries, if any

- Class, name, and quantity of hazardous materials involved

- Kind of incident and nature of hazardous material involved

- If a reportable quantity of hazardous substance is involved, name of the shipper and quantity of the hazardous material discharged

CHEMTREC is the acronym for Chemical Transportation Emergency Center, located in Washington, D.C. It has a 24-hour toll-free line and has evolved to provide emergency personnel with technical information and expertise about the physical properties of hazardous products. If you call CHEMTREC at 800-424-9300 or the National Response Center at 800-424-8802, they work closely together and by calling either one, they will notify the other about the problem.

In addition to calling the NRC or CHEMTREC, drivers are responsible to help carriers make a detailed written report. The driver is particularly valuable in completing these reports so it is a good idea for the driver to write out a report a soon as possible, detailing what took place.

HOW TO USE THE HAZARDOUS MATERIALS TABLE

Column 1 has symbols with a specific meaning. These include:

+   Designated proper shipping name and hazardous class must always be shown, even if product does not match hazard class definition.

D   Proper shipping name is appropriate for describing materials for domestic transportation but may not be proper for international transport.

A   Subject to the regulations only when transported by air, unless materials are hazardous substances and hazardous waste.

W   Subject to regulations only when transported by water unless material is a hazardous substance, hazardous waste, or marine pollutant.

Column 2 shows the name of regulated materials in alphabetical order. On this table, the proper shipping names are always shown in regular type. The names shown in italics are not proper shipping names and can only be used with the proper shipping name.

Column 3 is the hazard class or division, and may have the word *forbidden*. When you see *forbidden*, never transport this material. The hazard class for the material is the indicator of what placards to use. To choose the proper placard, you must have three pieces of information:

1. Hazard class for the cargo

2. Amount being shipped

3. Amount of all HazMat in all classes on the vehicle

If you have the words **inhalation hazard** on the shipping papers, you must use a poison placard in addition to the others that are required.

Column 4 shows the **identification number** for each proper shipping name. These ID numbers are preceded by the initials UN or NA. The letters NA are only used in shipments between the United States and Canada. The ID number must also appear on the shipping paper, the package, and the cargo tanks and all other bulk packages.

Column 5 identifies the packing group, which is assigned to the material.

Column 6 shows the hazard label, which shippers must put on packages of hazardous materials. Some products require more than one label. If the word *none* appears, no label is required.

Column 7 lists additional provisions for this material. If you see a column 7 entry, refer to federal regulations for specific information.

Column 8, a three-part column, shows section and numbers covering packaging for HazMat.

Columns 9 and 10 do not apply to highway transport.

THE HAZARDOUS WASTE MANIFEST

Any cargo containing **hazardous waste** must be accompanied by a hazardous waste manifest, signed by the driver. This manifest is the responsibility of the shipper; and the driver will treat the hazardous waste manifest as any other shipping paper.

The carrier who accepts the hazardous waste cargo must make certain that the hazardous waste manifest is properly completed and a shipment labeled as hazardous waste may only be delivered to another registered carrier or to a facility authorized to receive and handle hazardous waste.

The carrier must maintain a copy of the hazardous waste manifest for 3 years following transport. Once delivered to the authorized hazardous waste facility, the facility's operator must sign for the shipment.

When to Use the "Dangerous" Placard

If you have a load requiring a flammable placard and then pick up 1,000 pounds of combustible material, instead of using two separate placards, such as "flammable" or "combustible," you will use the **"dangerous" placard.**

The two exceptions are (1) if you have loaded 5,000 pounds of hazardous material at one location, you must use the placard for that material; and (2) if the words "Inhalation Hazard" are on the shipping papers, you must use the material's specific placard *and* a "Poison" placard.

Blasting agents (1.6), Oxidizer (5.1), and dangerous placards are not required if the vehicle contains Class 1 explosives and you are using Division 1.1, 1.2, or 1.3 placards.

When the vehicle displays a Division 2.1 Flammable Gas or an Oxygen placard, you do not need to display a Non-Flammable Gas placard if you pick up that material and add it to your load.

STOP!

Displaying the wrong placard is as wrong as not displaying any placard.

Placards are used to communicate with and inform others. Incorrect information is just as harmful as no information and may place rescue personnel in danger.

OTHER INFORMATION NEEDED WHEN HAULING HAZMAT

Precautions during refueling—always turn off engine before refueling and someone must be in control of the fuel at the nozzle **(see Figure 32–6).**

Where to keep shipping papers enroute—they must always be in the pouch on the driver's door or where driver can reach them while seat belt is buckled—and in clear view. Shipping papers for loads containing HazMat should be tagged and on top of all other papers.

Where to keep papers when you leave the rig—they should be placed on the driver's seat or in a pouch inside the driver's side door.

Special inspections for rigs hauling HazMat—other than the pretrip and enroute checks, stops are required every 2 hours or every 100 miles to check tires and remove any tires that are overheated. If you have a flat or a tire noticeably leaking, only drive as far as you need to get it fixed.

Directions for hauling chlorine—you should have an approved gas mask in the vehicle and must also know how to use an emergency kit for controlling leaks in dome lid plate fittings on the tank.

What to do when approaching a railroad crossing—no matter what, if you are in a placarded vehicle or carrying any amount of chlorine or have cargo tanks used to transport HazMat (loaded or empty), you must stop no closer than 15 feet and no further away than 50 feet. Do not shift gears while crossing. Turn on your four-way flashers when stopping at a railroad crossing **(see Figure 32–7).**

HazMat route restrictions—some areas of the country require permits and special routing for carriers transporting certain materials. As the driver, you must know about these special requirements, so check with your company and always check routes before beginning a trip—you want to be permitted to travel on the roads you will be driving. Fines are costly against both the company and you as the driver.

▶ **Figure 32–6**
Always turn off the engine before refueling.

▶ **Figure 32–7**
When transporting hazardous materials, you must stop no closer than 15 feet and no further than 50 feet at a railroad crossing.

STOP!

Anytime you are hauling explosives (1.1, 1.2, or 1.3), you are required to follow a written route plan. The same is true when hauling radioactive materials: The carrier is responsible for telling the driver that the trailer is loaded with radioactive material.

SECURITY MEASURES FOR HAZMAT LOADS

The FMCSA encourages the following suggestions to prevent any tampering or any security breaches involving loads of hazardous materials:

- Use tamper-resistant or tamper-evident seals and locks on cargo.
- Identify preferred and alternated routing, including acceptable deviations. Make sure routing complies with local routing restrictions.
- If possible, alternate routes to frequent destinations.
- Minimize exposure in downtown or heavily populated areas and expedite the shipment to the final destination.
- Minimize stops en route; if you must stop, select locations with adequate lighting on well-traveled roads and avoid high crime or dangerous areas.
- Use an engine kill switch.
- Use tractor and trailer brake locking devices.
- If trailer is dropped, use a fifth-wheel lock when possible.
- Perform a quick walkaround to check your vehicle for foreign objects after all stops.
- Train drivers on how to avoid hijackings or theft of property. Keep vehicles locked when parked and avoid conversation about route, cargo, and destinations on open channels or with strangers.

TSA HAZMAT CONTACT INFORMATION

TSA HAZMAT Office—(571) 227-3200

TSA Media Contact—(571) 227-2829

TSA Contact Center—(866) 289-9673

Federal Motor Carrier Safety Administration (FMCSA) Media Contact—(202) 366-8810

SUMMARY

In this chapter, you have learned about the various classes of hazardous materials and your responsibilities as a professional driver when loading and hauling hazardous materials cargo. You have also reviewed your responsibilities of checking and then carrying shipping papers when hauling a HazMat load, as well as what to do when a spill or incident involving hazardous

OTHER INFORMATION NEEDED WHEN HAULING HAZMAT

Precautions during refueling—always turn off engine before refueling and someone must be in control of the fuel at the nozzle **(see Figure 32–6).**

Where to keep shipping papers enroute—they must always be in the pouch on the driver's door or where driver can reach them while seat belt is buckled—and in clear view. Shipping papers for loads containing HazMat should be tagged and on top of all other papers.

Where to keep papers when you leave the rig—they should be placed on the driver's seat or in a pouch inside the driver's side door.

Special inspections for rigs hauling HazMat—other than the pretrip and enroute checks, stops are required every 2 hours or every 100 miles to check tires and remove any tires that are overheated. If you have a flat or a tire noticeably leaking, only drive as far as you need to get it fixed.

Directions for hauling chlorine—you should have an approved gas mask in the vehicle and must also know how to use an emergency kit for controlling leaks in dome lid plate fittings on the tank.

What to do when approaching a railroad crossing—no matter what, if you are in a placarded vehicle or carrying any amount of chlorine or have cargo tanks used to transport HazMat (loaded or empty), you must stop no closer than 15 feet and no further away than 50 feet. Do not shift gears while crossing. Turn on your four-way flashers when stopping at a railroad crossing **(see Figure 32–7).**

HazMat route restrictions—some areas of the country require permits and special routing for carriers transporting certain materials. As the driver, you must know about these special requirements, so check with your company and always check routes before beginning a trip—you want to be permitted to travel on the roads you will be driving. Fines are costly against both the company and you as the driver.

▶ **Figure 32-6**
Always turn off the engine before refueling.

▶ **Figure 32-7**
When transporting hazardous materials, you must stop no closer than 15 feet and no further than 50 feet at a railroad crossing.

STOP!
Anytime you are hauling explosives (1.1, 1.2, or 1.3), you are required to follow a written route plan. The same is true when hauling radioactive materials: The carrier is responsible for telling the driver that the trailer is loaded with radioactive material.

SECURITY MEASURES FOR HAZMAT LOADS

The FMCSA encourages the following suggestions to prevent any tampering or any security breaches involving loads of hazardous materials:

- Use tamper-resistant or tamper-evident seals and locks on cargo.
- Identify preferred and alternated routing, including acceptable deviations. Make sure routing complies with local routing restrictions.
- If possible, alternate routes to frequent destinations.
- Minimize exposure in downtown or heavily populated areas and expedite the shipment to the final destination.
- Minimize stops en route; if you must stop, select locations with adequate lighting on well-traveled roads and avoid high crime or dangerous areas.
- Use an engine kill switch.
- Use tractor and trailer brake locking devices.
- If trailer is dropped, use a fifth-wheel lock when possible.
- Perform a quick walkaround to check your vehicle for foreign objects after all stops.
- Train drivers on how to avoid hijackings or theft of property. Keep vehicles locked when parked and avoid conversation about route, cargo, and destinations on open channels or with strangers.

TSA HAZMAT CONTACT INFORMATION

TSA HAZMAT Office—(571) 227-3200

TSA Media Contact—(571) 227-2829

TSA Contact Center—(866) 289-9673

Federal Motor Carrier Safety Administration (FMCSA) Media Contact—(202) 366-8810

SUMMARY

In this chapter, you have learned about the various classes of hazardous materials and your responsibilities as a professional driver when loading and hauling hazardous materials cargo. You have also reviewed your responsibilities of checking and then carrying shipping papers when hauling a HazMat load, as well as what to do when a spill or incident involving hazardous materials occurs. You have also learned the security measures necessary when loading hazardous materials and what you should do to maintain the safety of your cargo, your rig, and those around you when handling hazardous material loads.

KEY TERMS

CHEMTREC
Combustible
Containment rules
"Dangerous" placard
Explosive
Flammable
Hazard class

Hazardous materials
Hazardous materials table
HazMat Endorsement
HazMat Threat Assessment
    Program
Hazardous waste
Identification number

Inhalation hazards
Placards
Radioactive materials
Route restrictions
Shipping paper
Special HazMat inspection
Special routing

REVIEW QUESTIONS

1. As of January 31, 2005, the Transportation Security Administration (TSA) required _____ from applicants trying to obtain HazMat Endorsement on their CDL.

    a. a low center of gravity

    b. background information and fingerprints

    c. less fuel emissions

    d. greater braking efficiency on all rigs

2. According to the Commercial Motor Vehicle Safety Act of 1986, persons with a HazMat Endorsement on their CDL have to retake the HazMat Endorsement test _____.

    a. each time they renew their CDL

    b. every year

    c. only one time

    d. every 10 years

3. HM-126-F requires that carriers train HazMat drivers in _____.

    a. general awareness

    b. a, c, and d

    c. safety

    d. function specific

4. If you are hauling a HazMat load, you are required to use placards on _____.

    a. the front only

    b. the back only

    c. all four sides of the vehicle

    d. the sides only

5. Regarding the shipper's role in hazardous material handling, which of the following is not required of the shipper?

    a. Pack products properly.

    b. Label products properly.

    c. Certify on the shipping papers that the shipment has been prepared according to regulations.

    d. Notify the receiver of the goods shipping date.

6. Regarding the responsibility in handling hazardous materials, which of the following is not the carrier's responsibility?

    a. Transport the shipment to the proper destination.

    b. Ensure the shipper has correctly named, labeled, and marked the HazMat shipment.

    c. Report accident or incident involving HazMat to proper government agency.

    d. Notify the driver about HazMat shipment.

7. Which of the following is not the driver's responsibility regarding handling hazardous materials?

   a. Must haul any leaking cartons labeled *hazardous* if the dispatcher tells the driver to do so.

   b. Must communicate the risk by attaching proper placards to the vehicle.

   c. Must deliver products as safely and quickly as possible while obeying federal and state HazMat regulations.

   d. Required to keep all HazMat shipping papers in the proper place.

8. Regarding the driver's responsibility concerning loading and handling of hazardous materials, which of the following is not a correct action?

   a. Never open any packages during transport.

   b. No overhangs or tailgate loads for explosives.

   c. Do everything possible to protect the public.

   d. Smoking is permitted unless loading explosives.

9. Regarding performance-oriented packaging (POP), which of the following is not a required performance standard?

   a. no release of HazMat products during transport

   b. biodegradable upon discard

   c. no reduced characteristics during use

   d. the package contain nothing that could ruin the packaging

10. The hazard class of materials indicates _____.

    a. which items should be placed near the top of the load

    b. the required stopping distance for vehicles transporting HazMat

    c. the degree of risk associated with that material

    d. the required center of gravity for HazMat loads

11. Regarding the hazard class numbering system, the first number indicates _____.

    a. the division, such as flammable gas, flammable liquid, flammable solids

    b. the required stopping distance for rigs transporting HazMat

    c. the class of the hazardous material (explosive, gases, flammable solids, etc.)

    d. which item can be mixed in a shipment

12. Regarding the shipping papers for hazardous materials, which of the following is not included?

    a. the route the driver must take

    b. the proper description of the hazardous material

    c. the signature by the shipper's representative

    d. verification that the shipment has been prepared according to all regulations applicable

13. In case of an accident involving HazMat, which of the following is not the driver's responsibility?

    a. Warn people of danger and keep them away.

    b. If it can be done safely, contain the spill.

    c. Tell authorities the destination of the goods shipped.

    d. Contact the appropriate emergency response personnel.

14. If you are hauling HazMat merchandise and you notice something leaking from the vehicle, which of the following should you not do?

    a. Pull as far off the road as you can.

    b. Get the shipping papers and get away from the vehicle.

    c. Keep others away from the vehicle.

    d. Drive to the nearest fire station.

15. Regarding security measures for HazMat loads, which of the following is not recommended by FMCSA?

    a. Using tamper-resistant or tamper-evident seals and locks on cargo.

    b. Locking the doors of the tractor and leaving the engine running at a truck stop while you are away from the vehicle.

    c. Using an engine kill switch.

    d. Using tractor and trailer locking devices.

33 Transportation Technology

OBJECTIVES

When you have completed this chapter, you should be able to:

- Be more familiar with technology that is being used in today's trucking transportation industry.

- Be aware of the applications of some of this technology and its benefits.

- Make decisions regarding your personal purchase of additional technology to assist you in your goal of becoming a professional truck driver.

INTRODUCTION

Figure 33–1

Professional drivers have been using information technology for decades.

Although many outside the industry may not realize it, the trucking transportation industry in general, and professional drivers in particular, have been using information technology for decades **(see Figure 33–1).** Today, however, as technology has become generalized to the public at large, many more understand the value of computer applications, communications, wireless technology, and global positioning systems to streamline performance, record keeping, and the daily transactions required in transportation.

In many companies, when new drivers come on board, a portion of their probationary training is dedicated to learning the operation and applying high technology to their daily routines—from collections to the transmission of data about a load. For the owner-operator, the Internet has become more valuable, not only from a weather and road-conditions information perspective but also because more independents are relying on the Internet to identify their next load.

The human resources and recruiting function of many industry members also has been translated to computers and the Internet. Every year, scores of drivers are introduced to job prospects through Internet sites, such as driver.com, hiringtruckdrivers.com, classadrivers.com, newdrivingjobs.com, and bubbajunk.com **(see Figure 33–2).**

Figure 33–2

The Internet plays a big role in the recruiting process of professional drivers.

Without a doubt, today's new professional driver must be as savvy about technology as most white-collar workers, and lack of this knowledge may slow down career progress. Computer literacy is quickly becoming as important as driving the rig itself.

The purpose of this chapter is to provide an overview of today's transportation technology and its application to the day-to-day routine of the professional driver.

ABOUT QUALCOMM®

Many of the major carriers equip their fleets with **QUALCOMM** equipment. The following information will give you some insight into this company and its services.

QUALCOMM's first product was OmniTRACS®, a satellite-based data messaging service used by the trucking industry to manage fleets. This product was introduced in 1988 and is now the largest satellite-based commercial mobile system in the transportation industry.

This product was followed by the Code Division Multiple Access (CDMA) technology for wireless and data products, and in 1995, CDMA was introduced commercially, quickly becoming one of the world's fastest growing wireless technologies. In 1999, CDMA was selected by the International Telecommunications Union as the primary technology for third-generation (3G) wireless systems.

Since its beginnings, QUALCOMM has grown by developing and applying advanced technologies for wireless telecommunications products and services. A main focus has been the transportation industry where QUALCOMM products have increased efficiency and lowered costs.

As an example, QUALCOMM products and services enable drivers to communicate with dispatchers and fleet managers. These same products monitor vehicle locations and help drivers protect their cargo and provide superior customer service while they are on the road. In addition, QUALCOMM develops solutions that not only provide value and help improve operations, but also help secure and protect drivers and cargo.

ONBOARD RECORDERS

On September 30, 1988, the Federal Highway Administration published a final rule (53 FR 38666) to allow motor carriers, at their option, to use certain automatic **onboard recording (OBR)** devices to record their drivers' records of duty status in lieu of the required handwritten records of duty status. This provision is now codified at 49 CFR 395.15. Many motor carriers employing that technology found that their compliance with the hours-of-service regulations improved.

Part 395.15 reads, in part, as follows: "Authority to use automatic onboard recording device—A motor carrier may require a driver to use an automatic onboard recording device to record the driver's hours of service."

Information required with use of OBR includes a driver's hours of service chart, electronic display, or printout showing the time and sequence of duty status changes including the driver's starting time at the beginning of each day. Along with using the OBR to record hours of service, the driver shall have in his or her possession records of duty status for the previous 7 consecutive days available for inspection while on duty. These records shall consist of information stored in and retrievable from the automatic onboard recording device, handwritten records, computer-generated records, or any combination thereof.

However, the FMCSA also realizes new technologies are emerging and the narrowly crafted onboard recorder provision is becoming obsolete.

Before considering changes to the rule, the FHWA believes it would be prudent to demonstrate the effectiveness of more recent technology for ensuring compliance with the hours-of-service regulations. The FHWA also hopes to demonstrate the safety and economic advantages to the motor carrier industry when the technology is used to reduce the prescriptive paperwork and record-keeping requirements of the hours-of-service regulations (49 CFR, part 395).

The FHWA intends to carefully evaluate results of the pilot demonstration project. Should the results prove to be positive and the safety potential of the involved technologies confirmed, the agency will consider proposing revisions to the FMCSR.

GLOBAL POSITIONING SYSTEMS

The FHWA also believes **global positioning system (GPS)** technology and many of the complementary safety management computer systems currently being used by the motor carrier industry provide at least the same degree of monitoring accuracy as the OBRs allowed by the Federal Motor Carrier Safety Regulations, 49 CFR 395.15.

Accordingly, the FHWA announced a voluntary program under which a motor carrier with GPS technology and related safety management computer systems could enter into an agreement with the FHWA to use such systems in a pilot demonstration project to record and monitor drivers' hours of service in lieu of complying with the handwritten records of duty status requirement of the FMCSR, 49 CFR 395.8 **(see Figure 33–3).**

▶ **Figure 33–3**

Global Positioning System (GPS).

Consistent with current initiatives in reinventing government and regulatory reform, the project is intended to demonstrate whether the motor carrier industry can use the technology to improve compliance with the hours-of-service requirements in a manner which promotes safety and operational efficiency while reducing paperwork requirements.

ELECTRONIC PAYMENT

Comdata revolutionized the trucking industry in 1969 with the Comchek® paper draft, the first specialized form of payment to transfer money and information over the road safely, securely, accurately. This paper draft has grown into an impressive group of funds distribution services, all based on providing a one-card solution for fuel and purchasing.

One such service is a card honored at truck stops and service centers in North America. Developed initially for fleets to authorize and track fuel, purchase, and repair costs, this card today is the centerpiece to an unmatched group of services that enable transportation businesses and fleets to operate more profitably.

FUEL MANAGEMENT AND REPORTING

Several companies now offer a discount fuel network that includes discounts and data monitoring, providing reports that help pinpoint problems and track fuel usage.

COMMUNICATION
Satellite Communication

Volvo Trucks has introduced Volvo Link™, its unique satellite-based communications system, integrated into each truck and available for models 2000 and newer.

This package allows immediate access to current truck information and improves the efficiency of operations as well as the productivity of the driver through instant messaging capabilities between the driver and the dispatcher and 24/7 access to each truck in the fleet.

Volvo Link offers reporting to include mileage, fuel utilization, engine idle time, and engine running time. Each feature is easily customizable to every user's needs **(see Figure 33–4).**

▶ **Figure 33-4**

Volvo Link.

Onboard Laptop Computers

Many companies now provide **laptop computers** as a means of communication and business management for professional drivers. Independents often use at least one laptop onboard to schedule loads, plan trips, get up-to-the-minute reports on road conditions, send and receive email, and communicate with consignors and consignees regarding pickups and deliveries.

Much of today's drivers' paperwork is done via computer and many truck stops now have wireless access and internet ports so that drivers can do business during or after their meals.

A good laptop—one that is sturdy and easy to use—can save a driver valuable time and, at the same time, keep him or her connected with family members and friends while on the road **(see Figure 33–5).**

▶ **Figure 33-5**

A laptop can save a driver valuable time and enable him or her to stay connected with family and friends.

Beginning in 2000, all Class 3–8 Freightliner, Sterling, American LaFrance, and Thomas Built Buses, manufactured by the Freightliner Corp., will include the Truck Productivity Computer, a feature that combines an onboard computer with an AM/FM stereo and weather band receiver, compact disc player, vehicle information display, GPS, and interfaces to wireless systems—all fitting into the standard radio slot in a truck dashboard.

Freightliner also sells the Truck Productivity Computer device on the aftermarket for all truck makes. "This device is designed to deliver the mobile computing power necessary to succeed in the highly competitive North American transportation industry," said James L. Hebe, Freightliner's president and CEO.

Featuring a Hitachi SH4 166 MHz processor, the onboard computer is capable of performing 300 million instructions per second (MIPS), equivalent in power to many desktop computers. To interface with numerous computer peripherals, the Truck Productivity Computer has two universal serial bus (USB) connections for such devices as magnetic card readers, bar code scanners, printers, flat bed scanners, cellular telephones, digital cameras, and game controllers. The driver also can plug a keyboard into the USB and a second full VGA monitor for enhanced display and alphanumeric input.

The Truck Productivity Computer also can provide the driver with an interface for wireless communications systems such as those that transmit messages and data via satellite or cellular networks. Among the tasks the Truck Productivity Computer can accomplish when combined with the appropriate hardware and operating software are:

- Send and receive email and access the Internet
- Display pickup and delivery information and show turn-by-turn directions to locations
- Send confirmation messages and transmit location information to dispatch departments
- Download vehicle information using magnetic cards
- Transmit imaged documents
- Download and transmit information from bar code scanners or handheld computers

Besides functioning as the platform for various mobile computing and communications applications, the Truck Productivity Computer also serves as the gateway to information about the vehicle. Among other functions, the device will let the driver check miles driven for a whole trip or current leg, monitor fuel economy while driving, and record current oil pressure, water pressure, and other vital signs.

The device also features an integrated GPS unit for determining the precise location of the truck. GPS data can be fed into vehicle tracking software to communicate truck location information to dispatch. A separate GPS antenna is required.

Freightliner also planned to offer voice recognition capability that lets the driver "talk" to the computer. The device also has the capability to convert text memos to speech. The computer essentially will read messages aloud, so drivers never have to take their eyes off the road.

The Truck Productivity Computer runs on Microsoft Windows CE, a 32-bit operating system platform for a broad range of communications, entertainment, and mobile communications devices. With the proper software, the Truck Productivity Computer could also record driver hours of service.

Credit Card Voice Mails/Emails

Companies now offer plastic cards that can be used for fuel purchase and for sending and receiving email messages. One company—Comdata—offers CABCARD which allows drivers to keep in touch with family and friends while being on the road without tying up company communications resources.

Cell Phones

Cellular phones—as a concept and an alternative to landlines—began in 1947 when researchers looked at crude mobile phones and realized that by using small cells (range of service areas) with frequency reuse they could increase the traffic capacity of mobile phones; however, the technology to do it was nonexistent at that point in time. That same year, AT&T asked the Federal Communication Commission to allocate a large number of radio spectrum frequencies so that widespread mobile telephone service could become feasible and AT&T would have an incentive to research the new technology. Because of the FCC's decision to limit the frequencies, however, only twenty-three phone conversations could occur simultaneously in the same service area—not a market incentive for research.

In 1968, the FCC increased the frequencies allocation, increasing the capacity of the airwaves for more mobile phones. AT&T–Bell Labs proposed a cellular system to the FCC of many small, low-powered broadcast towers, each covering a cell a few miles in radius, collectively covering a larger

area. Each tower would use only a few of the total frequencies allocated to the system, and as cars moved across the area their calls would be passed from tower to tower.

In 1979, the first commercial cellular telephone system began use in Tokyo and in 1983, the first American commercial for analog cellular service was offered in Chicago, by Ameritech, but in spite of incredible demand, it took cellular phone service 37 years to become commercially available in the United States. By 1987, cellular phone users exceeded 1 million, crowding the airways. That same year, the FCC agreed that cellular licensees could employ alternative cellular technologies in the 800-MHz band, and with new research and its resulting new technology, the rest—as they say—is history.

Along with the ability to allow mobile users to communicate through the use of phone numbers, today's cellular radios also make it possible to access computers, send text messages to other cell users, and allow users to take and transmit photographs and send emails.

Today, almost all professional truck drivers carry cellular phones to keep in touch with dispatch and families and to use in emergency situations. In many cases, it has not replaced the citizens band radio but has become yet another communications tool for the professional driver and the trucking transportation industry.

Pagers

Dedicated radio frequency (RF) devices, pagers make it possible for the user to receive messages on a specific broadcast frequency over a special network of radio base stations.

The first pagerlike system was used in 1921 by the Detroit Police Department, but the first time the term *pager* was used was in 1959. A small radio receiver that delivered a radio message individually to those carrying the device, the first pager was Motorola's Pageboy I, introduced in 1974. It had no display and could not store messages, but it was portable and notified the wearer that a message had been sent.

By 1980, there were 3.2 million pager users worldwide. Pagers had a limited range, and were used in on-site situations (e.g., medical workers within a hospital).

By 1990, wide-area paging had been invented and over 22 million pagers were in use. By 1994, there were over 61 million pagers in use in the U.S. and today, probably three times that many are used by businesses and individuals. Today companies—particularly those with local P&D operations—use pagers to maintain communication between their trucks and dispatchers.

Walkie-talkies

In 1940, the first handheld two-way radio—called "The Handy Talkie"—was designed by Motorola for the U.S. Army's Signal Corps. Later, this technology was adopted for peacetime use when U.S. police departments began using "call boxes." In 1963, beat officers began to use the **walkie-talkie,** a miniature two-way radio. With 1.4 watts of power, the radio had a range of 10 miles, weighed less than 2 pounds, could attach to an officer's belt, and gave officers instant contact with the radio dispatcher and patrol cars. By 1967, call boxes were obsolete.

Today, Nextel offers walkie-talkie service from coast to coast and across borders. Through direct connections, users can speak to base dispatchers, friends, and families almost anywhere within the network available for the particular device being used **(see Figure 33–6).**

Citizens Band Radios

In 1958, the first CB radio was used in the United States. By the early 1970s, fuel shortages and the introduction of a 55 mph speed limit made the CB indispensable to those who made their living on the road. Drivers used CB to locate fuel and get advance warning of speed traps, hence, the adoption of codes and slang to avoid the ears of the highway patrol, often also fitted with CB.

▶ **Figure 33–6**

Walkie-talkie service is available from coast to coast and across the borders.

Due to the popularity of the CB with professional drivers and other travelers, the original twenty-three channels were expanded to forty in 1976. That year, more than 10 million CBs were sold in the U.S.

The introduction of eighty channel CB rigs sparked a renewed interest in CB, and now there are currently twelve mobile (vehicle mounted) sets, two handheld units, and one base set available.

Today, CB has as many different uses as there are users. Professional drivers get traffic reports and directions, farm workers coordinate work and keep in touch with each other, children share their homework, families and friends keep in touch when traveling, and community groups continue to use CB radios for organizing bicycle races and other cross-country events.

CAUTION!

Never discuss your load, your destination, or next stop on a CB radio—for security reasons.

BlackBerry

Developed by Research in Motion (RIM), based in Ontario, Canada, **BlackBerry®** provides wireless connectivity as well as access to a wide range of applications on a variety of wireless devices. It combines award-winning devices, software, and services to keep mobile professionals connected to the people, data, and resources that drive their day.

BlackBerry keeps you in the loop while you are on the go, with push-based technology that automatically delivers email and other data to your BlackBerry device. It is the tool you need to stay connected and take care of business when on the road. In addition to staying connected to your email, you can also access corporate data, voice, SMS messages, web-based information, and paging services from your BlackBerry device.

REGULATORY COMPLIANCE

A number of companies offer electronic regulatory compliance assistance services. These services include a wide range of services, from fuel tax preparation to employment records.

Permitting Services

Through a wide-ranging network, electronic services provide state, provincial, and local permitting, expediting permit needs so drivers can get on the road.

Fuel Tax Services

Fuel tax services electronically track fuel purchases in every state and then fill out necessary paperwork. Fully automated processing of fuel tax reports includes the use of GPS or dispatch data and electronic fueling records.

License Renewals

License renewal services electronically track and manage base state license renewals, IRP and single-state registrations, and IFTA permitting

Driver Log Auditing

Driver log auditing services electronically maintain driver logs so that carriers can avoid fines and reduce exposure to conditional ratings, including all major and minor violations.

Fleets simply submit driver logs—including fueling, roadside inspection, and random drug test information—and access any needed data via the Internet within 48 hours, eliminating paper record keeping and having all DOT compliance data a few keystrokes away.

▶ **Figure 33–7**

Fleets can now electronically submit their drivers' logs.

Because the system is Internet based, it offers a higher degree of flexibility than traditional paper-based systems. All information is viewable, but only to those individuals authorized to view specific information. The system offers access to a mountain of log data that can be organized into several key reports or downloaded and customized to fit a fleet's log management conventions **(see Figure 33–7)**. Plus, it offers routine audit trails on regulatory items important to a fleet including the number and percent of DOT critical log violations; summary reports of missing, duplicated, and/or incomplete logs; and any necessary driver counseling.

Trip Management

Volvo Trucks feature Volvo Trip Manager to track and report data on each vehicle—a software program that tracks and reports performance on each vehicle by providing comprehensive data such as engine usage, fuel consumption, speed, gear usage, and service information—all without the need for additional onboard hardware **(see Figure 33–8)**.

Features include:

- No additional onboard hardware required
- Data quickly downloaded from the vehicle to a PC using a serial port interface, the same interface as VCADS Elite
- Reports easily generated from a PC
- Available reports

This information can be used to generate:

- Reports that show trends as they develop
- Reports to identify exceptions so that follow-up effort is minimized
- Data to be exported to frequently used applications
- Updates, but not at the same frequency as engine product changes

▶ Figure 33–8

Volvo trucks feature Volvo Trip Manager to track and report data on the vehicle.

InfoMax™ from Mack Trucks is an onboard data logger that records everything management needs or wants to know about the truck—exactly how your trucks are performing, trip and life of vehicle summaries, maintenance and fault information, engine duty cycle, daily driver stop-and-go activities, plus a lot more. InfoMax™ Wireless is the tool that lets you extract this valuable, fresh-from-the-engine data.

Data are transmitted from vehicle to computer almost instantly, and completely automatically. You get only the data you want as often as you want. This system can be fully customized to fit the needs of your fleet. InfoMax™ Wireless is the first of its kind and a truly innovative use of the very latest in short-range wireless technology. There are no communication fees or licensing agreements. Manual downloading is eliminated, saving time and money. You can access vehicles on your lot anytime, anywhere and reprogram the parameters on all the trucks in your fleet.

Satellite Radio

Beginning in 2001, Freightliner Corp. and XM Satellite Radio developed new integrated wireless information and entertainment services that are compatible with Freightliner's Truck Productivity Computer.

Additionally, Freightliner distributes, markets, and merchandises XM Satellite Radio through its fleet-owner relationships, its dealer organization, and its network of 160 TravelCenters of America. XM radios were first offered in Freightliner's new models of Freightliner, Sterling, American LaFrance trucks, and Thomas Built buses, beginning in 2001.

SUMMARY

In this chapter, you have been able to review some of the technology now available in the transportation industry in North America. Some drivers simply use cell phones to keep in touch with dispatchers as well as home and family while they are on the road. Others use QUALCOMM products, not only for communication but also for business transaction, tracking and reports, and to access other wireless information. Laptop computers, built-in computers, and wireless telecommunications are also available in some of today's trucks.

The bottom line in transportation across North America is that knowledge of wireless communications products and the ability to use a computer are fast becoming skills required of today's professional truck drivers.

KEY TERMS

BlackBerry	Laptop computers	Walkie-talkie
Cellular phones	Onboard recording (OBR)	Satellite Radio
Global positioning system (GPS)	QUALCOMM	

REVIEW QUESTIONS

1. Regarding driving a rig, computer literacy is _____.

   a. not important

   b. somewhat important

   c. the most important part of driving the rig

   d. quickly becoming just as important as driving the rig

2. _____ introduced its first product in 1988, a satellite-based messaging service used by the trucking industry to manage fleets and develop solutions that not only provide value and help improve operations, but also help secure and protect drivers and cargo.

   a. QualHunter

   b. CommComm

   c. QUALCOMM

   d. QualBird

3. Federal rules allow motor carriers to use _____ to record their driver's records of duty status.

   a. automatic onboard recording devices

   b. only required handwritten records

   c. driver's memory (no need for a written record)

   d. telephone answering machine recording at driver's home

4. Some motor carriers with _____ technology and related safety management computer systems may use this technology to monitor driver's hours of service.

   a. cell phone

   b. global positioning system (GPS)

   c. walkie-talkies

   d. citizen band radios (CBs)

5. _____ is honored at truck stops and service centers and is the centerpiece to an unmatched group of services that enable transportation businesses and fleets to operate more profitably.

   a. Onboard recorders

   b. Global positioning systems (GPS)

   c. Satellite communications

   d. Electronic payment (credit cards)

6. _____ is integrated into some tractors and allows immediate access to current tractor information and improves the efficiency of operations as well as the productivity of the driver through instant messaging capabilities between the driver and dispatcher and provides 24/7 access to each truck in the fleet.

   a. Satellite-based communications systems

   b. Cell phones

   c. Electronic payment

   d. Global positioning system

7. Many professional drivers use a _____ to schedule loads, plan trips, get up-to-the-minute reports on road conditions, and send and receive email to communicate with family members, friends, and others in the transportation industry.

   a. GPS

   b. onboard recorder

   c. onboard laptop computer

   d. electronic payment card

8. Today, almost all professional truck drivers carry _____ to keep in touch with dispatch and families and to use in emergency situations.

   a. pagers

   b. onboard recorders

   c. cellular phones

   d. GPS

9. _____ provides wireless connectivity as well as access to a wide range of applications such as email, corporate data, voice, SMS messages, web-based information, and paging services.

   a. BerryBerry

   b. BlackBerry

   c. BlueBerry

   d. BerryVine

10. _____ are Internet based and electronically maintain driver logs so that carriers can avoid fines and reduce exposure to conditional ratings, including all major and minor violations.

    a. Office logs

    b. Driver log auditing

    c. Dispatcher logs

    d. Shipper logs

CAREER PROFILE

Dora and Gordon Colvin

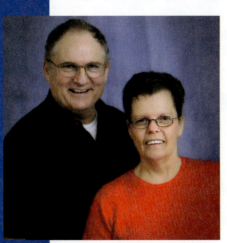

Used with permission of Accent Photography by Terra and Contract Freighters, Inc.

"You're going to find what you're looking for, whether you are looking for a bottom of the barrel job or a great career—you'll find it," remarks Dora Colvin. She and her husband Gordon, who goes by Butch, have been driving team for CFI since 1996. Each of them has driven over 1 million miles, and the pair was recently named Company Team of the Year for 2004.

Butch's dad was a truck driver, so he grew up around trucks. "My first memory was in a logging truck, and I've never done anything else," he remembers. He started driving professionally in 1961. Dora joined him in 1965, having gotten her commercial driver's license to ride with him in the truck.

"I hadn't seen my husband for a few weeks because he was working the wheat harvest. I went down to Oklahoma to meet him, and he was so tired," she recalls. "I couldn't see any reason for us to be just sitting there while he rested. When he woke up, we were in downtown Oklahoma City."

Owner-operators for 6 years, Dora taught during the school year and drove a truck with Butch in the summers, taking the kids along with them.

Life on the road can be lonesome, but cell phones have made it a lot easier. Butch would try to call home every night. "I would handle everything at home. I didn't want him to come home to a honey-do list," she says. "I would build it up for the kids, and we would celebrate when he came home."

"The kids worked on the truck with me when we were owner-operators," Butch reminisces. "We would spend quality time when I was home, even if that was the kids handing me wrenches. I hated to leave home, but I loved the machinery."

Now driving together, Butch and Dora enjoy going different places, seeing different sights, and meeting different people. "We spent so long with me in one job and with him in another," comments Dora. "This has been a great opportunity to spend time together."

The Colvins like the people they work with at CFI. "You're only as good as the people behind you," Butch remarks.

They also appreciate the recognition CFI gives its drivers. "When you do a good job, they let you know," states Dora. "They recognize achievement for the driver."

"We'll never forget the recognition from CFI because we've got the wall [of plaques] to prove it," adds Butch.

Apart from their life on the road, Dora authors children's books and is currently working on a cookbook for her mother. She also enjoys reading, crocheting, and writing poetry. Butch enjoys fishing in North Dakota and watching World War II movies. The Colvins reside in Udall, Kansas. They have been married for 41 years and have three children and four grandchildren, and their dedicated run, driving the same route for the same customer on a regular basis, allows them to see their family often.

"The thing we will remember the most is the fact that we've run all of these millions of miles together," they assert. "It has been tremendous—we've gone over 2 [million] here at CFI. Being able to spend our time together has been fantastic."

Used with permission of Contract Freighters, Inc.

34 Whistleblower Protections for Professional Drivers

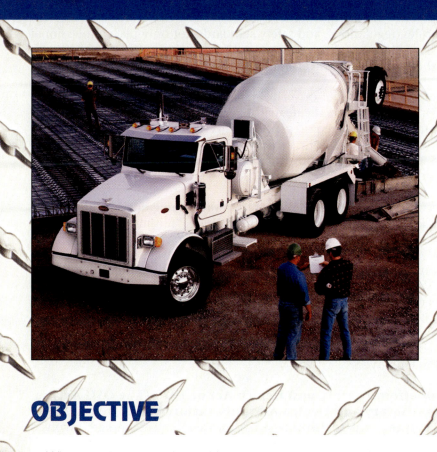

OBJECTIVE

When you have completed this chapter, you should be able to:

■ Know the necessary information about whistleblower protection.

INTRODUCTION

To the professional driver, following the rules that regulate the transportation industry and observing safety standards means the difference between continuing a career and losing it.

When any professional driver goes out on the road, he or she is automatically held to every transportation rule, regulation, and safety standard, whether it is enforced by city, state, or federal regulators. Not observing these rules, regulations, and safety standards not only place professional driving careers in jeopardy, but failure to follow these rules also can compromise the safety of that driver as well as others sharing the same streets and highways.

It also is the responsibility of the professional driver to make judgments regarding whether a truck meets safety standards or a load is within the regulatory guidelines. If a truck is overloaded, if the load is not properly secured, if the load requires special skills the driver may not have (such as the HazMat Endorsement on the CDL), or if the vehicle itself does not meet regulatory standards, it is up to the driver to stop at that point and either have these problems corrected or turn down the load.

Unfortunately, some employers expect drivers to look the other way when guidelines are not followed or equipment is substandard. Some employers take the attitude, "It is my way or the highway. If you do not like the loads we give you, go work elsewhere."

With whistleblower protections, however, any driver, mechanic, and freight handler at any company in the United States has the ability to comply with transportation rules and regulations—and to turn down improper loads or to avoid use of vehicles that do not meet safety standards—without fear of job loss.

There are actually two separate whistleblower protections for professional drivers, freight handlers, and other transportation employees:

1. Section 11(c) of the **Occupational Safety and Health Act of 1970 (The OSH Act)** authorizes the **Occupational Safety and Health Administration (OSHA)** to investigate employee complaints of **employer discrimination** against employees who are involved in safety and health activities protected under the act.
2. The second whistleblower protection—the Surface Transportation Assistance Act (STAA)—was passed in 1982.

OSHA WHISTLEBLOWER PROTECTIONS— WHAT THEY COVER AND HOW TO REPORT VIOLATIONS

Workers who have been discriminated against by an employer have the right to complain to OSHA and seek an OSHA inspection **(see Figure 34–1).** Some examples of discrimination are firing, demotion, transfer, layoff, losing the opportunity for overtime or promotion, exclusion from normal overtime work, assignment to an undesirable shift, denial of benefits such as sick leave or vacation time, blacklisting with other employers, taking away company housing, damaging credit at banks or credit unions, and reducing pay or hours.

Refusing to do a job because of potentially unsafe workplace conditions is not ordinarily an employee right under the OSH Act. (A union contract or state law may, however, give this right, but OSHA cannot enforce it.) Refusing to work may result in disciplinary action by an employer; however, employees have the **right to refuse** to do a job if they otherwise would be exposed to an **imminent danger** that poses the risk of death or serious injury. Call (800) 321-OSHA immediately to report imminent dangers.

▶ **Figure 34–1**

Professional drivers must know and follow the rules that regulate the transportation industry.

How Are Drivers Protected Under the OSH Act?

To be protected under the OSH Act, an employee must satisfy several criteria before he or she refuses to perform a job. If a driver believes an employer has treated him or her differently because they exercised safety and health rights, contact the local OSHA office right away. Most discrimination complaints fall under the OSH Act, which gives the driver 90 days to report discrimination.

GO!

If a driver believes working conditions are unsafe or unhealthful, he or she should call the employer's attention to the problem. If the employer does not correct the hazard or disagrees about the extent of the hazard, the driver also may file a complaint with OSHA.

Refusing to work may result in disciplinary action by the employer; however, employees do have the right to refuse to do a job if they believe in good faith that they are exposed to an imminent danger. "Good faith" means that even if an imminent danger is not found to exist, the worker had reasonable grounds to believe that it did exist.

Imminent danger is defined in the FMCSR as "any conditions or practices in any place of employment which are such that a danger exists which could reasonably be expected to cause death or serious physical harm immediately or before the imminence of such danger can be eliminated through the enforcement procedures otherwise provided by this act."

Before a hazard can be called an imminent danger, the following conditions must be met:

1. There must be a threat of death or serious physical harm. "Serious physical harm" means that a part of the body is damaged so severely that it cannot be used or cannot be used very well.

2. To be considered a health hazard, there must be a reasonable expectation that toxic substances or other health hazards are present and exposure to them will shorten life or cause substantial reduction in physical or mental efficiency. The harm caused by the health hazard does not have to happen immediately.

3. The threat must be immediate or imminent. This means that the driver must believe that death or serious physical harm could occur within a short time, for example, before OSHA could investigate the problem.

If an OSHA inspector believes that an imminent danger exists, the inspector must inform affected employees and the employer that he or she is recommending that OSHA take steps to stop the imminent danger. OSHA also has the right to ask a federal court to order the employer to eliminate the imminent danger.

As a general rule, the driver does not have the right to walk off the job because of unsafe conditions. If the driver does walk off the job and the employer fires or disciplines the driver, OSHA may not be able to protect that driver, so stay on the job until the problem can be resolved.

When Does a Driver Have a Right to Refuse to Do a Task Under the OSH Act?

The driver's right to refuse to do a task is protected if *all* of the following conditions are met:

1. Where possible, the driver has asked the employer to eliminate the danger, and the employer failed to do so.
2. The driver refused to work in "good faith." This means that he or she must genuinely believe that an imminent danger exists. The driver's refusal cannot be a disguised attempt to harass the employer or disrupt business.
3. A reasonable person would agree that there is a real danger of death or serious injury.
4. There is not enough time, due to the urgency of the hazard, to get it corrected through regular enforcement channels, such as requesting an OSHA inspection.

When all of these conditions are met, the driver must take the following steps:

1. Ask employer to correct the hazard.
2. Ask employer for other work.
3. Tell employer that he or she will not perform the work unless and until the hazard is corrected.
4. Remain at the worksite until ordered to leave by the employer.

If an employer discriminates against a driver, mechanic, freight handler, or other transportation employee for refusing to perform the dangerous work, contact OSHA immediately **(see Figure 34–2).** Acts of retaliation or discrimination prohibited by OSHA's whistleblower provisions include assigning undesirable tasks, blacklisting with other companies, evicting from company housing, damaging financial credit, demoting, denying overtime or promotion, disallowing benefits, disciplining, failing to hire or rehire, firing or laying off, intimidating, transferring, reassigning work, and reducing pay or hours.

How to File a Whistleblower Complaint with OSHA

OSHA Occupational Safety and Health Administration

▶ **Figure 34-2**

Occupational Safety and Health Administration (OSHA) investigates employee complaints against employer discrimination of employees involved in safety and health activities under the OSH Act.

1. If a driver believes his or her employer is discriminating against him or her because the driver exercised his or her legal rights, the driver should contact the local OSHA office immediately and within the legal time limit of 90 days. The complaint may be telephoned, faxed, or mailed **(see Figure 34–3)** to the OSHA office listed on OSHA's Web site at http://www.osha.gov

2. OSHA will conduct an in-depth interview with the driver to determine the need for investigation.

3. If the evidence supports the driver's claim of discrimination, OSHA will request that the employer restore the driver's job, earnings, and benefits.

THE SURFACE TRANSPORTATION ASSISTANCE ACT— WHISTLEBLOWER PROTECTIONS AND HOW TO REPORT VIOLATIONS

When the **Surface Transportation Assistance Act (STAA)** was passed in 1982, it included Section 405 to protect drivers, technicians, freight handlers, and certain other transportation industry employees from retaliation from their employers when they reported safety violations.

Specifically, Section 405 states that an employer is prohibited from firing, demoting, or in any other way discriminating against an employee who:

Figure 34–3

Complaints can be telephoned, faxed, or mailed to OSHA.

1. Refuses to operate a vehicle, which fails to meet federal, state, or local safety regulations

2. Reports a violation of vehicle safety requirements

3. Reports that he or she has been exposed to significant hazards

4. Testifies or otherwise participates in safety-related proceedings

When Do Whistleblower Protections Apply Under STAA Section 405?

To be protected by STAA, a worker must be in the private sector and must be a driver, freight handler, mechanic, or someone responsible for the maintenance and inspection of a commercial vehicle. The vehicle must:

1. Have a gross weight of at least 10,001 pounds

2. Be designed or used to transport passengers for compensation (excluding taxi cabs or vehicles having capacity of not more than six passengers)

3. Be designed or used to transport at least fifteen passengers, including the driver, and not used to transport passengers for compensation

4. Be used to transport hazardous materials in quantities requiring placarding under section 5103 regulations prescribed by the secretary of transportation

To be covered by STAA's whistleblower protections, the worker must also report the vehicle's condition to an employer, the Department of Transportation, or state or local police. If the worker violates safety regulations by driving the substandard vehicle, he or she is not protected by the law.

If a worker reports an unsafe vehicle or load that does not comply with regulations and the employer does not correct the problem or makes the correction and then disciplines the worker, the worker is protected by STAA. *(Note: Reporting a safety problem to a union representative, a mechanic, or coworkers is not considered when seeking whistleblower protection. The problem must be reported to the employer, the DOT, or the police.)*

What is Considered a Violation of Safety Standards or Federal Regulations Under STAA?

Every driver should have his own copy of DOT regulations, which should be available from every employer. In particular, health condition violations are very complex and each driver should be familiar with the exact wording of the laws before pursuing a complaint.

The most common violations of regulations or safety standards include:

1. Hours of service (DOT section 385.3). This regulation has been—and will continue to be—strictly enforced by the courts (as written in the STAA) for drivers who refuse a trip or a dispatch that violates hours of service regulations.

2. Refusal to speed to complete a dispatch is also covered and strictly enforced.

3. Failure to have the correct placards for HazMat loads.

4. Lack of safety inspections or uncorrected mechanical problems.

5. Lack of required safety equipment, including lights, falls under these protections. However, DOT rulings say that burned-out clearance lights are not safety violations and that stoplights have reflective qualities that substitute for required reflectors, making the lack of these reflectors a nonviolation.

6. Driver illness. If a driver is ill and unable to work, he or she must present a valid reason for this health condition to the employer and, having done so, the employer cannot demand that the ill driver operate a commercial vehicle.

7. State laws covering overweight vehicles, speeding, overlength or overheight vehicles are also included in the STAA regulations—and also include local ordinances involving routing or special height and width requirements.

Each situation the driver believes to be a safety violation must be reported to his or her employer and it must be noted that the condition involves a safety issue.

Along with violation of safety regulations, the STAA law not only covers the condition of the truck but also the environment in which the truck is driven, including driver illness, driver fatigue, bad weather, or poor road conditions.

What Are Considered Unsafe, Dangerous Conditions by the STAA Rules?

Weather and Road Conditions

If weather conditions make it unsafe to drive a truck and the driver refuses to drive, he or she is protected under STAA laws. In a court case, the court ruled that driving an empty bobtail on icy roads was unsafe and the driver acted reasonably by refusing to drive. Refusing to drive into bad weather also has been upheld by the courts.

> ### CAUTION!
> Remember: The hazardous situation—such as tornados, high winds, or icy roads—must definitely exist, not the driver's fear that bad weather may occur. (In cases of bad weather or road conditions, highway patrol travel advisories or other traffic alerts can back up a claim.)

But what about situations of dangerous road or weather conditions where others have made it through, but a driver sees the situation as too dangerous and refuses to drive? According to previous court cases, judges have ruled that it was "blind luck" that others made it through and survived while another driver refused to continue.

Two other cases to know about: In one case, the driver believed the load was too heavy to maintain highway speeds. The court ruled that this was an unsafe condition. Another driver claimed a co-driver was unsafe and refused to drive with that driver. The court ruled that an unsafe co-driver was an unsafe condition; however, the co-driver's unsafe habits required supporting testimony from other drivers who had driven with that co-driver in the past.

Driver Illness and Fatigue

The driver's health is a major consideration in safely operating a CMV, particularly professional drivers who are pushed to work long hours. To claim illness or fatigue as a reason to refuse a dispatch, however, the driver must give the employer a reason for the fatigue.

If fatigue makes it necessary for the driver to stop by the side of the road for a nap, it is not necessary to inform an employer before stopping—and this stop is also protected by STAA laws. However, the driver must notify the employer afterward about the reason for pulling off the road for a nap.

Drivers who also have had to wait an excessive period of time for dispatch have been upheld by the courts for refusing to go to work because they were suffering from fatigue—if the wait was excessively long and if the driver informed dispatch about his problems with fatigue.

If a driver becomes ill and cannot drive, he or she must specifically report the illness to the employer. A report stating, "I do not feel good" is not enough. The driver must be specific, such as "I have a migraine headache that affects my driving."

Do Not Go Home Without Telling the Boss!

The common mistake of a driver going home without reporting the unsafe condition to the employer leaves the driver unprotected by STAA laws. To get right to the point: *Never go home without calling in and reporting the specific safety problem to an employer.*

When making this report to an employer, the driver must identify the safety violation (vehicle defects, weather conditions, unsafe road conditions, illness, or fatigue), tell why the condition is unsafe, and be able to verify that the condition existed at the time the driver refused to drive.

Once the report is made, the employer must take an adverse action toward the driver in order for the incident to be covered by STAA's whistleblower protections.

An adverse action could be a warning letter, harassment, lower paying runs, fewer runs, suspension, reassignment of duties, discharge, or loss of money. When bad weather and a need to rest caused one driver to spend the night in a motel, the court made the company pay motel expenses.

Because many of these actions are done in writing, the driver has an easier job of proving they happened. The more difficult part of the task is connecting these actions to having blown the whistle about safety conditions.

How To File an STAA Whistleblower Complaint

In any and every case, professional drivers should carry a camera to document information that could be useful. Drivers are also encouraged to photocopy any **vehicle condition report (VCR)** or other documents that may be needed to document a case of whistleblower discrimination. Some professionals also carry small notebooks to write specifics of important situations, including witnesses and other information to document violations or questionable events.

1. All complaints must be filed with the federal OSHA regional office in the area in which the driver works. (The telephone number will be listed in the phone book under United States Government **Department of Labor**—Occupational Safety and Health Administration.)

2. All complaints must be filed within 180 days (including weekends and holidays) from the time of the employer's adverse action. The complaint letter merely asks the driver to describe the unsafe condition, the driver's action, the employer's response, and the driver's contact information.

3. OSHA will investigate within 60 days and may want dates, names, and other available documentation (audiotapes, videotapes, photos, or notes).

4. If the case is found to have merit, OSHA will order the employer to reinstate the driver with back pay. (If the employer does not comply, DOT will provide the driver with an attorney.)

5. If OSHA does not feel the case has merit, the driver is notified by letter and can object to OSHA's findings. In this case, the driver's best alternative is to hire a labor attorney and, within 30 days, send a written objection to the company, the Department of Labor (DOL) Office of Administrative Law Judges, and the regional OSHA director (all of these addresses will be supplied in OSHA's letter of findings).

6. After filing the objection, the administrative law judge will conduct a hearing within 45 days. Drivers are encouraged to have an attorney to represent them at this hearing.

7. During this hearing, the driver is allowed to call witnesses, and these witnesses (which are often coworkers) are protected from adverse actions by the company. The judge will review the evidence and can question witnesses. Decisions are usually made within 30 days from the time the judge receives all requested materials.

Professional Drivers Are Also Protected by OSHA— What's the Difference?

Drivers are also covered by OSHA's Section 11(c)—or its equivalent in states where there is a state OSHA plan. The OSHA Section 11(c) whistleblower protection law only has a 90-day period in which to file a complaint while STAA whistleblower protections offer the advantage of a longer filing period of 180 days.

STAA also allows the worker to hire a private attorney to bring action (and pays attorneys' fees if the discrimination is proven), provides for reinstatement of a fired worker when the DOL determines the complaint has "merit" status, and provides back pay as well as damages. Under OSHA's Sec. 11(c), only the DOL can bring action.

SUMMARY

While the rights of all professional drivers, mechanics, freight handlers, and other transportation employees are actually covered by two whistleblower protections—OSHA and STAA—it is the driver's personal responsibility to know and understand the various whistleblower protections and how to report complaints or violations when they occur.

It is up to the driver to document each incident, to follow the guidelines completely, and to be responsible for notifying employers to report unsafe vehicles or situations.

The driver should also be familiar with the laws provided by the Department of Transportation regarding vehicular safety as well as determining what comprises unsafe driving conditions.

Finally, it is up to the driver to file a complaint with either OSHA or STAA, depending on the particular situation and event. It is also the driver's responsibility to provide documentation of the events leading up to refusal to drive a certain vehicle or refusal to work under certain conditions. The driver may also want to ask for coworker testimony if this is needed.

Ultimately, it is up to the professional driver to be informed and to remain informed about rules regarding vehicular safety and the best safety practices.

Updates can be found at http://www.osha.gov or http://www.fmcsa.gov, or by reading transportation publications, company newsletters, or going to websites created specifically for driver information.

KEY TERMS

Department of Labor
Employer discrimination
Imminent danger
Occupational Safety and
 Health Administration
 (OSHA)

Occupational Safety and
 Health Act (OSH)
Right to refuse
STAA Unsafe Conditions

Surface Transportation
 Assistance Act (STAA)
Vehicle condition report
 (VCR)
Whistleblower complaint

REVIEW QUESTIONS

1. Following the rules that regulate the transportation industry and observing safety standards is _____.

   a. not important

   b. the difference between continuing a career and losing it

   c. only for drivers who work for big companies

   d. only for drivers who work for themselves

2. Because of OSHA whistleblower protection, workers who have been discriminated against by an employer have the right to _____.

   a. receive double-time pay for working under dangerous conditions

   c. drive 15 hours straight without rest to make up for lost time

   b. free meals when working away from their home base

   d. complain to OSHA and seek an OSHA inspection

3. Realizing that refusing to work may result in disciplinary action by the employer, an employee _____.

   a. has the right to refuse to do a job if the employee otherwise would be exposed to an imminent danger that poses the risk of death or serious injury

   c. is guaranteed an increase in pay for identifying dangerous working conditions

   b. will receive free meals until the dispute is settled

   d. is guaranteed recognition at the next safety meeting

4. As a general rule, when unsafe conditions are observed by a driver, the best choice of action is _____.

   a. walk off the job

   c. go to lunch

   b. start a soccer game with the other employees

   d. stay on the job until the problem can be resolved

5. If a driver believes his or her employer is discriminating against him or her because the driver exercised his or her legal rights, the driver should contact the local OSHA office immediately or within the legal time limits of _____ days.

   a. 45

   c. 30

   b. 60

   d. 90

6. To be protected by STAA, if a driver reports an unsafe vehicle or load, the report must be made to _____.

   a. a union representative

   c. a technician

   b. the employer, the DOT, or the police

   d. a coworker

7. Which of the following workers in the private sector are not protected by STAA?

   a. drivers

   c. dispatchers

   b. freight handlers

   d. technicians

8. Every driver should have his or her own copy of DOT regulations, which should be made available by the _____.

   a. state highway patrol

   c. federal government

   b. local bookstore

   d. driver's employer

9. Regarding STAA law that covers the condition of the truck and the environment in which the truck is driven, which of the following is considered to be an element of the environment covered under STAA law?

   a. driver illness

   c. bad weather

   b. driver fatigue

   d. a, b, and c

10. To be protected by STAA law, if fatigue makes it necessary for a driver to stop by the side of the road for a nap, which of the following best describes the driver's responsibility for informing his employer?

    a. It is necessary to inform the employer before stopping.

    b. It is not necessary to inform the employer before stopping, but the driver must notify the employer later.

    c. It is necessary to inform the employer 50 miles before the intended stop.

    d. It is not necessary to inform the employer at any time about the stop.

11. Which of the following is not a recommended way to document information that could be useful to a professional driver in filing a STAA whistleblower complaint?

    a. Carry a camera to document information that could be useful.

    b. Photocopy any vehicle condition report (VCR) or other documents that may be needed to document a case of whistleblower discrimination.

    c. Tell other drivers about your experiences with your company.

    d. Carry a small notebook to write specifics of important situations.

12. While the rights of all professional drivers, technicians, freight handlers, and other transportation employees are actually covered by two whistleblower protections—OSHA and STAA—if a driver is involved in an incident where he or she may need whistleblower protection, who is personally responsible to know and understand the various whistleblower protections and how to report complaints or violations?

    a. driver

    b. state government

    c. dispatcher

    d. federal government

35 The Commercial Driver's License

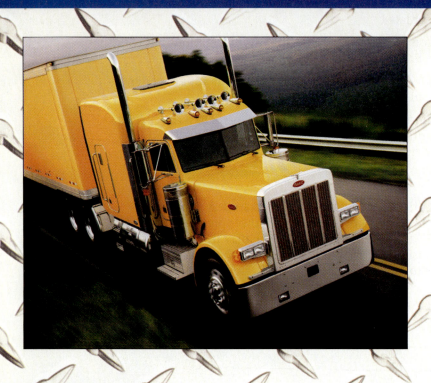

OBJECTIVE

When you have completed this chapter, you should be able to:

- Be familiar with many of the requirements for passing the Commercial Driver License test.

INTRODUCTION

Ⅰf you operate a commercial vehicle, the Department of Motor Vehicles (DMV) or Department of Public Safety (DPS) will require you to carry a commercial driver's license (CDL).

GO!

Over 8 million drivers have passed the knowledge and skills tests and obtained a CDL. Approximately 11 percent of these CDL drivers have been disqualified at least once.

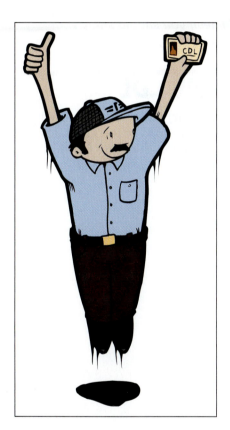

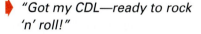
▶ *"Got my CDL—ready to rock 'n' roll!"*

▶ **Figure 35–1**

In most states a Commercial Driver's License (CDL) is required to drive a vehicle weighing 26,001 pounds or more.

In most states, a CDL is required for anyone who is driving a vehicle interstate or intrastate with a gross vehicle weight rating (GVWR) of 26,001 pounds or more. If you will be driving a vehicle designed to carry sixteen or more passengers or transporting hazardous materials, regardless of the GVWR, a CDL may be required **(see Figure 35–1).**

A commercial driver may have only one license and it must be issued by his or her home state. Examples of vehicles required by the DMV or DPS to be operated by a CDL holder are tractor-trailer, Greyhound bus, multiperson transportation van, taxi, dump truck, and electrician's truck.

As a potential professional driver, you should be aware of the requirements for the CDL.

Prior to taking the tests to pass the CDL, you should read and study your state's commercial driver handbook as well as test study books, videos, and audiotapes available from Thomson Delmar Learning, including *Pass the CDL Exam* workbook **(see Figure 35–2).**

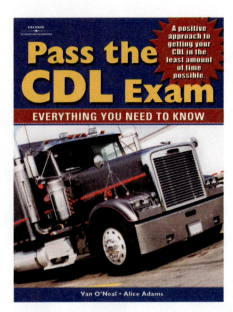

This chapter describes the process for taking the test for the commercial driver's license. Notably, several changes in the CDL requirements were made by the Federal Motor Carrier Safety Administration, effective September 2002. It is important to know these new guidelines.

If any driver violates the CDL requirements, the federal penalty is a civil penalty of up to $2,500 or, in aggravated cases, criminal penalties of up to $5,000 in fines and/or up to 90 days in prison. An employer is also subject to a penalty of up to $10,000 if he or she knowingly uses a driver to operate a CMV without a valid CDL.

▶ **Figure 35–2**

Prior to taking the CDL test, you should study your state's handbook and other test preparation guides.

INFORMATION REQUIRED ON THE CDL

While each state determines the license fee, the license renewal cycle, most renewal procedures, and continues to decide the age, medical, and other driver qualifications of its intrastate commercial drivers, drivers who drive interstate routes must meet the longstanding federal driver qualifications (49 CFR 391).

All CDLs must contain the following information:

- The words "Commercial Driver's License" or "CDL"
- Driver's full name, signature, and address
- Driver's date of birth, sex, and height
- Color photograph or digitized image of the driver
- Driver's state license number
- Name of the issuing state
- Date of issuance and date of the expiration of the license
- Class(es) of vehicle that the driver is authorized to driver
- Notation of the "air brake" restriction, if issued
- Endorsement(s) for which the driver has qualified

States may issue learner's permits for purposes of behind-the-wheel training on public highways as long as these permit holders are required to be accompanied by someone with a valid CDL appropriate for that vehicle and the learner's permits are issued for limited time periods.

NEW CDL RULES ISSUED IN 2002

In July 2002, the Federal Motor Carrier Safety Administration released new rules covering the commercial driver's license that went into effect September 30 of that same year **(see Figure 35–3)**. The new rules—which became part of the Motor Carrier Safety Improvement Act of 1999— include tougher penalties on drivers and states that do not comply with the provisions of the act.

Basically, the Motor Carrier Safety Improvement Act of 1999 amended Title 49 of the United States Code relating to the licensing and sanctioning of commercial motor vehicle drivers required to hold a CDL. This act also directed the DOT to amend its regulations to correct specific weaknesses in the CDL program.

The possible benefits expected from these new rules are fewer CDL-related fatal crashes and fatalities because of the additional CMV operators—and CDL holders, specifically—who will be suspended or disqualified for violation of the new disqualifying offenses and serious traffic violations covered under this rule.

The new rules state that a commercial driver can be disqualified if the driver's noncommercial license has been cancelled, revoked, or suspended as a result of convictions for traffic violations when driving a passenger vehicle. Disqualification can also occur if the driver has committed drug or alcohol-related offenses while driving a passenger vehicle.

▶ **Figure 35–3**

It is important to be familiar with the most current CDL rules.

CAUTION!

New disqualifying offenses include driving a commercial vehicle with a suspended or revoked CDL and causing a fatality through negligent driving in either a CMV or a passenger vehicle.

States failing to comply with FMCSA's guidelines on issuing licenses and maintaining proper legal databases will risk losing federal funding as well as the right to issue CDLs. If this occurs, drivers operating in that state will be forced to go to another state to get a nonresident CDL.

The new CDL rules include the following specific directives:

- Seven new provisions in the regulation address the following:
  - disqualification for driving while suspended, disqualified, or causing a fatality
  - emergency disqualification of drivers posing an imminent hazard
  - expanded definition of serious traffic violations
  - extended driver record check; new notification requirements
  - masking prohibition
  - disqualification for violations obtained while driving a noncommercial motor vehicle (CMV)
- The Motor Carrier Safety Improvement Act of 1999 requires the agency to withhold Motor Carrier Safety Assistance Program grant funds from the states if they do not comply with the regulation.
- A new masking prohibition does not prevent a conviction from appearing on a driver's record and requires making conviction information available to authorized parties.
- Applicants for an initial CDL, and those transferring or renewing a CDL, must provide state driver licensing agency personnel with the name of all states where previously licensed for the past 10 years to drive any type of motor vehicle, allowing state officials to obtain an applicant's complete driving record. The final rule limits this record check to CDL drivers initially renewing their license after the effective date of this rulemaking.

- States must maintain a CDL driver-history record noting an individual's convictions for state or local motor vehicle traffic-control laws while operating any type of motor vehicle. Information on these convictions and other licensing actions must be kept a minimum of 3 years. Disqualifying offenses range from 3 years to life.

- The Federal Motor Carrier Safety Administration may prohibit a state from issuing, renewing, transferring, or upgrading CDLs if the agency determined the state is in substantial non-compliance with the CDL licensing and sanctioning requirements.

- The new rule specifies applicants must pass both a knowledge and a skills test to obtain a new school-bus endorsement. The regulation requires the FMCSA to create a new endorsement CDL holders must obtain to operate a school bus.

- Under the new regulation, a driver may apply for a CDL from another state if the state he or she lives in was decertified and if the other state to which he or she applies elects to issue that license. States are authorized, but not required, to issue nonresident CDLs to such drivers.

- States with a school-bus licensing program meeting or exceeding FMCSA requirements may continue to license school-bus drivers with that program. States have the option to not require applicants for the school-bus endorsement to take the skills test when the applicant has experience driving a school bus and meets safety criteria.

- The regulations add these serious traffic violations: driving a CMV without obtaining a CDL; driving a CMV without a CDL in the driver's possession; and driving a CMV without the proper CDL and/or endorsement. Driver disqualification can result if a driver is convicted two or more times within a 3-year period.

- States must be connected to the Commercial Drivers License Information System (CDLIS) and the National Driver Register (NDR) to exchange information about CMV drivers and traffic convictions and disqualifications. A state must check CDLIS, NDR, and the current state of licensure before a CDL can be issued, renewed, upgraded, or transferred to make sure the driver is not disqualified or has a license from more than one state. Employers, including motor carriers, are authorized users of CDLIS data and, therefore, have access to an employees' or an applicants' driving record.

- New notification requirements necessitate that states inform CDLIS and the state issuing the CDL no later than 10 days after disqualifying, revoking, suspending, or canceling a CDL, or refusing to allow someone for at least 60 days to operate a CMV. Beginning 3 years after the final rule's effective date, notification of traffic-violation convictions must occur within 30 days of the conviction. Six years after the final rule's effective date, notification of traffic-violation convictions must occur within 10 days of the conviction.

- States whose CDL program may fail to meet compliance requirements, but are making a "good-faith effort" to comply with the CDL requirements, are eligible to receive emergency CDL grants.

- The FMCSA decided to merge all the CDL provisions into one final rule with one effective date because they were so closely related to one another.

CLASSES OF LICENSES AND ENDORSEMENTS

There are several classes of the CDL. They include the following:

Class A CDL—for driving combination vehicles where the combined GVWR is 26,001 pounds or more and the GVWR of the vehicle(s) being towed is over 10,000 pounds.

Class B CDL—single vehicles with GVWR of 26,001 pounds or more. These vehicles may also tow trailers with a GVWR of 10,000 pounds or less.

Class C CDL—any single vehicle, or combination of vehicles, that does not meet the definition of Class A or Class B, but is either designed to transport sixteen or more passengers, including the driver, or is placarded for hazardous materials.

Endorsements and Restrictions

Many drivers have a CDL that is "fully endorsed"—or that has all the endorsements so they can apply to work any job for any company. To be endorsed, drivers who operate special types of CMVs must pass additional tests to obtain any of the following endorsements on their CDL:

- T — Double/Triple Trailers (knowledge test only)
- P — Passenger (knowledge and skills tests)
- N — Tank Vehicle (knowledge test only)
- H — Hazardous Materials (knowledge test only)
- X — Combination of Tank Vehicle and Hazardous Materials

If a driver either fails the air brake component of the general knowledge test or performs the skills test in a vehicle not equipped with air brakes, the driver is issued an air brake restriction, restricting the driver from operating a CMV equipped with air brakes.

CDL KNOWLEDGE TESTS

You will also be required to take one or more knowledge tests, depending on what class of license and what endorsements you need. The CDL knowledge tests include the following:

- **General knowledge test**—taken by all applicants
- **Passenger transport test**—taken by all bus driver applicants
- **Air brakes test**—required if your vehicle has air brakes (and most of them do)
- **Combination vehicles test**—required if you want to drive combination vehicles
- **Hazardous materials test**—required if you haul hazardous material or waste
- **Tanker test**—required if you haul liquids in bulk
- **Doubles/triples test**—required if you pull doubles/triples

All drivers must take the knowledge test(s). You may want to take from one to six written tests, depending on the endorsements requested.

CDL SKILLS TESTS

If you pass the required knowledge tests, you are then eligible to take the CDL skills and performance tests.

There are three types of CDL skills tests:

- **Pretrip inspection test**
- **Basic controls skills test**
- **Behind-the-wheel road test**

You must take these tests in the type of vehicle for which you wish to be licensed.

Pretrip Inspection Test

The purpose of this test is to determine if you know whether your vehicle is safe to drive. During this test, you will be asked to conduct a pretrip inspection of your vehicle and/or explain to the examiner what you would inspect and why. You must demonstrate that you have a predetermined

▶ **Figure 35–4**

Pretrip inspection determines if you know whether or not your vehicle is safe to drive.

or set routine for effectively conducting a pretrip inspection **(see Figure 35–4).** You and your vehicle must pass the pretrip inspection test before you are allowed to take the behind-the-wheel road test.

Basic Controls Skills Test

The basic controls skills test includes up to seven exercises to evaluate your basic skills for controlling a commercial motor vehicle. These exercises are marked out by lines, traffic cones, or other boundaries and may include moving the vehicle forward, backing, parking, and turning maneuvers. The examiner will explain how each exercise should be done. You will be scored on how well you control the vehicle, how well you stay within the exercise boundaries, and how many pullups you make. (A pullup is when you pull the vehicle forward in order to correct your position and continue the exercise.) The basic controls skills test may include any or all of the following exercises:

- **Measured right turn**—drive forward and make a right turn around a cone, marker, or curb. Your right rear tires should come as close as possible to the marker without touching it.

- **Forward stop**—drive forward between two lines (the alley) and stop as close as possible to a stop line at the end of the 100-foot × 12-foot wide alley. After you stop, the examiner will measure the distance between the bumper and the stop line.

- **Straight-line backing**—tests your ability to back straight without touching or crossing boundary lines in an alley that is 100 feet long and 12 feet wide. The examiner will check if you touch or cross the boundaries. Pullups will be counted as errors.

- **Alley dock**—involves backing into an alley stall from the left side to simulate docking. The examiner will watch for pullups or crossing boundary lines or markers. When you stop at the end of the exercise, the distance between the rear of your vehicle and the stop line or dock marker will be checked.

- **Parallel park (sight side)**—involves parking in a space that is to your left. The space will be 10 feet longer than your vehicle. The examiner will check for pullups, hitting cones, and touching or crossing boundary lines. When you toot your horn at the end of the maneuver, the examiner will record the distance your vehicle is from the back, front, and curb lines.

- **Parallel park (blind side)**—in this exercise, the parking space is on the right side of your vehicle. The routine is the same as the sight-side parallel park.

- **Backward serpentine**—requires backing around cones or markers, beginning and ending with markers on the left side. The serpentine layout is a row of three cones. You are to back around the three cones in a serpentine or snakelike manner without striking the cones or markers. One correction or pullup is usually allowed. In some tests, you are allowed to exit your vehicle to check your position.

CAUTION!

A failure on any part of the skills test may cause you to fail the complete test, or points may be deducted for each error. Make sure you know how the examiner is going to score the test before you attempt the exercises.

Endorsements and Restrictions

Many drivers have a CDL that is "fully endorsed"—or that has all the endorsements so they can apply to work any job for any company. To be endorsed, drivers who operate special types of CMVs must pass additional tests to obtain any of the following endorsements on their CDL:

- T — Double/Triple Trailers (knowledge test only)
- P — Passenger (knowledge and skills tests)
- N — Tank Vehicle (knowledge test only)
- H — Hazardous Materials (knowledge test only)
- X — Combination of Tank Vehicle and Hazardous Materials

If a driver either fails the air brake component of the general knowledge test or performs the skills test in a vehicle not equipped with air brakes, the driver is issued an air brake restriction, restricting the driver from operating a CMV equipped with air brakes.

CDL KNOWLEDGE TESTS

You will also be required to take one or more knowledge tests, depending on what class of license and what endorsements you need. The CDL knowledge tests include the following:

- **General knowledge test**—taken by all applicants
- **Passenger transport test**—taken by all bus driver applicants
- **Air brakes test**—required if your vehicle has air brakes (and most of them do)
- **Combination vehicles test**—required if you want to drive combination vehicles
- **Hazardous materials test**—required if you haul hazardous material or waste
- **Tanker test**—required if you haul liquids in bulk
- **Doubles/triples test**—required if you pull doubles/triples

All drivers must take the knowledge test(s). You may want to take from one to six written tests, depending on the endorsements requested.

CDL SKILLS TESTS

If you pass the required knowledge tests, you are then eligible to take the CDL skills and performance tests.

There are three types of CDL skills tests:

- **Pretrip inspection test**
- **Basic controls skills test**
- **Behind-the-wheel road test**

You must take these tests in the type of vehicle for which you wish to be licensed.

Pretrip Inspection Test

The purpose of this test is to determine if you know whether your vehicle is safe to drive. During this test, you will be asked to conduct a pretrip inspection of your vehicle and/or explain to the examiner what you would inspect and why. You must demonstrate that you have a predetermined

Figure 35–4

Pretrip inspection determines if you know whether or not your vehicle is safe to drive.

or set routine for effectively conducting a pretrip inspection **(see Figure 35–4)**. You and your vehicle must pass the pretrip inspection test before you are allowed to take the behind-the-wheel road test.

Basic Controls Skills Test

The basic controls skills test includes up to seven exercises to evaluate your basic skills for controlling a commercial motor vehicle. These exercises are marked out by lines, traffic cones, or other boundaries and may include moving the vehicle forward, backing, parking, and turning maneuvers. The examiner will explain how each exercise should be done. You will be scored on how well you control the vehicle, how well you stay within the exercise boundaries, and how many pullups you make. (A pullup is when you pull the vehicle forward in order to correct your position and continue the exercise.) The basic controls skills test may include any or all of the following exercises:

- **Measured right turn**—drive forward and make a right turn around a cone, marker, or curb. Your right rear tires should come as close as possible to the marker without touching it.

- **Forward stop**—drive forward between two lines (the alley) and stop as close as possible to a stop line at the end of the 100-foot × 12-foot wide alley. After you stop, the examiner will measure the distance between the bumper and the stop line.

- **Straight-line backing**—tests your ability to back straight without touching or crossing boundary lines in an alley that is 100 feet long and 12 feet wide. The examiner will check if you touch or cross the boundaries. Pullups will be counted as errors.

- **Alley dock**—involves backing into an alley stall from the left side to simulate docking. The examiner will watch for pullups or crossing boundary lines or markers. When you stop at the end of the exercise, the distance between the rear of your vehicle and the stop line or dock marker will be checked.

- **Parallel park (sight side)**—involves parking in a space that is to your left. The space will be 10 feet longer than your vehicle. The examiner will check for pullups, hitting cones, and touching or crossing boundary lines. When you toot your horn at the end of the maneuver, the examiner will record the distance your vehicle is from the back, front, and curb lines.

- **Parallel park (blind side)**—in this exercise, the parking space is on the right side of your vehicle. The routine is the same as the sight-side parallel park.

- **Backward serpentine**—requires backing around cones or markers, beginning and ending with markers on the left side. The serpentine layout is a row of three cones. You are to back around the three cones in a serpentine or snakelike manner without striking the cones or markers. One correction or pullup is usually allowed. In some tests, you are allowed to exit your vehicle to check your position.

CAUTION!

A failure on any part of the skills test may cause you to fail the complete test, or points may be deducted for each error. Make sure you know how the examiner is going to score the test before you attempt the exercises.

Behind-the-Wheel Test

Once you have completed all other tests, you are ready for the behind-the-wheel test, also known as the drive test. It is the test where you show your ability to drive in traffic.

In this test, you demonstrate your safe driving skills over a route chosen by the examiner. As you drive, you must follow instructions given by the examiner. You must take the road test in the type of vehicle for which you intend to be licensed.

STOP!

Since safety is the highest priority, if you cause an accident or do not obey traffic laws during the test, you automatically fail the test.

During the test, you will drive over a preplanned course. The examiner will score certain driving performances in each location. Your application fee generally entitles you to several attempts at passing the behind-the-wheel test, which includes the following maneuvers and locations:

- Left and right turns
- Driving city business streets
- Intersections
- Railway crossings
- Left and right curves
- Two-lane rural or semirural roads
- Freeways or expressways
- Downgrades
- Upgrades
- Downgrade stopping
- Upgrade stopping
- Underpass or low clearance bridge
- Before downgrade
- Other railway crossing

These test locations offer a wide variety of traffic situations. They also require certain driving tasks to be done properly **(see Figure 35–5).** For instance, during each of the right turns, the examiner may grade your:

- Speed
- Position and lane usage—such as starting in the wrong lane, ending in the wrong lane, swinging too wide or swinging too short
- Mirror checks
- Signaling
- Canceling signal
- Gear changes
- Traffic checks

▶ **Figure 35-5**

The behind-the-wheel test examines your ability to perform various maneuvers in a variety of traffic situations.

The behind-the-wheel course is planned so that certain tasks or maneuvers are scored only at selected locations during the test. You may make ten right turns during the test drive, yet only four of the turns will be used as scoring locations. The examiner will not deduct points for a maneuver that is performed improperly if this occurs at a location other than the preselected location for the maneuver to be performed.

STOP!

There is one exception—an error that is grounds for immediate failure (GFIF) will be scored anywhere along the test drive course. Each state has its own special GFIF. When one of these errors is made, the test is stopped immediately.

Errors that may be grounds for immediate failure include:

- An accident during the test drive that involves property damage/personal injury
- Refusal to perform any maneuver that is part of the test
- Any dangerous action in which an accident is prevented by the actions of the examiner or others
- Passing another vehicle stopped at a crosswalk while yielding to a pedestrian
- Passing a school bus with its red lights flashing while the bus is loading or unloading
- Making or starting a turn in the wrong lane in traffic conditions
- Running through a red light or stop sign. This also applies if the examiner stops you from running a red light or stop sign
- Being unable to operate vehicle equipment properly or, after a short distance on the test course, it becomes apparent that you are dangerously inexperienced

Before you take your road test, make sure you know:

- How you will be scored
- What performances will be graded
- What makes up a passing score
- Grounds for immediate failure
- Rules for repeating the test in the event you fail your first attempt

More Information About Knowledge and Skills Tests

States develop their own tests which must be at least as stringent as the federal standards. Model driver and examiner manuals and tests have been prepared and distributed to the states to use, if they wish.

- The general knowledge test must contain at least thirty questions.

- To pass the knowledge tests (general and endorsement), applicants must answer at least 80 percent of the questions correctly.

- To pass the skills test, applicants must successfully perform all the required skills (listed in 49 CFR 383.113). The skills test must be taken in a vehicle representative of the type of vehicle that the applicant operates or expects to operate.

Third-Party Skills Testing

Other states, employers, training facilities, governmental departments and agencies, and private institutions can serve as third-party skills testers for the state.

- Tests must be the same as those given by the state.

- Examiners must meet the same qualifications as state examiners.

- States must conduct an on-site inspection at least once a year.

- At least annually, state employees must evaluate the programs by taking third-party tests as if they were test applicants, or by testing a sample of drivers tested by the third party and then comparing pass/fail rates.

- The state's agreement with the third-party skills tester must allow the FHWA and the state to conduct random examinations, inspections, and audits without prior notice.

Grandfathering Provision

States have the option to "grandfather" drivers with good driving records from the skills test according to the following criteria: The driver has a current license at time of application; and the driver has a good driving record and previously passed an acceptable skills test; or the driver has a good driving record in combination with certain driving experience.

Good Driving Record

A "good driving record" means a driver can certify that, during the 2-year period immediately prior to applying for a CDL, he or she:

- Has not had more than one license

- Has not had any license suspended, revoked, or canceled

- Has not had any convictions in any type of motor vehicle for major disqualifying offenses

- Has not had more than one conviction for any type of motor vehicle for serious traffic violations

- Has not had any violation of state or local law relating to motor vehicle traffic control arising in connection with any traffic accident, and has no record of an accident in which he or she was at fault

Driving Experience

"Driving experience" means the driver can certify and provide evidence that:

- He or she is regularly employed in a job requiring operation of CMV, and that either:
  - He or she has previously taken a behind-the-wheel skills test in a representative vehicle; or

- He or she has operated a representative vehicle for at least 2 years immediately preceding application for a CDL.

PASSING SCORES

The general rules set by the U.S. Department of Transportation on passing the CDL tests are as follows:

- You must correctly answer at least 80 percent of the questions on each knowledge test in order to pass.

- To earn a passing score on the performance tests, you must show you can perform all the required skills for your vehicle.

ONCE YOU HAVE A CDL

Drivers who have earned a CDL are held to a higher standard than other drivers. These standards include reporting any involvement in an accident to your employer, whether it involved a CMV or a personal vehicle.

Within 30 days of a conviction for any traffic violation, except parking, a driver must notify his or her employer, regardless of the nature of the violation or the type of vehicle which was driven at the time.

If a driver's license is suspended, revoked, canceled, or if the driver is disqualified from driving, his or her employer must be notified. The notification must be made by the end of the next business day following receipt of the notice of the suspension, revocation, cancellation, lost privilege, or disqualification.

Employers may not knowingly use a driver who has more than one license or whose license is suspended, revoked, or canceled, or is disqualified from driving. Violation of this requirement may result in civil or criminal penalties.

Reasons CDL Drivers Can Be Disqualified

Following are reasons a driver with a CDL can be disqualified:

STOP!

For conviction while driving a CMV, drivers must be disqualified and lose their privilege to drive for 60 to 120 days.

- Two or more serious traffic violations within a 3-year period, including excessive speeding, reckless driving, improper or erratic lane changes, following the vehicle ahead too closely, and traffic offenses in connection with fatal traffic accidents (90 days to 5 years)

- One or more violations of an out-of-service order within a 10-year period (1 year)

- Driving under the influence of a controlled substance or alcohol

- Leaving the scene of an accident; or using a CMV to commit a felony (3 years)

- Any of the 1-year offenses while operating a CMV that is placarded for hazardous materials (life)

- Second offense of any of the 1-year or 3-year offenses; or using a CMV to commit a felony involving manufacturing, distributing, or dispensing controlled substances

- States have the option to reduce certain lifetime disqualifications to a minimum disqualification period of 10 years if the driver completes a driver rehabilitation program approved by the state

- If a CDL holder is disqualified from operating a CMV, the state may issue him or her a license to operate non-CMVs. Drivers who are disqualified from operating a CMV cannot be issued a "conditional" or "hardship" CDL or any other type of limited driving privileges to continue driving a CMV

- For disqualification purposes, convictions for out-of-state violations will be treated the same as convictions for violations that are committed in the home state. The CDLIS will ensure that convictions a driver receives outside his or her home state are transmitted to the home state so that the disqualifications can be applied

REVIEW QUESTIONS

1. What commercial driver's license written knowledge tests will you need to pass?

   a. It depends on the type of commercial motor vehicle you wish to drive and the cargo you expect to haul.

   b. Everyone takes the straight truck test with hazardous cargo endorsement.

   c. Everyone takes the tractor-trailer test with hazardous cargo endorsement.

   d. b and c

2. Who sets the minimum standards for licensing and testing commercial drivers?

   a. states

   b. county where the testing is done

   c. city where the testing is done

   d. federal government

3. According to the Commercial Motor Vehicle Safety Act of October 26, 1986, a driver without a CDL may legally operate _____.

   a. a single vehicle with a gross vehicle weight rating (GVWR) of more than 26,000 pounds, as assigned by the manufacturer

   b. a trailer with a GVWR of more than 10,000 pounds if the gross combination weight rating is more than 26,000 pounds

   c. a vehicle designed to transport ten or fewer persons including the driver

   d. any size vehicle requiring hazardous materials placards

4. Regarding possession of a CDL, a driver must _____.

   a. have a license for each state in which he or she plans to drive

   b. have a license from the state where a load originates

   c. have no more than one license

   d. have a license from the state that is the destination of a load

5. For a first offense of driving a CMV while under the influence of alcohol or a controlled substance, a driver will lose the CDL for _____.

   a. 6 months

   b. 1 year

   c. 2 years

   d. 2 months

6. To legally operate a combination vehicle where the combined GVWR is 26,001 pounds or more and the GVWR of the vehicle(s) being towed is over 10,000 pounds, you must have a _____.

    a. Class B CDL   **c.** Endorsement H

    b. Class C CDL   **d.** Class A CDL

7. Which of the following CDL knowledge tests must be taken by all applicants?

    a. air brakes   **c.** combination vehicle

    b. general knowledge   **d.** hazardous materials

8. Which of the following is not one of the required CDL skills and performance tests?

    a. pretest inspection   **c.** basic control skills

    b. adjusting the fifth wheel   **d.** behind-the-wheel road test

9. Which of the following is not one of the exercises on the basic control skill test?

    a. measured right turn   **c.** backward serpentine

    b. straight-line backing   **d.** emergency stop

10. During the behind-the-wheel road test, if you cause an accident or do not obey a traffic law, _____.

    a. you may automatically fail the test   **c.** the examiner will discuss the situation with you, but you will not fail the test

    b. the examiner will take 10 points off your test score   **d.** b and c

Troubleshooting Guide

Find out your company's rules for drivers doing any type of repairs to their equipment. Find out what they expect of you. Follow your company's policy. Do *not* do any type of repair work unless you have been authorized to do so.

Warning. Before you jack up a cab-over-engine tractor cab, make sure you have been properly trained to do so. Always use the safety so the cab will not fall on you. Make sure nothing is loose and will fall from the cab or sleeper and break the windshield when the cab is jacked over. Lower the cab back into position very carefully.

If You See…	System Affected	What to Look For	What to Do
1. Ammeter shows continuous maximum charge	Electrical	Short circuit in wiring	Disconnect battery terminal until short has been repaired
		Points in voltage regulator or cutout sticking	Have mechanic repair
2. Ammeter shows discharge with motor running	Electrical	Loose connection or short in wiring	Tighten connection
		Battery installed wrong	Have checked by a mechanic
		Burned out or improperly adjusted generator or alternator	Have replaced or repaired by mechanic
		Loose or broken alternator	Replace or tighten belt
3. High engine temperature	Cooling	Low water level	Shut off engine, allow to cool to normal, add water
		Frozen radiator	Cover radiator, run motor slowly, add water as needed
		Broken fan belt	Replace fan belt
		Slow water or oil circulation	Have checked and repaired by mechanic
		Defective fan clutch or shutters	Have checked and repaired by mechanic
		Blocked radiator	Have checked and repaired by mechanic
		Defective thermostat or radiator hose suction side	Have checked and repaired by mechanic

If You See...	System Affected	What to Look For	What to Do
4. Coolant, oil, or fuel dripping	Cooling, lubricating, or fuel system	Check for source of leak	Have repaired by mechanic
5. Gauge reading out of proper range		Check the system that corresponds with the gauge	Have mechanic check gauge and appropriate system
6. Excessive exhaust smoke	Exhaust or turbo system	Air cleaner dirty Poor grade of fuel Return fuel link blocked, bent, or squeezed together Engine overfueled Fuel pump malfunctioning Pollution controls malfunctioning	Clean filter Let mechanic check and repair Have checked and repaired by mechanic
7. Black exhaust smoke	Engine, fuel system	Overrich mixture due to restricted air supply, poor fuel spray distribution, improperly adjusted fuel control racks, or overloading or lugging the engine	Clean or change filters, let mechanic check Shift to lower gear to keep engine speed up
8. White (sometimes gray) exhaust smoke	Engine, fuel system	Due to incomplete combustion in cold engine; should clear up when engine warms If it does not, look for misfiring due to worn injector spray holes, low cylinder compression, faulty cooling system, or low fuel volatility	Have mechanic check
9. Blue exhaust smoke	Engine or fuel system	Due to the burning of large quantities of lubricating oil as a result of worn intake valve guides, poor oil control ring action, worn blower or turbo shaft seals, or overfilled oil bath air cleaner	Have mechanic check

If You See...	System Affected	What to Look For	What to Do
10. Low pressure	Lubricating system	Oil has become diluted by fuel or coolant leaks	Let mechanic check
		High oil temperature	Let mechanic check
		Worn oil pump	
		Wrong weight of oil for type of weather conditions	Change oil
		Dirty filters	Clean or replace
		Worn bearings	Replace
		Oil and filter needs changing	Change oil and filter
		Oil leak	Let mechanic check

If You Hear...	System Affected	What to Look For	What to Do
11. Metallic click in time with wheel revolutions	Suspension, wheels, or tires	Wheel loose on axle	Tighten axle nut
		Loose wheel or tire lugs	Tighten lugs
		Piece of metal in tire	Remove metal or change tire
12. Dull thud in time with wheel revolutions	Wheels and tires	Flat tire	Change tire
		Loose wheel or tire lugs	Tighten lugs
		Rock between duals	Remove rock
13. Clanking noise in time with wheel	Tire on drive train system	Lock rim off tire	Change tire
		Loose driveshaft	Have tightened by mechanic
14. Dull thud or loud rap in time with engine	Engine	Burned-out main or connecting rod bearing	Shut off motor, contact garage for instructions
		Piston slap	
15. Air escaping	Tires, air system, or braking system	Punctured or damaged tire	Change tire
		Open petcock on air	Close petcock
		Air lines or fittings leaking	Repair lines, tighten or change fittings
		Brake application or relay valve sticking	Apply air to brakes several times
		Ice on brake valves	Apply heat if you have been taught how to do this
16. Snap or click when starting from dead stop	Drive train system	Loose universal joint bolts	Tighten bolts
		Excessive wear in universal joint or differential	Report to mechanic
	Fifth wheel	Worn or broken fifth-wheel lock	
		Loose or broken mounting bolts	

If You Hear…	System Affected	What to Look For	What to Do
17. Under floor noises	Drive train	Clutch trouble Bad throw-out bearing Bent driveshaft Broken teeth in transmission	Have mechanic check
18. Whine—harsh with high pitch	Drive train or engine system	Worn accessory drive gears Loose belts	Let mechanic check Tighten belts
19. Whine—short with high pitch	Engine	Ball bearing spinning in housing Generator or alternator malfunctioning Water pump malfunctioning	Have mechanic check Shut off engine immediately
20. Clicking sound in engine with loss of power, sluggishness, and overheating	Engine	Broken valve spring Worn timing gear	Have mechanic check

If You Feel…	System Affected	What to Look For	What to Do
21. Sudden loss of power	Brake, drive train, engine, or fuel system	Brakes dragging Clutch slipping Spark plug wire disconnected Overheated engine Vapor lock Blocked fuel filter Fuel pedal linkage failure	Have adjusted by mechanic Have adjusted by mechanic Replace wire Determine cause of overheating and correct it Let cool Change filter or have it changed Check linkage connectors
22. Engine surges	Fuel or engine system	Air in fuel system Worn gear on fuel pump Throttle linkage loose Low fuel supply Buffer screw not properly set	Have mechanic check
23. Brakes grab	Braking system	Grease or brake lining Improperly adjusted brakes	Have grease removed by mechanic Have readjusted by mechanic

If You Feel ...	System Affected	What to Look For	What to Do
24. Brakes do not hold	Braking system	Brakes out of adjustment	Have readjusted by mechanic
		Grease on linings	Have removed by mechanic
		Water or ice on linings	Drive short distance with hand brake set
		Low air pressure	Check for air leaks
		Air tanks full of oil or water	Bleed air tanks
		Master cylinder low on fluid	Fill master cylinder
		Worn brake linings	Have replaced by mechanic
		Hydraulic line broken	Repair or install new line
		Broken air line or fitting leaking	Repair or install new air line or fitting
25. Constant pull to right or left on steering	Tires, suspension, braking, or steering system	A soft tire	Repair or change it
		A broken spring	Drive carefully until can be replaced or repaired
		One front brake tight	Adjust or have adjusted by mechanic
		Misadjusted tandem or front axle alignment	
26. Tractor does not want to come back straight after lane change or turn	Steering/fifth wheel	Dry fifth wheel	Grease fifth wheel
27. Vibration in engine	Engine system	One or more cylinders not firing caused by defective spark plugs, shortened spark plug wires, or wires off spark plug	Change plugs or make necessary adjustments
		Sticky valve	Have repairs made by mechanic
		Broken valve	
		Blown cylinder head gasket	
		Vibration damper loose or worn	
		Unbalanced or damaged fan	
		Engine mounting loose or worn	
		Engine out of line in frame	
		Clutch out of balance	
		Drive line out of balance or line	
		Bad injectors	
		Air in fuel	

If You Feel...	System Affected	What to Look For	What to Do
28. Vibration in steering in time with rotation of wheels	Tire, wheel, or rim	Wheels out of balance	Have adjustments made by mechanic
		Bubble on side of tire	Change tire
		Broken lock rim on tire	Change tire
		Bent wheels or rims	Change tire
		Uneven tire wear caused by other defects	Have defects corrected by mechanic
		Tire mounted on wheel incorrectly	Loosen tire lugs and tighten evenly
		Loose wheel lugs, broken studs	Tighten lugs, have broken studs replaced
29. Gradual loss of power	Fuel or engine system	Fuel filter dirty or clogged	Clean or replace
		Throttle linkage worn	Let mechanic check
		Air filter clogged	Clean filter
		Fuel pump gear worn	Let mechanic check
		Dirty air filter	Clean or replace
		Cam lobes worn	Clean or replace
		Faulty valve	Let mechanic check
		Jelling fuel	Add antijell chemical to fuel
		Blocked or freezing fuel filter	Change fuel filter

If You Smell...	System Affected	What to Look For	What to Do
30. Burning rags	Drive train, engine, or brake system	Smoke or fire	Put out fire with fire extinguisher
		Overheated engine	Repair or replace part causing overheating
		Clutch slipping (engine will race)	Have adjusted by mechanic
		Hot or dragging brakes	Have adjusted by mechanic
		Hand brake not released	Release brake
31. Burning rubber	Brake system, tires, or electrical system	Tire on fire	Extinguish immediately and remove from vehicle
		Hot or dragging brakes	Have adjusted by mechanic
		Short circuit in wiring	Disconnect battery terminal
		Belt slipping or frozen pulley bearing	Tighten or replace
32. Diesel fuel oil	Fuel system	Any leaks in system	Have repaired by mechanic

If You Smell…	System Affected	What to Look For	What to Do
33. Burning oil (may also smell like burning rags)	Lubricating or engine system	Oil dripping on exhaust manifold or pipe Overheated engine	Find source of oil leak and wipe off excess oil Ascertain cause of overheating and repair or have repaired
34. Exhaust odor		Cracked manifold Loose connection in exhaust system Leaking muffler Improperly located tailpipe	Have repaired by mechanic Keep cab well ventilated until repairs have been made

Glossary

18-wheeler is the most familiar combination rig. The tractor has ten wheels and the semitrailer has eight.

2-axle dolly is attached to the trailer using the actual cargo. One end of the cargo rests on the dolly. The other end rests on the trailer.

2-axle float has a flat bed frame with two rear axles and no landing gear. It is used mostly in oil fields for hauling drilling equipment, pipes, and so on.

2-axle jeep dolly can be attached to the fifth wheel. The fifth wheel is between the tractor and trailer.

2-axle, double drop, low bed with outriggers has a double-top frame and two rear axles. Outriggers are attached to each side of the trailer to support wider loads.

45-degree angle parking an alley dock backing technique in which the rig is pulled forward at a 45-degree angle to the target, then backed in.

49 CFR Part 166 specification for hazardous materials that require special equipment or protection.

5-axle, removable gooseneck, low-bed detachable, two-axle dolly this low-bed frame has three rear trailer axles. A two-axle dolly is attached to the rear of the trailer.

Accelerator or accelerator pedal located just under the steering wheel, you can operate this pedal with your right foot to control engine speed. Make sure there is no looseness or sticking.

Accident packet given by most companies to drivers to help them handle their responsibilities at the scene of an accident. Packets usually contain basic instructions for handling the scene of an accident, a preliminary accident report or memo, and witness cards.

Agent a person or company that acts as the official representative of another, such as a consignee's agent.

Air application pressure gauge shows the amount of air pressure being applied to the brakes. When the brakes are not in use, the gauge will read zero psi.

Air blockage when air cannot reach the brakes. This is usually caused by water freezing in the air system.

Air brake application gauge indicates in psi the amount of air pressure used when the brake pedal is pushed.

Air brake system in an air brake system, pressure is used to increase the braking force. The compressed air can multiply the force of mechanical braking many times.

Air filter element keeps the air that flows through the vehicle clean and free of dirt particles.

Air intake system delivers fresh air to the cylinders. An air cleaner removes dirt, dust, and water from the fresh air.

Air operated release the device on a fifth wheel that allows you to release the locking mechanism on the sliding fifth wheel by moving the fifth-wheel release lever in the cab to the unlocked position.

Air pressure gauge tells the amount of pressure in the tanks. The maximum pressure is around 120 psi. The air compressor will build when the pressure falls below 90 psi (pounds per square inch).

Air reservoir provides air to your braking system. You should always bleed them each day to remove moisture.

Air starter using another vehicle's air supply to charge your starter.

Air suspension uses bags of air placed between the axle and frame.

Ammeter a gauge on the instrument panel that shows the current output of the alternator. It indicates whether the alternator is being charged by the battery or is discharging.

Antilock brake system (ABS) prevents the wheels from locking up by sensing the speed of each wheel electronically. The computer-operated system can apply the brakes 3 to 5 times faster than pumping the brakes manually. ABS keeps the rig from moving outside its lane while coming to a stop.

Arrester beds an escape ramp, 300 to 700 feet long, made of loose material (usually pea gravel).

Articulated vehicle a rig that has several parts connected by joints.

Articulation movement between two separate parts, such as a tractor and a trailer.

Atlas consists of maps of states, major cities, and areas. Some atlases may also include the location of permanent scales, low underpasses, size and weight limits, fuel taxes, designated routes, and state laws for access to the designated highway system.

Automatic transmission one that, when set for a certain speed range, will not exceed that speed and the engine automatically shifts through the gears until it reaches that speed.

Auxiliary brakes or speed retarders devices that reduce the rig's speed without using the service brakes.

Auxiliary lights include reflectors, marker lights, clearance lights, tail lights, ID lights, and brake lights.

When working, auxiliary lights make the rig visible to other highway users.

Auxiliary starter button available on some cab-over-engine (COE) models. It lets you start the engine with the cab tilted.

Average speed formula Average Speed = Distance ÷ Time.

Axles connect the wheels to the rest of the rig and support the weight of the vehicle and its cargo.

Axle temperature gauge shows the temperature of the lubricant in the front and rear drive axles. The normal reading is 150 to 200 degrees, but it can reach higher readings, up to 230 to 250 degrees for a short period of time.

Axle weight the load each axle is supporting. It can either be checked with portable scales by adding the weight of the wheel or at a weigh station by driving each axle over the scale.

Baffle a wall that has holes in it through which the liquid can flow in a tanker.

Bail-out area places you can use to avoid a crash.

Battery creates or receives and stores electrical energy.

Battery fluid on some vehicles the fluid level in the batteries needs to be checked or maintained.

Belly mount trailer a refrigerated trailer that has the refrigeration unit under the trailer.

Belted bias tires have body cords that run across the tread at an angle.

Bias ply tires have body cords running across the tire at an angle.

Bill of lading a contract between a shipper and a carrier.

Binders used to bind down loads on flatbed trailers. It is important to make sure that all cargo is packaged correctly.

Black ice a thin layer of ice clear enough to let you see the road underneath.

Bleeding tar tar in the roads that rises to the top, causing the road to be slippery.

Blind-side backing backing toward the right (blind) side of the rig.

Blocking pieces of wood nailed to the floor.

Blood alcohol content (BAC) the amount of alcohol in the bloodstream. Determines the level of intoxication.

Blowout when a tire suddenly loses air.

Braces and supports methods used to prevent loads from moving. Whether flatbed or drybox, a load must be blocked or braced to prevent movement on all sides.

Bracing pieces cut to fit and nailed or otherwise secured.

Brake fade occurs when the brakes overheat and lose their ability to stop the truck on a downgrade.

Brakes used to stop the vehicle. Make sure that you maintain air pressure and prevent leaks in brake lines. If the brakes are pulling, have them checked right away. Bad brakes are dangerous to you and other motorists.

Braking system used to slow or stop the rig. The braking system uses service brakes, secondary brakes, and parking brakes.

B-train a rig with two semitrailers pulled by a tractor.

Bulkhead a solid wall or steel divider that divides a large tank into smaller tanks.

Buttonhook turn a right turn that allows you to clear the corner by proceeding straight ahead until the trailer tires clear the corner then turning right.

Bypass system filters a small amount of the oil flow. It is normally used with the full flow system.

Cab the part of the vehicle where the driver sits. Keep it clean so that papers and trash do not obstruct your view or fall under the clutch, brake, or accelerator.

Cable antijackknife devices are mounted on the trailer and connected to the tractor. They keep the trailer and tractor in line.

Cab-over-engine (COE) tractor has a flat face with the engine beneath the cab.

Camber an alignment feature that is the amount the front wheels are tilted outward at the top. It is best for trucks to have positive camber.

Cargo doors are at the back or side of trailer where cargo may be loaded or unloaded. All hinges should be secure and rust and damage free.

Cargo retainer bars used to secure cargo and keep loose cargo from moving.

Cargo securement devices tie-downs, chains, tarps, and other methods of securing cargo in a flatbed. During inspection, make sure there is no damage and that they can withstand 1 ½ times any pressure from the load.

Carrier an organization that hauls cargo by truck.

Carrier bearings on trucks with a long wheel base, they join two driveshafts.

Carrier's time record a record maintained by the carrier that records a driver's duty status.

Caster an alignment feature that is the amount the axle kingpin is tilted backward at the top. It is measured in degrees. The axle should have a positive caster or tilt forward.

Cell phone a personal communications device operating on wireless technology

Centers for Disease Control (CDC) agency to be notified if a cargo spill is a disease-causing agent.

Center of gravity the point where weight acts as a force. Center of gravity affects the vehicle's stability.

Centrifugal filter a type of bypass filter in which the oil enters the permanent housing and spins the filter at a high speed, forcing the dirt and particles out of the oil for more efficient cleaning of the oil.

Centrifugal force the force that pushes objects away from the center of rotation. This force has the ability to push a vehicle off the road in a curve.

Chain control area a highway area on which it is illegal to drive without chains.

Charging circuit produces electricity to keep the battery charged and run the electrical circuits which include battery, alternator or generator, voltage regulator, ammeter or voltmeter, electrical wires, and battery cables.

Checklist list of parts of the vehicle to check or inspect.

Chemical Transportation Emergency Center (CHEMTREC) tells emergency personnel what they need to know to take care of a chemical problem. It also helps make the proper notifications and supplies the emergency personnel with expert technical assistance.

Chock a block (usually a piece of wood) put in the front or back of a wheel to keep it from moving.

Circuit breaker breaks an electrical circuit during an overload.

Class A fire a fire in ordinary combustibles such as wood, paper, and cloth.

Class B fire a fire in flammable or combustible liquids and gases such as gasoline, diesel fuel, alcohol, paint, acetylene, hydrogen.

Class C fire a fire in live electrical equipment. You must put it out with something that does not conduct electricity. After the electricity is cut off, extinguishers suitable for Class A or Class B fires may be used.

Class D fire a fire in combustible metals such as magnesium and sodium. These fires can only be put out with special chemicals or powders.

Clutch connects or disconnects the engine from the rest of the power train.

Clutch brake stops the gears from turning. To engage it, push the clutch pedal all the way to the floor.

Clutch pedal used when you start the engine or shift the gears. It has three basic positions—disengaged, free play, and engaged.

COD shipments shipments in which the driver collects payment on delivery for freight or cargo and freight.

Combination bypass/full flow filter oil from the full flow filter goes to the bearings, and the oil from the bypass filter returns to the oil pan.

Combination ramp and arrester bed this escape ramp relies on loose surface material to stop a rig. It has a grade of 1.5% to 6% and is 500 to 2,200 feet long.

Combination vehicle when you add a trailer to a tractor or a straight truck. It is also called a combination rig.

Combined axle weight the load of all axles (tandem or triple axles).

Commercial driver's license (CDL) required to operate commercial motorized vehicles.

Commercial motor vehicle (CMV) a motor vehicle or combination of motor vehicles used in commerce to transport passengers or property if the vehicle has a gross combination weight rating of 29,001 pounds or more inclusive of a towed unit with a gross vehicle weight rating of more than 10,000 pounds; or is designed to transport fifteen or more passengers, including the driver.

Commercial Vehicle Safety Act of 1986 (CMVSA/86) was passed to make sure all CMV drivers were qualified.

Common carrier a motor carrier that offers its services to all individuals and businesses.

Compressor squeezes the air into a smaller space. This increases the force the air exerts.

Computerized idle timer a function of the engine's electronic controls, it will shut down the engine in a prescribed amount of time after the truck has come to a halt.

Connecting carrier any carrier that transports freight to an interchange location and then transfers the cargo to another company to continue the shipment.

Contract carrier a motor carrier that is under contract to customers to transport their freight. The contract sets the rates and other terms of service.

Controlled braking putting on the brakes with a steady pressure just short of wheel lockup.

Conventional converter dollies used to change semitrailers into full trailers. The dolly becomes the front axle of the trailer.

Conventional tractors have a smoother ride because the driver sits between the front wheels and the rear wheels. Its main drawback is a longer wheelbase, making it difficult to maneuver in tight spaces.

Converter dolly a set of wheels with a fifth wheel used to connect a tractor to a trailer or a trailer to a trailer.

Converter dolly axle attaches to the front end of the trailer. This axle steers the second trailer in a set of doubles. The entire axle turns for steering.

Convex mirror a curved mirror that gives the driver a wide-angle view to the rear of the rig.

Coolant a fluid, usually a mixture of water and antifreeze, that circulates within the system. Coolant helps keep the engine cool and should be checked according to your truck's operator manual.

Coolant filter keeps the coolant system free of impurities.

Coolant level alarm lights up when the coolant level starts dropping, indicating a probable leak.

Coolant temperature gauge shows the temperature of the coolant in the engine block. The normal operating range is around 170 to 195 degrees.

Coolant temperature warning lights up when the temperature is too high.

Cool-down the period after stopping a rig but before turning off the engine.

Cooling system keeps the temperature down in the engine.

Countersteering turning sharply in one direction and then quickly turning back in the other direction.

Coupling joining a tractor to a trailer.

Coupling device device—called a converter gear or dolly—that makes it possible to attach one trailer to another or to a tractor. Check to make sure all parts are not damaged and are properly secured.

Coupling system connects the tractor to the trailer.

Cranking circuit sends electricity from the battery to a small starter motor.

Crosswind wind currents traveling from side to side—particularly dangerous on mountain roads.

Custom trailer and dolly for hauling large-diameter and long items   has a drop frame and two rear axles.

Customer relations   how you, as a truck driver, get along with customers.

Customer service   a vital part of the professional driver's job—in most cases, the driver represents the carrier to every customer he or she serves.

Dead axle   an axle that is not powered.

Defensive driving   driving to avoid or get out of problems that may be created by other drivers.

Deliver, or terminal, carrier   the carrier that delivers the shipment to the consignee.

Delivery receipt   a paper signed by the consignee or an agent of the consignee accepting the shipment from the driver. The driver keeps the receipt as proof of delivery.

Department of Homeland Security (DHS)   responsible for safety and security of all American citizens.

Department of Motor Vehicles (DMV)   assists in making state laws and regulations for motor carriers.

Department of Transportation (DOT)   administers federal regulations and interstate trucking operations.

Detention time or demurrage   detaining a vehicle beyond a given time. Payment is made to the carrier when delivery is delayed.

Diesel engine   has fuel injectors to supply fuel to the cylinders. The air intake system supplies the air to the cylinders. It does not have a carburetor.

Diet   the food a person eats.

Differential   transfers driving power to the wheels through the drive axle shafts.

Differential warning   flashes when the interaxle differential is in the locked position.

Disc brakes   a modern disc brake system usually has a fixed disc attached to the inside of the wheel. To slow down or stop, the linings are squeezed against each side of the disc. This looks something like a wide-jawed vice closing quickly on a spinning disk. It creates the friction that slows or stops the rig.

Distance formula   Distance × Speed = Time.

Documentation   the papers that accompany shipments and provide an accurate record of the cargo. It also serves as a contract for the transportation services.

Double clutching   a method of shifting in which you shift to neutral, then shift to the desired gears to match the rpm.

Double drop frame   these are low beds that can haul heavy and oversized equipment without going over the height limits. Since these trailers are low to the ground they may have bottom clearance problems at railroad crossings, curbs, and large potholes.

Downgrade   a steep downward slant in the road, usually around mountains or hill country.

Downshifting   when the engine needs more power, moving down the gears increases engine power while giving up some speed.

Drag link   transfers movement from the Pitman arm to the left steering arm.

Drain cocks   valves used to drain moisture from the air brake system reservoirs; should be drained each day.

Driveshaft   is a steel shaft that runs from the transmission to the rear of the vehicle.

Drive train   takes the power generated by the engine and applies it to the tractor's rear wheels. As the wheels turn, the rig moves.

Drive wheel skid (tractor jackknife)   a skid that occurs when the tractor drive wheels lose traction.

Driver awareness   a driver must be aware of his or her vehicle at all times and be constantly alert.

Driver image   the impression a truck driver makes on other people.

Driver reaction distance   the distance your rig travels during the time it takes to identify a hazard.

Driver's daily log, or driver's log   the most commonly used record of duty status for drivers.

Driver-side backing   backing toward the left (driver) side of the rig.

Driving time   all time spent at the controls of the rig. Written as a (D) on the log book.

Drum brakes   a metal cylinder that looks something like a drum that is bolted to each end of the axle. To stop the vehicle, the brake shoe linings are forced against the inside surface of the brake drums which creates the friction that slows or stops the rig.

Drum truck   hand truck used to carry drums. Never roll drums to load them.

Dry bulk tankers   used to haul dry bulk cargo. Dry bulk tankers have a high center of gravity that requires careful speed control, particularly on curves.

Duals   wheels with tires mounted in pairs on each end of the axle.

Dunnage   filler material such as sheets of plywood, padding, or inflatable bags used to fill voids in the load.

Dunnage and return   the weight of the dunnage will be listed on the bill of lading. If the shipper wishes it to be returned, this will be stated on the bill of lading.

Electric retarder   uses electromagnets to slow the rotors attached to the drive train. The driver turns it on or off with a switch in the cab.

Electrical system   provides electricity to power the charging, cranking, ignition, lighting and accessory circuits.

Emergency engine stop control   shuts down the engine. Use this control in emergency situations only. Many companies insist that it be reset by a mechanic after each use.

Emergency equipment   equipment needed during an emergency. For a CMV, the emergency equipment consists of a fire extinguisher, reflective emergency triangles, fuses if needed, tire change kit, accident notification kit, and a list of emergency numbers. It is also good to have extra food, drinking water, medicine, extra clothes and cold weather outerwear.

Emergency relay valve   relays air from the trailer air tank to the brake chambers. If there is a break in the lines between the tractor and trailer, the valve sends air from the trailer reservoir to the brake chambers.

Emergency stopping stopping quickly while keeping the vehicle under control.

Emergency triangles reflective triangles to be carried on all current commercial vehicles and required by law under FMCSR 393.95.

Employer–employee relations how you, as a truck driver, get along with your employer.

Engine block houses the pistons.

Engine brake retarder alters valve timing and turns the engine into an air compressor. It can be operated by hand with a switch on the dash or automatically when the foot is removed from the accelerator pedal.

Engine compartment area where engine is kept. Check to see that it has been properly serviced. Look for signs of damage or possible problems with the engine, steering mechanism, and suspension system.

Engine controls start the engine and shut it down.

Engine oil temperature gauge indicates the temperature of the engine oil. The normal operating temperature for engine oil is 180 to 225 degrees.

Engine shutdown the period of time from stopping the rig until the engine is turned off. Shutting down an engine requires a cooling off period. This prevents damage if the engine has a turbocharger.

Engine stop control knob used in some diesel engines to shut off the engine. You pull the knob out and hold it until the engine stops.

En route inspection a rig's control and instrument check while driving and a check of critical items at each stop.

Environment the area around the rig that you must see, hear, feel, and sense when driving.

Environmental Protection Agency (EPA) regulates hazardous materials.

Escape ramps areas used to stop runaway rigs by either sinking the rig in loose gravel or sand or sending it up an incline. They are designed to stop a vehicle safely without injuring people or damaging the cargo.

Evasive steering steering out of an emergency situation.

Exempt commodity carrier carriers that haul commodities, intrastate or interstate, exempt from regulations, such as fresh fruit (except bananas) and vegetables.

Exercise physical activity that elevates the heart rate, strengthens muscles, and burns calories.

Exhaust brake a retarder that keeps the exhaust gases from escaping which creates pressure that keeps the engine from increasing speed. It is controlled by an on/off switch in the cab or automatically by a switch on the accelerator or clutch pedal.

Exhaust pyrometer gauge indicates the temperature of the gases in the exhaust manifold. Maximum safe operating temperatures may be shown on the pyrometer name plate or listed in the operator's manual.

Exhaust system required on all motor vehicles and used to discharge gases created by the operation of the engine. These fumes could be deadly if they get into the cab or sleep berth. For safety, do not operate a vehicle with missing, loose, or broken exhaust pipes, mufflers, tailpipes, or vertical stacks.

Extreme driving conditions hazardous conditions created by weather such as snow, rain, or ice, or by difficult terrain such as mountains.

Fan belt a belt from the engine that drives the fan.

Fatigue being very tired from overwork, stress, or lack of sleep.

Federal bridge formula a formula used to figure permissible gross loads. It also requires minimum distances between the tractor and trailer axles.

Federal Motor Carrier Safety Regulations (FMCSR) federal laws that regulate commercial vehicle operation.

Federal regulations for hazardous materials transport federal laws that regulate the manner in which hazardous materials must be shipped.

Fender mirror is mounted on the fender of a regular long nose tractor. Requires less eye movement and makes it easier to watch ahead of you. Wide angle fender mirrors let you see more when you are making right turns.

Field of view the area that you can see either in front of you or behind you with your mirrors.

Field of vision everything you can see (front and both sides) while looking straight ahead.

Fifth wheel a flat disk mounted on the rear of the tractor that is used to connect the trailer to the tractor. The trailer kingpin fits into and is held in place by the fifth wheel.

Fifth-wheel antijackknife device prevents a collision between the trailer and the cab. It is automatic and restricts the rotation of the kingpin.

Fire extinguishers used to put out fires, usually marked by a letter and symbol to indicate the classes of fires for which it can be used. Every truck or truck-tractor with a gross vehicle weight rating (GVWR) of 10,001 pounds or more must have a fire extinguisher.

First aid immediate and temporary care given to a victim until professional help arrives.

Fixed or stationary trailer tandem axle assembly is a tandem axle that is placed to get the best weight distribution between the tractor and the trailer, but cannot be moved. Weight adjustments between the tractor and the trailer are then made by moving, or shifting, the load inside the trailer.

Fixed-mount fifth wheel the fifth wheel that is secured in a fixed position behind the cab.

FMCSR 392.4 prohibits driving while under the influence of any dangerous drug. These drugs include narcotics, morphine, heroin, codeine, and amphetamines.

FMCSR 397 regulations that deal with driving and parking vehicles with hazardous materials.

FMCSR 397.3 requires all vehicles carrying hazardous materials to comply with state and local restrictions on routes and parking.

FMCSR 397.5 the safe haven regulation that requires all vehicles carrying Class A or Class B explosives (Explosives 1.1 through 1.3) to be attended at all times.

FMCSR 397.9 controls the routes of HazMat carriers. Trips must be planned in the best interest of public safety.

FMCSR, Part 396, Inspection, Repair, and Maintenance of Motor Vehicles where you can find out-of-service regulations. By law you must know the requirements of FMCSR 396.9 (c), Motor Vehicle Declared Out-of-Service.

FMCSR 392.9 the part of the federal law that protects the driver by prohibiting the operation of a truck that is not loaded or secured properly.

Foot brake control valve (also called foot valve or treadle valve) this valve operates the service brakes on both the tractor and trailer.

Force of motion movement determined by the weight and speed of an object as it moves along.

For-hire carrier an organization that has as its primary business hauling cargo by truck.

Forklift used for loading pallets and heavy objects.

Four-axle, removable gooseneck, low bed with outriggers has a low bed frame, four rear trailer axles, and a detachable gooseneck and outriggers for wide loads.

Four-way flashers two amber lights at front and two amber lights or red lights at rear of vehicle. These are usually the front and rear turn signal lights, equipped to do double duty as warning lights. Make sure they are clean.

Frame the metal infrastructure of any vehicle—creates the underpinnings to support the rest of the vehicle.

Frame rails steel beams that run the length of the tractor and trailer.

Frameless construction the exterior of the van or tank is the weight-carrying part instead of the frame.

Freight bills bills prepared by the carrier from the bill of lading that must be signed by the consignee before the cargo can be unloaded and indicate whether the charges are prepaid or COD.

Freight broker a person or company that arranges for transporting freight.

Freight forwarder a person who gathers small shipments from various shippers and puts them together into larger shipments. These shipments then may go to a break-bulk facility where they are broken down for delivery to the consignees.

Fuel filters clean the fuel as it goes from the entry tube of the tank, through the tank and fuel lines, and into the injectors. To keep contaminants out of the fuel system.

Fuel gauge shows how much fuel is in tanks. Since the gauge is not always accurate, a driver should check the tanks visually before each trip and at stopovers.

Fuel system regulates the amount of fuel that is sent to the engine and how often it is injected into the cylinders.

Fuel system heater keeps the fuel system from freezing.

Fuel tank holds the fuel.

Fuel tax a tax that is paid by the carrier to each state; based on the number of miles driven in that state.

Full flow system all oil leaving the oil pump passes through an oil filter.

Full trailer is built so that no part of its weight rests upon the vehicle pulling and can fully support itself with its axles.

Fuse completes the electrical circuit and prevents overheating by breaking a circuit.

Gear box temperature gauge shows the temperature of the lubricant in the transmission. The normal reading is 150 to 200 degrees.

General knowledge test the written test all CDL applicants must take to see how much they know about the laws regulating the trucking industry.

Generators and alternators devices that recharge the battery when it loses electricity.

Glad hands connect the service and emergency air lines of the tractor to the trailer. The connections are secure when the glad hands lock.

Gooseneck used to rest the trailer on the ground to load heavy equipment.

Governor regulates the air flow to maintain the desired pressure. When the air pressure approaches 125 psi (pounds per square inch), the inlet valves open. They will close again when the pressure drops below 110 psi.

Gravity ramp escape ramp that has a loose material surface with a grade of 5% to 43%.

Gross combination vehicle weight rating (GCVWR) the total weight of a tractor, trailer, and load.

Gross vehicle weight (GVW) the total weight of a straight truck and load.

Gross vehicle weight rating (GVWR) the total weight of a tractor and all trailers.

Hand truck used to carry small loads from the trailer to a storage area.

Handling brake stopping the truck when the brakes fail.

Hazard any road condition or road user (driver, cyclist, pedestrian, or animal) that presents a possible danger to you or your rig.

Hazardous material material that may pose a risk to health, safety, and property while being transported.

Hazardous material shipping papers required and lists each item by the proper shipping name, hazard class, identification number, and packing group.

Hazardous materials endorsement an endorsement on a CDL that all drivers who transport hazardous materials must obtain.

Hazardous materials incident report a written report that must be filed within 15 days if there is an unintended release of hazardous materials.

Hazardous materials regulations standards set by the Research and Special Programs Administration (RSPA) Office of Hazardous Materials Transportation (OHMT) that regulate how hazardous materials are shipped.

Hazardous materials shipping paper a bill of lading that describes hazardous materials by the proper shipping name, hazard class, identification number, and the quantity being shipped. This form must be legible.

Hazardous waste manifest a form (EPA-8700-22) that describes hazardous waste and identifies the shipper, carrier, and destination by name and by the identification numbers assigned by the Environmental Protection Agency. The shipper prepares, dates, and signs the manifest. All carriers of the shipment must sign the paper. It must also be signed by the consignee. The driver keeps a copy.

Hazmat labels labels resembling small placards that are placed on packages near the proper shipping name and identification number.

Headerboard (headache rack) protects the driver from the freight shifting or crushing him or her during a sudden stop and/or accident.

Headlights two white lights, one to the right and one to the left on the front of the tractor—required on buses, trucks, and truck tractors. Used to illuminate the vehicle to help the driver see and help others see the vehicle. During an inspection, make sure they are clean and both high and low beams work.

Helper service a helper is to be provided for loading or unloading freight. The bill of lading specifies who will pay for the helper.

High center of gravity the bulk of the weight of the load is high off the ground.

Highway valve allows air from the hand valve to flow through the air line to put on only the trailer brakes.

HMR 177.810 requires drivers of vehicles containing hazardous materials to obey state and local laws for the use of tunnels.

Hours of service the amount of time you may spend on duty.

Household goods bill of lading used by moving companies for their shipments. This type of bill serves as a legal contract between the shipper and the carrier.

Hydraulic retarder a type of driveline retarder, mounted on the drive line between the engine and the fly wheel or between the transmission and drive axles that reduces speed by directing a flow of oil against the stator vanes. It can be turned on by hand with a lever in the cab or automatically by an accelerator switch on the floor.

Hydroplaning a road condition in which a thin film of water separates the tires from the road and the rig simply slides along on top of the water.

Identification (ID) number four-digit numbers used to identify all hazardous materials.

Idling letting the engine run while the rig is not moving.

Independent trailer brake (trolley valve) a hand valve that regulates the air flow to only the trailer unit and puts on the brakes. It is usually called the trolley valve and is normally on the right side of the steering column.

Individual wheel weight the load each wheel is supporting. It is usually checked by state or local officials with a portable scale.

Inner bridge the distance between the center of the rearmost tractor axle and the center of the leading trailer axle. Determines weight limits.

Inside delivery indicates the freight is to be delivered inside instead of unloaded at the curb.

Inspection routine list of steps you go through each time you inspect your vehicle so you do not forget a step.

Instruments and gauges make sure to check all instruments and gauges. In trucks with electronically controlled engines, the needles on all gauges will make a full sweep right after the engine is turned on to ensure all gauges are working.

Interaxle differential lock control locks and unlocks rear tandem axles. In the locked position, keeps the wheels from spinning. This position is used on slippery roads.

Interline carrier one that accepts or delivers shipments for only part of the trip. Another carrier either begins or completes the trip.

Internal combustion engine burns fuel within enclosed chambers called cylinders.

International Registration Plan (IRP) an agreement among the states and Canadian provinces for paying registration fees that are based on the percentage of miles operated in each state or province.

International transportation the movement of cargo from one nation to another.

Interstate between states.

Interstate operating authority issued by the DOT.

Interstate routes these routes have separate opposing traffic, limited access, and bypass many small communities.

Intrastate within the state.

Invoice a bill from the shipper that lists the goods, prices, and total due. This may be mailed to the consignee, or the driver may have to give it to the consignee if it is a COD shipment.

Irregular route an irregular route describes long-distance transport between a combination of origin and destination points using any suitable route.

Jackknife a type of accident in which the tractor and trailer turn to make a V shape.

Jifflox converter dolly used in the eastern United States, it is hooked behind the axle of a single axle tractor. This converts it to a tandem axle tractor. The tractor then can pull a loaded trailer.

Jug handle turn a right turn where you compensate for off-tracking by moving into another lane of traffic before entering the intersection. This type of turn is dangerous and sloppy.

Jump-starting using another vehicle battery to start a dead battery. You should always remember to observe safety rules, prepare the truck, and properly hook up the jumper cables when working on the battery.

Just-in-time (JIT) delivery system a method of shipping that gets rid of the costly overhead of warehousing stock.

Kingpin usually a 2-inch steel pin that is locked into the jaws of the fifth wheel to couple the tractor to the trailer.

Labels for hazard class; look very much like small placards and should be placed near the proper shipping name and identification number.

Landing gear on a trailer, used to support the load while it is not attached to a tractor.

Leaf spring suspension narrow metal strips of varying lengths bolted together and attached to frame hangers.

Lift axle an axle, usually kept in the raised position, that can be lowered when the vehicle is loaded to spread the load over more axles, reducing tire and axle wear.

Liquid cargo tankers rigs, consisting of a tractor and a semitrailer that is either oval, circular, or square shaped, that are used to transport liquid cargos such as gasoline, asphalt, milk, juices, and liquefied gas.

Liquid surge the wave action of the liquid cargo in a tanker.

Live axle supports the vehicle weight, sends power to the wheels, and is hollow.

Livestock transport trailer a type of trailer used to carry live animals. These trailers have either a flat floor or double drop frame design. They can have side or rear doors, or both. Slots or holes in the sides allow the livestock to breathe. Depending on the size of the livestock being carried, these trailers can be converted to have two or three decks.

Local pickup and delivery the driver operates in and around cities. He or she will usually be delivering freight to its final destination.

Local truck routes many cities and towns have designated routes for trucks.

Long-distance transport cargo is transported from a point of origin to one or more distant destinations.

Low air pressure warning alarm sounds or lights up when there is low pressure in the air brake system.

Low pressure warning signal tells the driver the air pressure has dropped below 60 psi. A red warning light will turn on, a buzzer will sound, or both will happen.

Lubrication system distributes oil between the moving parts to keep them from rubbing together.

Lug lever the device that unlocks locking lugs on a sliding tandem axle.

Lug tread deep grooves in the tire shoulders that run perpendicular to the sidewalls. These tires are best for the drive wheels.

Lugging occurs when the driver fails to downshift when the engine speed starts to fall below the normal operating range. In this condition, the tractor produces too little power and lugs, or struggles.

Maintenance policy guidelines companies set up that tell drivers and mechanics what their responsibilities are in servicing and maintaining their vehicles.

Malfunction when a part of system does not work properly.

Managing your speed adjusting your speed for the road, weather, and traffic conditions.

Maneuver to change direction while moving.

Maneuverability the ability of the tractor-trailer to change direction while moving.

Manual release the device on a fifth wheel that allows you to release, or unlock, the sliding mechanism by pushing or pulling a release handle.

Manual transmission one that must be shifted by the driver through the different gears. A clutch must be used.

Meet and turn a type of relay run in which two drivers start toward each other from different points and meet at a chosen mid-point. At the meeting place, the drivers exchange complete units or only trailers. Then each driver goes back to his or her starting point.

Motor carrier the person or company that is in the business of transporting goods.

Multiple-axle assembly two or more dead axles together. They spread the rig's weight over more axles. This reduces the amount of weight on any one axle.

Multiwheel low bed trailer with jeep dolly has a low bed frame and two rear trailer axles.

NAFTA (North American Free Trade Agreement) a trade agreement that allows the free movement of freight between Canada, the United States, and Mexico.

National network roadways that allow truck combinations to operate.

National Response Center helps coordinate the emergency forces in response to major chemical hazards.

National System of Interstate Highways also known as the Designated System or National Network. Consists of the interstates and many additional multilane, divided highways, such as the U.S. routes.

National Transportation Safety Board investigates accidents and offers solutions to prevent future accidents.

Nonsynchronized transmission one that does not have thin plates between the gears to assist in shifting. The driver must double-clutch.

Nose mount trailer a refrigerated trailer that has the refrigeration unit at the upper front of the trailer.

Nuclear Regulatory Commission (NRC) regulates hazardous materials.

Occupational Safety and Health Administration (OSHA) regulates hazardous materials.

Odometer shows how many miles or kilometers the rig has been driven.

Off-duty time illustrated as (OFF) on the log book. It is any time during which the driver is relieved of all on-duty time responsibilities.

Office of Hazardous Materials Transportation (OHMT) part of the Research and Special Programs Administration (RSPA) that classifies hazardous materials.

Office of Motor Carriers (OMC) part of the Federal Highway Administration (FHWA) that issues and enforces the Federal Motor Carrier Safety Regulations.

Off-road recovery using the roadside as an escape path and safely returning to the highway.

Off-tracking when the rear wheels of a tractor-trailer follow a different path than the front wheels while making a turn.

Oil filter keeps the lubrication system free of impurities.

Oil level alarm lights up when the oil level becomes too low for normal operation.

Oil pan bolted to the bottom of the engine is a container, or reservoir.

Oil pressure gauge indicates the oil pressure within the system. If pressure is lost, it means there is not enough lubrication in the system.

On-duty time illustrated as (ON) in the log book; this is the time the driver begins work, or must be ready to go to work, until the time he or she is relieved from work of any kind.

One-way check valve prevents air from flowing back into the compressor from the reservoirs.

Open dispatch the driver goes from the point of origin to a distant point.

Order notify bill of lading a bill of lading that permits the shipper to collect payment before the shipment reaches the destination. The driver must pick up the consignee's copy of the bill of lading before he or she delivers the shipment.

Order notify shipment one in which payment for the goods is made when the driver gets a copy of the Order Notify Bill of Lading from the consignee.

Ordinary trailer axle connects the trailer wheels to the trailer body.

Originating, or pickup, carrier the carrier that first accepts the shipment from the shipper.

Outer bridge the distance from the center of the steering axle to the center of the last axle in the combination. Determines weight limits.

Outriggers used for extra support of wide loads.

Overdriving driving at a speed that will not let you stop within your sight distance.

Overlength load cargo that is longer than the legal limit permits.

Oversteering turning the wheels beyond the intended path of travel or more sharply than the vehicle can handle.

Over-the-counter drugs drugs that do not require a prescription, but still may have important side effects such as drowsiness.

Over the road cargo is hauled on regular routes. Drivers may be away for a week or more.

Overweight load cargo that weighs more than the legal limit permits.

Overwidth load cargo that is wider than the legal limit permits.

Packing slip a detailed list of packed goods that is prepared by the shipper.

Pallet jacks used for loading palletized cargo.

Parallel parking parking in a straight line behind one vehicle and in front of another vehicle.

Parking brake used when the vehicle is not running. To check that it is working, put on the brake and engage the transmission to see if it holds.

Parking brake control valve a flip switch or push-pull knob that lets the driver put on the parking brake. Use this valve only when the vehicle is parked.

Parking brake system is used to hold the rig in place when it is parked.

Peddle run local pickup and delivery operation; the freight is usually hauled from the terminal to separate destinations in the nearby areas and freight is also picked up along the way and brought back to the terminal.

Pinion gear At the rear end of the propeller shaft is a short shaft with a small gear at the end.

Pitman arm connected to and moves the drag link.

Placards 10 3/4 inches square and turned upright on a point in a diamond shape. Federal laws specify when placards must be displayed on vehicles transporting hazardous materials.

Plane mirror a flat mirror for seeing to the rear of the rig.

Point of reference a stationary object that you spot or use as a target when you are driving.

Pole trailer carries long, narrow cargo. A pole trailer can be telescoped, or made longer or shorter to fit the load. Cargo may be poles, timbers, logs, steel girders, or concrete beams. Be careful because you could have problems with visibility and location of the steering axle.

Port of entry locations where the driver must stop and prove the carrier has authority to operate in the state.

Posted bridges many bridges have special weight restrictions. Do not cross a bridge if your rig's weight is more than the weight that is posted. Some fines are as much as $10,000.

Posttrip inspection a thorough check of the rig at the end of a trip.

Power skid a skid that happens when the drive wheels spin and the rear of the tractor moves sideways.

Power steering lets the driver control the tractor with less effort and stress.

Power steering fluid makes the steering easier to turn and should be checked during regular maintenance.

Prepaid shipments ones in which the transportation charges are paid at the shipping point.

Prescription drugs are drugs that are prescribed by a doctor.

Pressure points arteries that supply blood to the body.

Pretrip inspection a systematic parts and system check made before each trip.

Preventive maintenance servicing that is done at regular intervals on a truck.

Primary vehicle controls allow the driver to control the truck.

Principal place of business the main office of the carrier where all records are kept.

Private carrier an organization that uses trucks to transport its own goods in its own trucks.

Pro numbers preprinted numbers on freight bills that are often used to identify the freight bill.

Progressive shifting shifting before you reach the maximum governed rpm.

PSI pounds per square inch.

Public relations how you, as a truck driver, get along with the public.

Pusher axle nondriven axle mounted ahead of the drive axle.

Pusher tandem the rear axle is powered (live) and the forward axle is not powered (dead). The forward axle must have a drop center so the driveshaft can be attached to the live axle.

Pyrometer gauge that measures the temperature of exhaust gases.

Pyrometer warning lights up when exhaust temperatures are too high.

Quick release valve allows the brakes to release swiftly. When you remove your foot from the brakes, air escapes from the chambers into the atmosphere.

Radial tires have body ply cords that run across the tire perpendicular to the tread.

Radiator cap located at the top of the radiator. It keeps the coolant from overflowing.

Rear-view mirrors mirrors used to see on the sides and behind the vehicle. Should be at the proper angle and clean.

Receiver/consignee the person or company to whom the goods are being shipped or consigned.

Reflective triangle warning device carried on big rigs that is placed to warn other drivers when the rig is stopped. It is usually bright orange with red borders.

Refrigerated trailer used for hauling cargo that needs to be refrigerated.

Regular route refers to line-haul transport between given origins and destinations using assigned highways.

Regular run the driver operates between the same points on each trip and may or may not have a regular starting and finishing time for each period of driving.

Relaxation response a relaxation technique that calms the mind, body, and spirit. The relaxation response helps combat the ill effects of stress.

Relay run refers to a trip in which a driver drives for 10 hours and then goes off duty as prescribed by the hours-of-service laws. Another driver takes the unit on to the next point. This cycle may be repeated several times as the truck is driven from origin to final destination by several different drivers.

Relay valve makes up for brake lag on a long wheelbase vehicle.

Residential delivery The bill of lading will specify the address and method of collecting payment if the shipment is to a residence.

Restricted routes routes that you are not allowed to go on because the route is hazardous or prone to accidents.

Retention groove a groove in the fifth wheel designed to retain lubrication for the ease of turning of the fifth wheel.

Rib tread grooves in the tire tread that run parallel to the sidewalls. They are designed for highway speeds.

Rims part of the wheel that holds the tire in place. To prevent excess wear, loss of air pressure, or loss of a tire, rims should not be dented or damaged and should be rust free.

Rocky Mountain double larger than a standard double, but smaller than a turnpike double. The lead trailer is typically longer than the second trailer. Overall length is 80 to 100 feet.

Roll and rest a single driver takes the truck from origin to destination.

Rolling traction the friction occurring when one surface rolls over another.

Routine servicing tasks that can be done by drivers, such as add fuel, oil, and coolant, or drain the moisture from the fuel and air systems.

Safe haven an area approved in writing by local, state, or federal officials in which unattended vehicles carrying Class A or Class B explosives may be parked.

Safety valves keep the air pressure from rising to a dangerous level.

Sand piles mounds or ridges built high enough to drag the undercarriage of the rig.

Scanning looking far ahead, just ahead of the rig, and on both sides.

Scene the surroundings, or environment, in which the driver operates. It includes the road conditions, weather, scenery, people, animals, and other road users.

Scheduled preventive maintenance servicing that is based on time or mileage since the last scheduled maintenance.

Seat belt safety harness that holds you in the seat. You should always put your seat belt on before you start the vehicle.

Security the ability of a professional driver to protect him- or herself, the rig and the cargo being hauled against terrorist activity, theft, accident, and injury.

Secondary braking system can slow or even stop the rig if the service brake system fails.

Secondary collision a collision that results from either being involved in an accident or taking evasive action to avoid an emergency.

Secondary vehicle controls do not affect the rig's power or movement but help the driver's vision, communication, comfort, and safety.

Security seals seals shippers place on cargo containers that do not let the driver fully inspect the load.

Semiautomatic transmission one that is essentially a manual transmission, but uses electronic controls to automate some of the gear changes.

Semitrailer is the one most often used in a tractor-trailer combination. It has axles only at the rear of the trailer. The front of the trailer is supported by the tractor.

Service brake system is normally used to slow down or stop the vehicle.

Shipper/consignor the person or company who offers the goods for shipment.

Shock happens when something reduces the flow of blood throughout the body and could kill a person. Keep the person warm and quiet.

Shock absorbers reduce the motion of the vehicle body as the wheels move over uneven surfaces.

Sight distance the objects you can see at night with your headlights. Your sight distance is limited to the range of your headlights.

Signal or identification lights truck lights on top, sides and back to identify it as a large vehicle. It is important for these lights to be clean, working, and the proper color.

Single drive axles found on the rear of the tractor.

Single drop frames these are low beds that can haul heavy and oversized equipment without going over the height limits. Since these trailers are low to the ground, they may have bottom clearance problems at railroad crossings, curbs, and large potholes, but not as much of a problem as a double drop frame.

Skidding when the rig's tires lose grip or traction of the road.

Sleeper berth (SB) a berth in the tractor cab in which the driver can sleep. Its size and other specifications are determined by law.

Sleeper berth time time spent resting in an approved type of sleeper berth.

Sleeper operations the driver of a rig that has a sleeper berth can accumulate the required off-duty time in two periods as long as neither period is less than 2 hours.

Slides sliding assemblies for the fifth wheel and the tandem axle.

Sliding (adjustable) fifth wheel (slider) slides backward and forward. It can be locked into place to adapt to different loads. It greatly increases the flexibility of the total rig.

Sliding fifth wheels fifth wheels that are attached to sliding bracket assemblies and can be moved.

Sliding tandem used on semitrailers. Allows the trailer axles to be moved forward and backward on a track.

Sliding traction the friction occurring when one surface slides across another.

Sliding trailer tandem axle assembly is a tandem axle that allows the axle and suspension to slide, or move along, the frame rails of the trailer to make weight adjustments.

Smoothbore tank a tank that has no bulkheads or baffles.

Space management keeping a cushion of air around the rig at all times.

Spare tire additional tire used as a precaution in case something happens to the vehicle tires. Make sure they are properly secured, the right size, and inflated.

Speed the rate of motion of your rig.

Speeding driving faster than the legal or posted speed limit or driving too fast for the conditions.

Speedometer indicates road speed in miles and kilometers per hour and is required by law to work.

Splash guards (mud flaps) rubberized sheaths hanging behind the wheels that lessen the amount of water/mud kicked up in back of the trailer or truck. Make sure they are properly attached and not rubbing the wheels.

Splitter valve splits gears into direct or overdrive. This valve is controlled with a button on the top of the gear shift knob.

Spoke wheel made of two pieces. Difficult to balance and align the tires and rims. Make sure you check lug nuts often for tightness.

Stab braking first, apply the brakes fully. Then release the pedal partly when the wheels lock. Put on the brakes again when the wheels start to roll.

Standard double uses two semitrailers. The second trailer is converted into a full trailer by using a converter dolly.

Standard double rig a single axle tractor pulling a 28-foot semitrailer and a 28-foot trailer.

Starting routine steps used to start the engine.

Startup the routine followed for starting an engine.

State primary routes within each state, these are the major routes.

Stationary fifth wheel a fifth wheel that is placed to get the best weight distribution between the tractor's steer axle and the drive axle(s) of a properly loaded trailer, and is fixed in that position.

Steering arm the one on the right side attaches the tie rod to the wheels. The one on the left side is attached to the drag link.

Steering gear box transfers the turning of the steering shaft to the Pitman arm.

Steering shaft connects the steering wheel to the steering gear box.

Steering system allows you to steer the vehicle and should not have more than 10 degrees of steering wheel play.

Steering wheel connected to the steering shaft and controls the direction of the vehicle.

Steering wheel lash the rebound of motion of the steering wheel after it has been turned its maximum rotations.

Storage and delay charges an additional amount to be paid to the carrier if a delivery is postponed by the consignee or shipper or a shipment must be stored before it can be delivered. These terms are stated in the bill of lading.

Straight back parking an alley dock backing technique in which the rig is pulled forward so that the rear is facing the target, then backed in.

Straight bill of lading a contract that provides for delivery of a shipment to the consignee. The driver does not need to get a copy from the consignee when the goods are delivered.

Straight truck a single unit truck with the engine, cab, and cargo compartment all on the same frame.

Stress your body's response to difficulty, frustration, fatigue, or anger.

Suspension springs used to support a vehicle and its axles. Failure can have tragic results.

Suspension system supports, distributes, and carries the weight of the truck.

Synchronized transmission one that has thin plates between the gears called synchronizers. Allows shifting without double-clutching.

Systematic seeing a driver's visual search pattern that helps him or her know what to look at, what to look for, and where to look.

Tachometer displays the engine speed in revolutions per minute (rpm). It is a guide to knowing when to shift gears. The tachometer helps you use the engine and transmission effectively during acceleration and deceleration.

Tag axle nondriven axle mounted behind the drive axle.

Tag tandem the forward axle is live and the rear axle is dead. The dead axle tags along behind the live axle.

Tailgate delivery the freight is unloaded and delivered at the tailgate (the back of the truck).

Tailgating following too close behind a vehicle.

Tandem axle tractor a tractor with two axles.

Tandem axles two axles that work together. There are three types of tandem axles.

Tank vehicles endorsement an endorsement on a CDL that all drivers who transport liquids in bulk must obtain.

Tarp or tarpaulin is used to cover most freight and tied down with rope, webbing or elastic hooks. To do its job properly it should be tightly secured.

Technology ever-improving and expanding frontier affecting all aspects of transportation industry.

Thermostat a valve in the water jacket located at the point where the coolant leaves the engine. It opens to let the coolant go to the radiator for cooling after the engine temperature exceeds 180 degrees.

Through bill of lading a bill of lading used for shipments transported by more than one carrier that has a fixed rate for the service of all of the carriers.

Tie rod connects the front wheels together and adjusts their operating angle.

Tiedowns chains, ropes, and other implements used to secure cargo. Cargo should have at least one tie-down for each 10 feet of cargo.

Tire chains chain grids used on tires to provide additional traction on snowy, icy roadways. Tire chains are required during bad weather in some states.

Tire pressure amount of air pressure enabling tires to support their maximum weight. Check the manufacturer's instructions for proper air pressure.

Tire slides occur when the forces from weight and acceleration of the rig are greater than the tires' ability to maintain traction.

Tire tread the part of the tire that makes contact with the road.

Tires provide traction and reduce road vibration, transferring braking and driving force to the road. During inspection check tread depth, air pressure, and general condition of the tires. Bald or worn tires can cause a blowout, hydroplaning, or make the vehicle hard to stop. Tires with low pressure make the rig hard to handle and cause unnecessary wear.

Toll roads except for having to pay a toll, these roads are similar to the interstates.

Total stopping distance the driver reaction distance plus the vehicle braking distance.

Traction the contact between the tires and the road surface.

Tractor pulls the trailer and drives the vehicle.

Tractor parking valve a round blue knob you can push in to release the tractor parking brake.

Tractor protection system secures the tractor's air pressure if the trailer should break away from the tractor and snap the air lines.

Tractor steering axle supports and steers the front end of the tractor.

Trailer the freight hauling part of the vehicle meant to be pulled by a tractor.

Trailer air supply valve (also called **tractor protection valve**) in the open position, it provides air to the trailer brakes. In the closed position, it shuts off the air supply to the trailer.

Trailer brake control valve (also called **hand valve, trolley valve, or independent trailer brake**) operates the service brakes on the trailer only.

Trailer emergency relay valve used only in an emergency when the air supply is lost. If the air lines are crossed, the brakes will stay on.

Trailer hand valve brake valve in the cab used to operate the service brake of the trailer. To check it, apply the brake and begin to drive. If the unit moves, you have a problem and should stop immediately.

Transmission a case, or box, of gears located behind the clutch. It adjusts the power generated by the engine so it provides the right speed and torque for the job.

Transportation charges fees for transportation services.

Treadle valve (foot brake) controls the air that operates the brakes.

Tridrive axles three axles in the same assembly. They are used where a load carrying advantage is needed.

Trip time formula Trip Time × Distance = Average Speed.

Triple trailers are combination rigs that have three semitrailers pulled by a tractor.

Troubleshoot   search out the source of a problem and attempt to solve it.

Truck tractor   a vehicle used to pull one or more other vehicles, such as a semitrailer.

Turn signal lights   lights used to signal to other drivers that you are turning.

Turn-around   a driver travels for about 5 hours to a point destination and then returns to his or her home terminal. At the turn-around point, the driver might switch units or trailers for the return trip.

Turnpike double   a three-axle tractor pulling two tandem-axle semitrailers—nine axles in all. Turnpikes are most commonly used in the eastern states.

Twin-screws   the two drive axles of a tandem.

U.S. Coast Guard National Response Center   helps coordinate emergency forces in response to chemical hazards.

U.S. numbered routes   major through-routes. Those that parallel the interstates may be good alternatives in case of delays on the interstate.

Uncoupling   separating a tractor from a trailer.

Under the influence   refers to any driver operating under the influence of alcohol or drugs.

Uniform straight bill of lading   a contract that the parties cannot change. The goods must be delivered to the consignee or an authorized representative.

Universal joints (U-joints)   allow the cab to move in any direction and let the drive shaft change its angle of operation.

Unscheduled maintenance and repair   occurs when unexpected breakdowns or emergencies require immediate maintenance.

Upgrade   a steepening of the road, usually found around mountainous terrain or in the hill country; the opposite of a downgrade.

Upshifting   allows the rig to gain speed. Moving up the gears provides more speed but less power.

Variable load suspension (VLS) axle   allows adjustment of the weight carried by each axle. One type uses air or hydraulic suspension. The other type has springs.

Vehicle braking distance   the distance your rig travels from the time you apply pressure to the brake pedal until the rig stops.

Vehicle condition report (VCR)   a daily report filed with the supervisor by each driver that states the true condition of each truck he or she drove that day.

Visibility   your ability to see in front of you.

Vision   the ability to see, or sight.

Voltage regulator   controls the voltage produced by the alternator or generator. The regulator keeps the battery voltage from getting too high.

Voltmeter   gives an overview of the charging system. It tells the state of charge of the battery and whether the charging system is keeping up with the demands for electricity. During normal operation the meter needle should be between 13 and 14.5.

Warehouse receipt   a receipt kept by the driver to prove the shipment was unloaded at a warehouse.

Warm-up   the period of time after starting the engine but before moving the rig.

Weight distance tax   also called a mileage tax, ton-mile tax, or axle tax. A tax paid by the carrier that is based on the annual ton mileage.

Weight distribution   the balancing of a load which is determined by the location of the fifth wheel.

Wireless technology   communications technology that does not rely on wires, plug-ins, or electrical power.

Wheel load   the downward force of weight on a wheel.

Wheels   to be inspected with each trip, carries each tire, attached with lug nuts.

Index

X

Y